God's Viking:
Harald Hardrada

God's Viking: Harald Hardrada

The Life and Times of the Last Great Viking

Nic Fields

Pen & Sword
MILITARY

First published in Great Britain in 2019 by
Pen & Sword Military
an imprint of
Pen & Sword Books Ltd
47 Church Street
Barnsley
South Yorkshire
S70 2AS

ISBN 978 1 47382 342 6

A CIP catalogue record for this book is
available from the British Library.

Printed and bound in England by TJ International Ltd, Padstow, Cornwall

Pen & Sword Books Limited incorporates the imprints of Atlas, Archaeology,
Aviation, Discovery, Family History, Fiction, History, Maritime, Military,
Military Classics, Politics, Select, Transport, True Crime, Air World,
Frontline Publishing, Leo Cooper, Remember When, Seaforth Publishing,
The Praetorian Press, Wharncliffe Local History, Wharncliffe Transport,
Wharncliffe True Crime and White Owl.

For a complete list of Pen & Sword titles please contact
PEN & SWORD BOOKS LIMITED
47 Church Street, Barnsley, South Yorkshire, S70 2AS, England
E-mail: enquiries@pen-and-sword.co.uk
Website: www.pen-and-sword.co.uk

Contents

List of Illustrations		vi
A brief note on spelling and pronunciation		xv
Introduction		xvii
Chapter 1	War: *Stiklarstaðir, 31 August 1030*	1
Chapter 2	Rus': *Russia, 1031–4*	53
Chapter 3	Varangians: *Byzantium, 1034–42*	84
Chapter 4	Northland: *Norway, 1046–66*	160
Chapter 5	Conquest: *Stamford Bridge, 25 September 1066*	200
Epilogue		236
Appendix A	*Skald, saga, serpent slayer, son of Óðinn*	244
Appendix B	*Mosfell Archaeological Project*	260
Appendix C	*He, her, hero, heroine*	270
Endnotes		284
Abbreviations		332
Bibliography		334
Index		352

List of Illustrations

1. Norway at the time of Óláfr II Haraldsson. On the one hand, the upturned keel of mountains running south from Finnmark almost to Hedemark made vast areas of eastern and western Scandinavia virtually inaccessible to each other. Bonder communities, remote and inward looking, and resistant to change, would persist throughout the reigns of Óláfr and his half-brother Haraldr. On the other hand, the fractured geography of Norway's long coastline creates natural harbours and sheltered inlets, or fjords, which were ideally suited to the development of a muscular maritime culture. Moreover, this coastline is protected by a barrier of small islands, some 150,000 in number, which secures maritime traffic at almost every point from adverse weather and sea conditions. The exertion of kingly authority was thus feasible along the sea-fringe of Norway. Yet no king in Norway could survive except by force, and no king in Norway could domineer further than the reach of his ships.

2. The Byzantine empire at the death of Basil II. On Christmas Day 1025, Basil II died. For almost half a century he had been sole emperor. One of the greatest and most powerful Byzantine rulers, he had devoted his long life to the serious business of ruling. He had never married, spending most of his time on or near the frontiers, engaging and defeating the enemies of the empire. Everywhere the might of Byzantine arms was respected and feared. In addition, the treasury in Constantinople was full to overflowing with the accumulated plunder of Basil's far-flung campaigns. In fact, according to the contemporary courtier Michael Psellos (*Chronographia*, Basil II 1.31), the sum accumulated in the state's coffers amounted to 200,000 talents, a talent (Gr. τάλαντον) being equivalent to about twenty-six kilograms of silver. Little wonder, therefore, Constantinople, with its great stone defensive walls, its magnificent churches, its exotic bazaars and, most of all, the splendid court of the Byzantine emperor, cannot have failed to impress visitors from the far north, and they called it simply *Mikligarðr*, the Great City.

3. In 1882, using funds from the rising prosperity of the herring industry, the citizens of Lerwick, Shetland's capital and only town, chose to build a new town hall. Local scholars decided to grace the resulting Gothic Baronial building with a series of stained-glass windows commemorating Shetland's rich Norse heritage. The striking windows reflect the Norse warlords and adventurers who dominated Shetland during the viking age. In fair

weather, the archipelago of Shetland was two days away by sail from Norway, which needed only one night at sea. This particular stained-glass window depicts the hero of our story, a legendary character who lives on still in the northern sagas, the uncompromising warlord with a ruthless streak and big ego, HARADVS • HARDRADA • REX • NORVEGIÆ, Haraldr *harðráði*, king of Norway. (© *Nic Fields*)

4. Panoramic view of Stiklestad. Stiklarstaðir, as it is called in the sagas, was a farmstead in the lower part of the valley of Veraladr, some seventy kilometres northeast of Nidaros (Trondheim). It was here on 31 August 1030 that the fifteen-year-old Haraldr Sigurðarson earned his 'spurs' fighting along side his half-brother Óláfr II Haraldsson, the hardnosed evangelizing king who, in the year of life that was left to him, was seeking to regain Norway. The two armies probably met head-to-head on the flat ground where Stiklestad church stands today. Facing the king's motley muster was a bonders' host 14,400 strong and supposedly dwarfing the opposition by a ratio of about four to one. Óláfr was killed and his household warriors (*hirð*), scorning flight, fought to the last. His death was soon transformed into a sensational example of Christian martyrdom. The battles of Stiklarstaðir, where he was severely wounded but escaped, and Stamford Bridge, where he appeared to be on the verge of victory but fell (after three decades of warmongering), are apt bookends to Haraldr's adventurous and violent life. (*Sven Rosborn*)

5. Composite image depicting the Ledberg rune stone (Ög 181), Östergötland, Sweden. Some scholars believe the images on the front and back of the stone depict the final days of Þorgautr or Gunna, who are memorialized in the runic inscription. The first image is of a longship, viz. a journey overseas. In the second image a shielded warrior is walking to the left accompanied by a dog, viz. preparation for departure. In the third image the warrior is fully armed with spear and sword, viz. going into battle. At the top of the second side of the stone, the warrior's foot is being bitten by a wolf, and finally we see him legless with arms sprawled, viz. dead on the battlefield. Dated to the eleventh century, the warrior's nasal helmet is conical and similar in design to those shown on the contemporary Bayeux tapestry. The inscription reads: 'Bisi placed this stone in memory of Þorgautr   his father / and Gunna, both. Thistle mistletoe casket'. The last three words are perhaps a rhyming incantation, or *galdr*. (*Maksim*)

6. Practical and beautiful, Norse swords (Haithabu, Wikingermuseum) were carefully balanced for maximum effect as slashing weapons, and were designed to be used single handed. Their pattern-welded blades were double-edged and about ninety centimetres long. The finest blades were imported from the Rhineland; no Northman ever forged a blade like the Franks had done, and the quality of Frankish arms enjoyed high international prestige throughout the viking age. Great care was naturally taken of such prestigious weapons and this often found expression in the elaborate ornamentation of their hilts – wire,

inlay or thin plates of tin, brass, gold, silver and copper – which the Norse warriors often fitted themselves. The Norwegian scholar Jan Petersen detected no fewer than twenty-six dominant profiles for hilt furniture (here, from left to right, Petersen types Y, X, D, H, T: 2 (three of), unidentifiable). The hilt was formed over a tang from the blade, slotting over the guard, covering the grip, the end stopped with a pommel. (*Viciarg*)

7. Blade of a seventh-century Merovingian *scramasax* from Weingarten, Württemberg, alongside a conjectural reconstruction. *Scramasaxes* had a single-edged blade having an angled back-edge extending from the point to the thickened back of the blade for perhaps one third of its total length. The tang was usually set into a simple grip of bone, antler or wood; the guard was generally insignificant, or even non-existent, but some early *scramasaxes* had decorative pommels, boat-shaped or lobed. The shape and size of extant knives varies enormously; excavated examples commonly range from forty-four centimetres to seventy-six centimetres in length. The typical Saxon *scramasax* (OE *seax*) was broad, heavy and with an angled back sloping in a straight line towards the point; the Frankish version had a more curving blade and often had one or more fullers or shallow grooves on both sides of the blade, as in this example. Most of the Scandinavian *scramasaxes* were very broad-bladed weapons, slightly curved on the back and more strongly curved on the edge, with an acute point. (*Bullenwächter*)

8. (Left) Dane axe with a copper alloy socket (London Docklands Museum) recovered in the nineteen-twenties from the Thames near the Old London Bridge, and (right) a replica of a Dane axe based on an eleventh-century original housed in the Tower of London. It is said a Norse warrior, as he strode into the fray, spoke eager promises to his long shafted, broad bladed axe, the weapon with which he and his fighting comrades are most often associated with in the popular imagination. A Dane axe, narrowest at the socket and gracefully flaring out (unbroken by beard or angle) to around thirty centimetres at the killing edge, was a shock weapon designed to splinter shields and cleave helmets at close range. Such axes were certainly used in battle throughout the viking age – they can be seen wielded on the stone grave marker from Lindisfarne Priory, and on the best preserved of the Middleton Anglo-Scandinavian stone crosses (Cross B) a Norse warrior is shown seated on his high-seat surrounded by his implements of war: conical helmet, shield, sword, *scramasax*, spear, and axe. (*[left] mattbuck, [right] Grimr032125*)

9. (Above) the Gjermundbu helmet (Museum of Cultural History, University of Ósló), and (right) a full-scale replica (Pons, Le Donjon). The mid tenth-century original was unearthed in 1943 from a chieftain's grave on Gjermundbu farm in Ringerike, central Norway. This Norwegian helmet is the only one we can honestly say was a viking one. Made from four iron plates and a spectacle visor, surely this style of helmet was not only frightening to the foe but worrisome to the wearer too. For the spectacle visor would have

caught incoming spear tips and sword points and guided them right into the wearer's eyes. Yet the Gjermundbu helmet has clear evidence of battle damage (a sword blow and an arrow puncture), suggesting it was worn in earnest. (*[above] NTNU Vitenskapsmuseet, [right] © Esther Carré*)

10. The image of the viking longship with its fearsome dragon head is ingrained in the popular imagination. This is the prow end of the *Skidbladner* (ON *Skiðblaðnir*, named after the magic ship of the god Freyr), a full-scale reconstruction of the ship found in the Gokstad burial mound, now laid up at Brookpoint in Haroldswick on Unst, the northernmost island of the Shetland archipelago. Dated to 895/900, the Gokstad ship is representative of those that will have been used by the original viking raiders and the first generation of Norse settlers, as is demonstrated by the fact that replicas, such as this one, have crossed not only the North Sea but the Atlantic Ocean as well. Haraldr *hárfagri*, the Vestfold king who was striving to unite Norway under his rule, was said to have landed at Haroldswick (ON *Haraldsvík*) when he made his expedition to Shetland to clear out the vikings who were raiding the Norwegian littoral. The Gokstad ship is of that period. (*© Nic Fields*)

11. (Left) the Skuldelev 5 wreck (Roskilde, Vikingeskibsmuseet), and (right) the *Sebbe Als* from Augustenborg, Denmark, under sail, the first (launched 1969) of four full-scale reconstructions of the Skuldelev 5 wreck. Dating from around 1040 (and repaired 1060– 80), Skuldelev 5 was a small warship of the *snekkja* type, a predatory, rapier-like vessel probably more typical of the kind that was used by the Northmen on their raids. It was 17.2 metres long and 2.6 metres broad, and had been much repaired, which suggest it was a levy-ship. Constructed using oak, pine and ash, it was built in the Roskilde area. The ship was purpose-built for sailing in Danish waters and the Baltic Sea. It carried a sail estimated at 46.5 square metres and deployed twenty-six oars. (*[left] Casiopeia, [right] Steen Weile*)

12. Varangian rune stone (Vg 184), Västergötland, Sweden. On many of the Swedish rune stones there are references to men who died 'eastwards in Greece' (i.e. Byzantium). Up to the days of the Komnenian emperors many of the Varangians were Swedes, and in Sweden have been found a number of rune stones bearing the names of various men who died in the Byzantium empire, and had these stones raised in their memory. Of course, the Swedes commemorated on these memorial stones need by no means all have been Varangians, for these eastern adventurers would have included merchants, pilgrims, fortune seekers, and even plain tourists. This rune stone was raised in the cemetery of the church of Smula, but has been moved to the grounds of Dagsnäs Castle. It was raised in the memory of two brothers who died as warriors in the east. They may have been members of the Varangian Guard. The runic inscription reads: 'Gulli/Kolli raised this stone in memory of his wife's

brothers Asbjörn and Juli, very good valiant men. And they died in the east in the retinue'. (*Berig*)

13. A copy of the brightly painted rune stone at Pilgårds (G 280), on the Baltic Sea island of Gotland. The runic inscription reads: 'Hegbjörn raised this stone glaring (and his) brothers Röðvisl, Östen, Ámundur (?), who have had stones raised in memory of Hrafn south of Rufstein. They came far and wide in *aifur*. Vífill bade' The rune stone, which is dated to the last half of the tenth century, was raised by four Gotland brothers in memory of a fifth brother, Hrafn, who evidently lost his life far away in *eiforr* (rendered here as *aifur*), one of the frightening Dnieper cataracts Scandinavian peddler merchants (with their cargoes of iron weapons, furs and slaves) and professional mercenaries (with little more than their skills and services) had to traverse in order to reach Constantinople. Such memorial stones tell an intriguing tale not just of war but of trade and of fascination with objects from eastern lands. (*Berig*)

14. Varangian casual graffito scratched onto the marble balustrade, west gallery of Hagia Sophia. All the polish marble balustrades of Iustinianus' great sacred edifice are now covered with scrawled graffiti, scored by visitors down the centuries. Perhaps the most evocative of these is a series of rough scratches. Though most of it is indecipherable, this particular one concerns us. It is runic, and the opening letters (as read in 1967 by Professor S.B.F. Jansson) are the ending of a personal name: - A - L - F - T - A - N, which in full would have read Hálfdan, Half-Dane, both a royal and a common name in the viking age. Some time in the eleventh century, did a bored Varangian, having to stand through some interminable church service in a language he did not understand, idly scratch in his own tongue HÁLFDAN

WAS HERE for posterity? It is possible. It is also possible that this is the furthest example of runic writing outside of Scandinavia. (*Not home*)

15. Illumination (Biblioteca Nacional de España, Codex Matritensis Græcus, Vitr. 26-2, fol. 208 v.-a) from the Madrid manuscript of John Skylitzes' *Synopsis historión* offering a rare depiction of Varangians in full panoply. The scene is that of the deposition of Leo V the Armenian, assassinated in 820. The emperor's body is being taken to the Hippodrome. The soldiers in the background amongst the Great Palace buildings are identified as Varangians. At the time of this event there were, of course, no Varangians in imperial service, but as is usual in mediaeval illuminations, the illustration is based on contemporary figures (viz. second half of eleventh century). A number of the Varangians are shown with typical Byzantine helmets (with aventail) and shields, but they do have long shafted, broad bladed axes, and what appear to be mail coats (possibly reaching the elbow and knee), not

Byzantine-style lamellar corselets with *pteruges*. Other Varangians have shields of the kite shape variety, while others have spears rather than Dane axes. (*Alonso de Mendoza*)

16. Detail from the gold tesserae mosaic in Néa Moní on the island of Chios. Dated to around 1050, it depicts the *centurio* Longinius, the first gentile to recognize Christ's divinity, at the crucifixion. Dedicated to the Theotókos, the Mother of God, the monastery was founded by Constantinus IX Monomachos (r. 1042–55) as a thanksgiving gift to the monks who, when he was still an exiled nobleman, prophesied his ascension to the Byzantine throne. It has been argued that Longinius is portrayed as a contemporary senior officer of the Varangian Guard. There is no evidence to support making this notion any more definite than this may be a veteran Varangian adopting local military garb. After all, Longinius is dressed in stereotypical idealized Byzantine military style and is likewise shown with stereotypical idealized Byzantine physiognomy. (*Yorck Project*)

17. Two viking re-enactors meet head-to-head at *Wikingerlager 2013*, Ostbeskiden, Poland. The warrior on the right wears padded and quilted defensive jacket designed to be worn as independent body armour. As such it is made of several layers of cotton, linen or wool and faced with leather, and protects not only the torso but also the vulnerable groin and armpit areas, while a padded collar is an advantage too. The mailed warrior on the left is wearing a Byzantine style helmet complete with a nasal bar and ring mail aventail. Note well that unkempt hair and shaggy beards were atypical, the Norsemen taking care of their appearance, plaiting their hair and beards and washing frequently. With regards to experimental archaeology, manuscript paintings are an excellent source of detail. They can show the dimensions, style, and colour, mode of wearing and use, and so forth, for so many things, such as the fact that most probably Varangians wore a mixture of Norse and Byzantine gear, the latter becoming predominant the longer a man stayed in imperial service as his own equipment wore out or was lost. (*Silar*)

18. Basil II (r. 976–1025), illumination from the Basil II Psalter (Venice, Biblioteca Nazionale Marciana, Codex Marciana Græcus 17, fol. IIIr), circa 1017. The detail shows Basil as a Christian ruler (he receives the imperial diadem from the archangel Gabriel) and a Roman soldier (he receives a spear from the archangel Michael) triumphing over his many enemies (prostrate at his feet). It was he who totally subjugated Bulgaria, in addition to scoring victories over the Armenians, Georgians, Arabs and Italo-Normans. Unglamorous and one of the least attractive of all the emperors in terms of physical appearance, lack of cultural interests, and utter distain for the trappings of power, he was trusted by the army and people alike. At the beginning of his reign he suppressed two rebellions, on the second occasion with the aid of 6,000 Swedish mercenaries sent by Vladimir, prince of Kiev, in

return for the hand in marriage of Basil's sister Anna Porphyrogenita. Thus was the origin of the Varangian Guard. (*Alexandar.R*)

19. Lion of Peiraeus, Arsenale, Venice. This magnificent marble statue stood in time of the Byzantine empire at the entrance to the harbour of Peiraeus, but when Francesco Morosini captured Athens in the Turco-Venetian war of 1687, he had it removed to Venice as a memorial of his victory. There he had it placed in front of the naval stores where it still stands. Despite a number of weighty investigations by professional runologists, the various readings of the two Varangian inscriptions, in looping snake-like bands on the left and the right shoulders of the lion, are completely without substance, being based on the ingenuity (or imagination) of the investigators. Sadly, the effects of decay, weather and vandalism (including pockmarks from bullets) mean the runic scrolls are so worn that no one can read them. (© *Esther Carré*)

20. Illumination (Biblioteca Nacional de España, Codex Matritensis Græcus, Vitr. 26-2, fol. 212 r.) from the Madrid manuscript of John Skylitzes' *Synopsis historiôn* illustrating Georgios Maniakes (Gr. Γεώγιος Μανιάκης, ON *Gyrgir*) landing in Sicily in the summer of 1038 and defeating the Sicilian Arabs,. Here, he was assisted by a crack unit of Varangians, some 500 strong and led by Haraldr Sigurðarson. According to the poetry of our Norwegian prince (written to his bride-to-be) and that of the skalds in his retinue, Haraldr and his men played a crucial rôle in establishing a beachhead for Maniakes and his expeditionary force. Sicily had been conquered by the Arabs in the ninth century, administrated by the Fatimid rulers who eventually took charge of Egypt, and the emperor Michael IV was determined to recover this jewel for Constantinople. Yet it would be the armies of Robert Guiscard and his brother Roger de Hauteville, Norman knights who had already carved out for themselves dominions in the Lombard and Byzantine territories in southern Italy, which would win the island. (*Cplakidas*)

21. The daughters of prince Yaroslav (the Wise) of Novgorod and Kiev (r. 1015–54) in a fresco from the monumental cathedral of Saint Sophia, Kiev, built during his reign. The third from the left is Elisaveta Yaroslavna (ON *Ellisif*), who would marry Haraldr Sigurðarson on his return to Norway. He had by her two daughters, Maria (who was to die on the day – and, indeed, at the very hour, or so it was said – when her father had fallen on the field of Stamford Bridge) and Ingigerðr (later queen of Denmark and Sweden). Elisaveta had first seen Haraldr when the young prince-in-exile arrived in Kiev with his own retinue and broad ambitions. Haraldr is celebrated in Old Norse–Icelandic tradition as a winning war leader and a skilled specialist of the art of skaldic stanzas. In a poem addressed to Elisaveta in Kiev he complains that it is impossible to impress her, in spite of

his stupendous military triumphs; each stanza details one of these triumphs but ends with the refrain 'Yet the gold-ring-goddess from / *Garðar* lets me dangle'. (*Magnus Manske*)

22. (Above) the longhouse ruin known as Hamar 1, and (below) the reconstruction of the same longhouse located at Brookpoint in Haroldswick on Unst. The remains of longhouses, with a single room about twelve metres or so long, can be found all over the parts of the world dominated by the Norse. However, on Unst there are the ruins of sixty longhouses, the highest density of rural Norse sites anywhere within and without Scandinavia. Built around wooden frames on simple stone footings, the four exterior walls are of dry stone construction with an earthen core. The long walls are curved slightly inwards and, at first glance, the turf roof looks like an upturned boat. The roof is supported on the inside by a double row of wooden posts. The Northlands were dark, icy and chilly with long, long winter nights; around the solstice, the sun barely rises at midday. This was the time when folk stayed in their longhouses and songs were sung and tales were told and retold, entertaining the listeners, and even Haraldr Sigurðarson himself. (*[above]* © *Esther Carré, [below]* © *Nic Fields*)

23. Bayeux tapestry (Musée de la Tapisserie de Bayeux), scene 57, depicting the death of Harold II of England at the battle of Hastings, 14 October 1066. The *titulus* reads, in Latin, HIC • HAROLD • REX • INTERFECTVS • EST (Here King Harold is slain). This scene is so celebrated that it has become one of the iconic images of British history and the 'arrow in the eye' story, for many of us, is synonymous with 1066 and all that. The battle, ultimately, was decided by an anonymous archer who, like the Aramaic bowman at Ramoth Gilead, loosed one un-aimed shot. With the battle raging a Norman arrow sailed out of the evening sky and pierced Harold's eye and sank through the eye socket into the base of his brain. Only three weeks earlier, at Stamford Bridge, Haraldr III of Norway was slain by an English arrow that pierced his throat. (*Myrabella*)

24. The Derwent river at Stamford Bridge, looking downstream towards the defunct railway viaduct (currently serving as part of a cycle path) from the stone bridge that carries the A166 from York. Completed in 1727 by the East Riding County Council to a design drawn up by William Etty of York, the road bridge replaced an earlier mediaeval bridge that had crossed the river some 150 yards upstream. There is, of course, some controversy as to whether or not a village and a bridge existed at the time of the battle, the bridge that later Anglo-Norman sources record being defended single-handed by a giant Norwegian like a latter-day Horatius to give his comrades time to muster. The site of the battle would have been to the east (left) of the river on the rising ground now known as the Battle Flats. The battle was brutal, long and final. It was the biggest engagement on English soil since

Brunanburh in 937, and the two armies fought the whole day in scorching sun. (*Krystian Hasterok*)

25. Two monuments to the battle of Stamford Bridge have been erected in and around Stamford Bridge, East Riding of Yorkshire. The first monument (above) is located in the village itself on Main Street (A166), and consists of a marble plaque set into a redbrick wall and a freestanding, two–piece granite memorial. The memorial's inscription (on the bronze plaque) reads: THE BATTLE OF STAMFORD BRIDGE WAS FOUGHT IN THIS NEIGHBOURHOOD ON SEPTEMBER 25TH, 1066. The second memorial (below) is located at the battlefield site at the end of Whiterose Drive, and consists of a memorial stone and plaque detailing the events and outcome of the battle. The plaque points out that: 'This viewpoint overlooks the site of the Battle of Stamford Bridge, fought by King Harold of England against the invading Norse army of Hardrada'. If the truth be told, the Northumbrians actually had much more in common with the 'invaders' than their 'defenders', who after all were southerners. (*[above] Egghead06, [below] Æthelred*)

26. Monument of Haraldr Sigurðarson *harðráði*, king of Norway, by the Norwegian sculpture Lars Utne (1862–1922). The monument was put up in 1905 in the eponymous named square Harald Hardrådes, Gamlebyen in Ósló, the city that the king is traditionally held to have founded. The bronze relief on the granite monolith depicts Haraldr in full panoply and on horseback at the head of his army, while the Norwegian inscription reads: HARALD SIGURDSSON HAARDRAADE NORGES KONGE OSLO'S GRUNDLÆGGER 1015 – 1066 (Haraldr Sigurðarson *harðráði*, king of Norway, founder of Ósló, 1015–1066). Oddly enough, at Stamford Bridge his black horse stumbled and threw him, and later that fateful day he fought on foot and without his renowned byrnie nicknamed *Emma*. Just as in every Norse saga, the fate of a man can turn on small moments and misjudgements. (*GAD*)

27. *Valkyrie*, a striking bronze sculpture of a warlike valkyrie, riding a plunging horse and wielding a short spear. Designed and cast by the Norwegian sculptor Stephan Abel Sinding (1846–1922) in Paris in 1908, it is now located in the Churchillparken at Kastellet in Copenhagen. In later myths (and they appear as such in Wagnerian opera) the valkyries were represented somewhat romantically as the beautiful warrior handmaidens of the god of battle, Óðinn, who was also, of course, the god of poetry, thus closely connecting the two activities. It is hardly an exaggeration to say that Haraldr Sigurðarson, albeit a Christian king, would have known and respected them as demons of slaughter and death that devoured the slain on the red field of battle. After all, blood, battle (and poetry) were his life, and in 1066 he launched his final adventure – one that was to bring the viking age to a historical close, in spirit if not in fact. (*Zserghei*)

A brief note on spelling and pronunciation

In this book, I have tried to be consistent in so far as avoiding Anglicization, so, for example, the use of þ, the thorn symbol, instead of the familiar 'th'. Wherever practical, I have used the spellings that are most authentic and widely accepted by Norse scholars.

The Old Norse and Old English languages used letters that are no longer found in modern English. The most commonly used ones were: Æ or lower case æ ('eye'), Ð or lower case ð (the 'th' in 'the'), Þ or lower case þ (the 'th' in 'thing'), and Ö or lower case ö (rounded form of 'ea' in 'earth'). The letter g is hard (as in 'go'), except before i, y, where it is like y (as in 'yeast'). The letter s is always surd. The letter j before a vowel is semi vocalic, as for example in Björn.

Note that all personal and place names are stressed on the first syllable. The acute accent serves to mark long vowels, as for example in Knútr. I have not dropped the –r ending denoting the nominative singular ending for personal and place names, thus Haraldr *not* Harald.

Nicknames are a common feature of Old Norse texts and these are given in the original throughout but when first encountered are translated when the meaning is clear and makes sense.

Introduction

S aga is an Old Norse word, which originally meant simply a story. But from its association with the kind of story that Northmen liked to spin on long winter nights, it came to mean a story of heroism and endeavour, and of adventure on the high sea and, of course, over and beyond it. This story is one such saga, but it is a different story, not the usual viking one of sea-going raids, long-distance trading, and peaceful settlement, of ruthless roving raiders leaping over the gunwales of a longship, and tenacious travelling traders with sharp swords on their left hips. This story is about one particular man, one of the last great Norse warrior kings, the 'thunderbolt of the north', as the near-contemporary Adam of Bremen called him.[1]

He was Haraldr Sigurðarson, to give his name the proper spelling. He was not only one of the last but one of the most complex and remarkable warrior kings of Norway who has gone down in history under his most lasting nickname, one that has become commonly known – *harðráði*. What richness of adventure that name recalls, a name that will be spoken of as long as men have tongues to speak. Icelandic chroniclers were the first to dub Haraldr, without a hint of irony, *harðráði* (anglicized to Hardrada), which is difficult to translate into English but 'hard-ruler' is as near as we can get – in truth, a poor translation for want of a better. However, the nickname is not applied to him in any contemporary poetry that we know, nor even in historical prose, but, as Gabriel Turville-Petre explains, 'Norwegians and Icelanders of a much later age developed the suitable nickname *harðráði* … [which] seems to creep into chapter-headings and regnal lists probably during the latter half of the thirteenth century'.[2] Even so, there seems little doubt that the living Haraldr had been a hard, ruthless, unforgiving, egotistical, impious, absolute ruler, a king who 'surpassed all the madness of tyrants in his savage wildness' is how Adam of Bremen described him.[3] As we shall learn in due course, this Norwegian king was certainly tyrannical; he was *harðráði*.

Among Scandinavian warriors, Norwegian, Swedish, Danish or Icelandic, Haraldr Sigurðarson (posthumously called *harðráði*), as we have just pointed out, enjoyed a prestige second to none. In Haraldr's lifetime there was another notable contender for this martial crown, namely Rodrigo Díaz de Vivar (d. 1099), better remembered as *El Cid* (from the Arabic *Sayyi*, 'My Lord'). A mediaeval outlaw like Haraldr, Rodrigo too made a great success of his banishment, and few have matched them in posthumous literary fame. In 1637, for instance, Rodrigo Díaz had been brought back to life as Don Rodrigue, the hero of Pierre Corneille's high-minded tragedy *Le Cid*. Corneille re-imagined the mercenary warlord as a man prepared to sacrifice everything – love, happiness, and life itself – to satisfy the dictates of honour. The pen of Corneille reinvents Rodrigo as the exiled aristocrat of unimpeachable integrity and unflinching pride.

Rodrigo and the protagonist of our story, Haraldr, had much in common. No strangers to warfare and want, they were indeed perfect examples of *chevaliers sans peur*, but certainly not of *sans reproche*. By dint of superiority in battle and an instinct to advance, such men wind up being a warlord or even a king. They were true sons of their epoch. Courageous men, they were rash and short sighted, caring more for their own than their kingdom's honour.

What follows is a mere cross-section of a long, violent career, lived out by a flawed man, on a grand scale, a career that encompassed everything from the forlornness and uncertainties of exile to the heights of power and glory. Haraldr Sigurðarson was no stranger to the worst in man. War was his life; he lived with a sword in one hand, a firebrand in the other. Though war is still basically an unsavoury and dangerous, dehumanizing activity, this story, we shall discover, is of the type of warrior that one does not ordinarily encounter in this world. Haraldr's driving ambition was different from that of other men by dint of its sheer scope and magnitude. However, as an account of Haraldr's warrior career, this book is no more than a sketch meagre and inadequate, primarily addressed to readers who seek a brief biographical introduction to the life of an unfamiliar subject. Please understand too that I am merely repeating what I have read.

Chapter 1

War

To most people the viking age[1] is a period of history in which savage barbarians stormed out of the sub-Arctic wastes of uncivilized Scandinavia and spread throughout the Christian world in search of battle and booty. These savage barbarians were the vikings, who, when they had passed and taken the things they needed – even having their wicked way with the local virtuous maidens and leaving them in the lurch – left everything deader than the roots of any grass Attila's horses' hooves had ever scoured. God created and the vikings unmade. Or leastways so it may have seemed to the Christian commentators who first set up a stereotype, which survives to this day, in the contrast between the Nordic peoples as vikings, and so-called Christian Europe. At the end of this period it was expressed by Adam of Bremen (*fl.* 1075), for whom it was an inherent missionary assumption. Baptized northerners who respected the authority of the archbishop of Hamburg-Bremen, Adam's immediate boss, were as good as, or even better than anyone else for, he continues, 'having laid aside their natural savagery' the converts may say 'we believe that we will see the good things of the Lord in the land of the living'.[2]

Dispelling myths?

Like most things, human history is subject to fashion. As a reaction against the bad old predatory, piratical pigeonholing of the vikings, there has been a scholarly attempt to emphasize the non-violent aspects of their lives. In this way, there has been debate over the motives of the vikings and the nature of their impact upon western Europe, a scholastic tendency to play down the popular portrayal of violent men who steal what they will and rape who they will in favour of pioneering men in pursuit of profitable trading and peaceful settlement. Archaeology in such towns as York (ON *Jórvík*) and Dublin (ON *Dubh-linn*) has shown the truth in this, but one cannot ignore contemporary chronicle accounts of mayhem and violence. The fact that initial viking clashes pitted pagans against Christians influenced hostile western accounts. Immediate gain such as the acquisition of monastic wealth was one motive, and profit from blackmail was another.

To supposedly civilized, Christian lands the vikings brought nothing but violence and war, supposedly swarming out of the north like wolf packs, devouring everything in their path. This posture is particularly prevalent in the clerical accounts of viking raids, which give no real recognition of the motivation for the coming of the Northmen and their wreaking bloody havoc among the God-fearing Christians. Tens of men, sometimes well over a hundred, would suddenly appear out of nowhere, screaming, brandishing their swords and axes and generally sowing terror before settling down to a leisurely process of searching for treasure, collecting slaves, torture and destruction. However, we should not view this viking activity as anti-Christian in nature. On the contrary, monasteries, churches and their associated settlements provided soft targets as poorly defended and often isolated coastal 'honey-pots', housing portable rich metalwork in the form of eucharistic vessels and reliquaries and providing a ready supply of slaves of all ages and sexes (it is often forgotten that viking-age Scandinavia was at least partly a slave-based economy). Moreover, in moments of danger, many locals took their valuables to monasteries to hide them. After all, monasteries were often better heeled than many other communities, owning not only treasures but vast tracts of land too. The activities of small, savage war bands, and larger-scale conquest and settlement, are obviously very different matters. But Anglo-Saxon and Frankish annalists revile Norwegian raiders and Danish armies in exactly the same terms: they are all unspeakably evil heathen murderers, demons visible, a scourge sent by God.

As far as it goes, this is an appropriate assessment, for the repeated focus on such attacks should warn us against too peaceful an interpretation of the vikings. At the end of the day, the fact remains that violence, raiding, and martial prowess were prominent aspects in Scandinavian culture. Pagan ideology stressed the virtues of the masculine warrior and fearlessness in the face of battle. Being a warrior, after all, one had to be ready to die. Norse myth imagined the most virtuous men would enjoy an afterlife in Valhöll (called Valhalla by the Victorians), where they had the pleasure of killing each other anew every day until the end of the world.

Fighting farmers

The conduct of war in the viking age never ceases to exert a fascination, yet attitudes to war itself have change. Nowadays, the most terrible and adult of games, war, is regarded as an exceptional and undesirable event in the course of daily life, but in the viking age played a prominent, if not to say dominant, rôle in the pattern of everyday existence. Brute force was considered the legitimate way of resolving almost any dispute at all levels of Norse society.

With regards to Norse society, two kinds of training are in question: how a man learned to use weapons; and how men learned to fight in groups. The former lay almost exclusively beyond the scope of the military system. Men who were skilled in arms had been brought up using weapons and, in the Scandinavian tradition at least, to fight on shipboard as well as on foot, from their youth. As well as archaeology, the Old Norse sagas provide us with many details concerning viking-age warfare.

When the Northmen settled in northern England says the *Anglo-Saxon Chronicle* entry for 876, 'Healfdene [Hálfdan] divided up the land of the Northumbrians and they set about ploughing and cultivating it'.[3] Norse warriors became instant farmers. Indeed, the sagas tell us that farmers carried their weapons as they worked their fields. *Brennu-Njáls saga* says that one morning Höskuldr Þrainsson went out to work his field at his farm at Ossabær. He picked up his seed bag in one hand and his sword in the other and went out to sow the seeds. Alas, his sword proved insufficient protection against the five men who waited to ambush him.[4] The beloved foster-son of Njáll Þorgeirsson, Höskuldr was an innocent and non-violent man, not like the five killers who cut him down in cold blood, one of whom was Skarphéðinn Njálsson, the eldest son of Njáll. Nonetheless, even passive Northmen were constantly prepared to use their weapons, and kept them close at hand. *Hávamál*, a viking-age poem of commonsense advice, tells us never to be more than one footstep away from our weapon, no matter where or when.[5] Men even slept with their weapons hung on the wall next to the bed, ready for instant use should they be attacked in the dead of night, as we know from *Beowulf* and the Icelandic sagas.

Thus, in Norse society the societal structure made no distinction between martial and civilian life. All free Northmen had the right to own and carry weapons and, though not all of them were warriors, professional or amateur, they were familiar with their use and were expected to join in battle when necessary. Weapons were very much a part of everyday life in the viking age. Men were trained in warfare, though not trained in any meaningful sense of the word as we understand it, but who had learned their military skills in childhood and adolescence as a part of their total cultural environment. However, even if warlike virtues constituted the foundation of the morality and code of values, not all Norse men were natural born killers. Take, for instance, the beardless hero of *Brennu-Njáls saga*, Njáll Þorgeirsson, who never kills, never fights, and is only once shown to carry a weapon, a rather mundane short axe.[6] His neighbour and good friend Gunnarr Hámundarson, on the other hand, is the very model of the blond, blue-eyed viking, described chiefly in terms of his supreme and matchless physical and martial skills.[7] His two battles against vikings prove him to be the greatest of Icelandic warriors.[8] Undoubtedly, there were Northmen like Njáll and others like Gunnarr. Yet the majority of them would have been the types sandwiched between the two poles of peacemaker and bloodtaker.

Military power relies on the threat and enactment of warfare. Warfare ranges in intensity and scale in chiefdoms from raids to territorial conquest. At the lowest level a local chieftain would collect his own family members and his farm labourers, and call on those of his relatives and clients. As almost everywhere else in the pre-modern world, families were the social unit and the emotion centre. More so in the Norse world, where there was a relative underdevelopment of alternative social groups, namely the state, churches, cities and lordships that shared people with families elsewhere. Military organization, therefore, was essentially domestic in character and, as mentioned previously, all economic life rested on farming supplemented by fishing, fowling and hunting, with the household being the basic unit of production.

Clearly, Norse society was by and large militarized, causing military action and civil life to be closely intertwined, and warrior farmers, *bœndr* (sg. *bóndi*), would form a posse and take rations with them, from household stores, for the two or three days that the raid might last. Collectively, they might make one or two such raids per season, so it would not impose a great strain on farming manpower or food stocks. These would have been summer raids, between seedtime and harvest, sporadic and limited in size. Because all free men had the right to bear arms, it is important to understand that women too held an active position within this militarized society, more of which later.

It was because the sea was well and truly in their blood that to go *í víkingu* overseas was the real test of a Norse warrior's manhood. They knew they were sentencing themselves to a very harsh, unforgiving environment, but, though they had no romantic illusions, they knew there would be adventure of a kind – bullying winds, blistering sun, violent storm, fog, or the spoil to be taken in the settlements and monasteries in which they raided. In the mind of Northmen, raiding was very distinct from theft. Theft was abhorrent, one of the few acts that would condemn a man to a place of torment after his death. On the other hand, daylight raiding was an honourable challenge to a fight, with the victor retaining all of the spoils. A story from *Egils saga Skallagrímssonar* illustrates this distinction. While raiding a coastal farmstead, Egill Skallagrímsson and his men were captured by the farmer and his family, who bound all of the raiders. In the night that followed, Egill was able to slip his bonds. He and his men grabbed their captor's treasure and headed back to the ship. But along the way, Egill shamefully realized he was acting like a thief, saying, 'This is a poor sort of expedition, it's not warrior-like. We've stolen the farmer's property and he doesn't know it. We mustn't let a shameful thing like that happen.' So, Egill returned to his captor's house, set it ablaze, and killed the occupants as they tried to escape the fire. He then returned to the ship with the treasure, this time as a hero. Because he had fought and won the battle, he could justly claim the booty.[9] Raiding increased a man's stature in Norse society. A successful raider returned home with riches and renown, the two most important qualities needed to climb the social ladder.

Raiding was often a part-time occupation. A story from *Orkneyinga saga* describes the habits of Sveinn Ásleifarson. In the spring, he oversaw the planting of grain on his farm at Gáreksey. When the task was done, he went off raiding in the Hebrides and Ireland, but he was back to the farm in time to take in the hay and the grain in mid-summer. Then he went off raiding again until the arrival of winter.[10] One has the sense that Norse raiders also conducted legitimate trade while on their voyages. While Egill and Þórólfr were raiding in Kúrland on the Baltic one summer, they halted their raids, called a two-week truce, and began trading with their former victims. Once the truce was up, the viking brothers returned to attacking and plundering, raiding the places that seemed most attractive. That was what vikings did. The size of the raiding parties varied. Egill and Þórólfr, for instance, led separate groups of twelve men each from their shared longship.[11] A larger party is described in *Njáls-Brennu saga*. Gunnarr Hámundarson and Hallvarðr the White began their raiding party with two ships, one with forty oars, and one with sixty. At the end of the summer, they returned from their raids gorged with loot and with ten ships.[12]

With a regional or national levy (ON *leiðangr*, 'levying ships for war'), that is a specially mustered host led by a king (whether local or national) in person, the scale of ambition shifts from the small and limited to the big and (relatively) unlimited. With this size of force it is possible to fight pitched battles – if that is the word – and pillage whole regions rather than merely hamlets and homesteads, or at least threaten such action unless a geld is paid. This point is crucial in viking-age Scandinavia, where the character and goals of the warfare fundamentally changes from raiding and small-scale feuding aimed at settling scores and acquiring wealth to economically destructive campaigns motivated by territorial conquest. In the light of this, for example, it has been suggested that the Danish warship Skuldelev 5 (see Chapter 5) has been interpreted as a *leiðangr* ship on the basis it had been repeatedly repaired and had kept afloat after it was actually seaworthy. According to this interpretation, the ship was much more likely to be a *leiðangr* ship than the personal vessel of a chieftain or other high-status individual.[13]

It must be stressed, however, that little is known of the regional or national system of organization during the viking age, though it was usual in the later mediaeval period. This practice in Norway is mentioned in skaldic poems as early as the tenth century, though Judith Jesch counsels some caution.[14] Niels Lund, however, argues that even the armies of Sveinn I Haraldsson *tjúguskegg* (Forkbeard) and Knútr Sveinsson that conquered England in 1013 and 1016 respectively were simply old fashioned raiding armies on a large scale, rather than national levies. As opposed to a systematic levy or *leiðangr*, Lund continues, our Danish dynasts led a *lið*, 'a private military body which served a king or anybody who could afford it', small in size (occupying at most a few ships) but which could combine with other such groups to create the great armies occasionally seen in historic sources.[15] It has been proposed, however, that the *leiðangr* was the brainchild of Haraldr Sigurðarson, to which Kelly DeVries adds an observation of particular relevance to a topic we will be discussing later, namely Haraldr's invasion of England in 1066. DeVries suggests that 'it seems ludicrous to believe that someone like Harald Hardrada (*sic*), who had served in what was probably the most organized army in the world at the time, the Byzantine army, would abandon such a logical notion once he had returned to Scandinavia'.[16] This is possible. On the one hand, the armies of Sveinn and Knútr were multifarious coalitions of rapacious warlords, not instruments of a state. On the other hand, by the end of his reign Haraldr had successfully applied military force both to chastise his subjects and to intimidate his neighbours: twenty years of strenuous warfare had resulted in what can be recognized as a viable Norwegian kingdom.

All the same, whichever way we look at it, the army of Haraldr was not a professional standing army in one important respect. It did not train regularly as an army, that is to say, in large groups. It thus had no opportunity to practise what is known today as close order drill: marching in formation, changing formation, massed weapons tactics and so forth. Experience in battle counted as the only training any Norse army received in such actions. Drill formed, for armies that practised it – and outside of Byzantium drill was largely unknown in Europe between the breakup of the West Roman Empire and the late sixteenth century – the basis of tactical manoeuvre, discipline and unit cohesion, especially for infantry, and the workings of the field chain of command. Of course, the small size of Norse armies made command control easier, with individual leaders having a greater effect in a small army.

The younger the better

Whether the goal was slaughter or settlement, the Norse warrior was a very adaptable individual. He had the advantages of a wide range of practical skills learned from his rural background at home in small isolated hunting, farming and fishing communities – most Norse populations lived within one day's walk of the sea, so rowing and sailing brought farms into neighbourhoods. Hunting not only honed his skills with bow and spear, but also encouraged quick thinking and reflexes. He possessed sufficient basic ship-handling skills or familiarity with ships and the sea to enable him to offer unrivalled abilities as a seaman. He had a familiarity with domestic animals that allowed him to handle horses for riding or for pack transport and to slaughter cows, sheep or even horses for food. He could quickly throw up palisaded earthworks for protection, spades proving as crucial as spears. He had been trained to arms since boyhood, it being better to learn war early from friends and family, than late from foes. He was thus equipped with the necessary fighting skills and in most cases these had already been honed over a number of years of active service raiding overseas. It seems that the age at which a youth was expected to go campaigning was about fifteen, a male being considered to be an adult after he had passed fifteen winters. Certainly, in Norway, from the beginning of the eleventh century onwards, fifteen was the age of majority.

The excavations at Repton, South Derbyshire, conducted by Martin Biddle and Birthe Kjølbye-Biddle have revealed the remains of at least 249 men of a 'massively robust non-local population type, parallels for which can be found in Scandinavia' who were buried in a mass grave and showed almost no signs of a violent death. The burial site is close to a viking encampment, a *wintersetl*, constructed during the winter of 873/4. These vikings were members of the *mycel hæþen here*, 'great heathen army', which had built for themselves a small defended D-shaped enclosure (1.46 ha/3.65 acres) backing on the river Trent, which used the local monastic church (dedicated to Saint Wystan, a Mercian *æðeling* murdered in 849 in an intra-dynastic revolt) as a gatehouse through a double ditch and earth rampart. Forensic study has revealed that these bodies consisted mostly of 'non-local' males aged between fifteen and forty-five, who were almost certainly viking warriors buried in company with an important leader. Only one in five of the interred at Repton were women, probably locals. Further investigations uncovered many grave goods at the site, including axes, knives, a sword, ringed pins, and five dated (earliest 872, latest 874) silver pennies, all of which were of Norse origin.

As for that leader, he was laid to rest in a central furnished burial, which Biddle and Kjølbye-Biddle believe is that of Ívarr *inn beinlausi* (the Boneless). The absence of trauma wounds suggests that the interred had died from some kind of contagious disease. A permanent camp brought its own inevitable trials – in hot weather, dust and flies, and in winter, as may have been the case at Repton that winter, mud and misery. It should be pointed out, however, that a human body has large areas of soft tissue, from the groin to the lower ribs, in which serious and ultimately fatal damage can be inflicted. Such damage would, of course, be undetectable on the skeleton, our only present source of evidence for war wounds.

Indeed, one of the interred warriors (Grave 511) seems to have met a very violent death, presumably in battle and possibly with the Anglian locals. It appears that he had been killed by the thrust of a sharp implement through the eye, which had penetrated the orbital socket and gone into the brain, presumably caused by a sword point or spearhead finding a vulnerable spot on the head, which was unprotected by the helmet. And that is not all. For before or after death, this unfortunate warrior, who was aged between thirty-five and forty-five and stood 1.81 metres tall, had also received several cuts to the arm, and a great slashing blow to the top of his left femur, which would also have removed his genitals. Cuts to the lower vertebrae, inflicted from the stomach cavity, also imply he was disembowelled. He had been buried wearing a hammer of Þórr around his neck – a direct reference to the god – and with charms in the form of a boar's tusk and a jackdaw's leg.[17] Obviously, they had not helped him.

Nonetheless, fighting may often have been the business of rather older men than we might expect in the light of modern experience, more so if we consider the quotidian hazards of viking-age life: famine or dearth at least once a lifetime, a lifetime lasting some forty years for men (also for women though those who got past thirty would outlive men), some dreadful winters, many drownings at sea and deaths in battle.

By way of comparison, modern day statistics demand our attention. Assuming killed-in-action figures accurately represent age-groups, the average age of the United States infantryman (MOS [Military Occupational Speciality] 11b) fighting in Vietnam was twenty-two (nineteen is just an urban myth). British infantrymen in the Falklands/Malvinas War were of a similar age, twenty-three on average. Today's British infantryman is even younger: he has an average age of twenty. In fact, the United Kingdom was the only nation state in the European Union (pre-Brexit) and currently the only United Nation Security Council Permanent Member to recruit from age sixteen into the armed forces. The forces prefer young recruits aged between seventeen and twenty-six – in 2010, 29.8 per cent of recruits were aged under eighteen.[18] This was not only because they are fitter, but also because they are more biddable and prepared to take risks. Many are unemployable. They need under-educated teenagers. You can slap them around for a few months in basic training, break them down and build them anew as infantrymen, then hand them a gun and say go kill, and most of them, having forgotten their previous scale of values, will do it. You and I are far too urbane, too upstanding, too resentful – and, more to the point, too old – to go for this kind of thing any longer. But try hard to remember the typical seventeen-year-old in your high school playground and you will start to understand why adolescent males opt to join the army. It takes all kinds of people to make a world; fewer to make an army.

Returning to the Falklands/Malvinas, the youngest infantrymen fighting there were seventeen years old, two of whom, serving with the 3rd Battalion the Parachute Regiment, were killed in the brutal, bloody fourteen-hour encounter on the 700-metre high Mount Longdon (11–12 June 1982). This was a battle that turned out to be a classic infantry engagement even down to face-to-face fighting at ten metres or less, with frenzied, brutal, hand-to-hand combat necessitating the use of bayonets, rifle butts and sharpened entrenching tools. The 3rd Battalion the Parachute Regiment had the reputation of being a crack unit and it is noteworthy that the average age of the twenty-two paras killed during the battle of Mount

Longdon was just over twenty-two, the oldest was twenty-nine, and included seven teenagers, two of whom were the aforementioned seventeen-year-olds. It is also noteworthy that during the Falklands/Malvinas War, a relatively short war over a seemingly insignificant bit of inhospitable real-estate in the South Atlantic (unless one has experienced what it is to live outdoors in extremely cold temperatures, it is difficult to imagine just how horrendous it must have been), the rôle of infantryman was still fulfilled by foxholes, foot-slogging and fixing bayonets. And say what you will, even those of you who believe the real effectiveness of cold steel is open to doubt, combat for the battle-clad plain infantryman, grunt, jarhead, very much remains an up close and personal business.

Granted, modern warfare has become very complex, especially during the last century. Wars are won not by a simple series of battles won, but by a complex interrelationship among military victory, economic pressures, logistic manoeuvring, access to the enemy's information, political postures – dozens, literally dozens of factors. At a more mundane level, however, a modern infantryman's life still depends on the rifle – lugging it around twenty-four-seven, eating and sleeping with it, cleaning it incessantly and keeping ammunition close to hand. He would argue that the bayonet spoils the balance of the rifle and besides nobody expects ever to be in a situation where he would have to fix his bayonet and charge. Yet, in spite of everything, for the infantryman warfare still remains a situation in which there is dirt everywhere, exposure to the elements, hard labour, bad food, and the real possibility of people shooting at you. As any veteran will tell you, gentle reader, there is nothing as important in a battle as having a trusty, *tested* blade. The bayonet should feel like a partner, not a burden. I can go on but I think the point has been made.

In fact, the bayonet features prominently in Joanna Bourke's critique of modern militarism. For Bourke, the bayonet was an ideological means of infusing aggression into the soldiers in order to make them more willing ultimately to kill or be killed: as one Vietnam veteran noted to her, it was 'a charm to ward off fear'.[19] As a partisan of collective determination, Colonel Ardent du Picq plausibly claimed that no force ever withstood a bayonet charge.[20] This is not a matter of bovine stupidity, for victory could be won by plunging into the fray with the bayonet, or at least by the fear of it. As Napoléon once wrote, 'The bayonet has always been the weapon of the brave and the chief tool of victory', and its retention in more recent times should not be seen as an anachronism. The bullet and bayonet belong to the same parent, and certainly during the Falklands/Malvinas War the rifle was the principal weapon of the individual infantry soldier.[21] But unlike the rifle, the bayonet was a silent weapon with the power of direct, face-to-face killing. British infantrymen carried the L1A4 SLR short sword bayonet, with a blade length of 203 millimetres, and a number of them got to use the points of their bayonets for real. Before their assault on Mount Longdon on the night of 11/12 June, B Company 3rd Battalion the Parachute Regiment was ordered to fix bayonets by their company sergeant major on their line of departure at the base of the mountain.[22] The steel-winking eyes of the fixed bayonets that night certainly gave the vivid impression that the paras meant business. But I digress.

Team spirit

Besides adaptability, another key factor was flexibility. Viking war bands normally operated separately, but for big expeditions they were quite prepared to serve together. Such joint operations usually worked satisfactorily, although we can imagine with a certain amount of chauvinistic niggling. Thus, a viking army would consist of a series of smaller war bands each commanded by its own independent leader. Concerning the strength of these war bands, an investigation of our written sources, literary or otherwise, quickly demonstrates that the number of warriors in any one war band is expressed quite rarely in specific numbers. In such raiding warfare, war bands will have been small, mobile affairs: leaders and their followers, numbered probably only in the hundreds, and perhaps with arms and armour stripped to the barest essentials.

Whatever their size, these war bands were the building blocks for large-scale armies. As such, they were probably bound together by oaths of fellowship, and certainly pledged by oath to follow their leader. The evidence for these small war bands, which are variously called 'fellowships' or brotherhoods', can be found in contemporary annals and on rune stones. Danish runic inscriptions at Hedeby, Århus, and Sjörup record that those commemorated were *félagi*, or fellows, of those who raised and inscribed the stones.[23] In 861 the *Annales Bertiniani*, written by Prudentius bishop of Troyes and covering the period 830–82 in Carolingian Frankia, records that the vikings under Weland split up to take winter quarters '*secundum suas sodalitates*',[24] as if they had been an union of brotherhoods associated for the expedition. These independent war bands were, in turn, gathered into a larger army by means of their individual leaders being pledged by oath to follow more authoritative commanders or kings.[25] War bands and the leaders who raised them would come and go, with new bands joining successful armies. Here we can include the *mycel hæþen here*, 'great heathen army', which terrorized the Anglo-Saxon kingdoms from the mid-eight-sixties to the late eight-seventies.

Such roaming armies survived for years, winter and summer, living off enemy territory until the leaders' demands were satisfied, or scaled down, or negated by defeat. They gained or lost men based on their reputation, their ability to reward, and their supply of plunder. Nonetheless, they seldom disintegrated even after repeated defeats in battle; they included women, children, slaves, and livestock;

they were led by groups of chiefs, these armies being a combination of household warriors and clients obedient to senior chiefs, whether earls or kings, and until the eleventh century they were held together by the distribution of rewards in the form of movable wealth, most notably gold and silver rings and armlets, rather than by payment of regular wages. To cite only a single example of this, when the West Saxon force led by the *æðeling* Edward stormed the fortified camp at Benfleet (OE *Beamfleote*) of the viking leader Hæsten, it not only captured his ships, livestock and booty, but also the women and children of his followers. This included Hæsten's own wife and sons. All were carried off to London and Rochester.[26]

This manifest ability to maintain armies in the field for years at a time was one of the most singular features of viking warfare. When we pause to consider that warfare in this period was almost exclusively seasonal, it becomes apparent that this was so in part because even the most powerful rulers could command only a finite length of military service from their followers, but more because of the logistical constraints of supplying armies on campaign in hostile territory over any length of time, especially over winter.

Armed and dangerous

Weapons dictate tactics, and in this respect there is nothing to suggest that Northmen were particularly innovative in tactical matters, and their battlefield effectiveness seems out of proportion with their rather simple arsenal – it is not to any significant superiority in weapons that we should look for the secrets of their success. The Norse warrior's equipment was virtually the same right across Europe in our period of study, and between any two regions weapons usually differed only in details of design and quality (though some areas seem to show evidence of a traditional attachment to one weapon or another). Norse weapons were fairly simple, and except for the sword most could also be used in everyday life at home on the farm – an axe for cutting wood, spears and bows for hunting, and a single edged knife carried as a useful tool for performing a multitude of household, agricultural and artisan tasks. Only the sword was developed solely as a lethal weapon. So, each in turn.

The sword

The spear (ON *spjót*), unlike the sword (ON *svaerð*), has never held the same esteem nor has it been given names (the one notable exception being *Selshemnaren*, Seal's Avenger) or magical properties as bestowed onto the sword by the Northmen. Some were even said to have been made and presented to man by the gods. Take, for instance, Týrfing (ON *Týrfingr*), the wondrous dwarf-forged, albeit thrice-cursed, sword of Angantýr that 'never could be barred without killing a man, and with warm blood it would always be sheathed'.[27] This terrible sword could cut through anything, including iron and rock, but presumably not the magical shirt of Örvar-Oddr, more of which later. It was the dwarfs Dvalin and Durinn who made Týrfing at the command of Angantýr who held them prisoner. They cursed the sword before the king took it away. Týrfing was to bring bloody havoc to the king's kin, killing three of his descendents before it lost its magic powers.

In the words of an Englishman who was a rather curious blend of the mystic and the athlete, of the explorer and the linguist, of the antiquarian and the scholar, Sir Richard Burton:

> The history of the sword is the history of humanity... He, she, or it – for the gender of the Sword varies – has been worshipped with priestly sacrifices as a present god... Uniformly and persistently personal, the Sword became no longer an abstraction but a Personage, endowed with human as well as superhuman qualities. He was a sentient being who spoke, and sang, and joyed, and grieved. Identified with his wearer he was an object of affection, and was pompously named as a well-beloved son and heir. To surrender the Sword was submission; to break the Sword was degradation. To kiss the Sword was... the highest form of oath and homage... The Sword was the symbol of justice and of martyrdom, and accompanied the wearer to the tomb as well as to the feast and the fight.[28]

However that may be, in *Fóstbrœðra saga* it is written that in saga-age Iceland very few men were armed with swords.[29] A sword might be the most expensive item that a man owned. The one sword whose value is given in the Old Norse sagas (given by king Hákon Haraldsson *góði* to Höskuldr) was said to be worth a 'half a mark of gold'.[30] In saga-age Iceland, that represented the value of sixteen milk-cows, a very substantial sum. We have one saga episode that illustrates the value of a viking-age sword. Þuríðr Ólafsdóttir was married to a Norwegian scoundrel by the name of Geirmundr *gnýr* (Thunderer). He tried to sneak out of the marriage by sailing away from Iceland without her and their infant daughter, taking with him all his portable wealth. She turned the tables on him by taking his prized possession, his sword *Fótbítr* (Foot- or Leg-biter). She gave *Fótbítr* to her kinsmen Bollli Þorleiksson, the father of Bollli Bollason.[31]

Swords were heirlooms. The Persian traveller and geographer Ahmad ibn Rusta (*fl.* 900) visited the Rus' and described how, when a boy child was born, it was the custom for its father to present the child with a sword, saying something to the effect of: 'I leave you no inheritance. All you possess is what you can gain with this sword'.[32] With a mystic regard for their straight, broad-bladed, often beautifully ornamented swords, the Norse gave them names. In this warrior culture, therefore, a well-made sword was more than a tool – it was a most prized possession, almost an object of veneration, and could be passed down from father to son and used for generations. We are all familiar with, even if it is just through Wagner's version of this hero from his Ring cycle of operas, Siegfried, or Sigurðr *Fáfnisbana* to give him his Old Norse name, the most famous Germanic hero, whose most renowned and most oft-referred feat of valour was the slaying of the dragon Fáfnir.[33] Sigurðr has his sword forged from his father's old broken sword, and likewise the sword *Grásiða* (Grey-sides), which plays a major rôle in *Gísla saga Súrssonar*, is broken and repaired.[34]

Fascinating in our own era, a named sword resonates. Take, for instance, the mighty sword of king Hákon Haraldsson *góði* (the Good) given to him at his departure from England for Norway by his foster father, the Anglo-Saxon king Æthelstan (r. 925–39), a Christian. Known as Quern-biter (ON *Kvenbítr*), it was the sword with which Hákon is said to have cut a millstone in two.[35] At the battle of Fitjar the king, fighting against the champion Eyvindr *skreyjaof*, is said to have 'split him in two in the middle with his sword, through the byrnie, so that he fell in halves to either side'.[36]

Other sword names that show up in the sagas include: Gísli's aforementioned sword *Grásiða*, borrowed from a slave, broken in a duel, and then refashioned into a spearhead by smithy-sorcerer; *Jarlsnautr* (Gift of the earl); Steinar's sword *Skrýmr* (Boaster); Egill's two swords *Naðr* (Viper) and *Dragvandil* (Draw-wand, as in a wand for slicing);[37] Þórólfr's sword *Langr* (Long); Bersi's sword *Hvítingr* (White One), where 'white' often meant shining; Kári's sword *Fjörsváfnir* (Life-taker); Skeggi's sword *Gunnlogi* (Battle-flame).[38]

Some swords are mentioned in multiple sagas, spanning centuries. The sword *Sköfnungr* (Shinbone?) first appears in a *fornaldarsögur* set in the sixth century.[39] The saga ends with king Hrólfr *kraki* of Denmark dying in a battle and being buried with his sword *Sköfnungr*. It was renowned for supernatural sharpness and hardness, as well as for being imbued with the spirits of the king's twelve faithful berserker bodyguards who fell with him. Moreover, the sword, whose nature was dark, was not to be drawn in the presence of women, and that the sun must not be allowed to shine on its hilt. It is also said that any wound made by *Sköfnungr* 'will not heal unless rubbed with the healing stone which accompanies it'.[40] Skeggi Bjarnarson, the son of an early settler in Iceland, apparently broke into the Hrólf's burial mound in Denmark and took the sword *Sköfnungr*.[41] Later, Skeggi returned to Iceland with the legendary sword, sometime in the tenth century. Next we learn that Kormákr tried to borrow *Sköfnungr* from Skeggi for a duel.[42] By the beginning of the next century, *Sköfnungr* was in the hands of Eiðr, Skeggi's son.[43] By this time, Eiðr was an old man. His kinsman, Þorkell Eyjólfsson, asked to borrow *Sköfnungr* to avenge the death of Eiðr's son. The sword was still in

Þorkell's hands as he was transporting timber on a ship in Breiðafjörðr around the year 1026. A squall capsized the ship, and all aboard was lost beneath the waves.[44] *Sköfnungr* washed up on an island in the fjord. Þorkell's son Gellir came into possession of the sword, and as an old man, Gellir travelled abroad: to Norway, to Rome (on a pilgrimage), and then to Denmark, where he died and was buried as a Christian. Gellir had the sword with him, and it is said that 'the sword was never recovered after that'.[45]

Another named sword was *Brynjubítr* (Byrnie-biter), so named because it was apparently accomplished at biting through ring mail, which had been brought to Iceland from Constantinople before the end of twelfth century, in all probability in 1195 or 1196, by a person known as Sigurðr Oddsson *grikkr* (the Greek).[46] Later in his life this Icelander had participated in dramatic local events, by which time he had already acquired his nickname. Sigurðr's most notable achievement in the civil wars of the Sturlungs – one of the five great families locked in a struggle for power that finally led to the collapse of the Icelandic commonwealth – had been to save a wealthy farmer by herding him into a church 'and then he stood before the church and proclaimed that he would defend it, as long as he was able to stand'.[47] While not of the highest rank in Iceland, Sigurðr was evidently remembered as a valiant man and a defender of Christian values. Although the Varangian Guard is not mentioned in connection with Sigurðr, he had clearly served in Constantinople (under either the last two Komnenoi or Isaakos II Angelos) in some way and had brought home a fine Byzantine sword as proof.

For those who do not acknowledge that the Old Norse sagas have any historical significance, Androshchuk refers to a historical sword (amongst others) as once belonging to Offa (r. 757–96) mentioned in the will of Æthelstan *ædeling*, son of Æthelred II (r. 978–1016). Offa's 250-year-old sword (whether it was indeed his sword is of course not possible to establish, but that is what was believed) was bequeathed to Æthelstan's brother, who was soon to become king of England himself.[48]

The Icelander Bolli Bollason carried his father's sword, *Fótbítr* and used it to avenge his father's death. This was a particularly fancy sword, 'now inlaid with gold at the top and shank, and gold bands wound about its hilt',[49] though we are told that when *Fótbítr* was in the possession of Geirmundr *gnýr* it had 'a hilt of walrus ivory… no silver overlay',[50] which suggests Bolli had dandified it, most probably when he was in Constantinople serving with the Varangian Guard. Archaeological evidence also supports this kind of long and continued use of sword blades. One such example is a blade made during the migration era, centuries before the viking age, which had been fitted with an eleventh-century cross guard. This evidence suggests that sword blades several centuries old continued to be maintained and used.

Other swords came from foreign lands. About Hákon Haraldsson *góði* (d. 960), the illegitimate son of the Norwegian king Haraldr *hárfagri* (Fine-hair) and the foster son of the Anglo-Saxon king Æthelstan, we read:

> King Æthelstan had Hákon baptized and instructed in the true faith... In later times he was called Æthelstan's foster son [Hákon *Aðalsteinsfóstri*]... King Æthelstan gave Hákon a sword whose hilt as well as haft was of gold. Its blade was most excellent and with it Hákon cleft a millstone to its centre, whence it was called Quern-bite. *That was the best sword that ever was brought to Norway* [emphasis added]. Hákon wore it till his dying day.[51]

Whether foreign imports or home produced, swords in the viking age were typically double edged, with both edges of the blade being sharp. Swords were generally used single handed, since the other hand was busy holding the shield. Blades ranged from sixty to ninety centimetres in length, although seventy to eighty centimetres was typical. Late in the viking era, blades became as long as one hundred centimetres. The blade was typically four to six centimetres wide. The hilt and pommel provided the needed weight to balance the blade, with the total weight of the sword ranging from one to two kilograms. Typical swords weigh in at the lower end of this range. Blades had a slight taper, which helped bring the centre of balance closer to the grip.

Sword hilts are generally classified using a system devised by Jan Petersen and published in 1919. Since a given style was in use only during a given period, the hilt style can be used to help date a sword. For example, the Petersen type B hilt indicates that the sword was probably made between the middle of the eighth century and the early part of the ninth century.[52] The grips were made with a variety of materials, ranging from simple wooden grips wrapped with leather, to elaborately decorated grips wound with wire made from precious metals, or covered with embossed plates of precious metals. It is said that the grip of Geirmundr's sword was made from walrus ivory.[53] Bone or ivory would have afforded a good grip even when wet from sweat or blood.

While many highly decorated grave finds appear to tell a different story, the typical viking-age sword is assumed to have been fairly plain – few sword-bearing warriors could afford craftsmanship in precious metals, and the owner would surely judge the value of a sword by the quality of its blade, not the amount of its decoration.

Equally plain would have been sword scabbards. These were made from wood covered with leather and usually lined with oiled material to protect the sword from rusting; they usually had a metal chape to protect the tip, and sometimes metal reinforcement at the mouth. They were initially slung from a belt that ran over the shoulder, held in place by the waist belt; later in our period they were often hung directly from the waist belt.

Swords were used single-handed, combined with a shield or *seax* in the other hand. When delivering a blow care had to be taken not to strike directly onto the opponent's sword, as the steel – high quality by the standards of their age, but rather brittle by ours – could break easily. In fact, a Norse saga would remind its listeners that the expert swordsman did not strike fast and furiously, but took his time to pick his strokes carefully. In the work of Saxo Grammaticus he says:

> For of old, in the ordering of combats, men did not try to exchange their blows thick and fast; but there was a pause, and at the same time a definite succession in striking; the contest being carried on with few strokes, but those terrible, so that honour was paid more to the mightiness than to the number of the blows.[54]

As a result the sword was more of a bludgeon, used to hack at the parts of a warrior not covered by his shield, notably his head or forward leg. Thus, when Egill Skallagrímsson (of whom we shall hear anon) fought the berserker Ljot, he 'caught Ljot just above the knee, slicing off his leg, and Ljot dropped dead on the spot'.[55] Other blows could disable your opponent and expose him to the kind of wounds sometimes found on viking-age mortuary remains – repeated cuts on the bones of the head, arms and legs. Moreover, the heavy pommel not only acted as a counterweight to the blade but at close quarters could be used to deliver a disabling blow to the head or chin.

Contemporary Muslim writers let us know how highly appreciated the 'Frankish' swords were, because of their beautiful and well-made blades. A good sword needed iron of a particular variety with a particular concentration of carbon, a particular kind of heat applied in a particular way as it was woven, beaten, cooled, heated, beaten again, and folded. This time-consuming, labour-intensive and agonizingly meticulous process resulted in swords that were not only powerful weapons, but costly status symbols and family heirlooms. A good sword had a name, pedigree, and reputation. The poorly made sword not only reflected ill on its maker, but endangered the life of its owner. The legendary hero Beowulf (pronounced 'Bay-uh-wulf') suffered the failure of two swords. The first during the fight with the man-eating monster called Grendel; the second during his fight with the fatal fire-breathing, snake-like dragon (OE *wyrm*), which cost him his life:

> Inspired again / by the thought of glory, the war-king threw / his whole strength behind a sword-stroke / and connected with the skull. And *Nægling* snapped. / Beowulf's ancient iron-grey sword / let him down in

the fight. It was never his fortune / to be helped in combat by the cutting edge / of weapons made of iron. When he wielded a sword, / no matter how blooded and hard-edged the blade / his hand was too strong, the stroke he dealt / (I have heard) would ruin it. He could reap no advantage.[56]

A good sword came at a cost of intense and careful labour. A good sword needed iron of a particular variety with a particular concentration of carbon, a particular kind of heat applied in a particular way as it was woven, beaten, cooled, heated, beaten again before being decorated with runes, inlays of precious metals or stones and presented to a particularly demanding customer.

At the beginning of the viking age, iron smelting technology and steel making techniques were primarily small-scale endeavours. Even in areas where the process was semi-industrialized, the furnaces were small. This resulted in units of trade iron and steel that were not of sufficient size to create an entire sword blade, so blades were assembled from several pieces of iron and/or steel forge-welded together. If the metal was all the same alloy, the result is what the archaeologists call 'piled' structure, but smiths in the Roman and Migration/Vendel periods quickly realized that multiple alloys could be combined for decorative effect, in the process today known as pattern welding. Apparently, this welding technique balanced the flexibility of steel with the strength of iron, though as better quality steel came available, the technique, which involved a process that was long and complicated, became less common.

A forge-welded centre bar of several thin rods of malleable wrought iron was tightly twisted together, and the two edges hammer-welded into place along each side of the centre bar to give the blade a hard cutting edge and point. Depending on the way the twisting and forging was done, different repeating and often highly decorative patterns could be formed within the structure of the metal. Thus, in the eloquent words of Simpson:

> During this process a pattern would emerge along the central section, where the intertwined strips of steely and plain iron would show up in patterns of light and dark like eddying waves, coiling snakes, twigs, or sheaves of corn.[57]

It should be noted that more recent thinking (informed in part by experimentation) suggests that if anything pattern welding created a weaker weapon than a single piece of good steel, and that this process was likely to be intended more for decoration than function.

As furnaces became bigger and at the end of the viking age, smiths were beginning to operate them on power from waterwheels. These larger, more efficient smelting operations improved the quality and quantity of raw material used in sword production, so that a blade could be made from a single unit of steel. This, of course, removed the laboriously achieved patterns that resulted from the previous construction method.

Important trade traffic already existed between the Baltic Sea and northern countries on one hand, and the kingdoms and principalities at the Black Sea and the Caucasus on the other hand. In the mid-ninth century Ibn Khurradadhbih, a Khurasani *bon vivant* who headed the *barid*, the 'Abbasid postal and intelligence service of the caliph al-Mu'tamid (r. 870–92), relates in his work about Rus' merchants bringing blades from the regions of the Rhine, for instance the famous Cologne swords, to Constantinople, and even making the crossing of the Caspian Sea to disembark on its southeast shore to 'carry their goods on camel back [...] to Baghdad'.[58] There is the flavour of fact in all this, although some say (unconvincingly) that the author had confused the Rus' with Jewish Khazars. Indeed, occidental swords with the name of the far-famed Frankish blade smith *Ingelrii* forged into their blades have been excavated as far east as the Volga. The name clearly became associated with a workshop that had a long production life.[59]

Ibn Khurradadhbih also describes an alternative route to Byzantium (*bahr ar-Rum*), by which the Rus' merchants would convey furs (black fox and beaver) and (presumably Frankish) swords, paying a tithe to 'the emperor of the *Rum* (i.e. Byzantines)'.[60] Franklin and Shepard suggest that Ibn Khurradadhbih is here referring to the Byzantine city of Kherson close to the mouth of the Dnieper, which was the capital of the Khersonese theme and the principal Byzantine commercial centre on the northern shores of the Black Sea.[61] Although this is our only reference to Rus' making it all the way to the political and cultural centre of the caliphate, because of the nature of his work Ibn Khurradadhbih was very well informed. The Northmen themselves imported Frankish blades, which were mounted by local Norse sword cutlers, just as they imported ready-made swords from Carolingian workshops. This is mirrored in references in skaldic verse to *vigra vestœnna ok valskra sverða*, 'western spears and Frankish swords'.[62]

It is worth considering that the Scandinavian countries in our period of study were not able to forge sword blades of a quality equal to the blades of the Carolingian smithies. It is even possible that certain swords unearthed in Scandinavia or the Baltic regions have some relation to Constantinople. But very likely there is more influence from Byzantium on the northern sword material than vice versa. Old Norse literature as a rule gives only little information as to the origin of the swords. Famous swords mentioned and praised in the prose sagas and the skaldic poetry almost always are gifts from foreign princes, war booty or the like. Some of the returning Varangians took with them part of their military equipment or so it seems, because in a few cases swords brought home from Byzantium are mentioned, such as the aforementioned sword *Brynjubítr* in the *Sturlunga saga*.

Swords brought from Scandinavia to Constantinople are to be found in Old Norse literature. *Heimskringla* preserves the story of the sword *Hneitir* (exact sense uncertain, but something like 'Cutter') of Óláfr II Haraldsson *inn digri*, which the king had thrown away on receiving his mortal wound on the battlefield at Stiklarstaðir. The sword, with a grip wrapped about with gold, was picked up by a Swedish *bóndi* who had broken his own sword. He survived the battle and made good his escape, eventually getting back to his farm in Sweden, and the sword was to remain in his family for a number of generations. Eventually, sometime during the sovereignty of John II Komnenos (r. 1118–43), the sword was taken to Constantinople by a Swede. This Swedish warrior entered the Varangian Guard, and the emperor, who had been informed about the famous sword, gave its owner 'gold for tenfold the value of the sword'. The emperor than had the sword hung as a sacred relic above the altar of Saint Óláfr's, the chapel in Constantinople the Varangians had built as a thanks offering for their part in the victory at the battle of Beroë in 1122.[63] We also have the direct testimony of Eindriði *ungi* (the Young), whom we shall come across again, as recorded by Einarr Skúlason in his *Óláfrsdrápa*:

> The Lord of Kings [the emperor] / let the maker of danger [the sword] / in the storm of points [battle] / stand above the gold–encrusted altar.[64]

As to the origin of this sword the Norse literature says nothing, only that it was a very old one, taken from a burial mound, and that in the dim distant time of myth and legend it had been the property of some heroic king.

The spear

Óðinn brought war into the world: battles were begun by throwing a spear at the hostile army, dedicating the battle and its butcher's bill to him. Thus, in Old Norse mythology spears are closely associated with Óðinn and afterlife (e.g. according to the eddaic poem *Grímnismál*, the walls of Valhöll were constructed from spears) and they are also one of the attributes of the *valkyrjur*, valkyries. Óðinn did not carry a sword himself. His weapon was the spear, *Gungnir* (Swaying One), which never misses its mark. He was stuck, too, by a spear when he was hanging on Yggdrasil,[65] the mighty and eternally green ash tree that echoes the World Tree motif found in many cultures, willingly engaging in what was some sort of test or discipline that endows him with abnormal power, the sort of self-torment/ sacrifice that in other cultures shamans undergo to achieve occult wisdom.

To Northmen, the spear was therefore a weapon of great symbolic value, not only in connection to the supreme god but as the symbol of the armed, free man too. Moreover, of all the weapons man has invented, the spear is the one most universally used during our period, and in a very real sense it was the weapon of the ordinary. Whereas the sword was a weapon of military and political elites, the *sine qua non* of physical brutality that we call heroic combat, the spear was pretty much a common workaday weapon. This was due to it being the weapon for ultimate action at all times and to its very simplicity of design. Requiring only relatively little iron, the spear was cheap to purchase, functional and, above all, effective.

As the main arm for most Northmen, high and low alike, the spear, unlike the javelin, was usually employed as a far-reaching stabbing weapon and as such it would rarely have left its owner's hand on the field of battle – remember, a spear, once hurled, leaves the warrior defenceless. Besides, if it was his main weapon, would he really want to throw it away? No, for the spear was a valuable weapon. For some warriors, it may have been their only weapon.

The simple term 'spearhead', however, embraces a great range of shapes and sizes, complete with socket ferrules (either welded in a complete circle or split-sided) to enable them to be mounted on the shaft and often secured with one or two rivets and/or binding. Earlier spearheads were about twenty centimetres long, while later ones were as long as sixty centimetres. In *Laxdœla saga*, Helgi Harðbeinsson had a spear with a blade 'a full ell in length (about fifty centimetres), with iron wound around the shaft'. He thrust the blade through the shield of Bolli Þorleiksson, and through Bolli himself.[66]

Some spearheads had 'wings' on the head, two sideway projections useful for a variety of tricks, such as hooking behind a shield rim to pull the shield away, or to hook the body of the opponent. Possibly a Carolingian invention, a 'winged' spear is called *krókspjót*, barbed spear, in the Old Norse sagas. Grettir Ásmundarson used a barbed spear with a blade so thin and long that he was able to pierce all the way through Þórir and into Ögmundr with a single thrust, right up to the wings. Both men were killed by the thrust.[67] The spearheads were made of iron, and, like sword blades, were made using pattern welding techniques during the early part of the viking age.

Without entering into the refinements of typology, it can be said that for use as a stabbing weapon, practical experience tells us that the width of the blade was important. A wide blade actually prevents the spearhead from being inserted into the body of an enemy too far, thus enabling the spear to be recovered quickly, ready for further use. In our period of study the most common designs of spearhead were the broad, the leaf, and the diamond or lozenge. The broad-headed spear was known as the 'ox tongue'. It had the twofold function of stabbing with the point and slashing with the sharpened edges. The leaf-shaped blade was employed as a stabbing weapon and was commonly thrown. The last blade shape, the diamond, had a much heavier head and was mainly used for throwing against armour such as ring mail. The addition of a midrib gives greater longitudinal strength to a spearhead, increasing its effectiveness at piercing shields and armour during hand-to-hand spear play.

It is difficult to say with any certainty what the best length for a spear was, but commonsense dictates that it would have been mainly between two to three metres long, with twenty- to sixty-centimetre heads. Any shorter and the chief advantage of keeping the enemy a whole pace away is gone; any longer and it becomes awkward and too wobbly to use accurately with one hand. Of course, for our Norse warrior it also had to be light enough to wield one-handed (usually over arm in a thrusting manner) and used in conjunction with a shield. Apart from the obvious use of being able to dispatch a foe beyond arm's reach, the spear has the real advantage that a minimum amount of expensive iron is used in its construction.

True, a spear could easily be made by pulling up a straight sapling, or by tearing down a branch from the parent trunk and stripping it of twigs and leaves, one end then being sharpened and charred in a fire. Ash wood (as frequently mentioned in the prose sagas and skaldic poetry) was the most frequently chosen because it naturally grows straight and cleaves easily. It is both tough and elastic, which means it has the capacity to absorb repeated shocks without communicating them to the handler's hand and of withstanding a good hard knock without splintering. This makes it useful for oars and axe handles, and a splendid choice for a spear shaft. However, some fruit woods, such as the Cornelian cherry, have good qualities too. It goes without saying that the inherent weakness of its wooden shaft was the main drawback of the spear in battle. In order to sustain some lateral damage in use, shafts have to be at least twenty-two millimetres in diameter. The sockets on the surviving viking-age spearheads suggest that the shafts were typically round, with a diameter of two to three centimetres. Once the spear was made, its ashen shaft smooth and polished and fitted with a head, it could provide long service with minimum maintenance. Additionally, spears were also used for hunting, thus providing a dual-purpose, versatile implement for our Northman.

The seax

Those Northmen who could not afford a sword, and here we are assuming that it was the majority of them, were armed with a spear and either a long-bladed knife – commonly the single-edged, tanged *seax* (*scramasaxos* in the Latin of Gregory of Tours),[68] a favourite of the Anglo-Saxons too – or a single-handed axe (the gravestone from Lindisfarne Priory graphically shows a line of seven Norse warriors brandishing swords and one-handed axes). Compared with swords, *seaxes* were typically more crudely fabricated. Rather than being crafted by skilled, specialized blade smiths, *seaxes* were probably made at home – almost all households had their own smithies where everyday working tools could be forged.

Blades of *seaxes* tended to be sturdier, heavier and thicker than sword blades. They were certainly cheaper to purchase, thus providing a sturdy all-purpose useful tool in the fields and in the home and an effective second line weapon.

The main characteristic of the *seax*, despite obvious differences in local manufacture and, of course, length, was the shape. The back of the blade did not run parallel to the cutting edge but broadened out from the hilt for just over half of its length and then turned inwards to meet the cutting edge at the point, which was sharpened to allow thrusting. The guard, if any, was insignificant, the grip of perishable material such as wood, horn or bone, and the short tang invariably was without a pommel.

With regards to its offensive fighting function, a *seax* could have been used both for stabbing downwards and thrusting upwards. Its sharp wedge shape gives it great piercing strength. A cutting blow would smash flesh and bone beneath mail. On an unarmoured body, a cut would prove to be crippling or deadly. Likewise, its sharp point would make thrusts devastating to the human body. In fact, the design of the point was such that it could be slipped under the sternum to pierce the heart before reappearing at the base of the clavicle. Unless slashing, the *seax* was best held in the downward guard position with the cutting edge facing outwards. The distinction between knives intended primarily for personal use (carried by both sexes, and virtually all ages), and those for martial use is necessarily an arbitrary one, though a quite small blade, while handy about the person, can be used to cause fatal injuries, whereas a blade 127 millimetres long or more properly belongs to the field of battle. The longest blades are 540 to 760 millimetres, the equivalent length to a sword. Yet even in its longest forms, the seax allowed a warrior to fight in close.

That the *seax* was a very effective weapon is demonstrated by its widespread popularity in the Old Norse sagas. In *Heiðarvíga saga* Þorsteinn Víga-Styrsson followed Gestr Þórhallason to Constantinople, where he had joined the Varangians, so as to exact revenge for the slaying of his father, Víga-Styrr. Having tracked down his quarry, he approached him with 'a *seax* under his cloak with which he struck at Gestr's head'.[69] Again, in *Grettis saga Ásmundarsonar* we hear of the Varangians setting out on expedition from Constantinople, and before their embarkation an arms parade is held at which every member of the unit is to produce his weapons for inspection. At least one Varangian produces a *seax*.[70] The *seax* in question was that of one of the most emblematic outlaws in Old Norse literature, Grettir Ásmundarson, which he had named *Kársnautr*.

One of the more memorable descriptions of the use of a *seax* in a fight occurs in *Brennu-Njáls saga*, at the fight on the river Rangá. Kolr Egilsson thrust at Kolskeggr, brother of the great warrior Gunnarr Hámundarson, with his spear while Kolskeggr had his hands full dealing with other opponents. The spear went through Kolskeggr's thigh. Kolskeggr stepped forward and cut off Kolr's leg with his *seax*, and he asked, 'Did that hit you or not?' Kolr replied that it was what he deserved for not shielding himself. He stood looking at his leg stump. Kolskeggr said, 'You don't need to look: it's just as you think, the leg is gone. Then Kolr fell down dead'.[71]

A knife or axe would have been carried constantly at the belt, the *seax*, in particular, housed in a scabbard of folded leather and worn across the belly, blade uppermost so as to prevent the weapon from resting on its cutting edge, with the hilt at the right, to make it easy to draw. The *seax* was certainly a handy reserve weapon, easily drawn to finish the fight. Indeed, even those who could afford a sword preferred a *seax* over it for fighting, even heroes and anti-heroes. In *Grettis saga Ásmundarsonar*, for instance, Grettir Ásmundarson preferred his *seax*, called *Kársnautr* (Kárr's gift), which he took from the grave of the not altogether dead Kárr the Old. The walking dead Kárr attacks Grettir while he is collecting valuable treasure, but Grettir defeats and decapitates him.[72] In the Old English poem *Beowulf*, Grendel's even nastier mother, to fight Beowulf, 'pulled out / a broad, whetted knife [OE *seax geteah*]',[73] likewise Beowulf himself, to despatch Grendel's mother, 'drew a stabbing knife [OE *wæll-seaxe gebræd*]/ he carried on his belt, sharpened for battle'.[74]

The bow

Like most cutting and stabbing weapons, the bow had evolved, and remained in daily use, as a weapon for hunting – it was probably to be found in most Norse households – but it could equally be used in war. As already mentioned, the Northmen did not enjoy any great technical superiority over their foes; however, they did make greater use of the bow than, say, the Anglo-Saxons, Scots or Irish, for example. Bow-armed warriors were invariably to be found operating in collaboration with the shield wall, whereby they would loft arrows into the ranks of the opposition. Perhaps the experience of Northmen in sea battles taught them the advantages of such close co-operation.

Constructed from a single straight wooden stave (viz. not glued together from several layers), a Norse bow typically had a D-shaped cross-section with the flat side pointing to the front, and was tapered at the ends. Both the archaeological record and the sagas tell us that Norse bows were made from the wood of the European yew (*Taxus bacata*), ash (genus *Fraxinus*), or elm (genus *Ulmus*). Typically, they were 1.6 to two metres long. A complete bow found at Hedeby was made of yew and was 1.915 metres long. This is what is called a 'self-composite' bow, that is to say, the bow stave exploits the natural differences in texture within a single piece of yew wood. Today, it is housed with the Archäologisches Landesmuseum, Schloss Gottorf in Schleswig.

The estimated draw weight of our tenth-century bow is ninety pounds (40.8 kgf), and the effective range of this weapon was about 200 metres. This is a draw weight comparable to that of later mediaeval longbows, and one which imparted to the arrow a short range penetrating power sufficient to penetrate iron mail and wooden shields. After fitting the arrow to the string the archer drew the bow while lifting it, until the drawing hand reached his cheek; he then loosed quickly – holding a drawn bow tires the archer and impairs his aim. Exposure to undue damp soon limited the effectiveness of the bow, and could even place it out of action.

Similar bows made of elm were also found at Hedeby. Apparently, some bows had a reinforcing wrapping of linen, leather, or even strips of sinew. The finds at Hedeby also included arrows. The shafts are seventy to eighty centimetres in length and eight to ten millimetres in diameter, and carried the three-feather fletching, which stabilize an arrow's flight by spinning it.

Iron arrowheads came in various styles, ranging from trefoil points to plain leaf shape and barbed designs. Those heads with sharply pointed pyramid sections concentrated their impact into a tiny area, which meant they could burst open the rings of mail. It is worth drawing to the reader's attention the fact that both of the kings killed during the campaigns of 1066 fell to arrows in the chinks of their armour – one by an arrow in the throat,[75] the other by the famous arrow in the eye.[76] These bowshots at random remind us of the death of Ahab, killed in battle when 'someone drew his bow at random and hit the king of Israel between the sections of his armour'.[77]

Socket fittings to take the shaft were common, though an alternative to the socketed head was the tanged head, forged in one piece with a spike that was driven into the end of the shaft. Both the arrowheads and the fletching of arrows were doubly secured, by glues such as birch pitch and by strong thread whipping. Although the fashioning of arrows was thought to be a pastime fit for a warrior, in fact it seems often to have been done by the women of the household.

Although a bow was not the cheapest of weapons, the written evidence suggests that bowmen were usually too poor to afford sword, helmet and body armour. But the Norse sagas also speak of great men who preferred the bow to any other weapon. The tale of the battle of Svölðr mentions one Einarr þambarskelfir (Gutshaker), who stood beside Óláfr Tryggvason. After he had narrowly missed jarl Eiríkr Hákonarson, one of the opposition leaders, his bow was snapped by an arrow hit. The king asked him:

> 'What cracked there with such a loud report? Einarr answered, 'Norway out of your hands, sir king'. 'Hardly so great a break', said the king. 'Take my bow and shoot with it' – and he flung his bow over to him.
>
> Einarr took the bow and at once drew the head of the arrow behind it and said, 'Too soft, too soft is the king's bow', and threw the bow behind him, took up his shield, and fought with his sword.[78]

Even kings took great pride in using the bow. Haraldr III Sigurðarson used a yew bow at the battle of Níza (more of which later), a feat celebrated in verse by the king's chief skald Þjóðólfr Arnórsson:

> The valiant king of Uppland drew his bow all night; the lord caused arrows to shower against the white shields. The blood drenched point inflicted wounds upon the mail-shirted men, where arrows lodged in shields; the volley of spears from the dragon [ship] increased.[79]

Bowstrings were usually made of a strong twisted cord of hemp or flax. The saga hero Gunnarr Hámundarson of Hliðarendi was the sort of man who attracted trouble not because he was a troublemaker but because he represented a challenge to the young guns in the district, men of inferior worth who envied his greatness and plotted to bring him down. And this they do. One night they gathered at Hliðarendi, forty in number, and besiege him in his home. For a long time he fought them off with his bow and arrows, wounding eight men and killing two, until his bowstring was cut by one of the assailants. When he bent his bow Gunnarr always hit his mark with his swift arrows, however difficult the target may be. So he turned to his wife, Hallgerðr, and asked her for two locks of her long, beautiful hair to plait into a bowstring for him. But the beautiful, wilful and wicked Hallgerðr, with her husband on the edge of annihilation, flatly refused:

> 'Does anything depend on it?' she said. 'My life depends on it', he said, 'for they'll never be able to get me as long as I can use my bow'. 'Then I'll recall', she said, 'the slap you gave me, and I don't care whether you hold out for a long or a short time'. 'Everyone has some mark of distinction', said Gunnarr, 'and I won't ask you again'.[80]

Gunnarr knew that without his bow he was doomed, but he would not ask his wife's help twice. At any rate, the point of the digression, if this tale is to be believed, is that a bowstring could be made from the long tresses of a woman's hair.

Body protection

A number of male high status graves (mainly rich chamber graves) from the late viking age, which are distributed all over Scandinavia but are especially prominent in Denmark, show common features as to the character of the grave goods, consisting of horses, riding equipments, arms (but no byrnies and helmets), food in containers, and objects of leisure.[81] The most frequent finds of protective armour are fragments of ring mail that could have belonged to byrnies, aventails, coifs, the coif being a tight fitting mail hood made as one with the byrnie to protect the head. Likewise, though no actual fragments of helmets have been identified in the archaeological material, a number of mounts have been found that have been interpreted as deriving from a helmet (or helmets).

The helmet

Most of you are doubtless familiar with the 'spectacle' helmet unearthed from a mid tenth-century chieftain's cremation burial, an accidental find made in 1943 on a farm called Gjermundbu in Haug, a district within Ringerike in central Norway. In fact, this Norwegian helmet is the only one we can honestly say was a viking one in origin and date, though fragments of similar eyepieces have been found in Russia, which suggests its widespread use.

The helmet had been constructed of four iron plates held together by two iron bands riveted to the skull of the helm, with a wide iron band encircling the base of the helm. Harking back to the heroic age of Vendel Scandinavia, the addition of a spectacle visor might seem to provide better protection to the eyes and upper face. Unfortunately, this extra ironwork merely serves to direct incoming spear tips and sword points into the wearer's eyes, surely not what the designer intended. Yet the Gjermundbu helmet has clear evidence of battle damage (a sword blow and an arrow puncture), suggesting it was used in earnest fights. So either the viking-age warriors who used these helmet types did not perceive any additional risk from the spectacle visor, or the additional risk was thought to be worth the benefits offered by the extra ironwork. As a final point, the mail rings attached (by means of punched holes) to the rim of the Gjermundbu helmet doubtlessly once belonged to an aventail.

From around the year 900 use of another pattern of helmet became widespread throughout Europe. This was the *spangenhelm*, not unlike the Gjermundbu helmet but with a more pointed dome, a straight nasal bar in front to protect the face, and in-fill plates of iron, hardened leather, or even horn. Rune stone carvings show that this type of helmet was worn by many Norsemen.

Following not long after the *spangenhelm* came the development of a similar conical helmet beaten from a single piece of iron but with a riveted–on nasal bar not unlike the helmet from the Olmütz find. A leather-lined mail coif could be attached to the helmet's rim, a practice that became common in the eleventh century.

Nonetheless, the *spangenhelm* continued to be worn (we can see them on the Bayeux tapestry) as its construction would have been quicker and cheaper than a helmet drawn over a stake by hammering a single sheet of metal. Many warriors would also have worn padded caps to give a comfortable fit and extra protection against blows. These caps would have been made from thick woollen cloth or leather. Although a helmet was a lot cheaper than body armour, it is likely that only the wealthier sort owned one. Others had to protect their heads with caps of thick leather or fur, which are often depicted on the Gotland picture stones.

The byrnie

As usual, the question of body armour is a thorny one. This was a highly desirable possession, since the wounds of edged weapons could quickly prove deadly. A cut just a centimetre deep could easily lead to tetanus or blood poisoning, and penetration wounds, which could carry dirty clothing or other debris into the body, were lethally vulnerable to infection. Replica byrnies weigh in the region of twelve kilograms and are fabricated from more or less 30,000 rings. The twelve kilograms of iron in a mail shirt represented a treasure in the viking age. Thus, mail shirts must have been very rare. Anyone who could have afforded one would certainly have wanted one, but probably few people could afford that much iron. Fortunately, mail was durable and was handed down from man to man, and had the added advantage that it could be repaired by the owner when damaged.

Found too in the Gjermundbu burial was a mail shirt, the best preserved of its kind in Scandinavia. Found in eighty-five fragments, in its original state the shirt would have had a length of fifty-five centimetres from shoulder to hem with around four rings per square centimetre, which suggests that it was a short one, possibly only extending do the wearer's hips. The sleeves of the shirt were short too. It had been constructed out of iron rings with an anticlockwise lap, oval rivet hole and high domed rivet head with a prominent oval tail of wire with a sub-circular profile. These were associated with alternating rows of rings of an unknown closure type, circular in shape but with flats on the external circumferences and wire of a sub-rectangular profile. The thickness of the wire used to make the riveted rings was between 1.09 and 1.68 millimetres, each with a diameter of between 7.4 and 8.3 millimetres and weighing around 150 milligrams, while the dimensions for the unknown rings were 1.2 to two millimetres and 8.35 respectively. All in all, though, this made both types of iron rings on the thin side. From this data it is clear that the rings were small and sat very close together, thereby providing the wearer with good protection. Today the Gjermundbu mail shirt is housed with the Universitet Oldsaksamling, Óslo (inv. C27317).

Mail worn by Northmen was almost certainly the 'four-on-one' pattern, where four solid rings were connected by a single riveted type. This was made by cutting thin strips of soft wrought iron from a hammered sheet and forging it into a thin rod, one end being thinner than the other. This would then have been heated until it glowed cherry red and swiftly drawn through first a series of punched holes in an iron block. Re-heating and drawing repeatedly through a series of holes of decreasing diameter forced the wire into an approximately rounded profile.

Though long and tedious, the process did wonders for the grain flow in the iron; making the material stronger than if it had not been hot drawn.

The next task was to wind the wire round a rod and, using a sharp chisel, cut the wire into rings. The rings were then driven through a conical hole in another iron block that made the ends overlap. Half of the rings were set aside and the rest were flattened at their ends with a small hammer and punched, and a second punch was used to drive a hole through the soft iron. These were the riveted rings. As butted rings, that is rings that were simply bent into shape and butted together without a means to hold them shut, were not strong enough to stand up to the rigours of combat, the other half of the rings were heated at their ends and forged together in a hammer-welded joint to make a solid ring. The natural wearing of the iron drawing block, the winding and handling tended to flatten their original sub-circular profile. As the mail was assembled, a riveted ring was linked to four of the welded rings, a tiny rivet being driven through the holes to close the link. The rings were linked into rows then joined into panels of manageable size and weight, before being linked together to make the final garment. As the panels were linked, alterations to the four-on-one pattern were made to shape the mail to the contours of the body and to provide freedom of motion in places such as under the arm. Rings were dropped or added to rows as needed to shape the finished mail.

Wrought iron rusts very slowly, so proofing would not have been necessary. As a final point, mail shirts became longer as time progressed. The Gjermundbu mail shirt, it will be recalled, was hip length with short sleeves. Later, as we might infer from evidence such as the Bayeux tapestry, the sleeves reached the elbow and the hem reached the knees or just below.[82] These long mail shirts or byrnies (ON *brynja*, OE *byrne*), often with an integral hood, were split to the groin at the front and back to facilitate riding. In this final period of the viking age additional pieces were also added to the original, simple T-shaped mail corselet: coifs or mail hoods covered the head, and aventails – rectangular flaps – were fastened across the face with laces or hooks to protect the area not covered by a helmet.

Before leaving mail shirts, it is worth stating that mail did not provide a complete protection; mail was only a secondary defence. If one were to draw the edge of a sword across the arm of a combatant wearing a mail shirt, the sword would not bite; the rings would protect against a cut. However, if one were to take that same sword and strike a powerful blow against the arm or shoulder of the combatant, the rings would not prevent the skin from being bruised, or the bones from being broken. Mail does little to absorb or dissipate the force of a blow (viz. blunt trauma), and the force passes right through the rings. Thus, to take an obvious example, without some form of padding to cushion and spread the impact, the crushing force of a Dane axe would still break major bones, and force split rings deep into the flesh beneath. Both before and after the viking age, fighting men wore padded garments under their mail to help absorb and spread the force of a blow, to prevent crush injuries and to stop broken rings from being forced into the flesh.

Typically, these garments consisted of two layers of wool or leather stuffed with fleece, animal hair, cotton or rags, then sewn together and quilted. Later known as a *gambeson* or *aketon*, the garment itself was difficult to pierce and remarkably effective in deadening a blow.

However, there is no archaeological evidence that such quilted garments were worn during the viking age, nor any mention of them in Old Norse literature. Yet when you stop to consider the simple fact that a mail shirt was flexible enough for relative freedom of movement and was only effective against cuts, mail must have chaffed the skin of the wearer even with an undergarment and it offered only minimum protection against heavy blows. By reason of commonsense, therefore, a well-equipped warrior might well add a similar garment as a shock absorber under his byrnie, a safety feature that also added greatly to his comfort. By way of comparison, it is well known that a Latin knight wore two separate linen undershirts over his bare back, over which he wore a *gambeson*, which was made up of layers of cloth, tow or rags quilted on to a foundation of canvas or leather, and then covered with an outer coat of linen, cloth and silk. On top of this he wore his hauberk, which hung down to about mid-thigh.

The shield

Yet the plainest – and quite probably the oldest – of all forms of body protection, must have been the wooden shield. All warriors, regardless of station or rank, carried one, and in Old Norse literature the shield, of all defensive armour, is far the most prominent. For instance, the night before Stiklarstaðir all the king's men, regardless of rank or station, settled to sleep under their shields in the open.[83]

A basic and effective form of defence against any edge or pre-gunpowder projectile weapon, the shield was an integral and necessary part of a warrior's equipment in our period of study – and of his fighting technique. Needless to say, he would not have lasted very long in a battle without one.

A typical Norse shield was made from a single layer of flat narrow planks butted and glued together with an unlikely sounding but apparently effective rubbery mixture of cheese, vinegar and quicklime. It was bossed with iron and rimmed with rawhide binding strips to keep the shield board from splitting when hit edge on. There is negligible archaeological evidence for iron-rimmed shields, although in *Grettis saga Ásmundarsonar*, it is said that a berserker carried an iron-rimmed shield to a duel against Grettir.[84] Surviving shields are made from light, springy wood from conifers (spruce, fir, pine), but not all cases. Literary evidence contradicts and suggests that shields were made from linden (genus *Tilia*), a tough but flexible wood. The word *lind*, linden, is used to mean 'shield' in poems such as *Völuspá*,[85] and the term *lindiskjöldr*, linden shield, is used in some sagas. Linden certainly has advantages over other species of wood for shield use. It is lightweight and does not split as readily under impact as do other types of wood. For extra resilience against impact weapons, sun-dried, stretched leather might be added to the outer surface. As well as strengthening the shield rim, the rawhide binding strips would have secured the leather to the underlying board.

Tests conducted by Hurstwic using a replica viking-age axe against a replica viking-age shield have demonstrated the truth of this. First used in the demonstration was a shield without leather stretched across its face. With its first blow the axe split the shield board from one end to the other, and the fragments were held in place by the rawhide binding. The second blow destroyed the shield. The same test was then conducted on a shield with leather stretched across its face. The first blow penetrated the shield, but did not split the shield board. Even after four solid blows, the shield was still intact, without any splits. It remained usable, proving the benefit of leather facing on the shield board. It was not until the sixth blow that the shield failed. It is reasonable to suppose that no one used wooden shields without some more effective form of strengthening.[86]

Simple colour washes were presumably more common than complex motifs, but the latter are found in the literary sources, where the shield boards are described as painted with bright colours, intricate swirling or quartered designs, and animal motifs. The shields from the Gokstad ship burial, sixty-four in number, two overlapping shields to each oar port, were painted plain yellow and black alternatively; one of the fragments of the Oseberg tapestry shows one with a cross design; the shields of Óláfr II Haraldsson's army at Stiklarstaðir supposedly bore crosses in various hues on a white background; and picture (i.e. representational) stones on the island of Gotland show many with radial wavy lines or divisions. Even if a shield was not decorated, it is highly likely that it would be sealed with oil so that it repelled and resisted water. A shield that soaked up water from rain or sea spray could easily double in weight, becoming as heavy and waterlogged as to be nearly useless.

Cut through the centre of the shield board was a circular opening. Covering this opening was a more-or-less hemispherical hollow iron boss of fifteen centimetres diameter (including flange), which had a thickness of three millimetres. Broad-headed iron nails passed through the flange and were either flattened or clenched (bent over) on the reverse side of the shield board to hold the boss in place. Usually hammered out of a single piece of iron, the boss afforded security to the left hand on the inner side, which was gripping a handgrip. In the form of a wooden crossbar, this handgrip was plausibly bound with cloth or leather, though a sheathing of iron was another possibility. A single handgrip behind the boss allowed the shield to be moved about freely, and the boss itself could be used to punch the enemy. As well as the handgrip, there was a leather strap that allowed the shield to be slung around the upper body.

Typically, shields were some eighty to ninety centimetres in diameter. Some were larger, such as the Gokstad shields, which were made of white pine and ninety-four centimetres in diameter. Based on surviving remnants, some shields appear to have been as small as seventy centimetres in diameter. Presumably, when a man made a shield for himself, he sized it to fit his torso size and fighting style. A shield needs to be big enough to provide the desired protection but no bigger. A shield too small exposes additional lines of attack that an opponent might exploit, while a shield too large slows the defensive responses and exhausts the fighter unnecessarily. Shields may have been big across, but they were barely a centimetre thick, most surviving examples being in the range between six millimetres and twelve millimetres thick, the thinner versions obviously so for lightness.

Needless to say, in battle shields would splinter, they would split, and they would be shredded by arrows, by spears and by swords. The motif of shields being 'ground away by weapons' occurs both in Old Welsh, Anglo-Saxon and Old Norse literature. In the Welsh heroic poem *Y Gododdin*, for example, we have an evocative description of a shield after battle: 'As much as his hand could grip / there did not return of it'.[87] It would seem to us that the safety factor offered by such a flimsy piece of equipment must have been no more than an illusionary one. It is almost needless to add, that shields did not last long in combat.

In battle the shield was initially carried at arm's length in order to break the force of any weapon striking it and to keep away from the body any weapon that pierced it. For in fighting it was held close to the body so that it was not easily knocked aside. In this neutral, relaxed position, the shield protected from neck to knees. The head and the lower legs were exposed and unprotected. Thus, the head and lower leg were likely targets, and indeed studies of skeletal remains show that many battle injuries occurred to the head and legs.

That is not to say that the shield was never employed as an offensive weapon. The rim was often used to strike at a spear shaft to snap the head off or to knock the spear aside. As has been mentioned, the boss was forcibly thrust into an opponent's face or chest to throw him off balance. Even when the shield had been rendered to matchwood, the boss could still be used as an armoured fist.

In the desperate struggle with bow, spear and sword, warriors attempted to protect themselves with the large circular shield carried in the left hand. This afforded some shelter from missiles, spear thrusts and sword slashes. It was their primary defensive aid, as very few men at the time could afford to equip themselves with helmet or body armour. Skilfully handled, a wooden and leather shield would have deflected a sword blow or absorbed the impact from a spear, it could be used as an effective offensive weapon too, but it did not offer complete defence. Agility was the surest weapon of the lowly bondsman.

Availability

Because iron was difficult to produce during the viking era – the raw material, iron ore, was extracted from bogs – it was expensive. As a result, items such as swords, helmets and byrnies were expensive too and thus not that common. Anyone who could afford a sword, helmet and byrnie would certainly want them, but not too many people could afford them. Swords, helmets and byrnies were prized and carefully preserved, repaired as needed and passed from generation to generation. As a result, a typical fighting man was armed with nothing more than a shield and an axe, or perhaps a shield and spear. A poor man might simply use the wood axe from the farm, if he had nothing else available. Besides, in the chaos and clutter of close combat a shorter chopping weapon, one made for severing limbs and spilling guts, would be more useful than a much longer weapon like a sword, which had to be drawn with the warrior's right hand across his body and behind his shield, a potentially dangerous manoeuvre. A thrust through his right armpit, for instance, would have severely damaged lungs and possibly heart.

All the same, battle gear would have been as individualistic as the warriors themselves, the aforementioned Grettir being big and hugely strong and looking much like a troll in appearance.[88] The sagas say that a warrior might hold a second weapon at the ready in his shield hand, while fighting with his primary weapon in the other hand. In *Fóstbrœðra saga*, Þorgeirr held a shield and an axe in his left hand while he fought with a spear in his right hand. Later in the fight, he threw down his spear and took up the axe in his right hand, using it to cut through Snorri's spear shaft, and then through Snorri's head.[89]

Nasty, brutal and not very short

Weapons set the parameters of war and battles, within the boundaries established by the purpose of the conflict. They determine what is and is not possible. At the same time, understanding the tools of war is not the same thing as understanding war. Weapons are not so important, nor their form so determinate of the conduct or outcome of war, as is commonly assumed. War is a sociological phenomenon, and weapons are merely tools facilitating its practice. With that thought in mind, we turn from the material aspect of viking warfare, the toolkit of the warrior, to the actual business of battle itself.

Battlefield tactics would have been relatively uncomplicated, being as they were an affair of bow and arrow, shield and spear, axe and sword. Units in our period of study (and throughout the early mediaeval period) would not really be capable of battlefield manoeuvre. Battlefield manoeuvre is probably a rather overestimated feature of battle of any period; was not it the great military analyst Carl von Clausewitz who said that any troops trying to manoeuvre in the face of the enemy were disordered? Even so, there was probably even less battlefield manoeuvre in our period. Warriors would draw up and advance straight forward.

Thus, a battleline (of Northmen, at least) almost always consisted of a dense array of warriors defended by large circular shields held close together, a solid formation of wood, metal and muscle commonly known as the *skjaldborg* (OE *scildweall*), shield wall. In this manner, the warriors stood side by side and held their shields rim to rim, or even overlapping. The latter did not allow for wide swings with sword or axe, so the front rank was perhaps limited to thrusting or parrying the opponents' spears. Those immediately behind the front rank were able to strike and thrust over the shoulders of their comrades. In this respect, the terrain could be decisive, the side holding the higher ground having an advantage. Certainly, with the blunt, horrific simplicity of shield wall combat, it was unlikely that an army would deploy so that the opposition overlapped a flank to a large degree. Thinning but lengthening the shield wall, as at Stiklarstaðir, was preferable.[90] Having said that, however, a battleline spread too thin was one easily broken, so it would have been sufficiently deep enough to prevent the enemy being able to slice straight through it. In offensive weaponry, therefore, the spear and shield combination was supreme.

Once deployed and closed up in their respective shield walls, opponents would have been within but a short distance of each other. They would square up and face one another. Without doubt an uncanny silence fell, as the two sides eyeballed each other. A knot of well-equipped warriors and fluttering banners would mark the centre of each battleline. Then one or both sides would begin to grind slowly forward. Now the cacophony would begin: shouts, battle cries, chants, vows, boasts and taunts. The *Hávamál* says that Óðinn himself raises the battle cry:

> … if I am to lead / old friends to the fray: / under buckler I chant / that briskly they fare / hale and whole from battle: / hale wherever they are.[91]

Here Óðinn stands alongside his comrades as they chant and advance into battle. Obviously, by yelling under shields, the sound is amplified, much like the *barditus* of Germanic warriors mentioned by Tacitus: 'they raise their shields to the mouth (*objectis ad os scutis*) so that the sound, being reflected, gets fuller and heavier'.[92] A thing not uncommon in pre-modern warfare, such testosterone fuelled behaviour doubtlessly ensured that the psychological impact was felt before the armies actually opened the battle. Indeed, one key feature of such warfare is that two such formed bodies of warriors do not simply crash straight into one another. There is a phase where the two sides will attempt to psych-out their opponents, to establish a moral advantage allowing a charge to be pressed home. Hurling of insults and challenges will have been part and parcel of this, as well as the exchange of actual missiles, and attempts to disorganize or otherwise physically shake up the enemy. Because of all this, it does not seem unlikely that warriors went into battle with a certain amount of 'Dutch courage'; the Welsh heroic poetry frequently makes reference to warriors filled with fresh mead. 'War is the province of danger; therefore *courage* is the soldier's first requirement', Carl von Clausewitz maintained,[93] though I have a feeling that he did have the alcoholic variety in mind.

As well as the hurling of insults and the like, a battle often opened with archery, then following this with a volley of thrown spears, in an attempt to physically soften up the opposition's shield wall before the armies locked in close quarter fighting. The opposition would have ducked in an attempt to catch the lethal rain of arrows and spears on their shields. A shield wall was exactly what the name implies, it being formed by the man on the right overlapping his shield leftwards, typically by a width of up to half a shield, boss to rim, and so on and so forth, the overall effect being much like scales on a fish. The advancing enemy would see a line of coloured wood and grey metal, eyes glinting between helmet and shield, and the only flesh on display being the lower legs.

Next came the close contact phase, which seems to have consisted of short periods of stabbing, smiting, hacking and hewing (with the right arm), while pushing, punching, barring and blocking (with the left arm), followed by a welcomed break to draw breath, to rest limbs, to rearrange the shield wall. For instance, in accounts of Gate Fulford and Stamford Bridge, two battles we will be dealing with in some detail, chroniclers mention repeatedly that the fighting lasted 'long in the day', 'was stoutly contested' and 'continued steadfastly', and was 'a very hard fight on both sides'.[94]

The idea that battle was made up of short, furious bouts of close quarter fighting between longer spells of rest and recuperation, these pauses in the fighting growing longer or more frequent – or both – is the best way of reconciling the accounts in the primary sources of very long battles with the practicalities of hand-to-hand combat. After all, close quarter exchanges of this nature were not only savage but a most exhausting process, for the energy used in holding and directing a spear, swinging an axe or engaging in the cut and thrust of swordplay was massive.

Many kinds of fighters appear in the Old Norse sagas: heroes and cowards, bullies and berserkers. Many of them are capable fighters. Those that are seem to be familiar with weapons and ready to use them effectively. Still, it was not like *Starship Troopers* where all the soldiers, males and females, were either heroes or cowards, but fortunately all the cowards were weeded out in basic training. Battle in our period of study was a grim process of ugly attrition, hammering away at one another until sheer exhaustion or weight of numbers swung the balance. It clearly called for strength, endurance, flexibility, and a drench of sweat, and in one saga we are told of a warrior keeping himself in constant training by walking in a byrnie.

Obviously, where one man bashed another to bloody bits, it was no place for the chickenhearted and dependable comrades were a must. A warrior had to be sure of those who stood to each side of him (especially on his unshielded right-hand side) in the shield wall. And when your enemy was doing the same thing, it all came down to who was the stronger, who had the strongest backs and the stoutest hearts. It would be well for us to remember that the shield wall was only as strong as its weakest link. We are reminded of the opening scenes of *The Battle of Maldon*, a poetic account of the defeat of Byrhtnoth (pronounced 'boorch-noth'), the *ealdorman* of Essex, and his army in 991, and the bard's description of how Byrhtnoth told his shire levies as they stood the boggy ground and awaited the dreaded Northmen to cross the causeway:

> How they should form up and hold the position, / and he asked that they should hold their shields properly, / firmly with their fists, and not be at all afraid.[95]

Afraid or not, eventually the will of one side would collapse and their shield wall would implode. Once this happened all united effort was over. It was now, with the broken side fleeing for their lives that the slaughter really began.

More can be said. For example, re-enactment experience suggests that formations can be taught basic proficiency in spear and shield warfare very quickly. Mastery of the basic moves – open order, forming ranks, advancing from column to line and turning about (in which the shield is passed over your head) – can be learnt in a day. In terms of basic drill, ordinary fellows could be turned into fighters 'over a period of about six weekends'.[96] But the Achilles' heel of the shield wall was neither basic moves nor basic drills. To create a fighter who would stand firm in a compact shield wall was another matter. Where a few days and a good instructor might suffice to train a reasonably good spearman, many years and a whole way of life were needed to produce a proficient one. Learning the skill sets would have been done by apprenticeship starting in early childhood. The hours spent honing particular actions, learnt from older hands, meant that by the time a fighter reached adulthood many of the skills and reflexes probably had become second nature.

The human factor

Brigadier General S.L.A. Marshall (1900–77), in his seminal work *Men against Fire*, emphasizes the importance of comradeship as a means of overcoming mass inertia on the modern industrial battlefield:

I hold it to be one of the simplest truths of war that the thing which enables an infantry soldier to keep going with his weapons is the near presence or the presumed presence of a comrade. The warmth which derives from human companionship is as essential to his employment of the arms with which he fights as is the finger with which he pulls a trigger or the eye with which he aligns his sights.[97]

In a moment of sociological insight, he insisted that the infantry soldier 'is sustained by his fellows primarily and by his weapons secondarily'.[98] Soldiers, who are invariably members of a citizen army, require 'some feeling of spiritual unity'.[99] As the Pacific War veteran Eugene Sledge wrote of his own combat experience:

War is brutish, inglorious, and a terrible waste. Combat leaves an indelible mark on those who are forced to endure it. The only redeeming factors were my comrades' incredible bravery and their devotion to each other... That *esprit de corps* sustained us.[100]

In consequence, soldiers form a close and self-contained group, that is, they acquire and foster a sense of comradeship that dominates every aspect of their existence. Such comradeship is, to a certain extent, a negative state, a protective shrinking within a cocoon of intense intimacy with fellow soldiers as an essential means towards self-preservation and the maintenance of sanity in a world gone mad.

There were three distinct components to what military theorist would now term fighting power. The first was physical, involving the weapons and equipment used; the second, so closely related, was conceptual, and concerned the evolution of military doctrine; and the third was human, and centred on the myriad of complex factors that made men fight, even at great personal risk. Of the three, the human component (in truth, a matter of manliness) of fighting power is always more difficult to define than its fellows in the trinity. It can neither be counted nor calculated, nor it be accurately assessed through drill books, training manuals or pamphlets on doctrine, not that Northmen would have been interested in such reading matter.

Whether authentic or not, the reported words of Óláfr II Haraldsson *inn digri* on the eve of his twentieth and terminal battle, that fought in 1030 on a day of high summer at Stiklarstaðir (today's Stiklestad) when the sun turned black, near Nidaros (ON *Niðaróss* – '(at the) mouth of the river *Nið*' – today's Trondheim), showcases nicely the conception in these tribal battles of the vital importance of cooperative tactics and group cohesion. Here is the story of Óláfr:

I shall request all men to arrange themselves in groups so that kinsmen and acquaintances stand together, because then everyone will best shield his comrade if they know one another.[101]

The common Old Norse term to describe what soldiers of my generation called the 'buddy-buddy system' was *eaxlgesteakka*, 'shoulder comrade'. It was the Greek military writer Onasander who wrote, in the mid-first century, that a general should station 'brothers in rank beside brothers; friends beside friends; and lovers beside their favourites'.[102] Thus, as Óláfr knew all too well, his men would draw courage and confidence from the proximity to other obviously warlike and well-armed family, friends and neighbours. Instructively, in emphasizing friendship, the king was in line with modern western military doctrine, that is, the importance of close personal bonds in forming unshakeable group cohesion.

Take, for instance, *Infantry Training* (1944), one of the most important and useful documents to be produced by the British army during the Second World War. It includes extensive material on sophisticated infantry tactics but, nevertheless, it too stresses the importance of existing social ties to military performance. When describing the structure of platoon sections, it states that these small units are organized into two or (more unusually) three groups, one or two rifle groups and one Bren gun group.[103] The manual recommends that 'Groups are formed from friends as far as possible, in order that friends keep together and fight together'.[104]

In harsh reality, when the crunch came, comrades were closer than friends, closer than brothers. Their relationship was different from lovers. Their trust in, and knowledge of each other, was total. They performed duties together that bonded men, bonded men forever. The horrors of war could evoke what C.S. Lewis identified as 'the deepest of worldly emotions' – not romantic love, but rather 'the love of man for man, the mutual love of warriors who die together fighting against the odds, and the affection between vassal and lord'.[105]

As that cool repository of Norse worldly wisdom, which sensibly confines itself to this world and ignores the life to come, advises:

> The unwise man thinks / that he ay will live, / if from fighting he flees; / / but the ails and aches / of old age dog him / though spears have spared him.[106]

The shield wall holds steadfast only it has sufficient morale and courage to stand and face the fight. This requires warriors in ample numbers, as well as with enough practice and experience fighting together to be able to trust their fellows to stand with them, rather than break and run away. From Sjörup comes a stone that commemorates a warrior for his heroic defiance in defeat. The epitaph opens with a simple memorial formula: 'Saksi set this up in memory of his comrade Asbjörn Toki's son'. Then it breaks into heroic verse: 'He fled not at Uppsala / But kept on fighting while he could hold a weapon'.[107] As it clearly says in the *Hávamál*:

Cattle die, kinsmen die / you yourself shall die / I know one thing which never dies / the reputation of each dead man.[108]

The stanza above strongly suggests that a man's reputation was as integral to his fate as the time and place of his death: that reputation *was* Norse immortality. Your choice, then, was whether you took that death wound in the back or face on, and how you chose determined whether you would be remembered as a hero, a villain – or not at all. In fact, this stanza would pass muster anywhere, at anytime, yet it goes without saying that there was no place for the squeamish in the shield wall.

In essence, the strength of the shield wall and consequently the possibility of success depended on the motivation of the warriors to keep a tight formation during battle and to keep advancing through the ranks while others fell. Thus, in skaldic verse a common kenning – an Old Norse compound expression – for a fighting man was *runnr*, 'tree', who it is hoped, would stand in battle firm as a tree.

A warrior's motivation had to be internal. Comradeship was by way the strongest motivation – not wanting to let his fraternal comrades down, in the positive sense, not wanting to appear a coward in front of the men he respects above all others, in the negative sense. The esteem of comrades was not replaceable; we should conceive of this comradeship as a male brotherhood. Today we recognize this as combat cohesion, a special bonding that implies that men are willing to die for the preservation of the primary group, or the code of honour of the primary group. Acting as a 'force multiplier', at moments, survival and victory depend on the intense cooperation of all ranks during combat. More broadly, cohesion comprises horizontal bonding (viz. the relationship among peers), vertical bonding (viz. relationships up and down the chain of command) and organizational bonding (viz. the values of the society in which soldiers are embedded).[109]

Combat cohesion roused a feeding frenzy among military historians and social scientists during the nineteen-seventies and eighties, and it would be discourteous to ignore the feast. It is an old topic – the question of cohesion was central to the writings of both Niccolò Machiavelli and Carl von Clausewitz on war – but the modern daddy of small group cohesion is S.L.A. Marshall (in spite of the fact that over the last two decades or so he has been the focus of intense critique and sometimes outright rejection),[110] with the new zeal kindled by more recent conflicts such as the Vietnam and the Falklands/Malvinas wars.

It is widely recognized both within the armed forces themselves and in scholarly analysis that small group cohesion is essential among combat soldiers, for without that sense of solidarity and mutual obligation, individual soldiers are likely to save themselves or to run away. It is a striking and extraordinary fact that, despite the evident attractions of desertion, soldiers have often preferred to fight and die together.

So for our Northmen, endurance and self-control were vital traits, and success lay in keeping the battleline intact. As long as a tight formation was maintained, it would be almost impossible for the opponent to break through the wall of shields. Breaking up the battleline, whether in a fervent rush forward to engage the enemy or in uncontrolled flight, would inevitably lead to defeat. Before the battle of Ilevollene (27 May 1180), just outside Nidaros, Sverrir Sigurðarson, pretender to the throne of Norway (r. 1184–1202), related a parable to his men:

> A *bóndi* accompanied his son to the warships and gave him counsel, telling him to be valiant and hardy in perils. 'How would you act if you were engaged in battle and knew beforehand that you were destined to be killed?' The son answered, 'Why then should I refrain from striking right and left?' The *bóndi* said, 'Now suppose someone could tell you for certain that you would not be killed?' The son answered, 'Why then should I refrain from pushing forward to the utmost?' The *bóndi* said, 'In every battle you fight, one of two things will happen: you will either fall or come away alive. Be bold, therefore, for everything is preordained. Nothing can bring a man to his death if his time has not come, and nothing can save one doomed to die. To die in flight is the worst death of all'.[111]

The greatest test of a man was to fight to the bitter end, even in the face of certain defeat and death. It was this belief that caused Northmen to be bold and adventuresome. There was nothing to lose and everything to gain by being bold, since, as is said in *Heiðarvíga saga*, there is truth in the old saying that there is no slaying of a man destined to live.[112]

On a large scale, the Old Norse myths deal with the gods' battle against irreversible fate, as the chief god Óðinn wanders in the land of the giants seeking wisdom and especially knowledge about the fate of the world. Likewise, the protecting god of thunder Þórr moves in the same territory, slaying giants (who are not the lumbering, slow-witted creatures of later fairy tale) who are, nevertheless, fated to overcome and destroy the world. This noble yet vain struggle against fate resembles the struggle of mortal men in battle. Man is fated to die, but his heroism in resistance is comparable to that of the gods as a struggle to avoid an inevitable end.

In the academic literature, cohesion is typically understood to persist in primary groups all the members of which engage in regular face-to-face relations so that all individuals know each other personally. In other words, group cohesion is inversely related to group size. In emphasizing the importance of small group cohesion in battle, and the consequences of the action of a single warrior, Judith Jesch notes that men are regularly praised for not fleeing. Accounts on the rune stones like 'he fled not' and 'he fought while he had a weapon' and at the other end of the scale 'he lost his life because his companions fled' provide insights into the qualities that were valued and honoured in battle. One praised act of bravery that brought honour was 'feeding the beasts of battle', that is, killing the enemy.[113] This was war up close and personal; war in small scale, war centred on the individual and a small closely-knit group of fellow warriors bent on surviving the day.

Surviving the day not only meant facing the enemy, but mastering the extreme physical and emotional challenge posed by death, which is, of course, what war is all about. The noise alone would have been incredible – shouts, screams, war cries, and the desperate cries of the wounded and near dead in several languages all competing with the clashing of thousands of weapons. In the press, braced hard against the blood-smeared shields of one's foes, it was possible to physically feel the ebb and flow of battle. When deaths or crippling wounds created gaps in the shield wall, experienced warriors probably gave ground in order to maintain the battle line. Hardened warriors would have known the penalties for allowing the enemy to break into the shield wall. Stepping back and closing up the gaps, whilst maintaining a continuous front, was preferable to flight and being cut down from behind. The difficulty of creeping backwards in close formation might be offset against the fact that the advancing side would have the bodies of the dead, dying and wounded to negotiate.[114]

If you have read Homer, devotee of the spoken word and founding father of Hellenism, then you will know that if he has taught us anything, it is that the human being is a frail vessel, a fleshy animated flagon of blood and loose guts just waiting to be spilled in the dust and din of battle. Of course, usually death is pushed to the fringes of things you do in the modern world. Most people face their end pretty much alone, with a few family members if they are lucky. On the battlefield, even today, soldiers face death together, in their prime. If anyone dies, he is surrounded by the best friends he believes he will ever had. This truism has remained a constant fact throughout the history of warfare, and was very much so for our Northmen.

The numbers game

Paper strengths are of little use for practical purposes in any period of military history. This is nicely illustrated in a communiqué written by Berthier to Napoléon, then First Consul, from Dijon in April 1800, at the opening of the Marengo campaign. Berthier, as the nominal general-in-chief of the Army of Reserve, estimated that he would cross the Alps with 'at most 30,000 men of infantry; calculation of general-in-chief and not that of as clerks; what you can better appreciate than anyone else'.[115]

Having said that, apprising the numbers of combatants involved in any early mediaeval conflict is an exceedingly woolly task. It can safely be said that there is always a tendency to exaggerate both the size of armies and the number of casualties. It was certainly possible in the early mediaeval period to put a sizeable army in the field, even if only for a limited time, but it could not be greater than the population from which it was drawn. It is clear the chroniclers liked to tell a good story, yet few literary sources specify the size of armies and those that do are accounts prone to hyperbole.

Obviously, all such figures must be treated with suspicion, yet according to the testimony of one Icelandic *littérateur*, Snorri Sturluson, the king's army at Stiklarstaðir numbered only 'three thousand [3,600] men, which was considered a large army'. Indeed, it was considered large enough even to be divided into three 'battles': Swedes on the left (480 picked men supplied by their king Onund Jakob), Dag Hringsson's men (1,440 strong) on the right and Óláfr's personal retainers (*hirðmaðr*), Uppland and Nidaros men (1,440 strong) in the centre.[116] Dag Hringsson's father is said to have been of the Uppland kings banished for their part in a conspiracy against Óláfr Haraldsson more than ten years before. Dag had followed his father into exile in Sweden. It was there he met the king, who promised full restitution of his father's lands in Norway if he would join him with all the fighting men he could muster. And so Dag did. Anyway, it may be an understatement on Snorri's part, but there is nothing improbable about the figure of 3,600, and presumably many of Óláfr's men were proficient warriors, skilled practitioners of violence. Such armies could be tiny, when measured against twenty-first-century expectations.

Simply put, to use an old adage, the saga says what it means, and means what it says. One thing, at all events, is clear; the army opposing Óláfr's more professional and experienced force was largely composed of *bændr* and labourers and outnumbered his men four times over.[117] Yet this should not obscure the fact that these *bændr* were men whose commonplace occupation was working the land and sea as farmers and fishermen, men who normally engaged in farming (meat and barley), fishing (herring) or related craft activities such as ship building, house building and smithing – iron production stayed in the hands of farmers, not of specialist iron-masters; their compensation for poor soils and intractable terrain. This was the elemental economy that provided the food, and thereby the energy, which fuelled all social activity.

The fugitive

araldr Sigurðarson was the half-brother of Óláfr II Haraldsson – Óláfr *inn digri* (the Stout), as he was called in his lifetime – the hardnosed evangelizing king of Norway who would be recognized as a saint within a year of his violent death. Óláfr's father, Haraldr *grænski*, had died shortly after Óláfr was born. After his death Óláfr's mother, Ásta Guðbrandsdóttir, had married Sigurðr *sýr* (Sow) Hálfdanarson, a petty king in Hringaríki, part of the district known as Uppland, and it was there that Óláfr grew up.

Since the age of twelve Óláfr Haraldsson had been a viking, harrying the Baltic and much of northern Europe. He had fought in England for several years, first on the Danish side and then with the English, changing sides like any canny mercenary as pay and conditions dictated. He was leader of those who overran East Anglia, and said to be responsible for the destruction of London Bridge, the origin of *London Bridge is Falling Down*. He had returned to Norway in 1014, and by the following year he had been crowned king, having defeated *jarl* Sveinn Hákonsson at Nesjar.[118] He was the first Norwegian king to succeed in joining eastern Norway to what was otherwise a mainly west Norwegian kingdom. He also introduced (and enforced) new legislation and a new respect for the king's justice and the rule of law, which proved popular with the *bændr*, farmers, but obviously not with the regional big men, those petty kings and jarls who had previously lorded it with impunity over their pocket domains. Jarls were semi or fully independent regional lords and, as with the *bændr*, some held lands by odal (ON *óðöl*) right of inheritance, others ruthlessly fought their way to power. In the early period there is little clear difference between powerful jarls and the many petty kings who flourished in Norway.

In England Knútr I Sveinsson viewed these developments with growing concern. He had put a regent, his brother-in-law, *jarl* Úlfr Þorgilsson, on the throne of Denmark to rule the kingdom on his behalf while his attentions were engaged in England; and he had secretly been using English wealth to undermine Óláfr's authority in Norway. Subsequently, in 1025, Knútr claimed that he should be the king of Norway, with the result that Óláfr, in alliance with the Swedish king Onund Jakob, started waging war against Denmark. The final clash took place at the mouth of the Helgeä river in eastern Scania the following year. Though the outcome of the battle is disputed, which was fought on both land and sea, it did crucially weaken Óláfr's position. It was the end of Óláfr's territorial ambitions in Scandinavia and the beginning of his political troubles at home. Knútr was able to form an alliance with the alienated Norwegian jarls – who were happy to hail him as a deliverer from tyranny – and in 1028 Óláfr was forced to flee overseas to his brother-in-law, prince Yaroslav (ON *Jarizleifr*) of Novgorod and Kiev (called later 'the Wise'), whence he would return in 1030 in an unsuccessful – and for him, fatal – attempt to regain the throne of Norway.

Those informative years

Before continuing with Haraldr's story and his involvement with his half-brother's political affairs, let me take you back to his childhood. Sigurðr *sýr* Hálfdanarson was the father of Haraldr, and he was born in the year in which Óláfr was fighting his way to the Norwegian throne. As he grew, Haraldr displayed traits of a typical unruly boy with wild ambitions, ones well suited for the cut-and-thrust of Scandinavian kingship, and admired his half-brother Óláfr as his rôle model. Rumbustious and belligerent, he thus differed greatly from his two older brothers who were more like their father, down-to-earth and mostly concerned with maintaining the family estate.

On first meeting their royal half-brother, the three boys were asked in turn what he would like to own. Grain fields were Guþorm's choice, while Hálfdan chose cattle and so many as would surround the local lake when they were watered, but when it came to Haraldr's turn:

> 'Housecarls', he replied. The king asked, 'And how many?' 'So many that they would eat up all of my brother Hálfdan's cows at a single meal'. The king laughed and said to Ásta, 'In him you are likely to bring up a king, mother'.[119]

One does not have to take this anecdote at face value in order for it to have meaning. We are fittingly reminded of an anecdote concerning the young Napoleone di Buonaparte (as he was known at that time). Letizia, his mother, recalled that when she gave her children paints to use on the wall of their playroom, all the other children painted puppets but Napoléon alone painted soldiers. Snorri Sturluson (1179–1241), himself a Christian, was a great saga writer, and accordingly he often mixed fancy and fiction with fact and fidelity. While hardly to be considered other than an apocryphal anecdote, his account of Haraldr's first meeting with Óláfr does at least have a ring of plausibility, which should not lead us to reject the kernels of fact that may lie within. Unlike his father, but like his half-brother, his boyhood hero, Haraldr was very much interested in military matters. Remember and mark this fact.

Haraldr was a prince – of that we are sure – but not one in the way we envision today. There were few, in any, trappings of office, and he may have lived a very athletic and rugged life in his youth, as did most Norwegians of that time.

Armed and angry farmers

Haraldr's life and career would be intimately connected with warfare, but the first – and in some ways the most important – of his conflicts was against his fellow Norwegians.

Having added Norway to his North Sea empire, Knútr Sveinsson was content to leave a Norwegian, *jarl* Hákon Eiríksson, on the throne as regent and returned to the peace and prosperity of England. The following winter, however, Hákon was drowned in the Pentland Firth.[120] There were various rumours about his untimely end, but it is probable that he perished on his return from a visit to England, during which he became betrothed to Gunnhildr, Knútr's niece. In his place Knútr sent his son by Ælfgifu of Northampton, Sveinn Knútsson, to rule in Norway under his mother's guardianship. The news of these events eventually reached Kiev.

Haraldr's royal half-brother, Óláfr Haraldsson, was of the opinion that Norway could be won back most quickly by a decisive success in the district where his enemies were the strongest, namely the Trøndelag. Early in 1030, therefore, the exiled king set off along the frozen Russian rivers to the coast, and when the sea-ice broke up sailed to the Baltic island of Gotland (to be carefully distinguished from the mainland Götaland) with a small detachment of 240 warriors. In Sweden, the king, his brother-in-law Onund Jakob, lent him another 480 picked men, and with this ragtag little army he crossed the mountains and forests of the northern Norwegian hinterland into the valley of Veraladr (Veldal), hoping to rally support on the way. But little support materialized. The *bændr* on whom he had relied to answer his call, those farmers great and small on whom he had helped with his legal enactments and strict dispensations of justice for high and low alike had in the meantime turned against him.

One man did not let him down, however – Haraldr Sigurðarson, his half-brother, now a strapping fifteen-year-old and itching to swing a sword in the showdown scrap that everyone knew lay ahead. Óláfr demurred:

> 'It seems advisable to me', said the king, 'that my brother Haraldr be not in this battle as he is still only a child'. Haraldr answered, 'By all means I shall take part in it, and if I am so weak as not to be able to wield a sword, then I know what to do: let my hand be tied to the hilt. No one is more

minded than I to strike a blow against those *bœndr*. I mean to be with my comrades'... and Haraldr had his will to be in the battle.[121]

Like other Norse kings, Óláfr surrounded himself with skalds; at Stiklarstaðir he had three Icelandic skalds in train, including Þormóðr *kolbrúnarskáld* (Coal-brow's-skald), who would die of his battle wound that day, but his favourite Sigvatr Þórðarson was on pilgrimage to Rome.[122] These skalds Óláfr is said to have brought within his shield wall, bidding them mark the event well and immortalize it later. From their verse and other such traditions and legends as were associated with the battle Snorri Sturluson composed one of his consummate narrative pieces.

Fact or fiction?

The authenticity of Óláfr's last battle as a historical event has been brought into serious question. Those modern commentators that doubt the battle actually took place point to the fact that the near contemporary sources that mention the death of Óláfr Haraldsson say the warrior king was simply murdered. Thus, according to the *Anglo Saxon Chronicle*, the king was killed by his own men while he slept.[123] Adam of Bremen writes that Óláfr was killed in an ambush, and so does John of Worcester.[124] After the king's canonization it was felt that the saint could not have died in what was seen as cowardly circumstances. Rather, Saint Óláfr must have fallen in a large-scale land battle fighting on behalf of Christianity.

But what about *Heimskringla*? The title of this majestic work means 'Orb of the World' (*kringla heimsins*), the opening two words of the text (and thus called by the editors since about 1682), with which Snorri Sturluson grandly locates Scandinavia, and the homeland of the dynasty which is to be the subject of his celebrated collection of biographies of the kings of Norway. *Heimskringla* is a series of sixteen sagas about the Norwegian kings, beginning with the saga of the legendary Swedish dynasty of the Ynglings (who Snorri claims were descended from the Norse deity Freyr, the shining god of fertility, peace and plenty who was also known as Yngvi), followed by accounts of historical Norwegian rulers from Haraldr *hárfagri* (Fine-hair) up to the death of the pretender Eysteinn Meyla in 1177. A real historiography by the standards of the time, the *Heimskringla* is primarily concerned with facts, though the author permitted himself to arrange the details to fit the desired image of the king in question and to create an interesting story. The exact sources of Snorri's work are disputed, but included earlier kings' sagas, such as *Morkinskinna* ('Rotten Vellum'),[125] *Nóregs tal konungr* ('List of Norway's kings', commonly known as *Fagrskinna*, or 'Beautiful Vellum') and the twelfth-century Norwegian synoptic histories and oral traditions, notably many skaldic poems.

As we shall discover, *Heimskringla*, written either in the twelve-twenties or twelve-thirties, records the travels of Haraldr Sigurðarson to Kievan Russia after the death of his half-brother Óláfr Haraldsson and his rôle as a member of the Varangian Guard that served the Byzantine emperor in Constantinople. The story of Haraldr's service as a Varangian, though Snorri created an idealized picture of this difficult and domineering character, is corroborated by a Byzantine source from the end of the eleventh century, *Advice for the Emperor*. Written in Greek, this work succinctly describes the deeds of a captain of the Varangian Guard named *Araltes* (Haraldr), the brother of king *Julavos* (Óláfr) of Norway, who served the emperor Michael IV from 1034 to 1042. Yet for the sake of entertainment, Snorri might see fit to occasionally include an episode of dubious reliability, and he has no qualms about presenting conversation and speeches that had no absolute historical foundation. Thucydides, long before Snorri, made it clear that he intended his work to be 'useful'.[126] Snorri no doubt intended that too, but he also intended it might serve *til skemmtanar*, for entertainment.[127]

The battle

If we are to assume there was an actual battle, the fateful engagement took place on a day of high summer at Stiklarstaðir (Stiklestad), a farmstead in the lower part of the valley of Veraladr, some seventy kilometres northeast of Nidaros (Trondheim). Waiting for the king was an army led by Hárekr of Þjóttu, Þórir *hundr* (the Hound) from Bjarköy and Kálfr Árnason, a man who previously served Óláfr. The bonders' army consisted of 'no less than hundred times a hundred' according to Snorri Sturluson,[128] which in long hundreds means 14,400, and not 10,000.

The traditional date of Stiklarstaðir is 29 July (viz. 'the fourth kalends of August' in Snorri Sturluson's words),[129] but some accounts report an eclipse of the sun, which is reliably recorded for the summer of 1030, on 31 August to be precise.[130] Of course, the day of the eclipse may have been shifted to enhance Óláfr's saintliness. His feast day is 29 July, the canonical day of the battle of Stiklarstaðir. On the other hand, Jacqueline Simpson suggests the date discrepancy may have derived from misinterpretation of an original text of *Óláfs saga helga*, which would have probably given the date in the customary mediaeval form as '1029 years and two hundred and nine days since Christ's birth'. Reckoning in 'long hundreds' (as 249 days) from 25 December would actually give the date of 31 August, the day of the eclipse,[131] while reckoning in 'continental hundreds' (or 209 days) from 1 January would give the date of 29 July, which is found in Theodoricus Monachus' *Historia de antiquitate regum Norwagiensium* and Snorri's *Heimskringla*.[132]

To a cold eye it might appear that Óláfr set death or victory on a desperate throw of the gaming dice and it is interesting to find that Snorri, in general so favourable to him, shows him returning to his lost kingdom with everything he had formerly reprobated, a part-alien and part-pagan army of mercenaries. Against him, we read, were none but Norwegians. In essence, this was entirely an internal dispute, as neither Knútr nor the Danes took part in the battle; Óláfr had been killed by his own subjects. But in all likelihood Stiklarstaðir reflected the permanent realities of Scandinavian politics; pressure and interference from Denmark and Sweden, and Norwegians divided in factions: the crushing of the power-broking jarls would have to wait until Haraldr Sigurðarson was king. Stiklarstaðir is one of the incantatory names of Norse history. Yet it was too important to be left to historians, so passed into the hand of the legend maker.

We may assume that the battle was a bloody struggle of men who fought on foot, men who hacked and stabbed at their foes to the limit of their strength and courage. This is assumed because the actual details of the battle are wanting, but when the day was done Óláfr was dead and once more Norway had broken from a Norwegian's hand to a hand of an outsider. This fact is a timely reminder to us historians that viking-age kingship was about power, and power was about men – particularly warriors – and wealth. A powerful *regional* leader could by force of arms intimidate weaker *regional* leaders and demand from the latter military and financial support. We should not assume one nation, one king or, even less, one state, one king, any more than titles conferred power. It was not enough to claim a kingdom, it had to be held, and it had to be made secure. Thus, power was not conferred; it was grasped and done so with an iron grip.

A good tale is worth telling time and again, and if told often enough it eventually becomes difficult to see the difference between the reality and fiction. Indeed, because the army that killed him at Stiklarstaðir was made up of his own countrymen, skalds and saga writers portrayed his death as the great betrayal of a king by his kingdom, generously oiled by the bribes and promises of his Danish rival Knútr.

Let us take, for instance, the most celebrated (and accessible) account of Stiklarstaðir, namely that of Snorri Sturluson. His account is deliberately heroic and (it is believed) highly fictitious. The day, he informs us, began in epic style. Óláfr woke early and called on the vindictively minded skald Þormóðr to intone a pagan poem to rouse the host. This was the old *Bjarkamál*, which told of the doomed stand of Hrólfr *kraki* of Denmark and his champions at Lejre. Their courage whetted, so went the tale, Óláfr's men advanced to the place of slaughter. It was at this point that Óláfr wondered whether his half-brother Haraldr was not too young and weak for what lay ahead, and as we know already Haraldr's replied that if nothing else would serve, his hand would be tethered to his sword hilt. The armies were harangued by their leaders, and the leaders harangued each other. Then to a shout of '*Fram, fram, bóandmenn!*' in one army and '*Fram, fram,*

Kristsmenn, krossmenn, konungsmenn! ' in the other, the unequal struggle began. The weather was bright and the sun shone from a clear sky, but as blows were traded and the dead men fell, sky and sun grew red, and before the battle ended it was dark as a moonless night. The king, whose *hirð* was collapsing one by one, fought with ferocious fearlessness and no thought of flight. Two of his skalds, his standard-bearer, and his marshal fell near him. In turn, the king was brought to bay with his back against a rock and died of three fearful wounds. Some say Kálfr Árnason dealt him his last wound, some say a different Kálfr. The king's sanctity was revealed forthwith by the miracles wrought by his still wet blood.[133] The king's body was carried away and buried secretly in the sandy banks of the river Nid just south of Nidaros.[134] So much for the legend.

The chosen ones

Before we continue mention should be made of the *hirð* of Óláfr. Mustering some sixty strong, their service and wages were regulated by special laws. They were housed in a great dormitory within the king's residence, many sharing a dormitory with the king himself. Thus they lived with their chief and ate at his table. He protected them, and naturally in return they protected him. They were expected to follow him through thick and thin, serve him during good times and bad, and to fight by his side in battle, where their presence was often the decisive factor. To put it in an Old Norse perspective, it was the duty of a chieftain, called *góði* (pl. *góðar*), to provide food and drink for his followers, just as it was the duty of a warrior to provide food and drink, as skalds like to say, for the beasts of battle. These were the unwritten rules of the game in Old Norse culture. Indeed, it was expected for a viking-age ruler to have a personal military following in permanent attendance – a *hirð* (pronounced 'heerth').

The loanword *hirð* 'king's retinue', (later) 'royal court' comes from the Old English word *hired*, and is earliest and most convincingly attested in Norwegian contexts, namely in court poetry of the early eleventh century with reference to the personal retinues of great men, especially the kings of Norway.[135] The earliest attestation appears to be in a verse of the young Icelandic skald Gunnlaugr *ormstungu* (983–1008), which refers to a *hirðmaðr* of *jarl* Eiríkr Hákonarson of Lade (ON *Hlaðir*).[136] Thereafter, around 1016 the Norwegian court skald Sigvatr Þórðarson uses *hirð* twice referring to troops of Óláfr II Haraldsson,[137] and throughout the rest of the eleventh century it is common in such contexts.

The chosen men of the *hirð* were the king's closest companions. They guarded him day and night, ate with him and attended him constantly. Thus, the *hirð* did not only have military significance, and we should not think of it merely as a 'tool' to be used in times of need, it also fulfilled important representational and protective functions. Moreover, a band of retainers constituted a brotherhood with a code of honour that bound them together as tight as ticks, and in addition to the duties to the chief, the retainer had responsibilities towards his comrades. By its very nature, a band of retainers could be used to build and exercise power. They were also expected to die fighting when their chief had fallen.

Evidently, this was the scenario that played itself out at Stiklarstaðir, and once again, legend plays its part in the sacred memory of the battle. In 1901, the Norwegian poet and novelist Per Sivle (1857–1904) composed the poem *Tord Foleson*, about Óláfr's standard-bearer at the battle. Þórðr Fólason, to give him his name in Old Norse, was able to firmly plant the banner before he fell beneath it mortally wounded, and there it remained standing throughout the battle, even after the king had received his death-wounds and fallen upon the blood spattered grass of the battlefield.[138] It was kept erect and replaced by the local populace for centuries, and a memorial stands at the site today. The most famous line of the poem, *Mannen kann siga; / men Merket det maa* ('If the man he falls / the standard must remain'),[139] is inscribed on the memorial in the northern Norwegian village of Stalheim.

Óláfr's death

Turning to Óláfr again, the circumstances surrounding his death on the battlefield are confused. Almost every source concerning Óláfr gives a different version of the event, mentioning various weapons and assassins. In *Óláfs saga helga* in *Heimskringla*, for instance, four persons are listed as striking at the king: Kálfr Árnason (a man who previously served the king), Kálfr Arnfinsson (the cousin of Kálfr Árnason), Þórir *hundr* (the Hound) and Þorsteinn *knarrarsmiðr* (Shipbuilder). Kálfr aimed at the left side of Óláfr's neck, Þorsteinn *knarrarsmiðr* at the left leg, and Þórir *hundr* thrust a spear up below Óláfr's byrnie and pierced his belly – this was the spear called *Selshemnaren*, Seal's Avenger, which had killed his nephew Ásbjörn Sigurðarson *selsbani* (Slayer of Seal) – but it is not explicitly stated whether Kálfr Árnason or Kálfr Arnfinsson slashed the king's neck.[140] Elsewhere, however, we apparently learn the truth, for *Magnús saga góða* 'reveals' Kálfr Árnason as the killer,[141] while *Orkneyinga saga* has Kálfr Árnason confronted by the Orkneyman Rögnvaldr Brúsason in Kievan Russia five years after the battle and accordingly 'repented of (his share in) the great crime of having deprived king Óláfr *helgi* of his life and kingdom'.[142]

As an aside, some twenty-odd years later Haraldr would exact a bloody revenge for his half-brother's death. On one of the king's raids on Denmark, Kálfr Árnason was assigned to command the ship's crew that was to make the first landing on the island of Funen (Fyn). With assurance that Haraldr would speedily bring up the main force up in support, Kálfr led his men ashore only to be left in the lurch when attacked by a strong Danish force. Quickly overwhelmed, Kálfr was just one of the many Norwegians cut down by pursuing Danes as they fled back to their ship. Presumably having seen Kálfr slain on the sand, Haraldr's purpose was accomplished and he brought the main force ashore to start the serious business of raiding with fire and sword.[143] Thus, like a Norse Uriah, Haraldr saw Kálfr advance into the forefront of battle that he might die of an undefended back. For those of you unfamiliar with this biblical tale, Uriah the Hittite was the soldiering husband of the beautiful Bathsheba. King David sees her taking a bath; he lusts after her and orders her to get to his bed. She falls pregnant and David gets rid of Uriah by telling his commander, Joab, to put him in the front line where he is sure to be killed. And so it came to pass.[144]

Even so, whomever was the actual perpetrator – though Haraldr clearly saw Kálfr Árnason as the prime suspect – the general message is that Óláfr's death was dishonourable and heroic, a calvary in truth. In Christianity martyrdom is central. To sacrifice oneself, immolate oneself. Did not Jesus Christ do that? He became flesh and subjected himself to the most awful cruelty. Betrayal, torture, death on the cross. As a pagan, Óláfr had lived the viking life: sailed, raided, plundered, fought, fornicated, murdered, plotted, versified and played games. As a Christian, however, his human frailty or vigour had nothing to do with his eventual sainthood; it was enough that he had authority while alive, had been betrayed and brutally killed, and worked miracles afterwards. A hero and martyr is not an abstract prototype or a model of perfection but a human being made of contradictions and contrasts, weakness and greatness, since a man is many men, which means angels and demons combine inextricably in his personality.

On the run

The defeat and death of a beloved brother was a blow that would have finished most mortals. For the young Haraldr it proved a merely a temporary setback. Still, having experienced the pendulum of fortune he was forced to become a fugitive. He had been severely wounded in the day's fighting at Stiklarstaðir, but managed to escape from the corpse-strewn field into the surrounding forests, where he was hidden in a remote farmhouse while his wounds were healed. As soon as he was fit to travel he was smuggled out of Norway into friendly Sweden, and from there he made his way to Kiev where he was given asylum by prince Yaroslav. The journey on the road to Stamford Bridge had begun.

The court of Yaroslav, while partly a refuge for Haraldr, also offered positive appeals. Before Stiklarstaðir Haraldr was a royal prince; at Kiev he was a dispossessed adventurer. For it was from this point that Haraldr life as a wandering mercenary began in earnest. He gathered a considerable following (reputedly 500 strong) of loyal and disaffected men, and together they served many masters during the next fifteen years or so. As he slinked from Norway as a hunted nobody later tradition has Haraldr composing the following verse:

> Though endless woods I wend my / way now, honoured little. / Who knows but my name will be / noised abroad thereafter?[145]

Having survived his recent brush with death, Haraldr's life changed forever. The consciousness of having defied death undoubtedly contributed to his growing sense of infallibility, and his perception that he was a warrior destined for greater things. It was not predetermined, of course, that Haraldr Sigurðarson was to play this historic rôle. Haraldr was necessarily oblivious to what was to come. The refugee came to Kiev as a defeated prince and a series of military adventures followed, some impulsive others profitable. Stiklarstaðir was the first significant milestone in Haraldr's career and he probably looked back on it with mixed feelings. We are obliged to leave Haraldr in the paid service of Yaroslav.

Régime change

Following Óláfr's death at Stiklarstaðir, Norway would be ruled for five years by Sveinn Knútsson. Behind his throne, as *éminence grise*, stood his Mercian mother Ælfgifu of Northampton, Knútr's consort, now being suitably rewarded for her years of faithful concubinage. Her rule turned out to be an abysmal failure. She increased taxation, demanded greater services and made the Norwegians abide by Danish laws. Obviously, the Norwegians did not care for this new, brash foreign ruler, and she was a woman to boot; they soon found themselves longing for the days of Saint Óláfr. They had killed a perfectly good Norwegian king only to have a bad Anglo-Danish puppet foisted on them. Ælfgifu's rule of Norway was short-lived but long remembered for her harshness, as well as the bad harvests. The expression 'Ælfgifu's time' (*Álfífuþla*, she was known as *Álfífa* in Old Norse) was subsequently to become a synonym in Norway for any period of poverty and repression.

In *Ágrip af Nóregskonúngasögum* ('Epitome of the Sagas of the Norwegian Kings'), the following verse is attributed to her contemporary, the skald Sigvatr Þórðarson: 'Ælfgifu's time / long will the young man remember, / when they at home ate ox's food, / and like the goats, ate rind'.[146] Little wonder, therefore, Norwegian resentment inevitably erupted into violence. The revolt was underpinned by a Christian cult that now began to develop around the sacred memory of the late king Óláfr. Ælfgifu and Óláfr may once have embraced as lovers in England, or so it is said; as bitter enemies in Norway, he had been defeated and killed by her husband's Norwegian allies. Now in death the saintly Óláfr returned to haunt the lady of Northampton and would eventually bring about her downfall. Magnús Óláfsson, who had been left behind for safety and tutelage with Yaroslav in Kiev when his father set off on his winter journey to defeat and martyrdom, was now the best hope for the Norwegians, and thought was given to his return and restoration. He had been named after Carolus Magnus (ON *Karlamagnús*), the Frankish emperor Charlemagne, the first western ruler to challenge the supremacy of Byzantine emperors. Norwegian emissaries left for Kiev, met Yaroslav and Magnús there, and brought back the boy triumphantly to Norway. Five years after Stiklarstaðir, Saint Óláfr's eleven-year-old son was crowned king of Norway, thereby restoring Norwegian independence. In 1042, following the sudden death of Sveinn's half-brother Hörða-Knútr, Magnús was also crowned king of Denmark.

Chapter 2

Rus'

Nobody denies that the Swedes developed long-distance trade routes through Russia, down the Dnieper to the Black Sea and Byzantium, but Russian historians have stressed the Slav rôle in the origins of the old Russian state, minimizing the Scandinavian contribution. The truth, as usual, lies somewhere in between. Northmen may not have laid the foundation of the Russian state, or even cities such as Kiev and Novgorod, but they established a network of proto-urban centres to support their trade, which later served as bedrock for the emerging Kievan state. They provided rulers for a time though it is likely that Scandinavians who lingered in these cities intermarried with the local people and began a long process of cultural assimilated in Slav society, as they were in Normandy and Ireland. After all, the Norse were great 'cultural-chameleons' and seem to have quickly taken on the characteristics of the dominant social influences. This was a people who rode camels to Baghdad in order to trade with the 'Abbasid caliphate, became the personal guard of the Byzantine emperor, merged with the Irish aristocracy, emerged as the dukes of Normandy and became the mercenaries for the kingdoms surrounding the Irish Sea. The ability to assimilate themselves with alien cultures was one of their more notable features.

No Swedes please, we're Slavs

The Swedes had encountered in the Slavs an equally advanced society but one that lacked any true unity and it was this factor that allowed them to initially dominate. By the late tenth century, the nomenclature of the ruling house, burial evidence, and the written sources all imply that a Rus' culture had been shaped with the Slavic element predominating. Take, for instance, the son and successor of Igor I (r. 912–45), Sviatoslav (r. 945–72). In name and appearance this Kievan prince had departed from his Norse heritage, having openly adopted the style and appearance of a steppe khan. The year before the Pečenegs took his head (whether with or without Byzantine connivance) at the Dnieper cataracts, Sviatoslav had signed a treaty with John I Tzimiskès at Dorostolon (Silistra) on the Danube. The contemporary Byzantine historian and chronicler Leo Diakonos records his physical appearance:

Sphendosthlavos [Sviatoslav] crossed the river in a kind of Scythian [Rus']
boat; he handled the oar in the same way as his men. His appearance was
as follows: he was of medium height – neither too tall, nor too short. He
had bushy brows, blue eyes, and was snubbed nosed; he shaved his beard
but wore a long and bushy moustache. His head was shaven except for
a lock of hair on one side as a sign of nobility of his clan. His neck was
thick, his shoulders broad, and his whole statue pretty fine. He seemed
gloomy and savage. On one of his ears hung a golden earring adorned
with two pearls and a ruby set between them. His white garments were
not distinguishable from those of his men except for cleanness.[1]

This meeting between the Byzantine emperor and the Kievan prince is illustrated
in the Madrid manuscript of John Skylitzes' *Synopsis historiôn*.[2] Similarly, the
Russian *Primary Chronicle* tells us that

on his expeditions he carried neither wagons nor cooking utensils, and
boiled no meat, but cut off small strips of horseflesh, game or beef, and
ate it after roasting it on the coals. Nor did he have a tent, but he spread
out a horse-blanket under him, and set his saddle under his head; and all
his retinue did likewise.[3]

The eastward movement of the Swedes ranks, according to T.D. Kendrick, 'as the
most important adventure of the vikings in constructive politics and was certainly
the most fateful and significant part played by them in the great drama of European
history'.[4] Russian scholars are of a different opinion. The roots of the problem
lie in the identity of a people called *Rus'* (Gr. 'Ρῶς, Ar. *ar-Rus* or *ar-Rusiyyah*)
who appear in the Russian *Primary Chronicle* – Russia's oldest national chronicle.[5]
Between 860 and 862, according to the *Primary Chronicle*, the inhabitants of central
European Russia invited a number of men

who were known as Rus' (OES Русь), just as some are known as *Svie*
[Swedes], others *Nurmane* [Northmen, Norwegians], others *Angliane*
[Angles of southern Jutland] and others *Gote* [Gotlanders], to bring
order to their country.

Three brothers came: Rurik, the eldest, settled in Novgorod, a new settlement
established town south of Staraja Ladoga, while the other two (who died within
a few years) settled in Beloozero and Izborsk. On account of these Varangians
[Scandinavians] the district of Novgorod became known as 'the land of the Rus".[6]
Here we can compare the testimony of Liudprand of Cremona, through whose reports

to his master we are indebted for many details of the Constantinopolitan court of the time.[7] He is, for instance, in no doubt as to the origins of the Rus', stating bluntly 'the Rus', whom we with another name call Northmen'.[8] This clear identification of the Rus' with Northmen is repeated in his subsequent account of Igor's foray of 942.[9]

This is just a simplistic summary of a rather complicated story told by a much later chronicler who was more than a little muddled by geographical terms and historical events, indeed there is reason to believe that the term Varangian was not known in Russia before the last half of the tenth century when it came into use there as applied to the Scandinavian warriors who took service with the Russian princes or with the Byzantine emperors, and distinguished the latter from the old line of Scandinavian colonists who, by the year 1000, must have 'gone native'. Nonetheless, the entry for 6368–70 [860–2] contains several points of interest about the Scandinavian involvement in the Slavic territories prior to and at the beginning of the formation of Kievan Russia. Firstly, the mention of these particular Varangians being known as Rus' and coming from beyond the sea ties these people to the Swedes. The sea discussed in this entry is the Varangian Sea, or the Baltic Sea, and beyond this sea from the Slavic territories is Scandinavia and the home of the Swedes.

The Old East Slavonic term Rus' (pronounced 'Roos') is a problem too. It has been suggested that it derives from the Old East Norse word *róðr*, 'oar-way', or from the Finnish/Estonian words *Ruotsi/Rootsi*, which previously referred to the people from Sweden but currently denotes the country itself. There are other alternatives too, and the etymology of the name Rus' is still a matter of scholarly debate.[10] As Eric Christiansen so elegantly puts it:

> *Rhos* might be Swedes to the Franks, but Swedes were often called Northmen; and Northmen were Danes; and Danes, to the poets, were usually Jutes; and Jutes, to Asser the Welshman, were Goths; and Goths, said Jordanes and Isidore of Seville, came from Scandinavia; and so on.[11]

It is almost needless to add, that the narrative of the 'calling of the princes', which was written down a long time after the event, has inspired a larger volume of controversial literature than any other disputed point in Russian history.

Over the course of several generations, the territories of modern day Russia and Ukraine would become Kievan Russia. The question that now arises is how big a rôle did the Swedes play in transforming the fractured Slavic populations into a unified political entity by the tenth century? It is not my intention to enter what has been inelegantly labelled the 'pro-Normannist / anti-Normannist dispute' (though this debate has cooled somewhat since the break-up of the Soviet Union).[12] Suffice it to say that interpretation of the past is inevitably informed by the character and nature of the society making the interpretation. Needless to say, the Scandinavian origins of Russia are as complex as they have long been controversial.

The late Carolingian *Annales Bertiniani*, kept in the west Frankish court, contains the first written reference in a western source to the Rus'. Here, a group of Swedes who called themselves Rus' (*qi se, id est gentem suam, Rhôs vocari dicebant*) had visited Constantinople on a mission of friendship in the year 838.[13] The following year, unable to return the way they had come through Russia, they found themselves in the court of Louis *le Pieux* (r. 814–40) at Ingelheim (Mainz) on the Rhine with an embassy from Constantinople. It was at this point that Louis and his counsellors perceived that these Rus' were in fact Swedes (*gens sueoni*), a fact that seems to have been enough for the Frankish emperor to suspect that they had come as spies to the Byzantine empire as well as to his own, not for the sake of friendship as they claimed – the Swedes and their northern brethren were already detested and feared in Frankia – but to assess the wealth and vulnerability of his kingdom. He therefore decided to detain them until it could be established conclusively if they were to be trusted or not. In a response letter to Constantinople he reported his decision, stating that if they were found to be trustworthy and a suitable occasion presented itself, he would help them home to their *patria*. Otherwise, he would return them to Constantinople so that the emperor Theophilos (r. 829–42) could deal with them as he saw fit. Nothing more is heard in the matter.

A Byzantine copper coin from the reign of Theophilos, found in grave Bj632 excavated at the international trading town of Birka, lends some support for such an interpretation of this literary reference.[14] Furthermore, the *Annales Bertiniani* entry names the king of these Swedish visitors to Ingelheim as *Chaconos*, a name that may correspond to the Norse name Hákon;[15] it is known that a Swedish king, Hákon Hræreksson, was ruling in 844. The oldest evidence of direct Scandinavian involvement in Russia comes from the market place of Staraja Ladoga, dating back to around the second half of the eight century. Situated closest to Scandinavia, it is the earliest known trading post in old Russia. Even so, archaeological evidence also shows that Scandinavians had reached the area around Lake Ladoga as early as the sixth century. In search of costly furs, Scandinavians founded small trading colonies on the eastern Baltic coast in present-day Estonia, Latvia and Lithuania. It was during the mid eighth century that a new commodity made its entrance on the eastern trade route – 'Abbasid silver.

Dnieper portage

Thus, the Swedes (and others) came to Russia for the purposes of trade, long before Rurik was invited to Novgorod, and they developed there two great arteries of trade, one along the Dnieper and the other along the Volga, Europe's longest river. The Dnieper was the route to the Black Sea and Byzantium, while the Volga, led to the Caspian Sea and the Islamic world. The first, the way to Constantinople, is described by the *Primary Chronicle*:

> Starting from Greece [Byzantine empire], this route proceeds along the Dnieper, above which a portage leads to the Lovat. By following the Lovat, the great lake Ilmen is reached. The river Volkhov which flows out of this lake enters the great lake Nevo [Ladoga]. The mouth of this lake [river Neva] opens out into the Varangian [Baltic] Sea.[16]

The southern part of this route is described in greater detail by Constantinus VII Porphyrogenitus (r. 913–59) in a handbook (circa 950) devoted principally to foreign peoples and compiled for the instruction of his fourteen-year-old son Romanos so that foreign nations 'shall quake before thee as one mighty in wisdom'.[17] In fact, it served as an education for of all his successors and so of us. The scholar emperor provides a seemingly authoritative account of the trade route the Rus' used to get from Kiev to Constantinople. The Rus' gathered together from their various strongholds at the fortress of Kiev, standing high above the point where the northern river ways flow into the broad stream of the Dnieper. Preparations could not begin before the ice melted, in early April, while sailing conditions were most favourable in the Black Sea in June and July. The Rus' were required by treaty to leave Constantinople in the autumn, so they had a tight timetable. As for the journey itself, the Rus' took at least six weeks to make it down the Dnieper, for there were a succession of hazardous cataracts (Gr. καταρράκτες) to negotiate (a sixty-kilometre stretch of cataracts south of the river's junction with the Samara, around which the Rus' were obligated to portage their boats) and the hostile Pečenegs to be fought off.[18]

What little we know about these Turkic-speaking horse nomads is summed up in Constantinus' description of them as an insatiably greedy lot of barbarians who for good money can be bought to fight other barbarians and the Rus'. When doing so they employed those very peculiar and characteristic tactics employed since time immemorial by every Turkish nation – Huns, Avars, Kumans, Khazars, et cetera – namely extremely fluid horsemen using the old devices of simulated flight, of shooting while fleeing, of sudden charges with spine-chilling, wolf-like howling. They lived between the Volga and the Ural rivers under Khazar suzerainty; according to Ahmad ibn Rusta, the Khazars 'raid the Pečenegs every year' to collect the tribute due to them.[19] In turn, mounted on fast steppe land horses, the Pečenegs made their sudden raids on towns and villages, plundering them, damaging the crops, and herding off the inhabitants into slavery. Falling to a predatory band of Pečenegs could result in the cruel fate that befell prince

Sviatoslav in early 972, when they slew him near the cataracts and 'took his head, and made a cup out of his [close-shaven] skull, overlaying it with gold, and they drank from it'.[20] Trade in this part of the world was most likely a very violent business.

Of the nine notorious Dnieper cataracts (the term used in this account is *phragmós*, 'blockage, obstacle, barrier') that traverse its river bed and precipitate its waters, Constantinus has preserved the names of the seven he knew about in their Slavonic (*sklavistí*) and Scandinavian (*rhôsistí*) forms. They are, according to the emperor: 'Sleep not' (Gr. `essoupê*, OES *ne sŭpi*, ON *sof eigi*); 'Island-waterfall' (Gr. *oulvorsí*, OES *ostrovĭnyj pragŭ*, ON *hólmfors*); 'Roaring-[waterfall]' (Gr. *gelandrí*, OES ?, ON *gjallandi*); 'Ever-rushing' (Gr. `aeiphór*, OES *neyasyt'*, ON *eiforr*); 'Wave-waterfall' (Gr. *varouphóros*, OES *Vlŭnĭnyj pragŭ*, ON *bárufors*); 'Laughing' (Gr. *leándi*, OES *Vĭruchi*, ON *hlæjandi*); '[At the] rapids' (Gr. *stroúkoun*, OES *Na bŭrzŭ*, ON *strjúkandi*).[21] The emperor, a palace-dweller, probably drew upon an official report of a Byzantine diplomat who had been despatched to Kiev on a diplomatic mission.

We read of one of these, *eiforr*, on a brightly painted rune stone at Pilgårds, on the Baltic Sea island of Gotland, where it is rendered as *aifur*:

Hegbjörn raised this stone glaring (and his) brothers Röðvisl, Östen, Ámundur (?), who have had stones raised in memory of Hrafn south of Rufstein. They came far and wide in *aifur*. Vífill bade....[22]

The rune stone, which is dated to the last half of the tenth century, was raised by four brothers in memory of a fifth brother, Hrafn, who evidently lost his life in that frightening, insatiable, boulder strewn torrent. The crew were led by Vífill, whose name, incidentally, means 'beetle'. This stone offers us a vivid glimpse of five Gotland brothers and their captain on the make, carrying furs and swords and slaves, no doubt, to the markets of the east where they could exchange them for Arabic silver to be banked in buried catches at home on Gotland.

Trade between Sweden and Kievan Russia was important from the early ninth century and was at that time largely conducted from Birka. As Birka declined, the Gotlanders took over and in the eleventh century the trade from Gotland was concentrated on Novgorod, which lay on the major route between the Baltic and Constantinople. The short legendary history of the island, called *Guta saga*, written in the thirteenth or perhaps the fourteenth century, contains one of the classic descriptions of this route: The Gotlanders 'travelled up by the watercourse called the Dvina, and onward through Russia. They travelled for such a distance that they came to the Byzantine empire'.[23] Two fragments of a rune stone from Hallfrede in Follingbo parish, southeast of Visby, carry an inscription which has been interpreted as: '... (after) Uddgæir. He died in *Hulmgarþr* [*Hólmgarðr*]'.[24]

It should be noted that the custom of erecting inscribed gravestones became prevalent in Sweden only in the eleventh century, so that early survivals of runic inscriptions mentioning Russia are comparatively rare. Two of the six such survivals, both from Gotland, have been mentioned above. Two others (one of the early and the other of the late eleventh century) remark the activities of Swedish adventurers in Russia, which is referred to as *Garðar*, 'the kingdom of fortified towns'. Of the two remaining, one, dating from the late eleventh century, mentions the death in Novgorod of a certain Sigviðr, a captain of a ship, while the other, of about 1100, is a monument to one Spialboði, who 'met his death in Novgorod in Ólafr's church [*í Óláfs kirki*]'.[25] In both instances, Novgorod bears the later familiar name of *Hólmgarðr*, while the latter informs us that the Swedes in Novgorod had their own church dedicated to Saint Ólafr of Norway. The church stood in the commercial market of Novgorod where, for instance, the merchants from Gotland had their own market. This implies a permanent Swedish presence in the town, perhaps because it was a location where Northmen tended to congregate in their travels through Russia. Saint Ólafr had a special connection with Novgorod since prince Yaroslav was not only the brother-in-law of Ólafr II Haraldsson, but he also fostered and tutored Ólafr's son Magnús at his court in Kiev.

It was along the Dnieper route that the towns of Kiev (ON *Kœnugarðr*), Smolensk (or its pre-eleventh-century predecessor at the nearby archaeological site of Gnëzdovo), Novgorod (ON *Hólmgarðr*) and Staraja Ladoga (ON *Aldeigjuborg*) are situated, and it is along this route that quite a considerable body of Scandinavian archaeological material has been assembled, mainly originating from central Sweden.[26] In fact, at strategic locations along this route have been identified fortified settlements with many Scandinavian features and a considerable military presence. Gnëzdovo, for example, was once a fortified settlement situated on the junction of the Dnieper and the Dvina, and has been identified with *Miliniska*, which Constantinus VII Porphyrogenitus called a town of the Rus'.[27] Here a permanent garrison manned by mainly Scandinavian warriors controlled the trade route between the Dnieper and the Western Dvina, and provided the base from which tribute was taken from the surrounding local inhabitants. To date, the archaeological site of Gnëzdovo has revealed the greatest quantity of Scandinavian objects found in Russia.[28] However, these fortified settlements housed more than just Scandinavian warriors. At Staraja Ladoga, for instance, the population was polyethnic: a mixture of long-distance merchants, craftsmen, and local fur-traders.[29]

The Russian princess

Along the Dnieper and through these rapids, there came, in 957, the great Olga (ON *Helga*), widow of Igor, on her way to Constantinople to meet Constantinus VII Porphyrogenitus. The meeting of this Swedish-born princess from Kiev and the emperor of Byzantium was accompanied by great grandeur, an indication of the importance attached to her visit by the imperial authorities: there were banquets, gifts of gold, and pageants of colour and sound as bright banners fluttered and the voices of two church choirs sang. At the moment when she was presented to the emperor, 'the princess of Russia', as the Constantinopolitans described her, did not bend a knee or bow from the waist to the new Constantinus in the new Rome: she slightly if perceptibly inclined her head. She was put in her place by being seated, as the Muslim state guests had been, at a separate table.

The Russian *Primary Chronicle* has a different, richly embroidered version of this state visit. When the delicate subject of baptism was brought up, Olga told Constantinus:

> That if he desired to baptise her, he should perform this function himself; otherwise she was unwilling to accept baptism. The emperor concurred, and asked the patriarch [of Constantinople] to instruct her in the faith. The patriarch instructed her in prayer and fasting, in almsgiving and in the maintenance of chastity. She bowed her head, and like sponge absorbing water, she eagerly drank in his teachings… After her baptism, the emperor summoned Olga and made known to her that he wished her to become his wife. But she replied, 'How can you marry me, after yourself baptizing me and calling me your daughter? For among Christians that is unlawful, as you yourself must know'. Then the emperor said, 'Olga, you have outwitted me'.[30]

Thus, if the *Primary Chronicle* can be believed at this point, we must accept that it was during her visit to Constantinople that Olga was converted to Christianity. The details are indeed arguable, but there can be little doubt that Olga returned to Kiev a Christian.

Olga's fierce son, Sviatoslav, who we have met already, had no interest in Christianity – he is said to have told his mother that his soldiers would mock him were he to become a Christian – but he was restless to extend the sway of the Rus', particularly in the land of the Bulghars on the Danube. Although the first of the rulers of Kiev to bear a Slavic name, Sviatoslav acted with the ruthless adventurousness of his Norse ancestors and always with an eye for international business. Where better to establish a new centre than at the commercially important location at the mouth of the Danube?

As we have seen, Sviatoslav penetrated deep into the Balkans, as far as the border of Thrace and, hence, as far as the border of the Byzantine empire. Puffed with success, he turned his army on the empire itself. The result was a crushing defeat for the Rus'. To make peace, Sviatoslav and John I Tzimiskès met at the edge of the Danube. The emperor rode to their meeting wearing golden armour and accompanied by a magnificent retinue, while Sviatoslav came as an oarsman, sitting on the bench of a boat, differentiated from the other Rus' oarsmen only by the cleanness of his garment and by a bejewelled gold earring; a figure ridiculed by the Byzantines but eminently worthy of his viking ancestors. So, as we have said, on his way home Sviatoslav was slain by Pečenegs and with him died the ambition of the Rus' to commercially control the lower Danube.

Mast of pine, planks of oak

It is our bookwise emperor Constantinus VII Porphyrogenitus who provides the exotic details of the construction of the boats that the Rus' buy from the local Slavs. These were made from one log hollowed out, the μονόξυλα, the Rus' fitting them out and adding to them so they could hold cargo and crew.[31] They had to be manoeuvrable along a swift-flowing and often dangerous river and capable of sailing over open sea when they reached its mouth. Inevitably, scholars disagree a good deal over the technology of the boats the Rus' used.

In order to navigate narrow or very shallow stretches of water, the vessels used on these voyages would certainly have been no larger than the Skuldelev cargo carrier (Skuldelev 3) found in the waters of Peberrenden channel in Roskilde Fjord, Denmark. Built of Danish oak around 1040, this small, elegant trading ship 13.8 metres long, 3.4 metres wide amidships, and weighing two tons (plus 3.5 tons ballast), has a draught of eighty-six centimetres without the rudder. Decked fore and aft, there is a large open hold amidships with a volume of ten cubic metres, which would have held around 4.5 tons of cargo.[32] It, along with the other spectacular Skuldelev wrecks given to us by the salty world of marine archaeology, had been scuttled in a narrow stretch of the fjord in order to prevent raids upon Roskilde by Haraldr III Sigurðarson during his bitter war with Sveinn II Estriðsson. The Skuldelev finds are excellent examples of three different types of ship (two warships, two trading ships, and one coastal vessel), built in various parts of the Norse world at the end of the viking era.

Skuldelev 3 has been the inspiration for a number of full-scale replicas, notably *Roar Ege*, the first full-scale reconstruction to be undertaken at Vikingeskibsmuseet, Roskilde, and launched in 1984. Under a single sail (hand woven in a double thickness of raw wool) of thirty-six square metres and with a crew of five to eight, this fine little vessel has achieved speeds of 8.5 knots, and when sailing at an angle to the wind, could beat as close as fifty-five degrees to the wind with a leeway of five to six degrees in calm conditions. As a matter of interest, it took several dozen people two years to build *Roar Ege*, in part because Norse era construction techniques had to be re-invented. A largely identical replica, *Sif Ege*, was undertaken at Frederikssund and launched in 1990.[33] In 1994 and 1996, the reconstructed Swedish viking-age ship *Aifur* made a voyage from Sigtuna on Lake Mälar in Sweden to the Black Sea port of Kherson in the Ukraine. The venture, called Expedition Holmgård, was an attempt to navigate the 'road of the Varangians to the Greeks', as is mentioned in the Russian *Primary Chronicle*.[34]

The *Aifur* was a vessel 9.5 metres long, 2.2 metres wide and its hull weighed around 2 tons without ballast. Its construction combined features from different viking-age boats found in the Baltic region. It was constructed as a typical small cargo boat, suitable for all-round use on rivers, lakes and other reasonably sheltered waters. It carried a single nineteen-square-metre sail, its rigging being inspired by the picture stones from Gotland, a rich source of information with respect to the viking vessels of the period 750–1000. For example, the Lärbro Stora Hammars I and the När Stenkyrka Smiss I picture stones both depict a warship with a dragon stem post and decorated sternpost, and an intricate system of reefing lines attached to its sail, while the Alskog Tjängvilde I picture stone depicts a ship remarkably similar to the Oseberg ship complete with the ubiquitous chequered sail.[35]

The *Aifur* was manned by a sequence of crews, each consisting of about nine people. It should be noted that they were all volunteers, who participate at their own expense and under their own terms.

In 1994, the *Aifur* crossed the Baltic Sea and sailed up the rivers Neva and Volkhov to Novgorod. The distance covered was 1,382 kilometres. The effective time was 307 hours, of which sailing time 192.5 hours and rowing time, including manual towing, 114.5 hours. In 1996, the ship continued from Novgorod and journeyed further upstream. The river Lovat from Kholm upstream was not navigable due to a very low water level, and the portage over the first watershed therefore became far too long to be practicable – horses were not available. However, the crew continued on the rivers Usvyatya, Dvina and Kasplya, crossing the second watershed by putting the vessel on simple wheels, made on site. Including Novgorod to Svetlylahirske on the Dnieper, the distance covered was 1,568 kilometres. The effective time was 415.5 hours; of which sailing time 113.5 hours, rowing – including manual towing – 264 hours, and manhandling over land thirty-eight hours.

The total distance covered, during the 113 days of Expedition Holmgård, was 2,950 kilometres. The average distance per day was 26.1 kilometres. The average speed was 4.1 km/h, with 42 per cent of the time being spent sailing, 53 per cent rowing, and 5 per cent dragging the ship over land. During the Baltic Sea crossing, on the lakes Ladoga and Ilmen, and on the Dnieper dams, the *Aifur* proved to be a good sailing vessel before the wind and to a certain degree also capable of tacking – while the Gotland picture stones show that ships were rigged to sail mainly before the wind or with the wind abeam, experimental archaeology additionally informs us that they handled surprisingly well close to the wind too. Rowing and sometimes sailing downstream on the Dnieper also worked quite nicely. However, although the *Aifur* was fairly small, the rivers Lovat and Kasplya were navigable only with great effort and difficulty. In particular, the Lovat runs for approximately 540 kilometres, and the journey demonstrated that boat travel was not a viable option on its middle and upper reaches. What is more, the adverse stream on this shallow river with its many rapids was especially demanding.

The experience gained from Expedition Holmgård shows that only very light vessels would be suitable for the northern part of the historic passage. Even so, it is probable that the upper Lovat and the upper Kasplya may be navigable only after snowy winters and only for a short period each spring. And even then, the traveller on the Lovat would have to master the river's strong current and many dozens of rapids. Where exactly the northern section of the 'road of the Varangians to the Greeks' was situated is, in fact, unclear. What is clear, however, is that the popular image of viking crews rolling boats long distances on rollers became a thing of fantasy.

Understandably, Scandinavians scholars discussing the viking voyages to the east have shown an obsession with clinker-built boats. It is easy to overlook the obvious. Scandinavians were travellers by land too. It is not the author's intention to cast doubt on the feasibility of boat travel along the northern section of the 'road of the Varangians to the Greeks'. However, it should be emphasized that by travelling by horse and sledge on the frozen plain and on the solid ice of rivers and marshes, long distances have been covered in northwest Russia historically in a relatively short time. Indeed, in the Norse lands winter sledges were the preferred means for transporting cargo overland. In some ways, overland transportation was actually easier in winter. Frozen lakes, rivers, and marshes made some of the routes very much easier than in summer, and a horse-drawn sledge could carry heavier loads than a cart. Old Norse accounts of viking-age winter travelling, such as in Snorri Sturluson,[36] support the winter version of the 'road of the Varangians to the Greeks'. Likewise, Muslim geographers and historians contribute tantalizing information about the use of skis and dog sleds by peoples of the north. Alternatively, locally made, light, flat-bottomed boats have been standard on the eastern rivers in historical times and things were surely not different in our period of study.

To complete the story, it should be added that the southern section of the 'road of the Varangians to the Greeks' is not questioned. The Dnieper between Smolensk and the Black Sea was a huge, wide river. Two problems have been much discussed by scholars: the ever-present military threat to travellers presented by the nomadic tribes, for example the Pečenegs, and the hazardous rapids (of which the *eiforr/ aifur* was one) which were situated between today's cities Dnepropetrovsk and Zaporozhe. However, these rapids disappeared in the nineteen-twenties when the Dnieper hydroelectric dams were constructed, and all opportunity for negotiating them is unfortunately lost.

Volga portage

The second route exploited by the Swedes was to the east, and here there was no possibility of settlement on the same scale, as large towns had long been established to control the fur trade. This control was exercised by the rulers of the Khazars and the Bulghars in the region of the Volga, who exacted a toll on merchants. The Khazars were Turkic-speaking pastoral nomads closely related to the Volga Bulghars, their tributary subjects. Their khaganate occupied a strategic key position at the vital gateway between the Black Sea and the Caspian, where the two monotheistic superpowers representing Christianity and Islam confronted each other. It acted as a buffer protecting Byzantium against invasions by the vigorous peoples of the northern steppes – Bulghars, Magyars, Pečenegs and the like – and, later, the Rus'. Thus the Khazars had become the dominant power in the Volga– Pontic steppe–Caucasus region by the middle of the seventh century, and though technically allied with the Byzantines, they played a major rôle in trade between this region and the Islamic world for the next three centuries. The conversion of the Khazar military élite to Judaism sometime in the early ninth century did not seem to affect the relationship with either Constantinople or Baghdad.[37] Likewise, this conversion did not affect the composition of the Khazar khaganate, which remained multiconfessional, multilingual and multinational. The 'real' Khazars who ruled it were probably always a minority – as the Austrians were in the Austro– Hungarian monarchy. Even so, the Baghdadi al-Mas'udi (d. 957) says that in the Khazar army:

> Today, around 7,000 of them serve as the king's mounted archers. They carry a shield and wear helmets and ring mail. They also have lancers equipped and armed like other Muslim soldiers… The king of the Khazars is the only ruler of these eastern countries to have a paid army.[38]

Likewise, Muhammad ibn Hawqal (d. 986), another much travelled Muslim geographer: 'This king has 12,000 soldiers in his service, of whom when one dies, another person is immediately chosen in his place'.[39] Here we have an important clue to the Khazar dominance: a permanent professional army, which, in peacetime, effectively controlled the ethnic patchwork, and in times of war served as a hard core for the khaganate's armed horde.

There is an intriguing piece of evidence, the so-called Khazar Correspondence,[40] an exchange of letters, written in Hebrew in the mid tenth century, between Hasdai ibn Shaprût, the Jewish foreign minister serving Abd ar-Rahman III (r. 912 – 61), the 'Umayyad caliph of Qurtubah (Córdoba), and Joseph, khagan of the Khazars or, rather, between their respective secretaries. The authenticity of the correspondence has been the subject of much heated debate but is now generally accepted with due allowance made for the vagaries of later copyists.[41] With this in mind, there is a passage in Joseph's letter which deals with topical politics, and is rather obscure:

> With the help of the Almighty I guard the mouth of the river [the Volga] and do not permit the Rus' who come in their ships to invade the land of the Arabs... I fight heavy wars with them [the Rus'] for if I allowed it they would devastate the lands of Ishmael even to Baghdad.[42]

The Volga was obviously a vital artery for the Khazars, and likewise for others. Little wonder, therefore, Turkic peoples, such as the Khazars and the Bulghars, living and trading along the Volga formerly referred to it as *Itil* or *Atil*, 'big river'.

Generally speaking, the version of history that makes its way into the history books can be incomplete. This is why archaeology can be extremely useful to corroborate literary sources of historical events. Material evidence is a powerful check on speculation, deceit and inaccuracy. Yet we still need to be vigilant because archaeology favours 'glitter', as metals are better preserved than organic materials. Traded or taken 'items', such as slaves, cattle, cereals and of course furs can be archaeologically invisible. This 'glitter' has biased our view of the commodities of exchange and trade. Most slaves taken from the British Isles, for instance, seem to have ended up on the Volga river route to eastern Islam. The *Laxdæla saga* mentions an Icelandic chief who visited a slave mart off the coast of Sweden. There he purchased an expensive, aristocratic Irish girl from Gilli the Rus' who was said to be 'the richest of merchants trading there', and who did his buying and selling in a plush tent 'dressed in costly clothing and wearing a Russian hat'.[43] Gilli obviously got his nickname from his trading in Kievan Russia: his name is Hiberno-Norse (cf. OI *gillae*, 'boy'). Likewise, the scale of the fur trade was in fact huge. In addition to the pelts received by the Bulghar king in tribute, middlemen – like the Rus' merchants encountered by the envoy Ahmad ibn Fadlan – brought the furs they had brought or collected as tribute to the great market on the Volga, where merchants from Khurasan and Khwarazm gathered to buy them. Ahmad ibn Rusta says the Bulghars paid two-and-half dirhams per marten pelt,[44] but the price must have varied considerably according to type, rarity and quality. The pelt of a black fox, for instance, was 'the most sought after and expensive of furs'.[45]

Forty beads were found within the Hrísbrú Farm longhouse, Mosfell valley (Mosfellsdalur) in southwest Iceland, the largest number of such finds recovered within an Icelandic longhouse of the viking age. Most likely all these beads were imported and 95 per cent of them are made of glass, as opposed to locally produced beads, which were generally made of stone or organic material. Glass was not produced in Scandinavia, but bead workshops did exist that re-melted imported glass from other regions to make new beads. The raw material imported to Scandinavia took the form of glass rods, glass tesserae, and broken blown glassware probably originating from Frankish workshops.

According to Ibn Fadlan, one of the only cotemporary ethnographic observers of viking-age Scandinavians, green glass beads were the most highly prized ornaments to the Northmen, who would buy them for one *dirham* each and display them on necklaces around the necks of their women.[46] Indeed, four of the glass examples deserve our special attention as they are identified as 'eye beads' originally from the eastern shores of the Caspian Sea.[47] Similar 'eye beads' have also been at found at sites across Scandinavia.[48] Glass beads were valuable trade goods in the viking age, and these archaeological finds are consistent with the wealth and status of the inhabitants of the Hrísbrú farmstead. With its coastal port at Leiruvogur,[49] the Mosfell valley was in commercial and cultural contact with the wider Scandinavian and European worlds and beyond, such as the Caspian Sea. In all probability, these four 'eye beads' were imported into the Scandinavian world from Asia along the Volga trade route.

From the Volga bend it was possible for merchants to strike out across the thirsty desert to reach the silk route to Baghdad and China somewhere near the Aral Sea. It was probably in this area that the Swedes came into contact with Muslim travellers such as Ibn Fadlan who gives the first picturesque (some would say over picturesque) descriptions of the Rus' and their bizarre customs. It is always helpful to listen to the authentic ring of contemporary accounts, in particular those of encounters between different peoples. It is a truism that historical works that date from later periods reshape history and reflect the changing attitudes of different historical milieu, retrospectively imposed, but often enough such later sources are all that has survived. So, with Ibn Fadlan and his contemporary account we are lucky.

Journey among warriors

Although many tend to equate 'Islamic' with 'Arabic', and the Arabic language was widely used (for example on coins), the 'Abbasid caliphate was ethnically diverse. The 'Abbasid dynasty, based in its newly found capital of Baghdad (then and now the capital of Iraq), saw the flowering of Arabic and Islamic culture on a scale not seen before. Baghdad, the City of Peace (Ar. *Madinat-al-Salam*), rapidly became the largest and richest city west of China, rivalled in wealth and size only by Qurtubah (Córdoba), the capital of al-Andalus. The privileged position of warriors in the early conquest communities in Iraq, Syria and Egypt, coupled with extra tax burdens on unbelievers, encouraged conversion. The *mawali*, subject peoples who had converted to Arab monotheism, went out of their way to 'Arabize' their own family histories and traditions. Thus, though the 'Abbasid dynasty saw a sizeable increase in Arabic literature, it was the former non-Arabs and the Persians in particular, who were the main proponents of this cultural revolution.

The work of Ibn Khurradadhbih contains the earliest attestation of the name Rus' in the Muslim literature. However, from Theophilos' embassy to Louis *le Pieux* in 839 it can be inferred that the Rus' appear to have been known to the Byzantines at least a few years before Ibn Khurradadhbih is believed to have written his work; the final version of his *Kitab al-masalik wa' l-mamalik* was completed in 885, though it contains material dating back to the first decades of the ninth century, possibly from the archives of the *barid*.

Muslim writers comment on the fact that at least some Rus' warriors decorated their bodies. Ahmad ibn Fadlan, or Ahmad ibn Fadlan al-'Abbas ibn Rashid ibn Hammad, to give him is full name,[50] notes of Rus' warriors he came across on the Volga in 922 that they 'are dark from the tips of their toes to right up to their necks – trees, pictures, and the like'.[51] A word of caution, however. The word used in the original Arabic is obscure and is more commonly used to describe the decorations inside of mosques. Additionally, Ibn Fadlan described many other aspects of the Rus' merchants that are not supported by other sources. That these descriptions of body decorations do not show up in early mediaeval Scandinavian sources should make us somewhat wary about vikings commonly wearing tattoos. The use of cosmetics, on the other hand, is not so questionable.

Writing just four decades after Ibn Fadlan, a Sephardic Jewish merchant from Turtušah (Tortosa) by the name of Ibrahim ibn Ya'qub notes the use of indelible cosmetic in the trading site of Hedeby (Haithabu near Schleswig: ON *Heiðabý*, *haiþa bu* in runic texts) at the base of the Jutland peninsula, what is now north Germany but then the southern frontier of Scandinavia. This was used by both men and women 'to enhance the beauty of their eyes'. However, he was none too impressed with the town. For although, at 24 hectares (60 acres) in area, Hedeby was the largest Scandinavian town of the time, and one of the most important Scandinavian commercial centres, Ibrahim ibn Ya'qub found it a far cry from the Hispano-Arabic elegance, organization and comfort of distant Qurtubah (Córdoba) where he resided. Hedeby was noisy and filthy, he wrote, with the pagan inhabitants hanging animal sacrifices on poles in front of their houses, which were both the stave-built (horizontal as well as vertical) and the wattle-and-daub varieties. The inhabitants of Hedeby subsisted chiefly on fish, 'which are plentiful there'.[52]

Ibn Fadlan too had harsh words for northern hygiene (or lack of it). Speaking of those Rus' he had encountered by the Volga, he observed 'they are the filthiest of all God's [Allah's] creatures', and although he acknowledged that they washed their hands, faces and heads every day, he was appalled that they did so in a communal basin 'with the dirtiest and most polluted water you can imagine',[53] an ancient Germanic custom that caused understandable revulsion in a pious erudite Muslim scholar from Baghdad, who typically performed ablutions only in poured or running water. But he was no Qur'an-thumping moralizer, for his descriptions are straightforward and free from religious rhetoric, and, unlike later Muslim writers, he does not pass judgement on the bizarre (for him, at least) customs he witnessed.

And so to Ibn Fadlan himself, an appealing, cultured character that turns up in the most unexpected places and in the most unexpected guises. He was a *faqih*, an expert in Islamic jurisprudence, *fiqh* – jurisprudence, along with the allied study of Arabic linguistics, was the meat and bones of Islamic science. He served as secretary of an embassy from the court of caliph al-Muqtadir (r. 908–32) to the ruler (Ar. *malik*) of the Bulghars of the middle Volga region (a distinct group). The mission was 'to instruct him in law and acquaint him with the rules of Islam according to the *Shari'a*, and to construct a mosque and build a *minber* from which he could proclaim al-Muqtadir's name throughout his kingdom'.[54]

The Bulghars were a Turkic-speaking branch of the people whom the Khazars had split in the seventh century. One group migrated west, where they assimilated with Slavs and founded what became modern Bulgaria, west of the Black Sea; the others turned north toward the middle Volga region, where they continued to chafe under the rule of their powerful Jewish overlords, the Khazars, whose domination of the north Caucasus and Caspian region marked the northern limits of 'Abbasid power with its empire based on the river Tigris. In seeking assistance from caliphal Baghdad, the king of the Bulghars, who had embraced Islam as the official religion of his people, was seeking a distant alliance against the Khazars – the king had 'also beseeched him [the caliph] to build a fort to protect him against the kings who opposed him'.[55] Presumably in order to avoid Khazar lands, the caliph's delegation took a lengthy and circuitous route to the Bulghar capital, passing well east of the Caspian Sea via such cities as Bukhara and Khwarazm.

In his account, the Bulghar king treats Ibn Fadlan as an Arab, though some scholars prefer to see him as a non-Arab Muslim.[56] Incidentally, it was Ibn Fadlan's account that inspired the late Michael Crichton's (*Westworld*, *Jurassic Park*, et al.) first novel, *Eaters of the Dead* (1976), which was the basis of the film *The Thirteenth*

Warrior (1999), starring Antonio Banderas as an improbable – and clean-shaven – Ibn Fadlan.

It is important to bear in mind that most Islamic chroniclers were by training religious scholars or administrators, as was Ibn Fadlan, not military men or social anthropologists. As such, their experience lay primarily in the administration of the law and the state, and they were skilled in court politics and in handling rulers. They talked about what interested them, as did Ibn Fadlan, and they saw history through the prism of faith. For these pious and cultured gentlemen, history was the unfolding of God's will for the world and the inevitable victory of Islam. Therefore it is not appropriate to expect them to display any specialized military insight in their work. After all, they had moved laterally into writing history and geography from a deep study of the Qur'an, the *hadith* and the *Shari'a*.

Finally, as Judith Jesch warns us, we should not generalize from Ibn Fadlan's account about practices elsewhere in the Norse world. Everywhere the Scandinavians went, she maintains,

> ...they developed new ways of living which owed something both to the culture of the immigrant vikings and to that of the country in which they found themselves, so that no two areas colonized by Scandinavians were alike. They [the Rus' met by Ibn Fadlan] are likely to have been a select band of merchant-warriors who, like other touring professionals, may not have behaved the same way when abroad as they did at home.[57]

Barbarian traders with big swords

Commerce forged the link between the men of the north and the men of the book. It is therefore necessary to pause for a moment here to view the known descriptions of the Rus' as given by our Islamic sources.

Ahmad ibn Rusta describes the Rus' as sporting excellent swords, which he says came from Khurasan. He says too they wore baggy trousers that were tight below the knee,[58] a style that probably reflected the eastern influence in their wardrobes and is confirmed by illustrations on picture stones from the Baltic Sea island of Gotland.[59] It is for this reason that the Rus' were nicknamed 'the people with the trousers made from a hundred spans of cloth', suggesting that they were well known for needing large amounts of fabric to make such garments. He also comments upon their martial abilities:

> If an enemy makes war against them, they attack together, and never break ranks. They form a single fist against the enemy, until they overcome them... They have great stamina and endurance. They never quit the

battlefield without having slaughtered their enemy. They take the women and enslave them. They are remarkable for their size, their physique and their bravery. They fight best on shipboard, not on horseback.[60]

It is not known where Ibn Rusta obtained his information – he drew on a number of sources, both contemporary merchants and travellers and written works from the mid to late ninth century – but its reliability is not in question.

A near contemporary of Ibn Rusta, Ahmad ibn Fadlan, tells us that in the year 922, when he came across a band of Rus' armed merchants encamped by the Volga, they 'carry axes, swords, and daggers and always have them to hand. They use Frankish swords with broad, ridged blades'.[61] This is a description of men in a state of constant alert, always looking over their shoulders, as if they were living in perpetual expectation of being attacked, and not only by outsiders either. As Ibn Rusta clearly paints in his vignette of Rus' society:

They never go off alone to relieve themselves, but always with three companions to guard them, sword in hand, for they have little trust in one another. Treachery is endemic, and even a poor man can be envied by a comrade, who will not hesitate to kill him and rob him.[62]

The account of the civil servant, philosopher, and historian Ibn Miskawayh (932–1030) describes the Rus' in similar terms, albeit on the field of battle:

[The Rus'] are a formidable nation, the men huge and very courageous. They do not recognise defeat; no one turns back until he has killed or been killed. It is their custom for each to carry his weapons and hangs tools on his body, such as an axe, a saw, a hammer and similar implements. The warrior fights with a spear and a shield. He carries a sword and a spear and a knife like a dagger. They fight on foot, especially these invaders.[63]

Clearly based on eyewitness testimonies, this vivid description relates to the Rus' raid and occupation of Bardha'a (Barda, Azerbaijan), in 943. To reach their target, the raiders had obviously crossed the Caspian Sea. In the same account, Ibn Miskawayh also mentions that the swords carried by the Rus' 'are in great demand to this day for their sharpness and excellence'.[64] He, however, fails to mention their provenance.

Similarly, it is the military prowess of the Rus' that seems to have impressed Izz ad-Din ibn al-Athir (1160–1233), the court chronicler of the Zengid dynasty and arguably the greatest of all mediaeval Islamic historians, for his references to them deal exclusively with their military activities.[65] Unlike Europeans, Muslim chroniclers bore no grudge against the Rus', and thus the Muslim reports are more detached and, in the eyes of many scholars today, more credible. With this in mind, it is appropriate to note that these Muslim portrayals of the costume, weaponry, war gear, fighting skills and the funerary customs of the Rus' have resonance with the known burial rites of viking-age Scandinavia, or more specifically pertaining to the cult of Óðinn,[66] and with the finds from Birka and Gnëzdovo.[67]

Constantinople or bust

Writing on the extent of the influence and involvement of Scandinavians in early Russian towns and states, Paul Foote and David Wilson stress the priority of trade: 'Northern influence in Russia was primarily mercantile. The Scandinavians came to Russia in search of trade and any political power and control which they gained there was incidental to their main purpose'. Noting that there exists both archaeological and literary evidence for this trade, Foote and Wilson go on to describe how the Swedes in Russia from the first half of the ninth century onwards, coming first as merchants and later as mercenaries, played a part in the founding or consolidation of the states of early mediaeval Russia. The Swedes controlled a number of towns for the purposes of trade and military power, but the military power was not exerted for its own sake but for the development and control of the rich 'north-south commercial routes through western Russia from the Baltic to the Black Sea'.[68] Russia turned out to be a land of opportunity, the highroad to the golden city of Christendom.

Unlike Rome, Constantinople developed into a manufacturing centre, producing high quality textiles, leather goods, arms and armour, carved ivory, fine ceramics, glass items, mosaics, and enamelled metal. Moreover, by the tenth century, Byzantine merchants had largely settled into their roles as speculators. They were businessmen who were content to reside in the confines of Constantinople and let others come to them,[69] the city's location astride major trade routes making it an advantageous centre of long-distance trade. Trade between the north and Constantinople mostly constituted an exchange of raw materials for finished goods. With the mention of raw materials, we should understand that the main desirable features in items for long-distance trade are that they should be light, unbreakable or otherwise imperishable, and in the customer's eyes, luxurious. Among the raw materials of the north that meet such criteria, furs are outstanding. To the winter pelts of bear, fox, marten, ermine, squirrel, beaver and otter might be added the feathers of over wintering geese and the down of eiders. These items of a high-value, low-bulk nature would have been of primary interest to Swedish merchants.

It is believed that the first Swedes reached Constantinople in 838, their merchants seeing the magnificence and tasting the luxury of the Queen of Cities, which they knew as *Mikligarðr*, the Great City. This simplest and most evocative of titles lives on in the modern Icelandic *Mikligarður* and Faroese *Miklagarður*, which certainly throws a whole heap of doubt on a recent argument that supposes *Mikligarðr* meant 'City of the archangel Michael' (or 'City of Michael'). This is quite simply absurd. Bad arguments, like good ones, come and go. Constantinople, the wealthiest and most fascinating city of the Mediterranean world, and the centre of a sophisticated culture was throughout its history exposed to the attacks of neighbouring tribes and those from further afield, including the Rus'.

Twenty-two years later the first rulers of Kiev, Askold and Dir, made their bold attempt to plunder the treasures of the city, having already ravaged the shores of the Black Sea and the Sea of Marmara. For the next hundred years or so Byzantine-Rus' relations alternated between armed conflict and treaties of friendship. In 907 the Rus' were back again, this time under Oleg the Prophet (r. 882–912), prince of Kiev. He apparently swept down the Dnieper and over the Black Sea with a huge fleet, 2,000 vessels no less, but he was to make peace and conclude a treaty with the Byzantines. In fact, after the siege of 860, wars were waged in 907, 941, 944, 969–71, while treaties were concluded in the years 861, 907, 911, 945, 957, 971.

In fact the *Primary Chronicle* records the terms of four treaties between the Rus' and Constantinople, namely those of 907, 911, 945 and 971. They incorporate lists of names of Rus' envoys and merchants who negotiated the agreements. Most of them are interpreted as Scandinavian names lightly Slavonicized: forms of Hrœrekr, Karl(i), Vermundr, Ingjaldr, Hróarr, Óláfr, Sigbiörn and others. Equally important is the fact that there appears to be no Slav names among them, though there are a couple that have been identified as Estonian. Evidently, they are also pagan, because while the Byzantine signatories take their oath on the treaties by kissing the cross, these Rus' envoys swear by their weapons or by their gods *Perun* and *Volos*, which are presumably Fenno–Balto–Slavic renditions of Scandinavian gods in connection with the translation from Greek. Nevertheless, nearly half a century and several battles and treaties later, victory for the Orthodox Church seemed in sight: as we have seen, in 957 princess Olga of Kiev (widow of Igor I) was baptized on the occasion of her state visit to Constantinople (unless she had already been baptized once before her departure, which again is controversial).[70]

By the treaty of 907 the emperor gave the Rus' baths and supplies as they required. As merchants they could receive a monthly allowance for six months, including bread, wine, meat fish and fruit, and nautical equipment for their homeward journey. In return, the Rus' were required to have their cargoes registered and sealed by the relevant Byzantine officials, reside in one suburb (the Saint Mamas quarter), enter the capital by one gate only, unarmed and in groups of no more than fifty, escorted by an imperial officer. Once in the city they could conduct their business without paying dues, but could buy no more than fifty bezants' [a gold coin] worth of silk per man. They were to go straight back to Kiev without wintering on the Black Sea. Obviously, while within the empire the Rus' were 'not to commit acts of violence in our [viz. Byzantine] towns and our territories'.[71]

It was the usual Byzantine bureaucratic wonderland, tolerable only because the emperor was extremely powerful and there was no easier way of getting gold and silk. Still, if the treaty of 907 only dealt with conditions for everyday trade in Constantinople, the next treaty, namely that of 911, allowed the possibility of Rus' mercenaries serving 'the Christian emperor',[72] as Haraldr Sigurðarson was later to do. By this date the Kievan Rus' had extended their control of western Russia to incorporate Novgorod and were pressing towards the fat lands of the south. Among other matters, the third treaty, that of 945, ensured proper documentation and authorization of Rus' envoys and merchants, a sensible, practical provision to enable the Byzantine authorities to tell friend from foe. 'Henceforth envoys and merchants sent by the Rus' shall take with them a certificate to the effect that a certain number of ships have been dispatched. In this way we can be assured that they come in peace'.[73] Only four years earlier, under Igor I (r. 912–45), the Rus' had once again made further attempts to take Constantinople.[74]

The Russian *Primary Chronicle* describes Igor as a greedy, foolish and sadistic ruler. In 941 he had attacked Constantinople with an enormous fleet, apparently 10,000-ships strong.[75] According to John Skylitzes, who also says the Rus' fleet consisted of 10,000 ships:

> The atrocities they [the Rus'] had committed before they were defeated exceed the horror of a tragedy. They crucified some of their prisoners and staked others out on the ground. Others they set up as targets and fired arrows at them. They drove sharp nails into the heads of any of the prisoners who were priests and burnt down not a few sacred churches.[76]

In the end the Rus' were overcome by a mere fifteen retired *semifracta chelandia* or 'half-size' galleys.[77]

A miracle, perhaps, but from all their sides, these plucky superannuated vessels spewed Greek fire upon the Rus'. The Rus' were so struck with horror when their ships burst into quenchless flames that they threw themselves into the sea. But this liquid fire burned even more violently upon water, and those who were not mercifully drowned, weighted down by their armour, were melted like tallow while attempting to swim in the inflammable water. Liudprand of Cremona, whose stepfather was then the envoy of Hugues d'Arles, king of Italy (r. 926–47), at the Constantinopolitan court, gives mention of this terrible naval battle. According to Liudprand, not only the prows of the ships but even their broadsides were furnished with siphons for spewing Greek fire, which meant they 'threw the fire all around'. He continues, saying that God had favoured the Byzantine navy with good fortune with regard to a gentle wind and a calm sea.[78] The Russian *Primary Chronicle*, in its description of the same battle, says:

> Upon seeing the flames, the Rus' cast themselves into the sea-water, but the survivors returned home [where] they related that the Greeks had in their possession the lightning from heaven, and had set them on fire by pouring it forth, so that the Rus' could not conquer them.[79]

Likewise, Leo Diakonos testifies how terror-struck the Rus' warriors of his day were by this 'liquid fire', for 'they had heard from the elders of their people how the immense army of Igor, the father of Sphendosthlavos [Sviatoslav], had been reduced to ashes by the Romans [Byzantines] in the Euxine [Black Sea] by means of this Median fire'.[80] In the Madrid manuscript of John Skylitzes' *Synopsis historiôn* we have an illustration of the same naval battle, but without the terrible Greek fire. Nonetheless, the Rus', in boats reminding us of their famous *monoxyles*, are jumping into the sea, while the Byzantines are attacking them with long swords.[81]

Such fiery discomfort was once again visited upon the Rus' when they attacked Constantinople in 1043 and perished under the Greek fire:

> Ar-Rum [Byzantines] shot fire at the Rus' ships. The Rus' did not know how to extinguish the flames, and many of them were burned to death or drowned.[82]

The courtier and chronicler Michael Psellos informs his readers that he himself witnessed the Rus' attack 'standing at the emperor's side'.[83] He witnessed, too, the traumatic effects of Greek fire, the Rus', 'being unable to see now, threw themselves into the water, trying to swim back to their comrades, or else, at a loss what to do, gave up all hope of escape'.[84] According to Psellos, to face the Rus' attack only a few derelict vessels could be found to be armed with Greek fire to oppose them.[85] However, the success of the Byzantine fleet (as he himself witnessed and recorded) suggests that Psellos exaggerated its weakness for literary purposes. According to Kekaumenos, probably writing in the ten-seventies, the Byzantine fleet was still the 'glory of *Romania*' in his own day.[86]

Indeed, the Christian king Sigurðr I Magnússon *Jórsalafari* (r. 1103–30), during his stay in Constantinople around the year 1110, became acquainted with the Greek fire, and Old Norse literature describes it as something new and terrible. Before leaving Constantinople, Sigurðr gave all of his ships and many treasures away to the emperor, Alexios I Komnenos. This is lauded in the sagas as an act of generosity, but was in reality a successful business transaction on the part of

Sigurðr who sold his ships easily at a high price to Alexios who desperately needed each vessel to strengthen the imperial navy.[87] As for the king, he planned to return to Norway by land, but few of his men accompanied him as many were to stay behind to take up service for the emperor in the Varangian Guard.[88]

Even though the attacks of the Rus' on Constantinople were all unsuccessful, the metropolis turned out to be a source of wealth to many of them when the emperors began to employ them in the Varangian Guard. Another important stream of recruits for the Varangian Guard, as we shall discuss anon, was represented by the Norsemen from Scandinavia whose fascination with Constantinople is reflected in the sagas of the Icelanders, *Íslendingasögur*, and kings' sagas, *konunga sögur*, which all depict Constantinople as a city of opulence.

Further a field

The Old Icelandic saga *Yngvars saga víðförla*, which describes (albeit heavily fictionalized and geographically muddled) the last viking campaign in the Caspian in 1041, relates how the hero Ingvarr and his companions coming down the Russian rivers encountered heathen 'pirates' (*illgerðamenn*) who used fire weapons. Covering their ships with reeds to disguise them as islands, they attacked Ingvarr's ships. The Greek fire was projected from 'a brass [or bronze] tube' by means of 'blowing with smith's bellows at a furnace in which there was fire and there came from it a great din'. The result was 'a great jet of fire', which hit one of the Norse ships, 'and it burned up in a short time so that all of it became white ashes'.[89] The mention of bellows and a furnace, the brass or bronze tube, the great din, and the emission of fire can leave little doubt that the origin of the story lay in some Norse's harrowing experience with Greek fire.

This large but spectacularly calamitous military campaign was launched from Sweden by Ingvarr the Far-Traveller (ON *Yngvarr víðförli*), who travelled down the Volga to the Caspian Sea with a fleet of thirty fully manned ships. He and his followers apparently took part in the civil war battle of Sasireti, eastern Georgia, in the spring of 1042. It was to meet its doom deep in Asia somewhere near the Caspian Sea in the land of the Saracens (ON *Særkland*), and resembling a runic roll call of oblivion a set of nearly thirty Swedish rune stones commemorates men who travelled out or died on this expedition, most commonly using the phrase *með Ingvari*, 'with Ingvarr'. Presumably, some returned to tell the tale, but obviously many members of the expedition perished, including its leader, and were commemorated at home.

Though the exact number of inscriptions associated with this event cannot be determined for certain, a total of twenty-six rune stones, mostly located in the Lake Mälar region of Uppland in Sweden, are now known, with greater or lesser degrees of certainty, to have been erected in the mid-eleventh century to commemorate the deceased participants in Ingvarr's (disastrous) military adventure,[90] one of the last viking-age expeditions to the east.[91] Short, formulaic phrases carved on the stones name twenty-six warriors who went with Ingvarr. Take, for example, the stone at Gripsholm, Södermanland:

> Tóla had this stone put up for her son, Haraldr, Ingvarr's brother. / Like men (*drængila*) they journeyed for distant gold / and in the east they fed the eagle. / In the south they died, in *Særkland*.[92]

This inscription, commissioned by a woman, Tóla, occupies the body of a snake – the elaborate decoration of the stone suggests wealth – and begins in prose but turns to heroic alliterative verse to describe the adventurer's exploits. It is likely – though cannot be proved – that the two men shared a father, but not a mother, although it is also possible that the word 'brother' is used metaphorically and that they were 'brothers in arms'.

On the other hand, the word translated 'like men' is the adverb *drængila*, 'behaving like a *drængr*', the latter noun of shifting meaning but implying the concepts of bravery, loyalty and manliness. Thus a worthy free man was expected to face challenges with courage and equanimity. Worrying or complaining did nothing to improve the situation and only diminished a man. The most explicit formulation for the Old Norse term *drængr* comes from the *Skáldskaparmál* ('The Language of Poetic Art') section of Snorri Sturluson's *Prose Edda*:

> Young men without their own farms are called *drængr* while they are acquiring wealth or fame for themselves; those who travel between lands are called *drængr* on the move (*fardrængr*), those in the service of chieftains are called king's *drængr* (*konungs drængr*), and they are also called *drængr* who serve powerful men or landowners; men who are manly and promising are called *drængr*.[93]

Here we find the classic statement of the position of a *drængr*: a young, often unmarried, man (as opposed to the settled *bóndi*) without a permanent residence of his own who makes his way in the world by serving his social superiors. Anyway, returning to the epitaph for Haraldr. The expression 'to feed the eagle' is a heroic way of saying 'to kill men in battle', since it was well known, at any rate to skalds, that eagles gathered about the field of the slain in the hope of picking up easy fresh meat. *Særkland* is not a very precise place name, but is used to mean the land of dark-skinned peoples round the Mediterranean and in the Near East, and here refers to part of the Arab dominions, specifically the 'Abbasid caliphate of Baghdad.

That these Swedish rune stones are so numerous testifies that it was a large-scale and well-organized military venture.[94] It must be remembered, however, *Yngvars saga víðförla* was written in Iceland about a century and half after the stones were raised (it is ascribed to the monk Oddr Snorrason), which might explain why 'the four men named among Ingar's companions on the journey' are not the Swedes mentioned on the rune stones. Thus, in the saga they are Garða-Ketill (an Icelander, though 'Garða' identifies him as a visitor to or inhabitant of *Garðaríki*, Kievan Russia), Hjálmvígi (possibly a German), Valdimarr (who seems to have been a Russian), and Sóti (whose home country is not specified, though it is probable that he was a Swede).[95] In other words, all are from different countries, forming a sort of international team. The saga itself states that it was told at the royal court in Sweden and from there came to Iceland. Before it left Sweden, the saga was performed in different parts of the country by different saga-tellers. It therefore circulated in several oral versions, each saga-teller contributing to the tale – by adding details, creating new episodes, new characters even, and changing the interpretation of the events he recounted.[96]

Before we leave this subject, it is important to understand that the whole runic corpus – some thousands of inscriptions – is the only written source from the viking age that records what the Scandinavians wanted to say about themselves (as opposed to the chronicles of their neighbours or descendants). Thus, viking-age runic texts – the vast majority of the three-thousand-odd examples carved on to memorial stones – provide extraordinary insights into the lives and deaths of those Scandinavians who commissioned them and whom they commemorate. The rune stones taken as a group confirm what we expect vikings to do: travelling, trading, fighting, getting rich, and getting killed. A word of caution, however. The majority of these rune stones belong to the period 960–1100, and 90 per cent of those are to be found within the modern boundaries of Sweden: over 50 per cent, which include those discussed above, in Uppland.

Russia, 1031–4

The exile

We continue the story of Haraldr Sigurðarson in 1030, which for him was a year of suspense and shock. His personal valour, his restlessness, his concern for glory, his cunning and resourcefulness, his skill as a military leader and his dedication to himself were all to be put to the ultimate test over the following decade or so.

Anyhow, the next chapter of Haraldr's saga opens with his escape, then only fifteen years old (according to the Icelandic skald Þjóðólfr Arnórsson), in disguise, after the death of his half-brother, Óláfr II Haraldsson (later Saint Óláfr) on the fateful field of Stiklarstaðir.[97] The king had died in his quest to reclaim the Norwegian throne, which he had lost to the Danish king Knútr Sveinsson two years prior, but Haraldr was destined to survive and become one of the most travelled Northmen.

Indeed, Óláfr's defeat and death at Stiklarstaðir was to make exiles of Haraldr Sigurðarson and his close ally Rögnvaldr Brúsason, grandson of the formidable *jarl* Sigurðr of Orkney slain at Clontarf sixteen years previously. Both friends, having survived the defeat, were wanted men with prices on their heads and therefore needed to seek a safe and friendly haven far from the new régime that now ruled Norway. It was Rögnvaldr who carried young Haraldr away from the battlefield and smuggled him to a remote farmhouse in eastern Norway, where Haraldr was left to recover from his battle wounds. Once mobile, possibly in the autumn, he was then secretly escorted over the frontier into Sweden.[98] In fact, Haraldr was to be sustained by his loyal companion Rögnvaldr, who opted to share his exile and fight alongside him. Quitting Sweden the following spring, the two Scandinavian rulers-to-be sailed east to Russia and took refuge in the court of Yaroslav in Kievan Russia (the sagas' *Garðaríki* or *Garðar*, 'the kingdom of fortified towns'),[99] who 'received them most heartily for the sake of king Óláfr the Holy'.[100] The party's exile in Russia was not a time of idleness, and both men were to gain valuable military experience and leadership skills in the service of the Kievan Rus' prince.

Man of art, man of war

Yaroslav I (r. 1019–54), later known as Yaroslav the Wise, lord of Novgorod and Kiev, was one of the greatest princes of the viking age, revered as a patron and founder of learning and literature in Kievan Rus' during his thirty-five-year reign. He is perhaps the best known of all Kievan rulers to western historians. A shrewd and energetic ruler – he was one of the sons of grand prince Vladimir, a serial polygamist who had sired numerous offspring – Yaroslav was always careful to foster his ancestral connections with Scandinavia. He had married Ingigerðr Óláfsdóttir (referred to as Irina, Eirene in Russian and Byzantine sources), the daughter of the king of Sweden, Óláfr *sköttkonungr* (d. 1022). She was originally, according to Snorri Sturluson, pledged to Óláfr II Haraldsson, but was married in 1019 to Yaroslav, leaving Óláfr to marry her illegitimate half-sister.[101] Ingigerðr (d. 1050) would be canonized as Saint Anna of Novgorod (where she is buried) by the Orthodox Church, Anna being the name she received as a nun. Their daughter, Elisaveta Yaroslavna of Kiev, would latter marry Haraldr on his return to Norway; Yaroslav's contacts with the Norse kingdoms were obviously close and calculated. At Kiev, Haraldr would have met up with his nephew Magnús Óláfsson, now the rightful heir to the Norwegian throne.

Yaroslav was also a man of war. In 1037, having ground down those olden foes the predatory Pečenegs (who thereupon never were a threat to Kiev) the previous year, he celebrated his victory and the God who granted it by sponsoring the first Russian cathedral. This is, of course, his church of Saint Sophia in Kiev, magnificent enough to have been mistaken as a copy of Hagia Sophia in Constantinople, though architecture-wise, its model could have been the thirteen-domed oaken Saint Sophia in Novgorod built by his father. He asserted Kievan power with similar success in the northern marches of his vast dominion, brought the Chudes back under his sway, and pushed his frontier further to the west. Kievan hold on the Dnieper trade route was now absolute, making it an important source of revenue. With the state coffers now bulging, Yaroslav was able to buttress and beautify Kiev. The heart of the town, henceforth properly to be styled the city, was walled about with an earthen rampart, studded with bastions and pierced with gateways, while within rose churches, other than Saint Sophia, monasteries and schools. Other celebrated monuments of his reign such as the Golden Gate of Kiev were destroyed in December 1240 during the Mongol invasion of Kievan Russia, but later restored.

The Norseness of the Rus' had been quietly eroded with the adoption of Slavonic customs, assimilation and intermarriage, the change of language and religion, and the massive influence of Byzantium carried the process even farther. During his long reign Yaroslav only clashed once with the Byzantines, when he ill-advisedly sent his eldest son, vice-regent Vladimir Monomakh of Novgorod (r. 1036–52), to intimidate Constantinople in 1043. He lost his fleet, which was bad, and his illusions about the relative power of Kiev and Byzantium, which was good.

Brothers' war

Back in 1014 Yaroslav, when ruling Novgorod as vice-regent, had refused to pay tribute to Kiev and only Vladimir's death, in July 1015, prevented a war between father and son. Nevertheless, the Russian *Primary Chronicle* says that Yaroslav had felt himself so greatly under threat from Vladimir that he 'sent across the sea and brought Varangians' to beef up his local forces early in 1015.[102] In the event, he would have need of these Scandinavian mercenaries, but against his one of his many siblings instead of an irritated father.

During the next four years Yaroslav waged a complicated and bloody war for Kiev against his half-brother Sviatopolk I of Kiev, who was supported by his father-in-law, Bolesław I Chrobry of Poland. During the course of this struggle, other siblings (Boris, Gleb, and Sviatoslav) were liquidated and to follow their father into the budding Russian calendar of saints. The *Primary Chronicle* accused Sviatopolk of planning those assassinations, calling him the 'Accursed', while the Old Norse saga *Eymundar þáttr Hringssonar* is often interpreted as recounting the story of Boris' assassination by the Norwegian mercenaries led by Eymundr Hringsson (more of him below) and in the service of Yaroslav. However, the victim's name is given there as *Burizaf*, which is also a name of Bolesław in the Old Norse sources. It is thus possible that the saga tells the story of Yaroslav's struggle against Sviatopolk (whose warriors were commanded by the Polish father-in-law), and not against Boris.

Yaroslav defeated Sviatopolk in their first battle, in 1016, and entered Kiev in triumph while Sviatopolk fled west to Poland. But Sviatopolk returned in 1018 with Polish troops furnished by his father-in-law and reinforced with German, Magyar and Pečeneg mercenary bands, seized Kiev, and dislodged Yaroslav back into Novgorod. But both brothers were the losers, the real victor being almost certainly Bolesław who paid off the mercenaries with the plundering of Kiev.

Meanwhile, Yaroslav was back in Novgorod raising new revenues to pay for Scandinavian mercenaries to renew the war. In the spring of 1019 Yaroslav finally prevailed over Sviatopolk, who again took flight, although he is said to have fallen ill and died before reaching Poland.

Before Yaroslav could firmly establish his rule over Kiev, he had to face another challenge from another of Vladimir's numerous sons. This was Mstislav, whose power base lay at Tmutorokan, a region on the northern shore of the Black Sea where the Taman peninsula is today, from where he had carved out his own impressive dominion around the Sea of Azov. Mstislav moved north of the steppe sometime around 1024 and based himself at Chernigov within striking distance of Kiev. Once again, according to the *Primary Chronicle*, Yaroslav 'sent across the sea for Varangians' to face Mstislav's 'Kasogians and Khazars' recruited from his subject peoples around the Sea of Azov and supplemented with Servians.[103] The Servians were presumably Slavs from around Chernigov, and it was these who played a greater part in defeating Yaroslav's northern army in a bizarre battle fought at night in a thunderstorm. Mstislav, in his hour of victory, apparently made a telling remark: 'Who does not rejoice at this? Here lies slain a Servian and here a Varangian, and yet the *druzhina* is unharmed'.[104] The *druzhina* (itself derived from the Old East Slav word *drug*, 'friend' or 'companion') was effectively the homegrown warrior retinue of a Rus' prince.

After his defeat Yaroslav withdrew back to the north and yet, for whatever reason, Mstislav did not pursue his flight, but instead conceded Kiev to his brother while retaining Chernigov. In 1026 the two met again near Kiev, and formally agreed to a division of the lands of the Rus' along the line of the Dnieper, those to the east for Mstislav and those to the west for Yaroslav. 'Thus they began to live in peace and brotherhood', praises the *Primary Chronicle*,[105] until around the year 1036 when Mstislav died without issue, leaving Yaroslav as sole ruler over all the lands of the Rus'. Allegedly, he left a testament warning his heirs against engaging in fratricidal wars.

Serving Yaroslav

Yaroslav figures prominently in the Old Norse sagas under the name Jarizleifr the Lame; his legendary lameness (probably resulting from an arrow wound) was apparently corroborated by the Soviet scientists who examined his remains in 1939.

Haraldr was to remain with the Kievan ruler for at least three years, taking part in various military campaigns. We do know that Haraldr took part in Yaroslav's campaign against the Poles (ON *Læsir*),[106] which the *Primary Chronicle* dates to 1031,[107] the Kievan prince taking advantage of Poland's disordered state after the death in the previous year of his old enemy Bolesław Chrobry. Haraldr possibly fought against other Kievan enemies and rivals such as the Chudes, as well as the Pečenegs and other steppe nomads. According to *Orkneyinga saga* Yaroslav took Haraldr, along with Rögnvaldr Brúsason, 'into his service as defenders of his country,[108] while *Nóregs konunga tal* gives a little more detail, saying that Yaroslav made Haraldr a 'captain of his army and hired all his men as mercenaries'.[109] But what was the Kievan prince prepared to pay Haraldr and his men, mercenaries to a man?

Fortunately, we have the good example of Eymundr Hringsson, son of a Norwegian petty king, who decided to escape the tyranny and harsh treatment in Norway – Óláfr II Haraldsson had just seized control of all of Norway, deposing eleven regional kings in the process – and to win 'wealth and esteem' in the service of a foreign prince. The foreign prince in question happened to be Yaroslav, lord of Novgorod. Of him Eymundr demanded payment for mercenary service in the form of an ounce of silver for every man and a further half ounce to every captain, and that he and his men were prepared to serve the Novgorodian prince as long as they were paid. In other words, no pay, no play. There was to be no long-term relationship between Eymundr and Yaroslav. A warlord of a freebooting mercenary band generally wanted paying promptly, and in hard coin too. But this was apparently too high a price and Yaroslav refused. So, like any enterprising boss worth his salt, Eymundr then offered Yaroslav a workable compromise:

> Instead of silver, beaver and sable skins and other goods which abound here, in your land. Their value shall be estimated by us and not by your warriors. And if there be booty you can grant us pfennigs [ON *penningar*, sg. *penningr*]. If we are idle you shall grant us less goods.[110]

Yaroslav readily agreed.

Today, the quickest and most efficient way to recruit mercenaries is through the services of prime movers that have an intimate knowledge of the current mercenary market. Usually, the prime mover is either an official organ of a fully recognized government which works covertly through the agency of others or, alternatively, he is an entrepreneurial mercenary leader who first negotiates the contract with the employer and then recruits and leads the men to fulfil it. In a sense, Eymundr fulfilled the rôle of the entrepreneurial mercenary leader. We can safely surmise that the agreement between him and Yaroslav also included a definition of the nature of the enterprise for which the Norwegians were being hired. The terms of service were therefore negotiated on contractual basis, and in some detail. If violated by the employer, the mercenaries could, and would, refuse to march or fight.

It being the essential tenet of the mercenary to fight for whosoever will pay him, obviously Eymundr and his men had little interest in local politics and were strictly mercenary in their motivation. In better ordered times, of course, the support of a retained mercenary force, even under a short-term contract, required a more formal arrangement of remuneration. Failing that, as was the case here, plunder would almost always have supplied some component of the reward for mercenary service. Naturally Eymundr, as their leader, had a patriarchal duty to look after the men in his mercenary band, and they were bound by custom to serve him no matter the circumstances. He was the one who negotiated his band into the service of Yaroslav, and was the source of power and decisions within the band. Thus, a warrior rewarded by a lord found himself in an enduring social bond. We are guessing here that there was a similar contractual arrangement by which Haraldr and his men entered the service of Yaroslav.

Having spent three or four campaigning seasons under Yaroslav's command and travelling widely throughout the eastern lands, Haraldr eventually went south to Constantinople with the intention of enrolling in the famous Varangian Guard. By doing so he must have said farewell to his familiar comrade-in-arms Rögnvaldr Brúsason, who 'remained in *Garðaríki* when Haraldr Sigurðarson went to *Mikligarðr*'.[111]

Chapter 3

Varangians

T he history of the Varangian Guard is a remarkable story, both of survival and success. There can be few, if any, mercenary units that have produced such a sustained record of combat performance. The fame of the Varangian Guard, its romantic, even cutthroat reputation, has meant its members are so often portrayed as a hired band of axe-happy hooligans. Admittedly there were those who excelled at violence, and so their quotidian actions were brutally direct. All that mattered to such types was the immediate. The past was of no consequence to them, the future of even less. Their minds were entirely in the here-and-now. But they would have been in the tiny minority in this élite unit.

The term élite alone conjures up notions of favouritism, privilege, superiority, and standards that are unobtainable by the majority. In its purest form, the term élite translates into 'the choice or most carefully selected part of a group'.[1] Sociologists and political scientists generally recognize four types of élite: an élite of *birthright*, an élite of *merit*, a *functional* élite, and a *power* élite. The third type, the functional élite, is what concerns us here, and this group is composed of individuals who hold particular positions in society essential for its efficient and effective operation. This bureaucratic élite is made up of key civil servants, and it can also include a military élite.

From the twentieth century onwards, in the case of military elites, the issue does not necessarily centre upon cultural, economic, or political power. Rather, most often, it relates to the relationship of a given group within its own *institution*. Today, therefore, élite soldiers are carefully selected, rigorously trained and well led so as to perform to a higher standard than the conventional. Not surprisingly, the creed of the US army Rangers contains the conceptual definition of a military élite, based upon the premise: 'My country expects me to move farther, faster and fight harder than any other soldier'.[2] However, the creation of a *corps d'élite* has at least one detrimental effect on an army: the draining-off of the best soldiers from line regiments undoubtedly weakens their value and fighting qualities. Historically, however, the concept of a military élite, for sociologists and political scientists in any case, has centred upon their impact on the *politics* of a society.[3]

It is remarkable – though never remarked – how few writers have been soldiers in wartime. Rudyard Kipling, who wrote of soldiers and soldiering as well as anyone ever has, was never himself a soldier. I believe I am correct in saying that

Ernest Hemmingway was never a soldier, although he drove an ambulance and was wounded in combat. The American author and combat veteran James Jones (1921–77) – *From Here to Eternity* (1951), *The Thin Red Line* (1962) – was a writer of the rarest kind. He knew soldiers because he had been one, and knew war because he had been there. Only a man who has himself been to war could so eloquently render the emotion of a soldier crossing the boundary between life and death. Indeed, when you read his books you quickly realize that he describes the cruelty and horror with the detachment of a soldier who has shut down his emotional responses completely in a war zone... as soldiers always do, because otherwise they would not be able to survive. He once wrote that 'an élite unit is only élite when the majority of its members consider themselves already dead'.[4] Their lives were a trial-at-arms, antechamber only for the life to come, that life to come that was possible only to those who had kept the true faith. That is the full evolution of the soldier. It could be argued that Varangians thought they were already dead, and dying on behalf of the Byzantine emperor was what the Varangian Guard was all about.

Terminology

Though the term Varangian Guard is a modern usage, it is necessary to understand the meaning of the word 'varangian', before entering upon a detailed description of the Varangian Guard. Scholars agree that the word 'varangian', *væringjar*, derives from the Old Norse word *vár* (pl. *várar*), loosely meaning 'pledge' in reference to a band of men pledged to stand together and support each other loyally, observing a common code of conduct, and sharing out profits fairly amongst themselves.[5] Thus, Varangian Guard was *væringja-lið*, *lið* being in this case a 'host'.[6]

What must have appealed to the emperors about the Northmen was their long warrior tradition. Likewise, we need to understand the distinction between the designations Rus' and Varangian, which are often used ambiguously and slovenly. In the contemporary Muslim literary sources Varangians and Rus' are portrayed as two different groups within northern martial society.[7] While the Rus' consisted of men, women and children and formed a community built on warfare and trade, the Varangians were groups of warriors serving in the retinues of different lords, princes and kings, and, of course, the emperor of Byzantium. The Byzantine written sources use the word Βάραγγος, *Várangos*, to denote Norseman, but after the ninth century their service in the Byzantine military changed its meaning to that of Norse mercenary.[8]

One final point. Our word 'sources' perpetuates the French metaphor of springs, as in springs of water. At times the springs of the evidence for the Varangian Guard not only flowed rather brackishly but were tainted at their very origins. According to Blöndal/Benedikz the Varangians were divided into the 'Varangians within the City' (οι εν τη πόλη Βαράγγοι), who guarded the emperor and escorted him in his tours outside the palace, either within the capital or on his campaigns, and the 'Varangians without the City' (οι έξω της πόλεως Βαράγγοι) who were stationed in key posts in the themes. The authors claim that the term 'without the City' means throughout the empire, and this provides the basis for claiming that there were Varangian garrisons established in select areas across the empire.[9]

To a reader outside the rough and tumble of Byzantine history, their hypothesis may be compelling. Unfortunately, their hypothesis is not susceptible of anything like proof, and subsequent research has shown it to be incorrect. The existence of Varangian garrisons is not supported by evidence from the Byzantine written sources, and we can safely presume that there were no thematic Varangian units. To pick just one of the several examples Blöndal/Benedikz offer as regional Varangian garrisons we chose Cyprus. The authors suggest the possibility that a victorious navy contained some Varangians, who might have been employed to set up a garrison in Cyprus (at Paphos).[10] Shortly thereafter, the authors treat conjecture as fact, and proceed to invent an influx of new Varangian recruits sailing to reinforce the *nonexistent* Varangian garrison at Paphos.[11] This will not do. The authors present the reader with *no* evidence for any of their assertions, which, in truth, are pure speculation. Neither large nor disbursed geographically, the Varangians were a relatively small group of Scandinavians, and later English, employed as a mercenary bodyguard. In this capacity they were quartered near the emperor, that is to say, stationed in Constantinople as part of the tagmatic forces.

Enter the Swedes

The Swedes were just as active as their Nordic neighbours the Norwegians and the Danes but, as previously discussed, the Swedish viking age is closely associated with the east: the Baltic, Russia, the Byzantium empire, and the 'Abbasid caliphate. Swedish vikings (Swedes from Kievan Russia, in fact) had been fighting in the service of the Byzantine emperor throughout the tenth century. Indeed, the first Scandinavian mercenaries are mentioned in 902 as part of a military expedition to Crete, while a treaty of 911 (more of which later) between the Rus' (Gr. Ῥῶς), those of Scandinavian origin settled or active in old Russia, and Constantinople, contains a clause concerning those of the Rus' who wished to enter military service under the emperor.[12]

It has been noted that the principal incentive for a Rus' to be baptized was a desire to enter the service of the emperor, and that Varangians were encouraged by imperial authorities to become Christian.[13] Among the Rus' in Constantinople there was one detachment, which Constantinus VII Porphyrogenitus in his *De ceremoniis* refers to as 'baptized *Rhôs*'. On 31 May, in the year 946, a unit of 'baptized Rus' with banners, holding shields and wearing their swords' were standing as guards of honour in the Great Palace of Constantinople during the reception of envoys from a Muslim potentate.[14] They are listed among other naval detachments standing guard at the palace that day, including Dalmatians, and quite probably belong to the same unit of *Rhôs* that took part in the Lombard campaign of 935. It remains only to speculate whether they made up a separate squadron or were selected for the occasion from among a larger (and religiously mixed) detachment of Rus' mercenaries serving in the imperial navy. It is reasonable to guess that, since only Christian foreigners (viz. 'barbarians') were eligible for employment in the palace guard, the second possibility seems more likely.

In 949 we find Rus' crews manning Byzantine ships at Dyrrhachium (Dürrës, Albania) and along the Dalmatian coast, while 629 Rus' took part in the abortive armada sent by Constantinus VII Porphyrogenitus in the same year.[15] Rus' are also recorded at the battle of al-Hadath (Adata), northern Mesopotamia, in 954. The Byzantine forces were commanded by Bardas Phokas, the father of Nikephoros Phokas, the future emperor. The contemporary Muslim poet Abu ar-Tayyib al-Mutanabbi (d. 965) alludes to these mercenaries in his poem on the battle, which he presented to the victor that day, Sayf al-Dawla of Aleppo:

And how do the Byzantines and the Rus' hope to demolish [al-Hadath fortress] when the stabber [Sayf al-Dawla] is her foundation and pillars.[16]

The earliest named Scandinavian to take service in Constantinople was Þorkell Þjójstarsson, as far as can be traced. He spent some seven years about 950 in travel and adventure and, as he expressed it, 'was now a henchman of the king of *Mikligarðr*'.[17]

Passing from manuscripts to monuments, our next consideration concerns rune stones. Literacy in Scandinavia was largely limited to the runic alphabet and was typically used for relatively short inscriptions, which not only included rune stones, but also personal names scratched on individual items, graffiti and charms (as runes – literally, 'that which is secret' – were linked with magic, as well as providing a functional alphabet). The runic tradition, at least in the viking age, reached its culmination in Sweden, where the total collection of rune stones is outstandingly rich, in the true sense of the word. There are a couple of thousand monuments of this kind from the viking age, contemporary sources, and original documents no less.[18] But the ones that interest us at present are those containing the phrases *grikkfari*, 'the Greece-farer', and *a Grikklandi*, 'in Greece' (viz. Byzantium). There are over thirty runic inscriptions in all mentioning voyagers to Greece, with most *grikkfara* hailing from Uppland in Sweden. This is not surprising, for in Uppland most opportunities were on offer to gather news and information about the wealth of Constantinople and to organize the trading expeditions on a princely level. While some of them won gold, while others died there, not all of these Swedes necessarily joined the Varangian Guard. Some might have been merchants selling their wares, others mercenaries selling their services to the regular army of the Byzantine empire. The Swedish rune stones attest the social status deriving from time spent among 'the Greeks', and the emperor's gold was clearly one of the attractions for Swedes as for other northerners heading for Byzantium.

The most likely example of a Swedish Varangian, and probably a high-ranking one to boot, is Ragnvaldr Ingvarsson. His runic inscription is to be found carved over two faces of a large natural boulder beside a wooded path named Kyrkstigen ('church path') in Ed, just north of Stockholm. It was carved by his order, in memory of his beloved mother, Fastvi. Ragnvaldr (Rögnvaldr) was a name reserved for those belonging to the higher echelons of Norse society (he was a member of the Jarlabanke clan), while the stone advertises that he *a griklanti uas lis forunki*, '(he) in Byzantium, was commander of the retinue'. In full, the inscription reads:

> SIDE A   Ragnvaldr had the runes carved in memory of Fastvi, his mother, Ónæmr's daughter, (who) died in Eið. May God help her spirit.
>
> SIDE B   Ragnvaldr had the runes carved; (he) was in Greece, was commander of the retinue.[19]

Clearly, Ragnvaldr used his mother's memorial stone to boast of his own achievements, that is, he commanded a unit in the Varangian Guard.

By piecing together the evidence from five other Uppland rune stones,[20] it can be surmised that Ragnvaldr died together with his father Ingvarr and uncle Ingifastr, but the location and date of this family tragedy are not known. Omeljan Pritsak, however, suggests that they died in the Rus'-Byzantine war of 1043, for which Vladimir Monomakh of Novgorod, the eldest son of Yaroslav, had recruited Varangians.[21]

Saint Vladimir's gift

The institution of the Varangian Guard was apparently well established by the year 1000, since we find an Icelander, Kolskeggr Hámundarson, who 'went to *Mikligarðr* and became a mercenary'. He was to settle there, marrying a local girl, 'and became a leader in the Varangian Guard and stayed there until his death'.[22] This is, of course, according to the Nordic tradition. In Byzantine literary sources, however, the Varangian Guard (Gr. Τάγμα τῶν Βαράγγων, *Tágma tôn Varángôn*) does not seem to appear until 1028, the first regnal year of Romanos III Argyros (1028–34), the emperor Bolli Bollason had loyally served.

It was, according to Blöndal/Benedikz,[23] the emperor Basil II (r. 976–1025) who formed theVarangians into a regular *tagma* of his personal lifeguard, having received as many as 6,000 Scandinavian mercenaries from Vladimir (ON *Valdamarr*), prince of Novgorod, grand prince (*archon* is the corresponding Greek title) of Kiev and sovereign of Kievan Russia (r. 980–1015) who, as part of the deal, was to convert to orthodox Christianity (which his father Sviatoslav had roundly rejected) and marry Basil's sister, the *porphyrogénnêtê* princess Anna, a mature spinster by now, an honour the royal princess tried hard to avoid. According to the Mesopotamian scholar Izz ad-Din Ibn al-Athir, Anna 'refused to hand herself over to one whose faith differed from her own',[24] which is quite understandable, yet there was also the rumour of the 800 or so concubines and slave girls the prince apparently maintained in various Kievan Rus' towns. The Russian *Primary Chronicle* does not tell us what happened to these ladies. Before his conversion he had enjoyed an international reputation as a womanizer. The *Primary Chronicle* simply says – but with evident disapproval – that 'Vladimir was overcome by lust for women'.[25] The contemporary Ottonian cleric and chronicler, Thietmar of Merseberg (975–1018), was more direct: '*erat enim fornicator immensus et crudelis*'.[26] So Vladimir too started life as a pagan, like his father, and he too, like his grandmother Olga, ended up as a repentant sinner, accepted baptism and was eventually canonized. In his youth Saint Vladimir seemed to have followed Saint Augustine's handy motto: Lord give me chastity, but not yet. That being said, Olga's baptism, around 957 did not cut much ice, even with her own son. Vladimir's baptism, in 989, was a momentous event, one of those abrupt turns that make the study of history so fascinating.

In the words of an earlier chronicler, Yahya ibn Sa'ïd of Antioch (d. *c.* 1066), an Egyptian Melkite Christian:

> Emperor Basil later sent a Metropolitan [Theophylact, the former Metropolitan of Sebaste in Byzantine Armenia] and bishops to them [viz. the Kievan Rus'] and they baptized the king [prince Vladimir] along with all who lived in his land. He also sent his sister [Anna] to him; she had many churches built in the Rus' lands.[27]

It was rumoured too that the pagan Vladimir had investigated other faiths before his conversion to the Orthodox faith. For instance, it is said he had sent a ten-man delegation to the king of the Volga Bulghars, but Islam was rejected because 'drinking is the joy of the Rus', we cannot exist without that pleasure'.[28] Whether or not the use (or abuse) of alcohol was the real issue here, having married the purple-born Byzantine princess, the future Saint Vladimir spent the rest of his life converting the Kievan Rus' to Christianity and building churches. The celebrated Varangian Guard appears to have made its first entry on historical stage by way of an association with a Christian conversion and a marriage contract.

The truth of such a claim is difficult to establish: the origin of the Varangian Guard is veiled with some ambiguity. What we do know for certain is that between 976 and 989 the régime of Basil II was shaken by the insurrection of his former generals Bardas Skleros and Bardas Phokas. Both men were members of the military aristocracy of Anatolia and, as local strong men, were able to muster local forces strong enough to directly challenge the central authority in Constantinople and score several victories over the imperial forces. Basil had to go to considerable lengths to suppress both rebellions, even enlisting the aid of Vladimir at the price of offering his purple-born sister Anna – a privilege previously unheard of for any 'barbarian' ruler.

One emperor, two rebel generals

The Phokas clan had its origin in Kappadokia and for several generations had enjoyed high repute in the empire as soldiers. The father of Bardas Phokas was that Leo who had won military fame under Romanos II (r. 959–63), the father of Basil. His uncle Nikephoros was an even greater soldier and was himself to ascend the throne in 963, when he married Theophano, the mother of Basil. Actually, this was the second time Bardas Phokas had rebelled against his lawful monarch, which came to a head on 15 August 987 when he proclaimed himself emperor at Chresianus and promptly marched on Constantinople. Soon after, with Phokas absent, Basil II destroyed his army at Chrysopolis with the aid of those 6,000 Scandinavian mercenaries.[29] Apparently, these mercenaries, according the testimony of Michael Psellos:

> [C]ame upon them [the rebels] unexpectedly, when they were off their guard, seated at table and drinking, and after they had destroyed not a few of them, scattered the rest in all directions.[30]

The following year, with his surviving men, Phokas tried to take Abydos – the key to controlling the Hellespont – which Basil came to relieve.[31] Phokas, after twice falling from his horse, rode forward and issued a challenge to single combat (which Basil was unlikely to take up). Phokas then suffered a sudden dramatic stroke, falling dead from his horse mid-battle, which was unfortunate for him. His body was cut in pieces and the head presented to Basil.[32]

It was back in 971 when Bardas Phokas had rebelled for the first time. This was against John I Tzimiskès (r. 969–76), with the help of his brother Leo (the younger) and their father. He was actually proclaimed emperor at Caesarea in Kappadokia, but the rebellion was crushed by another warlord and rival, Bardas Skleros, and the whole Phokas family was sent into exile on the island of Chios.[33] Believe it or not, Phokas was brought out of exile by Basil, now emperor, to counter the rebellion of Bardas Skleros,[34] who had won two battles against Basil in 978 at Pankaleia and Basilika Therma. The rebel Skleros went on to capture Nicaea (İznık) and besiege Constantinople. The following year, at Aquae Seravenae (24 March 979), Phokas defeated his hated rival in single combat, splitting Skleros' head with a sword. So ended the first revolt against Basil.

Skleros survived and escaped to the 'Abbasid caliphate where he was to become a prisoner in Baghdad, until his captors released him in 987. With Baghdadi support, he proclaimed himself emperor again. Phokas was sent against him, but he too betrayed the emperor, first inviting Skleros to a parley, then treacherously clapping him in irons and declaring against Basil himself.

On the death of Phokas, Skleros, now almost blind, was released by Phokas' widow. He submitted to Basil and was allowed to retire, dying soon afterwards (6 March 991). Apparently, he advised Basil not to allow too much power to governors and generals, and admit no woman to the imperial councils.[35] From this moment on Basil became his own general, in so doing dispensing with the military elites that had been the mainstay of governance in the first years of his reign. Basil's intimate knowledge of the characters of individual soldiers and his supervision of promotions would further reduce the risk of challenges to his positions, as would his preservation of the strictest military discipline. Basil's martinet-like stance probably sprang from a mixture of personal proclivity and political calculation. In all probability the formation of the Varangian Guard played a part in Basil's strong-arm style of government; the Scandinavian mercenaries, after all, had been an instrument of his political ascendancy. In the words of Michael Psellos:

> Basil was well aware of the disloyalty among the Romans, but not long before this a picked band of Scythians [i.e. Rus'] had come to help him from Taurus. These men, fine fighters, he had trained in a separate corps, combined with another mercenary force, divided by companies, and sent them out to fight the rebels.[36]

It must be emphasized at this point that the distinct impression we get from the Russian *Primary Chronicle* is that Vladimir was only too happy to be rid of these Scandinavian mercenaries. For the prince sent messengers ahead of what appears to be a dangerous band of freelancers each bearing the following communication:

> See, Varangians are on their way to you. Do not keep them in the City [Constantinople] for then they will only give you trouble, as they have

given me, but divide them up into many places, and do not let one man come back here again.[37]

In 977, when the fratricidal war erupted between Yaropolk and his younger brother Oleg, Vladimir had fled to his kinsman Hákon Sigurðarson of Lade, ruler of Norway, to enlist mercenaries to aid him to win the princely crown from Yaropolk. When his father, Sviatoslav, died at the hands of the Pečenegs, Vladimir and his brothers fought savagely among themselves to enlarge the third share of Kievan power he had appointed for each of them. Yaropolk slew Oleg, and then perished in his turn, and it was the third son Vladimir who, with the help of these Scandinavian mercenaries, survived this fratricidal feud to succeed to all the lands of the Rus'.

Mercenaries face the chances common to every soldier of being killed by the enemy. In addition, however, they must reckon with the possibility of being bilked of their pay or massacred to avoid its payment; of being used as cannon fodder by an employer whose distaste for 'money-grubbing foreigners' may exceed the enemy's; or of being abandoned far from home when defeat or political change erases their employer or his goodwill. As Xenophon and the Ten Thousand learned, in such circumstances the road home may be long – or as short as a shallow grave. Vladimir may have wanted to get the Scandinavian warriors out of his own hair, but in doing so eventually there came into being the élite body of heavily armed northerners famous for using long shafted, broad bladed axes, which they 'bear on their shoulders'.[38]

Union of man and axe

It is a truism that human beings have never needed much in the way of technology to kill each other but it is equally true that it never hurts to have better weapons than one's potential opponents provided, and here is the rub, one knows how to use them.

They say every picture tells a story. If we were fortunate enough to be able to review a unit of Varangians at Constantinople in 1042, or perhaps at Herakleion a decade later, we would appreciate that they are combatants defined by a personal weapon, one with which they were singularly accomplished in handling. In the case of the Varangians what we would see is the two-handed battleaxe. Commonly known as the Dane axe – more properly called a *breiðox*, broad axe – this was a fearsome weapon of immense force, and so particularly decisive in close combat, the area in which most of the fighting took place in contemporary battles.

Varangians would have been taught to wield their axes over the left shoulder to avoid an opponent's shield. In this way, a Varangian held his axe in a left-handed grip to strike an opponent's unshielded right side. According to the Anglo-Norman chronicler William of Malmesbury, writing in 1125 or thereabouts, the signature weapon of the Anglo-Scandinavian professional retainers known as housecarls was borne on their left shoulder. Here is the evidence of William of Malmesbury: 'on their left shoulder they carried a Dane axe, with an iron [-headed] spear in their right hand'.[39] Pictorial evidence in the form of the Bayeux tapestry also shows combatants using their Dane axe two-handed with a left-handed grip, the blow about to fall on the opponent's unshielded side.[40]

The weapon, however, possessed one major disadvantage: when the Dane axe was held in both hands the shield could not be carried to protect the Varangian and, naturally, such a large weapon was always used in two hands. In expert hands it shattered shields and sliced through opponents from helm to hip. As in all hand-to-hand weapons, from the dagger to the spear, judgement of distance was the great secret with the Dane axe. Contrary to popular – and often even learned – opinion there would have been no frenzied hacking, no dramatic swings, no brute force and ignorance. The aim was not to make a great display of brutality but to actually kill with simple, short, straight strikes, slow and sure. With the heavy, razor-sharp blade of a cleaver – chop – chop – chop – chop – sharpened steel meeting flesh and bone.

Cruel and mortal

The axe-head itself was about the same breadth (width and height) as that of a present-day wood splitting axe, but distinctly lighter and thinner as it was designed to cleave human flesh and bone not hardwood. Raffaele D'Amato, citing David Nicolle as his source, proposes a length of 120 to 140 centimetres for the haft of those Dane axes depicted in the Bayeux tapestry, though archaeology supports the belief that the haft of a Dane axe was probably around 110 centimetres in length, with a weight around 1.73 kilograms. By way of comparison, a regulation cricket-bat measures 96.5 centimetres and weighs up to 1.36 kilograms. D'Amato also provides dimensions for the axe-head, namely eighteen centimetres from the back to the blade, and seventeen centimetres from point to point across the blade,[41] probably the Petersen type L or M, which is most familiarly rendered in the hands of the Anglo-Scandinavian housecarls in the Bayeux tapestry.[42] As the broad, thin cutting edge of the blade was backed by a thick body for resiliency, the Dane axe was a particularly devastating weapon in skilled hands. It could strike hard against a man in armour, or seriously compromise a shield with its sheer force. It would have been wielded two handed, like its wood splitting cousin, for control and power.

Whereas most swords in some way or another balanced the thrust, cut and slice, a Dane axe's primary method of attack was based on percussive cuts. The shape of an axe-head would focus momentum into a fairly small area and could transfer the shock through the mail and padding that many fighters would have been wearing. Because of this, the balance of most axes would have been much further forward than most swords.

It is easy for us to assume that axes, due to their forward balance, are slow and clumsy. The Dane axe had far more versatility than one might gather from a casual glance. With the off hand near the butt of the haft and the dominant hand closer to the axe-head, this weapon could be wielded comfortably and easily. The dominant hand could shift around to change techniques easily. In closer-in fighting, the dominant hand could shift further towards the head, allowing very fast strikes utilizing more of a punching type of hit, but at the expense of sacrificing some power. At a greater distance, the dominant hand could slide slightly further down the haft mid-swing, in the same way one would split wood, to not only cover the extra distance but to add momentum for much more powerful strikes. Requiring *skill* to wield efficiently, the Dane axe was a precise extension of the wielder's arms.

In addition to simple attacks, the shape of the head presented multiple offensive options. If an opponent was to parry the haft of the axe, the head could easily hook and tear down the opposing weapon. Should the wielder overreach with the blade, he could even hook an opponent and yank him down. It could even perform limited thrusting, outreaching most swords and yet, given the weight and size of the weapon, thrusts with the Dane axe would have been more like hitting with a battering ram than like the piercing attacks of pointed weapons.

The Dane axe was not difficult to recover from an attack, either. The head was heavy enough to cause significant damage, but because it was a two-handed weapon, the off hand could easily be used as a brake, so that if the wielder missed the opponent, the weapon remained in front where it could still be used to defend. The only concern – and this is true of all axes, large and small – was maintaining edge alignment on any strikes that were not directly downward because the edge was so far away from the haft that it wanted to naturally face down. The wielder could not have held the haft too loosely, or it would have rotated this way.

It is often believed that a Dane axe was a purely offensive weapon. While it is unfortunate that there is very little surviving evidence to detail how an axe like this was used historically, a basic understanding of larger hafted weapons can be applied to this weapon, and one can begin seeing that this is as effective at defence as it is with offence. Much like with a larger poleaxe, the haft could be used to deflect and stop outright oncoming attacks, and this axe's ash haft was more than substantial enough to take some serious damage. The wood would have certainly been more easily damaged than metal, but it could easily have been replaced after extensive use. By keeping the axe within the wielder's zone of control, the portion of the haft from his forehand towards the axe-head could be used to knock aside an oncoming blow, which would then leave the blade in a perfect position for a follow-up attack. A downward cut could be caught on the haft between the hands, which could easily flow into a strike with the butt of the haft, leading directly into a downward strike with the blade. The wielder could even catch and set aside a sword blade with the top of the wide axe-head.

A helmet was proof against sword and spear. A hard strike from a Dane axe, on the other hand, may have broken it, and at least was likely to have caved it in somewhat and stunned the wearer. Ring mail was proof against most sword cuts, but would have yielded to any thrust. It was also not proof against an axe. Mail would have allowed crushing/cutting injuries. Scale armour is covered by the remarks appertaining to helmets. Leather would have yielded to anything but the lightest sword cut. In effect, any blow to the body or head with an axe was lethal. Yet an axe large enough to be more useful than a sword in the crush of hand-to-hand combat was too cumbersome for an ordinary man. The size and weight of this weapon, of course, indicated the type of man who wielded it. The Dane axe was a weapon that suited the northerner's bulk and statue, weight and strength. An enemy who presented himself at a range of less than an axe-length to a Varangian was in very serious trouble.

In passing, it is interesting to note that, like swords, axes were sometimes named; female names were apparently favoured, Óláfr II Haraldsson, for instance, wielding one christened *Hel* after the Norse goddess of the shameful dead of all the nine worlds, the monstrous daughter of Loki who was half woman of peculiar beauty, half week-old corpse.[43] Indeed, R. Ewart Oakeshott writes of how Norsemen would name their battle axes with colourful cognomens, such as 'witch of the shield' or 'battle witch', demonstrating that these warriors held a certain amount of reverence for these arms; the terms 'fiend' and 'witch' were kept exclusively for axe names, whereas swords and spears had separate adjectives for their names.[44]

Maximum effort

There can be no doubt that the warrior whose weapon was the Dane axe would have required exceptional physical strength, but there was more to war than standing tough in a shield wall. Moreover, the Dane axe was not his only weapon, of course, because a Varangian also carried side arms, certainly a sword in battle and, at the very least, a long-bladed knife. He clearly used, and was proficient with, a spear. That said, there is another aspect to this Dane axe with wider implication, however, and it lies in the practicality of handling a weapon that demanded not only physical strength but a masterly level of skill in its handling, especially in the hands of warriors standing side by side in action. The warrior engaging with an oncoming enemy and concentrating on strenuous two-handed work with his own weapon would have been at risk of grievous injury (or worse) from any miscalculation or incompetence on the part of a fellow Varangian fighting beside him. In axe-play, intelligence was more important than strength or brawn. Likewise, without continual practice of basic techniques, the Varangian would not have developed the strength, flexibility, or automatic response needed to maintain the skill effective in battle.

In actual fact, we do not know much about the battle tactics and formations of the Varangians. It is possible that they fought in pairs when they came to grips with the enemy, as did those housecarls mentioned above. The one on the left, using his sword or spear, would employ his shield to deflect incoming blows. This enabled the one on the right to risk his person more boldly, which he did by striding in, striking with a lethal cutting-edge at the end of a long-handle up to a couple of metres in length, to shred his man from shoulder to belt. Tostig Godwinson was slain at Stamford Bridge with one of these terror weapons, which split his helmet, skull and neck to the shoulder blades. Allegedly, according to the contemporary Latin poem of Guy d'Amiens (d. 1075), it was Tostig's own brother, Harold, who dealt the killing blow, after which he 'hewed off his brother's head' and buried it apart from the rest of his body, a canonical sin. William, duke of Normandy, then is summoned to avenge this 'vile crime'.[45] Norman propaganda worked on this theme. Thus, William de Poitiérs points his accusing finger at Harold, saying 'you stained yourself with your brother's blood; for fear that his power might diminish yours'.[46] This action alone, therefore, justified the Norman conquest of England, William of Normandy being the righteous instrument of God's justice.

Even against mounted targets, this was a terrifying and highly effective combination, the pair working perfectly as a killing team, as the Normans were to discover at Hastings. In fact, the Dane axe terrified them. Writing within a decade of Hastings, William de Poitiérs calls them 'murderous axes', which 'easily penetrated shields and other protections',[47] while that cinematic work of art, the Bayeux tapestry, portrays a moustachioed housecarl striking his Dane axe deep into the head of a panicked warhorse.[48] Housecarls could deal terrible head-splitting axe blows to man and horse alike. Wace, a Jersey-born Norman poet (Jersey was then part of the duchy of Normandy) who became a canon of Bayeux cathedral, describes one English warrior, undoubtedly a housecarl, who 'held a very fine Norwegian axe [viz. Dane axe], its blade more than a full foot in length,' who pushed to the front of the battle 'where the Normans were at their densest' and, putting all his strength into a blow meant for a knight's head, missed and decapitated the man's horse. Everyone who saw gaped.[49] One Norman knight described by Wace was so filled with fear at the prospect of losing his favourite horse that he considered hanging back, but abandoned the idea as dishonourable.[50] Armed with a good Dane axe, a housecarl need fear neither man, devil nor armoured knight – if he could hit him. But to be sure of getting a solid strike, the housecarl had to wait until his target was almost upon him: an arm's length at most. It was best not accomplished in the company of rough fellows – even friends – who were continually jostling you about.

Much ado about an axe

This is a fitting moment to tackle a Greek term that is so misleading (to us moderns at least) that we must come to grips with it before proceeding further. A recurring problem with our contemporary Byzantine literary sources is an unashamed attempt on part of their authors to demonstrate their knowledge of the literature of classical antiquity such as Homer, Herodotos, Thucydides and Polybios, and their familiarity with classical Greek terminology, whence the use of the term ῥομφαία, *rhomphaia*,[51] for the Varangian two-handed battleaxe. Similarly, when Anna Komnene uses the term 'swords', ξίφη, and qualifies them as 'single-edged', ἑτερόστομα, she probably means the axes of the Varangians. Indeed, the odd reference when she actually says 'axe-bearing [πλεκανοφορος]' is an unaccountable lapse on her part.[52] Again, Michael Psellos in his last reference to the Varangians describes them as bearing 'single-edged battle axes [αζινας επεροστομος]'.[53]

In spite of being acknowledged by some modern commentators (and I am not talking of the lunatic fringe), the Varangian *rhomphaia* is a complete fiction, a literary contrivance, an example of the borrowing of the style and words of the classical past, what scholars call 'atticism'. Otherwise the formula is varied only a little: 'bearing' (φεροντες) or 'brandishing' (κραδαινοντες, rather than επισειεοντες of Psellos, but the meaning is very much the same) on their shoulders the *xiphos*. So, our two Byzantine authors describe the Varangians as brandishing on their shoulders a weapon for which the names *rhomphaia* and *xiphos* are used, and which is often described as 'single-edged' (επεροστομος) or 'heavy-iron' (βαρυσιδηρος) or both.[54]

This brings us to Michael Psellos and his vivid account of the occasion when he saw for himself the bodyguards protecting the rebel emperor Isaakos I Komnenos:

> Those then were the warriors who rounded off that circle of shields, armed with long spears and *single-edged battle-axes* [emphasized added]. The axes they carried on their shoulders and with spiked ends of the spears jutting out before and behind them the intervals between the ranks were, so to speak, roofed in.[55]

Again, Michael Psellos witnessed the Varangians protecting their emperor, in this case Michael VII (r. 1071–8):

> Well, the guards banged on their shields all together, bawled their heads off as they shouted their war-cry, clashed sword on sword, with

answering yells, and went off to the emperor thinking he was in danger; then, forming a circle about him, so that no one could approach, they carried him off to the upper parts of the palace.[56]

Here we should note the rather quaint terminology used by Psellos above when he refers to the Varangians, namely the 'Scyths from the Taurus'. Hence the Greek term *Tauroskuthai* was at that time a synonym for 'Varangian'. Thus, Michael Attaleiates writes: '*Tauroskuthai*, who in common speech are called *Rhôs*'.[57]

In fact, *Scythia* is a geographical concept of impressive durability. As a name for the part of Europe north of the Black Sea from the Danube to the Don, it was already well-established when Herodotos wrote about it in the fifth century BC. A thousand years later, it had the same meaning when Jordanes wrote about the Goths in the middle of the sixth century.[58] During these first Christian centuries, it is certain that the term 'Scythians' had started to be attributed to any group beyond the Danube coming into contact with the Roman world. For instance, the Goths are said by Prokopios to have been called Scythians previously, because all groups who lived in that area were called Scythians.[59] In our own period of study, the Russian *Primary Chronicle*, under the year 907, mentions the Varangians first among the peoples that the Greeks counted as being part of *Scythia*.

The Varangians are frequently referred to in the Byzantine chronicles as 'axe-bearing warriors'. Their Dane axes were wielded when and wherever their emperor needed them, and this included service on the walls of Constantinople. The best records of the Varangians manning the walls date from the Fourth Crusade (1202–4), the notorious crusade that did not fight Muslims but instead ended, after the second siege of the city, with the conquest and sack of the Queen of Cities.

Recounting the events of the first siege of his beloved city (July 1203), of which he was an eyewitness, Niketas Choniates reports that when the crusaders tried to enforce a landing at the imperial pier on the Golden Horn near the Blachernai quarter they were driven back by the great bravery of the allies of Byzantium, who included 'the Pisans and the axe-bearing barbarians'.[60] Niketas' history is the only complete Byzantine account of the Fourth Crusade. Not surprisingly, it gives a very different slant on events to that found in western accounts. In his splendid eyewitness account Geoffroi de Villehardouin recalls it was English and Danes who manned the fortifications on that day, namely Niketas' 'axe-bearing barbarians', and that 'the fighting was very violent, and there was a hand-to-hand fight with axes and swords, the assailants mounted on the wall and prisoners were taken on both sides'.[61] He also recounts that on 18 July, the day the Latins sent four envoys to the reinstated Isaakos II Angelos (r. 1185–95, 1203–4), Englishmen and Danes were posted at the city gates and all along the road to the Blachernai palace, fully armed with their formidable Dane axes. Villehardouin himself was one of the four envoys.

It is commonly said that imitation is the best form of flattery, yet when it comes to the Dane axe there is a hitch. The Dane axe, as we have discussed in detail, was a brutally effective battlefield weapon with a long haft and a wide, hacking blade, but its use demanded both good physique and long practice. For these reasons the method and the success of the Varangians were not easily imitated and gradually their numbers would have declined as further recruits from the northern world were not forthcoming. Indeed, the steadfast service by the Varangian Guard does not seem to have lasted much beyond the restoration of Byzantine power under Michael VIII Palaiologos (r. 1259–82). There is, however, a reference of 1329 to 'the Varangians with their axes' who were accustomed to guarding the keys of any city in which the emperor was staying, and another remembers that in 1351 the Varangians greeted the emperor in their own language of English.[62] There is no mention of them in action during the 1394–1402, 1411, 1422 and 1453 sieges by the Ottoman Turks. Besides, the Byzantine empire by this time was little more than the environs of Constantinople.

The cash nexus

Now let us consider more closely what motivated Northmen to take the road to Constantinople and thereby sign up with the Varangian Guard to fight on behalf of its employer, the Byzantine emperor. Given the nature of our sources, such a question is of course unanswerable, except in a few individual cases.

Before proceeding any further, however, we need to understand that the true mercenary employs his fighting skills as a commodity. A paymaster buys the skills for a set amount of time. When the time is up and the payment received, the relationship between mercenary and master is terminated. With particular regards to a Norseman serving the emperors of Byzantium, we need also to understand that this was a man who went out to prostitute himself and his talents in serving another race. He was not one of them. The words 'paid' and 'foreign' are thus the principal characteristics of the traditional definition of the true mercenary. Which begs the question, why throughout history certain individuals should want to fight for someone whom most had never met or knew little about is among the most difficult questions facing military historians of any period.

By way of a convenient and contemporary contrast, the Anglo-Scandinavian housecarls, the *corps d'élite* of kings from Knútr Sveinsson to Harold Godwinson whom we have met already, were not exactly mercenaries in the accepted sense of either being paid for military service or serving a foreign power, but they do seem to have had a corporate contract with their lord. Under this they had been initially maintained and paid (*stipendia et donativa*), in peacetime as well as in time of war, by means of a system of national taxation, the *heregeld*, which had been first been imposed by Æthelred II. However, in the reign of Edward Æthelredsson (the Confessor) this tax was abolished,[63] and the housecarls began to be paid for directly out of the royal coffers. Some housecarls were used to garrison a network of fortified towns (OE *burhs*, whence the modern word 'borough') to defend the kingdom of England,[64] the rest being based at court where they formed part of the king's personal retinue or *hirð*. These were carefully selected men of large statue, impressive physical fitness and very competent in handling the sword, spear and, of course, long-handled battleaxe. However, though they specialized in war, their services were not limited to it. The *Anglo-Saxon Chronicle* describes them as tax collectors too, which further reinforces the idea that they were the king's strong-arm men or enforcers. Thus, for example, the reference to the heavy-handed reaction of Hörða-Knútr (OE *Harðacnut*) to the murder of two of his housecarls within the minster of Worcester in 1041 while trying to collect taxes – in response, he 'had all Worcestershire ravaged for the sake of his two housecarls'.[65]

The term itself presents certain difficulties, for it was apparently used by contemporary writers in both a special and a general sense. The term is, of course, Norse in origin,[66] as is the institution which it describes, but from the reign of Knútr onward the word 'housecarl' is generalized to embrace almost any kind of household warrior or retainer. We encounter English as well as Danish housecarls.[67] In addition to the royal housecarls there were housecarls in the retinues of important lords who cannot have differed greatly from the household troops of the previous age.[68] Correspondingly, outside of England we find housecarls serving Scandinavian lords. There is, for instance, an eleventh-century rune stone that describes Hæra, the deceased, as having been the *húskarl* of a local Swedish lord named Sigröðr.[69] Now, *húskarl* is the word used by Haraldr III Sigurðarson in his ironic comment on how Einarr *þambarskelfir* has more followers than a *jarl*,[70] clearly indicating that jarls could also have *húskarlar*. Finally, we see the *húskarlar* in their fighting rôle, although on the other side, at the battle of Áróss in 1043. Magnús I Ólafsson *góði* is said by the skald Þjóðólfr Arnórsson to bring it about 'so fewer grew the / húskarlar of the *jarl* there'.[71]

As just indicated, the term *húskarl* was also borrowed into Old English as *huscarl* (pl. *huscarlas*), where the collocations link it very strongly with the king himself. Accordingly, the term *huscarl* is used in a special context to describe a unique, closely knit organization of professional warriors who served the kings of England from Knútr to Harold and became the spearhead of the royal army.

The sources disagree as to the exact time when the royal corps of housecarls was first established in the kingdom of England. The Old Icelandic source *Flateyjarbók* discloses that Sveinn I Haraldsson *tjúguskegg* introduced them into England, dividing the organization into two groups, one with its headquarters in London, and the other in northern England.[72] But scholars have tended to be sceptical of this account and to accept the testimony of the Danish historians Sven Aggesen (*fl.* 1150) and Saxo Grammaticus that the housecarls were established in England as an organization by Sveinn's son Knútr, probably around the year 1018.[73] From the time of their inception, they constituted the most highly trained and battle-ready force available to the rulers of England. They first appear in English sources in a charter of 1033, where Knútr grants land to 'his *huscarl* Bovi',[74] and thereafter they are occasionally mentioned in the *Anglo-Saxon Chronicle*, where they are described, as we have just mentioned above, as serving as tax collectors as well as soldiers.[75]

Mercenaries are soldiers for hire. They fight for their pay rather than under forcible recruitment or the usual claims of patriotism, justice, politics, or high ideals. Mercenaries have existed since the appearance of organized armies and have played an important part in wars for thousands of years. In this respect, standard definitions of 'mercenary' come down to little more than 'paid foreign soldier'. However, when dealing with the Varangians it should be noted that the word 'mercenary' carries none of the negative connotations it has gained from later centuries. It is essentially the equivalent of 'professional', which is one who is paid for his work.

The useful typology of paid military service in state-level societies that Stephen Morillo proposes terms a soldier 'unembedded in society of his employer' who 'sells his services according to the best offer among potential military employers', he is the 'classic mercenary',[76] and a soldier embedded in the moral economy of his society but for whom, nonetheless, market forces play an important rôle in their choice of military profession, the stipendiary soldier.[77] Understood in this way, the relationship between the mercenary and his master is primarily commercial, while that of other categories of paid soldiers is not. By Morillo's definition then, we can interpret housecarls as professional paid fighters as opposed to a species of mercenary, that is, men who offer their services to those who would pay the most, providing loyalty of sorts for a required period of time.

The relationship between mercenaries and their employers is always fraught. The hosts tend to regard their employees as a bunch of unprincipled, armed thugs who are leeching off them in their moment of greatest need and whose loyalty is suspect. After all someone, possibly the enemy, might come up with a better employment offer and business is business. It has not been unknown in history for mercenaries to change sides at a critical moment. For their part, mercenaries tend to treat their employers with open contempt. After all, if they had any balls they would not need to hire mercenaries. This attitude is not helped by the fact that the only locals most of the mercenaries are likely to meet are the hustlers and the harlots who hang around encampments. However, the real problems arise when the fighting ends. It occurs to the civilians that the mercenaries are now the strongest power in the land and it occurs to the mercenaries that the civilians might think their pay now an unnecessary expense. The situation can be even worse if the mercenaries' side lose. Any armistice deal is unlikely to include clemency to foreign soldiers of fortune, let alone back pay.

In one sense, the Varangian Guard stand as an example of the desire on the part of rulers to construct a force deliberately separate from society, what Morillo defines as 'unembedded political armies' as opposed to 'unembedded economic mercenaries'.[78] The main concern here is that the Varangians' stress on their loyal service to their lord, loyalty which would distinguish them as stipendiaries from true mercenaries by stressing that they were not fighting for profit, even though they serve for pay. 'I am the good shepherd', John has Jesus declare:

> The good shepherd lays down his life for the sheep. The hired hand is not the shepherd who owns the sheep. So when he sees the wolf coming, he abandons the sheep and runs away. Then the wolf attacks the flock and scatters it. The man runs away because he is a hired hand and cares nothing for the sheep.[79]

The same sort of sentiment *vis-à-vis* the good shepherd and the unreliable hireling is expressed by Beowulf when an aged king reflecting upon his career, in particular upon the service he rendered his kinsman and lord king Hygelac 'fifty winters' earlier, boasting:

> The treasures that Hygelac lavished on me / I paid for when I fought, as fortune allowed me, / with my glittering sword. He gave me land / and the security land brings, so he had no call / to go looking for some lesser champion, / some mercenary (OE *weorðe gecýpan*) from among the Gifthas / or the Spear-Danes or the men of Sweden.[80]

As said previously, a mercenary in the truest sense of the word is one who offers his services to those who would pay the most, providing loyalty of sorts for a required period of time, leaving as soon as his period of service had ended. Yet to many of us, the idea of a mercenary and the type of service he engaged in seems almost alien and a touch distasteful. In the main, civilians are terrified of these violent men.

This is no new thing. Throughout history, one thing remained constant – mercenaries were always feared and distrusted, and frequently hated, by their employers. The Florentine Niccolò Machiavelli (1469–1527), for example, famously disparaged mercenary armies totally, eloquently arguing in *Arte della guerra* that since professional soldiers profited from war, it was in their interests to perpetuate it whether it was in the interests of the city state which hired them or not. Indeed, he gives a number of examples, including that of Francesco Sforza, where mercenaries actively undermined or overthrew the polity which employed them.[81] In *Il Principe*, his rejection was even more forthright and speaks directly to the question of cohesion:

> Mercenaries and auxiliaries are useless and dangerous. If a prince bases the defence of his state on mercenaries, he will never achieve stability or security. For mercenaries are disunited, thirsty for power, undisciplined, and disloyal; they are brave among their friends and cowards before the enemy; they have no fear of God, they do not keep faith with their fellow men; they avoid defeat just so long as they avoid battle; in peacetime you are despoiled by them, and in wartime by the enemy. The reason for this is that there is no loyalty or inducement to keep them on the field apart from the little they are paid, and this is not enough to make them want to die for you.[82]

Instead of mercenaries, Machiavelli advocated the citizen army, like that of Rome, Sparta, or the Swiss, because he believed that the republican sentiments of its soldiers would motivate them to fight for each other and for their state, as opposed to mercenaries who fought only for their own individual remuneration.[83] Though the views of Machiavelli were not without foundation, an earlier 'golden age' of highly motivated, patriotic citizen militia armies is now perceived to have been in large measure a historical myth.

Klio, the muse of history, is rarely generous in her attentions to men of small consequence. Yet the mercenary, paid soldier or hired man appears right though history – he is no random occurrence or anomaly and has played a rôle in the wars of history, and has been romanticized, reviled and feared. Greek hoplite mercenaries fought for the Persian empire during the classical era and, like the Varangians, were entrusted with the protection of the ruler, his satraps and empire. Likewise Machiavelli's 'Switzer', the Swiss *reisläufer*, was the epitome of the professional infantryman in his day. Although the pike (5.5 metres long in the case of the Swiss) was thought of as a defensive weapon (particularly against armoured horsemen), the Swiss would charge the enemy – even cannons between their discharges – at the run in close order with pikes, a pretty neat trick. Little wonder, therefore, that their services were very much in demand, particularly by the popes of Rome. This emphasizes the belief that only an outside force with no territorial or dynastic connections, unbiased by local politics could form a truly loyal and incorruptible force.

In theory, therefore, this system of hiring Northmen had two major advantages: loyalty to the patron, the emperor, and maintenance of a high level of military skills based on the use of disciplined foot warriors wielding sword, spear and axe. A marriage of circumstances (whether happy or not is another matter) took place.

Axes for hire

The most common and explicitly stated motivation for journeys southward to Constantinople, naturally, is the desire for paid employment in the military service of the emperors there. Scandinavians and English (viz. Anglo-Scandinavians) of the tenth, eleventh and twelfth centuries found steady employment as professionals in the Varangian Guard, an élite fighting unit composed almost entirely of such northern European mercenaries, and, in a later literary reflection of this, the Old Norse sagas contain many tales of Scandinavian characters who find such work within its ranks. The saga writers usually present this mercenary service as a fairly typical career option for adventurous young men. With independent verification of the existence of these Norse fighting men both in Byzantine texts and in some archaeological evidence, primarily runic inscriptions, this economic motivation is one grounded in historical fact rather than spun out of literary fancy.

The most direct example of this motivation to fight in the emperors' battles is found in two passages in Snorri Sturluson's *Magnússona saga*, which bookend the account of the travels of Sigurðr I Magnússon *Jórsalafari* (Jerusalem-farer) to Byzantium and the Holy Land. Shortly after Sigurðr and his two brothers have been elected joint kings of Norway after the death of their father, Magnús III Óláfsson *berfœttr* (Barefoot), during a disastrous skirmish in Ireland, an expedition to the distant south led by a certain Skopti Ñgmundarson returns to Scandinavia, and the men become very popular on account of the fantastic stories they tell. Sigurðr is chosen and ultimately leads an expedition of sixty fine ships to the Mediterranean. After spending some time in the Holy Land, during which time the king of Norway assisted the king of Jerusalem, Baldwin I, in the taking of Sidon and Beirut,[84] the expedition sails to Constantinople and is given a grand welcome by the emperor, Alexios I Komnenos.[85] His meeting with the emperor is presented as a kind of competition between the two rulers in terms of prestige, and after some time in the city spent impressing the emperor, Sigurðr sets off for home. The Norwegians were described as determining to sail to Byzantium with the express purpose of going 'into military service [with the emperor]' for pay; once there, a large part of them do just that.[86] These Scandinavian saga characters then consider such mercenary service a good source of income or even a means to 'acquire great wealth' and thus a good motivation for far-travel south.[87] Other, named saga-characters make the same judgment.

One such character is Eindriði *ungi* (the Young). He is introduced in *Orkneyinga saga* when Rögnvaldr (Karli) Kolsson (d. 1158),[88] *jarl* of Orkney, is visiting the Norwegian king Ingi Haraldsson by invitation at Björgvin (Bergen) one summer:

Eindriði *ungi* arrived from Constantinople that summer; he had been in long service there, and was able to tell many things from there; and it was thought good entertainment to inquire from him about things in that part of the world. The *jarl* conversed frequently with him.[89]

Eindriði's one explicitly stated motivation for travelling to and spending time in Constantinople is mercenary service. Though he finds great popularity as a far-traveller upon his return to Norway, it would be only conjecture to suggest that he fights in the distant south with the purpose of gaining fame at home in the north. The offhand manner in which the saga writer mentions Eindriði's Byzantine employment indicates the Varangians' status as a commonplace of saga literature.

Even so, the description of Eindriði's homecoming reception in Norway, like that of Skopti Ñgmundarson, suggests that the Mediterranean empire is truly remote and exotic, to both the contemporary saga-audience and also the eleventh- and twelfth-century Scandinavians described in the narrative. The imaginative distance indicated by this exoticism – along with the geographical distance – ensures that few enough Northmen travel south for this mercenary service for their southern stories to be received with great interest back home in the north. Eindriði *ungi* figures in an earlier text as a source of information on Varangian activities in the Byzantine empire. In the *drápa* Einarr Skúlason composed about Saint Óláfr, the *Óláfrsdrápa* or *Geisli*, the skald cites Eindriði as the source of a story concerning Saint Óláfr's sword *Hneitir* in the possession of a member of the Varangian Guard,[90] and Snorri Sturluson cites both Eindriði and Einarr in his version of the events.[91]

Clearly, Eindriði was conducting a recruiting drive for the Varangian Guard in which he had risen to a senior rank. At Eindriði's urging, Rögnvaldr, too, travels south to the Mediterranean, leaving in the summer of 1152. The *Orkneyinga Saga* is an anthology of great stories, and the most exciting episode is the crusade by sea of Rögnvaldr to Jerusalem, Constantinople and Rome. Indeed, most of the account of his three-year expedition concerns events that occur before he reaches Constantinople – in Galicia and Narbonne, on the Mediterranean Sea, and in the Holy Land. In Rögnvaldr's own skaldic verses describing his decision to steer to Constantinople, he speaks of earning *máli*, soldier's pay,[92] from the Byzantine emperor, and 'reddening the mouths of wolves',[93] indicating that he and his men intend to earn their pay in battle. Indeed, when they reach the great city the emperor there, Manuel I Komnenos (r. 1143–80), gives the Orcadian *jarl* and his followers 'a great deal of money'.[94] However, for Rögnvaldr the mercenary motivation is not strong enough to keep him in the southern empire for longer than a year; he sets off for home that same winter.

Rögnvaldr shows himself aware of the financial benefits of mercenary service, and he has been made an offer, but his reason for refusing or cutting short mercenary service in Constantinople is not stated. Perhaps Rögnvaldr is in this decision similar to those men who see the threat of bloodshed or loss of life as too great a risk for what is really a business venture.[95] The popularity among Scandinavians of serving in the Varangian Guard demonstrates, naturally, that this is not true of all men. Blöndal/Benedikz suggest that Rögnvaldr and his principal followers or companions lose interest in serving in the Varangian Guard once they realize they will be subordinate to Eindriði *ungi*, who has 'clearly reached high command among the lifeguard section of the Varangians' and with whom the *jarl* is at this point 'on very cool terms'.[96] Our *jarl* was certainly no coward. He was a man of many warlike and peaceful talents, as accomplished with sword and shield as with pen and lyre.[97] He earned particular fame for his crusade, or cruise, to Jerusalem, having enjoyed sea battles and troubadour-life in equal measure. In any case, the swashbuckling Rögnvaldr has an earldom back home to look after, so he can hardly stay away from the north indefinitely.

Another Varangian of interest is the Icelander Þormóðr Eindriðason. His entrance into the Varangian Guard after he flees to the south, which is due to violence, is unique in that the emperor initially refuses to employ him due to his diminutive size. When, however, the emperor sees Þormóðr behead a large bull with a single blow, he remarks that the man can probably use his sword on things other than livestock and admits him into the Varangian Guard.[98] We shall assume that among the Varangians, some men took nicknames, abandoned their past lives and asked – and expected – no questions. The Varangians were never expected to become settled, and to a degree assimilated into the social life of the local population. Much like everything else in life, there were exceptions of course. We have already made mention of the Icelander Kolskeggr Hámundarson, who married a local girl and settled in Constantinople, and his compatriot Þormóðr, because of his violent past, perhaps did the same.

Beyond the merely monetary aspect of entering the military service of the Byzantine emperor, which was very important in that Varangians were very well paid (after all, they were mercenaries), to serve in the Varangian Guard became a kind of tradition for the Scandinavians. The impression of the good pay received by the Varangian Guard made on visitors to the Great Palace of Constantinople is shown by Liudprand's comment in *Antapodosis*: 'The palace at Constantinople is guarded by numerous companies of soldiers in order to secure the emperor's safety, and every day a considerable sum of money is spent upon these men's pay and rations'.[99] This was, possibly, one of the primary attractions for Northmen in entering the service of the Byzantine empire.

Take, for instance, the twenty-four inscriptions from the runic corpus that clearly indicate that the man being commemorated 'was' or 'died' *i/með Grikk(j) um* 'among the Greeks' or went out *til Grikk(j)a* 'to the Greeks'.[100] Unfortunately, they rarely specify what it was he did out there, but many of these men are likely to have been active in Byzantium as mercenaries. It is clear from several inscriptions that a voyage to *Grikklandi* could be extremely profitable. Thus, two inscriptions indicate that the commemorated *gulli skifti* 'divided gold' among the Greeks.[101] It seems, on occasion, Byzantium pay earned by a relative who died out there did find its way back home. One clear example of money from the empire going to the deceased's heirs in Sweden has a son commemorates his father thus: *far aflaþi uti kri[k]um arfa sinum*, 'he earned money out among the Greeks for his heir'.[102]

Battle performance

The question of military effectiveness can be approached from a variety of angles. If one starts with the obvious criterion of performance in battle, the Varangians emerge with considerable credit. We shall therefore turn to the events around Dyrrhachium, then under siege by Robert Guiscard, the first Norman duke of Apulia and a man who, according to one mediaeval chronicler, 'performed many prodigies in magnificent style, abounded in wealth, and continually enlarged his territories, overshadowing all his neighbours'.[103]

The city of Dyrrhachium (Durazzo to the Italians, today's Dürreš) was very well-defended, built on a long and narrow peninsula which ran parallel with the coast but with a marshy lagoon separating it from the mainland. There were also two fortified outposts situated on the opposite mainland area and some 'four stadia' from it, both of them centred around two churches, the one dedicated to Saint Nicholas where Alexios I Komnenos was able to observe the Norman camp and the battlefield, and the other to the warrior saint archangel Michael, God's own standard-bearer, where the Varangians will seek refuge after their fighting retreat from the field of battle.

According to Anthony Kellett, 'motivation is, in essence, the "why" of behaviour, comprising the influences shaping a person's course of action'.[104] By contrast, morale is the spirit with which motivation may be sustained. Morale and motivation clearly overlap but respond to different forces. Although the terms are often used interchangeably, they are different; motivation explains why combatants fight, whilst morale reveals the spirit with which such fighting is undertaken. It was at Dyrrhachium that the Varangians gave a fine demonstration of their high motivation. They demonstrated that they could act mindlessly too. According to the contemporary chronicler Gaufredus Malaterra, the 'Angles [viz. English]', as he calls them, 'whom they [the Byzantines] called Varangians',[105] demanded of the emperor that they should lead the fight. Anna Komnene tells us that the emperor ordered the Varangians to dismount (they had obviously ridden to the battle), and advance in ranks a short way in front of the main battleline with their leader Nabites.[106] The Varangians were perhaps 1,400 strong. In their eagerness to do battle, their initial attack, on the Norman right, the seaward flank, was devastating. Against the frighteningly efficient onslaught of the Varangians wielding their long-shafted axes, the Norman right-wing, foot, and for once even the horse, collapsed. As Gaufredus himself acknowledges, these warriors with their 'plumed double axes, their favourite weapon, were at first a great obstacle to us'.[107]

The flight of one part of an early mediaeval battleline usually brought about the defeat of the whole. In this case, however, a rout was narrowly avoided, partly because a river blocked the further flight of the Normans, but due also to the valiant efforts of the Amazon wife of Robert Guiscard, Sichelgaita. Fully armed *cap à pie* and brandishing a spear, if Anna Komnene is to be believed, the warrior duchess (she likens her to 'another Pallas, if not a second Athene') left her position by her husband's side and rode towards the action, urging the fleeing men to stand and shaming them, by word and example, to rally.[108] Her valiant efforts were rewarded, as the battleline stiffened once again and the Varangians, their charge finally exhausted, now found themselves in an exposed position well in advance of the Byzantine centre. Meanwhile, Bohémond, on the left, had seen relatively little action. He was thus able to send cavalry to the Norman right-wing, where they fell on the now exposed Varangians and cut them down wholesale.

The battle was turned. A sortie from Dyrrhachium under Georgios Palaiologos was beaten off, and now some of Alexios' allies, notably the Serbian and Turkish contingents, began to desert the field. Panic was infectious, and as the imperial army slowly, then rapidly, dissolved in a general *sauve qui peur*, only the surviving Varangians continued to hold their ground. Being the sort of men that did not lightly abandon the field, the brave remnant of the formidable but foolhardy detachment finally sought shelter in the aforementioned chapel, dedicated to the archangel Michael, which stood nearby. The Normans, Anna Komnene says, immediately set the chapel on fire and the last of the Varangians either perished in the flames or were cut down as they attempted to escape, leaving 'not even a messenger' (as the proverb says) to tell the tale.[109] Only their commander Nabites managed to survive the day.

Of course, performance in pitched battles is only one measure of military effectiveness, but it is an important one that deserves further consideration. Dyrrhachium may have been a disaster for the Varangians, yet this was exactly their kind of fighting, the close combat with edged weaponry every Varangian was trained and armed for, and the outcome at Dyrrhachium would seem never to have been a foregone conclusion. What is obvious at Dyrrhachium is that no effort was needed to get the Varangians to go forward; the problem was to hold them in check. Their experience and the wisdom handed down from older generations of Varangians convinced them that aggressive audacity always got the best results. Boldness in the offensive established moral authority, which was the basic ingredient of prestige, the mystical abstraction that every élite unit knew made it possible for it to outperform others on the red field of battle. Such men were unquestionably happiest moving forward on the attack.

The battle of Beroë (Stara Zagora, Bulgaria) in 1122 against the Pečenegs was a case in point. The Pečenegs were just one of a long sequence of Turkic-speaking horse nomads, which had begun with the Huns and was to culminate in the Mongol invasion, who had spread westward across the vast billiard table known as the Eurasian steppes. The Varangian contribution in this engagement was crucial, and though this is the only direct piece of evidence of the Varangians in action we do have both Norse and Byzantine sources for the battle. First we shall look at the evidence of Snorri Sturluson, who says the Varangian contingent 'numbered four hundred and fifty [540] men'. He continues, saying:

> Thereupon the Varangians ran forward on the plain, and when the heathens [Pečenegs] saw that, they told their king [khan] that still another force of the Greek king [Byzantine emperor] was advancing – 'and', they said, 'this is but a handful of men'. Then their king said, 'Who is that princely man riding on a white horse in front of their band?' 'We do not see him', they said…. But as soon as they met, a fear and terror descended upon the heathen host so that they took to flight immediately, and the Varangians pursued with them. By that time the Varangians had gotten into the fortification made by the wagons, and then there ensued a great carnage.[110]

It should be noted that Snorri cites his source for his account as Einarr Skúlason,[111] whose poem *Geisli* was composed some thirty years after Beroë. The skald himself cites his source as Eindriði *ungi*,[112] who may well have been present in the battle, or spoken with comrades who were in it.

Next, we should look at the evidence of John Kinnamos, a Byzantine source nearer in chronological terms than Snorri; he was secretary to Manuel I Komnenos (r. 1143–80). He describes an invasion of the Pečenegs (who he calls *Skuthai*, 'Scythians'), against whom John II Komnenos (r.1118–43) led an army and encamped near Beroë over the winter, setting out against them in earnest in the spring.

> When the armies met it was doubtful for a while which of the two would win… The Romans [Byzantines] fought with great valour, and at length the Scythians were completely defeated… One unit, brave men, returned to their camp and would not think of flight, but rather risk their lives along with their wives and children, and fight in their fort of

wagons... A fierce fight now ensued, and many men fell on both sides. The Scythians used their wagons as a defensive palisade, and the Roman army lost many men. Now when the emperor saw this... he commanded the axe-bearers who stood around him (they are a Britannic people who of old served the Roman emperors) to attack them with their axes and to break the fort of wagons. This they did at once.[113]

Though Kinnamos implies the Varangian contingent at Beroë was composed of English (viz. his 'Britannic people'), the evidence obtained from the Varangian Eindriði *ungi* is worth closer inspection. *Geisli* states clearly: 'Four and a half hundred [480 + 60] / Norsemen (*Norðmanna*), who dared / to feed the ravens, / won great renown'.[114] The actual nationality of the Varangians involved at Beroë appears to weigh heavily in favour of a Norse composition.

Third, we have the evidence of Niketas Choniates, who describes the battle in very similar terms. He states that the emperor looked 'upon the icon of the Mother of God and, wailing loudly and gesturing pitifully, shed tears hotter than the sweat of battle'. After this he continues, saying it was the Varangians who, armed with 'long shields and single-edged axes', cleaved a path through the Pečeneg wagon laager, so exposing the entrenched enemy to eventual defeat.[115] The Pečenegs (whom Niketas also calls 'Scythians') had been broken, their frenzied fury snapped with the courage of the emperor's Varangians unexpected attack on their wagon laager and, to use the words of Haraldr's chief skald Þjóðólfr Arnórsson, 'courage is half the victory [*hugr ræðr hölfum sigri manna*]'.[116] The semi-ordered ranks of both sides were dissolving rapidly into a swirling chaos, clusters of disorganized men smashing and cutting each other. Butchery, now. The Pečenegs still outnumbered the Varangians, but it mattered not at all. As always, fleeing men fell like prey. In every sharp and severe showdown, the Varangians either killed, or were killed.

We must note that Niketas does not mention Saint Óláfr (viz. Snorri's 'princely man riding on a white horse'), but attributes the victory to the prayer made by the emperor to the Blessed Virgin. However, it would be natural for the Byzantines to attribute the victory to the Blessed Virgin and for the Norsemen to ascribe it to the divine intervention of their patron saint. Moreover, Snorri tells us that the 'heathen king was blind',[117] and the anecdote of the blind king who suddenly sees (our Pečeneg khan sees the man on a white horse leading the Varangians) is reminiscent of one of the miracles of Saint Óláfr.[118] Epiphanies of heroes and saints on white horses (in earlier Roman times usually Castor and Pollux) are found in battle accounts of many nations and periods down into the modern era, such as the appearance of Saint James careering on his milk-white steed at the battle of Otumba in Mexico on 7 July 1520.

A second related point is the way in which the discipline of the Varangians emerges as a decisive factor in many of the battles they fought. The sources also provide occasional clues as to the range of strategies by which discipline and morale were maintained, whether it be training exercises, stiff penalties for ill-disciplined behaviour, the promise of rewards for bravery and the prospect of booty, commanders using the language of comradeship to maintain a rapport with their men, or care for the wounded and the proper burial of those killed in battle.

As already intimated, however, performance in battle cannot be used as the sole criterion for gauging military effectiveness. First, the significance of an individual unit in individual battles needs to be assessed within a wider context, while, second, pitched battles were by no means the only form of warfare in this period. One example of the first point is provided by the Sicilian expedition, a subject we will be dealing with later. The imperial army that Georgios Maniakes commanded was as usual heterogeneous. Its strongest elements were not only a hard-hitting Varangian contingent, probably around 500 strong,[119] under Haraldr Sigurðarson, but also an equally important contingent of 300 mounted Italo-Normans under the brothers William and Drogo de Hauteville. It was on this campaign that William de Hauteville was to gain his moniker *bras-de-fer*/*bracca ferrea*, Iron Arm, by single-handedly slaying the Arab emir of Syracuse in battle; like the Varangians, the Italo-Normans were generally good at what they did. So too, both were fighting-men of mercenary type, but the similarity stops there. Therein lays an irony because the Normans were themselves a people descended originally from an originally Scandinavian settlement formally established on the Seine some one hundred and twenty-five years earlier.

Horse-soldiering?

Curiously enough, the Byzantist Warren Treadgold makes the rather bold claim that the Varangian Guard was a cavalry force, seemingly able to make a cavalry charge.[120] Yet, on what evidence this assertion is based is not made clear. As far as the present author is aware, and sadly for historical accuracy, there is not a wisp of evidence whatever for this: none. Not a jot or scintilla. A tremendous shame, but there you go. Horse riding is one thing, of course, and fighting from horseback quite another. Thus, one should discriminate between horseback riding and fighting from horseback. The latter demands special skills and technical preconditions. Horses are skittish creatures – those, like me, who do not work with them, easily forget it. Horses spook easily, tire quickly, require long training just to carry a rider – much less to carry one into battle – and, above all, do not like being injured. It is for the latter reason horses would 'refuse' in the face of an obstacle they could neither jump over nor go around.

To arrive, dismount, hammer, hew, slash and stab, then ride off was the normal *modus operandi* for the Varangians. As an aside, herein lies the rationality to refute the ill-founded thesis that the Anglo-Saxons actually fought from the saddle as trained cavalrymen in the way their Franco-Norman knightly opponents clearly did by 1066.

The horse in mediaeval warfare was used for two very different purposes: as a means of strategic (large scale, campaigning) transport; and as a weapon in battle. Now, in his account of the battle of Stamford Bridge (discussed later), Snorri Sturluson lays much emphasis on the rôle of English cavalrymen who charged the Norwegian lines, throwing their spears before them. The Bayeux tapestry shows the Norman knights at Hastings wielding their spears overhand rather than couching them beneath their arms as was customary in cavalry charges of a later period.[121] By throwing their spears, the knights sacrificed much of the impact of their charge, but the fact that Snorri describes English horsemen doing the same thing at Stamford Bridge would seem, at face value, to give considerable credibility to his account.

But can we trust Snorri's account of Stamford Bridge? If we did then the academic debate, which has raged almost incessantly since the early twentieth century, would be over and done with for good. But the act of trust is fraught with doubt. Although an excellent mediaeval historian, Snorri was by no means a contemporary observer. And earlier references to English cavalry forces are merely suggestive. Certainly, many Englishmen rode to battle and probably even pursued their enemies on horseback.[122] But aside from the thirteenth-century *Heimskringla* there is no evidence of their using cavalry in pitched battle. After all, the most striking fact about the English tactics at Maldon and Hastings was the absence of a cavalry force. For example, Byrhtnoth ordered his warriors to leave their horses, drive them away, and go forth on foot.[123] This may be taken as an additional illustration of the Anglo-Saxon practice of riding to the scene of the battle. The English *þegn* might use horses to take him to the battle but in the actual engagement his practice was, as at Maldon and Hastings (and Stamford Bridge, I might add), to fight on foot on the shield wall.

Cavalry are warriors fighting on horseback; infantry are warriors fighting on foot. This maintains the important but much neglected distinction between horses as strategic transport and horses as battlefield 'weapons', and in fact follows the common mediaeval usage.[124] Thus, soldiers who rode to battle but fought on foot fought as infantry, not as 'dismounted cavalry', an anachronistic term that can only confuse our picture of mediaeval warfare.

It must be said that, despite the wealth of recent scholarship on every aspect of the Norman Conquest, the firmly held view of Allen Brown that Hastings saw the clash of two very different techniques of combat still holds true. Ironically, William's army at Hastings was by no means a typical Norman army. On the contrary, it was a loose coalition of allies and adventurers from all over north–western Europe,[125] in addition to William's own Norman followers, much like the forces with which the Danish Sveinn I Haraldsson *tjúguskegg* and his son Knútr Sveinsson had conquered England half a century before. For William, the battle was an all–or–nothing gamble, God's judgement on his claim to England. The strategic situation meant that Harold could afford a draw, while William could not. Had the English held together for an hour more, or through one more Norman attack, they might have won the war without winning the battle. William's army was not going to get any bigger; Harold probably fought with only a part of his military forces gathered.[126] William, in a hostile country, without a firm base of operations, was also more likely to run into supply problems than was Harold. Finally, Harold was the sitting king, and a boxing analogy is here apt: the challenger has to win; the champion only has to not lose.

Finally, though the Bayeux tapestry shows Harold's housecarls and William's knights to have used the same equipment, the former fought on foot and the latter on horseback as their principal *modus operandi*.[127] Here, we should add that the hard core of William's army can rightfully be called knights, as a system of landholding, the feudal system, was already entrenched in Normandy: a pyramid of mutual obligation based on sworn loyalty and land tenure, the land grant providing the revenue that equipped the vassal knight to fulfil his military duties when summoned by his lord, and freeing him from most mundane daily concerns. This, of course, goes beyond the purely military definition of 'knight' as a fully armed and trained soldier, fully armed including mail hauberk, helmet, sword, shield and warhorse.

The English connection

While it would be reasonable enough to assume that the first warriors gifted by the prince Vladimir to the emperor Basil were of Swedish origin, there is plentiful evidence for later recruits to the Varangian Guard being drawn from the widest orbit of the Scandinavian world. The sometimes glorious, occasionally grotesque, and all too often untestimonied exploits of Haraldr Sigurðarson, between 1034 and 1042, suggest a guard dominated by the Scandinavian connection, Swedes and their Nordic brethren, the Norwegians, the Danes, and the Icelanders.

Just a few weeks after the battle of Stamford Bridge, another fought at Hastings was to eventually deliver a new influx of recruits to the Varangian Guard. After duke William of Normandy had forcibly taken over the kingdom of England, the great bulk of England's warring élite either lay lifeless with their king when night fell on Saturday, 14 October 1066, or subsequently had lost both status and a military rôle, or rather than chaff under the Norman yoke in their own land had fled to a hasty exile. The famous White Tower of London is a stark reminder of the military might that actually brought all this about. It appears that a number of these Anglo-Saxon and Anglo-Dane refugees left England and immigrated to the Byzantine empire. Their emigration was by sea through the Mediterranean. The Anglo-Norman chronicler Orderic Vitalis records one such example of migration from England:

> Some of them who were still in the flower of youth travelled to remote lands and bravely offered their arms to Alexios [I Komnenos], emperor of Constantinople, a man of great wisdom and nobility. Robert Guiscard, the duke of Apulia, had taken up arms against him in support of Michael [VII Doukas], whom the Greeks... had driven from the imperial throne. Consequently, the English exiles were warmly welcomed by the Greeks and were sent into battle against the Norman forces... this is the reason for the English exodus to Ionia, the emigrants and their heir faithfully served the holy empire, and are still honoured among the Greeks by emperor, nobility and people alike.[128]

Orderic's testimony, however, has been rather problematic for scholars because the author dates the English journeys to Byzantium immediately after 1066, which does not coincide with the dates for Alexios Komnenos' reign (1081–1118). Based on the sources available to him at the time he was writing, it is possible that Orderic mistook the dates when these events took place or that he was unaware of the dates of Byzantine history. On the other hand, the *Chronicon Universale Anonymi Laudunensis* sets the date for the arrival of the English in Constantinople in 1075.[129]

Jonathan Shepard, who defends the presence of the 'English' in the Byzantine empire, uses this as one of the dates of their arrival, over half a decade before Alexios' coronation.[130] Shepard also argues that there is evidence from the Exemption Charters in Byzantium from before 1081 of the presence of 'English' (Gr. Ἠγγληνοί) who are distinctively separate from the rest of the Varangians. Of course, we have to appreciate that any distinction between Anglo-Saxon and Anglo-Dane would have seemed piffling at the latitude of Constantinople; particularly so as all barbarous languages were much the same to the Byzantines. The earliest possible connection between the English and the Varangian Guard is a seal found in England of John Raphael (or Rafayl), the catepan of Italy (Gr. κατεπανίκιον Ἰταλίας, *katepaníkion Italías*) from September to December 1046, replacing the catepan Eustathios Palatinos and arriving with a unit of Varangians. It is conjectured that he was recruiting for the Varangian Guard on the occasion of an embassy to William I of England in 1070. Curiously enough, by the eleventh century, those we label the Anglo-Saxons were calling themselves the *Angelcynn* or the *Englisc folc*.

The number of *Englisc folc* who left home immediately after the Norman conquest is believed to have been relatively small. At first William kept many English nobles in place, not only to lend legitimacy to his rule, but also to provide the knowhow for running his new realm successfully. However, after the first rebellion against his rule in 1069, the king confiscated land and titles and handed them over to fellow Normans. After the second rebellion of 1075 few English nobles continued in power. The rebellions had failed, and all hopes of outside help to overthrow William had been dashed. A new generation of English nobility, growing up without a future in a Norman-dominated England, left to seek their fortune elsewhere.

Regardless of when they first emigrated, some of the émigrés did not wish to become a race of foreign mercenaries or vagabonds. With that, according to *Játvarðar konungs hins helga*, they decided not to accept imperial service:

> And when they came to talk of this, king Kirjalax [emperor Alexios I Komnenos] tells them that he knew of a land lying north in the sea, which had lain in old under the emperor of *Mikligarðr*, but in after days the heathen had won it and abode in it. And when the English heard that they took a title from king Kirjalax that land should be their own and their heirs after them if they could get it won under them from the heathen men free from tax and toll. The king granted them this. After that the English fared away out of *Mikligarðr* and north into the sea; but some chiefs stayed behind in *Mikligarðr*, and went into service there. Earl Sigurd and his men came to this land, and had many battles there, and got the land won, but drove away all the folk that abode there before. After that they took the land into possession, and gave it a name, and called it England.[131]

Dated to the fourteenth century, this Icelandic saga narrates the life of Edward Æthelredsson (better known to history as the Confessor) from the beginning of his reign to the political conflict that led to the Norman invasion. It informs that when the Anglo-Saxon and Anglo-Danish rebels, fighting against *Vilhjálmr bastarðr* ('the bastard', i.e. William I of England), became sure that the Danish king Sveinn II Estriðsson would not aid their rebellion any longer, they agreed to leave England for *Mikligarðr* (Constantinople). The English force consisted of 'three earls and eight barons who were their leaders, and the foremost of them was Sigurd earl of Gloucester (*Sigurðr eorl af Glocestr*). But they had three hundred and fifty ships, and aboard them a great force many picked men'.[132] This account is supported by the description in the *Chronicon Universale Anonymi Laudunensis* where the English who did not wish to submit to William's rule set out in 235 ships to Constantinople to serve in the forces of Alexios I Komnenos. The *Chronicon* describes these men as nobles assigning them with titles such as *comes* and *barones*.[133] The émigrés made their way to Constantinople by an adventurous journey via Spain and Sicily. Historians suggest that both these sources are based on an original from the same century written by a monk from Lâon, a theory based on the vernacular origins of much of the material.

To return to those English who did not want to as mercenaries in the Byzantine army, they were allowed to settle by the emperor in some area along the Black Sea coast, Alexios seemingly benefiting from his request by gaining back a lost territory without having to use his own forces. Shepard argues (I think convincingly) that the English settlement on the shores of Black Sea was also of significance for the expansion of Byzantine control. The empire regained its influence on these regions around the year 1100, the same time the English led by Sigurd conquered their new land, as indicated by *Játvarðar konungs hins helga*. The mention of recovered Black Sea lands under Alexios appears in Byzantine written sources.[134]

However, as we clearly read in the passage above, other émigrés did decide to take on military service in Constantinople and became an important component in the Varangian Guard. Yet others would be forced to flee to the empire after supporting the abortive Danish invasion of northern England in 1069. All the 'English' who accepted employment in the Varangian Guard found many disaffected Normans and Frenchmen there already.

There is also evidence that Alexios began recruiting mercenaries from England in the later part of his reign, since there are records in the *Chronicon Monasterii de Abingdon* of a man named Ulfric (Wlfric) sent by Alexios to Henry I of England in an embassy sometime between 1100 and 1118. The *Chronicon* describes Ulfric as an Englishman who was also a '*Lincoliae urbis natives*',[135] but his mission in his motherland was of unknown origin, which it why it has been suggested that it was for the purpose of recruitment.

Though the records are few and far between, there is evidence from our various literary sources that the English became the most prominent part of the Varangian Guard by the twelfth century. Writing on the Macedonian campaign of 1122, the Komnenoi court biographer John Kinnamos says that the Varangians serving for the Byzantines were of the English race, and Niketas Choniates (whose *O City of Byzantium* provides one of the principal commentaries on this period) refers to them, under the year 1189, as 'the Germans [English] who carry on their shoulders the one-edged axes'.[136] The English Varangians appear once again in records of the Fourth Crusade as the defenders of Constantinople along with the Byzantine forces. Danes also appear alongside the English in the contemporary chronicle of a humble knight, Robert de Clari, who wrote: 'When he was inside, the sergeants who were in this storey – the English, Danes, and Greeks there – looked around and saw him, and they rushed on him with axes and swords and cut him to pieces'.[137]

Plodding on in our chronology, anxious to pick up what morsels of evidence are left, we arrive in the second half of the thirteenth century. At this time George Pachymeres (b. 1242) refers to the English in his chronicle as the 'axe-bearing Celts' at Nicaea (İznik), revealing also that the name of the captain of the guard at Thessalonica was a certain Henry, who conspired to free one of the emperor's most dangerous political prisoners.[138] Soon after the *De officiis* in the Pseudo-Codinus, which tells us that English was used for certain Christmas salutations to the emperor,[139] both the English and every other Varangian disappear from Byzantine records.

Vanity and violence

Inevitably, a haze of myth has shrouded the Varangian Guard. It has certainly been over glamorized in Icelandic tradition, mainly because the Icelandic saga-writers were inordinately proud of any young Icelanders who served in it and returned home dressed in exotic raiment and laden with royal gifts, honours, and of course tales, tales about the shimmering wonders of Byzantium and the Holy Land, hospitable emperors, seductive empresses, opulence and danger, which would have been meat and drink to the saga-writers. Icelanders, it must be said, were quite self conscious – Iceland was Iceland before France was France or England was England or Italy was Italy. In Iceland, everyone was employed in more or less the same enterprise. In Iceland, people customarily travelled about the countryside and were familiar with each other's homes and districts. It was a land of unity rather than diversity, where anything out of the ordinary stood out, is noticed, remarked upon, analysed and perhaps admired. Amidst the glaciers, ice, black sandy beaches, lava plains and green meadows of Iceland, the Norse civilization reached its apogee.

The case of Bolli Bollason is a good example, for when he returns to Iceland from the distant south dressed in the finest gear and garb, laden with all the honour, knowledge and riches he can carry, we must conclude that the saga-composer thinks rather well of this sort of far-travel southward. With their colourful clothes and splendid shields, the homecoming Bolli and his colourful cavalcade of eleven comrades are presented as carefree sons of fortune who had succumbed to the heady fragrance of Byzantine civilization. Much like the young Brythonic warrior Blaen celebrated in *Y Gododdin*, 'who took delight in gold and purple; / First pick of sleek steeds raced beneath him',[140] it does seem that a returning Varangian could be a *skartsmaðr mikill*, quite a dandy, and certainly Bolli for one earned for himself the nickname *prúði*, the Elegant.[141]

Bolli may have been a show-off with something to show, acting like a resplendent prince amongst wretched paupers. Yet, the trappings of rich costume served a practical purpose as well as satisfying an individual Varangian's vanity. He knew fine clothes and ostentatious displays of silk and gold were the conventional, outward marks of a warrior's standing and authority, which commanded the respect of onlookers. But he was not alone in this respect. By owning objects of foreign origin, certain people created a visual distinction between themselves and others within their society, in order to further underline their higher social standing. As befitted a warrior élite and to sustain the prestige of their paymaster the emperor, the Varangians probably sported splendid weapons and colourful clothes.

Contemporary observers comment on the great care Norsemen took over their general appearance. The mediaeval Icelandic law book *Grágás* calls for the most severe penalties for a man who makes someone dirty in order to disgrace him.[142] Indeed, evidence from both literary and archaeological sources shows that cleanliness, good hygiene, and regular grooming were a part of Norse life. The number of combs found on Norse sites shows a deep concern for grooming. Personal hygiene kits, some highly decorative, have been found in both male and female graves. These include tweezers for plucking superfluous hair and tiny spoons for removing earwax.

Only a person of status could afford to spend time on such activities. Consequently, a well turned out appearance would be the hallmark of the warrior of middle or high rank. Dress has always been an effective medium for the communication of social standing. Not only rank, but even marital status, descent and affiliation could be displayed by dress. Yet, in Norse society we get the impression that personal hygiene knew no social barriers. As it says in *Reginsmál*:

Combed and washed every thoughtful man should be / and fed in the morning; / for one cannot foresee where one will be by evening; / it is bad to rush headlong before one's fate.[143]

Again, from the *Hávamál*:

Washed and fed, a man should ride to the Assembly / though he may not be very well dressed; / of his shoes and breeches no man should be ashamed / nor of his horse, though he doesn't have a good one.[144]

John of Wallingford, the abbot of Saint Albans Abbey, wrote in his chronicles that the Norse invaders in England were far more attractive to Anglo-Saxon women since, unlike Anglo-Saxon men, they combed their hair daily, took baths weekly, and laundered their clothing regularly. A treaty negotiated in the year 907 between the Byzantine empire and the Rus' contained most of the usual provisions one might expect: Constantinople was obliged to give the Rus' merchants food, drink, and supplies for their ships. However, an unusual condition in the treaty was that Constantinople was required to provide baths for the Rus' 'as often as they want them'.[145]

Let's return once again to Haraldr Sigurðarson. He was one of history's showmen, a skilled propagandist and was fully aware of the power of imagery. Like Alexander with his silvery war helmet flaming in the sun, Caesar in his handsome scarlet cloak, Custer and his elaborately fringed buckskin uniform, MacArthur with a crushed hat and corncob pipe, or Patton in a burnished steel helmet and packing ivory-handled six-shooters,[146] he created an unforgettable image. The fastidious Haraldr was as vain as a bedizened bride, to be sure. But more than simple vanity motivated this eccentricity. He had a sure sense of what made effective military leadership and what gave an army identity and *esprit de corps*. He intended to be as conspicuous as possible, especially on the red field of battle, both to his own men and to the enemy. They saw a bright flash of ring mail. Enter Haraldr ablaze with the burnished byrnie *Emma* that proclaimed his identity. It was said by Snorri Sturluson that *Emma* was so long 'that it reached down to the middle of his leg', and 'so strong that never had weapon fastened on it'.[147] True or not, the wearer was Haraldr; his arrival had a simulating effect upon his weary men. It sounds like fiction, doesn't it? Yet, all wars are full of stories that sound like fiction. Commanders in history are notorious for being vainer than catwalk models, vainer than rock stars. And what about those ancient Spartans? Always combing their hair before battle.

On foreign things

It is time for a word or two about foreign equipment and influences. As the emperor's bodyguard, the Varangians would expect to be well equipped, namely complete with helmet – a conical skullcap with a long nasal guard – body armour, shield and a good sword as a bare minimum. And there was the Dane axe, of course. Nonetheless, those lacking in certain items of equipment would have been supplied (probably at a price) from the imperial armoury – probably a basic helmet, nothing too fancy, and a cuirass of mail or an iron lamellar *klibánion*. Likewise, those members who had their own gear would have, over time, gradually replaced items as their equipment suffered from wear and tear. In both cases, these would have been of Byzantine manufacture.

Armour made by combining numerous tiny plates (Gr. πέταλα, L *lamellae*) of metal, horn or hardened leather is called lamellar armour. Metal, of course, offered better protection, but was also heavier, less comfortable, and more expensive. If leather was used then the most preferred type was cowhide, and the preferred part of the hide was the animal's back, as this was the thickest. Although differing in minor details, lamellar armour was always constructed from more-or-less rectangular overlapping *lamellae* laced together in rows, which were then laced vertically, each row overlapping the one above so that the tops of the *lamella* heads were visible (viz. opposite to scale, which overlapped downwards). The *lamellae* had rounded corners to reduce the sharpness of their edges and to prevent damage to the lacing. Laces would have been cut as spirals from leather of suitable thickness.

The excavations in the Great Palace of Constantinople (Gr. Μέγα Παλάτιον) have unearthed a number of thin, iron *lamellae* from lamellar armour (more than 200 pieces) in six standard sizes, varying in width from three to six centimetres, the length being approximately twice that of the width. On more than half of the examples of each size the centre was beaten out from back to front to form a distinctive vertical ridge. Most of the *lamellae* were found melted together by fire. A coin with the representation of the emperor Manuel I Komnenos (r. 1143–80) was found melted together with some of them. All were pierced with perforations for being fastened by means of leather thongs; the regular arrangement seems to have been three along one end, one on the other and two along each side.[148] The thongs were pulled through the perforations and in this way the *lamellae* were laced together and presumably attached to a leather backing. The edge of each *lamella* butted against the centre ridge of its neighbour in the row. As well as strengthening the *lamellae*, the ridges presumably prevented excessive sideways shifting. Another problem would have been the risk of the *lamellae*, when the rows pushed past each other, slicing the lacing. The solution would have been to lace strips of leather between the rows of *lamellae* so as to cushion them and eliminate the slicing effect. In fact, Byzantine lamellar, when depicted in icons and manuscript illustrations, is shown with narrow bands spacing the rows.[149]

Usually, lamellar was made into a cuirass or corselet to which elbow length sleeves, calf length front split skirts and a rear skirt could be added, or alternatively, instead of sleeves and skirts, *pteruges*. Saint Michael as the guardian of Paradise in the gold and enamel plate from a bookbinding now in the treasury of Basilica di San Marco in Venice, from eleventh century, is dressed in a similar body armour, here made of square *lamellae*, just as the body armour worn by Basil II in his psalter in the Marcianum, Venice.[150] Good examples of this type of armour are seen in the illustrated Madrid manuscript of John Skylitzes' *Synopsis historiôn*,[151] all of them with close parallels in the psalter of Basil.

Though widely used across the Asia and the Near East, lamellar armour was very rare in Europe and would have been only available to those who travelled eastwards. For instance, the recent excavation of what is called the Garrison at the great international trading town of Birka near present-day Stockholm, has uncovered unique evidence for warriors and warfare, including finds of iron *lamellae* as well as ring mail.[152] These iron *lamellae*, of which eight different types have been identified, are without direct parallel in their time period, at least not in the neighbouring regions.

Birka was a packed gateway of mixed population – it was at one end of a trade route that extended to the Volga and burial customs suggest that nearly half the people there were foreign – where Mälardal Swedes, Götar from the south, Frankish, Frisian, and east Baltic visitors found it convenient to do business from the seven-fifties to the end of the first millennium. Until it gradually declined in importance towards the end of the tenth century, this urban-like settlement was a cultural melting pot operating as a hub in the trade of prestigious objects and sophisticated crafts. One can imagine men in small groups haggling and babbling in a welter of dialects.

Situated on the small island of Björkö in Lake Mälar, Birka was a fortified site on the northwest point of the island. The walls of the town were pierced with six gateways and studded with towers. The most prominent feature of Birka's fortified structures was its hill fort, which is called the Borg by Swedish archaeologists. There is an unexplained discontinuity between the construction of hill forts and other later mediaeval fortifications. Hill forts are frequent during previous periods, especially the Migration period, but in the sixth century they virtually disappear. An exception is the Borg at Birka.

This hill fort consists of a semicircular rampart, bound on the southwest by the rock cliff that drops steeply into Lake Mälar. Its rampart, of stone-faced rubble walls, measures approximately 350 metres in length and varies between two and three metres in height. It is pierced by three gateways. Originally, the rampart was crowned with a wooden superstructure, making it in all an imposing five metres in height. In close proximity to the hill fort, just outside the gateway designated the King's Gate, the Garrison was situated in a steep slope leading down to the waterfront. The location of the Garrison blocks the direct path from the water up to the hill fort and while the buildings in this garrison area were protected between two rock cliffs, just a few steps up the hill fort side commands a good view of the surrounding waters and of the town area. In addition to the rock cliffs, the Garrison was enclosed by a rampart crowned with a wooden superstructure. The most prominent structure of the Garrison was a hall building (19 m × 9 m), designated the Warrior's Hall by the archaeologists.[153]

In the light of this, therefore, it has been argued that mercenary, well equipped and well-trained warriors lived at Birka in addition to the civilian inhabitants, and it is possible that some of these either had previously served or travelled to the Byzantine empire or even further.[154] Occasionally, the Old Norse sagas do refer to *spangabrynja*, which has the sense of 'plate mail'. In *Grœnlendinga þáttr*, Símon was given some old *spangabrynja* as compensation for the killing of a kinsman. Whatever the armour might have been, the saga says that Símon was insulted by the offer, and he threw the *spangabrynja* to the ground as useless junk, resulting in another fight and more killings.[155] One wonders if *spangabrynja* might have been lamellar armour. Perhaps a roving Northman brought some home with him.

The reason why lamellar armour was so widely used in the east was that horsemen – prevalent as they were – needed a form of body protection that was flexible, comfortable and easier to move in when the horseman was mounted. In addition, it was easier to store and transport and required less customization for fit than plate armour, and it offered better protection than ring mail. Its principal defensive advantage over other types of armour was its capacity to absorb shock, by diffusing the energy of blows landing against it through the layers formed by the overlapping rows of *lamellae* and lacing sandwiched between them before penetration could begin.

Contemporaneous European ring mail, by contrast, was readily pierced by arrows and spears, and once pierced, the fractured links could become shrapnel that would exacerbate or infect the wound. Ring mail offered even less real protection against bladed weapons, which did not actually need to penetrate the armour to be deadly: haemorrhaging or brain damage due to blunt trauma could kill just as readily as lacerations or incisions. Additionally, lamellar armour had the further advantage of ease of repair, which could be undertaken by warriors even in the field. Individual *lamellae* could be recycled into new armour too.

That Varangians used their personal equipment together with Byzantine is logically deducted by the use of the Dane axe. Most would agree that a mixture of Byzantine and Norse equipment was in use, with a predominance of the latter in the first period of the service until it was replaced with gear taken from the imperial armoury when their own equipment wore out. There is, of course, no way of knowing the extent to which Varangians were actually influenced by Byzantine culture, particularly as regards to their weaponry and war gear, although it was usually characteristic of the mercenary employed overseas to bring his own style of arms and armour and afterwards to return home with those of the military organization for which he had served. The previously mentioned Icelander Bolli Bollason, peacocking his lusty self in strident apparel, demonstrates a likely Varangian taste for Constantinopolitan *haute couture*.

Much could be said of clothing for the Varangians. Without question, new recruits would have arrived in Constantinople decked out in Norse clothing. The basic material of Norse clothing was wool. Rich or poor, everyone wore woollen cloth – the quality varying according to social status – while the basic form of male dress consisted of a tunic, a simple shirt-shape cut straight and with added sleeves. The tunic reached the knee, and was worn over trousers. Trousers seem to have been cut in various shapes: full-length, straight and loose; tighter fitting in the manner of later mediaeval hose; knee length, with separate, cross-gartered leggings below; and – for the relatively wealthy, given the amount of material needed – in the baggy Rus' style. These garments made from woollen cloth and normally loose enough for easy movement, were often the only clothing a Norseman owned apart from a simple knee-length woollen cloak, and a leather waist belt, a pouch, and a knife belt to which small possessions might be slung.

Presumably, some form of undergarment or loin cloth would have been worn, but no archaeological evidence of this has survived. However, as the climate in the Mediterranean was much hotter than their homeland, Varangians presumably would have replaced heavy woollen garments with others made of lighter fabrics, locally fabricated, such as linen and cotton and cheaper grades of silk. Cotton, for instance, was widely worn in the Byzantine empire, and had reached southern Iberia with the Arabs, but there is no evidence for its use in Scandinavian clothing.

The same could be said of footwear. At first, the latter would have been of the leather shoe or ankle boot variety, commonly the 'turn-shoe' variety, high boots being a rare commodity among Norsemen (and English), but later Varangians may have picked up Byzantine military boots. Turn-shoes probably did not last long – perhaps a few months to half a year before they wore out and were replaced. They followed the patterns common to northern Europe from the fourth to thirteenth century – with either a central upper seam, or fastened with laces at the side, though the ankle-high style could have ankle flaps secured by toggles made from leather, wood or bone. The technique for making such footwear was a two–step process. First, the uppers were sewn to the sole, with the finished side in, and the rough side out. Second, the shoes were turned inside out. This put the seam inside the shoe, where it was less susceptible to wear. It also put the holes that resulted from the stitching inside the shoe, so the shoe was less likely to leak on wet ground. Standard waterproofing measures included either a fifty-fifty mix of beeswax and mutton fat, or a liberal dose of fish oil. Knee-high leg wrappings could also be worn as protection against cold, mud and thorns. Shoemaking was not only a specialist craft, but a home one too.

Shoe fastenings occasionally broke in use. In an unforgettable episode in saga literature, the shoe lace (ON *skópvengr*) of Skarphéðinn Njálsson broke as he ran towards an ambush, forcing him to stop and retie it. It did not slow him down any. In a bold move, he leapt onto the ice and slid across the frozen river to place his axe in Þráinn's skull.[156] A fellow Icelander Þorsteinn, son of Hallr of Síða, who, we are asked to believe, knelt and tied his shoe lace, calmly, as men fled after the fall of *jarl* Sigurðr at Clontarf, north of the Liffey near Dublin. The pursuing Irishmen asked him why he was not running away like the rest of them, 'Because I can't reach home tonight,' said Þorsteinn – 'my home's out in Iceland'. He was spared, lucky fellow.[157] It is often useful to be lucky.

A Varangian warrior probably loved display. Everything that gave brilliance and the sense of drama to life appealed to him. His sword was richly ornamented; his raiment was gilded and embroidered – he made a splendid show. We only have to remind ourselves again of the splendour of Bolli Bollason in his Constantinopolitan apparel of scarlet and gold-embroidered silk,[158] and the 'burnished byrnie' *Emma* of Haraldr Sigurðarson, likewise made in Constantinople, which covered him down to the calves.[159] Conceivably, Haraldr meant this as a satirical reference to Knútr's Norman queen and mother of Hörða-Knútr. Silk was a prized material throughout Europe during our period of study – a very expensive luxury that had to be imported over great distances from the east. Only the very wealthy could afford silk, which was in any case too vulnerable for everyday use in the robust daily life of even the richest Northmen. It was most often used for decorative braiding and embroidery; a Hedeby find of a half-finished piece of tablet weaving is believed by archaeologists to have originally included golden wefts and silken warps.

Bad company

Foreign influences could reflect ideological and political standing in quite a visible way, even if such are not always easy to interpret. Doubtless, there were fewer gentlemen in the Varangian Guard and more thugs, the unit attracting a distinctly less reputable element of freelance fighters, individuals of the worse kind, such as the hardscrabble men, coarse men, crude men, ribald men, and rude men. Men hungry for a fortune, greedy and insatiable types when it came to everything that could be stolen, consumed, drunk, sold or fornicated with. Brutal men, often. Even cruel men, on occasion. They must have come in all colours. All the same, it was undoubtedly regarded as a crack unit in the Byzantium army, for which only the best were admitted. The emperor wanted able-bodied warriors, not 'warm bodies', as military jargon has it. He needed hard fighters and hard livers; men proud of themselves, and preferably without family. He also needed these battle-hardened and weapon-trained men to be utterly loyal and absolutely unscrupulous.

War is a powerful generator of solidarity, comradeship fuelling soldiers' fighting morale. It also propels soldiers forward into war crimes and acts of mass murders. One example will suffice to best illustrate this valid point with regards to our Varangians and their military cohesion. In 1021 Basil II invaded Christian Caucasia, and his Varangians receive particular mention in this campaign for their cruelty. When Basil ordered every man, woman and child in a particular part of Georgia butchered, the Armenian chronicler Aristakes Lastivertsi (d. 1080) notes that this depopulation operation took three months, and that the Varangians were certainly not chary when it came to performing this grisly task.[160] Basil is generally held to have been the most effective and competent of the Byzantine emperors; we can also add that he was one most efficient and cruellest when it came to war. His Varangians played no small part in this.

The hefty Dane axe may have been the dreaded motif of the northern barbarian on a distant campaign, but even during peacetime it was the habitual Byzantine practice to use the Varangians for the nastier kinds of political skulduggery, the sort that scarcely any native soldier would touch. Such as, for example, the dragging of the patriarch of Constantinople in full vestments out of church during a service, as Isaakos Komnenos had them do with Michael I Keroularios; the patriarch had challenged the accepted interdependence of church and state. An ex-civil servant, more of an administrator than a cleric, Michael had ordered the blinding of the once powerful John the Orphanotrophos back in 1043.[161]

The *keroularioi*, or candle makers, were a craft guild in Constantinople; in this case Keroularios was probably Michael's family name, not his nickname. This was the same peppery and self-important Michael Keroularios who quarrelled with the pompous and equally self-important papal legate, Humbert de Mourmoutiers, cardinal of Silva Candida, who formally laid a solemn bull of excommunication directed against the Orthodox patriarch on the high altar of Hagia Sophia (16 July 1054), and the patriarch in turn issued an excommunication on the papal legate 'and all those who share his view'. This did not categorically include the pope but the history of the so-called Great Schism between Rome and Constantinople effectively dates from this time, even though the date is more a retrospective rather than an actual landmark in history.

The current dispute between the Orthodox and Roman Catholic Churches revolved around certain theological issues and ecclesiastical customs. Both Churches believe in the doctrine of the Trinity, one God with three aspects. However, one main theological issue is the Procession of the Holy Spirit and the Latin addition of the word *filioque* ('... and from the Son', a difference in the nature of the Trinity) to the Nicaean Creed (in Orthodox theology the Holy Spirit proceeds from the Father alone, as is the original creed). Amongst other lesser issues, the use of unleavened bread – azymes – for the Eucharist by the Latins (and Armenians) – to the Greeks the use of unleavened bread seemed Judaistic and disrespectful to the Holy Spirit whom the leaven symbolized – and correct phase of the moon for celebrating the greatest feast of the Christian calendar, Easter. The detailed story of such theological issues makes arid reading. Besides, to a post-Christian reader, it might seem that such controversies, if of course we are willing to wrestle with them, deserve to be treated with the irony of an Edward Gibbon. Nonetheless, the events surrounding the mutual excommunications of that year had more to do with the personal animosities between the stubborn patriarch and the arrogant cardinal.

To be excommunicated meant to be declared an outsider, to be separated from the community of the faithful and turned over to the Prince of Darkness. But 1054 came to symbolize the widening chasm between the Greek east and the Latin west (the excommunications were only lifted in 1965, when there was a meeting between pope Paul VI and the patriarch Athenagoras. Imagine that!). In theory, at least, after 1054 the Catholics viewed the Greeks as schismatics and heretics and as enemies of the faithful. Many (most?) from each party viewed the other in terms of simplistic and hostile caricatures. It was a religious age. And so it was that the First Crusade (1095–9) introduced two cultures to one another who shared a belief in Jesus Christ yet could not cooperate on how that belief should be interpreted.

Churches were often the focus of urban life. Today, I suppose, they are frequently quiet, ordered and puritanical places, but to envisage them in eleventh-century Constantinople we must imagine something altogether quite different: places of cacophony, chaos and colour. Food vendors, moneychangers and other tradesmen milled around outside the building, hawking their wares and their skills to the curious, the needy and the unwary. Performers looked for a chance to draw an audience for their songs, or to hear tales of derring-do and the strange. On any given day the crowd outside any given Constantinopolitan church buzzed with passing news as they swapped tales and related the latest gossip and intrigues. On this particular day, however, they were being offered the shameful sight of their beloved patriarch being manhandled by a bunch of boreal brutes.

According to the author of the Skylitzes *Continuatus*, Isaakos, who had been crowned by Michael Keroularios in Hagia Sophia (1 September 1057), 'revered him',[162] but after an initial period of mutual goodwill, the patriarch became arrogant toward the emperor and 'went so far as to wear sandals dyed purple',[163] which were the prerogative of the emperor. Obviously, Michael was a quarrelsome and contumacious power seeker; Isaakos, who had the support of the army, eventually acted against him. On the Feast of the Holy Archangels, 8 May 1058, the Varangian Guard were ordered to arrest him, along with his nephew, and confine them on the island of Prokonnesos. He died soon after. Incidentally, it was Michael Psellos who drew up the charge sheet (the *Accusation*) against the haughty patriarch, which included the damning ones of heresy and treason.[164] It was Michael Psellos who had led the delegates to offer the position of Caesar to Isaakos.[165]

And such behaviour was not the worst of it. For a Varangian was not at all coy when it came to the torturing of political suspects, like those accused of high treason or those who conspired against the emperor. Such was the fate of Korax the Theologian. After having forced a confession out of him, the Varangians publicly plucked out his eyes. He died three days later in prison.[166] Blinding had been the fate of Michael V Kalaphates (r. 1041–2) and his uncle the *nobilissimus* Constantinus, more of which later.

Putting the eyes out was one of the considerably more brutal forms of corporal punishment in the empire, and not just for commoners, either. Horrifying to us, of course, but to the Byzantines blinding was seen as more lenient than death, and conveyed the coded message that family ties were sacred but occupying the throne was not. In other words, the Byzantines judged that blinding rendered an individual unfit to rule.

Little wonder, then, the emperor's northern mercenaries were generally detested in the empire. Moreover, the elevated social position, large salary, well above that of other mercenaries, and high perquisites that went with the post were sure to make a Varangian the object of hate to ordinary citizens of the empire. Even their Christianity was incomprehensible, crude in its practices, barbaric in its language; and their free and easy ways with the local women were, without the shadow of a doubt, an added factor in the envy equation. Thus, the common Byzantine attitude to these outlandish interlopers from tiny kingdoms in the far north can be seen in a nursery rhyme: 'Frank, Marangian [Varangian], filth and dirt'.[167]

To emphasize his disapproval of the employment of mercenaries (in this case the Catalan Company employed by Andronikos II Palaiologos), as well as their actions, George Pachymeres quotes Plato. He writes:

> Plato correctly outlines the mercenary service in the *Laws*. He said that most of them become arrogant, unjust and violent and the most imprudent people apart from very few. Of all the Cardinal Virtues, which are possible to be witnessed in the citizens involved in civil wars, only the fourth one, which someone could call bravery, can be attributed as perfect to mercenaries because they wish to die in war only, not because of virtue, but only for the sake of salary; and for this, they are easily involved many times in reckless violence, being arrogant and against justice because they are unjust, arrogant against prudence because they are violent and being totally imprudent because of the absence of prudence.[168]

Although a clergyman, George Pachymeres possessed great secular knowledge and provides a reasoned and sophisticated analysis of past events. He was to sadly say of the arrival of the Catalonian expedition, 'O that it need not have been'.[169]

This company of mercenaries was organized in 1302 by Rutger von Blum (better known as Roger de Flor), a disgraced Knight Templar from Brindisi – and thus not himself a Catalan. However, it is thought that it may have originally contained a large number of Iberian warriors – although not all from Catalonia – who had fought together for Frederick II of Sicily (r. 1296–1337). The Catalan Company (*la Companya catalana*) was not small, probably numbering at least 6,500, about 4,000 of whom were foot soldiers of outstanding skill and ability, and whose name, *almogávares*, frightened even the most stalwart warriors of the time.[170] Their new employer was Andronikos II (r. 1282–1328, d. 1332), who was looking for experienced soldiers and could pay very well. The Catalan Company jumped at the opportunity to travel from the western to the eastern Mediterranean, arriving in Constantinople in September 1303.[171] There they met with almost immediate success, first when they sacked the island of Keos, off the coast of Anatolia, and then when they chased the Ottoman Turks from outside the Byzantine capital. Initially, this brought so much favour in Constantinople that Roger de Flor even married into the emperor's family, only to find that this placed him in the middle of their incessant quarrels and jealousies. Dark deeds were afoot, for he was murdered by them on 5 April 1305.[172] Leaderless and wanting nothing further to do with the Byzantine empire, but respected and feared by all in the east, the Catalan Company withdrew from Constantinople. The wandering Catalan soldiers of fortune – now with Byzantine and Ottoman recruits amongst their ranks – went on to terrorize the inhabitants of central Greece, and even to rule the Burgundian duchy of Athens from 1311 to 1388.[173]

One aspect of the poor press that mercenaries have received is that they are seen as the most brutal and degraded of soldiers. Cruelty, in particular is often seen as their defining characteristic. But this is hardly a special quality of mercenaries. In fact, throughout history mercenaries in all their varieties have been hired from time to time to perform someone else's dirty work. In 1381, to take one particularly interesting example, the merchants of Ghent employed a band of mercenaries so as to remove their immediate economic rivals, the four guilds of Bruges, the tailors, the glaziers, the butchers and the fishermen. We shall let Froissart, the event's narrator, take up the awful story:

> All who could be found were to be killed, with no exceptions… They [the mercenaries] went through the houses searching for those good people and killed them. More than twelve hundred of them died that night and there were a number of other murders, robberies and crimes which never came to light. Many houses were plundered and women raped and killed and chests broken open, on such a scale that the poorest man of Ghent became rich.[174]

Such barbarous acts did much to justify the typecasting of mercenaries as greedy, godless, cruel exterminators. Niklaus Manuel Deutsch (d. 1530), popular artist and dramatist, Bernese mercenary and statesman, once put into the mouth of a Swiss *reisläufer*, or mercenary, the following ditty:

If you pay us well / We'll move against your enemy / 'Til the very women
and little children / Cry 'Murder!' / That is what we long for and rejoice
in. / It's no good to us when peace and calm rule.[175]

Peace was antithetical to his *raison d'être*. The same could be said of that diabolical
Essex man, John Hawkwood (d. 1394). Franco Sacchetti tells of how, saluted by a
pair of wandering friars with the customary 'God give you peace!', Hawkwood had
snarled 'God take from you your alms!' Naturally, the friars protested that they but
wished well. 'How so?' asked Hawkwood. 'Is not begging your profession and is
not mine war? If you wish me peace how shall I live? So I say, God take away your
alms!'[176] Mercenaries were often the instruments of violence, but their employers
were princes and potentates who were well aware of their methods. The life of
these soldiers was often brutally short. They had few places they could call home
and few friends other than their comrades in arms. Civilians could not understand
their ways. A professional mercenary saw more combat than most citizen soldiers,
and unlike them, they needed a constant state of war to make a living.

Serve and protect

It should be said, of course, that the Varangians were never expected to be assimilated
into Byzantine society at all, since that might have made them politically suspect,
but were intended to be held apart as a mercenary centre of excellence for all the
Northmen's military skills. When vulnerability was a liability, their arrival and
organization as bands under the command of their own nobility meant they would
not be prone to the problems of discipline and loyalty usually associated with
mercenary forces. Both would they – unlike native soldiers – be distracted by local
loyalties at so great a distance from their original homelands and when their first
loyalty was the professional obligation to their paymaster the emperor. They were
seen as cutthroat thugs; but they cut throats only to the emperor's order.

Being isolated by origin, language and location from the local population,
the Varangians focused their loyalty on their patron. It was only when Haraldr
Sigurðarson involved himself in the palace *putsch* to topple the unpopular Michael
V Kalaphates on the night of 20 April 1042 (and then put his eyes out) that the
Varangians took an independent rôle in palace politics. This episode does not
entirely paint the Varangians as pillars of virtue, uncompromisingly loyal to the
incumbent emperor. There again, Haraldr Sigurðarson scarcely behaved as an
ideal bodyguard should. Haraldr was no textbook Varangian. On the contrary, he
was a wild-eyed military gambler of some sort.

However, it is probably true that the men Haraldr joined were actually a lot
more like loyal retainers than he was. They served where they signed on, and where

they served they kept their bargain. The Varangians might serve in the splendour of a Constantinopolitan court seething with intrigue, but, in the admiring words of Anna Komnene, they:

> ...regard loyalty to the emperors and the protection of their persons as a family tradition, a kind of sacred trust and inheritance handed down from generation to generation; this allegiance they preserve inviolate and will never brook the slightest hint of betrayal.[177]

This praise was in reference to her father's own seizing of the throne. Even a mercenary must have something to put his pride in, and so the Varangians continued to be an important feature of the Constantinopolitan court for over a century thereafter.

Accordingly, the Varangians were responsible for guarding the great bronze gates, known as the Chalke (Gr. Χαλκῆ), which barred the entrance of the Great Palace of Constantinople.[178] The Great Palace served as the main residence of Byzantine emperors to 1081 when Alexius I Komnenos chose as his main residence the palace of Blachernai. In spite of that, the Great Palace continued to be used as the primary administrative and ceremonial centre. In the glory days of Constantinople the Great Palace was the most imposing building in the city, with clearly defined secular as well as sacred functions. On one hand it demonstrated its material and political superiority over the wider Christian world, but on the other hand it had strong religious connotations. The secular connotations are relatively easy to understand: the palace was a visible manifestation of the glory of the empire, being the most important architectural achievement within the urban setting of the city. It was located close to the Hippodrome where the emperor was visible to the public, communicating with it through the representatives of the circus factions. In other words, the Hippodrome presented a visible and accessible aspect of imperial power in touch with the city's populace. The Great Palace, by contrast, symbolized an elevated, remote and secretive aspect of the imperial power, being a carefully confined and guarded complex accessible to a very select group of imperial dignitaries and foreign ambassadors. Just as the Great Palace was an earthly embodiment of the heavenly mansion, so the emperor was the vicar of God and his vice-regent on earth.

The Varangians were also responsible for the emperor's other properties such as his office and chief reception chambers in the palace of Blachernai, where they stood around his throne during receptions. The Varangians formed the guard of honour at the coronation of the emperor. They surrounded his throne at state receptions and protected his solemn processions to various Constantinopolitan churches on special sacred occasions. In church the emperor sat on a high throne, while behind him stood specially selected Varangians with their Dane axes. Their attendance on the emperor when he attended church in state is documented by John Kantakouzenos when he describes 'the so called Varangians with their axes' at the coronation of Andronikos III Palaiologos on 2 February 1325 in Hagia Sophia.[179]

Evidently, the idea was to strike fear into the hearts of possible assassins. In times of threat, the Varangians physically surrounded the emperor with a protective hedge of spears and axes, such as on the occasion when Alexios I Komnenos, having just escaped the conspiracy led by Nikephoros Diogenes, the son of the former emperor Romanos IV, held court in the camp where the attempt had taken place. In the words of his daughter Anna:

> When the sun peeped over the horizon and leapt into the sky in glory, all those members of the imperial retinue not infected with Diogenes' pollution, as well as the soldiers who had long served as the emperor's bodyguard, led the procession to his tent; some wore swords, others carried spears, others [i.e. Varangians] had heavy iron axes on their shoulders. At some distance from the throne they arranged themselves in a crescent-shaped formation, thereby surrounding the emperor. They were all moved by anger and if their swords were not ready to go to work, their souls certainly were. Near the throne on either side stood the emperor's relatives, and to the right and left were grouped the armour-bearers. The emperor, looking formidable, took his seat, dressed rather as a soldier than an emperor. Because he was not a tall man, he did not tower above the rest. Nevertheless it was an impressive sight, for his gold overlaid his throne and there was gold above his head.[180]

Here we witness the Varangians in action in their most common peacetime duty, protecting the emperor from danger.

In *Veraldar saga* Hagia Sophia is described as follows: 'Iustinianus ordered to erect in Constantinople the temple of God which is called in Greek Hagia Sophia and which we call *Ægisif* and this is the house most carefully made and the biggest in the entire world as far as we know'.[181] A brief reference to Hagia Sophia is found too in *Alfrædi íslenzk*: 'In Constantinople is the church which is in their language called Hagia Sophia and the Norsemen call it *Ægisif*. This church is the most magnificent and famous of all churches in the world both in shape and size'.[182] The presence of the Varangians in Hagia Sophia is curiously confirmed by a piece of casual graffito. All the polish marble balustrades of Iustinianus' great sacred edifice are now covered with scrawled graffiti, scored by visitors down the centuries. But perhaps the most evocative of these is a series of rough marks scratched into a marble balustrade in the west gallery of the church. Though most of it is indecipherable, this particular one concerns us. It is runic, and the opening letters (as read in 1967 by the great Swedish scholar Professor S.B.F. Jansson, a leading authority on runic inscriptions) are the ending of a personal name: - A - L - F - T - A - N, which in full would have read Hálfdan, Half-Dane, both a royal and a common name in the viking age. Sometime in the eleventh century, did a bored Varangian, having to stand through some interminable church service in a language he did not understand, idly scratch in his own tongue HÁLFDAN WAS HERE for posterity? It is possible. There are also other runic scrawls, and another in the south gallery mentions a certain Ári (or Árni), a very common name in Iceland. Five more possible runic inscriptions in Hagia Sophia were reported to the Norwegian Runic archive in 1997.

No more heroes

In the *Íslendingasögur* the focus is on the Icelandic heroes who sought their fortune in Constantinople at the time of the empire's greatest military victories in the tenth and the early eleventh centuries, when military emperors of the Macedonian dynasty were determined to regain the territories originally belonging to the Byzantine empire and prepared to pay foreign mercenaries well for their loyal service. However, the knowledge of the declining fortunes of the empire was clearly reflected by declining numbers of Icelanders serving in the Varangian Guard in the thirteenth century. This fact alone implies the awareness of Icelanders that Constantinople was no more a fast route to enrichment.

The Varangians were famous for their blind loyalty to the emperor in Constantinople. Still, loyalty, meaning the pledged word, may have been the Varangians' fulcrum, but they did support the sinister Mourtzouphlos ('the traitor',[183] as Robert de Clari contemptuously called him) against Alexios IV Angelos (r. 1203–4) in his bid for the throne, succeeding in that quest to rule as Alexios V Doukas (r. 1204). Mourtzouphlos, whose nickname referred to his bushy black eyebrows, would reign (and live) long enough to regret his treachery. On 28 January 1204 there was a quartet of emperors at Constantinople, while a fifth emperor, Alexios III Angelos (r. 1195–1204), who had fled from the crusaders back in July 1203, remained at large somewhere in the empire. Worse was to come, for on the day the city finally fell to the crusaders, Mourtzouphlos took to his imperial heels and slipped shamefully away across the Bosporus. As the philosopher put it, nature abhors a vacuum, any more than society can bear anarchy. In the small hours of 13 April, therefore, two candidates stepped forward for the 'captaincy of a tempest-tossed ship', as Niketas Choniates so elegantly expressed it.[184]

And so it was that a lottery was held and Constantinus Laskaris was the winner. He strongly urged the Constantinopolitans to resist the hated Latins, now at large on the city streets, and bluntly told the Varangians that if the crusaders triumphed, they would be out of a lucrative job. While the terrified public at large closed their ears to the new emperor's exhortations, the ravenous Varangians took advantage of their undeniable need for their services and demanded a pay rise. When, as dawn kissed the sky that day, they saw the crusaders gathering themselves, even the inducement of increased remuneration was not enough to steel their hearts for the coming fight and many Varangians, along with Laskaris, simply 'took flight to save themselves'.[185] These were the same Varangians who had recently held the city walls with such spirit. Rational perfidy and cowardice, perhaps, in the light of the situation, or a classic case of risk management, nonetheless it does look as if the Varangians had become unstable ballast. 'On that truly hateful day of evil name', as Niketas Choniates so passionately described it,[186] the sack of Constantinople was about to commence.

The Latins often regarded the Greeks, as they called the Byzantines, as mendacious, effeminate heretics. Witness the remarks of Odo de Deuil, chaplain to Louis VII of France, written about his experiences during the Second Crusade (1146–8), describing the Greeks as lacking 'all manly vigour, both of words and spirit... they have the opinion that anything done for the holy empire cannot be considered perjury'.[187] To the Byzantines, as Niketas Choniates graphically observed firsthand, the Latins were often just as distasteful:

> Between us and them the greatest gulf of disagreement has been fixed, and we are separated in purpose and diametrically opposed, even though we are closely associated and frequently share the same dwelling. Overweening in their pretentious display of straightforwardness, the Latins would stare up and down at us and behold with curiosity the gentleness and lowliness of our demeanour; and we, looking grimly upon their superciliousness, boastfulness, and pompousness, with the drivel from their nose held in the air, are committed to this course and grit our teeth, secure in the power of Christ, who gives the faithful the power to tread on serpents and scorpions and grants them protection from all harm and hurt.[188]

Truly, the crusades made perfectly clear the split between Latin and Greek. This was now a cultural, religious and political rift. They also demonstrated that the question of who spoke for all Christendom – the pope in Rome or the emperor in Constantinople – was often a violent and bloody dispute.

Drink, dainties and debauchery

Previously, we discussed how the Varangians' most prized asset as with all mercenary elites was not their skill at arms or fearsome reputation but the stainless banner of their loyalty, both to their chief and to their comrades. Of course, spotless loyalty has always been the primary, military virtue in every age, rated higher than either smartness or strength. The Varangian Guard probably rate as one of the most famous (or notorious) mercenary units in history, and their fascination undoubtedly derives chiefly from the incongruity of finding such warriors serving the true emperor of the Romans, the Christ Incarnate, in the Holy City of Constantinople, the Queen of Cities. Indeed, to its citizens the Varangians were renowned as men with long hair and beards, and to borrow the words of Ahmad ibn Fadlan, they were as 'tall as palm trees, fair and reddish'.[189] In a similar vein, Liudprand of Cremona (d. 972) speaks of the Rus' and the Northmen as the same 'northern race (*aquilonares homines*) of a ruddy complexion'.[190] Again, there is an excellent eyewitness description by Michael Psellos:

> There were Italians [viz. Italo-Normans], and Scyths from Taurus [viz. Varangians], men of fearful appearance, dressed in fearful garb, both alike glaring fiercely about them. They were not alike in other respects, for while the one tribe painted themselves and plucked their eyebrows, the other preserved their natural colour; the one made their attacks as the spirit moved them, were impetuous and led by impulse, the other with a mad fury; the former in their first onslaught were irresistible, but they quickly lost their ardour; the latter, on the other hand, were less impatient, but fought with unsparing devotion and a complete disregard for wounds.[191]

They were also said to drink too much.

The Varangian Guard was a war band of lusty, hard fighting, hard drinking ('wineskins', *vinbelja*, Snorri Sturluson calls them, a vinous remark that has made something of a career for itself through its neat quotability),[192] hard cased, axe-wielding, barbarian northerners. When the Varangians had their reins loosened, a wee bit, they transformed almost instantly into unbridled soldiery. In their case, alcohol was the point around which everything else revolved. Talking of the Rus' he had met on the banks of the Volga, Ibn Fadlan notes '[t]hey are addicted to alcohol. They drink it night and day. Sometimes one of them dies cup in hand'.[193]

We think of wine as something as healthy and normal as food, and also as a great giver of happiness and well-being and delight. Drinking wine is not a route to oblivion; it is as natural as eating. Accustomed as they were to beer and barley, the Northmen had soon developed a taste for wine, so much so that one raiding force sent 200 men to Paris to get hold of a supply so that they could spend some time in revelry and dissipation.[194] Wine produces different effects on different races. On the Varangian, we imagine, wine did only one thing – it brought out his most swinish tendencies.

Michael Attaleiates, a palace courtier at the time, has a tale of alcohol-fuelled violence involving the Varangians. Nikephoros III Botaneiates (r. 1078–81) and his secretary were once attacked on a staircase by some sottish Varangians who were meant to be on guard in the Great Palace. The unfortunate secretary was shot clean through the neck and died, but the emperor, a seasoned soldier, defended himself well and was helped by some members of the court until some Greek guards came to his rescue. The ringleaders were not put to death but sent away to distant garrisons outside the capital, and most of the soldiers were pardoned, which says much for this particular emperor's generosity.[195]

When it came to literature, the Byzantines were far less interested in satire, which was undoubtedly inhibited by the absolute nature of the imperial power. But this genre was not altogether neglected. For example, there is a curious fourteenth-century Byzantine satire *The Book of the Fruits*, a mock trial of the Grape in the court of king Quince in a pseudo-Aesopian quarrel among the fruits where the Varangians are depicted as standing beside the king and his lords all through the proceedings.

Whether or not the Varangians' new taste for wine went as far as resinated wine we do not know. Retsina was certainly not to the taste of all westerners, as Liudprand of Cremona testifies when he exclaims that 'the Greek wine, on account of being mixed with pitch, resin and plaster, was to us undrinkable'.[196]

Generally speaking, grave drunkenness is a thing of great ugliness and people do things they would not have done. Some Byzantine sources also tell anecdotes of the disastrous results of Northmen's drunkenness in the distant south.[197] Perhaps in anticipation of just such fiascos, the south faring Danish king Eiríkr I *ejegoð* (r. 1095–1103), who was visiting Constantinople, not only reminds the Varangians serving Alexios I Komnenos 'to be faithful to the emperor', but also warns them against excessive wine consumption.[198] We may remember that the Danes who slew archbishop Ælfheah of Canterbury at London on Saturday night, 19 April 1012, were 'very drunk' due to their consumption of wine 'brought there from the south', and that they brought the archbishop to 'their assembly' before beating him to death 'with bones and with ox-heads' because he would not pay them more money, and so made a martyr.[199] Here we should add that 48,000 pounds in silver had been paid to the Danes in their camp at Greenwich that very week: about twelve million coins if it was paid in money.

Yet the Norse warrior liked to drink his fill, and more. The court skald Þjóðólfr boldly tells Haraldr *hárfagri* in a song that though he found his veterans flocking too numerously to the mead bowl, he did not complain of their number when they were sacrificing limb and life in his war service.[200] The character of early mediaeval battle, whereby the warrior was dependent on those who stood beside him in battle, enhanced the importance of communal feasting and drinking in order to bond the group together. The feasting, boasting and storytelling carried out in halls, as recounted in the Old Norse sagas and elsewhere (e.g. in the heroic-elegiac poem

Beowulf, where the nameless Anglo–Saxon *scop*, poet, adopts a Nordic past that is partly historical for his English audience),[201] can be interpreted as a need to express this 'martial reliability'.[202] Thus, alcohol's rôle here, like taunting and war cries, was to bolster courage and comradeship. Indeed, Norse feasts must have been alcoholic to excess, if the stories are to be believed. Because of the impurities in the drink, there must have been some head-splitting hangovers the following morning. The proper way to drink was 'without restraint', according to some sources, and the stories suggest that was the rule. Still, the *Hávamál* poet recommends in several verses that one should drink with moderation.[203] Likewise, when Hárekr challenged Brandr to drink, Brandr declined, saying that he did not have such an excess of wits that he wanted to drink them all away.[204] In an Old Welsh context, one of the Gododdin warriors receives praise for moderation, as 'He was wise and refined and proud; / He was not rude to fellow-drinker'.[205]

The great passion of mercenaries throughout history is of course binging, not moderation, with more than a little help from wine and whores. But there was one thing that distinguished the Varangian Guard from similar formations: it was a regular élite unit fashioned to serve the needs of a secure, vital centralized state. Men of war to the bone, the weapons of battle came to their hands like tame dogs, and conformed to their hands like gloves. A common Northman took up a sword or an axe as he might take up a spade or a mattock – as a tool needing to be wielded for his survival and that of his family. There was, of course, a much darker side to the vocation. Not only were Varangians prone to looting, but, also, liable to commit other acts of improper violence such as intimidation, rapine and the use of deliberate cruelty. Such nasty habits were further exacerbated through gambling, drunkenness and lechery, off-duty pastimes which, incidentally, alleviated the hardships and perils of their dangerous occupation. Throughout history mercenary forces, albeit professional, were of a temperamental nature. To maintain (and exploit) their superior *esprit de corps* and cohesion they required a fully competent leadership that was strict, if not ferocious, in its control.

Duty and discipline

During offensives, the Varangians formed the vanguard, while in retreat, they took up the rear. Many times their fierce spear-cum-axe-work and stubborn endurance in desperate situations saved the day for the emperor. The wild bunch of northerners that had been accepted as hired swords by the soldier emperor Basil had evolved into a regular unit of seasoned veterans. They were accustomed to campaigning hardships in their former untamed lives, naturally, but now they were accustomed to cohesion in battle too. Also, of importance was the trust Varangians placed in their comrades and their commanders. A war leader, who is a soldier, can only teach his wisdom to men whose bodies have been prepared for adversity and their minds to resist fear. Then the spark can kindle the spark. And so with them.

Together with the tactical innovation of the Varangians' signature spear-cum-axe-work went considerable *esprit de corps* and, above all, a greater discipline than was normal in mercenary units. Being so close to the throne meant that discipline in the Varangian Guard had to be preserved at all times, and the men are represented as having their own laws and power to impose penalties on those who broke them, unless the emperor himself intervened. As Machiavelli was later to recognize, training and discipline was not enough to guarantee obedience – this had to be reinforced by the fear of harsh punishment. George Kedrenos has a story of one of the Varangians raping a local woman during a campaign in western Anatolia, where the Varangians were currently in winter quarters in 1034 (it is likely that Haraldr Sigurðarson was there at the time, as we shall discuss anon). She killed him with a 'foreign sword', which was in all probability the man's own weapon, and when this was known his comrades met together and decided that the brave lady should inherit the possessions of the dead man, while his body was treated as that of a suicide and thrown out with no burial rites.[206] John Skylitzes gives more details, saying the woman 'seized his Persian-type short sword, struck him in the heart and promptly killed him'.[207] This particular incident is illustrated in the Madrid manuscript of John Skylitzes' work, though the lady in question dispatches the rapist by using his spear and not his short sword (a case of artistic licence, perhaps).[208]

Lest we forget that the release of pent-up sexual tensions was a horrifying, if familiar, component of soldiering and remains so to this day. It seems, like the Swiss mercenaries that were the terror of European battlefields at the turn of the sixteenth century, the Varangians had a strict camp code of their own, and would punish by death or otherwise individuals who had offended the honour of the unit. We shall shortly witness another example of this rigorous disciplinary code when Haraldr Sigurðarson acts as judge and executioner of those Varangians who took the side of Michael V Kalaphates in the civil upheaval that resulted in his downfall. The Swiss mercenary bands also possessed the privilege of trying and judging their own members when they were found guilty of some offence. These men had to be subjected to a rigorous disciplinary code whose instruments were the drill sergeant and the drum head tribunal.

It was custom among the German *Landsknechts* (to use an example that is meaningful to most), the colourful and bitter rivals of the Swiss in the European mercenary business, that the process of mustering after recruitment was turned into a positive rite of initiation. The new recruits entered the mustering ground via a gateway formed for the occasion by two halberds stuck in the ground with a pike laid across the blades to form a crossbar – the tools of their bloody trade, so to speak.

They were then formally enrolled in the books of the unit, allocated their weapons and given their first pay, minus the appropriate deductions. They then formed a ring around their colonel, or *obrist*, in order to hear the articles of war. These documents contained a list of the senior officers, the conditions of pay, and the military and judicial codes. Essentially they specified that:

> [T]hose who flee from the enemy should be struck down by his comrades; those who desert will be considered without honour and will suffer punishment to body and life. No one is to burn and pillage without an order. Women and children, old people, priests and their churches are to be protected. No one should take anything in a friendly territory without paying for it. No one should hold a meeting without the permission of the Colonel. Mutinous soldiers should be reported immediately to an officer. Soldiers are not to assume that they are released from their duties should pay be delayed for any reason. In the camp, comradeship is the order of the day. The sins of gambling and drinking are to be kept within reasonable limits. Anyone who does not intervene in a fight immediately is considered guilty of fighting himself. Anyone, having given suitable warning, who strikes down someone causing unrest, will not be punished. The Lord's name is not to be taken in vain. Soldiers should attend church regularly.[209]

Thus, to take one article from those stated above, that of gambling. This was very popular among soldiers and was generally tolerated, albeit usually with some restrictions. The articles of war would, for instance, specify that it was not allowed during guard duty, that debts should not exceed the soldier's pay, or that their weapons should not be gambled away.

To the articles of war the recruits had to swear a formal oath by raising a hand with two fingers extended. Thereafter, they were in a world that allowed for considerable personal eccentricity and an unusual degree of closeness between officers and men, but which was controlled with great ferocity. Absences were checked through an unusually strict system of leave passports. A gallows not only marked every mustering centre and stopping place but was used as an off-limits symbol, on doors of dwellings exempt from billeting, for example. And when a man's behaviour, by cowardice or in any other ways, had soiled a unit's honour, he was judged not by civilian law, but by the *spiessgericht*, spear-law. Thus, a full trial under the penal law of the *Landsknechts* (*Malefitzrecht*) took place in the open air in front of the whole unit. After defending himself among his peers the decision, which could only be death or total acquittal, was given by a show of hands. The death sentence could then be carried out by running the gauntlet that allowed his 'honest' comrades, to the sound of drums and fifes, to finish his life with the points of their pikes. Any comrade who left a gap for the delinquent to escape 'would step into his shoes'.

It is clear that the *Landsknechts* regarded themselves as an 'order' with their own forms of administration and jurisdiction, as well as customs and habits such as the right to participate in decisions and shape their daily lives. These qualities provided strong internal cohesion. Much like our future *Landsknechts*, the Varangians appear as a fascinating enigma, through a glass darkly: men of fierce, self-sacrificing courage, whose lives centred on the concept of honour but who seemingly had no notion of fair play; men seen by some of their contemporaries as of imposing statue, great martial skills, courage, commitment, discretion and discrimination, and by others as no different from barbarians with their butchering, blinding and binging. Clearly, these professional warriors were born and raised in a different world and fought a different type of warfare to that of their Byzantine employer, and we must now return to the Byzantine scene in the time of Haraldr Sigurðarson.

Byzantium, 1034–42

The mercenary

Now here is an interesting fact. Most tyrants have been rather small men – Caesar, Hitler, Mussolini, Stalin and Franco as well as Napoléon. And what of Haraldr III Sigurðarson *harðráði* himself, seated in the high chair of the royal hall in Nidaros, surrounded by his armed following? He was, in the words of Snorri Sturluson:

> [A] handsome man of stately appearance. He was light blond, with a blond beard and long moustaches, with one eyebrow higher than the other. His hands and feet were large, and both well proportioned. His height was five ells. He was ruthless with his enemies, and given to harsh punishment of all opposed him.[210]

It appears, therefore, our Haraldr was strikingly fetching (in a sort of Nordic way), brilliant, but prey to sadistic tendencies. Still, there was much more to success as a war leader than simple popularity. Furthermore, grizzled warriors generally preferred a hard man who knew what he was doing than a genial incompetent. Even today, all professional soldiers look for and admire a brave and intelligent leader, truth be known, and will even put up with abuse from him providing that at a critical moment he displays courage and leadership. I know this to be a fact… in combat, then and now, forces without leadership – at all levels – will always fail.

These days we perhaps know Haraldr Sigurðarson best as the inheritor of 'seven feet of English soil', but what concerns us most in this chapter is that prior to being king – or tyrant, as his critics would have it, in the sense given to the word by Plutarch, that is, an absolute ruler – of Norway Haraldr had an interesting (and lucrative) career as a Varangian.

Before the year 1066 the Varangian Guard was chiefly composed of Scandinavians, some of whom were political exiles. Certainly, fitting the latter bill is the most famous of these Scandinavians, at least according to later Old Norse saga tradition – his life story is told in no fewer than six sagas – is Haraldr Sigurðarson who was to invade England in the early autumn of 1066, and, as it turned out, was to go to his own death at Stamford Bridge. Along the road to Stamford Bridge lay the throne of Norway, but this is somewhat anticipating events and we must return to the young Haraldr and spool backwards to the start of his activity in the Varangian Guard.

Joining the professionals

Though Haraldr was (and still remains) unquestionably the best known of all the Varangians, he was neither the first Varangian nor the last. Just as any other potential recruit, Haraldr went the usual Varangian way, floating down the Russian rivers (in his case, just the Dnieper), across the Black Sea, and so on to Constantinople. Once enlisted in the feared and famous Varangian Guard to do battle against the enemies of *Miklagarðskeisari*, the emperor of Constantinople, he could have expected to land in Sicily or southern Italy, to fight in Anatolia and Bulgaria, to possibly die in the red sands neighbouring the Caspian Sea and so too on the marshy banks of the Euphrates. The size of the corps he was seeking to join probably numbered just more than 5,000 men, a small but lethal body of men that represented part of the élite core of the Byzantine army.

It should be remembered that the primary function of the Varangians was defensive, to guard and protect the emperor in Constantinople. Yet, the Varangian Guard was much more than just a palace guard, for it was the invariable rule when the emperor took the field in person, his Varangians were present in strength. While we know something about their ethnic composition and weaponry, we know very little about their actual deployment and rôle in battle. Their distinctive weapon, as we have discussed in detail, was the long-shafted Dane axe, even before the English joined their ranks. What we do know for certain, however, was that they were professional warriors.

Let me explain. When referring to the various main types of arms-bearing men, warrior is defined as a man whose vocation is war, while the soldier has war as his profession.[211] According to this definition, the warrior fights for personal recognition and therefore fought as an individual rather than as a member of a disciplined battle order. In turn, the soldier is part of a clearly defined military strategy where honour on a personal level is subordinated. On a more practical note, the warrior supplied his own arms and armour, while the soldier acquired them from the lord or king. When dealing with a martial context like that of the Varangian Guard, these definitions become too blunt, as the Varangian construct incorporated significant elements of both. The Varangian Guard was not, in the modern sense, a professional force that rehearses on the parade ground, but with regard to vocation and the concept of personal and military honour, these arms-bearing men were clearly warriors but their organization, system of rank, and advanced forms of warfare techniques, which included fighting in battle formation, signify the soldier. Consequently, these men are defined as professional warriors, the military élite of a martial society devoted to, and living by, their vocation. So, this was the professional outfit that Haraldr was hoping to join.

Haraldr's motives

Though Haraldr is given no explicit motivation in the written sources, Byzantine or Old Norse, for his decision to travel to the distant south, his first actions upon reaching Constantinople are sketchily summed up by Snorri Sturluson as follows:

> And when Haraldr arrived in Constantinople and had a meeting with the queen [empress Zoë] he took military service with her and right away in autumn sailed with some galleys (*galeiðr*) together with the fleet into the Greek Sea (*Griklandshaf*).[212]

Zoë, was 'born in the purple', the niece of a warrior emperor, the daughter of another, and destined to be wife of three more, beloved of the ordinary people of Constantinople. The question begs itself to be asked, therefore: Would the extraordinary and exalted Zoë Porphyrogenita have granted an audience to a young barbarian prince cast out from the far north?

On the other hand, Haraldr first enters the pages of the *Morkinskinna* disguised as his own emissary. In this semblance, the prince is able to praise himself more thoroughly and state his own case more vigorously than would have otherwise befitted his rank.[213] The story continues. For in his youth, Haraldr voyaged to Constantinople and entered the service of the emperor, doing so under the assumed name of Norðbrikt. As the *Morkinskinna* imparts, Haraldr did so because 'foreigners who are the sons of kings tend to be mistrusted'.[214] The common man needs no disguise, since he is by his very nature anonymous.

If mercenary service was not Haraldr's original motivation, it certainly swiftly eclipses any other possible ones he might be conjectured to have had in travelling to Constantinople. Besides, he had to eat, and so did his fellow Norse travellers. It is only idealized heroes who tend to have no bodily needs, and Haraldr was neither a demi-god nor a romantic hero. He was an exile, an adventurer, and to Haraldr and his followers food was all-important, and they were not ashamed of their need for it. It was an adequate motive for warfare. Thrust out from Norway, he urgently needed to find a master in whose service he and his men could fill their bellies. Yet, he guarded himself against the characteristic pitfalls of an émigré existence, and instead, turned the hard school of his exile into a challenging and productive experience.

Haraldr was to do little else than fight during his time in the Byzantine empire. Indeed, he was to fight on nearly every frontier of a still large Byzantine empire, from the Euphrates to Sicily, even finding the time to bathe in the purifying waters of the Jordan, as was the custom of pilgrims. Haraldr also donated generously to the shrines of the Sepulchre, the True Cross and other hallowed sites, it being said that the amount of money he piously donated was beyond counting.

Returning immediately to the military method of gaining nonmaterial favour, Haraldr then freed all the roads in and around the Jordan valley, killing brigands and highwaymen, such as Bedouin who preyed on the potentially rich pilgrimage routes.[215] In all likelihood, Haraldr probably turned a quick profit by providing a protective escort for pilgrims to Jerusalem.[216]

The profit Haraldr garnered in the Holy Land may have been spiritual. *May* is the word. For during his eight years of mercenary service in Byzantium Haraldr amassed a fortune from pay and booty, for Snorri Sturluson blandly describes him garnering 'an immense amount of treasure' on these campaigns, much of which he secretly ships to his future father-in-law prince Yaroslav in Kiev for safekeeping.[217]

Despite Snorri's assertion that Haraldr signed up with the empress Zoë, Byzantine and other Norse sources agree that he entered the service of the emperor Michael IV (r. 1034–41). However, the separate *Haralds saga* relates that he did not wish it to be known in Constantinople that he was a royal prince, because the Byzantines did not take very kindly to men of such exalted status becoming mercenaries, and so he assumed the name Norðbrikt.[218] Yet the late eleventh-century Byzantine work known as *Advice for the Emperor* contains no hint of the 'crownless prince in disguise', and its author knows his true name and lineage. In his brief and dry biography of Haraldr, who he calls *Araltes* in his native Greek, he also adds that the Norwegian prince 'brought with him a company of five hundred men of good family'.[219] The Old Norse source *Nóregs konunga tal* does not specify the size of Haraldr's company, however it does identify its ethnicity when it reports the prince arrived in Constantinople 'with a great crowd of Norwegians'.[220]

When the young Haraldr set his eyes on Constantinople it was already the most venerable of cities in Christendom – perhaps of all the cities in the world. Founded by Constantinus I (r. 306–37), Constantinople flourished even more under Iustinianus I (r. 527–65), and was to do so again under the Macedonian dynasty (843–1071). The Byzantine capital was a political, administrative, cultural and religious megalopolis – a grandiose city full of magnificent palaces and public monuments. In 1034 it had no peer.

Haraldr's life had adapted itself to the scale and pace of a farmstead, so his first impression of Constantinople must have been one of dizzying speed and neck craning size. The Icelandic skald Bölverkr Arnórsson, the brother of Þjóðólfr Arnórsson, describes the young Haraldr Sigurðarson watching the gleaming roofs of the city on his approach down the Bosporus:

> Fresh gales drove our gallant / gallery scurrying shoreward – / with armoured prows and poops our / proud ships rode to harbour. / Of *Mikligarðr* the golden / gables our famous prince saw. / Many a mere-ship fair-sight / moved toward the high-walled city.[221]

As the future king of Norway was to soon find out, even at night Constantinople shimmered; it was one of the few cities in the empire to boast street lighting. Not only was it a striking city, it was a rich one. This was a fabulous city of golden opportunities, an emporium of golden dreams, ruled by a potential employer rich in worldly wealth and furniture, fat in foodstuffs and padded in soft raiment. This was the city prince Haraldr intended to seek his fame and his fortune. He had seen many towns and settlements in recent years, but he had never visited so mighty a place as Constantinople (there was none like it in the mediaeval world). History does not record Haraldr's initial reaction to Constantinople, but one can imagine his engaging sense of marvel at the size, scale and splendour of this great metropolis. We do know from memoirs written by visitors who had set their eyes on Constantinople for the first time that it appeared like something out of One Thousand and One Nights, a fantastical creation whose architecture and monuments were completely unfamiliar to them.

Pirate hunter

Earlier, we indicated that the Varangian Guard followed the emperor to war, both as a bodyguard and as an élite unit of his campaigning army. However, the Varangians were considered skilled, practical seamen, and part of them served in the imperial navy. From what is recorded of Haraldr Sigurðarson we can deduce that his first period of imperial service will have been spent in this capacity.

Snorri Sturluson, as does the separate *Haralds saga*, states that Haraldr, as soon as he set foot in Constantinople and entered the service of the empire, 'sailed with some galleys together with the (imperial) fleet into the Greek Sea [Aegean]'.[222] Undoubtedly, as mariners well versed with the habits of pirates, Haraldr and his seafaring war band were employed in the capacity of pirate hunters. Since the death of Basil II the waters of the eastern Mediterranean had once again become infested with pirates. The separate *Haralds saga* states that Haraldr was to pay the emperor a hundred (i.e. the Norse hundred of twelve tens) marks for each pirate vessel that he seized, and that he could keep any booty above that for himself and his men. One accusation levelled against him later on was that he had swindled the emperor by holding back more monies than his due.[223] This we can well believe.

There was trouble from pirates in other parts of the empire during the first years of the reign of Michael IV, and it is likely that Haraldr and his men were used in the naval operations to clear them off the seas. John Zonaras mentions a great Arab fleet from Sicily and North Africa made raids on the Aegean islands, and even attacked the mainland of Greece and Anatolia, where they captured the town of Myra (Demre), the site of the original tomb of Saint Nicholas (d. 343).[224] George Kedrenos repeats this, and adds that these Arab corsairs concentrated their felonious activities in the Cycladic archipelago and the shores of Thrace.[225] The Byzantines, under the command of the *stratêgós* of Kibirriotes, won a victory over these pirates, destroying many of their vessels and selling those of the crews not executed into slavery.

We have one of Haraldr's own verses, composed in Norway many years after his return from Byzantium, in which he makes reference to his fights against the Arabs:

> Another time it was that / I reddened swords far from my homeland; / the sword sang in the town of the Arabs [*Serkja garði*] / – but that was long ago.[226]

Since *Serkir* is often used in Old Norse as a synonym for Arabs and Arabic-speaking peoples generally, and likewise to the use of *Særkland* for any land of the Islamic conquest, it is possible to surmise that Haraldr is alluding to his war service in Anatolia, where there was much fighting against Arab pirates during the first four years of the reign of Michael IV,[227] and where a principal Byzantine general was a man who enters the life of our Norwegian prince in other ways, Georgios Maniakes.

With Maniakes

The Byzantine empire sough to recover Sicily then held by Arab Egyptian Fatimids, who controlled the island by means of the cadet dynasty of Kalbits. The Sicilian expedition sailed in the early summer of 1038. It had been put under the command of the greatest of living Byzantine generals, the gigantic Georgios Maniakes (known as *Gyrgir* in the Old Norse written sources), still glorious from a series of Syrian triumphs six years before, which had rescued the empire at a time of great peril. For the expedition he was created *stratêgós* of Longobardia, and furnished with the best imperial soldiery to be had.[228] Among them was certainly Haraldr Sigurðarson, just back from his (profitable) pilgrimage to the Holy Land (he is presumably the first Norwegian prince to go there).[229] Other 'exotics' included 300 Normans from Salerno commanded by two sons of Tancred de Hauteville, William and Drogo, sent by the Lombard prince Gaimar V of Capua-Salerno who was the suzerain of the Normans of Aversa and a vassal of Byzantium,[230] and the Lombard Ardouin, a former vassal of the archbishop of Milan.

Maniakes was, in character and accomplishments as in physique, well over life-size, in truth, one of those colourful near-geniuses thrown up at intervals through history that seem to have the world at their feet, only to lose it again through some compensatory defect that betrays them in a moment of crisis. Michael Psellos, who knew the man personally, has left us a fearsome description:

I have seen this man myself, and I wondered at him, for nature had bestowed on him all the attributes of a man destined to command. He stood ten feet high [viz. very tall][231] and men who saw him had to look up as if at a hill or the summit of a mountain. There was nothing soft or agreeable about the appearance of Maniakes. As a matter of fact, he was more like a fiery whirlwind, with a voice of thunder and hands strong enough to make walls totter and shake gates of brass. He had the quick movement of a lion and the scowl on his face was terrible to behold. Everything else about the man was in harmony with these traits and just what you would expect. Rumour exaggerated his appearance and the barbarians, to a man, lived in dread of him, some because they had seen and marvelled, others because they had heard frightful tales of his prowess.[232]

The military prowess of this magnificent monster was much respected in the capital, but this Turkish-born former baggage boy was a blunt man who had to survive under a régime increasingly given to palace intrigue, double-dealing, backbiting, suspicions, conspiracy, and treachery.[233]

His opposite number as commander of the fleet was a nonentity called Stephanos who unfortunately for Maniakes was far better connected to the real power behind the imperial throne. An erstwhile shipyard caulker,[234] Stephanos' main qualification, in fact, was that he was brother-in-law to the eunuch John the Orphanotrophos whose young brother now occupied that throne as Michael IV. Thus, Stephanos woke up one morning to find himself commanding ships instead of caulking them. Of Stephanos, Michael Psellos – reporting, as usual, at firsthand – writes:

I saw him after the metamorphosis, and there was nothing whatever about him in harmony or congruous with the part he was playing; his horse, his clothes, everything else that alters a man's appearance – all were out of place. It was as if a pygmy wanted to play Herakles and was trying to make himself look like the demi-god. The more such a person tries, the more his appearance belies him – clothed in the lion's skin but weighed down by the club! So it was with this man: nothing about him was right.[235]

Maniakes and Stephanos, both brilliant, at least in their own minds, each disdainful of the other. They must have hated each other. The difference was Maniakes *was* brilliant and Stephanos was nothing more than a hollow nonentity. Stephanos the pygmy and Maniakes the ogre was going to be a bad match with only one possible ending. This would happen, as we shall see, in 1041.

As for understanding the part Haraldr Sigurðarson played in the Sicilian campaign we are thrown back upon the evidence of the stanzas of the prince and his skalds. Haraldr composed a number of these for his future bride back in Kiev, Elisaveta Yaroslavna (ON *Ellisif*). In one of them:

> The ship passed in many places by Sicily (*Sikiley*); / it moved swiftly / at the men's instigation; / then were we fine and hopeful. / I do not think that the lazy man / would bother to go that way, / yet the Goddess of *Garðar* [i.e. Elisaveta] / will not look at me.[236]

Valgarðr à Vellir, probably a son or a near relative of Mörðr Valgarðsson (of *Brennu-Njáls saga*), who appears to have been in Haraldr's retinue during the last years in Byzantine service, also refers to the Sicilian campaign, and uses strong words about the horrors visited upon the locals by the war:

> The prince took a great force / south of the broad lands / where the ships quivered; / Sicily (*Sikiley*) was at length depopulated.[237]

So too does Bölverkr Arnórsson who appears to be describing Haraldr's part in establishing a crucial beachhead for Maniakes and his expeditionary force:

> The ship was filled with blood / by the cape where blood blew; / the ships ran to the shore, / the Lord [i.e. Haraldr] fought nobly, / he won sand under him to the south of Sicily (*sunnan Sikiley*) / for a great force (*liði miklu*), / where the bodies of the dead let the blood / pour on to the planks in the bottom of the ship.[238]

As we can surmise from this skaldic stanza the Sicilian landing was hotly contested by the Arabs, resulting in the Varangians under Haraldr taking heavy casualties.

Relations between these two incomparable men cannot have been harmonious, to say the least. Maniakes, a self-made man of humble foreign origins with all the merits and defects of such men, would be highly unlikely to get along with the blue-blooded and equally self-conscious northern prince. Moreover, a commander who made so much of the punctilio of military discipline was unlikely to take kindly to the free-and-easy Norse attitude to camp life. A tale from the stylus of Snorri Sturluson has clearly got its roots in this fact. He tells us of an occasion when Haraldr and his Varangians wanted to pitch their tents on high ground rather than in the slough below. The ensuing heated quarrel between the Byzantine generalissimo and the Norwegian prince was tipping towards bloodshed when wiser heads stepped in and suggested drawing 'lots as to who was to be the first in riding or rowing or choosing a berth in harbour or selecting a place for pitching their tents'. Snorri concludes his tale with Haraldr winning the draw through deception, the outwitted Maniakes thereby yielding to the decision that 'the Varangians should have the first choice in all matters under dispute'.[239]

Within two years of campaigning in Sicily, Maniakes had reclaimed virtually the entire island from an Arab enemy possessed of superior numbers and interior lines of communication – he had gained victories at Rametta in 1038, a stronghold in the eastern part of the island, and Draginai (now Troina, to the west of Etna) in 1040, taking Messina in 1038 and Syracuse in 1040, which had the largest concentration of Greek-speaking people.

However, the expedition lost all hopes of final victory in 1041, mainly because of a quarrel between Maniakes and Stephanos. Maniakes never attempted to hide his contempt for Stephanos, who merely antagonized his brother commander by the gap between his high position and his non-existent abilities. Matters came to a head when Maniakes heard that Stephanos had allowed an Arab fleet to escape through the Byzantine naval blockade. Exasperated, the army commander publicly reproached the fleet commander, his volcanic anger manifesting itself when he assaulted him physically with his riding crop, calling him a careless coward and double-crosser as he thrashed him across the head and shoulders.[240] The supremely useless Stephanos, who was determined on revenge, complained to his all-powerful relative in Constantinople, and in short order Maniakes was recalled in disgrace and imprisoned. His successor, a eunuch called Basil Pedidiates, proved as incapable as Stephanos. The Byzantine army lost its momentum and its morale, and the retreat began, to finally leave Messina as the one remaining imperial possession on the island. In the meantime, the Italo-Normans had fallen out with the heavy-handed Maniakes over battle booty, deserting to the Italian mainland where they began to prey on Byzantine lands there, and Haraldr and the Varangians had been called back to Constantinople. As for the Varangians in the quarrel between Maniakes and Stephanos, they being warriors of an independent turn of mind it seems natural to assume that they took the side of the fleet commander.

While there is good reason to believe the Varangians having similarly resented the overbearing Maniakes and his short-changing habits, there is no question of Haraldr and the Varangians following the Italo-Normans ('Latin men' as Snorri calls them), either in their defection or the Italian insurrection they joined. Quite the contrary, as it is perfectly clear that when they were despatched to southern Italy they were fighting against the same Normans who had earlier been their brothers-in-arms in Sicily. Thus, this short stanza from Þjóðólfr Arnórsson, one of Haraldr's skalds: 'He who led the march at the grove / in the land of the Longobardians (*Langbarða*)'.[241] Paradoxically, in the light of this, it does not do to forget that the Varangians and the Normans were blood-brothers too.

Nothing more is known of Haraldr's part in this Italian campaign, other than he came out of it alive and with some honour on the evidence of his promotion to the *manglavitai*. However, before we move on to deal with his last Byzantine adventures we should pause and examine some of the anecdotes told of him during the Sicilian campaign. Personal prowess in arms, such as displayed by Haraldr when he established that aforementioned beachhead for Maniakes, greatly augmented the prestige of a prince, but skill as a strategist and tactician, as a besieger and commander in the field was a vital prerequisite for political success. As well as exaggerating his importance in Constantinopolitan affairs, Snorri Sturluson offers a highly coloured account of Haraldr's exploits on Sicily, crediting him with a series of unlikely time-worn stratagems.[242] These are folktales of unusual persistence often attached to the name of more than one Norse leader. They range from shamming death, to gain entry to a besieged city claiming the need for Christian burial (this ruse to gain entry into a besieged town by means of a fake funeral cortege is also attached to Ragnarr *loðbrók* as well as his son Björn *járnsíða*),[243] to the highly dubious use of sparrows as unwitting incendiaries.

In fact, the legend of the incendiary sparrows is a yarn also told of Haraldr's contemporary, the Norman Robert Guiscard in Sicily, and of the Danish warlord Guðrum at his siege of Cirencester (not that he ever did besiege the said town). It has been even told of the Kievan princess (later saint) Olga that she burned down a Slav town and had much of its populace killed or enslaved out of revenge (the pagan princess had not yet converted, after all) for the murder of her husband, prince Igor I, the previous year.[244] This itinerant folktale was later fathered on to Genghis Khan (r. 1206–27); he apparently offered to lift the siege of Volohai (a garrison city of the kingdom of Xi Xia) [245] in exchange for a thousand cats and 10,000 swallows. These bizarre tributes were duly handed over by the gullible Xi Xia commander, and the Mongols tied flammable materials to the tails of the cats and birds and ignited them. When the poor creatures were released, they fled home, setting the city ablaze, and Genghis Khan's army easily stormed the burning Volohai.[246]

Even if none of these tales are true, and surely incendiary birds is just the kind of mix of pointless cruelty and impracticality (the bird-on-fire weapon relies upon it homing instincts) that smacks of urban legend, they represent an interest in disinformation and trickery, which would not shame more systematic students of warfare.

Burning Bulgaria

We next find Haraldr Sigurðarson back in Constantinople preparing to take part in the emperor's final quelling of the Bulghar rebellion, a carefully planned operation that took place in 1041. It was during this campaign that Haraldr apparently earned the epithet 'burner of Bulghars' (ON *Bolgara brennir*), or so says Þjóðólfr Arnórsson.[247]

According to Gwyn Jones, 'burning towns came naturally to Harald',[248] and this pyromania was to be demonstrated to the full during the king's decade-and-a-half long campaign against Denmark with the incineration of Hedeby in 1051 standing out. It is described in an anonymous stanza attributed to *menn Haralds*, 'Haraldr's men':

> Burned down was at both ends – / bold methinks this deed was – / by Haraldr's valiant henchmen / *Heiðabýr* (Hedeby) altogether. / Dire damage to Sveinn [Estriðsson of Denmark] we'll / do, before dawn was I – / high flames out of houses / whirled – in the town's outskirts.[249]

It is also mentioned by the Icelandic skald Þorleikr *fagri*:

> How that to *Heiðabýr* the / hate-filled king then travelled, / that, he who heard not, needs to / have his shipmates tell him – / the time when, to no purpose, / toward king Sveinn's borough / Haraldr headed west – ah, / had it never been thus![250]

Fire was deadly in mediaeval towns, with their closely packed wooden houses: a fire started in one quarter of a town could easily spread throughout the town in a short time, and armies burnt whole towns, as well as numerous villages, to the ground in this period. Haraldr's men may not have been unduly worried about the misfortunes suffered by the people on the Danish shores; it was neither a sentimental age nor were Norsemen sentimentalists. But, as Þorleikr rightly points out, the razing of Hedeby by the 'hate-filled king' was surely a pointless exercise in vengefulness – and surely self-defeating, too, for a would-be king to destroy his hoped-for kingdom's major mart. War is, as Clausewitz would later theorize, the controlled use of force to bring about political ends. Uncontrolled force is as likely to harm as to help. That was Haraldr's nature; he was a man of extremes, a man who could resort to senseless destruction, a man with a turn for poetry and pyromania.

By way of a footnote here, the end of Hedeby is symbolically marked by the wreck known as Hedeby 1 found in the harbour there. Hedeby 1 met an abrupt end, apparently before it had reached the end of its useful life. The recovered hull only partly survives, and the charred strakes show that it was burned to the waterline. The favoured interpretation is that the ship was used as a fire-ship in an attack on the town. It had been filled with combustible material and sent out in flames into Hedeby harbour when the wind was from the right direction. Drifting into the harbour, it set alight any of the wooden structures on the shore with which it came into contact.[251] Although we cannot trace this specific event in the Norse sources, both the runic and the skaldic corpus refer to raids on Hedeby.

The Bulgarian campaign was the last military action in which Haraldr was engaged in imperial service. It was also to be the last for his boss, Michael IV. The emperor made a triumphant entry into his capital, dragging along behind him captured Bulghar chiefs. Michael Psellos, who was an eyewitness of the procession, describes the toll the strain of warfare had exacted from the emperor's never very robust body – he had long suffered from epilepsy – and it must have been clear to all, including himself, that he was a dying man.[252] Consequently, he set his own house in order, and with the consent of his wife and empress, the *porphyrogenita* Zoë (as the true representative of the Macedonian dynasty), named his nephew Michael, son of his sister Mária and Stephanos, he who had crossed the mighty George Maniakes in Sicily, as his successor on the throne. Michael IV passed away on 10 December 1041, and Michael V succeeded him. Popularly known as *kalaphates*, 'the caulker', in mocking reference to his father's former career with the tar brush, the parvenu emperor was that classic example of what becomes of a man when he wields power without responsibility (a recurring and dangerous problem even in our own day and age), that is to say, much like a boy with a peashooter, the temptation to use it can be overwhelming. Things were about to get ugly for Haraldr and his men.

Loyal liquidator

Tradition is a funny thing. Given enough time it seems to take on a life all of its own. As previously mentioned, there is a tradition that Haraldr was accused of withholding booty that rightly belonged to the emperor, as related by Snorri Sturluson, and he was incarcerated on this and other charges relating to the misappropriation of imperial funds.[253] We are then told how he was released from jail, which is said to have happened shortly before Haraldr and his Varangian companions involved themselves in the palace *putsch* that toppled Michael V Kalaphates (r. 1041–2), more of which below.

There is, of course, the possibility that Haraldr's old commander, the unforgiving Georgios Maniakes, might have had some part to play in putting Haraldr and his companions in prison. We last saw Maniakes himself incarcerated, having fallen foul of court politics. As mooted before, Haraldr and his Varangians may have taken the side of Stephanos in the acrimony that was to deprive Maniakes of his command. In 1042, having released him from prison, Michael V Kalaphates sent Maniakes to southern Italy to put down the Italo-Normans and then to reconquer Sicily from the Arabs. The situation for the Byzantines had deteriorated in his absence, having by this time lost all Italy except Bari, Taranto, Brindisi and Otranto.

The return of the formidable Maniakes was never going to bode well for Haraldr, especially when the new emperor shared a similar disposition towards the

Varangians, replacing them as his personal bodyguard, as the eyewitness Michael Psellos says:

> [W]ith new soldiers, Scythian [*Skuthai*] youths whom he had bought sometime previously. Every one of them was a eunuch. They understood what he required of them and they were well fitted to serve his desires. Indeed, he never questioned their allegiance, because it was to himself that they owed their promotion to the highest ranks. Some he employed in actual guard duties, while others were engaged in various tasks that he wished to be done.[254]

These castrated 'Scythian youths' were almost certainly Pečenegs by origin and their 'various tasks' undoubtedly nefarious in nature. Meanwhile, though they were no longer responsible for the emperor's personal safety and comfort, the Varangians were not disbanded but continued in use in the garrison of the capital.

Just to wrap up Maniakes' remarkable career. Arriving in Italy, Maniakes advanced once again, ruthlessly destroying everything in his path. However, while bravely battling against the Italo-Normans he heard that a certain Romanos Skleros had seduced his wife. This so enraged him that he stuffed the ears, nose and mouth of the poor unfortunate messenger with dung and tortured him to death. When recalled by Constantinus IX Monomachos in 1043 he rebelled and was proclaimed emperor by his army. An imperial force blocked the way at Ostrabos (Ostrovo) in Bulgaria. Maniakes fought at the head of his men and whoever was injured by his sword escaped 'with half or more of their body maimed, for he was known to be invincible and firm, a big and broad-backed man terrible in appearance but an excellent leader'.[255] Maniakes was winning the fray when fatally wounded. His severed head was taken to Constantinople and publicly displayed in the Hippodrome.

Anyway, to return to the subject in hand. Having sent Maniakes off to war again, Michael V turned to dispose of the only person who gave his rule authority, the dowager empress Zoë Porphyrogenita – her father was Constantinus VIII, her uncle Basil II, her grandfather Romanos II, her great-grandfather Constantinus VII Porphyrogenitus. Michael had always hated his foster mother, who he kept under constant surveillance, and about a year after his coronation he accused her of attempted regicide.[256] On 18 April 1042 a detachment of Michael's ruffian *Skuthai* dragged her from the women's quarters and she was shut up in a convent on Prinkipo (Büyükada), the Isle of the Prince in the Sea of Marmara. As Michael Psellos wrote, obviously filled with distaste, the old empress, 'the daughter of a most noble family, was dispossessed by a man sprung from the gutter'.[257] It is said that the 'rascally Michael', to the apt words of our eyewitness, gloated over her shaven tresses as she was bundled away from Constantinople. News of the undignified departure of the anointed empress of the old and tried Macedonian house shook Constantinople to its very foundations. Loyalty to the emperor was about to fade fast.

Constantinopolitans quickly took to arms and attacked the Great Palace itself. Michael Psellos, who was an eyewitness in the imperial residence, as the emperor's secretary, has left an excellent and vivid account of the subsequent events, and is indeed our chief witness as to the part played by the Varangians in the overthrow of Michael V. It at this time that Haraldr and his companions were released from prison, an action that was likely to ensure the support of the majority of the Varangians for the insurrectionists if, of course, they were personally much attached to Haraldr as we are led to believe by our Old Norse sources.

In what must have been a desperate act to save the emperor and his supporters from their encircling doom, Zoë was hastily brought back from her nunnery prison, vested anew in her imperial regalia and put on public display. But it was too late. The citizens, now backed by the Church and the nobility, refused to submit any longer to the misrule of the parvenu Kalaphates, remaining as they did firmly attached to the former legitimate dynasty. What is more, according to Michael Psellos, 'not even the foreigners and allies whom the emperors are wont to maintain by their side – I am referring to the Scythes from the Taurus [*Tauroskuthai*, viz. Varangians] – were able to restrain their anger... all were ready to lay down their lives for Zoë'.[258] After a period of terrible rioting in the city, on the evening of 20 April Michael was deposed, publicly blinded and exiled to the monastery of Eleimon on the eastern Aegean island of Chios, a retreat into the religious life being considered the proper place for a dethroned emperor. What God had given, He could take away too.

The Lord may have turned his back on Michael, but there is good reason to believe that the blinding of the emperor and his uncle the *nobilissimus* Constantinus was actually performed by Haraldr and his men. Was this a simple act of revenge on Haraldr's part, or was he merely a pawn in somebody else's game of thrones?

As the eyewitness Michael Psellos wrote – and not without a lightly malicious touch, I might impart – of the Varangian detachment that performed this unpleasant duty, 'bold, resolute men who did not shrink from anything'.[259] Though the author himself actually witnessed the blinding of the deposed emperor and his loyal uncle, Michael does not mention Haraldr Sigurðarson at all. On the other hand, according to the Old Norse sources, this Varangian detachment was commanded by Haraldr, Snorri Sturluson even claiming that it was Haraldr himself who boasted on his return to Norway that he personally blinded the emperor. Snorri includes the description of this gruesome act as written in the *Sexstefja*, a *drápa* in honour of Haraldr composed by the skald Þjóðólfr Arnórsson:

On both eyes blinded was then / Baleful strife was started / Greekland's great lord by the / greedy-wolf-brood's-sater. / Over in the east, a / ill mark Norway's ruler, / Magnús' kinsman, made on / main sworn Greek king's countenance.[260]

If true, then it seems that Haraldr would stop at nothing, even if it meant acting as a political bully rather than a professional soldier. Another honorific *drápa*, this one by the Icelandic skald Þórarinn Skeggjarson, goes as far to make the unsavoury suggestion that Haraldr 'gained even more of the glow-red gold' as a result.[261] He was also apparently the agent of punishment by hanging of those Varangians who had loyally remained by the emperor's side, so that '*eru Væringjar færi* [the Varangians are fewer]'.[262] Our authority for this is a half-stanza composed by Valgarðr á Vellir preserved in *Nóregs konunga tal*; Valgarðr himself is thought to have served alongside Haraldr during the later period of his Byzantine service. By all accounts, no adventure was too exacting or repugnant for him. For him, it was the nastier (and the more lucrative) the better.

A quick exit

Haraldr Sigurðarson was the classic example of the princely émigré turned professional mercenary. Having been seriously wounded at Stiklarstaðir in the vain attempt to restore his half-brother Óláfr to the Norwegian throne, the young Haraldr had made his way first to Kievan Russia and then to Constantinople where he joined the Varangian Guard and quickly rose to a senior position within its organization. According to Snorri Sturluson, Haraldr arrived there at 'with a great host of men',[263] and in truth, as we shall discuss below, these may have been all he ever commanded. Þjóðólfr Arnórsson refers to eighteen battles fought before he returned to Norway, and it is assumed that these would have been the major engagements in which he and his companions took part as Varangians serving Michael IV:

All have heard that Haraldr / had – often the folk-leader / urged the storm-of-arrows – / eighteen fierce-fought battles. / Glorious king! With gore the / grey eagles' talons you did / redden, wherever you harried, / home here that you journeyed.[264]

Thus, he was to be one of the leading figures (though not its leader) in the Varangian Guard for the next eight years, fighting for the emperor in the Aegean, Anatolia, the Holy Land, Sicily, southern Italy, and Bulgaria before being forced to flee Constantinople.

If we are to believe the Old Norse sources, his exit was actually a spectacular escape and abduction of a Byzantine princess, Mária, the beautiful maiden niece of empress Zoë, after he had exceedingly irritated the empress – which, in fact, was not a difficult thing to do. What was not possible, however, was to run off with the empress' niece when she had no brother and neither of her two sisters had ever married. The only Mária known in the Constantinopolitan court circle at that time was the sister of Michael IV and widow of Stephanos, and she hardly qualified as a maiden.

This, of course, may be a vivid story that was not true. On the other hand, it is possible that Haraldr had some affair in Constantinople with a noblewoman called Mária; it was a common enough name there. Haraldr's apparent amorous exploits must have been generally known in Europe. In the early twelfth century William of Malmesbury gave a passing comment to a similar *affaire du cœur* Haraldr ostensibly had in Constantinople, which suggests the type of tall tale that was current about him as early as this:

> Olaf was succeeded by Harald Harvagra [Hardrada?], Olaf's brother, who had once, as a young man, been in military service with the Byzantine emperor. By the emperor's order he was thrown to a lion for seducing a woman of quality. He choked the great beast by the sheer power of his muscular arms.[265]

As we have discussed previously, Haraldr was not thrown to the lions but thrown in prison, probably for embezzling, only to be released during the civil disobedience that ended in the ousting and blinding of Michael Kalaphates.

Snorri Sturluson has the puzzling statement in his *Heimskringla* that after an emperor's death 'it is custom there that... the Varangians are permitted to have *pólútasvarf*, that is, they had the right to go through the palaces of the late emperor 'where are kept his treasures, and every one may then freely help himself to whatever he lays his hands on'.[266] Snorri has interpreted the term *pólútasvarf* as 'palace-plundering', but he may be in error here, since it appears to come from a Slav word for the collection of tribute or taxes (perhaps with forcible intention). Thus, there is a comment by Constantinus VII Porphyrogenitus in his *De ceremoniis*, where the emperor describes the tax-collecting methods of the Kievan princes: 'At the beginning of November they go on a tax-collecting expedition, which is called by them a circular journey [... εἰς τὰ πολύδια ἃ λέγεται γύρα]'.[267] As we know, before arriving in Constantinople Haraldr had served Yaroslav of Kiev, and Saxo Grammaticus makes a rather critical observation regarding Haraldr's character, saying that he was '*homicidi crimine damnatus*',[268] a remark that might be connected with some act of violence during a tax-collecting expedition. Alternatively, having brutally removed Michael V from the throne, Haraldr may have seized the moment to acquire a little more wealth for himself before the new emperor (in this case, the sisters Zoë and Theodora) had time to get a grip on what must have been an exceedingly chaotic situation in the capital. None of which is more than speculation, of course, but we are well aware of Haraldr's fondness for acquiring gold, gold that he planned to put to good use in the future. And that future lay in Norway.

Haraldr was now in his late twenties. He had known no profession other than that of arms for his entire adult life. He was totally inured to his own discomfort, but uneasy in the rôle of underling to autocratic authority. In the *Advice for the Emperor* it states clearly that Haraldr asked the emperor, Zoë's new husband Constantinus Monomachos – she married him on 11 June 1042, seven weeks after the recovery of the throne – for leave to depart, been refused it, and then took it upon himself to go anyway.[269] Snorri Sturluson describes the actual departure in dramatic detail:

> That same night Haraldr and his men… went to the place where the galleys of the Varangians were anchored. They captured two of them and rowed out into the Golden Horn, and when they came to where the iron chains were stretched across the entrance of the harbour Haraldr ordered his men on both vessels to take to their oars; and those who did not row were to run back to the stern, each with his sleeping bag in hand. So they ran the galleys up on the iron chains. And as soon as they were fast and the momentum was spent, Haraldr ordered them all to run forward. Then the galley on which Haraldr was, plunged forward and through this teetering slid down from the iron chain; but the other galley hung fast on the chain and broke in two, and many were drowned there while some were rescued. In this fashion Haraldr escaped from *Mikligarðr* and sailed into the Black Sea.[270]

In all likelihood this tale of nautical derring-do is correct in its essentials. There was a boom drawn across the mouth of the Golden Horn to defend this natural harbour from enemy shipping, which consisted of an iron chain supported on wooden rafts. According to the anonymous late Byzantine source *Patria*, Tiberius II Constantinus (r. 578–82) is said to have built a fortress (Gr. Φρούριον) at the confluence of the Golden Horn and the Bosporus, though this has been disputed by scholars.[271] Indeed, Tiberius III Apsimar (r. 698–705) and his successor Anastasius II (r. 713–15) are named as possible founders of the fortress, who are also noted as having restored the maritime fortifications of Constantinople. No matter whether it was the second or the third Tiberius who had what was known as the Kastellion of Galata constructed, it was from this harbour fortress that the legendary chain could be stretched to the opposite (southern) shore.[272] The iron chain itself is not mentioned until the 'Umayyad siege of 717, and it was described as thick as a man's arm.[273] The tenth-century chronicler Leo Diakonos mentions the two ends of the chain 'fastened to enormous logs' as the tower of *kentenarion* on the (southern) side of Constantinople and 'a tower of *kastellion*' on the northern shore of the Golden Horn, which was secured as part of the preparations by Nikephoros II Phokas (r. 963–9) against a possible Rus' amphibious assault from the Black Sea.[274] In addition, at least from the time of Manuel I Komnenos (r. 1143–80), there was a similar boom across the Bosporus.[275] It is also known that the same ruse was employed some thirteen-hundred years before by Caius Duilius (consul 260 BC) to escape from the grand harbour in Syracuse,[276] as it was in more recent times by the torpedo ram HMS *Polyphemus* (active 1881–1903) during a simulated attack on Berehaven Harbour, 30 June 1885.

Anyway, safely into the open waters of the Black Sea with a close-knit band of battle seasoned Varangians, Haraldr Sigurðarson now headed for home, a place he had not seen for some twelve years. The first port of call on the return was Kiev to claim from Yaroslav the promised hand of his daughter and to recover his accumulated loot.

From player to king

In the service of Byzantium, Haraldr had enjoyed all sorts of escapades, and while doing so had earned for himself a reputation of being one of the most energetic, enterprising, redoubtable and ruthless warriors of his age. He also acquired for himself a loyal band of hard-bitten adherents. It is Snorri Sturluson who remarks that after Haraldr has been in Constantinople only a short time, the Varangians become deeply attached to him, and in battle they band together. 'And at last Haraldr became the leader of all Varangians.'[277] The men's immediate attachment to the Norwegian Haraldr suggests they too were Scandinavians.

Still, we need to be aware here that, apart from Snorri's self-assured statement, there is no evidence for Haraldr having taken command of the Varangians. Quite the opposite, in fact. For the Byzantine source *Advice for the Emperor* supplies precise details of the ranks that Haraldr (or *Araltes* in his Greek name-form) held as an illustration of how it was both unnecessary and undesirable to promote foreigners, however able they might be, to positions of the highest rank. By way of recognition for his services in the Sicilian and Italian campaigns, Haraldr was first appointed *manglavités* (Gr. μαγγλαβίτης) and later promoted to that of *spatharokandidátos* (Gr. σπαθαροκανδιδᾶτος) on his return with Michael IV from the suppression of the Bulgarian uprising in 1041. The *manglavitai* were armed with a club or *manglavion*, which they carried in procession to clear the way for the imperial retinue. They were commanded by a *prôtospatharios* ('first of the imperial sword-bearers'), an officer of high court rank. The *spatharokandidâtos* was second in rank after the *prôtospatharios*.

In fact, the ceremonial commander of the Varangian Guard was called the *akolouthos* (Gr. ἀκόλουθος); the 'acolyte' to the emperor, due to his constant proximity to the emperor, and his place was to stand immediately behind him in processions or behind the throne at audiences. However, it should be understood that this was a court title rather than a military rank. The military commander of the Varangian Guard, according to Anna Komnene, was commonly known by the generic Greek terms *hegemon* or *archon*.[278] On the other hand, the officer in command of the *manglavitai* held the rank of *prôtomanglavitês* (Gr. πρῶτομαγγλαβίτης), but neither of the two positions held by Haraldr in Constantinople approached such seniority. Indeed, their comparatively modest status is unmistakably acknowledged by the author – now normally accepted as one Kekaumenos, a retired Byzantine general writing in the ten-seventies – of the *Advice for the Emperor*, when he observes with obvious approval that *Araltes* 'did not complain about the titles of *manglavitês* or *spatharokandidâtos* he had been honoured with; but instead, as king [of Norway] he showed good faith and brotherly love towards the Romans'.[279] The terms *manglavitês* and *spatharokandidâtos* were in origin positions or ranks in the emperor's bodyguard, but came to be used as honorific titles in the Constantinopolitan court.

There is no reason, however, to doubt Snorri's claim for Haraldr being popular among his fellow Varangians. One such admirer of Haraldr that we know of was Bolli Bollason, who is probably the most well-known Icelandic Varangian. Bolli's decision to travel south was independent of any Norse lord, and in truth he travelled south against the wishes of Óláfr Haraldsson, whose guest Bolli is at the time of his departure; the Norwegian king lets Bolli depart with a bemused comment about how self-willed Icelanders are. In *Laxdæla saga* Bolli expresses various desires motivating his far-travel, but only a short time after arriving in Constantinople he joins the Varangian Guard and distinguishes himself with excellence and bravery. The narrator comments that no Northmen entered the Varangian Guard before Bolli,[280] but this cannot be true and is probably a literary gesture to enhance Bolli's excellence. It may, however, indicate that the saga-writer believes the Varangians who welcome Bolli into their company are Rus'.

Bolli died sometime when Haraldr was king of Norway, as is recorded at the end of *Sneglu-Halla þáttr*. The tale makes reference to Bolli's military prowess (obviously he was no fop), in ironic contrast to the tale's protagonist:

> Haraldr learned of the deaths of two of his men (*hirðmenn*) from Iceland, Bolli the Elegant and Sarcastic Halli. He said of Bolli, 'The warrior must have fallen victim to spears'. But of Halli he said, 'The poor devil must have burst eating porridge'.[281]

Halli, the hero of this tale, was an impudent Icelander with a quick wit and a talent for verse. Unlike his fellow Norwegians, who derided them as colonial bumpkins, suet-landers (*mörlendingar*), suet-fiends (*mörfjandi*), or laughed at them for preferring buttered porridge (*grautr*) to proper food, Haraldr always had a soft spot for Icelanders and so too for skalds, so little wonder the Icelandic skald Halli became a favourite with the Norwegian king. He slips out of a number of tough spots, like leaving the king's parade to eat buttered porridge, or reciting a ribald poem about Þóra the queen to her face,[282] thanks to his ability to weave skaldic verses at the drop of a spoon. Hence the king's witty reference to Halli's possible cause of death.

As for Bolli, he was already in the employ of the Byzantine emperor when he joined Haraldr's band, possibly attracted by its growing reputation for profitable plundering or accepting a personal invitation. Bolli, after all, had known Haraldr's half-brother Óláfr Haraldsson upon whom he had made a very good impression.[283] Bolli had been born in 1006 to Guðrún Ósvífursdóttir, the winter after the killing of his father Bolli Þorleiksson. Having married Þórdís, the daughter of Snorri Þorgrímsson *góði* of Helgafell, either in 1024 or 1025,[284] Bolli went abroad the following year, leaving his little daughter Herdís to be fostered by her grandmother Guðrún. It could have been the example of his close kinsman Úlfr Óspaksson (the nephew of Guðrún and future marshal of Haraldr),[285] which led him to go abroad to Byzantium. There he spent 'very many winters',[286] before returning home to Iceland. It is probable that, if we are to accept *Sneglu-Halla þáttr* has some truthful base, the brave Bolli may have ended his life in the same way as his father and many other Icelanders, and fallen before the spears of his enemies.

Haraldr, too, was to return to his homeland, the young prince being destined for greater things than a rootless existence of freelancing and freebooting. Looking back at him down the perspectives of history we can see that the decisive turning point of this particular phase of his life came one night in the autumn of 1042, when he hoodwinked his lord and master the emperor and slipped out of Constantinople in a ship weighed down with a king's ransom, a visual corollary of the brilliance (and bloodiness) of his achievements. Disrespectful, yes. For if he was a servant of the emperor, it was only as the jackal serves the lion; he had struck his own bargain, this for me, that for you. Still, to a man like Haraldr wealth was the *vin ordinaire* of existence, but power was champagne. He was in the empire business, not the money business. Else, how explain the fact that he was soon to muscle his way back into Norway pregnant with purpose.

Chapter 4

Northland

Long voyages, by land and by sea, trade, piracy, and violence have generally been thought of as the main characteristics of the viking age, carried out by men with rough hands used to the plough and the wood-axe as well as the sail-sheet, the steering-oar, and the sword-hilt. For these navigators life on the stormy seas was anything but idyllic. Many men perished, the victims of drowning, cold or damp. In bad weather water constantly penetrated the vessel, restless winds and seas threatening to engulf it. The only recourse the crew had was to bale the water out.

No one really knows what set the Northmen on their course. Population pressure in the fjords of the Scandinavian peninsulas has been suggested, but there were large unexploited areas in the hinterland. Travel was undeniably easier by boat than on land, and the Northmen were certainly familiar with the sea. They were to use their nautical knowledge to trade, raid and settle in locations all across Europe and beyond. Then, as in ages to come, it was a point of contention whether the Northmen were better endowed by their greedy and termagant gods for commerce or slaughter. Of course, generalizations are never the whole truth, but robbing your richer neighbour was a simple way of redressing the perceived injustices of nature. Men want land to farm, wealth to make life splendid, or at least bearable, and some of them want dignity and fame. Here there is no mystery. It hardly needs saying that want, greed, self-interest, profit, advantage, describe or qualify it as one will, is endemic in human nature.

Which brings us to trade, and trade's dark sister piracy. Both were essential to the Northmen, for they practised both assiduously; to ignore one or the other is to look with only half an eye or less. When circumstances favoured they were happy to be wandering traders, portable scales and weights being as much as their panoply as spears and shields, but when seas were undefended and settlements lay open to their sleek serpent ships, then they became rough dealers. After all, it did not take much to make a trader into a raider – or vice-versa. In the wise words of the *Hávamál*:

> Betimes must rise / who would take another's / life and win his wealth; // lying down wolf / never got the lamb, / nor sleeping wight slew his foe.[1]

It would thus be wrong to give the impression that overseas adventures were narrowly focused: trading could soon turn to into raiding, while raiding could dissipate itself into settlement, albeit, more often than not, at the insistence of the sword blade. Of course, as always, raiding and trading were never really mutually exclusive activities, and the vikings – warriors, explorers, merchants, pirates – were a powerful people with clear ideas and solutions.

Lest we forget that many of these raiding-cum-trading voyages were undertaken by men whose everyday work was that of a farmer, *bóndi*. The responsibility of running the farm fell to the wife when it happened, as it might, when her husband in the busy times of sowing and harvesting found himself in Russia or in Greece, or in a ship held up by calms or contrary winds in the Aegean or the Sea of Marmara. Runic inscriptions pay suitable homage to many women for their good work. A fine testimony is given to a wife at Hassmyra in Västmanland. In poor prosaic translation the inscription reads:

> The good farmer Holmgöt had the stone erected in memory of Odendis, his wife. Never will there be a better housewife at Hassmyra to take care of the farm. Balle *rauða* (the Red) cut these runes. To Sigmund Odendis was a good sister.[2]

Note that the lady in question was the one who took 'care of the farm', a solid reference to the centrality of women in viking-age Scandinavian society. Indeed, this runic inscription reflects a Scandinavian social pattern, in which women were more the equals of men than in other parts of mediaeval Europe. Examples of influential women may be found in *Landnámabók* and in several of the Old Icelandic sagas, for example *Laxdæla saga*.[3] Still, for man or woman, farming was not an easy option to follow in viking-age Scandinavia.

Between a rock and a hard place

A good deal of the work of Adam of Bremen deals with viking-age Scandinavia, and the fourth book of his *Gesta* is a *Descriptio insularum aquilonis*, 'Account of the islands of the north', which makes Adam the earliest known German geographer. Because he was anxious to credit the Bremen archbishopric with Christianizing the rough inhabitants of the far north, Adam spent much labour on describing the geography of that part of the world. Here the Saxon cleric explains that Norway was only suitable for pastoral farming because of its high mountains and cold climate, thus 'the land produces the most powerful fighting men, who are not enfeebled by any luxury of produce and so are more likely to take the fight to other nations than to be molested by anybody'. He continues:

Thus they are forced by daily lack of commodities to travel the whole world, bringing back from their forays a plentiful supply of the riches of all countries, and so they sustain the penury of their own.[4]

He was not alone in this appraisal of Norway; all outside observers agreed it was a poor country, blighted by rain, snow, acid soils and darkness. In a world where life has managed a toehold, that life there was *tough*. And adaptable too. Warlord-infested, war-ready Norway was the ideal reservoir for anybody looking for experienced and ruthless fighters, this cold, high, stony land with long winter nights and endless summer days that grew only one crop thickly, a breeder of pirates and tyrants. Even today, less than 10 per cent of the Fenno-Scandian landmass is cultivated; in Norway, one per cent of the modern kingdom's area. Grain, deciduous trees and fruit will not thrive outside those enclaves.

To be brief about the matter, the domesticate economy of viking-age Scandinavia was heavily characterized by animal husbandry, and cattle as the most important of the livestock. That importance is reflected in the language: the word for cattle and the word for money are identical, *fé*.[5] Cattle were the only way you could maintain, show, and trade wealth in this winter locked, craggy land. A man was only as good as his herd. Cattle are the oldest form of wealth, and still one of the most sensible. They produce their own interest, in the form of calves; they supply milk, blood, horn, leather, and meat – but meat is not part of the deal very often. You do not want to eat up your capital. What you want is to grow your herd.

Similarly in Scandinavia, cattle were raised for many purposes. Dairy cows provided dairy products that could be consumed fresh, but more importantly, they were turned into foods such as cheese, butter, and *skyr*,[6] curds, which could be stored over the winter months when cows stopped producing fresh milk. It is still eaten in Iceland today; many visitors find it unattractive at first, but the taste for it grows with use. It is thick and pasty, with a clean, sour flavour. When served with cream and sugar, it was a dish fit for a king. Second in importance to viking-age farmers were sheep. Sheep were raised for their fleece, their milk, and their meat. However, both sheep and cattle were small animals by today's standards, the sheep springy, the cattle multi-coloured and unshapely, yielding less meat and milk. Cereals such as barley (the main crop), rye and oats (introduced after 800, probably from the Slav lands to the south) were sporadically cultivated in so grudging a climate, and farming was augmented by fishing, fowling and hunting. Most of the barley harvested would be malted to brew beer (more work for women), and most days households would live on grain crushed, soaked and heated with butter or whey to form *grautr*, the dish Icelanders were supposed to find irresistible, and others unavoidable.

Before we leave this particular topic, we should talk very briefly about one of the new techniques associated with archaeology, namely palaeoclimatology. Armed with pollen analysis, lava and ice-core sampling, specialists in this field can offer a reasonably clear picture of the changes and constant features of the northern climate over the first millennium of the present era. Hence the discovery that for most of the viking-age temperatures and rainfall were not dramatically different from what they are today, which has had a sedative effect on theories inspired by the vision of a lush and sunny Iceland. So Hrafn-Flóki Vilgerðarson was not far wrong when he returned to Norway from this island nestled below the Arctic Circle and named it *Ísland*, ice land. Moreover, he had little good to say about the place, it being, after all, mostly a desert land of ice sheets, glaciers, and cooled lava. Nevertheless, one of his crew, Þórólfr, reported that every blade of grass dripped with golden-hued butter, an attractive image at a time when butter was the means for long-term storage of excess dairy production, representing wealth and easy living. For his optimism, Þórólfr earned for himself the nickname *smjör*, Butter.[7]

To stay alive in Scandinavia was harder work than in warmer parts of Europe, and demanded fiercer exploitation of natural resources: iron, timber, and a vast reserve of forest and upland wild life, surrounded by seas full of fish. The Norse farmer was offered a choice: to live strenuously at home, or leave for new, richer pastures.

The Norse sword was then the longest and the Norse arm the strongest, land being the only wealth, and its ownership the sole foundation of power, privilege, or dignity. As no man could win or hold possession without the strong arm to defend it, every freeholder was a warrior, every warrior a freeholder, each and everyone kitted out and hardy. It should therefore be no surprise that the Northmen were a race of hardy farmers and fishermen who knew all the arts of the crofter and all the wiles of the sea. It goes without saying of course that the sword arm was a saleable commodity, and Northmen, perhaps salted with a greater measure of ruthlessness and duplicity than was the norm, were the epitome of the fighting adventurer throughout most of this period. They readily left home and stained swords with blood, rather than staying at home and keeping them shiny, unsullied by blood or the grindstone. The Northmen had a fitting name for a fellow like that, a *kolbítr* (coal-biter), a scathing reference to an idle person who always sits by the fire.

If this was their hope, then some were ready to try their luck in a military market where the top buyer in our period of study was of course the Byzantine emperor. He certainly paid well, offering forty gold pieces per annum to Varangians. Thus it is that the Varangian Guard is one of the very few mercenary units whose history can be counted in centuries. The length of its existence (though not the number of battles in which it fought) is only surpassed by the Papal Guard. But where the Swiss had only to journey over the Alps into next-door Italy, the Northmen had to travel far beyond their known inhospitable world.

Arabic silver, Byzantine gold

For safekeeping Gotlanders (as did Northmen in general) buried their wealth in hoards, many of which they never returned to retrieve. It is presumed that most hoards were buried in the ground as a security measure, but for some reason the owner or owners failed to return and collect them. No fewer than 50,000 Arabic silver *dirham* coins of the eight to tenth centuries have been found on the Baltic Sea island, compared with only 35,000 in all the rest of Scandinavia put together.

In Scandinavia the demand for silver was constant as it had no indigenous source itself. In particular, silver coins, which the Scandinavians themselves did not mint, were much coveted (in Sweden, for instance, coins were not minted until the late tenth century). T.S. Noonan has concluded that while a portion of this great number of coins would have been obtained through raids, bribes, payments to mercenaries, such as Varangians, and other non-commercial factors, most of them were accrued through trade.[8] Thus, silver was the main lure that brought Gotland merchants deep into Russia, silver that had been mined in the Hindu Kush and Afghanistan and minted in Baghdad, Cairo, Damascus, Isfahan and Tashkent to a degree of purity and consistency in weight which could not be bettered anywhere in Europe, let alone in Scandinavia.

Dirhams are useful source material, for besides quotations from the Qur'an, they display the place and time of their minting, and sometimes a personal name or other more specific information. There was no real substitute for the *dirham*, and when the supply faltered, as in the eight-thirties and eight-fifties, or ceased, as a money-substitute silver could be fragmented and traded by weight, without asking anyone's permission: hack-silver appears in hoards wherever trading was brisk throughout the period.

Gotland may be famous for its Arabic silver coin hoards, but the hoard from Oxarve (now in the Royal Cabinet of Coins, Stockholm) is the only one to date in Scandinavia, let alone the island, that contains solely Byzantine coins in a large number – 123 silver *miliaresia*, to be exact, which is equivalent to just over ten gold coins, the annual pay of an ordinary ranker in the Byzantine army.[9] Though the coins date between 945 and 1055, 90 per cent of them are from the end of the period, the reign of Constantinus IX Monomachos (1042–55). If this is indeed the pay of a Varangian returning from Byzantine employ, he would have been a near contemporary of Haraldr Sigurðarson.

Of the vast treasure that Haraldr himself collected from the empire, barely a coin must remain un-melted – only twenty Byzantine coins have been found to date in all Norway. Of course, as we cannot be sure that all hoards have been uncovered, coin hoard data must always be interpreted with caution. Silver, compact and valuable, lent itself well to long-distance travel and was easily recycled, alloyed, and refined. Little wonder, therefore, silver was one of the most widely used forms of durable, movable wealth and became an important medium of exchange.

As a final point at this juncture, in Scandinavia the economy was not monetized but multilayered, with barter at the lowest level and something approaching a commodity, supply-and-demand economy at the highest level of long-distance exchange where items were fed into the economic system. With this in mind it is perhaps not surprising those Byzantine coins from Oxarve, which were only valid as coins within the empire, could not be used as coins in Scandinavia. But the metal value of the coin together with its imperial image certainly rendered these coins an exceptional exchange value outside Byzantium. These coins did not lose value as no tax was put on them. The mainstay of the Byzantine economy pre-1092 was the pure gold *nomisma* (literally 'coin'), a small thick coin struck at seventy-two from a Roman pound (327.45 g) of gold. A slightly lighter (by one-twelfth) but otherwise identical coin was first struck under Nikephoros II Phokas (r. 963–9). This was called *tetarteron nomisma* (literally '[lacking] a quarter coin'), and the older coin became the *histamene nomisma* (literally 'full weight coin'). In practice, it was not important to distinguish the two types as payments were made by weight, not number, of coins. Under Michael IV (r. 1034–41) the purity of Byzantine gold coins was gradually adulterated, falling to 26 per cent by the accession of Alexios I Komnenos in 1081. Finite supplies of metals for coinage meant that Byzantine emperors were more reticent about letting large amounts of coins leave the empire than their Islamic neighbours.

The fictionalization of fact

Not only the hirsute owner of a fine line in hairstyles, Haraldr *hárfagri* is also credited by mediaeval historiographies – in our context especially the kings' sagas (viz. *Morkinskinna*, *Fagrskinna* and *Heimskringla*) – to be the first king of all Norway. According to these sagas, it was under his long rule (d. 933) that Norway enters into the full daylight of history. Spuriously the son of Hálfdan *svarti* (the Black), a petty king of Ringerike in south-eastern Norway, it was Haraldr, while still a youth and after a savage struggle with the independence-loving old noble families and wealthy farmers, who brought the whole realm under his steely sway: and according to the same unification mythology, it was his descendants who reigned as kings throughout the following centuries.

Of course, there is always another story. But it is the stories told by the strong, the stories of kings, which are believed in the end. More recent research has raised doubts about the trustworthiness of these traditions, questioning whether Norway as the exclusive property (viz. family land, or *óðöl*) of the *hárfagri*-dynasty was indeed a viking-age achievement, or rather a mediaeval construction. The earliest reference to *óðöl* is in the *Bersöglisvísur* ('Out-spoken Verses') of Sigvatr Þórðarson, addressed to the young king Magnús I Óláfsson *góði* in around 1037. There, it means the private land of the *bœndr* threatened by confiscation or damage; according to Sigvatr (and later skalds), a king who interfered with *óðöl* was a tyrant,[10] which would account for the legend of how Haraldr *hárfagri* had caused the emigration to Iceland by a general seizure of such estates in the ninth century. Exactly who Haraldr had been, and if indeed he brought the whole of Norway to heel, are now questions of some complexity and much learned debate, particularly so among state-formation addicts. This hegemony (if that was what it was) may have been a fairly loose one at times, but this discussion shall not concern us here *per se*; suffice it to say that Haraldr, a conquering over-king or not, probably began the political consolidation of Norway, a process that was continued by his (unrelated) successors.

Equally, it has been pointed out that it was not until the accession of Haraldr Sigurðarson that we can begin to talk about a stable dynasty, his sons, grandson, and great-grandsons succeeding him in due order. Though Haraldr's predecessors claimed to be descendants of Haraldr *hárfagri*, their lineage is questionable at best.[11] *Haralds saga Sigurðarsonar* only traces his lineage to his father and (half)-brother.[12] The view held by most scholars today is that the *hárfagri*-dynasty ended with Haraldr Greycloak Gunnhildarson in 976 when he was enticed to Denmark with Norwegian help and cut down in the Limfjord. As such, an argument can therefore be made that the accession of Haraldr Sigurðarson established a new dynasty, for his connection to Haraldr *hárfagri* is a reconstruction carried out after his death; as Haraldr *hárfagri* was his political forerunner, so also he must be his common ancestor. Thus, Óláfr Tryggvason and Óláfr Haraldsson, along with Haraldr Sigurðarson, had their lineages reconnected to the *hárfagri*-dynasty in the mid-twelfth century, an ugly and troubled time, a period of vicious civil war when a large number of pretenders fought for the Norwegian throne.

Originally nicknamed *lúfa*, (Mop-hair), legend has it – it is impossible to verify – that, rejected by the proud Gyða for not being the lord of all Norway, Haraldr made a solemn vow neither to cut nor comb his hair till he had brought the whole land under his sway or else die in the attempt to do so. But after he had fulfilled his vow, not only did he marry the lady (and many wives besides), but had his curls cut, cleansed and combed too, and was called thereafter *hárfagri* (Fine-hair) for his magnificent head of silky hair.[13] The legend, twisted and ornamented over time, undoubtedly exaggerated the reality. But there can be little doubt of Haraldr's existence as a powerful *local* ruler in Norway. He had at least nine sons – some accounts say twenty – who reached manhood. What was unquestionable, of course, was Haraldr being the father of the ill-famed fratricide Eiríkr *blóðøx* (Eric Bloodaxe). What is not commonly known, however, is that Eiríkr was also the maternal great-grandson of Sigurðr *ormr í auga* (Snake-in-the-Eye, viz. a menacing gaze like that of a snake, such is mentioned in the eddaic poem *Rígsþula*),[14] one of the sons of Ragnarr *loðbrók*.

Nomenclature

The people of the Scandinavian peninsulas shared a common (Northern) culture and as a group could be regarded as Northmen or people from the North. It is equally clear according to Alfred Smyth, that contemporary Northmen recognized differences between, and divisions within, their own cultural and political sphere.[15] The Northmen spoke Old Norse, which they called *dönsk tunga* (L. *vox danica*), the Danish tongue, but no one is quite sure why they referred to their language as such. With minor variations, this language was spoken throughout the Scandinavian lands during the viking age. During this period, language was no barrier to communication across the Scandinavian lands; from the vast white island of Greenland (so named by Eiríkr *rauða* to make it sound more enticing to prospective settlers, a practice still known to land developers) to the Baltic Sea, nearly the same language was spoken throughout. However, there is evidence that, despite the common language, a man's homeland could be identified by his speech. Some scholars today would go further and say that by the start of the Norse era, significant differences already existed between East Norse (Sweden and Denmark) and West Norse (Norway and the North Atlantic settlements such as Iceland) dialects.

Though not nomadic, Northmen were a people on the move. From the first memorable raid on Saint Cuthbert's monastery on the tidal island of Lindisfarne in 793, until the battle of Stamford Bridge just outside York in 1066, the vikings of Norway, Denmark and Sweden were the most powerful and influential people in northern Europe. Understandably, the aspect of Norse society that most captures the modern popular imagination is the viking raids. But that, of course, is another very long story, which will be touched upon later. What does concern us here, however, is the fact that the pagan, pre-Christian past was not far away. The new world religion, Christianity, took a long time to penetrate the hearts and minds of the Northmen.

As for that powerful and emotive word 'viking', there is still less than full agreement as to the original meaning of the two Old Norse nouns *víking* (feminine) and *víkingr* (masculine). In the written record they certainly mean, *víking*, piracy or piratical raid, *víkingr*, a pirate or raider, and *í víkingu*, on viking raids.[16] The first element of the words, *vík-*, has been explained in various ways. A viking was one who lay up or lurked in or came from a bay, fjord, or creek (*vík*), an element preserved in place names such as Reykjavík, Iceland (Smoke Bay), Lerwick, Shetland (Mud

Bay), and Uig, Lewis (Bay). On this basis it has been suggested that the term may have originated with pirates who haunted such inlets, from which they emerged to waylay passing vessels. Alternatively, he was a man of the camp (OE *wîc*, *wîcing*, cf. L *vicus*), an element preserved in place names such as Wijk bij Duursted, Holland, Quentovic, France, and Ipswich, England. On this basis it has been suggested that the term may refer to a warrior, or a man of the town, specifically a seafaring man or trader. Reference to the Old Norse verb *víkja* made him a fast mover, or one who turned, receded into the distance, made a detour or a tour away from home, which should not surprise us given his strategy was one of mobility, surprise and speed. Whichever interpretation is followed, the origins of the word 'viking' seem to refer to an activity rather than a specific people or ethnic group.

Even so, *wîcingas*, viking, is the word frequently used by the Anglo-Saxon sources to describe raiders and settlers from Scandinavia, while the Carolingian sources prefer *Nordmanni*, Northmen. Both words include, without differentiation, Danes and Norwegians. Until the mid-ninth century it is possible to make a broad distinction between Norwegians, who settled northern and western Scotland and the Northern and Western Isles and were active in the Irish Sea, and Danes, who raided the North Sea and Channel coasts, but thereafter the distinction becomes blurred. If anything, it was the Irish annalists who were a lesson to all with their division of Norse invaders into fair foreigners, Norwegians (OI *Finngaill*), and dark foreigners, Danes (OI *Dubgaill*), which perhaps gives a reflection of predominant hair colouring, but sadly it was a lesson no one bothered to heed. Though some argue that it seems more appropriate to see 'fair' and 'dark' as terms for 'old' and 'new', the Irish annalists were probably correct with Norwegians and Danes; the second term, according to Colmáman Etchingham, 'most commonly denotes Vikings active in Britain, who were primarily Danes and intervened in Ireland in 851–2 and 875–7'.[17]

Thus, the Welsh chroniclers, for example, made no such clear distinction. The Danes coming in by way of England and the Norwegians by way of Ireland were pretty well all black: black Gentiles (MW *y Kenedloed duon*), black Northmen (MW *y Normanyeit duon*), black host, black pagans (MW *y paganiaid duon*), black devils, and the like. Still, at the end of the day the shocked victims (Christians) of a quick-in quick-out viking raid could not be expected to inquire too nicely into which island or promontory, what fjord or mountainside whence sprang these black-hearted northerners (non-Christians) who seemed to 'haunt the tide'. So, when it all comes down to it, the modern use of the term viking is a convenience. Without it, we would need a bulky three-part phrase referring to a specific activity, by people from a specific geographical region and living in a specific time period, such as, for example, pirate, Danish, ninth century.[18]

At this point it needs to be mentioned that the viking adventure in Russia was part of a great Scandinavian enterprise that stretched north and west across the

Atlantic, south into the Mediterranean and east into Russia and beyond – but that is the historian's overview, armed with the luxury of hindsight. For the individual boatload of well-equipped, weapon-handy vikings, the pattern was much smaller, local and personal. There was no grand scheme behind the process of raiding and settlement in clannishly divided Ireland, to take one geographical example; it must have happened piecemeal, its attractions spread by word of mouth, family by family along the Norwegian seaboard. A single summertime's hit-and-run up and down the Hibernian coastline could have made all the difference if the harvest came in under expectations. This brings us to the constant need for land to farm and for waters to fish. Thus it was that Ireland became a talked-about destination, and only later was a political dimension added, when the kingship of Dublin was created. Dublin would remain a Hiberno-Norse stronghold – the Irish triumph of 902, which gave them Dublin, proved short lived – until its seizure by the Anglo-Normans (really Cambro-Normans), led by Richard fitz Gilbert de Clare (better remembered under his cognomen of Strongbow), in September 1170.

Serving both Christ and the pagan gods

The process of Christianity used to be conceptualized as one of conversion, effectively the replacement of one set of ideas with another, but it is clear that what happened was in fact more nuanced and prolonged. In one sense, there is no doubt that Scandinavia in the eighth century was a 'chow mein' of tribal territories each with its own traditional beliefs, and yet only three and half centuries later took its place on the European political stage as the three Christian states of Norway, Sweden and Denmark. However, the degree to which this outward transformation reflects deep social change and actual spiritual practice is less clear.

The young were presumably brought up Christians of sorts; but their religion was probably only skin-deep. As for the old, well old beliefs died hard to say the least, and the values and customs of Christendom meant little to them compared to those of the gods they had worshipped and sacrificed to and obeyed since they were old enough to think. So many pagan and Christian ideas existed side by side in Norse society.

To cite an example of this, if we take the testimony of the *Landnámabók* we hear of the Icelander Glúmr, who still prays in a genial way to a Christian cross, with the words 'A blessing on the old ones, a blessing on the young'. This tallies well with the half-Christian, half-heathen expressions found in much eleventh-century Norse poetry. There were other Icelanders less committed, like Helgi Eyvindarson *inn magri* (the Skinny), one of Iceland's first settlers and a man who had received baptism.[19] He exemplifies the comfortable overlap between pagan and Christian beliefs; Helgi called his farmstead *Kristnes*, that is Christ's headland, and 'believed in Christ, and yet made vows to Þórr for sea voyages and in tight corners and for everything that struck him of real importance'.[20] A sensible fellow.

This episode reminds us of the story of Hallfreðr and his shipmates who are keen to leave Norway (recently Christianized) and reach a land where the old ways persist. They decide to leave their destination up to the whims of their traditional and trusted gods, declaring that they will give offerings to Freyr if they get a wind for Sweden (still a pagan land), or to Þórr or Óðinn if the wind carries them straight to Iceland.[21] The Norse sources show that the appeal to chance decided matters that educated Christians usually left to reason.

Everyone who knows anything about Northmen knows who Þórr is, anglicized as Thor, and they know he is not the blond, beardless man depicted in motion pictures and comics. The myths and poems tell us he is red-haired and bearded, strong, by far the strongest of all the gods, and easy to anger. He is the powerful protector of gods and of men. He is straightforward where his father Óðinn is cunning, good-natured where his father is devious. Þórr was undoubtedly the most popular god of this period (as attested by place names, personal names, runic inscriptions, and hammer symbols in stone and metal), a patron of farmers, fishermen and warriors. This was the god of the moment, the one you could trust, the one to placate. The hammer pendants worn by men and women, and often buried with them, were charms against misfortune, like crosses, as an anti-Christian symbol. Þórr was something of a larger-than-life character and was not particularly bright. He was also a serial rapist and pulverizer of giants and giantesses, the herculean wielder of the phallic hammer Mjöllnir, the dwarf-made lightning-maker, and protector of his sisters. His following seem to have drawn strength from his strength; however it was used or abused. He alone kept the loyalty of his followers for centuries after they had accepted to be washed with the waters of baptism, and still cherished him in folktales as a sort of Desperate Dan.

At least one of the sons of the aforementioned Helgi Eyvindarson sons might be also of 'mixed faith' if not a Christian. He obviously doubted the belief in Þórr, for when Þórr's 'oracle guided him [Helgi] north of the island [Iceland] Hrólfr asked Helgi whether he was planning to sail to the Arctic Ocean if Þórr told him to go there'.[22] In Hrólfr's opinion, unlike that of his father, following Þórr's advice was not obligatory; on the contrary, it might be absurd or even harmful.

Another sensible fellow like Helgi was Örvar-Oddr (Arrow-Odd). When he travels to the Holy Land, like a good pilgrim he bathes in the river Jordan. However, though a baptized Christian, Oddr still wears a magic shirt woven in silk and embroidered with gold. The magic immunity of the shirt protects him from cold, fatigue, fire, hunger and of course from the bite of iron, the protective virtue of which is unchanged by his immersion in the sanctified waters of Jordan.[23] The Jordan's 'seal of approval' on Oddr's magic shirt is nevertheless in keeping with the saga's easy and accommodating dovetailing of heathenism and Christianity.

The supernatural plays an important part in the story of Oddr, and is frequently recognizable as the familiar magic of the folktale – those arrows that return to their shooter, his inviolable shirt, his encounters with giants and monsters – while our hero is actually nicknamed for his magic arrows. But it would be wrong to see *Örvar-Odds saga* as nothing more than a fairytale. A darker side to the narrative gradually emerges as the near-tragic entailment of Oddr's preternaturally extended lifespan becomes clear: he must stand by as his closest companions die before him. When he was an infant, a *völva* or 'staff bearer' – a seeress – predicted that he would be killed by his own horse Faxi, at the place he was born (instead of on the sea or in battle as a good viking should), after a lifespan of 300 years.[24] Before he leaves to go a-viking, Oddr kills his horse, buries it deep, and leaves home vowing never to return. Heavy with years (and glory) and mighty homesick, he indeed returns home. While walking over the grave of Faxi, he mocks the old prophecy only to trip over the skull of his dead horse. Out slithers a snake, the bite of which leaves him dead. Thus, the prophecy was fulfilled.[25]

Indeed, the bizarre manner of Örvar-Oddr's demise has a parallel in that of the Kievan prince Oleg the Prophet, who likewise receives the prophecy that he will suffer death from the skull of his own horse. Prophecies can seldom be avoided, no matter what elaborate attempts of avoidance are made. However, the general sentiment among the Northmen is best expressed by the *Hávamál*:

> Don't say, 'It's been a good day' till sundown. / Don't say, 'She's been a good wife' till she's buried. / Don't say, 'It's a good sword' till you've tested it. / Don't say, 'The ice is safe' till you've crossed it. / Don't say, 'The beer is good' till you've drunk the last of it.[26]

In other words, believe no prophecy until it bears fruit, a prudent, realistic, and somewhat cynical view of human affairs and the world.

We can also go as far to say that sometimes Norsemen would receive baptism to improve trade with the Christian peoples; sometimes they would accept it only for the sake of the presents handed out to new believers; sometimes the new faith was embraced in prudent obedience to a king. Even if the convert attended church while on dry land, he often continued to sacrifice to his old gods when sailing the seas.

In this respect it may be of interest to hear what the monk of Saint-Gall (usually identified with Notker the Stammerer) in the Frankish empire said of the process when a group of Norsemen were baptized at the court of Louis *le Pieux*, the loyal son and pious successor of Charlemagne.[27] When the gifts failed to suffice for all, they tore the presented fabrics into smaller pieces and divided them amongst themselves. We are told by one of those Norsemen present:

'I have gone through this washing business here twenty times already, and I have been dressed in excellent clothes of perfect whiteness; but a sack like this is more fit for clodhoppers than for warriors. If I were not afraid of my nakedness, for you have taken away my own clothes and have given me no new ones, I would soon leave your wrap and your Christ as well.'[28]

Norse pagans called Christ (*Kristr*) White Christ (*Hvitakristr*), probably because those baptized into his service wore white clothes, *albæ*, on first taking that service.

The Old Norse sagas suggest that after the Icelanders accepted Christianity, baptized Christians continued to observe some of the pagan ways. *Eyrbyggja saga* tells that Þóroddr and his men were lost at sea and presumably drowned. At their funeral feast, Þóroddr and the others walked in to the room, all soaking wet. The saga author comments that if drowned men attended their own funeral feast, it was a sure sign that Rán, the goddess of the sea, had accepted the drowned men. Thus, the guests at the feast thought the appearance of the men was a good omen. The author adds that at the time of the saga, many baptized Christians still held pagan beliefs.[29]

The stranger-god

There is probably nothing harder to grasp, for those of us brought up within a monotheistic tradition of religion and spirituality (of whatever religious persuasion, or none), than the mental world of paganism (as Christians called it). Its two most important features were that religion – for which the Northmen had no one-word equivalent – was a matter of cult acts rather than of dogma, faith or belief; and that the world was full of gods – humanoid but superhuman, polymorphic but individual, strong but not invincible, violent, ardent and passionate – the chosen defenders against the immediate threats of nature and man. The gods were powerful beings with whom it was necessary to come to an accommodation in order to survive and prosper, but one did not have to entirely trust them or even like them in the process. To foster the two-way trust that was needed for such a relationship, Northmen frequented sacred places, ate and drank in the gods' honour, and offered gifts and sacrifices in return for luck and protection. They made offerings to the larger group of gods, the *Æsir*, for victory, and to the smaller, the *Vanir*, for good harvests and fertility.[30] In return, they expected that their prayers would be answered.

In Rouen, the great chief Rollo (more about him later) is apparently resting at peace in the cathedral; but his conversion from paganism to Christianity may have been less than perfect. According to the chronicler Adhémar, writing a century later:

[A]s his death drew near he went mad and had a hundred Christian prisoners beheaded in front of him in honour of the gods whom he had worshipped, and in the end distributed one hundred pounds of gold round churches in honour of the true god in whose name he had accepted baptism.[31]

The uneven, plodding and imperfect acceptance of the new god side-by-side with vigorous cults of the old ones can be explained by the fact that the Norse remodelled themselves on patterns they found among the people they pillaged and tormented, in so far as these patterns were *useful* to them: Frankish and Saxon influences in their dress, brooches, swords, belts and harness is obvious, down to small details. One example of this is the Frisian trefoil sword belt buckles, which after having been imported or looted by Northmen were transformed into brooches worn by their women, thus undergoing a rather radical transformation and cultural redefinition.[32] The Northmen did not rush to fill a vacuum, but were adopted to reinforce what was already there: kingships, lordships, cult of war, festivity, funerals and poetry. Widukind of Corvey, a well-informed contemporary source (*c*. 970), reported that 'the Danes had been Christian of old, but all the same they used to serve idols with gentile ceremony', because they believed that 'Christ was indeed a god, but there were other gods greater then he'.[33] If Widukind was right, the stage at which other gods ceased to be gods would come much later.

Unlike Judaism and Christianity, there was little connection between the Norse paganism and morality. A Northman lost the favour of the gods not by breaking some universal commandment, but by offending the gods themselves in some way. Thus, particularly with regards to the last, Norse paganism must be seen in the context of a Norse world in which the line between men and gods was at best blurred. Jewish and Christian polemic worked hard and very successfully to ridicule paganism, and even now, influenced as we are by outdated nineteenth-century romantic reconstructions of Germanic–Nordic myth, we tend to picture the different gods and goddesses that defined any form of polytheism in the terms their opponents chose: a range of larger-than-life characters, with dubious habits and morals, family tensions worthy of a soap opera and a range of fabulous powers usually used (like thunderbolts) irresponsibly and to the disadvantage of humankind. This was a wilful representation. Polytheism was much more nuanced and complex than its monotheistic critics saw, or wanted to let on. Good romping tales of divine peccadilloes were only part of the picture. The point was that the range of divinities, their different characteristics, responsibilities and family relationships represented an ambitious attempt to classify the world, to explain (and dispute) the nature of power and social relations, to understand the cosmos and humanity's place in it.

For the Northmen, the true god was a living man with a single eye, a travelling cloak, a broad brimmed hat, and this man, Óðinn, knew the secrets of every heart and the destinies of all men and women. On his earthly travels, Óðinn appears under various disguises and names such as *Heriafoðr*, 'Father of war bands', *Alðafoðr*, 'All-father', *Yggr*, 'Terrible', *Grímnir*, 'Hooded One', *Harbarðr*, 'Grey Beard' – he had other names, too many to list in this place – but usually as a one-eyed old man, cowled and hooded.[34] The facial scars Óðinn retains from his self-mutilation make him (in some accounts) recognizable when he appears in his wanderer aspect, though he often pulls hood or hat down over his face in an attempt to disguise his features. Disguised as a member of one of the lowest rungs of Norse society, dependant on the goodwill of his 'fellow men' (which he traditionally ascertains through *Hávamál*, stanzas 2–4), he goes about largely unnoticed, discovers the wilful pride of kings and bestows blessings with one hand while taking them away with the other. He only reveals his true nature at the last moment (if at all) and just before he disappears again. In *Ynglinga saga* and *Völsunga saga*, among other sagas, he appears in the guise of a harmless old man with drooping hat and dark (often grey) cloak as well as a staff to replace his trusted spear (though sometimes he carries that one as well). Yet harmless he was not.

He had been hanged from a tree, had been pierced by the point of a spear, had suffered hunger and thirst, had died, and had been reborn.[35] He could also raise the dead.[36] He was revered as the 'god of the hanged'.[37] Even kings could be sacrificed to him by being hanged and pierced with a spear, as was king Víkarr.[38] The sacral king, like the shaman, served as a link between human society and the gods. The king could perform the correct ritual to make good things happen or bad things cease. If the king failed to set matters right, he could be held responsible and pay for his failure with his own life.[39]

It is also unlikely to be a coincidence that several of Óðinn's names refer to him as the god of the gallows, and some of the myths relate how he could wake the hanging dead and interrogate them about the future. Hanging people are shown on several picture stones from the island of Gotland, and a tree full of hanging human bodies is also depicted on one of the fragments of the tapestry from the Oseberg ship burial in Norway. Obviously, there is a disturbing similarity to aspects of Christian myth, that is to say, a god hanging on a tree, pierced by a spear, thirsting, yet all this had happened a long time before Jesus Christ. With that, Óðinn demands particular attention, since this deity helps to shed light on Norse paganism and within the context of early Christianity.

As the head of the Norse gods, Óðinn lends a monotheistic quality to Norse paganism and can be interpreted as a proto-Christ figure. Óðinn is the first god to live and die on earth, and the only god to live 'until the end of time'.[40] Most importantly, he is the creator of mankind itself; Óðinn is said to have fashioned

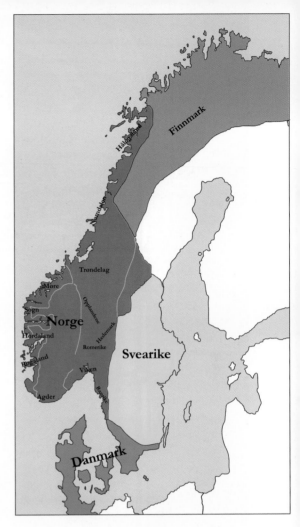

1. (Right) Norway at the time of
Óláfr II Haraldsson.

2. (Below) The Byzantine empire at
the death of Basil II.

3. (Above) A stained-glass window housed in Lerwick's town hall, which depicts HARADVS • HARDRADA • REX • NORVEGIÆ, Haraldr *harðráði*, king of Norway. (© Nic Fields)

4. (Below) Panoramic view of Stiklestad. (Sven Rosborn)

5. (Right) Composite image depicting the Ledberg rune stone (Ög 181), Östergötland, Sweden. The inscription reads: 'Bisi placed this stone in memory of Þorgautr … his father / and Gunna, both. Thistle mistletoe casket'. The last three words are perhaps a rhyming incantation, or *galdr*. (Maksim)

6. (Below) Practical and beautiful, Norse swords (Haithabu, Wikingermuseum) were carefully balanced for maximum effect as slashing weapons, and were designed to be used single handed. Their pattern-welded blades were double-edged and about ninety centimetres long. (Viciarg)

Das Langschwert war die typische Waffe des Kriegers in der Wikingerzeit. Prunkschwerter waren darüber hinaus Zeichen eines sozialen Ranges.

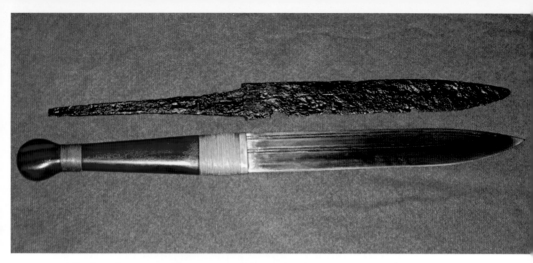

7. Blade of a seventh-century Merovingian *scramasax* from Weingarten, Württemberg, alongside a conjectural reconstruction. (Bullenwächter)

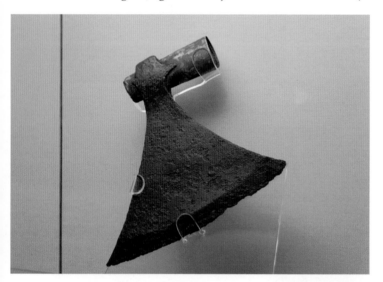

8. (Above) Dane axe with a copper alloy socket (London Docklands Museum) recovered in the nineteen-twenties from the Thames near the Old London Bridge, and (right) a replica of a Dane axe based on an eleventh-century original housed in the Tower of London. ([Above] mattbuck, [right] Grimr032125)

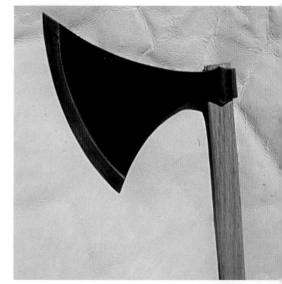

9. (Above) the Gjermundbu helmet (Museum of Cultural History, University of Oslo), and (right) a full-scale replica (Pons, Le Donjon). ([above] NTNU Vitenskapsmuseet, [right] © Esther Carré)

10. This is the prow end of the *Skidbladner* (ON *Skiðblaðnir*, named after the magic ship of the god Freyr), a full-scale reconstruction of the ship found in the Gokstad burial mound, now laid up at Brookpoint in Haroldswick on Unst, the northernmost island of the Shetland archipelago. (© Nic Fields)

11. (Above) the Skuldelev 5 wreck (Roskilde, Vikingeskibsmuseet), and (left) the *Sebbe Als* from Augustenborg, Denmark, under sail, the first (launched 1969) of four full-scale reconstructions of the Skuldelev 5 wreck. ([Above] Casiopeia, [left] Steen Weile)

12. Varangian rune stone (Vg 184), Västergötland, Sweden. On many of the Swedish rune stones there are references to men who died 'eastwards in Greece' (i.e. Byzantium). (Berig)

13. A copy of the brightly painted rune stone at Pilgårds (G 280), on the Baltic Sea island of Gotland. The runic inscription reads: 'Hegbjörn raised this stone glaring (and his) brothers Röðvisl, Östen, Ámundur (?), who have had stones raised in memory of Hrafn south of Rufstein. They came far and wide in *aifur*. Vífill bade…' (Berig)

14. Varangian casual graffito scratched onto the marble balustrade, west gallery of Hagia Sophia. The opening letters (as read in 1967 by Professor S.B.F. Jansson) are the ending of a personal name: - A - L - F - T - A - N, which in full would have read Hálfdan, Half-Dane, both a royal and a common name in the viking age. (Not home)

15. Illumination (Biblioteca Nacional de España, Codex Matritensis Græcus, Vitr. 26-2, fol. 208 v.-a) from the Madrid manuscript of John Skylitzes' *Synopsis historiôn* offering a rare depiction of Varangians in full panoply. (Alonso de Mendoza)

16. (Right) Detail from the gold tesserae mosaic in Néa Moní on the island of Chios. Dated to around 1050, it depicts the *centurio* Longinius, the first gentile to recognize Christ's divinity, at the crucifixion. (Yorck Project)

17. (Below) Two viking re-enactors meet head-to-head at *Wikingerlager 2013*, Ostbeskiden, Poland. The warrior on the right wears padded and quilted defensive jacket designed to be worn as independent body armour. The mailed warrior on the left is wearing a Byzantine style helmet complete with a nasal bar and ring mail aventail. (Silar)

18. Basil II (r. 976–1025), illumination from the Basil II Psalter (Venice, Biblioteca Nazionale Marciana, Codex Marciana Græcus 17, fol. IIIr), circa 1017. The detail shows Basil as a Christian ruler (he receives the imperial diadem from the archangel Gabriel) and a Roman soldier (he receives a spear from the archangel Michael) triumphing over his many enemies (prostrate at his feet). (Alexandar.R)

19. Lion of Peiraeus, Arsenale, Venice. This magnificent marble statue stood in time of the Byzantine empire at the entrance to the harbour of Peiraeus, but when Francesco Morosini captured Athens in the Turco-Venetian war of 1687, he had it removed to Venice as a memorial of his victory. There he had it placed in front of the naval stores where it still stands. (© Esther Carré)

20. (Above) Illumination (Biblioteca Nacional de España, Codex Matritensis Græcus, Vitr. 26-2, fol. 212 r.) from the Madrid manuscript of John Skylitzes' *Synopsis historiôn* illustrating Georgios Maniakes (Gr. Γεώγιος Μανιάκης, ON *Gyrgir*) landing in Sicily in the summer of 1038 and defeating the Sicilian Arabs,. Here, he was assisted by a crack unit of Varangians, some 500 strong and led by Haraldr Sigurðarson. (Cplakidas)

21. (Below) The daughters of prince Yaroslav (the Wise) of Novgorod and Kiev (r. 1015–54) in a fresco from the monumental cathedral of Saint Sophia, Kiev, built during his reign. The third from the left is Elisaveta Yaroslavna (ON *Ellisif*), who would marry Haraldr Sigurðarson on his return to Norway. (Magnus Manske)

22. (Above) the longhouse ruin known as Hamar 1, and (below) the reconstruction of the same longhouse located at Brookpoint in Haroldswick on Unst. ([above] © Esther Carré, [below] © Nic Fields)

23. (Above) Bayeux tapestry (Musée de la Tapisserie de Bayeux), scene 57, depicting the death of Harold II of England at the battle of Hastings, 14 October 1066. The *titulus* reads, in Latin, HIC ● HAROLD ● REX ● INTERFECTVS ● EST (Here King Harold is slain). (Myrabella)

24. (Below) The Derwent river at Stamford Bridge, looking downstream towards the defunct railway viaduct (currently serving as part of a cycle path) from the stone bridge that carries the A166 from York. (Krystian Hasterok)

25. Two monuments to the battle of Stamford Bridge have been erected in and around Stamford Bridge, East Riding of Yorkshire. The first monument (above) is located in the village itself on Main Street (A166). The second memorial (below) is located at the battlefield site at the end of Whiterose Drive, and consists of a memorial stone and plaque detailing the events and outcome of the battle. ([above] Egghead06, [below] Æthelred)

26. Monument of Haraldr Sigurðarson *harðráði*, king of Norway, by the Norwegian sculpture Lars Utne (1862–1922). The bronze relief on the granite monolith depicts Haraldr in full panoply and on horseback at the head of his army. (GAD)

27. *Valkyrie*, a striking bronze sculpture of a warlike valkyrie, riding a plunging horse and wielding a short spear, located in the Churchillparken at Kastellet in Copenhagen. (Zserghei)

man and woman out of two tree trunks on a beach.[41] Snorri Sturluson has this to say of Óðinn: 'But his greatest work is that he made man and gave him a soul that shall live and never perish though the body decay to dust or burn to ashes.'[42] It is interesting, although perhaps not surprising, that Snorri endows Óðinn with this life-giving power while also mentioning death. Óðinn is a god of the dead, and he acquires his magical abilities by undergoing a symbolic death – sacrificed by himself to himself – and returning to life. His animal is the raven, a bird associated with corpses, and he gives them the ability to communicate so that they can act as his servants.[43] Those who are fortunate enough to die a glorious death join Óðinn in the warrior paradise of Valhöll.

Little wonder, therefore, Norsemen lived in a world where Christianity had difficulty in establishing its relevance to their everyday lives in the far north. For this reason, the pagan philosophy of life lived on in the minds of the people despite royal attempts to suppress it. It was a religious system that dealt in questions, myths and metaphors rather than in creeds and the tenets of belief. There was no single text giving a definitive statement of pagan ethics, and even the modern scholar has to study many different brief statements and observations scattered across the literature, the eddaic poem *Hávamál* being the single text that contains the fullest discussion of ethical issues.

Hávamál, or The Sayings of Hárr (viz. the many-faced one-eyed Óðinn), is a mixed bag of poetical proverbs and magic lore, and perhaps represents the purest literary example of the ethics of the vikings. He is the wisest of the *Æsir*, and had given his eye for more wisdom: before he could drink a draught from the wondrous well of the wise giant Mímir, in which boundless wit and wisdom are hidden, Óðinn had to pawn one eye as a pledge. He is often depicted as a one-eyed greybeard, strong, wise, crafty, and cruel. He is the god of knowledge and of war, or, more precisely, of victory. He did little fighting because he was primarily a strategist, planning conquests as much by guile as by force. Accordingly, in the *Hávamál*, Óðinn (OE *Wôden*), the foremost and oldest of the gods of the northern pantheon, gives wary, even cynical, advice to us mortals on how to behave and manage in order to lead a wealthy and worthy life in a male-dominated social world: trust no one (and bear in mind that no one ever refuses a gift); don't get ripping drunk (it makes you look foolish); don't neglect the minutiae of social etiquette (always provide visitors with water and a towel); always keep your weapons within reach (you never know when you will might need them). With its pearls of worldly wise wisdom, of laconic humour and of noble sentiment, the *Hávamál* is the kernel of the spirit of the vikings. As a final point, there is an ongoing discussion about whether or not the name Hárr ought to be construed as 'One-Eye' instead of 'High One', in which the former interpretation, derived from the Gothic word *Haihs* ('one-eyed'), seems to be slowly gaining ground.

While Christianity was a universal religion propagating a doctrine of eternal salvation, Norse paganism was an ethnic religion without either a hierarchical priesthood or any other permanent institutions. In comparison to organized Christianity, Norse paganism was more diverse, changeable, local, and decentralized. The decentralized nature of paganism presented less potential for control of materialized ideology and centralization of social power.

The essence of Christian doctrine, as we well know, was the renunciation of the material world, the idea that made the great break with the classical age. So, rather than having Pauline conversions on the road to Nidaros, it seems the Norwegian kings were alive to the political and economic advantages of being part of European Christendom. It was a matter of cold-eyed *realpolitik*. The Christian establishment in Europe, consisting of both the Church and kings exercising their rule in close coordination with the Church, had achieved a nearly monopolistic control of trade and politics in the European world. It was evident that good political and economic relations with Christian Europe depended on at least a semblance of Christian conversion, and so this semblance was achieved and good relations secured, but this does not mean a deep and meaningful transformation of religious consciousness, nor a wholesale rejection of the pagan spiritual heritage.

So it calls for special pleading to describe Norway (along with its far-flung satellites of the North Atlantic littorals and archipelagos) in any meaningful sense as a Christian kingdom. Accordingly, on one side we witness the unity of the Christian new order and its hand-in-glove partner Norwegian imperialism, and on the other, individualistic paganism and local independence. Norse Christianity was at best rudimentary and heavily laced with superstition. The Christianization of Norway no doubt sprang from circumstance, ambition, and all the freaks and hazards of nature and of human behaviour, as much as from religious conviction.

Besides, during the viking age the ruler of Norway, despite his sole sovereignty, his taxes, and his new men, was merely the 'king of an army' rather than a territorial king. Even at this period, chieftains still led their own armies and chose whom they fought for. In his rôle as war leader, the Norwegian king was but *primus inter pares* of a nobility whose *raison d'être* was belligerent independence. Thus it would appear that the Norwegian kingdom that emerged under Haraldr Sigurðarson was the product of military muscle applied both to its subjects and to its near neighbours, a launching pad for Haraldr's wider ambitions to rule over as much of England, Sweden and Denmark as he could get.

This brings up an intriguing question of Haraldr's take on Christianity, for it is possible to argue that it was associated with blood-soaked nationalism. One could go so far as to argue that Haraldr Sigurðarson was pure pagan in his belief, even if he was baptized, and certainly in some ways, considering his series of extravagant adventures in the course of his lengthy exile, he looks like a barbarian warlord from the heroic age of Vendel Scandinavia.

Here is not the place to discuss the ambivalent nature of Haraldr's beliefs. What *is* important in the context of our argument is the fact that Haraldr was certainly a Christian born and bred, but his piety is highly questionable. Like a pagan warrior, he looked for omens in the natural world.

Fatalism and foredoom

Like most 'bad guys', the vikings are the victims of cultural stereotyping. In the popular imagination they provide the comic book archetypal pagans: marauding shaggy war bands living and dying by the sword, with no respect for person or property, and least of all for the hallowed monasteries and clerics of Anglo-Saxon England and Carolingian Frankia. They worshipped violent and unforgiving gods who inhabited the dark places of far-off northern Europe and they sacrificed animals and humans with complete disregard for Christian ethics. The Norse warrior aspired to the glorious death to join Óðinn's zombie army of *einherjar*, 'those who fight alone'. Valhöll, the hall of the slain, was a product of the cult of Óðinn. Here he presided over the ultimate expression of the gift economy, providing the chosen with all that was good on an unbelievably lavish scale, a place where they were assured of sex, mead, boar meat and battles every day until they joined in the cosmic final war of gods against brute giants and monsters, *Ragnarök*, the Fate of the Gods (no mere twilight).[44]

As explained by Snorri Sturluson, *Ragnarök* meant a comprehensive mutual destruction of gods, giants, and monsters in a final cataclysm that would end the world and presumably, mankind. That *Dies iræ*, when the sun and moon shall be devoured by the ravenous wolves Skoll and Hati, the stars shall fall out of the sky, the great cosmic tree Yggdrasil shall tremble, the sea shall boil, and the huge fiery giant Surtr shall set the world on fire so that everything shall be reduced to cinders. That will be the end. But after that, a new immortal world would appear, inhabited by six divine beings, including Báldr, the beloved second son of Óðinn and Frigg and invulnerable god of the summer sun (he was accidentally killed by a dart made of mistletoe thrown by his blind brother Höðr, a ruse at the instigation of the faithless Loki), an antitype of Christ the redeemer. Meanwhile, from the remains of Yggdrasil step a man, *Lif*, Life, and a woman, *Lifthrasir*, Life's Yearning. They will restock the dewy, fruitful earth; rebirth always follows death. Wagner made an opera out of this, and in the eleventh or twelfth century it inspired the poem *Völuspá*, 'The Prophecy of the Seeress'.

Carvings on the Gotland picture stones, usually dated to the eighth century, reveal that this was a current belief in the east Baltic at the time,[45] and the symbols of resurrection carved on the Sparlösa stone in Västergötland include a hall and a rider which may refer to it. The later sources put together the hall, valkyries and horse, which make up the earlier myth, with a daily routine of feasting (an abundance of strong words and strong drink), fornication and fighting until the great final war that brings the current world to an end.

At any rate, the point is this. Men could be defied even without the benefit of Christian polemics, though to do so they first had to feed Óðinn's pets: the eagle, the raven, the wolf, alias the gore-swan, the hostility-gull, and the watcher.

On the other hand, the scholarly world, faced with an acute lack of archaeological evidence for pagan hordes, has created an alternative stereotype of the peaceful immigrant and trader eager to take on all the trappings of the host society, including its religion. In Anglo-Saxon England, within the space of a single generation, pagan fighters had become Christian farmers. Christian burial was rapidly adopted,[46] many choosing to be buried in churchyards. By the tenth century their once ferocious leaders were commissioning stone crosses and establishing private chapels on their new estates. Meanwhile back in the home world, a Scandinavian king did not have absolute power. He was constrained by the law, which he must both uphold and obey. The free farmers (*bœndr*) of the individual regions included wealthy, powerful men and often firm in their traditional outlook, and they could and sometimes did take on an independent line and opposed a king by force if they disliked his policies. As this social class was a very broad one ranging from impoverished peasants to men of wealth and local authority, the latter could rely upon a wide spectrum of support in their opposition to the crown. Moreover, whilst *bœndr* could be sailors, hunters, traders or raiders they were still fundamentally cultivators of the land, and as a consequence intimately tied to the natural world around them.

Leftover pagans?

Eiríkr Haraldsson *blóðøx*, more commonly known as Eric Bloodaxe, is worthy of mention here, by way of a lengthy footnote to enduring paganism. Indeed, it is worth setting the scene a little here. The court skalds that followed kings from the mid-tenth century onwards seldom use the word king, *konungr*, of their patrons before the ten-twenties: they preferred to flatter them with titles indicating military roles or martial qualities. If the praise of his old enemy the warrior poet Egill Skallagrímsson can be taken as a model, the laudable pagan king excelled in five ways, all military: first, he breaks up and scatters gold to his warriors, regardless of expense; second, he fights in person, with devastating effect, indifferent to danger; third, he has a skald to advertise his fame and generosity and victories; fourth, he holds his land 'in his talons', by force and fear; fifth, Óðinn, the corpse-collector, approves of him, valkyries and ravens attend him.[47]

Thus, the clichés of skaldic verse are the eagerness of kings for war, for crossing the sea, for meeting foreign foes, for laying waste to the countryside, for feeding the 'beasts of battle' – that is, battlefield scavengers such as eagles, ravens and wolves devouring the corpses of the slain.[48] These are the achievements of any successful pirate, rather than a mirror for princes. This is the gold-giving warrior king, proud of his pagan origins and by no means metamorphosing into an honorary Christian. Eiríkr lived most of his life a pagan, a true son of Óðinn. He probably died a pagan too.

We do know that Eiríkr *blóðox* was the best loved son of Haraldr *hárfagri* who succeeded him as king of Norway (if indeed his father had unified it into a single kingdom), was a victorious sea-king in his youth and also in later life, but grim, unkind, and violent of disposition; the chilling cognomen is thought generally to refer to the savage feuds he conducted – and won – with many of his numerous brothers (strictly speaking half-brothers) in the dynastic struggles that came with their father's declining years.[49] Hence Eiríkr is called *fratrum interfector*, 'brother-killer', by Theodoricus Monachus,[50] though *Nóregs konunga tal*, on the other hand, ascribes the cognomen to Eiríkr's violent reputation as an international pirate.[51]

Norsemen were all warlike, but Eiríkr *blóðox* was a special case; he enjoyed homicide as a family activity. Little wonder, therefore, after a stormy year or two the Norwegians finally sent a message to his fifteen-year-old half-brother, Hákon Haraldsson *góði*, who returned to Norway generously armed and equipped by his foster father, Æthelstan of England, to be set up as king by a powerful group of landowners opposed to the strong and wilful Eiríkr. The takeover was expertly stage-managed, and with his support dwindling away Eiríkr sailed westwards from Norway with his ships, his movables and treasure, his wife Gunnhildr, daughter of Gormr *gamli* (the Old) of Denmark,[52] and a small army of friends, family and supporters who had stuck by him. Having fled from his kingdom, Eiríkr eventually landed in northern England, where he became the last Scandinavian king (r. 947–8, 952–4) of York, or *Jórvík* as he would have called it. A great warrior but pitiable statesman, he was steered, like Ahab and Macbeth, by the masculine will of Gunnhildr. She is described as 'a very beautiful woman, shrewd and skilled in magic, friendly of speech, but full of deceit and cruelty'.[53]

Eiríkr *blóðox* was an ambitious and unsuccessful king. He had to flee Norway after losing the support of the free farmers, *bændr*. History was to repeat itself when he was king of *Jórvík*. The accounts of his last struggle are confused. Some written sources say Eiríkr was killed during a viking raid in Spain after being driven out of Northumbria,[54] others claim he fell in England in a battle against a certain Óláfr, sub-king to Eadred, king of Wessex and Mercia (r. 946–55),[55] others again that he lived in England until his death.[56] The best English authority for the period simply states that the Northumbrians expelled Eiríkr in 954.[57] Another

English source, Roger of Wendover (d. 1236), a monk of Saint Albans, reports that Eiríkr was betrayed into the hands of his enemies and killed by a certain earl Maccus (Magnús?), son of Óláfr, 'in a lonely place called *Steinmor*'.[58] This was the wild and desolate heights of Stainmore in County Durham, where the old Roman road that runs from York to Catterick to Carlisle (today's A66, more or less) crosses the northern Pennines and drops into the broad valley of the Eden. If true, it seems Eiríkr was crossing this rolling waste of heather and rushes and rough grass in a bid to reach the relatively safety of the Hebrides. The identity of Eiríkr's fatal opponent, Maccus Óláfsson, is uncertain, but the name appears in the dynastic lists of the Norse rulers of the Isle of Man and it may well have been that he was acting as an ally of Eadred. The death of Eiríkr was a momentous event, as the kingdom of Northumbria had fallen and would never rise again. As Symeon of Durham expediently reminds us: 'Here the kings of the Northumbrians came to an end, and henceforward the province was administered by earls'.[59]

A fierce and rough warrior, Eiríkr had few redeeming features besides his pig-headed bravery. He was baptized when acknowledging Eadred as his overlord, but in the magnificent lay *Eiríksmál*, composed by an unknown skald probably at the behest of his widow Gunnhildr *konungamóðir* (Mother of kings),[60] there is not one slightest hint of Eiríkr being a Christian king. Indeed, in this eulogium of an unpopular, though brave, king, the Norse pagan ethos prevails absolutely. The images of the lay invoke the warlike ideals of Eiríkr's rule, the pagan's ultimate hope for eternal life, the nature of his mortuary beliefs, presided over by the shamanistic figure of Óðinn.

Óðinn always had high hopes of him, and was ready to receive the fallen king into Valhöll. Recognizing king Eiríkr from afar, Óðinn bids two mighty heroes of the olden times rise up and welcome him: *Ragnarök*, the Fate of the Gods, is approaching, and heroes such as Eiríkr will be needed for the impending cosmic last battle with the most evil of Loki's offspring, Fenrir, the grey wolf of destruction.[61] His death wounds displayed, Eiríkr draws near, and with him are no fewer than five kings slain in battle, a worthy retinue for his apocalyptic apotheosis. 'Kings five there are,' says Eiríkr, 'them all I shall name thee: am I the sixth myself'.[62]

Five dead kings for Óðinn

Much of the scholarly discussion has centred on the ending of the poem and the 'five kings' who accompany Eiríkr *blóðøx*. The argument that one expects the names of these kings to have been mentioned leads to the conclusion that the poem is incompletely preserved, which is the commonly held view.[63] On the other hand, if the expression 'five kings' is regarded as a conventional poetic device and does not refer to historical kings, the poem has an appropriate ending and we should not expect anything else to follow.[64] Of course, the processes of literary composition are in their nature remote from mathematical proof, and the vast and fertile field of saga is notoriously one in which the searcher can find almost anything he or she pleases. But death comes to kings as it does to all men, and it is interesting to remark one thing here: the expression 'five young king lay on the battlefield' occurs in the verse description of the battle at *Brunanburh*, the tenth-century 'battle of nations' where Celts and Norse clashed against the West Saxon and Mercian shire levies in a vicious daylong engagement fought not so many years before (937).[65] As well the bodies of five kings, which had been 'put to sleep by swords', the Celtic–Norse confederation left seven earls and a son of Causantín mac Áeda (Constantine II) king of the Scots on the field of the slain. It seems that by the end of the day, many a northern and overseas invader lay in his gore, 'torn by spears, shot over his shield', left as carrion for wolves, ravens and eagles.

If we choose to ignore the objection concerning the chronology, can we identify the battle called *Vínheiðr* in *Egils saga Skallagrímssonar* with *Brunanburh*? If so, then it was at this crucial English battle that the two brothers, Þórólfr and Egill Skallagrímsson, together with their own following of 300 warriors, played a decisive part as Norse mercenaries (we are in pre-Varangian Guard times here) in the army of Æthelstan (ON *Aðalsteinn*) of England and his younger half-brother Eadmund, who later succeeded him. The king in his preparations for the northward march against his Celtic and Norse enemies had sent word throughout north-western Europe that he wished to hire mercenaries. He probably did this through recruiting agents. In any case, Egill and Þórólfr, had been made aware of this whilst in Friesland and, we are told, were singled out by the king as suitable commanders for the entire mercenary force.

The part played by the hired Norse warriors in this fight receives no mention in the *Anglo-Saxon Chronicle* account, which instead highlights the contribution of the West Saxon and Mercian contingents – after all, the monks who wrote the *Anglo-Saxon Chronicle* attempted to distil the important events of each year, as they saw them, into single short paragraphs. *Egils saga Skallagrímssonar* stresses the experiences of the Skallagrímsson brothers in the fight and how their professional code determines everything from their equipment to the way in which they confront death. Egill won fame and fortune that day, but Þórólfr was to forfeit his life. Æthelstan, with Egill's help, had won a great victory. Þórólfr was to be buried with honours, while the king took off one of his arm rings and presented it to Egill, who was additionally rewarded with two chests of silver. Thus was the battle of *Vínheiðr* concluded, according to *Egils saga Skallagrímssonar*. Of course Egill Skallagrímsson was of a rather different stamp than most men, indeed a far more interesting figure than most, and further will be said later of his colourful but complex life.[66]

Brunanburh is one of the most well known viking-age encounters. Although the Wessex kings had established their supremacy over the lowland zone, the peripheral areas of Britain, and in particular those under Celtic or Norse cultural domination, had not abandoned hope of independence. Yet the resulting broad anti-English alliance had made strange political bedfellows of several lesser kings whose domains encircled the Irish Sea (the battle is known as *helium Brune* by the Welsh and Irish annalists), clearly having its roots in reactionary opportunism rather than enduring bonds of trust and friendship. These lesser kings included Owen king of Strathclyde and Óláfr Guðröðsson king of Dublin (OE *Ánláf*, OI *Amlaíb mac Gofraidv*). The latter, the claimant to the kingdom of York, was a man of mixed Norse and Celtic descent who according to *Egils saga Skallagrímssonar* was the prime mover of the allies. These also included the wild Gall–Gaels of the Western Isles, renegade Christians who had come to 'out-viking the vikings'. The grand plan, it seems, was to turn Æthelstan out of the north and the Danelaw – as the Danish-settled Midlands were now called, an area in which people lived according to a different set of rules, conventions or habits than elsewhere on the island, some of which survived into the Domesday survey (1086) – and if possible to dethrone or kill him.

In fact, the Norse of Ireland and the northern kingdoms of Britain shared quite a long history of deadly antagonism. The Hiberno–Norse ruthlessly battered Strathclyde and Alba in the eight-sixties and the eight-seventies, even toppling Strathclyde's power-centre, *Alt Clut* or Clyde Rock at Dumbarton, in one of the greatest sieges of the period.[67] Long-lived Causantín mac Áeda (r. 900–43) turned back Norse inroads against Alba in 904, and later battled Ragnall, a scion of the dynasty of Ívarr in Ireland, at *Tinemore* or Corbridge in 918. Causantín's martial efforts, perhaps executed in accordance with a Northumbrian alliance, failed to prevent Ragnall's ascension over York the following year.[68] Regardless of Causantín's motives, surely a united Dublin–York sea-kingdom caused some alarm for Alba.

Soon after his coronation in January 925 Æthelstan met the Hiberno–Norse king of York, Sigtryggr (OI *Sitric Caech*), at Tamworth in Mercia, and gave him his sister in marriage, procuring Sigtryggr's adoption of Christianity as part of the bargain.[69] But when Sigtryggr died early in 927 it became clear that Æthelstan had never intended an independent Hiberno–Norse kingdom of York to continue. He invaded the kingdom, expelled Sigtryggr son Óláfr and his brother Guðröðr, and entered York, demolishing the Norse fortifications and seizing huge booty, which he distributed to his army. It was a historic moment, for a southern king had never directly ruled in York before, and entries in their chronicles show that even Anglo-Saxon traditionalists north of the Humber viewed the turn of events with much trepidation. Obviously an Englishman in Northumbria did not see the world in the same way as an Englishman in Wessex, and might be happy to serve a Hiberno–Norse king rather than the hated *Suthangli*.

York was only the beginning. That summer Æthelstan rode north, attacked Bamburgh and drove out the North Saxon *eorl* Ealdred Ealdulfing, who had ruled north of the Tees almost like an independent king. Ealdred became Æthelstan's man and was reinstated as the *eorl* of Bernicia. The Ealdulfings made alliances with anyone who held power in the north, and would continue to rule in these parts until after the Norman Conquest.

It was these events, acerbated by Æthelstan's northern expedition in 934 when he systematically lay waste areas of Causantín's territory and forced his submission, which made the formation of a coalition to withstand Æthelstan's imperial pretensions imperative. Hatred of Æthelstan was the motivating factor for the anti-English alliance, and the instigator was Causantín, whom the English remembered as 'the hoary-headed traitor'.

A German cleric resident in Christ Church Canterbury went to the Old Testament and Joshua's slaughter of the kings of the Amorites for his parallels:

> Holy king Æthelstan... / who God set as king over the English, sustained by foundation / of the throne, and as leader of [His] earthly forces / plainly so that this king himself, mighty in war might be able / to conquer other fierce kings, treading down their fierce necks.[70]

And this he did. The battle was evidently spectacular in scale and brutality, for as the *Annals of Ulster* recounts:

> A great, lamentable and horrible battle was cruelly fought between the Saxons and the Norsemen, in which several thousands of Norsemen, who are uncounted, fell, but their king, Amlaíb, escaped with a few followers. A large number of Saxons fell on the other side, but Æthelstan, king of the Saxons, enjoyed a great victory.[71]

It was also reported in chronicles from Wales and Scotland.[72] This indicates the scale of the battle and the political tensions which were brewing in its wake across North Britain and in Ireland. Nonetheless, we possess few undisputedly factual details of this mighty clash, except that the combined might of Dublin, Alba and Strathclyde fell in bloody defeat at the day's end. Causantín and Óláfr evaded death and fled to their lands. The English victory was unambiguous.

During Æthelstan's reign the new royal title of *rex to(tius) brit(anniae)*, 'King of all Britain, appeared on his coinage, the first ruler of an independent world of *Britannia* since the days of Magnus Maximus, along with the first representation of any English king wearing a crown instead of the diadem usually worn on previous coin portraits. High-flying title aside, Æthelstan's victory at *Brunanburh* did not prevent the defeated Óláfr Guðröðsson recovering his ambitions and returning to York. The seasoned and battle-scarred Dublin king regained control of the kingdom of York shortly after Æthelstan's death at the end of 939 and expanded the kingdom's boundaries southward to Watling Street. The Northumbrians resented southern English authority, and so York passed smoothly to Óláfr's cousin, Óláfr *Cuarán* (the Red) Sigtryggsson, upon his death in 941.[73] But Æthelstan's death had thrown everything into the melting pot. It led to a fifteen-year struggle for power in Northumbria where the last energies of the Northumbrian kingship attempted to resist the trend of English history and the military power of Æthelstan's successors, his young half-brothers Edmund and Eadred. Between 939 and 954, seven different kings ruled in York, Scandinavian and English, in nine separate reigns. In reality, Dublin Hiberno–Norse rule lacked long-term stability and, as we have seen, would eventually dissipate all together with the fall and death of Eiríkr *blóðox*.

On the location of the battlefield of *Brunanburh* there is a lot of fierce debate amongst scholars in academic milieus, with forceful claims made for Burnswark in Dumfriesshire and Bromborough on the Wirral amongst thirty-odd other widely various contenders, most of whose names begin with *B-*, contain *r* and often *u*. Rich in high-ranking casualties but not in tactical or topographical information, the primary sources indicate the year, the leaders, and of course the victors; these essentially are the only real certainties that can be reliably gleaned there from. The *Anglo-Saxon Chronicle* gives little clue regarding the battlefield, though interestingly enough *Egils saga Skallagrímssonar* provides us enough basic detail to its terrain. The saga says 'the battlefield was a flat moor with a river flowing on one side and a large wood on the other', while a town (possibly *Brunanburh*) lay 'to the north of the moor'. It was in this town that Óláfr Guðröðsson 'settled... along with most of his troops'.[74]

However, there is nowhere on the map by the name of *Brunanburh* (or by its many and varied spellings), and none even in the *Domesday Book*.[75] Even the early mediaeval chroniclers refer to the battle under a variety of spellings – sometimes in the same document. Apart from the battle poem's *Brunanburh*, there is the *Brunandune* in the chronicle of Æthelweard, followed by Henry of Huntingdon's *Brunesburh*, Roger of Hovedon's *Brunnanbyrg* or *Bruneberih*, the *Brunnanburch* of the Chronicles of Melrose, and the *Brumford* or *Brunfort* of Ralph Higden of Chester. Somehow, the chronicler Geoffrey Gaimer had got hold of the name *Bruneswerce*, perhaps a variation of Symeon of Durham's *Brunanwerc*. Nevertheless, the sense in each case is something like 'Bruna's fort' or 'Bruna's stronghold'. The search for the whereabouts of *Brunanburh* continues to provide historians with a lively game.

Two evangelical kings of Christ

There are various ways to approach the concept of 'state' within the context of later viking-age Scandinavia. According to Löfving, 'a necessary qualification for a state society is, at least theoretically, a monopoly on violence in order to exercise justice', while 'state formation... requires a homogeneous ideology of society, and the rulers must have sufficient knowledge and resources in order to exercise government'.[76] While it is clear that state-formation in late viking-age Scandinavia went hand in hand with the development of the notion of kingship, it is less obvious exactly what rights and privileges were enjoyed by Scandinavian kings in this period. For a state to function the centralization of authority is also a prerequisite, with the development of a network of administrators directly under the king's jurisdiction scattered throughout the kingdom in towns and royal estates. Central to much of this is the notion that even as early as the later viking age kings were binding their vassals to them by the granting of land in return for various, especially military, services.

That said, however, the introduction of Christianity into Norway offered a number of political advantages for royal power. It could be used to break down the opposition against the idea of a national kingdom and to legitimize the subordination of local communities under the crown. The method used by the first missionary kings was a simple albeit blunt one. It was considered necessary to make the local chieftains accept the new doctrine; after which the rest of the population would follow suit, or so it was hoped. If the chieftains accepted Christianity, this would automatically place them in a subordinate position to the king. He was the leader and protector of Christianity; all others were subject to him; he had the 'whip hand' in political relationships. In places where the royal position of power was weakest, administrative, power-political and ideological points of support – towns – were established, such as Nidaros in Trøndelag. Here, coins were minted in royal mints, with the issuing king depicted on the obverse side and a Christian cross on the reverse. Having made their choice of one god over many, the convert kings confirmed their position of power and soon established episcopal sees in these towns. On the other hand, we must not forget that the conversion of Norway was a lengthy, complex and subtle process, recently scholarship clearly demonstrating how gradual, indecisive and ambivalent the infiltration of Christian culture was.

They say converts are the worst. Óláfr Tryggvason of Norway (r. 995–1000), one of the most spectacular vikings of the age, who would first make his tempestuous entrance upon the European stage at the momentous battle fought near Maldon in 991,[77] is credited in the Icelandic sagas with the forcible conversion of Orkney to Christianity in 994, he himself having been baptized that very year in England.[78] This was a year before he made himself, in defiance of the claims of Sveinn I

Haraldsson *tjúguskegg*, master and pacifier of his own country, which he was to pitilessly hold for five violently evangelistic years. Óláfr was, strictly speaking, a convert himself, before he became a renowned converter of others. In this respect, Óláfr is credited, deserving or not, with the 'macro-conversion' of Norway,[79] yet he and his kingly like were certainly no milk and honey Christians but blood and iron ones. To use that old saying, there is nothing like the converted, and Óláfr himself appears to have been very persuasive. He is known to have threatened people with mutilation or death if they refused baptism; just as fire and sword wrought more conversions in the Merovingian kingdom, in Germany, and in England, than did peaceful, missionary activity so too in the far north. In spite of everything, however, the conversion of Norway was a process that had begun before Óláfr's return and one far from complete at the time of his death.

Óláfr's brutally short, evangelizing reign ended at the battle of Svölðr in the year 1000. It was here that *jarl* Eiríkr Hákonarson, son of *jarl* Hákon Sigurðarson whom Óláfr deposed, and Sveinn I Haraldsson *tjúguskegg* of Denmark, a former ally, defeated him and divided Norway between them. Wounded, Óláfr leapt overboard from his blood-soaked warship the *Long Serpent* (ON *Ormr inn langi*), followed by those of his retainers who were still alive.[80] Snorri Sturluson mentions the rumours of Óláfr's survival,[81] as does the Icelandic Benedictine monk Oddr Snorrason, who reports sightings of the king in Rome and Jerusalem, where he had gone on pilgrimage to pay penance for his sins.[82] It is these rumours that Hallfreðr subjects to extended debate in his memorial poem, eventually concluding that the king cannot be alive – 'the ruler died in / ruthless struggle in Southland'.[83]

Óláfr Tryggvason is one of the most written-about characters in all of saga-literature and concerning whose life and evangelizing efforts a whole host of stories and episodes sprang up in the centuries following his apparent death at Svölðr. He was also important as the forerunner of his namesake the saint, the erstwhile Óláfr II Haraldsson, in the way John the Baptist had been a precursor of Jesus Christ. Energetic warriors and missionaries, both Óláfrs were killed in battle. Little wonder, therefore, the battle of Svölðr itself quickly became a favourite topic of skaldic poets and authors of kings' sagas. Yet, its causes, and even its location, remain the subject of much scholarly debate. As for that post-battle division of the spoils, Sveinn of Denmark retained direct control of the Vík, the area in which Danish influence was always the greatest. Óláfr of Sweden was given control of Ranríki in the southeast and four provinces in eastern Þrándheimr, most of which was effectively ruled by Eiríkr Hákonarson's brother Sveinn Hákonarson as the Swedish king's vassal. Eiríkr Hákonarson ruled the western provinces of Þrándheimr and coastal provinces – in other words most of Norway – although it would be a mistake to underestimate Danish influence during this time.

At any rate, it is not really until the martyrdom of Óláfr's distinguished successor and namesake Óláfr *helgi* that one can safely speak of a Christian Norway. Yet many of his fellow Norwegians were certainly not overly enthusiastic about Christianity, which, in sober truth, had been rammed down their throats by the two proselytizing Óláfrs, and the old heroic ideal of uninhibited and unabashed self-assertion and the martial values appealed to them far more than Christian ethics. So the conversion of Norway was no simple and comprehensive business as the missionary stories imply. For a long time there were mixtures of paganism and Christianity. Indeed, as late as the turn of the thirteenth century it was possible for a Norwegian in Björgvin (Bergen) to cut on a stick: 'may you be in good health and spirits / may Þórr receive you, may Óðinn possess you'.[84]

The two Óláfrs used the cross to cow chieftains and consolidate royal support, but met with constant and in the end successful opposition from their chief men. Their desire to secure control had intruded on landholders' traditional rights, and their championship of a particular religion, the foreign import Christianity, had been seen as a disguised attempt to change social and economic patterns that had existed for centuries. Certainly, it would not have been lost on Haraldr Sigurðarson that his half-brother Óláfr had been deposed twice (the second occasion, for him, fatal) partly because of his religious convictions and partly on grounds of power. Look at Hákon Haraldsson *góði*, for instance, who was a less aggressive Christian, and *jarl* Hákon Sigurðarson of Lade, a full on pagan who ruled longer and more successfully than any of them; he may have been ousted by Óláfr Tryggvason but he had had twenty good years by then. So was conversion worth it?

Óláfr Haraldsson was a rather harsh ruler and prone to rough treatment of those who stood in his way. On becoming ruler of Norway in 1015 he picked up where his evangelizing forerunner and namesake Óláfr Tryggvason had left off, bringing Christianity to his domains on the sharp edge of his sword. He seems to have committed most of his worse atrocities in the name of Jesus Christ, and indeed to have won his canonization as a direct result of those acts, which were the very antithesis of all that Jesus Christ had taught. Here is his story.

Óláfr Haraldsson spent his youthful years raiding as a viking, but before he took the throne at the age of twenty-one, he was apparently baptized in England,[85] his principal stomping ground. Old Norse sagas and skaldic poetry even go as far to suggest that Óláfr led a successful river-borne attack which pulled down London Bridge with grappling irons,[86] though this is not confirmed by Anglo-Saxon sources. As king, he began the conversion of Norway to Christianity. His predecessor Óláfr Tryggvason had already inducted Christianity as the 'official state' religion in Norway, but in practice, Christianity had not taken root.

In the Fjord district of central Norway, for instance, the farmers kept a gold and silver idol of Þórr. The idol was hollow, and every day, the farmers fed the idol with bread and meat as an offering. Óláfr was discontented with the farmers for their pagan practices. One night, he caused their ships to be damaged and their horses to be run off. At dawn, the angry farmers approached the king, carrying the glittering idol. The king said, 'Behold the true God comes in the east with great light'. The farmers turned to see the sun rising in the east. Meanwhile, one of the king's henchmen struck the idol with a club, so that it fell to pieces, and as it did 'out jumped mice... and adders, and snakes', so well nourished by the sacrifices that they were 'as big as cats'. The farmers took fright, and fled to their horses, which could not be found, and to their ships, which were filled with water. The king pointed to the weakness of the god of the idol, and said that the farmers could either convert to Christianity on the spot, or do battle with the king and his men. The farmers all accepted the Christian faith.[87]

On another occasion, as the free farmers of the Sogn district mustered to face him, the king sent men into the deserted settlements and farmsteads to torch their homes. He resorted to slaughter the men as they tried to save their property.[88] According to his skald Sigvatr Þórðarson, the king burned more settlements than he built. On another occasion, when the Swedish king Óláfr *sköttkonungr* had despatched emissaries to collect taxes in the disputed borderlands between the two kingdoms, Óláfr Haraldsson had a full dozen of them hanged as a feast for the ravens.[89]

Óláfr's dealings with pagans showed that, beneath the Christian rhetoric, he ultimately believed in brute force to achieve his will. Even in the teeth of their opposition the king was impatient with any show of compromise or moderation, and insisted that a true ruler knew how to *force* his subjects to come to heel. Resentment of the king and his standpoint was both individual and collective. His main enemies were powerful local chieftains and free farmers. They joined forces with Knútr Sveinsson of Denmark, and his Norwegian vassal, *jarl* Hákon Eiríksson, and expelled Óláfr from Norway in 1028. With a devoted clique of skalds, Christians and gangsters, Óláfr fled to prince Yaroslav in Kiev. Encouraged by the message that Hákon Eiríksson had died, Óláfr returned from his exile two years later, raised a small army in Sweden, and crossed into Norway.

Here, at Stiklarstaðir, he encountered a much larger army of armed and angry chiefs and freeholders. This fact in itself reveals the limited extent of Christianity in Norway at the time. And so it was that at Stiklarstaðir Óláfr Haraldsson was a Christian king pitted against the allied forces of conservative paganism in Norway. With the two armies drawn up facing each other in hostile array, Óláfr led his much smaller army into battle with the rallying cry '*Fram, fram, Kristsmenn, krossmenn, konungsmenn* [Onward, onward, men of Christ, men of the Cross, men of the King!]'.[90] Indeed, as the headlong charge rolled downhill, we need not doubt Óláfr's personal courage.

Meeting the enemy head-on, unflinching, was sometimes more important than strategy, because it validated authority and rank. Indeed, it is a fundamental truth that a leader would not succeed unless he risked leading from the front, and like any self respecting leader, Óláfr was to be found front and centre in the shield wall and trading blows with the best of them. His personal retainers (*hirðmaðr*) fought like furies to the finish, while his half-brother, Haraldr Sigurðarson, was wounded but escaped.

From sinner to saint

In some sense Óláfr Haraldsson succeeded where Óláfr Tryggvason had failed. However, as we have discussed, Óláfr Haraldsson's stern methods of ruling led to his expulsion in 1028, whence he fled to Novgorod. In 1030 Knútr's Norwegian regent, *jarl* Hákon Eiríksson, was lost at sea. Óláfr therefore seized the opportunity to win back Norway, but had to face the opposition of the ruling jarls and chieftains, and he eventually died in the battle of Stiklarstaðir the same year. The new ruler, the Danish Knút Sveinsson, did not elevate the nobility who had killed Óláfr to its former power. As a consequence, the Norwegian nobility elevated the memory of the expelled Norwegian king and brought Óláfr's son, Magnús Óláfsson, from Kievan Russia to rule over them. As a tribute to his accomplishments, Óláfr Haraldsson was locally canonized very soon after his death, already in 1031.

Stiklarstaðir is a central event in Óláfr Haraldsson life. Snorri Sturluson, for instance, devotes no fewer than thirty-eight chapters of his Saint Óláfr's saga in *Heimskringla* on said battle. The death of the king that day was his birth as a saint. Miracles attributed to Óláfr are said to have been reported within hours of him being laid low on the field of Stiklarstaðir. Óláfr's body was exhumed – according to some sources it rose to the surface of its own accord – five days more than the twelvemonth after his death and brought to the church of Saint Clement in Nidaros, where it was found to be uncorrupted, with hair and nails still growing. It was then that the slain king was canonized as Saint Óláfr, patron saint of Norway.

Within thirty years the king's burial place had become the 'metropolitan city of Northmen',[91] goal of pilgrims from Dublin to the Dnieper, and so full of wealth and shipping that to win it was halfway to winning Norway. How quickly he fell from grace, and then rose like a dove to sainthood, continuing his work long beyond the viking age as *perpetuus rex Norvegiae*, 'Norway's eternal king'. This is somewhat ironic, both because of his early career as a ruthless viking, raiding all around the North Sea coasts, and because of his equally ruthless (though finally failed) attempts to subjugate Norwegian jarls and chieftains to his Christian hegemony. A lesson of politics.

Óláfr Haraldsson may have been an unpopular ruler and his Christian faith may not have been to the Norwegians' tastes, yet his local canonization was in 1164 confirmed by pope Alexander III (r. 1159–81), making him a universally recognized saint of the Roman Catholic Church. Yet it is hardly unexpected to find that different literary sources describe Óláfr in different ways. On the one hand, the liturgical texts in prayers, lessons, and chants, with many biblical allusions, place Saint Óláfr among the Old Testament leaders of people, such as Moses or Jacob. Likewise, many of the common liturgical texts present king Óláfr as one of the martyr kings, as a courageous champion of *Hvitakristr*, the White Christ.

The earliest Old Norse texts about the life of Óláfr Haraldsson were *vitae* of the saint written in Latin in the twelfth century. The *First Saga of Saint Óláfr* was written somewhere between 1160 and 1200, of which only six or seven short fragments survive. However, the thirteenth-century *Legendary Saga of Saint Óláfr* is clearly heavily based on it, which was the most important source for Snorri Sturluson's version of the saga in his *Heimskringla*. Even earlier than the *vitae* is the skaldic poem *Glælognskviða* ('Sea-Calm Poem') by the Icelander Þórarinn *loftunga*, which is dated to around 1052. It is here that we hear for the first time of the intact corpse of Óláfr Haraldsson and the nine miracles performed by Saint Óláfr. One is the killing and throwing onto a mountain of a sea serpent still visible on the cliff side. Another took place on the day of his death, when a blind man regained his sight after accidentally rubbing his eyes with hands stained with the blood of the martyred king.[92]

According to the Old Norse sources Saint Óláfr was, together with the Mother of God (Gr. Θεοτόκος), the patron saint of the chapel of the Varangians. This church is believed to have been located near the church of Hagia Irene in Constantinople. The icon of the Madonna *Nicopea*, presently in Basilica di San Marco in Venice and alleged by scholars to have been the icon traditionally carried into war by the Byzantine emperors,[93] is also believed to have been kept in the Varangian chapel in times of peace. The Madonna *Nicopea* has been identified with that taken by the crusaders in a cavalry skirmish outside the walls of Constantinople in 1204, as recorded by the eyewitness Geoffroi de Villehardouin.[94] However, that holy relic was given to the Cistercian abbey of Cîtreaux in the county of Champagne, from whence de Villehardouin hailed. As for the chapel itself, the oldest Varangian one that we know of from Byzantine sources was dedicated to the *Panagía Varangiotissa* and this was the one, if we are to believe Snorri Sturluson, probably built after the Byzantine victory at Beroë in 1122.[95]

The king

I
t is certain that what prompted Haraldr Sigurðarson to return to Norway was the news that Magnús Óláfsson, his nephew and the son of Óláfr II Haraldsson, had been recalled to the kingdom and had been made king. Knowing Haraldr, we can safely assume that he must have considered himself much more capable than his nephew. Not only that, he must have felt that it would be much more profitable for himself if he were to return home and rule there with a king's authority, rather than to stay as a mercenary officer in the army of another ruler, however attractive Constantinopolitan life may have been.

And so it was in 1045 that Haraldr made his way back to Scandinavia, entering Sweden the same year and Norway the following year. All exiles long for their native ground with fierce intensity. More so in Haraldr's case, for his undisguised objective was to become king of Norway, if necessary by waging war against Magnús I Óláfsson *góði* (r. 1035–47). Magnús was understandably reluctant to acquiesce to his uncle's bullish plans for régime change. Everything was about to change.

From renegade adventurer to reigning prince

In preparation for such a war Haraldr opened negotiations with Magnús' Danish enemy, Sveinn Estriðsson, and the Swedish king, Óláfr *sköttkonungr*, who was Sveinn's ally and the grandfather of Elisaveta Yaroslavna, Haraldr's Kievan wife.[96] In the face of this triple threat Magnús, through adroit diplomacy, reached an understanding with his uncle and in 1046 they agreed to share Norwegian royal power. The wise nephew may not have liked the partnership with the wily uncle, but he was poorly placed to protest, let alone to resist. The following year, on 25 October, Magnús took his last breath and Haraldr became the sole ruler of Norway.

It was perhaps fortuitous then that Magnús passed away when he did. In an age shrouded in conspiratorial darkness, it is tempting to speculate that Magnús was assassinated. Usually in cases involving the sudden death of powerful figures, rumours of malfeasance spread with incredible speed, and root themselves as fact in the collective imagination. History, the emotional jury, would have returned a verdict of murder. Yet, as suspicious as the timing of this particular death may seem, Haraldr did not have anything to do with his nephew's demise, at least not according to the original written sources.[97] Even Adam of Bremen and Saxo

Grammaticus, no friends to Haraldr, do not try to tie him to his co-ruler's death. According to Saxo Grammaticus, for instance, Magnús died because he fell from his horse while he was running after Sveinn Estriðsson of Denmark.[98] History, the sober judge, has concluded that the nephew died by chance.

It is easy to detect a motive for Haraldr wanting to kill Magnús. At the best of times co-rule over any political entity breeds jealousy and discontentment, especially when that political entity is one as large as the kingdom of Norway, and especially when the two rulers have been brought together by the threat of war, with neither trusting the other. Be all that as it may, Haraldr, who must have long held the view that he was the only throne-worthy candidate, had successfully made the transformation from mercenary warlord into worldly monarch. Thus, the skald Þjóðólfr Arnórsson says of Haraldr, at the end of *Sexstefja*, a formal praise poem that traces the course of the king's life: 'May the high one, Ruler of retinues / Cheerfully leave his inheritance and family estate / To his sons: that is my wish'.[99] What Haraldr had inherited from his father was a share in the estate of a pocket sized kingdom in the hills of Hringaríki. What Þjóðólfr meant by 'his inheritance' was the whole of Norway, which he had acquired from his nephew by buying one share with his chests of Byzantium gold, and winning the other by hard fighting. A little more than seventeen years after his enforced exile Haraldr was back where, at least in his own view, he belonged. The son of a small-time king had become the king of Norway. And so began Haraldr's Norwegian period. It was to last for two decades.

Looking for trouble

In it all there was to be little of benefit to Norway, and much that was to be essential to benefit Haraldr. Yet Norse rulers always showed more zeal in robbing other peoples' kingdoms than in uniting their own; the frontiers of Norway were not the limits of the arena across which Haraldr now aimed to manoeuvre. For Haraldr was not the type of man who, just because he was now king, would embark upon a peaceful and retiring life. He had spent most of his life in harness, and he had defied the odds time and again. He went on to enjoy the rest of his life at war, ending his long career of violence as Haraldr III Sigurðarson, king of Norway, the last great viking invader of England, felled by an anonymous English arrow at Stamford Bridge in that fateful year of change, 1066. Power attracts the worst and corrupts the best. Whichever Haraldr was it is hard to say. Perhaps he was neither, for in my opinion he was a complicated character.

The more complicated a character is the more interesting he is, but at the same time the more dangerous he is, and Haraldr was certainly dangerous, fighting for two lands that did not want him. Haraldr was born to war and grew up in it. Perhaps the Norwegian king would have turned his attentions to England earlier had he not been embroiled in a long and wasteful war with Denmark.[100] As the twelfth-century Norwegian Benedictine monk, Theodoricus Monachus, rightly wrote of him:

> Haraldr was a vigorous man, farsighted in his decision-making, quick to take up arms, jealous of what was his and covetous of what was another's; and so he waged war against Sveinn [Estriðsson], in the hope of wresting from him the kingdom of Denmark.[101]

Haraldr was meant to be a warrior, not to rule. Once he was crowned king of Norway Haraldr proved to be a less effective ruler than a warrior, being far more interested in pursuing confrontation on the red field of battle than in conducting the higher affairs of state.

A mediaeval Christian king had to deal with all the mundane problems of governing, the minutiae of running a mediaeval Christian kingdom, and Haraldr was terrible at it. Now a good pagan king, on the other hand, as portrayed in that tale of the old Scandinavian lore, *Beowulf*, should be generous, brave and just, a man of martial accomplishments. He fights primarily for fame, for the glory of becoming the number one Germanic hero, and secondarily he battles for gain, for treasure he can give away, so as to show his largess at bestowing gifts. So a good prince, the *Beowulf* poet reminds his listeners, is 'a wrecker of mead-benches, rampaging among foes... giving freely while his father lives so that afterwards in age when fighting starts / steadfast companions will stand by him / and hold the line'.[102] Likewise, as the Norse skalds insist, the good king was a dissipater, not an accumulator: 'wealth-wounder', 'silver-foe', 'ring-tosser', was the winner, not the ruler who hid his winnings, as Eyvindr *skáldaspillir* (the Plagiarist) complained of Haraldr Greycloak Gunnhildarson.[103]

This brings us back to Haraldr. No one studying the life of Haraldr would find him to be a particularly Christian king. His glory has little to do with worship, unless it be justified self worship, and he fights primarily for glory, to increase his fame (and power), to show that he occupies the foremost place among all warrior kings. When Haraldr goes forth to battle, he is on the quest of reputation, but not of Christ or the truth. As we will discuss later, Haraldr does not die so as to advance the truth of Christian values but so as to maintain his own glory, the fame of a warrior king who seeks heroic immortality.

A terror by land and sea

It is a characteristic of wars that they are apt to last considerably longer than the combatants expected. In general, both warring parties expect to win. In the event, they are wrong more than half the time.

The wasteful campaigns that thereafter sought to make two unwilling kingdoms into one would drag on till 1064. Haraldr invaded Denmark and Sveinn invaded Norway; the two kings circled each other like Turkish wrestlers seeking a hold and the war went nowhere for nigh on two decades. On what was essentially a sorry tale of coasts raided, farmsteads burned, and husbands slaughtered, and their womenfolk carried off, the royal skalds exercised their full powers of invention to shed splendour and even humour. Thus, the skald Valgarðr á Vellir celebrates Haraldr's raid on Denmark in 1047:

> Shoved out for you a ship was, / shield-surrounded, battle- / eager Yngvi-scion, your / own to win, from Sweden. / High, then, to mast's head you / hoisted the sail as you / scudded past level Scania, / scaring women, near Denmark.

Giving the impression that the kingdom was a soft target, he then goes on to crow over what made the Danish women afraid, setting down his what were his memories in naked and violent words:

> Down-cast, away drifted / Danes who lived still, scattered / in flight, while fair maidens / fell in our power. / With fetters fastened, women / followed you down to your vessels; / cut chafing chains the flesh of / chattel maidens cruelly.[104]

As Edmund Burke would later say, the problem with war is that it usually consumes the very things that you are fighting for – justice, decency, humanity. Quite true when you consider many more perish in war than profit from it. In the case of our hero, as we said before, he exhibited more zeal in robbing other peoples' kingdoms than in uniting or defining his own.

Finally, on 9 August 1062, the outnumbered Haraldr defeated the Danes at a great naval battle fought off the mouth of the river Níza (today's Nissä in south-western Sweden, close to the Norwegian border) in Halland. Haraldr had 180 ships, *halft annat hundrað*, while Sveinn had 360, *þrimr hundruðum*.[105] Apparently Haraldr's new flagship had seventy oars (viz. thirty-five pairs of rowing benches),[106] and the king's principal skald Þjóðólfr Arnórsson uses both *naðr* 'snake' and *ormr* 'serpent' of Haraldr's *dreki* (pl. *drekar*) 'dragon'. He also says Haraldr's *ormr* has a *fax*, 'mane', while the prow is an *orms munnr*, 'dragon's mouth'. With the king at the tiller, he continues in this poetic vein, saying:

> Onward, Northmen urge the / iron-mailed great dragon, / like as, with outspread wings, an / eagle, on hail struck sea-stream.[107]

It was an impressive sight.

A warship of this class would be the king's flagship in dynastic wars, as when Óláfr Tryggvason of Norway, on the *Long Serpent*, battled Eiríkr Hákonarson, *jarl* of Lade, and Sveinn I Haraldsson *tjúguskegg* of Denmark, at the battle of Svölðr. The longest ship currently preserved from the viking age is Roskilde 6, discovered in February 1997, with a reconstructed length of more than thirty-seven metres (width 3.5 metres). Built around 1025, such a splendid ship would almost certainly be the property of royalty, and it is tempting to link the find to Knútr I Sveinsson, who then ruled Denmark and southern Sweden from England. The ship's sail has been estimated at 200 square metres, and with its thirty-nine – maybe forty – pairs of oars, this aquatic leviathan must have been a splendid sight. A true saga ship, it could easily carry a hundred warriors, and without doubt would have had its bellicose image enhanced by a fine dragon-head prow.

A dragon-head prow epitomizes the popular concept of a viking ship, and rightly so. An apparently tenth-century Icelandic law (as copied into *Landnámabók* in the fourteenth century) prohibited ships with dragon-head prows from entering harbour, lest the frightening appearance of the ship threaten the tranquillity of the *landvættir*, land spirits. As the law clearly stated, the ship's crew should 'unship them before they came in sight of land, and not sail near the land with figure heads with jaws gaping and wide or grinning muzzles, which would terrify the *landvættir*',[108] and presumably others on the island. The *landvættir*, which had lived there before men, were offended by any form of violence.

Sea battles in the viking age were fought on stationary ships and were more like land battles waged on floating islands upon which the contending forces engaged in close combat, that is, attempted to board the enemy vessels and cutting down their crews with the sword or the axe. With that, the battles had three parts. First, steersmen on each ship manoeuvred for the most favourable position, relative to both friend and foe. Battles were fought in protected fjords, or in the lee of an island where marksmanship would not be spoiled by rocking decks. Missiles (such as arrows and spears) were fired as the ships closed and drew together. Sails were furled, and it is possible that masts were un-stepped. Ships were tied together, creating floating islands. Opposing crews tried to board the outermost ships in the tied-together fleet, with the goal of clearing the deck of the enemy. Hand-to-hand fighting on the decks of the ships determined the outcome (an undertaking fraught with danger in itself because of the confined space). When the outermost ship was cleared, it was cut loose and set adrift, to make it possible to board the next ship making up the 'island'. Small boats swarmed around the battle to kill any combatants that tried to save themselves by jumping overboard. At Svölðr, for instance, a survivor *sá Trönu ok báða Naðra fljóta auða* 'saw the two 'Serpents' [*Short Serpent* and *Long Serpent*], the swift *Crane* too, float crewless'.[109] Obviously, it was far harder to run away from an enemy onslaught on board ship than on land. Thus, battles on sea were far more dangerous and fiercer then battles by land, for on sea there was no recoiling or fleeing. Driven from their decks, the vanquished were engulfed in defeat.

Back at the river Níza, the fight having emptied seventy ships of the Danes – *á einni svipstund*, 'in a twinkling of an eye' according to the skald Þjóðólfr Arnórsson – their fleet broke ranks and, as the skald Steinn Herdísarson says, *heit und blés blóði á sæ*, 'hot wound(s) spouted blood onto the sea'.[110] Badly beaten, Sveinn Estriðsson survived the day by jumping overboard, barely making it ashore ahead of the Norwegians hunting for him (again, according to Þjóðólfr Arnórsson).[111] This 'scurvy' means of escape brought derision from at least one of the skalds present, Arnórr Þórðarson *jarlaskáld*:

> Crewless floated the fearless / friend-of-Jutes' [Sveinn's] swift warship,
> / ere that the *æðeling* fled, with / all its warriors fallen.[112]

Nonetheless, Sveinn was back in Denmark the following winter with undiminished revenues and the approbation of his people. It was the remarkable brutality of Haraldr, the wanton destruction, the ruthless butchery that kept Sveinn on his throne. In the spring of 1064 (*Morkinskinna* dates it to 1065), after lengthy and tortuous argument, Haraldr finally made unconditional peace with the Danes, recognizing Sveinn as their rightful king. The man who had virtually lost all the battles had effectively won the war, and Sveinn would outlive Haraldr by eight years.

Sveinn claimed Denmark through his mother, Estrið (Estrið being the Danish form of Ástríðr), the daughter of Sveinn I Haraldsson *tjúguskegg*, and half-sister of Knútr Sveinsson and also the half-sister of king Óláfr *sköttkonungr*. Sveinn was the son of the disgraced *jarl* Úlfr Þorgilsson who was defeated (possibly, as the written sources cannot agree as to which side he was fighting for) at the Helgeä river in eastern Scania (1026), and later cut down in his pride and treachery in the church of Saint Lucius in Roskilde (ON *Hroiskelda*) on the orders of Knútr Sveinsson for having, in secret concert with queen Emma, had elected as king of Denmark his son Hörða-Knútr, whom Knútr promptly deposed. Little wonder, therefore, Sveinn felt obliged to adopt his mother's name Estrið (whence Estriðsson and not Úlfsson – generally speaking, a child would take a metronymic rather than the more common patronymic when the father was unknown, deceased or less prominent than the mother).

It is worth noting that Sveinn's aunt Gyða became the wife of the most powerful warlord in Anglo-Scandinavian England, *eorl* Godwin Wulfnoðsson of Wessex (d. 1053), and so was mother to the Godwinson brothers, Harold and Tostig. In 1069

Sveinn would cross the cold North Sea at the head of a large fleet to join the English opponents of William I, variously known as the Bastard or the Conqueror, claiming England as rightful successor to Knútr – despite the fact the rebellion was led by Edgar *æðeling*, the last surviving male of the royal house of Wessex who had been passed over in 1066 due to his youth and the political supremacy of Harold Godwinson. The following year Sveinn would take York, the second city of England, but his invasion was not, as it happened, destined to succeed. He made peace with William and returned to Denmark.[113] William then began the systematic destruction of opposition in an episode known as the 'Harrying of the North' in the winter of 1069/70. The aim may have been as much to render the area unattractive to Sveinn as to punish the rebels.

Sveinn may have been a fairly ineffectual war leader, but five of his sons succeeded in turn. Fascinatingly, his bones were dug up at Roskilde and reconstructed by F.C. Hansen in 1914. He was tall (over two metres when the average was below 172 centimetres) bore the marks of his adventures as a self-made king: three broken ribs, an awkward twist to the back, head skewed to the right, reminders of hard fighting. With his big flat head, receding forehead, beetle brow, long nose and slight overbite, he looked majestic if he stood still, but walked knocked-kneed and flat footed;[114] in *Haralds saga Sigurðarsonar* a rough-tongued farmer's wife calls him a 'wretched king... He is both halt and a coward'.[115] His brain capacity was above average and Adam of Bremen, who knew him well, found him an intelligent and persuasive talker. His affability, lechery and wit were celebrated by Icelanders over a century after his death, and the dynasty kept his memory green in Denmark.

Domestic issues

Having muscled his way to the kingship, Haraldr would have to convince the Norwegian nobility that he was the right person to rule Norway alone. To establish domestic alliances and consolidate his power, he married Þóra Þórbergsdotter of one of the most powerful Norwegian families. Yet savoir-faire was not one of his strong suits, much preferring ruthlessness towards individual opponents or potential enemies. The primary opposition to Haraldr's rule would be the descendants of Hákon Sigurðarson, from the powerful dynasty of jarls of Lade (ON *Hlaðir*), which lay just a couple of kilometres east of Nidaros, who had controlled northern Norway and Trøndelag with much autonomy under the Norwegian king. Hákon had even ruled the whole of Norway (nominally under the Danish king) from 975 until 995, when he was killed during the takeover by the southern king Óláfr Tryggvason. Even after Hákon's death his offspring held a certain degree of sovereignty in the north, and at the beginning of Haraldr's reign the family was headed by Einarr *þambarskelfir*, the extraordinary archer who had fought beside Óláfr Tryggvason when the kingdom fell from his hand at the battle of Svölðr. Einarr, however, was still held in high enough regard by the victorious *jarl* Eiríkr Hákonarson to be given his sister Bergljot in marriage. While the family had maintained good relations with Magnús, Haraldr's absolutism and consolidation of his kingship soon led to conflict with Einarr.

Although the relationship between Haraldr and Einarr was poor from the start, the altercation did not occur before Haraldr went north to his court in Nidaros. One time in Nidaros, Einarr arrived at Haraldr's royal residence, and in an overt display of power was accompanied by 'a great host – eight or nine warships – and a crew of some five hundred [viz. six hundred] men',[116] obviously seeking a showdown. Haraldr was not to be provoked by the incident, composing some lines of verse in which the king casually claimed 'the mighty chieftain' will be made 'to kiss the axe's thin lips'.[117] Although the sources differ on the circumstances, the next event nonetheless led to the 'axe-kissing' the king had promised in his poetry, which threatened to throw Norway into a state of civil war. When the news was brought to Einarr's wife, Bergljot, she cried out for vengeance: 'Now we feel the want of my kinsman, Hákon Ivársson [her great-nephew]. The slayers of Eindriði [her son] would not be rowing down the river [the Nid] if Hákon stood here on the banks'.[118]

Although the remaining descendants of Hákon Sigurðarson considered open rebellion against the king, Haraldr eventually managed to negotiate peace with them, and secured the family's submission for the remainder of his reign. With the death of Einarr, and of his son Eindriði, the jarls of Lade had outlived their rôle as a focus of opposition, and Trøndelag was definitely subordinated to Haraldr's national kingdom.

Before Níza, Haraldr had been joined by Hákon Ivársson, great-grandson of *jarl* Hákon Sigurðarson, who distinguished himself in the sea battle and gained the king's favour. Reportedly even considering giving him the title of *jarl*, Hákon Ivársson was greatly offended when Haraldr later backed down from his promise. With a strong hold over Uppland, Hákon was granted the revenues of Värmland by the Swedish king Steinkel. In early 1064, Hákon entered Uppland and collected their taxes, the district thus effectively threatening to renounce their loyalty to Haraldr. The revolt of Hákon and the *bændr* in Uppland may have been the main reason why Haraldr finally had been willing to enter a peace agreement with Sveinn Estriðsson. After the agreement, Harald resided in Ósló for the winter and sent tax collectors to Uppland, only to find that the *bændr* would withhold their taxes until Hákon arrived. In response, Haraldr entered Sweden with an army and quickly defeated Hákon. Still facing opposition from the *bændr*, Haraldr embarked on a campaign to crush the areas that had withheld their taxes.

Due to the remote location of the region in the interior of the country, Uppland had never been an integrated part of the Norwegian king's realm. Using harsh measures, Haraldr burned down farms and small villages, and had people maimed and killed. Starting in Raumarike, his operation of fire and sword continued into Hedemark, Hadeland and Hringaríki. Since these districts contained much of the best farming and pasture land in Norway, Haraldr strengthened his economic position by confiscating farming estates. By the end of 1065, with the stern hand of Haraldr making itself felt, there was peace of sorts in Norway, as any opposition had been killed, chased into exile or silenced.

Chapter 5

Conquest

Befone we examine the last adventure of Haraldr Sigurðarson, we need to pause and consider viking activity against Anglo-Saxon England and Carolingian Frankia.

The growth of royal power in Denmark around the end of the eighth century under the strong king Godofred, contemporary and rival of that eminent expansionist Charlemagne, has plausibly been linked to the beginning of viking raids, as lesser political leaders and rivals for power were driven overseas to seek fortune and prestige. Likewise, the strong rule of his son Hörik I Godofredsson (r. 827–54) was probably a factor in the resurgence of viking raids.

The Northmen were not the first foreigners nor, for that matter, the first pagans to attack the British Isles and Frankia They were much like the Romans and the Anglo-Saxons before them – pagan, exploitive, persistent – but unlike their invading predecessors the Northmen eventually became assimilated. Moreover, their horizons were different: they reached Ireland and other parts of the British Isles (and places beyond) untouched by these earlier invaders. Unlike the Roman and Anglo-Saxon invaders, the Northmen also had the misfortune, as they would have seen it, of having their deeds reported by a uniformly hostile 'press'. These unlettered far-northerners left no contemporary written accounts of these events: nothing left to challenge the native annalists and chroniclers, who naturally viewed these invasions with fear and horror.

It can be argued that the reason for the widespread and genuine terror that these raids produced was a result not of deliberate 'terror tactics' but of the fact that their seaborne raids from unknown and distant lands could not be countered and retaliated against in the usual ways. After all, violence was still very much a standard tool of international politics, and with that the rulers of the English and Frankish kingdoms also led their followers on regular military expeditions with the aim of securing wealth either in plunder or in land. For among them it was the practice for annual assemblies to be held, in which the kings and the nobility would, among other things, decide upon the target for a military campaign in which they would all join later in the year. The resulting spoils of war played an important part in enhancing the power of the most effective of the English and Frankish kings. Thus, in the eyes of the English and Frankish rulers, the viking raids were unprovoked: they had not raided Norse cattle; they had not burned

Norse homes; and they had not enslaved Norse women and children, or murdered Norse old folk.

After all, bloodshed and cruelty were commonplace in war and peace all through Christendom. It is certainly surprising that Northmen should have been singled out as especially evil, or deliberately depraved, when it is not recorded in the habitually unsympathetic Christian sources (nearly all the work of clerics) that they ever executed in cold blood over 4,000 disarmed prisoners of war, as did Charlemagne in Saxony; or perpetrated genocide, as did Cædwalla of Wessex on the people of the Isle of Wright;[1] or order the massacre of all foreigners in their kingdom, as did Æthelred II;[2] or mutilated thousands of prisoners, as did Basil II in Bulgaria.[3] No doubt they would have done so, if they ever commanded the time, the resources and the administrative machinery. In their case their predatory and mobile conduct was geared to looting, blackmail and enslavement, and for all the harm they did in burning, enslaving and impoverishing westerners, 'war crimes' were the prerogative of those thought nowadays as the champions of civilization and Christianity. The one god of the Christians was not adverse to large-scale devastation and wholesale slaughter, any more than were Óðinn or Þórr. These people were not as nice about distinction between various shades of morality as we are; our notion of 'humanity' was alien to both sides.

With buoyant speed

One of the reasons the vikings were so scary and effective was that they were marching over alien territory. Without local loyalties to obsess on, and without vulnerable families in the war zone, they went where they pleased. And they killed, tortured and burned whatever they found. That made their war bands much more flexible and effective than the local militias that were tied to home turf. The point I am trying to make is that the peculiarity of the viking raids was symptomatic of their origin in a classic confrontation between a sea power and land powers. They were able to strike at their land-based opponents at almost any point they chose while remaining largely immune across the sea to any such counterattacks. They were operating outside the geographic reach of their homeland. In this respect, the typical viking craft was a low, sleek, clinker-built vessel driven by sail and oars, and the crew member was also the warrior, gave the vikings the mobility to suddenly come over the horizon and easily prey on the coastal and riverine regions of Europe.

Clearly the construction of these craft is of importance here, and good evidence comes in the shape of a fourth-century boat deposited at Nydam Mose, southern Jutland. Deliberately sunk, the boat was laden with war booty, including over a hundred swords. Built of an oak felled in 310–20, the boat was some 23.7 metres long, 3.5 metres broad and 1.2 metres deep. Warrior oarsmen, twenty-eight in number, propelled this open vessel, while a steersman controlled it by means of a large steering-paddle on the starboard ('steer-board') side. The boat shows an early well-developed hull of clinker construction. It is the first physical evidence of the success of this 'shell' type of construction; with overlapping planks firmly secured to the stem at each end providing a light, strong but flexible, seaworthy hull.

A seaworthy hull does not only have to keep afloat under extreme conditions, but also requires some control over its destination, as demonstrated in many accounts of Norse boat journeys. Built from the bottom up, the keel-less hull was built from eleven broad oaken planks, and was furnished with barb-shaped oar-locks, fourteen per side, lashed to the gunwales. The overlapping strakes were fastened with iron clinch-nails. Experimental archaeology tells us that something like 700 kilograms of these nails were needed to make a 15.5-metre hull and, in round about terms, iron was as expensive as silver is to us today. The hull was rendered watertight by jamming pieces of tarred wool into the overlaps between the clinker-laid planks. There was no deck but the transverse timbers were shaped in a way that made them suitable for supporting loose floorboards.[4] The Nydam boat had no mast and therefore did not carry a sail.

The Nydam boat could go up shallow rivers, overcome tidal bores, and even risk the open seas. Prokopios tells us that Angle warships of his day 'do not use sail for seafaring, they only use oars',[5] and, to all intents and purposes, the Nydam boat was a sleek, seagoing rowing boat. But this forerunner of the Norse warship known as a 'longship' had too major drawbacks: the absence of a keel rendered it less manoeuvrable in swift currents and adverse winds; it had no sail. Nevertheless, all its technical features would live on in the longship (viz. oars, low freeboard, broad amidships, dragon-headed prow), with the most important development being the transformation from rowing to sailing ship, which of course still is propelled by oars alone. During swift attacks on foreign shores rapid manoeuvring without the dependence on the wind was absolutely crucial.

The classic features of the viking-age sailing ship can be seen in the Gokstad ship: light in the water, graceful to the eye, speedy at full sail, and easy to beach. Though this virtually complete viking ship was buried in the late eight-nineties, the Gokstad ship could have been fifty years old at that time, which would mean that it could be a ship of the early viking period. The ship measures 23.33 metres long, 5.25 metres broad amidships, and 1.95 metres from the keel to a line from starboard to port gunwale amidships. Built entirely of oak, except for the decking, mast, and yards, it probably weighed as much as eighteen tons and probably drew ninety to ninety-five centimetres, a very shallow draught. The most remarkable part of this ship is its keel; carved from a single oak timber, it measures 17.6 metres long and tapers in depth from forty-two centimetres amidships to thirty-seven centimetres at its ends. The oak tree from which the keel was shaped must have been at least twenty-five metres high and, of necessity, straight. Craftsmen fashioned this keel so that it formed a gentle arc about twenty-five centimetres deeper in the centre than fore and aft and they created thereby a shallow ship.

Once the keel was laid, then the bow and stern posts, each a single piece of oak, were affixed to it by wooden nails. With the keel and end posts in place, it appears that the siding was then attached to them and, only after that, nineteen frames and cross-beams were stretched across the ship to keep the sidings in place. Each side was constructed of sixteen strakes (planks), each overlapping the one below it (i.e. clinker-built). The oar-strake on each side had sixteen circular oar-holes, which could be closed by wooden shutters when the ship was under sail. Above the topmost strake a thick gunwale was placed. A shield rack along the gunwale permitted thirty-two shields to be hung overlapping on the outside: the remains of all sixty-four shields were found at the Gokstad site. Decking was placed on, but not attached to, the cross-beams. The ship was steered by a long rudder, which was not placed at the bow but, rather, was fastened to a piece of wood, called the wart, on the starboard (steerboard) quarter.

The mast has not survived in its original state, and its height and, consequently, the height of the sail are not known with any certainty. Whatever its precise height – somewhere between ten and thirteen metres – the mast was set into a heavy housing on the keel amidships; from this housing it could be removed as conditions required. The sail was rectangular in shape or, perhaps, closer to being a square (possibly eleven square metres). Probably checked or striped and made of coarse wool, the sail hung from a yard; lines attached from the bottom of the sail to points along the gunwale provided the necessary ability to reach (i.e. sail across the wind) and to tack (i.e. sail on the wind).

Even so, there was no such thing as *the* viking ship: there were, indeed, many kinds of viking ships, varying not only in length (from about six metres to about thirty metres) but also in means of power (oars or sail/oars). Norse sagas, skaldic poetry and rune stones mention a variety of names for different types of ships, yet it is difficult to match names to categories, but the main division was between trading vessels and warships. The building method was identical for both classes, but the dimensions clearly demonstrate that they were meant for different functions.

Trading ships (described by terms such as *knarr*, *knörr* and *hafskip*) were built to give plenty of room for cargo, to be manoeuvred by a few men, and to cope with bad weather. Characterized by a heavier construction, they were beamier, with a length-to-width ratio of only 4:1, had higher gunwales, and an open hold in the middle with deck planking and oars at bow and stern only. They were meant to be driven mainly by sails; it must have been tedious to row them with such a small crew.

As previously mentioned, a warship (described variously as *snekkja*, *drekar* and *langskip*) was built to be swift and manoeuvrable, to carry many men, and to move quickly even without sails. It did not have to be completely seaworthy; raids were made in summer, and there was time to wait for good weather if open sea had to be crossed. The speed was achieved by a 7:1 ratio of length to width, manoeuvrability by a curved keel, which allowed it to turn around its central axis. To guarantee a high speed without sails there was room for many rowers on a straight deck running along the full length. There were probably so many crewmen that the oars could be manned day and night. If so, then the crew of a warship probably numbered more than twice the number of oars, and as each warrior took along his whole equipment, space must have been very tight. On the other hand, trading ships had a smaller number of men, but more than half of the ship was filled with trade goods. Thus, to name two well-known examples, the 16.3 metre long Skuldelev 1 – a completely seaworthy trading ship – could be sailed by just five to eight men, whereas the thirty-metre warship Skuldelev 2 had a crew of thirty or so.

Slaughter to settlement

The earliest documented foray by the vikings is that upon the monastery of Lindisfarne (8 June 793), when it was plundered and some monks were slain.[6] Situated at the end of a causeway, off the coast of the northern Anglo-Saxon kingdom of Northumbria, Lindisfarne was a spiritual, cultural and intellectual powerhouse. Not for nothing is it still known as Holy Island. For those Anglo-Saxons who heard of it, the sacking of Lindisfarne was an offence against God, learning and the sense that the Anglo-Saxon kingdoms were safe from external threats. Far away in the court of Charlemagne, the Northumbrian monk and scholar (he taught the Frankish monarch rhetoric and dialectic), Alcuin of York (d. 804), eloquently recorded his profound shock at the events that had unfolded off the Northumbrian coast in a letter he wrote to Æthelred, king of the Northumbrians:

> It is nearly 350 years that we and our fathers have inhabited this most lovely land, and never before has such a terror appeared in Britain as we have now suffered from a pagan race, nor was it thought that such an inroad from the sea could be made. Behold, the church of Saint Cuthbert spattered with the blood of the priests of God, despoiled of all its ornaments; a place more venerable than all in Britain is given as a prey to pagan peoples.[7]

The cause, Alcuin moralized, was the failure of the monks to live up to their monastic ideal; God was punishing them for their unfaithfulness to Him.

Allowing for the rhetoric of the moralist, the possible distortion of events in the transmission, and the piety of a native Northumbrian, it still remains abundantly clear that this event struck deep to the heart of Alcuin, not merely for what it was but also for what it portended. Still, allowing for regional variations and twilight zones, modern scholars distinguish four discernible phases to the viking raids.

During the first phase (790–840) the vikings used their shallow draught ships, which were ideally suited for surprise raids on coastal and riverine locations. Indeed, it was thanks to their shallow draught that the ships could sail far upriver, so even in-landers so far from the sea were within range of the raiders. Furthermore, the shallow draught made for fast and easy disembarkation during a raid. Another relevant characteristic was the ship's side-mounted rudder, fixed to the uppermost plank at the right rear and controlled by a single helmsman by means of a horizontal tiller bar. The rudder itself was deeper than the keel, and on approaching the beach it was simply taken aboard. When the ship was beached, a warrior could be certain that if he jumped out near the stem, the water would scarcely be over his knees. The crew could leave the ship and join the raid quickly and confidently. Hedeby 1 and Skuldelev 2 are both about thirty metres long, Roskilde 6 over thirty-seven metres in length, and none of these surviving longships are more than 3.7 metres wide or have a draught of much more than one metre. This means they were all about ten times longer than they were wide and could have sailed close enough into the shoreline for the crew to be able to jump out and wade ashore with ease. These are characteristics we have come to expect associated with viking amphibious warfare methods and this is precisely what these three ships were built for – the rapid transport of raiders, the ability to penetrate far up rivers and into fjords, and instant landing on any shore.

Gone as swiftly as they had arrived, the fleets were modest in size and manned by personal war bands that employed hit-and-run tactics. These raids were habitually seasonal and isolated, occurring along the coasts of England, Frankia and Friesland. The year 840 and the death of Louis *le Pieux* are generally viewed as a watershed. With the Frankish nobility at one another's throats, the Frankish empire became a viking hunting ground.

The second phase (841–75) saw a marked increase in activity, with the raids multiplying in number, size, intensity and speed. Arriving unexpectedly, the war bands secured booty, either killing or enslaving their victims, and left straight away. They met no or little organized resistance, which accounted for their immense success in this period. In 843, for the first time, the Northmen wintered on foreign soil, at the monastic island of Noirmoutier, just south of the mouth of the Loire, which was the centre of the salt and wine trade.[8] The establishment of winter bases (*wintersetl*) and the requisitioning of local horses meant that they could now spread their activities farther afield. For example, in 864 they secured their boats on the Charente and travelled cross-country by horse as far as Clermont in the Auvergne. Not for nothing has Eric Christiansen listed the spade as a key weapon in the viking armoury;[9] the Roman penchant – rigorously applied – for pitching a fortified camp at the end of each day's march (usually at midday, and not thereafter) is well known, but that of the viking not so. Yet the context of over wintering also had more sinister overtone—quick plunder in the spring.

As the Northmen were not a single unified people it meant that it was possible to hire one band of vikings to defend against other bands of vikings. This could be done with one-off official payments, such as that made by Charles *le chauve*, king of the West Franks, in 860 to the viking leader Weland to attack a rival viking fleet at Oissel on the Somme. Weland, however, subsequently accepted an even larger amount from these vikings to break off his assault, and joined forces with them before again making his peace with Charles, only to be killed by his own men the following year. The story of Weland demonstrates the instability of a relationship based on one-off payments.

The inflow from the Atlantic deterred mediaeval navigators from making a regular passage out of the Straits of Gibraltar, though it did not deter vikings (and others) from entering the Mediterranean. It comes as little surprise, therefore, to find that during this phase the Mediterranean receiving the attention of the Northmen. In the autumn of 844 a fleet of fifty-four longships sailed up the Guadalquivir and sacked Ishbiliyya (Seville), although it received a bloody repulse at the hands of a relief force sent from Qurtubah (Córdoba) – later Islamic sources have captured vikings hung from palm trees – and the survivors returned to the Loire valley where they settled. This attack on Ishbiliyya was obviously memorable event as it is mentioned by the Muslim geographer Ahmad ibn Abi al-Ya'qubi (d. 897/8), who reports that the sea raiders were 'the Magus (*al-majus*), who are called the Rus' [*ar-Rus*]'.[10] The Persian word *magus*, probably familiar to us from the magi of the gospels, is a term usually used in Islamic sources to describe the followers of the Zoroastrian religion, which was based on the recognition of the dual principle of good and evil or light and darkness, in Iran and Mesopotamia. However, here the term is used in the pejorative sense of 'unbelievers'. At any rate, in the autumn of 859 a second fleet of *magi*, this time under Björn *járnsíða* (Ironside, probably a reference to his byrnie) son of Ragnarr *loðbrók*, penetrated either further, raiding al-Andalus, or Islamic Spain, North Africa, Provence, Italy – heading for Rome, but mistakenly sacked the northern Italian town of Lúna (Luni) instead, which amounts to sacking Carlisle believing it was London – and then back to al-Andalus where it was finally defeated in the neighbourhood of Gibraltar. Only twenty of the original sixty-two ships returned to Noirmoutier in 862. The Northmen had found the followers of Allah formidable foes.

In England, desultory raiding continued but began again more earnestly in 865, when a large force, described as the 'great heathen army',[11] led by two brothers of Björn *járnsíða*, Ívarr *inn beinlausi* and Hálfdan, wintered in East Anglia. By remaining on foreign soil, the vikings increased the political threat to local rulers. It was for this reason that many Anglo-Saxon and Frankish kings bought off the vikings in an attempt, which often proved to be futile, to remove them from their kingdoms.

In the third phase (876–980) the vikings were out for more lasting gain. As well as increasing their hold on lands in England and Frankia, they also permanently settled in Ireland, which had never been visited, much less subjugated, by Rome's legions, Man, the Hebrides, Orkney, Shetland, the Faeroes and Iceland, changing the political geography of these lands. Although the Northmen occasionally met with strong opposition, in England the *mycel hæþen here*, which was now the focus of Norse activity in the west, conquered the kingdoms of East Anglia and Northumbria and reduced Mercia to a fraction of its former size (865–79).

It is clear that – to start with at least – the force that landed in East Anglia possessed a size and a degree of unified command that caused it to have a devastating effect on its opponents. Yet the *mycel hæþen here* was unable to subdue the Wessex of Alfred (r. 871–99), with whom in 878 a truce was made, which became the basis of a treaty (Treaty of Wedmore, signed summer 886). This was a treaty between equals, as Alfred implicitly acknowledged that the whole of eastern England from the Tees to the Thames estuary was in Danish hands and that English law did not apply there (*Denelagu*, Danelaw). Although hard pressed by fresh armies of vikings from 892 to 899, Alfred was finally victorious over them, and other Northmen who tried their luck in his kingdom. For example, the *Anglo-Saxon Chronicle* records how in 896 a group of six viking ships raiding the south coast were surprised by a larger fleet of Anglo-Saxon ships while most of the crews were ashore. An engagement ensued, partly on ships and partly on the shoreline, and the raiders were defeated, with most of them killed or subsequently captured and executed. Only two ships escape, one supposedly with just five survivors, and the men on the other 'very much wounded'.[12]

Something similar may lie behind a mass grave found in June 2009 on Ridgeway Hill north of Weymouth, Dorset. The burial pit, which was in a disused Roman quarry, contained fifty-four dismembered skeletons and fifty-one decapitated heads, which had been piled separately at the edge of the pit. The skeletons were all of males, almost all aged from their late teens to around twenty-five years old, with a handful of older individuals. Radiocarbon dating of three individuals found that they dated to sometime between 970 and 1025, while isotope analysis of tooth enamel from ten skulls found that the men came from all over Scandinavia, including one from north of the Arctic Circle. All of them had been stripped of everything of value (there were no associated finds) and beheaded from the front with a large, very sharp blade. They had not been cleanly killed, as many of the victims had suffered multiple blows to the jaw, cranium and vertebrae. One man had his hands sliced through, suggesting that he had attempted to grab the weapon as it was being swung towards him. They had no obvious battle wounds and were most likely captives.

This situation is illustrated by a well-known story from *Heimskringla*. It is set in Norway in the year 986 and concerns the aftermath of the semi-legendary battle of Hjörungavágr, where *jarl* Hákon Sigurðarson, ruler of most of Norway until his murder in 995, defeated (he is reputed to have offered up one of his sons to secure victory) the fleet of the Danish Jómsvíkings, the famed members of a bachelor brigand community that feared no man and dared all. They had come north with a great fleet to wrest Norway from *jarl* Hákon. Vagn Ákason, a leading Jómsvíking who had gained admission at the tender age of twelve,[13] had been made captive, together with thirty of his crew, and brought ashore in shackles.

> Vagn and his men all sat together on a log. Þorkell (Leira) [a chieftain from Vík] wielded a big axe and hewed down the man who sat on the end of the log.
>
> Vagn and his companions were tied in such a fashion that a rope was slung around the feet of all of them, leaving their arms free. Then one said, 'Here I have a dagger in my hand, and I shall stick it in the ground if I am conscious when my head is chopped off'. He was beheaded, and the dagger dropped from his hand.
>
> Next to him sat a handsome man with long fine hair. He swept his hair forward over his head and stretched out his neck, saying, 'Don't sully my hair with blood.' A man took hold of his hair with a firm grip. Þorkell swung his axe, but the viking swiftly jerked his head back, so the man holding his hair was forced forward, and the axe fell on both his hands, shearing them off, so that the axe struck the ground.[14]

To cut a long story short, eighteen men were beheaded and the remaining twelve, including Vagn, received quarter. Although the actual existence of the mercenary brotherhood of the Jómsvíkings is very much doubted in academic circles, and despite the preposterous heroics in the face of certain death, the picture rings true. This brings us back to the executions in Anglo-Saxon England. Fifty or so is a realistic number for the crew of a warship conforming to a model of thirty pairs of oars, such as Hedeby 1 (*c.* 985) and Skuldelev 2 (*c.* 1042). So the mass grave itself clearly represents the aftermath of a single execution event, namely a boatload of Norse raiders, which had been carried out by local Anglo-Saxons. As there are more bodies than skulls, it is suggested that a couple of the heads – perhaps of high-ranking individuals – were kept to be put on public display.[15]

In reality, the spirit of Wessex was so little broken that Alfred's son and successor, Edward the Elder (r. 899–924), was able to commence the re-conquest of Danish England. Before his death the small Danish states on old Mercian and East Anglian territory had fallen before him, which meant that all lands south of the Humber were once more in Anglo-Saxon hands. The more remote Northumbria resisted longer, largely under Hiberno–Norse kings from Ireland, but Eadred (r. 946–55), the son of Edward the Elder who succeeded his brother Eadmund (r. 939–46), finally liquidated the Scandinavian power there in 954 when the last independent king of York, Eiríkr *blóðøx*, was driven out and fell in battle in an attempt to win back his kingdom. But that is a story we have already touched upon.

From bad to worse

The fourth and final phase (980–1016), when England ultimately becomes part of the North Sea empire of Knútr Sveinsson, coincides with the reign of Æthelred II (r. 978–1016), the unfortunate king who was accorded in the twelfth century the unflattering nickname of *unræd* ('no counsel/wisdom', or perhaps 'ill-advised'), as a bitter contrast to the meaning of his actual name, 'royal counsel/wisdom'. The pun then could mean that Æthelred was given bad advice, did not take advice, or simply that he was unwise; it could mean worse, that he was guilty of acts of evil. Certainly *unraedas* were what England was plagued with: all these disasters befell us through *unraedas*, 'bad policies', says a contemporary chronicler in 1011, and does so again in 1016.[16] The pun is a clever one and there is no reason to think it only arose nearly two centuries later, as some have thought. The nickname is quite in keeping with the irony displayed by our chronicler. Undeniably, having acquired the poorest reputation of any English king, Æthelred has popularly been remembered as 'Ethelred the Unready'. According to the authors of the satirical *1066 and all that* he was 'the first Weak King of England and was thus the cause of a fresh Wave of Danes'.[17]

And what of this 'fresh Wave of Danes'? The fourth phase can be sub-divided into four stages. The first stage (980–91) of this phase saw the resumption of viking activity in England after a lull of twenty-five years, though with mainly local effects, while the second stage (991–1005) witnessed heavier attacks.

These heavier attacks can be seen as the effects of a single large viking army on English territory from its arrival with ninety-three ships in 991 under the future evangelizing king of Norway, Óláfr Tryggvason, until the famine of 1005 forced it to return to Denmark. It was this army that fought *ealdorman* Byrhtnoth at Maldon, and received tribute (the notorious Danegeld) in 991 (10,000 pounds in silver), 994 (16,000 pounds), and 1002 (24,000 pounds) – note how the figures steadily increase.

Hoards of coins of this period are widely known in Scandinavia and indeed, more late Anglo-Saxon silver coins have been found there than in England. The raids were no longer mere plundering attacks, but destructive forays designed to achieve the maximum damage and to extort the largest amount of Danegeld possible – astonishingly large, these tributes reflect not only the designs of the Danes but also the wealth of England. It should be said that contemporaries did not criticize Æthelred for paying the geld so much as for paying it too late, after the damage had been done.

The third stage (1006–12) of this fourth phase saw two invasions. The first, in 1006, was only stopped by a massive payment of tribute in 1007 (36,000 pounds in silver).[18] It was at this nadir of his fortunes that Æthelred was cajoled into action. In 1008 the king ordered that a fleet be built, but local rivalries limited its usefulness, and it did not prevent the arrival in 1009 of another immense viking army led by one of the most successful freelance vikings of the day, the Dane Þorkell *inn hávi* (the Tall). Þorkell harried much of southern England, and only ceased after the payment of tribute in 1012 (48,000 pounds in silver), in addition to supplying him and his men sufficient food and wine. For reasons unknown, Þorkell suddenly decided that it is more profitable to eat at the king's table than to steal food from it. He struck a deal with Æthelred. He and his men would defend Æthelred's realm in return for being fed and clothed, thereby becoming a valuable, if unpopular, ally of the English royal house, checking the progress of the Danish invasion of 1013.

From the sublime to the ridiculous there is but one step. The *Anglo-Saxon Chronicle* narrative for the year 1013 shows that Þorkell's army, like that of the Danish, ravaged the country 'as often as they pleased',[19] in spite of Æthelred payments and supplying of provisions: Þorkell's forty-five ships seem to have been scarcely less fatal to the English now than in the days of their hostility. Whichever side he fought on, Þorkell was an independent warlord first and a dependable ally a long way second.

This brings us to the fourth stage (1013–16), which again saw two invasions, both of which culminated in the conquest of England. Led by Sveinn I Haraldsson *tjúguskegg* of Denmark, the first invasion arrived in 1013, the year the English kingdom that had existed since Æthelstan's day finally came apart. Virtually a king without a country, the thought of engaging the dreaded Sveinn in battle apparently did not thrill Æthelred, and caused him to vacate his throne in favour of a safe haven in Normandy. Ironically, it was Þorkell's mercenary fleet that carried him there.

Sveinn's son would return with a second invasion force in 1016 and go on to rule England. The son was of course Knútr I Sveinsson *inn ríki* (the Great), known to modern English historians as Cnut and to ordinary Englishmen as Canute, who by 1027 could in his letter to the English people title himself *Rex totius Angliae et Denemarchiae et Norregiae et partis Swavorum* – he was king of Denmark 1014–35, England 1014, 1016–35, Norway 1028–35, and part of Sweden (probably Skåne, in southern Sweden) 1026–35.[20] By the by, the five Skuldelev ships (now resurrected and on display) mirrors the 'nationality' of the political reach of Knútr's North Sea empire – two were built of Danish wood (Skuldelev 3 and 5), two were built in Norway (Skuldelev 1 and 6) and one ship (Skuldelev 2) was built in Ireland.

Knútr had first come to England with his father back in 1013, and following Sveinn's untimely death in the first weeks of 1014, barely a month after winning the crown of England, returned to Denmark before renewing his claim to England. In the meantime, Æthelred had been invited back to England – but on terms. He had to promise to govern his people 'more justly than he did before... and to be a gracious lord to them and reform all the things which they hated'.[21] The blinding or killing of nobles, desertion of his troops, failure to pursue a policy to its end: so many entries in the *Anglo-Saxon Chronicle* indicate that the king had acted with cruelty and folly. Nothing illustrated this more than the massacre of Saint Brice's Day (13 November) in 1002 when the panic-stricken, paranoiac Æthelred 'ordered slain all the Danish men who were in England',[22] or (in the words of a royal charter of 1004) a 'most just extermination' of 'all the Danes who had sprung up in this island, sprouting like cockles amongst the wheat'.[23] The justification was the Danes intended to kill the king along with all the members of the *witan*. A total ethnic cleansing of all the Danes in England would have been quite impossible, as Danish settlers had been established in eastern England since the ninth century and, since the reign of Edward the Elder, had been increasingly intertwined with English society and its ruling elites. The most likely scenario is that, in 1002, Æthelred ordered the deaths of prominent and recognizably distinct Danish settlers who had arrived in England during the previous decade. But as often happens, events got out of hand. In Oxford, for instance, the Danes there had taken refuge in the church of Saint Fritheswide, where they were burned alive by a mob inflamed by the government's anti-Danish rhetoric. It is sad to say that even today certain things do not change. Hatred is still ugly.

Æthelred had no luck: he was unlucky to become king in the way he did (a royal murder had brought him to the English throne); unlucky that Danish attacks should come so hard on the heels of his accession; unlucky in the strength, skill and staying power of the Danish leaders who attacked him. Even so, the successful viking-age kings had contributed to their own luck. And the English, as they were to show later, could still fight and win under a good war leader. Æthelred's brief period of glory was over by the following year. In the spring of 1015 the king's son Eadmund Ironside (the nickname was probably contemporary and referred to his bravery), who was about the same age as Knútr, quarrelled with his father and struck out on his own. Other English leaders decided to throw in their lot with Knútr. Æthelred tried to raise another army, but with the air full of rumours of betrayal, he abandoned his levies and retired to London where he spent the winter of 1015/16. There Eadmund joined him. The way was now clear for Knútr to strike the final blow. He closed in on London with all his army only to learn that Æthelred had passed away on Saint George's Day (23 April) 1016.

Eadmund was acclaimed king. He devoted the following six months to a courageous but finally unsuccessful struggle to prevent Knútr from gaining mastery of England. No fewer than six battles were fought during these months. The last of them, fought on 18 October at Assandun, 'the hill of ash trees', now Ashingdon a few kilometres north of Southend, proved a decisive defeat for the English army. Even so, Knútr agreed a division: Eadmund was left with Wessex; Knútr took the rest of the English kingdom, including London. Such a partition would in all likelihood have proved unworkable, but following the death of Eadmund on Saint Andrew's Day (30 November), *feng Cnut cyng to eall Engla landes rice*.[24] The passing of the brave Eadmund was a most convenient turn of events for Knútr, but there is no contemporary suggestion of foul play. There remained the legacy of war to be paid. Two years later, in 1018, the last and biggest Danegeld was paid to Knútr. England had to raise 72,000 pounds in silver, in addition to which the truculent citizens of London had to provide another 10,500 pounds. This enormous sum went to pay off the bulk of Knútr's invasion army, mercenaries in the main.

The last phase of viking raiding has produced different theories from historians and archaeologists. From around 965, the Arab trade routes into Russia and beyond began to suffer from an acute shortage of silver, due to the exhaustion of the silver mines that had previously supplied the Islamic world. This was a major problem, as the availability of Arab silver had fuelled a far-flung trade network in which the products of eastern and northern Europe, including slaves, were exchanged for Arab coins. These became the silver armbands and ingots that supported gift-exchange, tribute and the rewarding of Norse warriors. At the same time that the supply of Arab silver faltered, the growing power of the Kievan Russia made it more difficult for Norse adventurers to seize precious metals as booty. The decline in the eastern trade routes may also help explain the presence of Swedish vikings in the fourth phase of attacks on England, since they were no longer benefiting from the eastern trade that they had previously dominated. This shutting off of the silver supply from the east was simultaneously accompanied by more silver becoming available in western Europe, due to the discovery of new silver sources in the Hartz mountains in the nine-sixties; this caused Norse raiders to target western Europe again, to compensate for the lack of silver moving into Scandinavia from the east.

Enter the Normans

The Normans who had given shelter to Æthelred were, ironically, themselves descendants of vikings. Charles *le simple* (r. 898–923), king of the West Franks, had ended the raids on his kingdom by granting large swathes of land around Rouen (then called Neustria) to the vikings led by a man named Hrólfr (Treaty of Saint-Clair-sur-Epte, signed autumn 911). Like Huiglaucus who ruled the Geats (a people occupying what is today southern Sweden), he was such a huge man that no horse could bear his weight, so he had to go everywhere on foot; for that reason he was known as *Göngu*-Hrólfr, Hrólfr the Ganger.[25] History would get to know him better as Rollo.

Rollo, a son of *jarl* Rögnvaldr of Möer, found himself exiled from Norway for breaking the ban on raiding within the realm of Harald *hárfagri*. Rollo and his followers, old campaigners who were survivors of the raid to England in 892 to 896, operated along the Seine at the turn of the tenth century, so much so that Charles was forced to come to terms. Legend has it that Rollo treated the act of making homage with something less than the respect due to Christian majesty. When the moment came for him to kiss the royal foot he bent down and grasped it and then, straightening to his full height, hauled the foot up to his lips. The king, naturally, fell flat on his back, much to the merriment of Rollo's men. Even if this story has no better foundation in fact than the fertile and impish imaginations of later historians, what is not beyond dispute is the dawn of the duchy of Normandy (ON *Northmandy*) – though its early rulers were styled by the Frankish title of count (*comes piratarum*, 'count of the pirates', viz. vikings) rather than *dux*, duke.

Boisterous antics aside, in return Rollo pledged his allegiance to Charles, was then baptized the following year as well as gaining Gisèle, the king's daughter, in marriage, and thereafter he and his successors defended the mouth of the Seine against other viking visitors. Normandy so swiftly adopted the language and institutions of the Franks that it was transformed from a Scandinavian stronghold into a feudal Frankish province within little more than a generation and there is, for example, no evidence of the Norse tongue in use after 940. It has left few traces in the French language except for nautical words (e.g. *bâbord*, port [side], *tribord*, starboard, *quille*, keel, *havre*, haven) and place names (e.g. those ending *-bec*, *-bu*, *-dique*, *-tot*). Nevertheless, daring, vigour, drive, vitality and the warlike trait invariably – and not at all unreasonably – associated with the Northman does appear to have passed down to his Norman descendant in the thrust of Norman conquest southwards into Italy and Sicily, eastwards to Antioch and, of course, over the Channel to England. Rollo's great-great-great-grandson was duke William of Normandy.

The invader

Histtory is never as neat and tidy as we would wish, but the date is not entirely arbitrary: the year 1066 changed the kingdom of England forever. The Norman Conquest has always been recognized as one of the great watersheds in English history. The consequences were dramatic and far-reaching for monarchy, ruling élite, language of government, social system, architecture, and landscape. However, one consequence of that fateful year often overlooked was the spectacular shift in England's position in Europe. Instead of remaining within the orbit of a greater Scandinavian empire, England was dragged into mainland continental politics, with new enemies to fear.

Game of thrones

England on the eve of the Norman Conquest remains a subject of confusion and obscurity. The kingdom is ruled by Edward, an elderly and ailing king, sometimes known as the Confessor because of his piety. It is a prosperous and peaceful kingdom, secure in the knowledge that it is separated from the more troubled mainland of Europe by the English Channel. The kingdom is divided into earldoms, which are ruled by nobles, and it is these nobles who think about the future of the country. Most prominent of the earls is Harold Godwinson, *eorl* of Wessex, who is very popular with the people and who has been virtually running the country since the start of the king's illness.

When Edward passed away on 5 January 1066, there were a number of claimants to the now vacant English throne, a rich prize with all its prestige and perquisites. Contemporary pro-Norman chroniclers, such as Guillaume de Jumièges and William de Poitiérs, vigorously state that Edward had nominated William, duke of Normandy, as his successor as early as 1051. This meant that the kingdom of England had become William's and his alone, by hereditary right. William himself claimed that Harold, *eorl* of Wessex, had been sent to him in 1064 to confirm Edward's grant. However, evidence from the *Anglo-Saxon Chronicle* and the Bayeux tapestry suggests that Edward entrusted the kingdom to Harold on his deathbed, a decision that was ratified by the *witan*, the assembly of England's leading nobles or *þegns*. Another rival was Edgar *æðeling*, the son of Edward the Exile, whose presence at the English court was a reminder of his direct descent from the old Anglo-Saxon royal family exiled in 1016. There was also a wildcard in the pack, Harold's dissident younger brother Tostig Godwinson, erstwhile *eorl* of Northumbria. And then there was of course Haraldr III Sigurðarson *harðráði*, king of Norway.

Tostig (ON *Tósti*) had been sent into exile in the autumn of 1065 and spent the winter in Flanders. The *eorl* of Northumbria at the death in 1055 of the previously very popular *eorl* Siward (the Danish warlord best remembered, thanks to Shakespeare, for his martial exploits against Macbeth),[26] Tostig was the first man from southern England to govern the northern earldom.[27] Though brave, shrewd, and hard, Tostig tried his damnedest for ten years to govern this distant and difficult earldom but failed. In short, he possessed all the attributes of power and riches necessary for unpopularity, and was widely considered by his subjects as a villain. The reputation was possibly overdrawn. Siward had been a Scandinavian by birth, a similarity that he had in common with many of the Northumbrians; they considered Tostig a 'southern foreigner'. He was ousted from office and exiled from England along with his family and retainers following a violent uprising in Northumbria for which it seems he was partially to blame. Though done reluctantly by Edward, Tostig being a favourite of the elderly king, his disposition was to set in motion the train of events that were not only fatal to Tostig himself but also to the Anglo-Saxon (really Anglo-Scandinavian) kingdom of England.

As we well know, Haraldr Sigurðarson was a violent adventurer, and in 1066, as in the past, he showed his propensity to ill-considered action. His reign in Norway had meant twenty years of strenuous warfare against his neighbours and subjects, financed by a dwindling stock of Byzantine gold. It was to end in a bid for the only card worth having: a reliable tax base overseas.

Seeing one another across the battlefield, it is reputed that Haraldr of Norway said of Harold of England, 'A little man that was, and proudly he stood in his stirrups'... and when asked what he was prepared to offer king Haraldr 'for his pains', king Harold wittedly replied 'seven feet of English soil or so much more as he is taller than other men'.[28] How right Harold was, in a way. Skilled in the laconic form of apothegmatic repartee he may have been, but we should very much like to know when it first occurred to Harold Godwinson that he might succeed Edward as king of England. Was it shortly after the sudden death of the king's half-nephew, Edward *æðeling* (also known as Edward the Exile), in 1057? Perhaps. In the end we shall never know for certain, however long we chew the bones.

Two things are certain, though. First, in twenty years of marriage Edward had failed to produce a single heir, and this failure had inevitably caused an aura of uncertainty to hang over the delicate matter of the royal succession. Second, Harold's own claim to the throne of England was somewhat questionable, being the Confessor's brother-in-law (through his sister Eadgyða) though without a claim by descent. What he had in abundance, however, was wealth, power and supporters. When he ascended the throne of England, Harold married Ealdyð, the widow of Gruffydd ap Llywelyn, king of Gwynedd, daughter of Ælfgar, the previous *eorl* of Mercia, and sister to Edwin, *eorl* of Mercia, and Morkere, *eorl* of Northumbria. This marriage secured an alliance with the only rival family to the Godwinson dynasty in the kingdom, and it seems also to have led to peace between the powerful northern English earldoms and their new southern king.[29]

Crowned the very day of Edward's funeral, Harold II Godwinson would reign, in the laconic words of the *Anglo-Saxon Chronicle*, *xl. wucena. ænne dæg*, 'forty weeks and one day'.[30] His reign was not only brutally short but bloodily eventful too.

Haraldr's claim

Destined to be a victim of his own vaulting ambitions, Haraldr Sigurðarson had claimed, and indeed was attempting to make good his claim, to be king of England as well as of Norway. Actually his claim to the English throne was little more than a slender pretext based on an ambiguous treaty drawn up some thirty odd years previously, but it mattered not to a man whose every *raison d'être* was war and the warrior's way. Haraldr's claim was based on a treaty entered into between Hörða-Knútr of Denmark (r. 1035–42) and England (r. 1040–2), and Magnús I Óláfsson *góði*, Haraldr's kinsmen and predecessor as king of Norway (r. 1035–47) and the last Norwegian king to rule Denmark (r. 1042–7). Having took each other for foster-brother and pledged everlasting peace, it was apparently agreed that if either party should die without a male heir the survivor would inherit the deceased's domain.[31]

Hörða-Knútr, from Hörða in Jutland, was Knútr Sveinsson's son by his lawful wife, Emma of Normandy, and therefore his only legitimate heir. However it was Knútr's illegitimate son, Harold I Harefoot (r. 1035–40), the second issue of his Mercian mistress Ælfgifu of Northampton, who was recognized as king in England in 1037, he being the preferred candidate (he was half-Mercian) of the powerful northern magnates of said kingdom. Thus, Hörða-Knútr was at the time not yet king in England (whose name is usually spelled Hardecanute in English histories), although he did become king on his half-brother's sudden (and suspicious) demise in 1040.

There is a story, which may be fanciful, that before Ælfgifu became the mistress of Knútr, she had been the lover of Óláfr Haraldsson during one of his stints as a fighter in England. The story continues, saying that Ælfgifu's affair with the Knútr was the main cause of the enmity that subsequently arose between him and Óláfr. What is known with greater certainty is that during her relationship with Knútr two sons were born, Harold Harefoot, destined to succeed his father as king of England, and Sveinn Knútsson, who would rule as king of Norway under her own regency between 1030 (after Óláfr had been killed at Stiklastaðir attempting a comeback) and 1035. Sveinn is a back-story character in the first act of *Macbeth*, where Shakespeare calls him 'Sweno, the Norway's king'.[32]

And here is another interesting story, one with a whiff of sexual scandal. In *Encomium Emmæ Reginæ* ('A Book in Praise of Queen Emma', also known as *Gesta Cnutonis Regis*), composed in the early ten-forties by a Flemish monk in Saint Omer at the request of Emma of Normandy, Knútr's widowed queen and bitter rival of Ælfgifu of Northampton, an allegation is made about the pedigree of Harold Harefoot. It is claimed that Harold, rather than being Ælfgifu's child, was actually the son of a servant girl, who, as a newborn baby, had been smuggled into Ælfgifu's bedchamber so that he could be passed off as a child of her union with Knútr. The rumour about Harold's lowly parentage was evidently widespread; it also found its way into four versions of the *Anglo-Saxon Chronicle* for the year 1035,[33] the year he became king of England. In the next century the rumours were repeated in more detail by the cleric chronicler John of Worcester.

Here, interestingly enough, John says it was the other bastard son, Swegn (i.e. Sveinn), who was smuggled into the royal bedchamber, Ælfgifu having 'ordered the newborn child of some priest's concubine to be brought to her, and made the king believe that she had borne him a son'. Whilst of Harold Harefoot he wrote in the same paragraph that:

> Harold claimed to be the son of king Canute by Ælfgifu of Northampton, but that is quite untrue, for some say that he was the son of a certain *sutor* [cobbler], but that Ælfgifu acted in the same way as she had done with Sveinn. But because the matter is open to doubt, we have been unable to make a firm statement of the parentage of either.[34]

Sveinn, then, is supposed to be the bastard son of a fornicating priest; Harold the offspring of a common cobbler. Which brings us to the rather compelling argument that the eponymous lady depicted in the Bayeux tapestry with a priest is none other than Ælfgifu of Northampton. The Latin *titulus* above the two woollen figures is enigmatically short but suggestive. All it says is UBI UNUS CLERICUS ET ÆLFGYVA (Where a priest and Ælfgifu...).[35] According to J. Bard McNulty, who first proposed that the eponymous lady depicted in the Bayeux tapestry with a priest was Ælfgifu of Northampton, the reason for her portrayal at this point in the tapestry was to undermine the Norwegian claim to the English throne.[36]

Returning to the contentious issue of the Danish and English crowns, Hörða-Knútr in turn was to die childless two years after his half-brother Harold Harefoot, apparently of an excessive consumption of alcohol.[37] So now, in 1042, the thrones of both Denmark and England were dangerously vacant, and the pathetic brood of the great Knútr Sveinsson was exhausted. The succession in Denmark had already been decided by the aforementioned treaty between Hörða-Knútr and Magnús I Óláfsson *góði*. There was only one other legitimate claimant: Sveinn Estriðsson son of Estrið, the half-sister of Knútr. As Knútr's nephew he was the rightful heir by blood to Denmark; but Magnús gave him no time to advance his claim. He came sweeping down from Norway with a formidable fleet and simply took possession.

In the meantime, the English promptly chose an English ruler, Hörða-Knútr's older step-brother, Edward (r. 1042–66), better known to posterity as 'the Confessor'. Edward was the issue of Emma of Normandy and her first husband, Æthelred II, and had been in exile on the continent. And so the English crown reverted to the Anglo-Saxon line.

Danish rule had lasted twenty-eight years, and it had not only brought peace for the first time in decades but had brought a good deal of Scandinavian cultural to England too. In the military sphere this was reflected in the rising use of the Dane axe instead of the spear, and the introduction of a professional standing military force, the housecarls, as the core of the royal army. This group of warriors formed part of the king's household but were not tied to him by land grant or the traditional giving of gifts, as was the case with Scandinavian housecarls, but by salary. It is possible that the earls began to create their own bodies of housecarls after the reign of Knútr, though this remains a matter of scholarly debate, as it may be that the term came to mean any senior noble's household rather than a military body. Nonetheless, there may have been as many as 3,000 royal housecarls under Harold II Godwinson at Hastings on Saturday, 14 October 1066.

Yet institutional continuity and the ordered exploitation of England by Knútr and his sons should not blind us to the fact that the Danish conquest was a brutal affair. The English hostages whose hands, ears and noses Knútr had cut off in 1014 could have testified to this effect.[38] Likewise the farmers who lost their livelihood, and in many cases their lives:

> Before you, young as you were, / You burned men's farms. / You often
> made the farmers / Sound the alarm for the destroyer of houses.[39]

So said the Icelandic skald Óttarr *svarti* (the Black) in his praise poem for the king. There were executions, confiscations of property, banishments, extortion, unjust taxation, and many acts of injustice. In some ways Knútr looks like a barbarian conqueror from the heroic age of Scandinavia. It is of interest in this connection that the Old English epic *Beowulf*, which celebrates such a warlord, survives in a manuscript copied, probably, during Knútr's lifetime. Though some scholars have gone so far as to suggest the work was actually composed in the king's honour, there is now a general recognition that a late ninth- to early eleventh-century genesis for *Beowulf* is quite possible due to the strong cultural, mercantile and political interaction between English and Danes during these centuries. The poem itself was preserved by only one manuscript dated to around the year 1000. Manuscripts are fragile and easily destroyed by time or fire: the *Beowulf* manuscript (Cotton Vitellius A. xv), which is now housed in the British Library, has scorch marks on it.[40]

Knútr after all was a man to fear. A man who cut off body parts for no reason, and liquidated all the major secular leaders he did not trust. But the influence of the Church was such that he became respected and admired as a king who was just, who was a conscious emulator of the great kings of Wessex, a pious man who endowed the Church. The picture of him (one hand on his sword, he donates a gold cross to Christ) in the *Liber Vitae* of the New Minster, Winchester, sums it up: the big tough flaxen-haired young warlord (only around twenty-years-of age when he became king), former 'terrorist' turned the Lord's Anointed, it shows how easily he could move from the world of Scandinavian paganism to that of Christian European kingship. Indeed in 1027 he went on a pilgrimage to Rome. Knútr, incidentally, never tried to order back the flowing tide. In fact, far from a sign of folly, the story was to prove the king's sense and humility, showing flattering courtiers that even the greatest king cannot control the waves, that earthly authority has its limits. The story was later distorted to make Knútr appear arrogant.

Knútr ruled England until his death on 12 November 1035. Between 1017 and 1035 there is record of Knútr being absent from the kingdom on no more than four or five occasions, and each time fairly briefly. What is apparent therefore is the dominant proportion of his reign that Knútr spent in England, and how this would appear to signal England rather than Denmark as the centre of his Scandinavian empire where before its contacts had been more closely tied to Carolingian Europe and Rome. Indeed, Knútr seems to have thought of England as a source of wealth, manpower, and skills on which he could draw for the prosecution of his greater ambitions in Scandinavia.

Returning back to the year 1042, naturally Magnús claimed *both* Denmark and England under the terms of the aforementioned treaty and until his death five years later was regarded with understandable apprehension by the English government of Edward. Edward had spent his exile in the court of his cousin Robert, duke of Normandy, and was open to Norman influence, which henceforth gained ground in England. He married the daughter of Godwin, *eorl* of Wessex, one of the most powerful lords in the land, but they did not produce any children, which was to have dire consequences for the realm in years to come.

Edward struggled to impose his wishes on his powerful earls, especially Godwin, Leofric of Mercia and Siward of Northumbria. Anglo-Scandinavian politics and intrigue aside, it was, of course, not to be. The situation went from bad to worse after a series of deaths left Godwin's sons Harold, Tostig, Gyrth and Leofwine ruling all the earldoms of the kingdom apart from Mercia. It seemed that the king became a mere figurehead from this time on. Little wonder, therefore, in 1066 England appeared vulnerable; vulnerability arouses the predator in most men. In Norway, his intermittent war with the Danish kingdom now over, Haraldr was looking for a new outlet for his energies, and the English succession crisis provided it.

The beginning of the end

The story told by Snorri Sturluson of how Haraldr, Varangian officer turned Norwegian king, inherited 'seven feet of English soil' is well known. What is not so well known is Snorri's story of Haraldr's last act before sailing for England in the summer of 1066. The king opened his half-brother's tomb and trimmed the saint's hair and nails. He then locked the tomb again and threw the key into the river Nid; 'nor has the shrine of holy king Óláfr been opened since that time'.[41]

Ahead of what must have been a final act of filial piety, Haraldr had prepared to make good his claim to the English throne by putting timber, sailcloth and men together and assembling a war fleet at Björgvin (Bergen). With the full war fleet assembled, armed and ready for the enterprise of England, the Norwegian armada must have looked an impressive sight. One of the Bergen rune sticks bears the brief inscription in runic characters: *Hér ferr hafdjarfr*, 'Here sails the sea-bold one'.[42] One easily imagines a sea-king, sunburned, salt-stained, storm-beaten, swaggering and clinking with iron, his face bearing the scars of battle, his longship gilded, carved, painted, visible from afar with raised mast and glittering weathervane above the dyed sail (in skaldic poetry and sagas dark blue [or black], red and purple sails are common),[43] his natural sphere the shore-less salt highway, his trade war and fighting his delight, sowing death and desolation, looting and burning settlements, enslaving the natives and turning a profit.

The rune stick (ON *rúnakefl*) is precisely that: a roughly whittled piece of stick, only twenty-five centimetres in length, cut from a juniper tree and split lengthwise. Juniper, which belongs to the cypress family, is the most widespread of conifers. This was also the case in our period of study. Juniper grew where no other trees were found, from the arid mountain slopes of the Mediterranean to the windswept coasts of the Faeroes, even by the icy sea in treeless Greenland, which very much reminds us of the scale of Norse exploration. In the words of Eric Oxenstierna, the Norsemen 'were the first people to visit four continents of this globe, a staggering fact, made all the more astounding when we take into consideration how far off the beaten track their Scandinavian homeland was'.[44]

The four continents referred to here are Europe, Asia, Africa, and North America, while this particular piece of juniper was excavated at the site of Bryggen in Bergen, and is dated to the period 1248 to 1332. Where it was split the surface was not properly smoothed; the bark side undressed, apart from trimming off a couple of twigs at the knots. Nevertheless, it had been decorated with ships on both the round and flat side. In addition, it bore the above-mentioned runic inscription. On the flat side are seen the prows of forty-eight ships, in a line abreast, overlapping each other and gradually decreasing in size towards the right side. In this way, the viewer gets the distinct impression of looking at a mighty war fleet, longships lying side by side, bobbing and bumping at anchor, ready to sail. The ships are tall and sweeping. Some carry carved figureheads or weathervanes on their prows, and others, resembling the stem of Skuldelev 5, are elegantly curved. The strakes of the clinker-built hulls are also shown.

Dating from around 1040 (and repaired 1060–80), Skuldelev 5 is a small warship of the *snekkja* type, a predatory, rapier-like vessel probably more typical of the kind that was used by the Northmen on their raids. It is 17.2 metres long and 2.6 metres broad, and has been much repaired, so that Ole Crumlin-Pedersen found it 'hard to believe that any prominent mid-11th century person who was keen about his reputation would have had such a ship for his personal use'.[45] Yet a ship of this size required a crew of about thirty warriors. Crumlin-Pedersen concludes that Skuldelev 5 was a levy-ship, of the type for which the twelfth-century Norwegian laws indicate that *bœndr* had to provide materials for their construction and maintenance as well as manning them. However, Niels Lund's interpretation of Skuldelev 5 is probably closer to the mark than Crumlin-Pedersen's. Lund compares it with the ships mentioned in runic inscriptions and owned by one or two men who took them on expeditions such as that led by Ingvarr the Far-Traveller, also in the mid-eleventh century.[46] Skuldelev 5 is made from oak, pine and ash, and was built in the Roskilde area. The ship was purpose-built for sailing in Danish waters and the Baltic Sea. It carried a sail estimated at 46.5 square metres and deployed twenty-six oars. A full-scale replica of Skuldelev 5, *Helge Ask*, has been constructed using archaeological data and traditional shipbuilding methods. Under sail, with a good breeze, *Helge Ask* has reached speeds of circa fifteen knots, and under oar power, even when rowing into the wind, can make a respectable 5.5 knots.

Ole Crumlin-Pedersen, a leading authority on mediaeval ships, has estimated that for a typical twenty-metre longship, approximately fifty-eight cubic metres of oak was required. This is equivalent to eleven oak tree trunks, each a metre in diameter and five metres long, along with a single eighteen-metre long trunk for the keel. Oaks of this size and of sufficient quality would be difficult or impossible to find today. To put this in some perspective, the keel of the Gokstad ship, which dates from the late eight-nineties, required a tall, straight-grown oak about twenty-five metres tall.[47]

What of Haraldr himself? Although the carving dates from a later period, the dragon-heads and weathervanes on the prow of some of the ships have parallels in the viking age. Unquestionably, this rune stick would have fitted Haraldr and his invasion of England admirably. When he, colossal in his prime, slipped across the North Sea with warlike intent, he did so with around 7,500 Northmen.[48] It is said he had nearly 240 ships.[49] He picked up allies in Shetland and Orkney, including two sons of the *jarl*, and at the mouth of the Tyne on 8 September, 'as they had previously arranged',[50] joined the twelve ships of Tostig Godwinson and the Flemish mercenaries hired by him.

Tostig's wife was Judith de Flandre, whom he had married in 1051. Her pedigree was impressive. She was the daughter of the late Baldwin IV Fairbeard (d. 1035), half-sister of the current, very influence count of Flanders, Baldwin V, and aunt of Mathilde de Flandre, queen consort of Duke William of Normandy (the Conqueror), who happened to be Judith's first cousin through her mother Eleanor of Normandy. Although everything else in Tostig's life eventually disintegrated, his marriage with Judith remained steadfastly solid.

At any rate, so the campaign narrative goes on, the combined fleets of Haraldr and Tostig then proceeded darkly down the English coast, slashing at the coastal towns on their route – at Cleveland, Scarborough, and Holderness.[51] At fifty-one years of age, thirty-six of them since he had been proved in the furnace of war on the field of blood at Stiklarstaðir, Haraldr was at the height of his powers, determined to sit upon the throne of England and determined to bring about a reestablishment of the North Sea empire of Knútr Sveinsson, the king who had taken Norway from him at the battle of Stiklarstaðir, the king had made his half-brother a martyr and a saint. To borrow those erudite words of that brilliant orientalist, T.E. Lawrence:

> All men dream, but not equally. Those who dream by night in the dusty recesses of their minds wake in the day to find it was vanity; but dreamers of the day are dangerous men, for they may act their dreams with open eyes, to make it possible.[52]

Not so for this particular dangerous man on this particular occasion. For it would be an unfulfilled, fatal day dream (we shall tell why at the appropriate moment).

The forgotten battle

When Haraldr invaded England, sailing into the Humber and up the Ouse, he landed at a place called *Richale* (now Riccall).[53] This settlement lay fifteen kilometres downstream of York, or *Jórvík*,[54] as Haraldr would have known it, a traditional Scandinavian bastion. The first organized resistance he was to meet was at Gate Fulford, baring the crossing of the Ouse just three kilometres south of York.[55] There, 'on Wednesday, the day before Saint Matthew's Day',[56] that is Wednesday 20 September, he faced the combined forces of the brothers Edwin, *eorl* of Mercia, and Morkere, *eorl* of Northumbria, who had to fight the Norse invaders without the bulk of the English strength, which is still being force marched northward by their lawful king, Harold Godwinson.

Though most often perceived as hit-and-run roving raiders, Norsemen in the tenth and eleventh centuries were, in fact, well armed and skilled professional warriors. According to Gwyn Jones, much of their success had to do with their significant tactical experience when on the defensive.[57] Given the opportunity, they always chose a strong defensive position, either on a hill or behind a stream or between two woods. This would be the case at Gate Fulford.

Gate Fulford as a battle is not as well known as the battle of Stamford Bridge (ON *Stafnfurðubryggja*, OE *Stantfordbrigge*) that occurred just five days later and has often tended to overshadow it. Haraldr arrayed his army with one end of his line 'on the bank of river, the other... further up on land and extended to a ditch'. Beyond the ditch lay marshland, 'deep and broad and full of water'. The battlefield, then, was a flat avenue between the river and impassable wetlands. The brothers Edwin and Morkere had chosen this ground well – even if their force was inferior in numbers to the Norwegian king's, they had flat ground on which to form their shield wall, and their flanks were well protected. The same, of course, applied to Haraldr. He placed his raven banner *Landøyðan* by the river and marshalled his best warriors there, spreading his least reliable troops, probably those of Tostig himself,[58] thinly on the right flank, beside the ditch and swamp.[59] The scene was thus set for the battle of Gate Fulford.

The two armies clashed. Casualties immediately accumulated underfoot. The English 'fought so bravely at the onset,' wrote John of Worcester, 'that many of the enemy were overthrown'. He continues, recording that 'after a long contest the English were unable to withstand the attacks of the Norwegians'.[60] It seems that Norwegian pressure began to bite, and, at last, the English line broke. John and Snorri Sturluson agree that panic spread, and men fled for their lives. The earls had been roundly defeated and much of the English army was hacked to pieces while trying to escape, John simply recording that 'more [English] were drowned in the river than slain in the field',[61] Snorri making more of a meal of it, saying that some of the English 'fled up or down along the river, but most leapt into the ditch. There the bodies of the fallen lay so thick that the Norwegians could walk dry-shod over the swamp'.[62] It was to be Haraldr's last victory.

It had been a long and extremely bloody encounter in which the balance of fortune fluctuated between English and Norwegian as the day progressed. It must have been a matter of dead tired men who had used up their adrenaline long since slogging it out. Finally, the English army had collapsed in rout and the road to York lay open; Haraldr had shown his teeth. With the army of Edwin and Morkere quite literally drowned, Haraldr and Tostig advanced to York. They did not storm the city, but negotiated its surrender, agreeing to an exchange of hostages as a token of faith, which was possibly to take place at Stamford Bridge. Suddenly the Northumbrian *witan* was acting once more as it had in the heady days of Eiríkr *blóðøx*.

Believing he had nothing more to fear in the north, Haraldr made promises of 'complete peace'.[63] Clearly satisfied with the progress of his English campaign, he then graciously withdrew his men to rejoin his fleet downstream on the Ouse at Riccall. His men were great fighters; he had laid an admirable plan. Nothing could possibly go wrong. Success was certain.

So matters might have rested. But alas, the magic was to desert him at Stamford Bridge. The skittish pride of man makes him believe that any thing he creates he can control. Whether inanimate or animate, it is in the nature of man to make his own monsters. Created out of his own imperfections, he animates them with magic, and never truly knows what they will do. Though he was to earn the cognomen *harðráði*, Haraldr was not immune from the occupational disease of rulers: overestimation of the capacity to control events. When the ego tries to control events the ego can only lose control of itself. The *Heimskringla* can be an eerie, fascinating read, made poignant because we know what happened next. In the event, the business of Gate Fulford proved to be the key to the entire campaign.

The final reckoning

Historians continually ponder the eternal question of whether history makes great people or whether great people make history and how individuals can determine the course of history as well as the rôle of unexpected fortune. Haraldr's last campaign was beginning auspiciously. The battle of Gate Fulford had been fought on 20 September, and the Norwegians had received the allegiance of *Jórvik* on 24 September. All this they may have planned; events were to take a different and more rapid course. As Haraldr and Tostig turned in that Sunday night on or near their ships at Riccall, what they did not realize, of course, was that the army of Harold Godwinson was only about twelve kilometres to the west of them. In a breathless march from London, the English army had reached the river Wharfe in time to spend the night at Tadcaster, some twenty-three kilometres south of York.[64]

War is played out in space and time. Speed is crucial. As Napoléon was later to assert: 'Strategy is the art of making use of time and space . . . space we can recover, time never'.[65] If, to cite the most well-known example of this observable fact, Napoléon had been able to lead his army into the field two hours earlier at Waterloo, things might have turned out very differently. Commenting on this, Victor Hugo wrote many years later, 'A little rain, and an unseasonable cloud crossing the sky, sufficed for the overthrow of the world'.[66]

Monday dawned, a sunny morning, much like any other. At this point the battle god who had favoured Haraldr on so many fields (and waters) of conflict seemed to have turned away and ultimately resolved on his destruction, for he made what proved to be a grave error in judgement. The Norwegian king still had no inkling that the English king was within striking distance. Thus, secure in his confidence that the day would proceed without incident, with fine, clear weather and warm September sunshine, he allowed his men making what was a reasonably long march to leave their byrnies behind, taking only their weapons, shields, and helmets. He probably predicted that collecting the hostages would be a matter of a leisurely lope. A comforting conclusion, but one which was divorced from the actuality. He was about to get a surprise.

As Haraldr and his men were marching merrily towards York under a clean-swept autumn sky, shields over their backs and helmet dangling from their belts, they saw an enormous cloud of dust. Below this storm of dust came an approaching army, 'and it looked like gleaming ice as the weapons shone'.[67] The Norwegians were in trouble. The brightening sky Haraldr had looked at that morning – the brightening sky Harold had looked at – had been cloudless. Before the sun had set that day, a lot of men would be dead, dying or wounded.

The conduct of any war has always been subject to the unexpected, and the campaign of 1066 proved no exception. To the surprise of the Norwegians, and to Haraldr's considerable consternation, the English were to catch the invaders, in the words of the anonymous author of the compilation of kings' sagas known as *Morkinskinna*, 'very mirthful'.[68] In their happy state they probably thought about what they could do to the English, not about what the English might do to them. Soon they would be singing a different tune. Haraldr, with only two-thirds of his remaining force, and most of them unarmoured, had clearly not expected the sudden arrival of the king of England 'with all his army'.[69]

If, with all the benefits that hindsight affords us, we are looking for a moment from which the English expedition was doomed, it was here, as Haraldr's men headed happily towards York. This was apparently the occasion of the last two poems of Haraldr. The first verse reads:

> We stride forward, / fighting bravely, / though byrnie-less, / 'gainst blue-steel swords. / Helmets do shine – / I have not mine: / below in the ships / lies our armour.

As soon as he had spoken this verse, Haraldr said: 'This verse is poorly composed, and I shall have to make another and better one'. He made another, one rich in kennings and metrically perfect:

> Hide within the hollow – / high-born maid thus bade me – / of our shields we surely / shall not, in battle-tumult: / high she bade me hold my / head, the Hildr-of-combat,[70] / when in bloody battle / blades and skulls were clashing.[71]

On the eve of battle, even the most intrepid warrior is subject to feelings over which he has little control. However, this feeling of pending misfortune is heightened not just by the doom-laden prose and poetry of our literary sources, but by the fact that we can only dimly see the final hours of Haraldr's life.

The fighting began untidily and haphazardly. Haraldr sent three men on horses to ride like the wind to the fleet at Riccall for backup and byrnies. Things went very badly very quickly for the Norwegians. The English rushed upon them, eager to get to grips. The Norwegians were thrown into a wholesale panic – no other word will do. The unarmoured warriors could put up only token resistance before fleeing across the Derwent. The English brought them down at will, like foxes among chickens. Many, like the English only five days before, dived into the river in desperation. Even without armour scores drowned, their bodies choking the surface of the river. The battle was already going badly for the Norwegians.

The day's event at Stamford Bridge may be surrounded by fables and legends, but there is one particular incident worth mentioning, that is of the giant Norwegian who made his stand alone on a narrow wooden bridge across the Derwent, a tributary of the river Ouse. Centuries later a commander would have called him a 'forlorn hope', a long-odds chance hastily hoping that all will be held at all hazards, which once in a while did succeed. Our Norwegian goliath stood there as a sort of statement – allegorical, mythical, biblical, magical – that to try to cross the bridge was against nature, decency, reason even. Unlike his comrades, this hero apparently had chosen to wear his byrnie that day, the mail deflecting the arrows of the English. One after another all who challenged him were hacked down and hurried on to the afterlife having felt the bite of his Dane axe. At length, a lone Englishman decided to creep unseen beneath the planking of the bridge. With a mighty shove he sent his spear through a crack in the planking, up under the enemy's byrnie and deep into his groin, so despatching him off to Valhöll and allowing his comrades free passage across the river. The personal valour and skill of this individual Norse warrior is not mentioned in any of the Old Norse sagas, it actually being celebrated by the twelfth-century historians Henry of Huntington and William of Malmesbury as also by an interpolation of the same date into *Anglo-Saxon Chronicle* manuscript

C by a scribe whose native tongue was not Old English.[72] It is the latter, less circumstantial source that informs us he had kept his byrnie.

Much of this may be regarded as part of the heroic code – the hero stands alone, he defies his foes – but it is also reckless. It is in the twelfth-century sources we learn that the lone Norwegian defender had been given the chance to surrender but declined the English offer and, or so says William of Malmesbury, 'skewing up his face, taunted them with being men so feeble-hearted that they could not stand up to a solitary man'.[73] According to the version of Henry of Huntington (d. 1155), this one Norwegian stood his ground, 'hewing down more than forty of the English with a battleaxe, his country's weapon'. His stand on the bridge did have two results. First, this giant of a man delayed the English and very probably gave some encouragement to his comrades. Second, the axeman on the bridge made an impression on his opponents. Henry of Huntingdon continues, saying the diehard warrior was 'worthy of eternal fame'.[74] And so he was.

The best laid plans and the most apparently sure advantages could disintegrate by the luck of the draw. Indeed, plans are made of ceramic and improved plans are the most brittle of all. Yet a wrong decision is better than a delayed decision. Or to put it another way, it is best to do something, even if it is wrong. For it was at this point Haraldr decided to stand and fight, and drew up his army. But just as he was riding to inspect the men his horse fell and threw him off forwards. This incident is reported by the Old Norse sources. But while the anonymous author of *Ágrip af Nóregskonúngasögum*, who was obviously a cleric, and the Benedictine monk Theodoricus Monachus make Haraldr admit that it is a bad omen,[75] in the other three sources he comments that 'a fall is a good omen':[76] it seems he needs it to be, to remain consistent with the decisions he has taken so far. He needs to keep on pretending that he has a chance of winning the battle, in order to involve his men as much as he can in his desperate and crazy pursuit of his own way, however disastrous. After all, he had won every battle except his first. Of course, as we all know, the fateful 25 September would end in Haraldr's sanguineous and spectacular death.

'[T]hat day a very stubborn battle was fought by both sides', so says one version of the *Anglo-Saxon Chronicle*,[77] but the day was to go the English way.

Uncanny warriors

Before we pursue this narrative, we should note something of those Scandinavian warriors who English speakers call berserkers. We can interpret the iconography of the warriors who appear to be biting their shields, bursting to commit mayhem, as a reflection of a literally tradition enshrined in some of the Old Norse sagas that these are *berserkir*, which probably meant 'bearskin dressers'. The element *ber-* was sometimes interpreted as *berr-*, meaning 'bare', which Snorri Sturluson understood to mean that *berserkir* went into battle bare-chested, or:

> [W]ent without byrnies, and were mad as dogs or wolves, and bit on their shields, and were as strong as bears or bulls; people they slew, and neither fire nor iron would deal with them.[78]

This view is no longer generally accepted.[79] In fact, the word may imply that a *berserkr* went into the fray wearing the skin of a bear or assumed the ferocious qualities and strength of a bear. The same could be said of a wolf. For instance, one Icelandic saga calls the *berserkr* of Haraldr *hárfagri* 'wolf-skins (*úlfhéðnar*), for on them would no iron bite',[80] and the term *úlfhéðnar* (sg. *úlfhéðinn*) also appears in *Vatnsdæla saga*, which gives to understand that 'those berserks who were called *úlfhéðnar* had wolf-skin coats (*vargstakkr*) for byrnies'.[81] The tenth-century Norwegian skald Eyvindr Finnsson *skáldaspillir* attests such warriors with his line: 'This hero bore the grey wolf-cape in the one-eyed's storm'.[82] The 'one-eyed's storm' is a kenning for battle, the 'one-eyed' being Óðinn of course. These warriors, with the heads of wolves (and bears), are depicted on bronze panels for helmets and sword scabbards from sites in Sweden.[83]

This concept of immunity from iron may have evolved from a trance-like rage, or *berserksgangr*, during which the *berserkir* might receive wounds, but due to his state of frenzy take no note of them until the madness passed from him. Saxo Grammaticus explained how the *úlfhéðnar* would appear in battle:

> Their eyes glared as though a flame burned in the sockets, they ground their teeth, and frothed at the mouth; they gnawed at their shield rims, and are said to have sometimes bitten them through, and as they rushed into conflict they yelped as dogs or howled as wolves.[84]

A warrior who continued fighting while bearing mortal wounds would surely have been a terrifying opponent. Mediaeval Icelandic law prohibited *berserksgangr* – 'if a man goes berserk, he will be punished by the lesser outlawry' – and required those present to restrain someone in *berserksgangr*. Failure to do so incurred a penalty of one-half pound of silver and three years' exile.[85]

The most notorious lunatics of the viking age, these were the wild and enormously strong warriors who worked themselves into such a paroxysmal frenzy before battle that they barked and bayed, and did indeed bite their bucklers. Four of the warders that make up the Lewis Chessmen are biting their shield rims.[86] Equally, the berserker Ljot who fought Egill Skallagrímsson entered the duel 'howling horribly and biting his shield'.[87] Having shuffled off their humanity altogether, to become completely bestial, they were now ready to throw themselves into a fight with such reckless abandon, running headlong into a dozen spear points. As legions of the damned, jesting with fate, it seems as if they wanted to die there and then. Such possessed fighting men might have made them less than ideal dinner guests, but they were often kept by a Norse king (ON *konungr*), earl (ON *jarl*) or chieftain (ON *höfðingi*) about his court as useful in feud and fray, for all that they were antisocial, sociopaths even. Still, he would be lucky to get a couple of summers out of psychotic fellows such as these. However, they did have, when crazy-eyed and cloaked in others' blood, the distinct advantage of terrorizing an unsuspecting enemy.

There is of course vast scholarly disagreement as to the precise nature of the *berserkir*. Theories range from them being a mere literary plot-device or stock-villain, over frothing madmen and werewolves to élite warriors with a very real technique of inducing frenzy to aid battlefield-endeavours.[88] While it may be deemed unscientific to assume that they really were able to change their shape, it might be interesting to examine how those stories came to be and what they meant to contemporaries who believed in them. Famed killer and skald Egill Skallagrímsson was known to fly into a frothing rage from time to time, but it was his grandfather Úlfr, called Kveld-Úlfr, who was said to be a *berserkr* and a *mjok hamrammr*, which literally means 'someone who could change their shape by magic'. This is reflected in grandfather's name Kveld-Úlfr, 'evening-wolf', and hints at the assumption that he became a wolf during the night. Belief in werewolves was widespread in mediaeval times, and Kveld-Úlfr was the shape shifting berserker in the family.[89] Úlfr is indeed described as a wise man and formidable warrior – he was a Norwegian *hersir* – who even in old age managed to fly into a berserk's brutal rage and change his shape to become of hideous aspect and fight his enemies.

In one notable episode Kveld-Úlfr slew a number of men with a cleaver before reaching his opponent Hallvarðr and cutting through both Hallvarðr's helmet and skull and flinging him overboard in one movement. With regard to *mjok hamrammr* or *berserksgangr*:

> [A]s long as they're in the frenzy they're so strong that nothing is too much for them, but as soon as they're out of it they become much weaker than normal. That's how it was with Kveld-Úlfr; as soon as the frenzy left him he felt worn out by the battle he'd been fighting, and grew so weak as a result of it all that he had to take to his bed.[90]

Such men, like Kveld-Úlfr, were particularly powerful at night time, as was the nature of shape shifters.[91] And so it was that an Icelander called Oddr Arngeirson 'left his home at Hraunhofn [in far northeast of Iceland] one evening and the next morning appeared in Þiorsardal [in the south-south-west] to save his sister Þurid when the Þiorsardal people were going to stone her to death for witchcraft and sorcery'.[92] Stoning was the standard death for witches and wizards. Yet Óðinn himself was a shape shifter:

> When he did so his body would lie there as if he were asleep or dead; but himself, in an instant, in the shape of a bird or animal, a fish or a serpent, went to distant countries on his or other men's errands.[93]

This brings us back to Oddr who covered in one night no less than 240 kilometres across the icy wilderness of the interior of Iceland, which was a dangerous no-man's-land sporadically shaken by seismic activity and volcanic eruptions, so as to save his sister by sunrise.

Naturally, the *berserkir* have occasioned much debate amongst scholars.[94] Who were they? Are our sources reliable as an expression of pagan ideas or are *berserkir* a pure literary fiction? Following the scientific researches of Howard Fabing,[95] some scholars argue that berserkers employed a raw mushroom, namely *Amanita muscaria*, to give them reckless power in battle. Commonly known as Fly Agaric – the quintessential bright red cap with white worts of enchanted forests and faerie groves – this strong drug induces hallucinations, senseless rioting, prophetic sight, erotic energy, and remarkable muscular strength, in effect making man a beast of prey. Some hours of this mindless ecstasy are followed by complete inertia. Fly Agaric grows naturally, though only in symbiosis with birch and/or pine trees, in most of Scandinavia. This is all speculative. No contemporary or near contemporary Old Norse source mentions its use or of any similar mind-altering substances. Indeed, are we to believe that *berserksgangr* was simply a matter of synthetic rage?

On the other hand, the traditional way of looking at the *berserkir*, namely as warriors who in some way were associated with bears, is not entirely outlandish. It is impossible to tell whether they fought in bearskins or whether they were perhaps only transformed into bears by magic. However, this would not prevent them from roaring like bears when fighting the actual battles, which was probably rather frightening. Of course, the belief that these warriors were bears only has to do with the magical transformation: being a warrior of this special kind would demand that they were strong and savage like bears. Thus, there is no reason to imagine that these *berserkir* were ever thought of as bears in any essential way. Likewise, *úlfhéðnar* could be regarded as warriors whose character and fighting spirit showed certain wolfish traits. Animals and other natural species are, as was maintained by Lévi-Strauss many years ago, 'good to think [with]',[96] because they may illuminate how different groups of people are related to each other, namely in the same way as different groups of animals are related.

In his poem of praise for Harald *hárfagri* at the sea battle on the Hafrsfjord Þórbjörn Hornklofi says that berserkers and wolf-skins began the fight: 'Their *berserkir* bellowed / as the battle opened, / the *úlfhéðnar* shrieked aloud / and shook their weapons'.[97] Since Þórbjörn wrote these lines for the king and other eye-witnesses soon after the battle, they must be close to the truth. The fact that he pairs *berserkir* and *úlfhéðnar* adds weight to the argument that that both are animal-warriors and that his berserks, as their name says, are bear-warriors. Accepting that certain groups of warriors were thought of as bears does not necessarily mean anything else than accepting that players from a certain football club may be called lions or sharks or similar names. They are not thought of as lions or sharks, but when playing football they act like these animals in a metaphorical way. And so with *berserkir* and *úlfhéðnar* in battle.

Egils saga Skallagrímssonar says of Harald *hárfagri* at the Hafrsfjord he had twelve berserkers, 'men that iron could never bite', in the bow of his flagship, which was in the van.[98] Snorri Sturluson likewise has the king man his flagship with berserkers and bodyguards.[99] Berserkers thus had the rôle to open battles.

Also, Haraldr died

We will never know what went through the mind of Haraldr Sigurðarson as he stood and watched the fast approach of the English army, but he seemed to have taken a resigned, and rather realistic, view of the situation when he stated, 'we will put up a fierce fight for a time before we succumb'.[100] The smell was there: defeat. So it may have come to the king that, since die he must, the thing would be best done boldly. Standing on the boundary between life and death, the king then raised his treasured raven banner, *Landøyðan*, as a symbol to his men that they were to prepare for battle.

With a great shout the English army broke into a run, crossing the scant few metres between the two forces. At this point we have to imagine a terrible crash sounded along the battle line as the two armies smash into each other. Many men died before they could strike a blow.

Haraldr is said to have been struck by an arrow in the throat. 'That was his death wound'.[101] So death, when it came, was almost hushed. It struck out of the battleline, came from the English, with a hiss. Desperation often called for desperate, reckless measures. 'Filled with the rage of war',[102] almost on the verge of insanity, he had leaped forth in front of the scattered battleline, and finally fell while fighting fiercely two-handed and without armour. Running, fierce of aspect, into the open arena between the two armies, Haraldr must had been an irresistible phenomenon – in the grip of a berserk rage, blood and brain spattered, terrible and terrifying, possibly looking no longer fully human after all the chopping and cutting, determined to go down fighting. The vicious one-man assault was an undoubtedly brave, but predictably terminal, intervention in the battle of Stamford Bridge: a man can but die upon his death day. Haraldr had gone over the edge; the other edge, berserk.

We ought probably to presume, then, that far from being oblivious to the shadow of death, in his final charge the king realized that he was involved in a now hopeless battle. Now he knew he had entered the province of death. Quite clearly he had cast his shield away in great fervency (or in despair), no longer caring that it would mean his death. We can easily believe that Haraldr had been born without fear. He certainly did not dread death, for it was not really so difficult to face death if one knew that one had to die. More to the point, death on the red field of battle meant Haraldr would feast with Óðinn for all time. So, when he lost his life at Stamford Bridge in the flaming September sun he cheated death (I suggest) by embracing it *berserkr*-style, passing through death to heroized immortality.

To the cosmos, the death of one man could hardly have any more significance than that of a butterfly, but in the realm of mankind, a single death could be immortalized. Men's bodies fade away, but ink lives on. With this debonair disregard for death, Haraldr lives on still in the northern sagas and the chronicles of his enemies.[103] Crystallized in the perpetual memory the chroniclers achieved for him, Haraldr Sigurðarson forever lives larger than life, brilliant, rapacious, valiant, cruel, and the gusto turned up to eleven. It was the act of a hero of pagan legend, not of the ruler of a Christian kingdom.

Undeniably, dying of old age was not considered to be saga-worthy, even if examples of this occur even among the acknowledged Norse warriors. For example, the aging of the great viking heroes, such as Egill Skallagrímsson or Víga-Glúmr, is described in somewhat pathetic tones.[104] Aging and the resulting diminishing of male capabilities has unmanly connotations – drooling, palsied, quivering carcass, slow of thought and crippled in mind and body; the Northmen said of such men, 'he died as a cow in the straw'. According to the Norse world view the best qualities of human beings are masculine, and in Norse society men who grow old and can no longer carry out acts of physical aggression or defence are described in feminine ways. Norse thinking regarded death away from the battlefield and in the comfort of one's bed as an ignominy and a sin. And thus a 'straw death' was shameful; an Óðinn cultist would do well to kill in battle, and eventually be killed himself. As Haraldr appreciated, part of the warrior's reward for a good death is that others will long remember him. Remembrance is a real and valued form of immortality. This lust for a heroic, violent death is best expressed by John Dryden in his libretto for the semi-opera *King Arthur*, set to music by Henry Purcell and first performed in 1691:

> Brave souls, to be renowned in story / Honour prizing, / Death despising, / Fame acquiring, / Die and reap the fruit of glory.[105]

In brief, Haraldr chose to die in such a spectacular way because he would rather be seen (and remembered) to die bravely then live with the knowledge of his defeat.

This is the end

To finish the Stamford Bridge story. The death of the leader normally decided the outcome of a battle. And so it was at Stamford Bridge. In only half a day's fighting, the question of who would henceforth rule the kingdom of England was seemingly settled. However, though the death of Haraldr was the decisive moment, the fighting at the end of the day must have proven especially pitiful. Eysteinn Orri, having made a nineteen-hot-kilometre march in full battle gear, arrived with reinforcements from the ships, but his intervention served only to prolong the slaughter. Eysteinn picked up Haraldr's fallen banner, *Landøyðan*, and initiated a final counterattack with his near-exhausted men. 'It was even in the balance whether the English would fly', says *Morkinskinna*.[106] While for a moment the Norwegians appeared to almost breach the English line, Eysteinn was suddenly killed, leaving Tósti to lead the invaders against his own brother.

Those English that had not succumbed to wounds, heat exhaustion, muscle fatigue, or a host of other injuries still had to eliminate islands of half-broken resistance, namely those Norwegian warriors that had not given way yet. According to Snorri Sturluson, it was in one of these steadfast bands, the toughest of the tough, which Tostig met his end:

> But before this last battle began, Harold, the son of Godwin, offered quarter to his brother, Earl Tostig, and to all the Norwegians still alive. But the Norwegians all shouted together and said they would rather fall one upon the other than accept quarter from the English, and raised their war-whoop. Thereupon the battle started again.[107]

Though Tostig's death robbed the Norwegians of their last leader the calls to surrender were met with predictable scorn – from those who were left. It seems that Norse fatalism had not disappeared with paganism. Finally, the attackers broke through the survivors' shield wall and in a desperate, every-man-for-himself last stand, the English overwhelmed the Norwegians. Of the aftermath *Anglo–Saxon Chronicle* manuscript D has this to say:

> [T]he remaining Norwegians were put to flight, while the English fiercely assailed their rear until some of them reached their ships: some were drowned, others burnt to death, and thus perished in various ways so that there were few survivors, and the English had possession of the

234 of God's Viking: Harald Hardrada

place of slaughter. The king [Harold Godwinson] then gave quarter to Olaf [Óláfr Haraldsson] the son of the king of the Norwegians, to their bishop, to the jarls of Orkney [Paul and Erlend Þórfinnsson] and to all those who were left aboard the ships. They then went inland to our king, and swore oaths that they would ever maintain peace and friendship with this land; and the king let them sail home with twenty-four ships.[108]

And so it was, on the promise that none of them would ever return to set foot on English soil again, Harold allowed the remaining Norwegians to take some of their ships and flee. The survivors filled no more than twenty-four of the 300 ships which had landed only a week ago. On the night of 26 or 27 September Harold probably celebrated his victory in York. On the morning of 28 September William of Normandy landed at Pevensey. Had Hastings never occurred, Stamford Bridge would doubtless have gone down in history as one of the most significant and illustrious of English victories.

One man's misfortune is another man's fortune

The Greek goddess Nemesis was lame. In Greek mythology, she limped after men throughout their lives, to bestow a sudden change of fortune near the end. This myth gave comfort to those who had a hard time in life, and some unease to those who enjoyed good fortune, for Nemesis' hallmark was that she appeared unexpectedly, and changed things in the blink of an eye. She was the goddess of revenge, the personification of vengeful judgement.

Until he pushed his luck to the point where it could not possibly hold, Haraldr was always fortune's darling, enjoying her excellent endowment throughout his life. Not only had he enjoyed good health, but he had several children. A contemporary observer would not have been thought unreasonable if he or she had predicted the permanent occupation of the English kingdom by Haraldr III Sigurðarson. He was a young man at fifty-one, fit as a fiddle and every sinew of his body was still flexed for war, his favourite mistress. Matters, however, turned out differently; when the Norwegian king set foot on the squishy ground of England, he had exactly one week to live. Overestimating his abilities and underestimating fate, Haraldr had met his nemesis. Hubris, it will get you every time.

Not so William the Conqueror, who probably ranks as one of most lucky conquerors in history. He began as bastard duke of Normandy and ended up as king of the most well organized and richest kingdom in Christendom. William's claim is a study in itself, but we shall confine ourselves to say here that his claim is hedged by doubts regarding both the historical sources and the technicalities of English law. Edward the Confessor's intention with regards to the English succession has puzzled historians as far back as William of Malmesbury, and one recent historian, Stephen Baxter, has commented that Edward's 'handling of the succession issue was dangerously indecisive, and contributed to one of the greatest catastrophes to which the English have ever succumbed'.[109] Irrespective of whether he had a legitimate claim or not, William went on to conquer the English kingdom. Hence it is perhaps simplest to say that William succeeded by right of conquest. Unquestionably, during the course of the campaign, he held his ragtag army together through supply shortages, one of the hardest fought battles of the period, disease, and the pacification of a hostile population. He managed to exert more influence over the course of the battle of Hastings than his opponent, no mean leader himself. On 25 December 1066 William, duke of Normandy, was crowned William I of England at Edward the Confessor's abbey in Westminster.

Epilogue

Today's western leaders do not fall with tiresome regularity like mediaeval kings in a Shakespearean bloodbath. In reality, these politicos, who may or may not look upon the exercise of power merely as a convenient means to satisfy their voracious appetites, can take their countries into foreign wars for various reasons. Such reasons can include ambition, greed, moral or messianic fervour, or on a calculation of national advantage, which may or may not be flawed. Wars are no longer waged of course in pursuit of expansionist ends such as *lebensraum* or national frontiers. Wars are now waged for ideological reasons – the defenders (or exporters) of western liberal democracy versus the autocratic strong-arm charismatic leaders, or the cynical capitalist running dogs and their puppets (some with at least a pretence of democracy) who tag along in meek support versus the protectors of the people, take your pick. Under the present conditions, anyhow, it is hard to justify most wars that are not a purely defensive reaction to invasion. To be a citizen is *ipso facto* to assent to an organization that exercises a monopoly on violence – and to pay for its maintenance. In other words, something more powerful than us has taken control of our lives.

At the same time, today's generals manage the wars of politicos as well as they can. The best try to husband the lives of their dead tired and worried soldiers and to keep them under proper control. When it is all over and they are safe back home at their desks, it seems a common practice for them to immediately set down to write their own version of events in memoirs, to carve out their niche in history, to justify the decisions they took, and occasionally to take a sideswipe at a former colleague, proving that he was drunk, or crazy, or a traitor, or whatever, but that yours truly, the general writing the memoir, was the true hero.

Written in a roundabout way, the way generals do when they want to libel somebody without winding up in court, their memoirs are by nature subjective and complete adherence to truth should not be expected, especially if they had written memoranda with at least one eye on the future record. These literary generals tend to be of the belief that war and emergency encourage the ascent of men who are able to convert crisis into opportunity. Today we citizens are all more aware of the dark arts of the 'spin doctor', putting a positive gloss on events that have provoked controversy or disquiet, but this desire by generals to be known to men to come and, naturally, to cast oneself in a good light, is no recent phenomenon.

It comes as no surprise, therefore, to find that understanding the historic past can be incredibly challenging. Literary sources are only accurate as the knowledge of the author, and historical narratives can be influenced by political orientations and specific agendas. Even accurate depictions of historical events may not reveal the whole truth; how some people may have experienced a particular event may differ radically from how the majority of people experienced it. We need only think of the Lilliputians viewing the two ends of the same egg.

More immediately relevant is the question: was Haraldr III Sigurðarson even a Christian? So it has generally been assumed – he was, after all, the half-brother of a bona fide saint. Adam of Bremen gives a very unfavourable portrait of Haraldr, describing him as a kind of enemy of Christianity. He writes that:

> King Haraldr surpassed all the madness of tyrants in his savage wildness. Many churches were destroyed by that man; many Christians were tortured to death by him. (...) He also gave himself up to magic arts and, wretched man that he was, did not heed the fact that his most saintly brother [Óláfr] had eradicated such illusions from the realm and striven even unto death for the adoption of the precepts of Christianity.[1]

Of course, we should also note that Adam had personal contact with Haraldr's discarded Danish ally and subsequent lifelong foe, Sveinn II Estriðsson of Denmark, one of Adam's named informants whom he uncritically admires. Sveinn's view of his bullying enemy Haraldr was therefore almost bound to influence the hostile cleric. What is more, Adam has been proven to be highly tendentious or even directly unreliable, and we cannot rule out the possibility that, for reasons of partisanship, he simply invented Haraldr's heathenish habits.

So in this book we have dealt with Haraldr Sigurðarson. It was not an easy thing to do, because everything in human history is supposed to get judged and put in the good or bad boxes, and you really cannot do that with Haraldr. In fiction, for instance, there is always a villain. But real life does not fit into neat themes. To my mind Haraldr was dealt a cruel blow in adolescence, and certainly the dreadful experiences of his mid teens help to explain why, as a mature man, he was surpassingly harsh, ruthless and unlovable, a man whose life was spent in violence and war, and war seems to have brought out a brutal streak in this uncompromising, forceful man. Harsh, rapacious, courageous, possessed of tremendous physical stature and strength, it is a shame we cannot just let him be what he was, a puzzling character who was a prime predator. Haraldr exemplified all the ethos of old (heathen) Norse antiquity with its stern fatalism: brave warrior and born war leader, hardhearted mercenary and hard king, and once having tasted the sweet cup of war, warfare became the great content of his life.

Whatever else he was, he was, without doubt, a brilliant warrior. What Homer would have explained by ascribing divine ancestry to him, what Plato expressed by the metaphor of an admixture of gold in the clay of which the great man was made, Haraldr's contemporaries put down variously to uncanny luck or to strength and rapacity. Haraldr *harðráði* was particularly popular as a subject of stories in mediaeval Iceland, many of which seem designed to illustrate one or other of two contrasting sides to his character as it was traditionally remembered: his kindness and sense of humour (particularly when dealing with Icelanders and poets), and on the other hand his arbitrariness and harshness.

In *Morkinskinna* we find an anecdote concerning an Icelander who was in the court of Haraldr, entertaining the court for months. As the autumn came to an end, the Icelander fell silent, and the king asked why. The Icelander stated that he only knew one more story and that he dared not tell it because it was the saga of the king himself. Haraldr ordered the Icelander to save the story for yuletide. The Icelander eventually told this saga over the thirteen days of the Christmas feast. As the saga came to an end, the king asked where the Icelander had learned it. He replied that he had learned it over several years from a certain Halldór Snorrason who had been with the king on the campaigns recounted in the saga.[2] Haraldr was a Janus, a model of a two-sided man with a dark side that tarnished the bright and always a bit unpredictable. The two sides of Haraldr – the poet and the tyrant – cannot easily be reconciled.

In a warrior culture, no matter its point or place in time, nobility, even graciousness, coexisted comfortably with a capacity for mass murder. Haraldr was not only comfortable at war; he was also keenly sensitive to the appeal of poetry and even skilled in the art himself, having tasted the mead of poetry.[3] Because we feel a moral repugnance for tyrants we sometimes underrate their intellectual powers. 'No king of Norway was himself a better poet', in the opinion of Gabriel Turville-Petre, 'and none showed a deeper appreciation of the art than Haraldr did; none expressed his views about it in more forthright terms'.[4]

It is often said politics, promises and poetry are all lies. Politics, yes that is its nature. Not being the cleanest of human activities, nothing can be excluded in the world of politics. Promises, well that depends on who is giving them. But poetry, I do not think so. After all, the northern sagas were written about Norsemen by Norsemen for Norsemen, and therefore have a certain credibility and sympathy for their subject. Surviving poems show a wide range of topics and tones: respectful and reverent; boastful and proud; witty and humorous; threatening and defiant; vile and obscene. However, scurrilous or satirical poems were banned because of the injury they caused to the subject and to his reputation. Poems, being a divine gift from Óðinn (the highest of the gods), were thought to have special power. Poems had the power to bestow honour on a worthy man and to remove honour from a wretch. An adept skald could earn a valuable reward from a generous king, or save his head from an angry king, by creating a well composed poem. The world of the Norse poem was graphic.

The originality of Haraldr's mind was such that it could never be happy in peacetime administration, and there was a sense in which his intellect required war for its satisfaction. Without a doubt, the sagas dedicated to his life, especially the one written by Snorri Sturluson, are packed with poems delivered by many diverse poets that praise his heroism and stature. Snorri writes that the reason for his including so many poems in his saga, mostly delivered by Icelandic skalds, was that 'much about king Haraldr is incorporated in poems delivered by Icelanders before him or his sons'.[5] Facility with language, either in public speaking or crafting poetry was highly prized in Norse society. Poets, in particular, were held in high esteem not just for the aesthetic qualities of their art, which required deep knowledge of rhyme, metre and special poetic language, but also for the memorializing functions they served. Serving as a court poet abroad or reciting one's praise poems for kings or jarls, brought the promise of great reward. An especially potent combination was to excel not only in the art of poetry but also in arms. In this ilk are warrior poets such as Egill Skallagrímsson and even kings such as Haraldr III Sigurðarson *harðráði*, a poet of no small skill.

Haraldr was an accomplished 'old school' viking too, an exiled prince who had experienced, among other things, lush Mediterranean lands, exotic women and epic combat. But having claimed his northern inheritance, he squandered it, his reign in Norway being largely taken up with long-drawn-out warfare against neighbouring Denmark. The peace made in 1064 freed Haraldr for a project he had long been meditating: an invasion of England.

The enterprise of England ended in defeat at Stamford Bridge, and Haraldr's ambitions on the kingship of England were extinguished when death finally caught up with him on the red field of battle. As a consequence, on 25 September 1066 fortune's wheel brought down the great warrior king of Norway. To be honest, it was a rather tame end to an extraordinary career, but, after death, as in life, Haraldr would command attention.

Eternal fame notwithstanding, a credible king had to identify with the people and the kingdom he ruled, yet, as a true lover of war, Haraldr's wars were his own wars, made inevitable by his measureless greed for power, wars which never served the interest of his kingdom. No, his life was a fellowship with the old gods, and of those it was the terrible Óðinn in whom he most believed. The nobility of this attitude of mind is well caught by Robert Louis Stevenson in one of his fables, of the three men on a pilgrimage, the priest, the virtuous person, and the old rover with the axe:

At last one came running, and told them all was lost: that the powers of darkness had besieged the Heavenly Mansions, that Odin was to die, and evil triumph.

'I have been grossly deceived', cried the virtuous person.
'All is lost now', said the priest.
'I wonder if it too late to make it up with the devil?' said the virtuous person.
'O, I hope not', said the priest, 'And at any rate we can but try. – But what are you doing with your axe?' says he to the rover.
'I am off to die with Odin', said the rover.[6]

This was the proud spirit of fatalism and fellowship with Óðinn is implicit throughout Haraldr's warlike and wandering life.

For all his bellicose efforts, however, Haraldr was never able to re-establish Knútr's North Sea empire, a personal creation that did not survive Knútr's death, not even his nephew Magnús' rule over Denmark, a fantasy that finally ended when his body returned to Norway. In the words of a fine recessional:

Now travel home from south / In dusk, past famous commonwealths, / Ships downcast with this / High enterprising leader dead.[7]

The sequel to Stamford Bridge is easily told. For whatever reason (left unexplained in any of the sources), Haraldr's remains had not been brought back to Norway immediately after Stamford Bridge but one year after the battle. The dead warrior king was then brought to Nidaros and 'interred in the church of Saint Mary, the one he caused to be built'.[8]

With the death of Haraldr Sigurðarson, one would have thought there was nothing more to say; but it is not so. There is always a reluctance to close a story, especially a story worth telling. Thus we may ask ourselves the question: But what of Haraldr's celebrated battle banner *Landøyðan*? The most likely answer is that it was trampled into the bloody mire of the battlefield and lost. However, there is an intriguing alternative to its fate.

Godred Haraldsson *crovan* (d. 1095) was a Norse–Gael adventurer who fought for Haraldr at Stamford Bridge and survived that fateful day;[9] he went on to rule the Isle of Man. The epithet *crovan* perhaps derives from the Gaelic *crob bhàn*, 'white-handed' (crippled?), or *crò bàn*, 'white-bloodied' (pale?). Godred was likely an *Uí Ímair* dynast.

It was in the year 1079 when Godred made his third and final attempt to win the island and at what is now Skyhill, just west of Ramsey, he emerged the victor. His dynasty ruled Man (and the Hebrides) for almost two centuries as sub-kings of the Norwegian crown, Magnús III Óláfsson *berfœttr* (r. 1093–1103), the grandson of Haraldr, having brought a great war fleet west-over-sea in 1098 to secure formal sovereignty, by means of a royal cruise, over the sea-kingdom of Man and the Isles. The *Chronicle of Man*, compiled at the Cistercian abbey of Rushen on Man in the thirteenth century, records that the Norwegian king forced the men of Galloway, in southwest Scotland, to ship timber to Man for the construction of forts.[10]

Now, it has been proposed by John Marsden that Haraldr's banner survives to this day. At Dunvegan Castle on the Isle of Skye, there is displayed a cloth fragment known by the Gaelic name *Am Bratach Sìth*, the Fairy Flag. This piece of cloth has long been deemed the most prized possession of the *Clann MhicLeòid*, Clan Macleod, who are said to have held the castle as their primary stronghold since the fourteenth century. Several different stories relate how the cloth came into the clan's possession, ranging from it being a gift from the fairy folk to it having been brought back from the Holy Land by a crusading clansman. But one tantalizing morsel of folklore surrounding the flag remains fairly consistent: it has the power to save the Clan MacLeod in times of danger and has twice been unfurled to lead the clansmen to victory on the field of battle. The first occasion was at the battle of Bloody Bay fought sometime around 1480, and the second at the battle of Glendale fought some ten years later.

As unlikely as it might seem, there are a number of factors which suggest *Am Bratach Sìth* could in fact be Haraldr's *Landøyðan*. Firstly, the Macleod eponymous ancestor *Leòd* (ON *Ljótr*, 'ugly') descended directly from the Norse-Gael sea kings of Man and the Isles through a woman named Helga 'of the beautiful hair'. In reality, Helga's brother was none other than Godred Haraldsson *crovan*. The question is: could Godred have snatched up *Landøyðan* from the mud of Stamford Bridge and carried it off with him to present as a gift to his sister? Perhaps, in which case he would surely also have told her of its history and legendary powers. Most telling of all, however, is the fact that modern forensic examination of the Fairy Flag has determined it to be made of silk dating back at least to the seventh century and having originated in either Rhodes or Syria, each of which supplied silk to Constantinople where, as we well know, Haraldr served as a Varangian before becoming king of Norway.[11] Whatever one may think of it, it is a hypothesis worth the historian's attention.

It would be difficult to bring a chosen subject of history to an arbitrary end without a forward glance at one of the main characters who walked the northern stage. This was Magnús III Óláfsson *berfœttr*, who was to strut, like his larger-than-life grandfather, across the boards in no mean way, and was to die a warrior's death too.

We have just made mention of Magnús and his royal visit to Man and the Isles. History repeats itself, first as tragedy, then as farce, said Marx in reference to the two Bonaparte emperors. Indeed, Snorri Sturluson, when recounting the overseas activities of Magnús, provides a tale of pillage, depredation and vainglory loss. Certainly there is something bizarre about family history repeating itself, for the Norwegian king, just as it had for his grandfather Haraldr when he fell in England, the ease of his initial progress in his campaign to conquer Ireland resulted in him growing more adventuresome and then becoming more unwary. It was reported that during a raid ashore on Saint Bartholomew's Eve (23 August), Magnús and his men were ambushed by the Irish. Apparently the 'king and his men had little armour, for the king had gone ashore wearing a silk doublet and on his head a helmet, girt with a sword and with a spear in his hand, and he wore gaiters, as was his custom'.[12] Here we should make mention of the two popular versions as to why Magnús acquired his curious cognomen, berfættr. According to Snorri Sturluson it was due to his adopting the Gaelic dress of the Irish and Scots, which thus left the lower legs bare.[13] According to Saxo Grammaticus, however, he acquired the cognomen because he was once forced to flee from the Swedes in his bare feet.[14] One is inclined to favour Snorri's version.

Due to the king's aggressive nature and his many campaigns overseas, Snorri says he also had the cognomen styrjaldar-Magnús, Magnús the Strife-lover.[15] As Snorri also says of Magnús, he 'was a vigorous man, warlike and active, and in every respect more like his grandfather Haraldr [harðráði] in disposition than his father [Óláfr III Haraldsson]'.[16] In truth, Magnús was an old-style viking warlord, whose main achievements were a series of raids at home and abroad, mostly in Britain and Ireland. Irish annals indicate that Magnús was in Ireland by 1102, briefly taking the lordship of Dublin, before he made a pact with Muirchertach Úa Briain (ON Mýrjartak – he was the son of Toirdelbach Úa Briain and great-grandson of Brian Bórumha mac Cennétig), king of Munster and self-declared high king of Ireland.[17] He cemented the alliance by marrying his son Sigurðr (then either nine or twelve depending on the source) to Muirchertach's daughter Blathmin, said to have been five years old at the time. Magnús spent the winter on the Isle of Man, and the following summer joined with Muirchertach in an attack on Domnall Úa Lochlainn, a king in Ulster. They were badly defeated in battle at Mag Coba on 5 August, and according to Snorri Sturluson were awaiting supplies from Muirchertach in order to return to Norway when they were ambushed by a large army of Irishmen.[18] Irish annals relate that Magnús was killed by Ulstermen while raiding there, in County Down, in 1103. Thus ended Norwegian designs on Ireland.

Magnús was the last Norwegian king to fall in battle overseas. With his death, Blathmin's marriage was disavowed by the Norwegians, and in so doing indirectly undermined Muirchertach's proclaimed position as high king – though distinguished from petty kings, it is unclear what power the high king had over the other Irish kings (the depiction of Ireland in Old Norse sources as a land of petty kings certainly rings true). The office was ceremonial and religious rather than political. Brian Bórumha, who perished at the moment of victory at Clontarf, had taken the high kingship by force. After him the Uí Néill high king Máel Sechnaill mac Domnaill, whom Brian had displaced, reigned until 1022. After Máel Sechnaill there were a succession of inferior Brians, the 'kings with opposition', none of whom was powerful enough to rule what his ambition bade him covet. By the turn of the twelfth century these kings of Connacht and Munster and Meath and Leinster, the would-be high kings and their supporters and rivals, had, by their predatory marches and their petty wars, most effectively ruined Ireland. They had, in the expressive phrase of the Irish annalists, already made Ireland 'a trembling sod'. Muirchertach, despite his Úa Briain blood, was no more fitted than the rest to rule the lot.

Appendix A

Skald, saga, serpent slayer, son of Óðinn

It was the quaint mediaevalist socialism of William Morris (1834–96) that inspired him, with the collaboration of the Icelandic scholar Eiríkr Magnússon, to embark on the ambitious Saga Library project to translate from the original Old Norse fifteen sagas, of which only six were completed. They did, however, produce English translations of *Heimskringla* and *Völsunga saga*, the latter also including translations of eddaic verse, collectively known as *Poetic Edda*. Compiled around the year 1270 from earlier collections of poems, the *Poetic Edda* (along with Snorri Sturluson's *Snorra-Edda*, or *Prose Edda*, explication of them, a kind of primer for young skalds to encourage them to imitate those of the viking age) relates early Norse myths and traditional ways of thinking, and tales of ancient heroes and their exploits. The mythological poems in the *Poetic Edda* contain cosmogonic lore (as *Völuspá*, *Vafþrúðismál* and *Grímnismál*), didactic poetry mixed with narratives about Óðinn (as much of *Hávamál*), and mythological adventures (such as *Þrymskviða* and *Skírnismál*), which are partly alluded to in cosmogonic poetry. All in all, the tales are exciting, packed with action, and frequently contain valuable object lessons, a theme to which we will return. The primary manuscript of the *Poetic Edda*, the Codex Regius, now lives in the Árni Magnússon Institute in Reykjavík (GK 2365 4to).

Skald

The court of a warrior king or lordly noble would have given patronage to a court poet or skald (ON *skáld*), whose rôle was to extol the martial valour of the leader and his followers. The skald's job was thus to celebrate institutionalized violence for the delight of his military paymaster and his retinue, yet no less important was his job to praise his paymaster's hospitality and wider generosity. After all, a chief must be generous to his retinue so that they repay him with their loyal service, with their blood if need be. 'Well has the king fed us. I am fat still about the roots of my heart' said Þormóðr *kolbrúnarskáld*, the skald of Óláfr II Haraldsson (viz. Óláfr *inn digri*), inspecting the gobbets on the arrowhead he had just extracted from his vitals. Thereupon he leaned back and was dead.[1] He had fought beneath the Norwegian king's standard at Stiklastaðir.

Skaldic verses, therefore, unlike the anonymous eddaic poems, are often attributed to professional skalds whose names, dates and political allegiances are known. They record contemporary reactions to the facts or fictions of viking life, and more often than not, refer to battle, murder and sudden death. I cannot sum it up better than the Icelandic chieftain and man of letters Snorri Sturluson did:

> It is the practice of the court poets to praise most fulsomely the man they are reciting to, but no-one would dare tell in a man's presence anything about his exploits that everyone who listened – even the man himself – knew to be falsehood and invention. That would be mockery not praise [*háð, en eigi lof*].[2]

Of course, we who live in a more sceptical world, where public flattery has become accepted rhetoric, need not put too much trust in Snorri's argument. Yet it is unlikely that any professional poet, reciting for reward before a prince, would mention shameful acts of his or describe any of his defeats in anything but glorious terms.

Saga

Even readers who know very little of Old Norse literature will mostly have heard of the northern sagas, but far fewer have a clear idea of what actually constitutes a saga. In this appendix, for the benefit of readers who have little or no knowledge of Nordic tradition, we will look in more detail at the northern sagas.

The term saga, meaning both 'story' and 'history', is derived from the Old Norse–Icelandic verb *at segja*, 'to say', and denotes a lengthy prose narrative not unlike the modern novel. Indeed, the sagas are virtually an entire universe, complete with characters, events, and history of the viking age in Iceland and neighbouring lands. The world of the sagas is populated with heroes who made their mark on their surroundings and their times, and with warriors who travelled by land and by sea, living their adventures and battling against kings and jarls. However, do the Old Icelandic sagas provide accurate information about a viking period 250 years before they were written? It is indeed a question worth pondering.

So at this point we will take a rather long diversion, to look at the nature of these northern sagas, which are both more and less than a history. The best, indeed the majority, of them rest on a foundation of history and antiquarian speculation, but the superstructure is often shaped by arbitrary assumptions as to the nature of history itself. Though their matter has to do with events involving the fate of nations, the saga-composer saw history in terms of men and women and human destiny, and in terms of a story, a vivid narrative of clashing personalities and dramatic events. Ergo, sagas contain such timeless elements as passion, friendship, enmity, honour, deceit, betrayal, and revenge. If anything, they deal with living on the edge of civilization, the two contrasting contexts of a very basic fight for physical survival with the problems of building a functional society without an all-powerful authority that enforces law and order. This binary contrast invariably means sagas are very violent, bloody and anti-establishment. There is blood on almost every page, and bodies pile up in every chapter. Much like the western genre of our own time with its querulous cast of gunmen, cardsharps, desperados and prostitutes, sagas were not the fixed and immutable record of known facts.

Thus, as in a good western motion picture, saga conflict might include ambushes, cattle rustling, boundary disputes, declared semi-legal killings, clandestine undeclared homicides, and nocturnal farmstead burnings – setting fire to a house and burning a man in it to death was a well-known way of getting rid of an enemy in viking-age and mediaeval Iceland. There are skirmishers with outlaws and spontaneous free-for-alls in the law courts or in the drinking dens, intrigues and unholy decisions. The sagas in particular celebrate tough, shrewd heroes who do not shrink from conflict and from defending one's rights, who fight on against the odds and do not back down, even at the cost of death, all the good plot devices you remember from old westerns.

The Old Icelandic sagas are great tales with well-defined characters that talk and act with robustness and zest – heroes and villains, saints and kings, women of beauty, all displaying great human qualities, superhuman endurance, depth of sinister qualities as well as power, satanic hates and intrigues – all presented against an impressive background of smoky longhouses, dark forests and majestic mountains. But the sagas also explore enduring themes – questions that every society must ask itself about love, friendship, loyalty, hatred, jealousy, and betrayal. While 99 per cent of the public would accept some basis of remembered history in the sagas, research-minded scholars have their own doubts and speculations. Speaking for myself, I would rather side with the public.

Iceland was to be the child who outgrew the parent; its mature literary achievements were to be greater than those of the Scandinavian homelands as well as those of the Norse settlers in conquered lands. The defining characteristics of the 'Sagas of Icelanders', or *Íslendingasögur* (sg. *Íslendingasaga*), are anonymous authorship, concern principally with Icelandic characters (many of them historical figures), a narrative time frame falling between about 830 and about 1050, and composition roughly between 1200 and 1400, the time of Chrétien de Troyes, Dante and Chaucer. In thirty-one major sagas and scores of minor narratives called *Þáttr* (pl. *þættir*), literally 'a strand in a rope', *Íslendingasaga*-plots often centre on inter-familial feuding, a tendency that has resulted in their also being called 'family sagas'. They quote many skaldic verses to authenticate or otherwise enhance episodes in the narrative. Many of these verses are authentic, or at least demonstrably contemporary with the events they describe, literary relics from the tenth, eleventh and twelfth centuries recorded by saga-compilers centuries (or at the nearest, decades) later.

The great, intricately plotted saga of Njáll must be the most powerful and popular of the Icelandic family sagas. It survives in several manuscripts, the earliest from around the year 1300. The saga, however, dates from after 1271, as legal details in the saga refer to laws introduced to Iceland from Norway in that year – Iceland, as an alternative to social dissolution and anarchy, lost its independence to Norway in 1262–4,[3] eventually becoming an impoverished backwater. A complex tale of intelligent wisdom and insatiable revenge, this saga is set in Iceland around the time of the Icelanders' conversion to Christianity in the year 1000. The saga teems with memorable characters such as the heroic Gunnarr Hámundarson of Hliðarendi, a warrior without equal with an aversion to killing, the villainous, insinuating Mörðr Valgarðsson, and Njáll Þorgeirsson himself, known for his wisdom, his gift of prophecy, his skill at law, and his inability to grow a beard. The core of the story revolves around a ferocious family feud, which culminates in the burning of Njáll and his family in their farmhouse at Bergþórshvoll. Njáll, a Christian, is given the opportunity to escape but chooses death rather than a life of shame and perishes in his burning house along with his wife Bergþóra and their grandson.[4] It should be noted that surprising and burning your enemy in his home was one of the less common, but more spectacular methods of gaining redress. Flosi Þórðarsson, the leader of the party against Njáll, freely admits that burning the family in the house will be 'a great responsibility before God, for we're Christian men'.[5]

We might also add that while quite a few sagas conclude with the heroes converting to Christianity and heading off to Rome on a pious pilgrimage, this is usually the least memorable part of the story and reads rather like an advertisement for the Christian faith tacked on as a political necessity, providing a cover for the main body of the text just as health-warnings on packs of cigarettes only slightly disguise the cigarette companies' desire to cause profitable addiction. One could also compare the standard paeans to Marxist-Leninist Communist ideology that authors were required to insert into Soviet scholarship, even where the other contents had absolutely nothing to do with V.I. Lenin or Karl Marx.

Sagas were an individual's version and interpretation of facts, and could undergo shortening, lengthening, interpolation of new material, deliberate change, accidental manipulation, plain misunderstanding. It must always be remembered that sagas are not history as such, and so we cannot presume that any saga whatsoever can be believed through thick and thin. Full of stories of magical incidents and strange marvels, sagas drink from the spring wherein fact has not yet been filtered from fancy, the saga-writer composing not to narrate human events as they occur, but to make sure that we have the opportunity of living the emotions and the passions of our heroes even at the distance of centuries. Skalds spoke of their art as forging, brightening up, word-working, or building. So, forensic fixations about 'the facts' should be laid aside by the reader, as the saga-writer is trying to impart far greater truths. Thus *Yngvars saga víðförla*, to take one example that we have already met, with a known historical basis, includes realistic, plausible scenes, interspersed with encounters with giants, dragons and, of course, beautiful princesses.

Serpent slayer

Thus – to cite a single example – to illustrate this particular point, one instance we are all very much familiar with, the great viking freebooter Ragnarr *loðbrók* (Hairy-Breeks). The viking idea was that fame was everything, to be remembered for great deeds. Without a doubt, the career of Ragnarr depicts just the type of image on which the popular viking stereotype is based. Known to legend, but standing at the farthest edge of history, Ragnarr's origins and doings remain almost impenetrably obscure – he himself claimed to be descended from Óðinn. Royal genealogies or pedigrees are easily, frequently and demonstrably manipulated for what we would today call political propaganda - much like Timur-i-Lenk (Tamerlane) claiming highly improbable descent from Genghis Khan, virtually a prerequisite for any wannabe Central Asian strongman, while today for an unhappy comparison we need look no further than one of the world's current crop of self-styled strongmen leaders (in truth, a cartoon imitation of such, a great blusterer and long-tongued liar, a sociopathic man-child with delusions of godhead) who claims, untruthfully as it turns out, his father was from a certain northern European nation. Hitherto enemy kings may be retrospectively made into relatives; rivals and competitors made into brothers or cousins; the numbers of generations shortened or lengthened; and so on. They also manifestly include legendary and divine personages. Ragnarr's purported ancestors also included the mythological beings know as the *álfar* or elves (not at all elfin), his mother Álfhildr and all her bloodline being descendants of Álfuren *gamle*, better known as Álf the Old.[6] It could be of course claimed that such tales were told to enhance a man's right to a throne, as was perhaps true of Ragnarr. After all, when a man rises in the world, one of his first cares is to adopt an eligible ancestor.

It is not that we lack information about Ragnarr. On the contrary, there survives a superabundance of materials relating to his adventurous career. The trouble is that nearly all the literary sources are late and legendary. A good example is *Ragnars saga loðbrókar*, written around 1230 and centred upon the life and family of our hero with hairy breeches who was supposed to have lived in the ninth century and had already been incorporated, at length, into the Danish history of the Danish cleric Saxo Grammaticus.

Old legends can be very enduring, surviving because they are worth hearing and because they are continually being re-examined, reinterpreted and retold. Take, for example, the story of Arthur. There is Mallory's Arthur, the monarch of the Round Table dispensing Christian justice and charity in an idealized past, as well as Tennyson's, a pre-Raphaelite version full of colour, fabrics and Wagnerian backdrops, Hollywood's superhero and the Romano–British warlord of the archaeologist and the historian. They remind us that every age makes of Arthur what it will. Thus, what is important is the fact that Ragnarr, like Arthur, lies at the heart of a legend that seems set to enjoy some sort of permanence and universality.

Is it possible to distinguish two Ragnarrs, one historical and the other a creature of mythology? Ragnarr (and his many sons) were popular stuff of legend of mediaeval northern Europe, an international world of courts and courtliness, tournaments, sieges, stained glass, illuminated manuscripts, the ballads of chivalry and the architecture of castles. He still remains to this day, in popular culture, the most picturesquely named viking of all time, for his byname *loðbrók* refers to the special garments he had tailored for himself: 'they were shaggy breeches and a fur-coat, and when they were done, he had them boiled in pitch'. Once he donned this 'armour', 'he rolled in the sand'.[7] Apparently this process had the magic property of making him invulnerable, especially against the monstrous venom-spewing serpent he was meant to slay (a guarantee of wonders, some would say lies, to come).

Serpent is a word often used in mythology, religion, and folklore to denote non-specific reptiles, such as snakes, dragons, or sea monsters. Serpent is used as a poetic metaphor, or kenning, in the skaldic poetry of Iceland. It was a symbol of protection for warriors, a guardian of great treasures, and may have been a symbol of fertility and healing, as was the case in ancient Greece. In some instances, the serpent was an opponent of the gods. In Norse mythology, the serpent *Níðhöggr* chewed at the roots of the sacred tree, Yggdrasil, and the child of Loki called Jormungundr, the *Miðgarðsormr*, encircled the earth with his tail in his mouth and spewed burning black venom during *Ragnarök*. Óðinn turned himself into a serpent to enter the cavern where he found the mead of poetry. Fáfnir turned himself into a dragon to guard his treasure. The gods placed a serpent, its fangs dripping with poison, over the head of the mischief-maker Loki after they had bound him fast to a rock.

It was this heroic deed that won him the hand of his second wife, Þóra, maiden daughter of Herrauðr, who was a *jarl* in Götaland (always to be distinguished from the island of Gotland out in the Baltic).[8] In *Krákumál*, or 'Words of the Raven', the twelfth-century poetic monologue supposedly chanted by Ragnarr as he met his heroic end in Ælla's snake pit, the speaker states that he acquired the name *loðbrók* as a result of slaying a serpent in Gautland and so winning Þóra in marriage.[9]

Before she was carried off by an illness, she bore Ragnarr two sons: the elder was called Eiríkr, and the younger was called Agnar.[10] Later in life his third wife Áslaug (also called Kráka or Randalín), orphaned daughter of the legendary serpent slayer Sigurðr *Fáfnisbana* (another corpus of stories that merge legendary and romance motifs and themes) and the half-human half-supernatural Brynhildr (Wagner's Brünnhilde), ran up Ragnarr an invincible shirt, woven out of 'out of greyed woollen-hair', which he wore 'over his mail',[11] as a parting gift from her before he set sail for England. The strong, fierce, tragic Áslaug was the mother of his sons Ívarr *inn beinlausi*, Björn *járnsíða* (who was to even surpass Ragnarr in terms of his legacy), Hvítserkr – whose name White Shirt could be the cognomen of the brother named Hálfdan mentioned in the *Anglo-Saxon Chronicle* (OE *Healfdene*),[12] Old Irish (OI *Albann*)[13] and Frankish (Fr. *Halbdeni*)[14] texts – Rögnvaldr, and Sigurðr *ormr í auga*. Ragnarr's first wife was of course the celebrated shield maiden Lagertha. It was Ragnarr's great and only fear that his sons would become more famous than he was. We have only to think of Björn and his grand cruise around the western Mediterranean, or Ívarr and the 'great heathen army'.[15]

It comes as no small surprise, therefore, that attempts have been made to distil a historical Ragnarr from the superhero (complete with superhero costume) of saga tradition. So he survives to this day as a pseudo-historical character, a landless leader of landless men (viz. sea-king: ON *sækonungr*, cognate with OE *sæcyning*) with Danish royal connections. *Sækonungr* was a title given to such as ruled over armed hosts on board ship but had *no* lands. *Sækonungar* also bore the title of kings of hosts or war kings (rather: warrior kings, *her-konungar*), because all their subjects were warriors. Indeed, an authentic *sækonungr* was he who 'never slept under a sooty rooftree nor ever drank in a hearth-ingle'. In sum, a *sækonungr* was a mere leader of warriors, a shipboard king and not a proper ruler in the mediaeval sense of the word.

In this capacity Ragnarr led a fleet of 120 warships up the Seine to sack Paris – which was no bigger than the Île de la Cité – in March 845, assuming Ragnarr can be identified with the viking chief named *Reginheri* (also called *Ragneri, Reginerus, Ragenarius*) in contemporary Frankish chronicles. During this raid over a hundred Christians were hanged as an offering to Óðinn and the city sacked on Easter Sunday, 28 March.[16] As the halleluiahs of Easter turned into lamentations, Charles *le chauve* (r. 843–77), king of the West Franks, paid tribute to vikings to halt their smoking tracks of pillage and butchery and to be gone from his kingdom with all their loot.[17] It amounted to 7,000 *livres* (2,570 kg) of silver;[18] it brought Charles six years of freedom from invasion.

The same Frankish chronicles then go on to claim that Ragnarr and most of his men died or were stricken soon after the raid, as divine retribution for plundering Christian holy sites. And not by any illness, for Ragnarr suffered terribly from diarrhoea: 'All his entrails spilled onto the ground'.[19] It is not difficult to see this description as a deliberately exaggerated account of the symptoms of dysentery.

After the Paris adventurer, and assuming of course he was considerably less dead than we have been told, we subsequently find Ragnarr campaigning in Ireland in 851–2. Here he fought against the Norwegians who had founded what was to become the capital of Ireland, Dublin, a decade earlier, supposing Ragnarr can be identified with the Norse king named *Ragnall* occurring in certain Irish writings. Despite his invulnerability, however, Ragnarr met his end shortly afterward (856?), possibly while engaged in a freebooting expedition on the Isle of Anglesey or in north Wales itself.[20] Yet none of this seems in general fits the established story of Ragnarr as found in the saga-branch of the Ragnarr *loðbrók* tradition.[21]

These Old Norse sagas appear to reflect the revival of interest in the viking way of life that developed in the second half of the twelfth century. Thus, Ragnarr's antecedents, despite ingenious scholarly attempts to make bricks with very little straw, remain mysterious. According to the comprehensive survey of Frankish, Irish, English, Norse and Danish sources, clerical as well as secular, by Rory McTurk, Ragnarr can be seen as a wholly synthetic character made up of many elements, which loom vaguely through the mists of tradition. These various elements may be summarized as follows:

1. A serpent slayer and seducer of fair maidens.
2. A pirate chief who dies cursed, along with most of his men, after besieging Paris, and is remembered in a 600-line poem by Abbo Cernuus (the Crooked) of Saint-Germain-des-Prés, a young Neustrian Benedictine monk who glorifies the heroic defence of count Odo and his 200 companions.[22]
3. A historical family of freebooters active in the British Isles and Frankia in the eight-sixties and eight-seventies.
4. A fertility goddess who is called *Loðbróka* or *Loþkona*, who was originally identical with the Germanic fertility goddess *Nerthus* described by Tacitus in chapter 40 of his *Germania*.[23]
5. An actual assailant of the kingdom of Northumbria in 867, which eventually results in the death of its king Ælla.
6. A legendary hero who is thrown into a snake pit where he dies singing, much like Gunnarr of old in the eddaic poem *Völuspá* (though he played the harp with his toes too).[24]

This is the rather rickety historical hub that lies at the centre of a mass of legends and folktales, yet the existence of a historical Ragnarr is surely irrelevant to the power of the Ragnarr myth. Ragnarr, unlike the far-famed 'sons of Ragnarr', inhabits a common Norse legendary twilight zone, also occupied by giants, trolls, enchanters, monsters, and wise kings with beautiful daughters.

That said, from a political point of view the result is the great Danish king Regnerus Lothbrog of Saxo's ninth book; from another view point, without the politics, the result is the hero of Old Norse saga. Saxo wrote *Danorum Regum Heromque Historia* to provide the Danish kingdom with a glorious past and to hold up a mirror for his contemporaries by contrasting the high moral standards of bygone times with the sloppiness and degenerated manners of his own time - very much what Livy had done for the Romans of his day. He therefore stressed the heroic deeds and manly virtues of the Northmen and toned down their cruelty. Admittedly he described some cruel actions, but took care to show that they were justified. So, for example, Regnerus tortured to death his prisoners from among the followers of a certain Haraldus, who commanded some Danish support in his second of three attempts to usurp Regnerus' throne.[25] Likewise, Regnerus' son Inguar (viz. Ívarr *inn beinlausi*) was entirely right to punish the Anglo-Saxon king Ælla of Northumbria (d. 867), who had sent his father to his death.[26] This of course is the most popular version of Ragnarr's death, whereby he was thrown into a pit infested with venomous snakes and was (eventually, once stripped of his 'shirt of invincibility') bitten to death by them. With his dying breath, Ragnarr supposedly chanted a cryptic prophecy:

> The piglets would protest loudly / if the boar's plight they knew. / Death has been dealt to me, / snakes dig in my flesh-house / and savagely stab me, / besides the beasts I'll die now, / soon I will be a corpse.[27]

And so it came to pass.

The 'piglets' came to Northumbria and in revenge wrought a bloody havoc upon the kingdom. They captured Ælla in battle and, according to Saxo, Ívarr ordered the king's back 'to be carved with the figure of an eagle', and 'not satisfied with inflicting wounds, they [Ívarr and his brothers] salted the torn flesh'.[28] Saxo is not alone in having misunderstood 'the blood-eagle punishment'; some Old Norse written sources describe it as the cutting the ribs from the victim's spine and pulling his lungs out, spreading them across the shoulder blades in the manner suggestive of an eagle's outstretched wings. There is not a scrap of historical evidence that this gruesome ritual ever happened outside the ghoulish imaginations of later saga writers. As Roberta Frank has shown, these interpretations are based on a misunderstanding of a sentence by the skald Sigvatr Þórðarson (dated 1025–38) who wrote that 'Ívarr had Ælla's back be cut by an eagle', meaning that Ælla was left to be eaten by carrion birds.[29]

Theories that Ívarr *inn beinlausi* was a cripple and had to be carried about in a litter are the result of English literalism. Norse nicknames were usually candid, and Boneless (*beinfri*) is still used in Norway to describe a crafty, sly character, that is to say, 'No bones, you can't hear him coming'.

According to Irish chroniclers, a viking armed camp had been established at Dublin (ON *Dyflin*, from OI *Dubh Linn*, pronounced *Duvelinn*, 'black pool') on or close to the existing Irish settlement of *Áth Cliath* ('ford of the wattles'), situated at a crossing point of the Liffey.[30] Other such centres were soon established at *Hlymrekr* (Limerick), *Veigsfjörth* (Wexford), *Vethrafjöthr* (Waterford), and *Vikingalo* (Wicklow). The Northmen, thus, introduced towns to Ireland; the small settlements already existing near Celtic monasteries could scarcely merit the name 'towns'. Dublin's subsequent illustrious history should not distort its actual importance in the mid-ninth century: for its first few decades it was just another of the growing Norse towns. If one of these towns stood out, it was perhaps Limerick. However, Dublin's splendid harbour, its eastward prospect, and its potential for trade were to make it, in time, Ireland's principal town. Indeed, what the Irish called a 'ship-fort' (OI *longphort*, pl. *longphuirt*), the Dublin haven was to become the base from which Norse colonists on the Irish coast were united under a certain Óláfr (OI *Amlaíb*), apparently of the Norwegian royal house of Vestfold. In the eight-sixties Óláfr subjugated the Norse settlements of the Hebrides and Galloway while raiding deep into Ireland and Pictland, making him 'the greatest war-king West-over-the-sea'.[31]

Óláfr's staunchest ally and companion in the kingship of Dublin, his brother Ívarr (OI *Ímair*, OE *Ingware*), and a more colourful version of the story is that he was Ívarr *inn beinlausi*, and who is to say that is not true? Now, Ívarr *inn beinlausi* was one of the joint leaders of the *mycel hæpen here*, 'great heathen army'.[32] Numbering somewhere – and the estimates vary widely – between about 500 and 2,000 warriors, this was a group of hitherto uncoordinated bands of vikings that originated from Norway, Sweden and Denmark who came together under a unified command to invade the four Anglo-Saxon kingdoms that constituted England in 865, namely Wessex, Mercia, East Anglia, and Northumbria. Their intention was different from their predecessors' for theirs was not meant to be a summer's raiding; these vikings came prepared for a sustained campaign, intent upon winning English land for themselves. One of their accomplishments was the conquest of York, which the 'heathens' initially entered unopposed on All Saints' Day, 1 November 866, a major event in the Christian calendar. It is said that the remaining Roman walls had been allowed to fall into disrepair. The capture of York effectively brought the curtain down on the northern Anglo-Saxon kingdom, and the Norse presence became more firmly established from 876 onwards. York was to be their capital in the north, a Norse town to rival Dublin, Hedeby and Birka, but that lay in the future.

The identification is certainly inviting but rather difficult, for Ívarr *inn beinlausi* was no Norwegian but a prodigy among the Danes – he was, of course, one of the many sons of the legendary Ragnarr *loðbrók* – unlike Ragnarr, who is barely visible in the early morning mist, the sons of Ragnarr stand clear, their Nordic bodies visible in the midday sun of viking history. At any rate, true or not, from 850 to 954, the year Eiríkr *blóðox* fell, a united Norse kingdom, administered from Dublin and York, extended from the coastal settlements of the Irish Sea and across northern England to the east coast. The *Annals of Ulster*, which has the merit of being contemporary with the events recorded, refers to Ívarr (under 873, which was the year of his death) as *rex Nordmannorum totius Hiberniae et Britanniae*, 'king of the Northmen in Ireland and Britain', that is to say, he was the effective ruler of the Scandinavian enclaves in Ireland and England based on Dublin and York.

York, or *Jórvík*, became a notable North Sea port-of-trade, while Dublin was essentially an armed stronghold providing protection for traders and slavers. The two power-centres were linked by a number of routes, the most direct of which was via the Lancaster coast to the Ribble-Aire gap through the Pennines, which divided northern England effectively between east and west. However, it is reckoned the preferred route was by sea to the firths of Forth and Clyde and overland portage following the Antonine Wall, with its still serviceable Roman military road, across lowland Scotland. The sailing/rowing distance from Ireland was not extreme, though the hazards of tide-races, storms and sea-mists were not negligible.

Son of Óðinn

Of the various methods vikings employed to sow fear in the guts of their foes, perhaps none would have been as visually striking as the raven banner (ON *hrafnsmerki*), a triangular or semicircular war cloth flown by many renowned viking chieftains. The sons of Ragnarr *loðbrók* had a war banner called 'Raven'. Woven and embroidered by their three sisters in one afternoon, it was said that if the banner fluttered, the *loðbrók* brothers would carry the day, but if it hung lifeless the battle would be lost.[33] The magic weaved by the sisters seems to have finally worn off, for 'Raven' was evidently captured on the field of battle by the Anglo-Saxons.[34] The *Anglo-Saxon Chronicle* quite clearly states that they (the *loðbrók* brothers) called the banner 'Raven' (OE *ræfan*), not that it had the bird depicted on it, although it is usually assumed that it had. The raven device is associated with other Norse leaders in the British Isles, as for instance on the coins issued in *Jórvík* 939/40 by the Hiberno–Norse king Óláfr Guðröðsson. Both of these suggest a symbolic expression of the warrior ideology of feeding the ravens.

A very similar story is also told in *Encomium Emmæ Reginæ* (written around 1042), where the army under king Knútr carries a magical raven banner, normally of plain white silk but at times auspicious for victory displaying a raven 'opening its beak, flapping its wings, and restive on its feet, but very subdued and drooping with its whole body when they were defeated'.[35] As we can see, the strange thing is this banner, unlike that of the *loðbrók* brothers, does not have a picture of a raven woven or embroidered onto it. It is blank. The raven, however, magically appears in times or war, and its appearance predicts the outcome of the war. If it is to be a victory, the raven beats its wings and opens its beak, and is restless in its feet. Is it to be a defeat, however, the raven is quiet and drooping its whole body.

Prophetic or not, a banner played a decisive rôle in the actual battle, as the fighting was most fearsome closest to it. It was the symbol of resistance, warriors fighting as long as the banner was flying. Its loss was associated with great dishonour, yet this symbol was flaunted in the very front of the battleline. A banner also functioned as the point where men rallied round to reform and continue the struggle. To carry a banner was an especially honourable task, probably reserved for an experienced warrior. All that having been said, Sigurðr Hlöðvirsson *inn digri* died bravely, hacked down and hurried on to the afterlife apparently whilst bearing his raven banner 'woven with mighty spells'.[36] This particular banner ensured victory to the army it was carried before, but only at the price of the bearer's life.[37] So naturally, none were too keen to step forward and volunteer to be the banner bearer of the *jarl*.

The magical raven banner initially helped Sigurðr Hlöðvirsson win the battle of Skitten over the Scots. But later on, facing the Irish at the battle of Clontarf, everybody knew that none who held the banner escaped death, and the *jarl* consequently had to carry the dark scary thing himself. Twice had the banner bearer fallen, and the *jarl* had called on the Icelander Þorsteinn, son of Hallr of Síða, next to bear the banner. Þorsteinn was about to do so, when Amundi the White called out, 'Don't carry the banner – everybody who does gets killed'. 'Hrafn *rauða*', said the *jarl*, 'you carry the banner'. 'Carry that devil of yours yourself', answered Hrafn. The *jarl* said, 'Then it's best that the beggar and his bag go together', and with that he took up the banner, and was immediately pierced through with a spear.[38]

In the gruesome setting of the battlefield, a situation where men are all too easily reduced to the level of beasts of prey, or to carrion, it is essential to hold fast to the elusive concept of honour as a talisman against horror and despair. So it was to be a splendid and unnecessary death at Clontarf near the fortress of Dublin on that fateful Friday before Easter, Sigurðr meeting his doom under a heathenish banner in a holocaust reminiscent of the fabled encounters of old. In doing so, he not only protected his honour but also he escaped oblivion by earning for himself a slice of saga-fame. Likewise, Amundi the White was cut down while Hrafn *rauða* (the Red) was chased into the Liffey where he was in danger of being drowned by the rapidly rising tide. In dire straits he made a vow as follows: 'This dog of yours has run twice to Rome, Apostle Peter, and would run a third time if you let him'. He got across the river safely.[39] But did it really happen? Here, it should be noted,

is a salutary reminder that in any one saga practically all of the main characters
are historical, but the details of their larger-than-life actions and fairly copious
speeches, though related soberly enough, are either the property of the author or
variations of folk traditions that had grown up about the incidents.

In popular imagination, of course, it is the male warrior, with his iconic long
beard, large axe and razor-sharp sword, which is the hallmark of Norse society.
Battle is the domain of men, but women affect it in more ways than by being maiden
warriors or collectors of the dead. Magical raven banners were always woven by
the mother or sister of the warrior in question, with the magic woven into the
fabric as it was made to protect the son or brother. It was Eðna Kjarvallsdóttir,[40] his
sorceress mother, who made for Sigurðr with all sorcery her skill his brilliant but
baleful banner. 'The banner was wrought with cunningly executed handiwork and
elaborate art. It was made in the shape of a raven, and when floating in the wind
it resembled the raven flying'.[41] A pretty good trick. The raven is a bird of battle
since it feeds on the corpses of the slain, as every ornithologist knows. As the Norse
commonly said, 'To make war was to glut and gladden the greedy gull-of-Óðinn',[42]
and there was a touch of the uncanny about Sigurðr, who was more than happy to
revel with the heathen raven.

In Old Norse literature, the raven (ON *hrafn*) is the bird of combat and carrion,
and appears in almost every skaldic poem describing bloodshed and battle. In this
context the raven can be poetically paraphrased as 'the taster of the corpse-sea' and
the warrior as 'the raven's foot-reddener' as described in the praise poem for *jarl*
Þórfinnr Sigurðarson *inn ríki* of Orkney, the *Þórfinnsdrápa* composed by Arnórr
Þórðarson *jarlaskáld*.[43]

Of these raven banners, however, none captures the imagination quite
so much as that of Haraldr Sigurðarson. The king's raven banner was called
Land-waster (ON *Landøyðan*), and he fought victoriously under it for over two
decades. The name alone bears testimony to the banner's long active service
before it was raised on his very last battle in 1066. It was certainly the same
banner that features in a story from Snorri Sturluson telling how Haraldr and
his Varangians laid siege to a Sicilian town. We shall let Snorri enlighten us in
his own words:

> Two Iceland men were then with Haraldr. One was Halldór son of the
> *góði* Snorri [Þorgrímsson], who brought this account back to Iceland,
> and the other was Úlfr Óspaksson, grandson of Ósvífer the Wise (*inn*
> *fróði*). Both these men were among the strongest and bravest of men,
> and Haraldr's best friends; both had taken part in the games. Now
> when some days were passed the townsfolk showed more courage,
> and would go unarmed upon the town walls, leaving the gates open.

The Varangians observing this went one day to their sports with their swords under their cloaks, and their helmets under their hoods. After playing awhile they observed that the defenders were off their guard, instantly seized their weapons, and ran towards the gate. When the defenders saw this they went against them, fully armed, and a battle began in the gateway. The Varangians had no shields, but wrapped their cloaks round their left arms. Some of them were wounded; some fell, while all were in grave danger. Now came Haraldr with the men who had remained in the camp, to the assistance of his men. But the defenders had now manned the walls, from which they shot arrows and hurled stones at them. A severe battle ensured. Those who were in the gateway thought there was more delay in aiding them than they could have wished. When Haraldr arrived at the fortress gate his standard bearer fell, and he said 'Halldór take up the banner!' Halldór took up the banner, and said foolishly, 'Who is going to bear your banner if you follow it as feebly as you do now?' But these were words more of anger than of truth, for Haraldr was one of the boldest of men under arms. They now forced their way into the town, where a hard struggle ensued, which ended in Haraldr's victory and the capture of the town. Halldór was severely wounded in the face, the scar of which remained with him as long as he lived.[44]

Halldór Snorrason was one of Snorri Sturluson's ancestors. Anyway, somewhat reminiscent of the story of the raven banner that *jarl* Sigurðr Hlöðvirsson raised at Clontarf, though as far as we know the banner of Haraldr was not cursed. In Snorri's saga devoted to Haraldr, the Danish king Sveinn asks him at one point which of his possessions he valued most highly:

Sveinn asked Haraldr which of his possessions of his he valued most highly. He answered that it was his banner [*merki*], *Landøyðan*. Thereupon Sveinn asked what virtue it had to be accounted so valuable. Haraldr replied that it was prophesied that victory would be his before whom this banner was borne; and added that this had been the case ever since he had obtained it. Thereupon Sveinn said, 'I shall believe that your banner has this virtue if you fight three battles with king Magnús, your kinsman, and are victorious in all'.[45]

Scholarly conjecture suggests the raven was meant to invoke the power of Óðinn, who was often depicted in the company of his two helper ravens, Huginn and Muninn (the Old Norse words for *thought* and *memory* or *mind* respectively), who served as his eyes and ears. Snorri Sturluson, in the *Prose Edda*, says that at daybreak, Óðinn sends these two birds off around the world to gather the daily news from the land of men (ON *ór heimi*). At day's end, they would return to perch on their master's shoulders and whisper to him what they had seen and learnt. Since they embodied Óðinn's mind and thoughts, Huginn and Muninn symbolized his ability to see into the future.[46] In the *Poetic Edda*, it is written:

> The whole earth over, every day, / hover Huginn and Muninn; / I dread lest Huginn droop in his flight, / yet I fear me still more for Muninn.[47]

To Óðinn was attributed mastery of shape shifting and great magical powers, frequently described as the product of extreme asceticism. While considered by many to be firmly in the realm of mythology, others believe that he was an archetypal shaman chieftain, his memory living on in the Germanic and Norse lands being with the passage of time gradually reduced from legend to fantasy. Thor Heyerdahl (1914–2002), the Norwegian adventurer and ethnographer, advanced the theory that the people who eventually populated Scandinavia had their homelands in Scythia and possibly moved west through the Mediterranean, especially Greece and Italy, to thrust up through central Europe during the Migration Period.[48] Probably better known for his nautical adventures with the *Kon-Tiki*, *Ra*, *Ra II*, and *Tigris*, Heyerdahl's Óðinn hypothesis was subjected to fierce criticism by Norwegian scholars and as yet to be validated by any historian, archaeologist or philologist. All that we can positively say at this point in time is that some believe the name Óðinn or Wôden is cognate with the deity Varuna (literally 'The All-Enveloping Sky'), Hindu god of the underworld and of waters, hinting at a common Proto-Indo-European source. Varuna became Uranus (Gr. Οὐρανός), the Graeco–Roman deity.

The raven was a common symbol in many mythologies, sometimes as a sign of evil owing to its habits as a scavenger and sometimes as a sign of good. The ravens of European mythology are invariably messengers of the deities, or an alternate shape for various deities and spirits, the most widely known being the Welsh hero Brân the Blessed and the Irish goddess the Mórrígan, and of course the omniscient Óðinn, the one-eyed god who sees all.

In Greek mythology, ravens are associated with Apollo in his rôle as god of prophecy. They were said to be a symbol of good luck, and were the god's messengers in the mortal world. Of all the classical poets, the Augustan poet Ovid best preserves the details of the legend of why the raven is as black as night. He tells us that Korônis, the divine daughter of the Lapith king Phlegyas, was bathing in Lake Boebis, when Apollo spied upon her and coveted her. She became pregnant by the god. Her father, however, had promised her in marriage to her cousin Ischys, the Arcadian son of Elatos. The marriage preparations were in progress when a raven informed Apollo. In his anger the god scorched the snow-white feathers of this messenger of evil tidings which, thereafter, wore black plumage and was feared as a herald of disaster. Afterwards he repented, but the colour of a creature cannot be restored; further changes there can be, but there is no reverting to the original. Pangs of regret or not, it is worth remembering that Apollo shot down Ischys, while his twin sister Artemis slew Korônis and her innocent maiden companions.[49]

Ironically, the virgin Artemis, as well as being the mistress of wild things, was also the patroness of the young and the goddess of childbirth. However, when her brother Apollo saw the body of Korônis laid on the funeral pyre, he felt pity for his unborn son. Removing him from his mother's womb, he took him to the cave of Cheiron on Mount Pelion. There, Asklepios grew up and was instructed in the art of healing by the wise and gentle centaur, and so becoming Homer's 'blameless physician'.[50] Zeus would strike Asklepios down with a thunderbolt when the healer–hero brought the fair Hippolytos back from the dead, because in doing so he had transgressed the boundaries of mortality, rivalling the skill of the gods.[51] For Asklepios all that he had been taught by the horse-man Cheiron was not enough. Zeus eventually placed Asklepios in the heavens as the constellation of Ophiuchus, the snake bearer, who bestrides the sky between Sagittarius and Scorpius.[52]

In Irish folklore there is the extraordinary goddess named the Mórrígan, who appears to embody all that is perverse and horrible among supernatural powers. Primarily associated with fate, she delighted in setting men at war, and fought among them herself, changing into many frightful shapes and often hovering above fighting armies in the aspect of a raven to pick out the battle's victims. The Mórrígan has thus been likened to the valkyrie and the Norns of Norse mythology.

Appendix B

Mosfell Archaeological Project

Τ he use of the Icelandic corpus of literature in scholarly research is a contentious issue for historians and anthropologists in academic milieus. Yet it is the view of the archaeologists Jesse Byock and Davide Zori that the Old Icelandic sagas preserve a stable oral tradition that record memories of actual people and actual places, as opposed to being simply stories:

> Most archaeologists working in Iceland today avoid the sagas, dismissing them as fictitious writings. We take a different view. We employ Iceland's medieval writings as one of many datasets in our excavations, and the archaeological remains that we are excavating in the Mosfell valley appear to verify our method. Together, the written medieval sources and the archaeological discoveries offer new information about Iceland's earliest past and about the Viking Age in general.[1]

This site was the home of the Mosfell chieftains (*Mosfellsdælingar*, the people or men of Mosfell valley), a powerful viking-age family of leaders, warriors, farmers, and legal specialists. They worshipped the old gods and about midsummer 999 became Christian.

As the reader will gather by now, the accuracy of the sagas is a highly contentious subject. They are not histories in our sense of the meaning, but they are based on actual events and historical characters. It is likely the details were manipulated by the author to meet his literary needs. Regardless, specialists in North Atlantic and viking studies, such as Byock and Zori, believe there is a large body of genuine historical information in the Old Icelandic sagas, though they must be used with great care as a historical source.

MAP

The Mosfell Archaeological Project (MAP), led by Byock and Zori, is an ongoing scientific and archaeological excavation of the glaciated and once wooded Mosfell valley (Mosfellsdalur) in southwest Iceland.[2] The valley lies between modern Reykjavík and the Althingi (ON *Alþingi*) at Þingvellir, which was the political centre of viking and mediaeval Iceland. Their findings at one particular location,

Hrísbrú Farm at the north-eastern entrance to the valley,[3] include a large turf-clad longhouse, timber/stave church dating to the period of transition from paganism to Christianity, a burial ground exhibiting mixed pagan and Christian attributes, and a pagan cremation site on the adjacent mound of Hulduhóll.[4] Together these remains form the core features of a chieftain's farmstead.

In Old Norse, this type of longhouse is called an *eldskáli* or firehall, named for the long fire, *langeldr*, down the centre of the hall. In the case of the Hrísbrú longhouse, which was constructed before the year 940, the long fire is 5.37 metres long, making it one of the largest such hearths excavated in Iceland.[5] All the evidence suggests that it was a classic Icelandic viking-age longhouse with bow-sided walls built from turf and stone, a tripartite internal room division, and doors at opposite ends of the long axis. The house had an internal system of posts supporting the superstructure and dividing the rooms of the house into three aisles, a common feature of many Iron-Age longhouses across northern Europe. All rooms had internal wooden panelling. The house was divided into five separate spatial units including a central hall, two gable rooms, an anteroom, and a covered entryway attached to the western gable room.[6]

A proud nation with a unique form of government – 'among them there is no king, but only law'[7] – the political system of viking-age Iceland centred on the chieftain and his house. A chiefly longhouse functioned as a meeting hall for a chieftain's supporters and a chieftain used his hall for status display. Icelandic chieftains and wealthy farmers held feasts to display their generosity and ability to consume luxury goods. These were opportunities to show off their wealth and offer commensal hospitality that included consumption of expensive meat and beer. The sagas frequently record well-attended wedding and funeral feasts that cemented alliances and displayed the household's economic wealth. A chieftain's feast was a public statement of wealth and consumption capacity that served as an indication to allies and supporters (ON *þingmenn*) of the resources the chieftain could mobilize in times of stress.[8]

It should be emphasized that the mediaeval idea of representation was basically functional, that is to say that it regarded man as an economic rather than as a purely political animal in the narrower sense of the term, and this is exemplified in the social institutions of Norway, Sweden, Denmark and Iceland, to quote but four relevant examples. However, as alluded to above, in Iceland there was no king or courtly culture, no clerical hierarchy, no urban trade and commerce, no armies. It was a rural conservative society composed of some powerful leading men at the top, *bœndr* in various ways dependent upon the chieftains, hired labourers, both transient and permanently attached to one farm, and slaves. In brief, an Icelandic longhouse was a monumental hall that served as a private home, a feasting hall, and a materialized statement of the socio-political power of the occupant, a seat of business, of political brokering and conflicts, where power was exercised. Here was heat and light, rank and ceremony, human solidarity and culture.

What the sagas say

Egils saga Skallagrímssonar (written around 1230, by Snorri Sturluson himself, it seems, who was a descendant of Egill Skallagrímsson) and the *Íslendingabók*, 'Book of Icelanders', (written around 1120 by the Icelandic cleric and scholar Ari Þorgilsson) recount that in the years before and after the conversion to Christianity, Grímr Svertingsson, a prominent chieftain and the Lawspeaker or *lögsögumaðr* at the Althingi from 1002 to 1004, lived at Hrísbrú (Old Mosfell).[9] The Mosfell chiefs are said to have entered into marriage alliances with the chiefs at Borg, a day's ride to the north of the valley. This powerful family was descended from the Norwegian Skalla-Grímr Kveldúlfsson, the first settler or *landnámsmaðr* in Borgarfjörður and father of the Egill from *Egils saga Skallagrímssonar*. The two families were close enough to support each other, but far enough away not to compete for followers or natural resources.

An episode from *Egils saga Skallagrímssonar* offers insight into the functioning of an ancient alliance between Borg and Mosfell. Egill Skallagrímsson was originally from Borg. In his later years, he handed down his chieftaincy (*goðorð*) at Borg and his authority over men (*mannaforrá*) to his son Þorsteinn and moved to Mosfell to live with Grímr Svertingsson, who was the husband of Egill's niece and stepdaughter Þórdís.[10] Egill had raised Þórdís as his own child – the saga makes much of the deep affection between stepfather and stepdaughter.[11] He had married his brother Þórólfr's widow, and thus Þórdís and he were blood kin.

After Egill departed for Mosfell, Þorsteinn at Borg, found himself in a property dispute with his neighbour. He was not as big and powerful as his father and yet much easier to get along with; he has inherited the good looks and disposition of his two namesakes, Egill's uncle and brother. Still, this conflict was especially dangerous, because the neighbour Steinarr Önundarson had secured the alliance of two local chieftains, both of whom stood to profit if Þorsteinn were to lose the dispute. The matter resulted in a showdown of force at the local springtime assembly (*várþing*) where Þorsteinn found himself outnumbered. According to Icelandic law and custom, each spring assembly was run by three chieftains, or *góðar*, and for Borgarfjörður at this time, Þorsteinn was one of the three, while Steinarr's new partners, Einarr of Stafaholt and Tungu-Oddr (Tongue Oddr), were the other two chieftains. Thus, Steinarr now had the support of two out of three of these chieftains. If matters went against him, and surely they would, Þorsteinn stood to lose his lands, his chieftaincy, and perhaps his life. The saga describes the dramatic resolution of this crisis at the Borgarfjörður springtime assembly as follows:

> That day people gathered at the *þing* slope to discuss their lawsuits, the courts being due to convene in the evening to try the cases. Þorsteinn was there with his following and had the most say about how the assembly was to be conducted, just like Egill before him when he was in authority, and responsible for the chieftaincy. Both sides were fully armed.
>
> Then the people at the assembly saw a group of men come riding up by Gljufur river, their shields glinting in the sun, and as they rode into the assembly the man who led them was seen to be wearing a blue cloak. On his head was a gilded helmet, a gold-adorned shield was at his side, a barbed spear in his hand, its socket incised with gold, and about his waist a sword. This was Egill Skallagrímsson who had come with eighty men fully armed as if ready for battle, a choice company, for Egill had taken with him all the best farmers' sons in the Nesses,[12] those whom he thought most warrior-like.[13]

Mobilizing eighty warlike and prominent men would be no small task with the dispersed settlement pattern of early mediaeval Iceland. Moreover, costly weapons and apparel in this society were a clear indication of military prowess and success in warfare. The dramatic arrival of Egill's forces has changed the tide of the competitive military display in favour of Þorsteinn's side.

After his timely journey to Borg, Egill returned to Mosfell. Years later when he died (*c*. 990) in the Mosfell valley, Egill was first interred in a pagan burial mound within site of the farm.[14] Later, after Iceland had converted to Christianity, he was re-interred twice in Christian graveyards. His second burial (first reburial) was at Hrísbrú (Old Mosfell) in the early eleventh century. His third burial (second reburial) was at Mosfell (New Mosfell) in the mid-twelfth century.[15] But for the saga, we would know nothing of Egill's posthumous travels, which provides a wealth of information about the local solutions to religious changes from paganism to Christianity. Thus, the penultimate chapter in *Egils saga Skallagrímssonar* names Hrísbrú as the site where a conversion-period church was built in the Mosfell valley. The same passage, which jumps forward in time over a hundred years, also supplies information about when, why, and by whom the church was built, as well as the subsequent construction of a new church and graveyard:

> When Christianity was adopted by law in Iceland, Grímr of Mosfell was baptised and built a church there. People say that Þórdís had Egill's bones moved to the church, and this is the evidence. When a church was built

at Mosfell, the one Grímr had built at Hrísbrú was demolished and a new graveyard was laid out. Under the altar some human bones were found, much bigger than ordinary human bones, and people are confident that these were Egill's bones because of the stories told by old men. Skapti *prestr* (the Priest) Þórarinsson,[16] a man of great intelligence, was there at the time. He picked up Egill's skull and placed it on the fence of the churchyard. The skull was an exceptionally large one and its weight was even more remarkable. It was ridged all over like a scallop shell, and Skapti wanted to find out just how thick it was, so he picked up a heavy axe, swung it in one hand and struck as hard as he was able with the reverse side of the axe, trying to break the skull. But the skull neither broke nor dented on impact, it simply turned white, and from that anybody could guess that the skull would not be easily cracked by a small fry while it still had skin and flesh on it. Egill's bones were re-interred on the edge of the graveyard at Mosfell.[17]

It tells us that a viking-age church was to be found on Grímr's farmstead at Hrísbrú in the Mosfell valley; that it was built when Christianity was accepted into Icelandic law about midsummer 999 by Grímr Svertingsson, the chieftain at Mosfell and husband of Egill's niece and stepdaughter Þórdís, because he converted to Christianity; that the private church included a burial ground containing the remains of the warrior poet Egill Skallagrímsson; that his remains were moved there by Þórdís, whom we can assume was a newly converted Christian like her husband. Around 130 years or so later, as the owner of the Mosfell farmstead, the chieftain-priest Skapti Þórarinsson would have made the decision to move the farm and the graveyard to their new locations. At this time, the larger Mosfell farm was split into two farms: the new location was given the name Mosfell, while the old farm site was renamed Hrísbrú. The farmer who took over at Hrísbrú would have been Skapti's tenant.[18] The sources for Egill's post mortal peripatetics are also given by means of the formulaic phrases 'people say' (*sögn manna*) and 'the stories told by old men' (*sögn gamalla manna*), implying oral memory as the source – for example, in *Eiríks saga rauða*, narrative entertainment (*sagnaskemmtun*) is mentioned as a pastime for the long winter months.[19] Suffice it to say that Egill's burial is not a folkloric event claimed by numerous places. There are no traditions of Egill being buried elsewhere, not even in his ancestral seat at Borg in Borgarfjörður.

As for those abnormal bones and rather strange skull, it has been postulated that Egill was a victim of either Paget's disease or skeletal fluorosis.[20] Paget's disease (*osteitis deformans*) is a metabolic bone disorder characterized by abnormal bone re-growth. The re-grown bone is often larger, softer, and deformed compared to normal bone, generally affecting the skull, pelvis, leg and back bones. In modern

Scandinavia, the disease is not unknown, but it is uncommon. Fluorosis is a disease caused by an excessive intake of fluoride (the ionic form of the element fluorine). At high concentrations it can act as a poison, and chronic intoxication can have a range of outcomes, from fluoride stained teeth to full-blown skeletal fluorosis. Significant amounts of fluoride are emitted from Iceland's many volcanoes.

Was there a hindrance to pagan Egill being re-buried in a Christian context? It has been argued that a reburial such as this went against Christian law. While this may be true, Christian law and practice are not always the same, and discrepancies were particularly common in the decades immediately following Iceland's conversion to Christianity. The Icelandic narratives of the conversion period detail the tolerance of continued pagan practices on private farms. It is difficult to believe that the first generation of converts to Christianity in Iceland would have adhered closely to the complicated details of Christian law even if they had known what they were.

The reasons for the conversion have been much debated by scholars, but clearly the decision was made in the contexts of the general spread of Christianity and the formation of Christian monarchies in Scandinavia. Economic and cultural connections on which Iceland depended were threatened by ideological difference between Iceland and the Scandinavian countries. In particular, the Norwegian king Óláfr Tryggvason was applying pressure on Iceland to convert by threatening to cut off trade connections and by holding prisoner the sons of wealthy chieftains or *góðar*.

The pagan spirit lived on, and its persistence, even many generations after the 'change of faith', is demonstrated by the fact that Christian bishops practised polygamy and, in spite of canon law prohibiting clerics from using violence, rode on raiding expeditions in the days of Snorri Sturluson as freely as the big men of old. The passage from *Egils saga Skallagrímssonar* above in which Skapti tries to crush the skull of his ancestor with an axe clearly suggests that Skapti is no ordinary priest. According to the saga, he was apparently not very pious, did not exhibit the expected Christian veneration for the remains of the dead, and carried around an axe.

In fact, Egill was entitled to burial in hallowed ground: during his service as a mercenary for the Anglo-Saxon king Æthelstan (r. 925–39), we are told he (and his brother Þórólfr) had received *prímsigning*, 'as was the custom in those days both for merchants and mercenaries serving Christian rulers'.[21] *Prímsigning* is an Old Norse term meaning 'provisional baptism', adopted from the Latin *prima signatio*.[22] *Prima signatio* consisted of making the sign of the cross over non-Christians in order to cleanse them of the evil spirit. After being 'prime signed', pagans 'could mix equally with Christian and pagan and were free to hold any belief that suited them'.[23] Egill's own god, by the way, was the many-faced Óðinn, the shape shifter and rune-maker, lord of drink, wanderer, and god of poetry and of the slain. He was a god who gave something and took something.

In excavations from 2001 to 2005 the MAP team unearthed the well-preserved foundations of an early Christian church at Kirkjuhóll, which, according to all the evidence, had been in use (along with the accompanying graveyard) in the tenth and eleventh centuries. Byock and Zori postulate that an empty grave shaft under the floor of the chancel of the Kirkjuhóll church 'could have been the temporary resting place for the body of viking-age Iceland's iconic warrior-poet Egill Skallagrímsson'.[24] It had been disturbed by the digging of a hole that led into the grave. If they are correct, then this grave shaft would have been Egill's first reburial, it being emptied when his bones were dug up and moved to the new church built at Mosfell sometime in the mid-twelfth century. Sieving of the fill within the emptied shaft produced a fragment of very poorly preserved bone that appeared to be human.[25]

Now back to Egill's own tale. Clearly Egill was a man unfettered by conscience, absent any moral compass you or I might reckon by. His brain probably worked overtime, seeing the board at least six moves ahead. He was impertinent, headstrong, conceited; as reckless in word as in deed; impressive (if he pleased) on public occasions. He was certainly one of the most brilliant, picturesque, and, it must be added, capable killers that even the sagas can produce. Manifold and monstrous as were Egill's crimes, his astonishing ability and cool courage lend a sort of savage sublimity even to his bloodstained career, and, indeed the doggedness the herculean old man displays at the very end of his life is almost without parallel.

As we discussed above, Egill had become the settled farmer, a respected figure of authority and apparently the man of peace. But he rides up to the local assembly with eighty armed men, and, as we learn from the last pages of the tale, his battle days are behind him now but his killing days are not over, and his actions continue to invite speculation after his death. As Egill senses his end is near, he disappears one night with his lifetime's worth of wealth, made of two chests filled with silver, and two thralls (owned by Grímr Svertingsson) to help him bury it so nobody can enjoy it. Then, for old time's sake and as the last act of his violent life, the blind octogenarian berserker kills with his bare hands the two thralls to keep the location secret and stumbles his way back home where he dies peacefully shortly after. And then there is that weird farewell, Egill's bones are dug up years afterwards and wondered at for their bigness, beyond the wont of little men.

The great French romance writer of the second half of the twelfth century, Chrétien de Troyes, always strove to describe his hero as a perfect man. This seems also to have been the aim of the authors of some *Íslendingasögur*, who, like encomiasts, pass over all that is unworthy in their heroes, and concentrate on their nobler deeds. Expecting to be entertained and reassured, the crowd invariably want book heroes, historical characters recreated as they ought to have been rather than as they were. This was certainly not the intention of the author of *Egils saga Skallagrímssonar*. According to the saga, Egill was ugly and greedy, a ferocious killer of men – not only in battle or in single combat – and deceitful. On the other hand, he is described as a man who was deeply attached to his wife, to a favourite son, to his stepdaughter, and to his only friend, Arinbjörn Þórisson. With regards to the last, friendship was a social bond like kinship. It was seen less as a sentimental tie, more as a contractual one, bringing advantage to both sides and sustained by visits, gift-exchange and acts of support. Yet for Egill his friendship for Arinbjörn went beyond this, as witnessed by his great poem *Arinbjarnarkviða*, in which he praises his friend's nobility, truth and generosity.[26]

Egill is generally regarded as the finest versifier of viking-age Iceland,[27] which makes him all the more fascinating as by all accounts the man was a complete maniac. Egill is not only the beneficiary of Óðinn's gift of poetry, but also to some small degree an embodiment of the god. A dark, ugly, brooding character, haunted by rumours that his grandfather was a werewolf, the slightly mad, touchy Egill was not the sort of poet we think of in our post-romantic age. Then again, it is reckoned that a story plot is only as good as its villain, and our villain is certainly a colourful liquidator. His father tells Egill he will not be taking him to his grandfather's feast because 'you're difficult enough to cope with when you're sober'.[28] The sweet little boy was three. Unperturbed, Egill saddled up a horse and followed his family to the feast, close enough to follow, far away enough not to be seen. He reached the feast and his grandfather was so impressed by young Egill that he was allowed to stay. Egill then recited a poem to his grandfather, and was rewarded with three seashells and a duck egg.

At the tender age of six Egill murdered one of his little friends with an axe for cheating him in a ball game. The two households came to blows, and seven men were left for dead. When Egill returned home his father was not pleased, but his mother proudly declared 'that Egill had the makings of a real viking [*vera víkingsefni*] and it was obvious that as soon as he was old enough he ought to be given fighting-ships'.[29] His antisocial behaviour and asinine brutality would lead to his banishment. He participated in viking raids and adventures ranging across Iceland, Norway, Sweden and Denmark down to the east Baltic lands, Saxony, Friesland and England. His many and varied encounters, which are the brutal stuff of legend, included kings, sorcerers, berserkers and outlaws. Egill was a viking of most masterly magnificence, a word spinner, a traveller, immensely strong and resilient, contemptuous of lesser men, and aware of the nullity of human life. He was incredibly dangerous. A demon to frighten children with.

Violence was also a factor at Hrísbrú. This reality is observed in the skeleton of an apparent homicide victim. This skeleton of a man in his forties was interred immediately to the east of the chancel foundation.[30] The skull shows massive cranial trauma with a gaping wound in the left parietal and a slice of bone removed from the occipital bone. These wounds caused rapid death. The wound on the top of the head was probably caused by an axe, as evidenced by the size and the isolated region of the cut, while the wound to the rear may have been the result of either an axe or a sword. Possibly the killing was carried out by two assailants, and, given the nature of the blows that came directly down on top of the skull; the victim may have been executed.

Such evidence of violence at the Hrísbrú site is consistent with descriptions of feuds found in the Icelandic sagas. Indeed, these sagas envelop us in a society that is at once honour-bound and blood-stained, presided over by the laws of the blood-feud, where the kin of a person slain are bound to exact a price for the death, either by slaying the killer or by receiving satisfaction in the form of *wergild* (the 'man-price'), a fixed compensation. This Icelandic value system is best illustrated by Beowulf when he utters the first principles of the northern warrior's honour-code: 'It is always better to avenge dear ones than to indulge in mourning'.[31]

One saga in particular, *Gunnlaugs saga ormstungu*, offers an account that specifically describes the Hrísbrú site and corresponds, at least in a general way, to the archaeological evidence for violent death at the site. According to the saga, around the year 1010 Illugi *svarti* (the Black), a chieftain from the upper hills of Borgarfjörður and father of the renowned warrior poet Gunnlaugr *ormstungu*, raided his rival Önundr Eilífsson,[32] the Mosfell chieftain who followed Grímr Svertingsson, and caught and executed one of the kinsmen of Önundr, a man named Björn:

> In the autumn [*c.*1010] Illugi (*svarti*) rode from his home at Gilsbakki with thirty men and arrived at Mosfell early in the morning. Önundr [the chieftain at Mosfell] and his sons escaped into the church, but Illugi caught two of Önundr's kinsmen, one named Björn and the other Þórgrímr. Illugi had Björn killed and Þórgrímr's foot chopped off. Then Illugi rode home and after this Önundr sought no reprisal.[33]

Wound pathology certainly reinforces the brutality of feuds with its almost casual use of shock weapons. In viking-age Iceland there were all sorts of feuds, superb and dramatic as possible – some ferocious, others heroic – according to the sagas. The finest themes of vengeance can be witnessed there: hatreds that were decades old, mollified for a moment, but never totally snuffed out; abominable ruses; murders that took on the proportions of massacres and at times almost resembled an act of glory.

Scholarly scepticism about the Old Icelandic sagas is in part a political legacy. The mid-twentieth-century reinterpretation of the family sagas as thirteenth-century fictional creations was proposed by a group of Icelandic literary scholars known as the Icelandic School (*Íslenski skólinn*). This group emerged at the climax of Iceland's struggle for independence from Denmark, which Iceland declared unilaterally in 1944, and their theory became institutionalized, in the Icelandic educational system. It was and still is the accepted theoretical position among many researchers, particularly archaeologists.[34]

Yet it became clear to Byock and Zori that archaeology and sagas, especially the Icelandic family sagas or *Íslendingasögur*, could complement each other. Obviously, the texts and archaeology support each other in illuminating the economic life of these viking-age people centred on a settled pastoral life of livestock-raising, coastal fishing, and the gathering of wild foods in a challenging marginal environment.[35] Yet they could support each other in geographical and political landscapes too. In this way, the family sagas include invaluable information concerning the roles of chiefs and internal political processes, including wealth transfers, alliance building, conspicuous consumption at feasts, and élite gift exchange. For Byock and Zori (and like-minded others) the Old Icelandic sagas contain historical facts maintained intact in oral tradition. So it does matter what the sagas say.

He, her, hero, heroine

Perhaps we need to challenge the popular perception that viking warriors were necessarily large, aggressive and hirsute men, and that warfare was the quintessential masculine activity. In general, this was almost certainly the case, as supported by both the written sources and archaeological finds, but there are important exceptions. A more nuance view would recognize that even large, aggressive and hirsute men had mothers, and very likely sisters, wives and daughters. Moreover, the image of an armed female standing in a shield wall alongside other courageous Norse women and men is indeed alluring and fascinating.

In Old Norse literature, the sagas and skaldic poetry, women come to the battlefield in the form of sorceresses, of valkyries, and of shield maidens. The shield maiden has often captured the popular attention, on the one hand overturning the rules that polarize male and female, and on the other a sort of glorification of the female presence in a male world. And why not? Women usually did the cooking, fire-tending, fur-dressing, tool-sharpening, and hairdressing; fire-lighting, sword wearing, preening, boasting, and gambling with dice was for men. Prose and poetry being the work of males, women are invariably deceivers: inconstant, unscrupulous, over-talkative, quarrelsome, querulous, lecherous, capricious, and shameless, though not necessarily all these at once.

It's a woman's world

One common rôle of women in the sagas is as an inciter. The goading scene is a classic in the saga literature. Whereas men may strut and saunter across the saga stage, women are frequently found goading them to act, to take revenge, when the men might otherwise have been content to do nothing, or if they did, preferring material compensation to blood vengeance. The women are much harder than the men, even more eager to protect the family's honour. Perhaps this is due to the woman's passive, domestic rôle, which prevented her from acting herself.

In *Brennu-Njáls saga* Hildigunnr encourages her uncle Flosi to take blood revenge for the slaying of her husband, Höskuldr Þrainsson, by flinging her husband's bloody cloak onto Flosi's shoulders. Dried blood from the cloak rained down on Flosi. He responded, 'Cold are the counsels of women'.[1] Flosi later takes revenge for Höskuldr's death by burning Njáll and his family in their home. In *Laxdæla saga* the greatest of all saga heroines, Guðrún Ósvífursdóttir, is married four times, but the centre of the action is the 'love triangle' that ends when her third husband, Bolli Þórleiksson (he was the father of the well-known Bolli Bollason), kills her former suitor Kjartan Óláfsson, the son of Þórgerðr Egilsdóttir, the daughter of Egill Skallagrímsson. Guðrún incites her husband and her brothers to take revenge on Kjartan, who is in fact Bolli's beloved foster brother. For Bolli to kill his foster brother would be a despicable act, but Guðrún pulls out all the stops, saying to the men:

> With your temperament, you'd have made some farmer a good group of daughters, fit to do no one any good or any harm. After all the abuse and shame Kjartan has heaped upon you, you don't let it disturb your sleep while he goes riding by under your very noses, with only one other man to accompany him. Such men have no better memory than a pig. There's not much chance you'll ever dare to make a move against Kjartan at home if you won't even stand up to him now, when he only has one or two others to back him up. The lot of you just sit here at home, making much of yourselves, and one could only wish there were fewer of you.[2]

A woman might use the threat of divorce as a means to goad her husband into violent action. Divorce was relatively easy and could result in severe financial burdens upon the husband; once she was brought by her husband, a *brúðr* or bride retained the rights to her *konufé*, women's goods or portion. The alternative to divorce, however, could be dire. In this particular case, the consequent hostilities between the two foster brothers ended with Bolli killing Kjartan, and then he in turn being killed by Kjartan's kinsmen.[3] In old age Guðrún summed up her life in words that have become proverbial in Iceland: 'Though I treated him worst, I loved him best'.[4] As a young mother, Guðrún had brought up her son Bolli to wreak bloody vengeance on his father's killers, but she ends her life in Christian piety as a nun and anchoress in a completely different ethical world

After the burial of Ásbjörn Sigurðarson *selsbani* (Slayer of Seal), Sigrið (his mother) gives the spear that took his life to her brother-in-law Þórir *hundr* (the Hound), and with her words to this very powerful man, she not only demonstrates her own personal power, but also demonstrates how powerful viking-age women can be.

> 'Here is a gift I shall give you, and I wish it may serve you well.' It was a spear.
> 'Here is the spear that pierced my son Asbjörn, with his blood still on it. It will help you to remember that it came from the wound you saw on Asbjörn, your brother's son. It would be a manly deed if you parted with it in such

fashion that it stood in the breast of Óláfr the Stout [Óláfr II Haraldsson]. And now I say', she continued, 'that you will be called by everyone a vile wretch if you do not avenge Ásbjörn'. With that she turned away.[5]

The spear is called *Selshemnaren* (Seal's Avenger). The revenge is fulfilled three years later, in 1030 at the battle of Stiklarstaðir when Þórir *hundr*, along with two comrades, slays the king.

That is not to say that women never pick up a weapon and use it in anger. Two examples are related in *Gísla saga Súrssonar*. When the cowardly Eyjólfr the Grey and his men attack the outlaw Gísli Súrsson in overwhelming numbers, Gísli's wife Auðr stands by his side, armed with a club. In the first rush, Gísli kills a man called Helgi by cutting him in two, while Auðr strikes Eyjólfr so hard that he staggers back down the hill. Gísli turns to his wife and says, 'I knew I had married well but never realized until now good the match was'.[6] Gísli, who might otherwise have lived a peaceful and prosperous farming life with his well-loved wife, is forced to live by his wits in exile and outlawry. After he is eventually cornered and killed by Eyjólfr at Geirþjófsfjörðr (all fifteen men with Eyjólfr that day had been wounded or killed), Eyjólfr goes to the farm at Helgafell to visit Börkur, and his wife Þórdís, who is Gísli's sister. Understandably Þórdís does not want to offer hospitality to her brother's killer, but Börkur insists. During the meal, Þórdís recognizes Gísli's sword lying on the floor by Eyjólfr's feet. She intentionally drops a tray full of spoons, and bending down to pick them up, she grabs the sword and thrusts up at Eyjólfr from below, giving him a major wound. Börkur seizes Þórdís, and she declares herself divorced from him on the spot.[7]

As Christine de Pizan (b. 1364) – the only mediaeval woman, as far as is known, to have earned a living by her pen – would point out, it was men who wrote the books. Despite the odds sacked against her by her sex, Christine would become one of the most distinguished writers of her day. In the prologue of her *Le Livre de la cité des dames* (1404) on the lives of various heroines of Homeric legend, the Old Testament, Greek mythology, and Christian martyrology, Christine wonders why men 'are so unanimous in attributing wickedness to women' and why 'we should be worse than men since we were also created by God'.[8] At the end of her book, she places all these women behind the battlements and towers of her ideal city, saying that it is a refuge for all worthy women and they must defend it against their male enemies. Actually, the whole premise of the book was an argument against the vilification of women, then in vogue among male writers, and her ultimate goal in life was to encourage women to be in charge of their own lives. In her next book, *Le trésor de la cité des dames* (1405), she offers advice to a noblewoman on how to govern her lands when her husband dies. She also says a noblewoman will further good government in her realm by acting as a mediator between her barons and try to reconcile any differences between them. She continues:

But if her land is attacked by foreign enemies – as frequently happens after the death of a prince with under-aged children – it will be necessary for her to make and conduct war. She must keep the good will of her barons and lords so they are loyal and come to the aid of her child. She must also have the service of knights, squires, and gentlemen so they will boldly fight for their young lord. She must keep the affection of the people too, in order to help with her wealth and property. She must speak to her subjects, so they will not betray her, saying that the great expense of war will not, if it pleases God, last long.[9]

At the end of her life Christine took up the pen again and wrote a short poem in praise of the figure that, to posterity, stands out above all others of her time – another woman, Jeanne d'Arc. On Jeanne's involvement in the relief of beleaguered Orléans on 8 May 1429, which was the last pocket of Armagnac resistance north of the Loire, Christine happily declared:

No miracle was more clear, than that / God so aided and to all it was known. / Thru the inability of our enemies who / helped each other like dogs without breath, / so they were captured or put to death.[10]

For Christine, the teenage heroine was the epitome of all that she had written about. At the end of her poem she hoped that Jeanne would lead Charles VII on a crusade to the Holy Land. Jeanne's brief military career served as a model for female heroism ever after. It replaced the reality of the stalwart noblewoman defending her marital rights, with a new idea of the inspired common woman fighting in defence of more mystical virtues of independence and freedom.

Warrior women

There is something about the idea of women warriors fighting alongside men during the viking age, but does it have any basis in reality? Impossible to say. All we can say is that it makes for a good story and in the case of legendary warrior women like the vigorous, independent, fiery-hearted Lagertha (ON *Hlaðerðr*), there is probably some basis in fact. In *Danorum Regum Heromque Historia* the cleric chronicler Saxo Grammaticus mentions that in Denmark there were once women, 'forgetful of their true selves', who dressed themselves like men and spent their time 'cultivating warrior's skills'.[11] A gallery of such hoydenish characters are mentioned in his account, including not only Lagertha, but also Hetha, Visina, Vebiorg, Rusila, Stikla, Alvild or Gurith.[12] Saxo is notorious for having incorporated purely legendary material into his work – he derived the current (*c.* 1215) Danish royal family from a bear,[13] in the male line – so some scholars may dismiss his warrior women as the Scandinavian equivalent of the classical Amazons.

As a Christian, a cleric, and a man, Saxo did not approve of women warriors who strapped on weapons and went to war, that much is clear. Inevitably, like many churchmen, he saw only one rôle for women, the domestic trinity of dutiful daughter, dedicated wife and devoted mother. Despite women being relegated to a life of *purdah*, it does seem, however, our misogynist ecclesiastic had a soft spot for Lagertha, the shield maiden who has recently taken the firmest hold on the popular imagination. Her story continues to be retold, albeit on the small screen.

The remarkable embodiment of beauty, brains and bellicosity, Lagertha was the first wife of Ragnarr *loðbrók*, a shadowy, but possibly historical female figure. The story of her beauty and of her first meeting with Ragnarr is a captivating tale that has long passed into legend. Ragnarr thought Lagertha well worth wooing and winning, for she possessed, in the poetic words of Saxo, 'a man's temper in a girl's body',[14] and her career as a formidable *bellatrix* and courtship with Ragnarr is amply recorded by the Danish historian.[15] Saxo's florid Latin style often provides a contrast to the brusque tone of the Icelanders, and he makes comments himself where Icelandic authors do not. It is important to keep this consciously in mind, therefore, when reading Saxo. 'History' is perhaps not the best description of his work, as it is full of the supernatural and quixotic.

It is according to Saxo that Lagertha makes the transition from shield maiden, or *skjaldmær* (pl. *skjaldmeyjar*), to maiden king, or *meykondr*. Later on, when Ragnarr asks for her help against his enemies in a civil war, Lagertha 'in whose veins there still ran strong feelings of her former love',[16] comes quickly with her son, Fridleif, and second husband. She provides Ragnarr with a hundred and twenty ships. She encourages the warriors with her bravery and causes the enemy to panic in their shock. Returning to battle brings back her former ways, and in the night she sticks a spearhead in her husband's throat. She seizes the whole title and sovereignty, as she prefers to govern alone than share the rule with her husband (as the legend went). Here we can see echoes of the widespread folkloric image of a proud, independent and unapproachable woman warrior/ruler who refuses to marry any suitor of lower dignity than she (cf. Sigrið *stórrada* and the burning of her two suitors). As her own woman, Lagertha did not necessarily need a man anymore. As a powerful and bellicose warrior woman, Lagertha was a masterful killer, equally at home with swords and sex as weapons.

Yet Lagertha was not alone in the weird world of women warriors. There are ironclad amazons at the immense battle of Brádvellir in the year 750 or thereabouts. This was an event long remembered (and embellished) in Norse legend, in which the decrepit, crippled and cruel Danish king Haraldr *hilditönn* ('War-tooth') lost to his Swedish nephew Sigurðr *hringr* (Ring), a possible candidate for the father of the legendary warrior king Ragnarr *loðbrók*.[17] Haraldr cannot be wounded with bladed weapons, the carnage only ending when he is tumbled from his chariot and clubbed to death by Óðinn with his own club, who is present in the guise of the king's charioteer. As well as the one-eyed war god, the aforementioned Hetha and Visina, 'whose female bodies' nature had endowed with manly courage', and Vebiorg, 'instilled with the same spirit', lead war bands of men on the Danish side, with Hetha in charge of the right flank of Haraldr's army and Visina his standard-bearer. Saxo Grammaticus continues, claiming that 12,000 of Sigurðr's champions and 30,000 of Haraldr's were slain – not counting the commoners who fell. Visina and Vebiorg are among the dead, but Hetha survives the apocalyptic chaos to be given part of Denmark to rule under the victorious Sigurðr. She does not last long, however, because 'the Sjællanders, who had had Haraldr as their captain, though it a disgrace to be subject to a woman's rule'.[18] Apart from Lagertha, Saxo's women warriors do not succeed in the world of men.

Bizarre as the story of warrior women sounds, it is probably true. Stranger things, involving complete forces of warrior women, have happened throughout military history. Did not the saintly Jeanne d'Arc, so as to lessen the advances of the soldiers around her and so preserve her holy virginity, throughout her brief but brilliant military career wear male garb? There is some reason to think, therefore, that some of the women Saxo mentioned may have been flesh and blood and weapon-wielding warriors too. The woman warrior Rusila mentioned above (the name suggests red hair) has been identified by some scholars with the *Inghen Ruaidh* ('the red-haired maiden'), who is mentioned independently by the anonymous author of the twelfth-century *Cogadh Gáedhel re Gaillaibh* as one of the leaders of the Norse in Ireland.[19]

One of the most renowned warrior women in Old Norse accounts is Hervör from *Hervarar saga ok Heiðreks*. She retrieves her father's sword from his burial mound by supernatural means, and assumes the rôle of the son her father never had. As a surrogate son she adopts the clothing, manners and occupations of a male. After a time, however, she finds a husband. Until this point, Hervör was a maiden, not yet admitted to womanhood, but rather also like one who has no gender at all and might choose which identity she would adopt. Once married, she adopts the female social rôle of a woman and child bearer.

In *Laxdæla saga*, a woman named Auðr after being divorced by her husband (on the grounds that she behaved like a man and wore breeches of the kind appropriate to a man, hence her nickname, *Bróka-Auðr*, Breeches-Auðr) attacked him with her short sword while he lay sleeping. He was badly wounded, Auðr having 'struck with such force that the sword lodged in the wood of the bed'.[20] Freydí Eiríksdóttir, an illegitimate daughter of Eiríkr *rauða* ('the Red') and one of the heroines of *Grœnlendinga saga* and *Eiríks saga rauða*, wears men's clothes and is portrayed as the epitome of evil, being responsible for killing a number of fellow explorers and for personally taking the sharp end of an axe to five women whom her men had refused to kill.[21] She frightens off an attacking band of *skræling vár* by running after them, even though she is pregnant, and then, when surrounded by them, picking up a sword from a dead Greenlander, pulling out one of her breasts from her clothing and slapping it with the naked sword. The natives were terrified at the sight and ran off and took to their skin boats and rowed away.[22] All this murder and mayhem took place in the New World, Vinland to precise, at the site discovered by Freydí's brother Leif Eiríksson. Anyway, despite her heroism the Greenlanders decided to return to Greenland.

Conversely, once the Scandinavian countries were Christianized, any warrior tradition amongst women died out. The figure of the warrior woman predictably jarred in the traditionally masculine spheres of war, politics and religion, even in the headless polity that was Iceland. For that reason, the mediaeval Icelandic law book *Grágás* prohibits women from wearing male clothing, from cutting their hair short, or from carrying weapons, the punishment for cross-dressing being exile.[23] Saxo, writing around the eleven-seventies, speaks of women warriors in Denmark as belonging to a distant – almost legendary – past, the women of his day being written up as quiet, passive queens. Saxo obviously differs from *Grágás* in countless ways, but an interesting similarity between the two sources is that they both refer to warrior women, and in doing so portray them as having held a place in their contemporary time. Warrior women were not portrayed by Saxo as nonsense, and the calm assumption of our Christian cleric is that this represents a state of affairs that is decidedly pre-Christian.[24]

To reinforce this point regarding pre-Christian and Christian Norse women, we shall briefly turn to *Guta lag*, a set of laws from the Baltic Sea island of Gotland. This legal codex contains detailed laws covering a wide range of quotidian situations, from crime, to inheritance, to trading goods, and on how weddings were to be conducted. Indeed, when it came to marriage, the laws imply that these were arranged by one's parents. *Guta lag* notes that:

> If a man seduces another man's daughter or one of his wards into betrothal without the authority of her father or kinsmen, then he must pay forty marks to the complainant. If a man takes (i.e. takes in marriage) a woman or maid by force or violence, without the authority of her father or kinsmen, then those who prosecute her case shall decide between his neck or wergild, if the woman is Gotlandic; the authorities take twelve marks of the wergild. If the woman is not Gotlandic, then those who prosecute her case shall decide between his neck and ten marks of silver; the authorities take twelve marks [i.e. in coin] of the wergild.[25]

It has been assessed that twenty-four marks would have been the value of a wealthy farmstead on Gotland, so this fine was sizeable. As for the value of one mark (*mörk*), this was the equivalent of twenty-four *örtugar* (sg. *öre*), ounces, of silver.

Theft and adultery seem, to some extent, to have been regarded as more despicable crimes than killing, presumably because they were crimes that broke down trust in the farming community. Thus, *Guta lag* contains a schedule of monetary fines, curious in its scaling, for the touching of a woman: for touching her wrist or ankle, half a mark; her elbow or her leg between knee and calf, eight *örtugar* of silver; her breast, one *öre*; above the knee, five *örtugar*; higher than that, the 'touch dishonourable' or the 'madman's clasp', no fine payable under the assumption that a woman should have registered her protest at the first opportunity, if she was to receive maximum compensation.[26] Certainly, one noteworthy aspect of this law relating to what today we would call sexual harassment is that the woman appears to have been assigned some responsibility for protecting herself against unwanted advances, since the fines for these diminished according to the intimacy of the advance.

The opening words of *Guta lag* invoke Christianity and revoke heathendom:

> This is the first beginning of our law: that we should reject heathen ways and accept Christianity and all believe in one almighty God, and pray to him that he grant us good harvests and peace, victory and health. And that we should uphold our Christianity and our proper faith and the province in which we live and that we should each day do, in our deeds and desires, those things that are to the honour of God and which most benefit us, both in body and soul.[27]

It has been suggested that the Christian overtones of *Guta lag* are the direct result of a visit to Gotland by Óláfr II Haraldsson in 1030 or thereabouts and his conversion of the Gotlanders to Christianity. *Guta saga* does not, understandably, mention the visit in 1007, during which the twelve-year-old Óláfr intimidated the Gotlanders into paying protection money and subsequently stayed the winter.[28] It has been suggested that the visit described in *Guta saga* is actually the one mentioned in *Óláfs saga helga*, when Óláfr is said to have visited Gotland on his way *home* from Russia in the spring of 1030. However, Óláfr only seems to have stopped for confirmation of *jarl* Hákon's death and to await a favourable wind.[29] Besides, considering the exiled king was keen to make his presence felt in Norway, it does not seem very likely that Óláfr would have wanted to make a prolonged break in his journey at that time.

The visit to Gotland as an evangelizing king, if it did occur, can be placed between 1007, when Óláfr made his earlier visit as a predatory pagan, and 1030.

This missionary visit may have resulted in the introduction of Christianity to Gotland, or at least in the baptism of individual Gotlanders, but it is questionable whether a general conversion of the whole of the population resulted. Nevertheless, the importance of Saint Óláfr to the mediaeval Gotlanders is emphasized by their dedicating their church in Novgorod to his name.[30]

A sword is girl's best friend

It is certain that many of the women in the Icelandic sagas, like the women in Greek tragedy, play large and interesting roles. Turning from Old Norse textual sources to material evidence, there are three Danish and two Norwegian examples of women buried with military accoutrements (plus a number of possible examples from southern Sweden),[31] but of course these need not be interpreted as shield maidens.

The presence of weapons, most often knives, spearheads and arrowheads, has often been explained away, in more or less convincing fashion, as representing gifts or marks of transferred status in the circumstantial absence of a man, or as symbols of some kind. For instance, it has been argued that a spearhead (or an exceptionally large arrowhead) may have served the function of a magic staff, the deceased woman being a ritual specialist, perhaps involved in the practice of magic known as *seiðr*. The richest Norwegian ship burial, at Oseberg in Vestfold, was that of a woman surrounded by goods and travelling gear and apparently accompanied by her maid servant. Among the grave goods were two axes of very good quality, and it has been argued that these 'male objects' were intended as household tools used in the kitchen (for cutting joints of meat etc.).

Conversely, other interpretations are possible. After all, the depiction of various examples of different types of females, some wearing long dresses and spears, others with helmets and sword on three of the weaved fragments of the Oseberg tapestry is a valuable source in this respect.[32] Indeed, there is no reason why these 'male objects' should not be simply representing the processions of the dead while they were alive: women with weapons. It is interesting to note that the majority of such items are projectile weapons, that is to say, those that are less reliant on physical strength (as opposed to dexterity in handling) to wield effectively.

What is more, there is no reason why women who fought as men should not have been buried as women; there could have been dozens of temporary hellcats who ended up as goodly housewives, whose natural tools were now the distaff and flax, pots and pans, needle and thread, not the spear or the bow. Always, and this is the rub, the critical discussion is in the nature of 'it could have been', it's possible', 'why couldn't they have', and other such statements, but none point to any valid proof that women fought as warriors. There is also the current argument that the graves and their furnishings may actually provide more information about the people responsible for the burial, rather than about the dead. In other words, we should move away from the tendency to regard the grave contents as direct reflections of the roles that the deceased may have played during their lives, that is to say, not to view graves as 'mirrors' of the social status and ethnic identities of the deceased. The fact that 'the dead do not bury themselves' has very important implications for the discussions of past mortuary behaviour.[33]

In December 2012 an amateur archaeologist armed with a metal detector discovered a tiny silver figurine in a field near the village of Hårby on Fyn (ancient Funen), Denmark.[34] It has been dated to the year 800 or thereabouts. Partly gilded, while other areas are coloured black by niello, a mixture of copper, silver and lead sulphides used as an inlay, the 3.4 centimetre-high figurine, which would have been a pendant, undoubtedly represents a woman: she has a knotted ponytail and long garments characteristic of female figures in Norse art. What is curious is that she is bearing an upright double-edged sword in her right hand and a round shield in her left. Most experts conclude that the figure must be symbolic, rather than realistic, and are inclined to label her as a handmaiden of the war god Óðinn, one of his valkyries, 'choosers of the slain'. This I find hard to believe.

Any association between valkyries and swords is extremely rare. Literary texts suggest they were usually mounted on horses and equipped with byrnies and helmets and armed with spears when going about their duties on the field of the slain. Thus a stanza from *Hákonarmál*, composed by the skald Eyvindr Finnsson *skáldaspillir* presumably shortly after the death of king Hákon Haraldsson *góði* (d. 961), reads: 'The king heard what the valkyries said, mounted on their horses, cautious they were, wearing helmets they sat with sheltering shields by their side'.[35] This description of the valkyries is very similar to the depiction of armed women in pendants and figurines from the viking age.

A sword is an iconic image closely associated with masculinity, it being the weapon of choice, the prized possession, and the status symbol of the better sort of Norse warrior. More to the point, far from Wagner's beautiful maidens longing romantically for dead heroes, the valkyries of the viking age seem originally to have been terrifying demons of war, unleashed into combat and literally personifying the brutal essence of battle, devouring corpses on the battlefield like wolves and ravens; in this they resembled the Furies of Greek mythology with their manic thirst for retribution and blood revenge. We know of fifty-one individual valkyries, whose translated names embody what they really were: Sword-noise, Battle-weaver, Shield-scraper, Teeth-grinder, Killer, Silence, and the rest of the posse.[36]

Spinning spells

After the Hiberno–Norse defeat at Clontarf, an Icelandic poet portrayed the valkyries in their original form, in sombre power and dark magnificence, exulting in blood and weaving the web of war with human guts on a loom made from spears, while using arrows and swords as shuttles and weaving batons, and human heads as loom weights:

> A wide warp / warns of slaughter; / blood rains / from the beams cloud. / / A spear-grey fabric / is being spun, / which the friends / of Randver's slayer / will fill out / with a red weft. // The warp is woven / with warrior's guts, / and heavily weighted / with the heads of men. / Spears serve as heddle rods, / and arrows are the pin bearers, / we will beat with swords / our battle web. // Hildr sets to weaving, / and Hjörþrimul / and Sanngriðr and Svipul, / with swords drawn. / Shafts will splinter, / shields shatter; / the hound-of-helmets / devours shields.[37]

In this song of the valkyries, Randver's slayer was Óðinn, and the god's friends, the valkyries themselves of course. The 'hound-of-helmets' is a kenning for battleaxe. The textile itself is said to predict the outcome of a specific battle, and when the textile is complete the weavers tear it apart and the pieces are scattered in all directions.

The poem is preserved only in *Brennu-Njáls saga*, where towards the end of the saga some of the characters participate in Clontarf (called 'Brian's battle' here), but the outcome of this battle does not seem to fit the darkly prediction of the Irish enduring 'an evil time' very well.[38] History – and the saga too – tells us that it was Brian Bórumha mac Cennétig of Munster – Brian of the Tributes – high king of Ireland (OI *ard rí*), who won the victory, though he paid for it with his life at the very end of the battle. Since Clontarf ended in the tumbling of the Norsemen into the sea, the Irish (forgetting that an army of Leinster Irishmen fought beside the Norsemen on the losing side) regard it as the repulse of an invasion. Thus, the Norse invaders were driven off, leaving Sigurðr Hlöðvirsson *inn digri* (the Stout), *jarl* of the two North Atlantic archipelagos of Orkney (ON *Orkneyjar*) and Shetland (ON *Hjaltland*), on the field of the slain. So the poem might originally have been associated with a different battle, perhaps the Norse victory near Dublin almost a century before, in 919.[39] Even so, as magical acts, spinning and weaving have often been associated with the creation or foretelling of destiny. An Irish example occurs in the *Táin Bó Cúailnge*, where a seeress is seen carrying a weaver's beam and weaving a fringe. This is a magical act that enables her to prophesy the coming battle.[40]

Spinning and weaving, in general, were associated with a branch of sorcery called *seiðr* and seen as women's magic, first and foremost, despite the fact that Óðinn himself was a master of it.[41] The *Æsir* feared *seiðr*, and forbade its practice, except by women, on the grounds that it was dangerous to, and might even invert, male virility – men who performed it were stigmatized by life-threatening connotations of effeminacy, cowardice and a suggestion of passive homosexuality.[42] A man's effeminacy was inseparable from cowardice in the Norse way of thinking, and together they indicated that a man was not fully a man. The worse defamation of all was to say that a man was not merely effeminate, but in fact played a woman's part in a homosexual relationship. *Seiðr* was taught to the *Æsir* by the *Vanir* deity Freyja ('Lady'), the gorgeous golden-haired goddess of love in the guise of a promiscuous tease, but only Óðinn among them dared to practice *seiðr* – because he desired to control its great power: the power to know the future. Thus, the enraged Loki calls Óðinn *argr*,[43] a derisive term used for men who engaged in homosexual intercourse as the passive partner, as well as men or women who practised *seiðr*. The contradiction of this female magic's embodiment by the highest male god lies at the root of Norse sorcery's terrible power.

With witchcraft in their eyes, and sorcery in every movement, the female Norns (ON *Nornar*) who lived under the great cosmic ash tree called Yggdrasil, were supernatural powers often seen in the metaphor of weaving *men's* fate, whose life strings, whatever they may be, were spun, measure and cut by them.[44] Their caprices, where one corrects or spoils the others' endowments, are often seen in Old Norse literature, when beauty, bounty and beastliness can be given together. Presumably, the association of women with man's fate was a permutation of earlier concepts of women as fertility symbols; the goddesses of fertility controlled the growing and flowering of crops and livings things on earth. By the thirteenth century the Norns were named Past, Present and Future (*Urðr, Verdandi, Skuld*) – probably a recent innovation – and in popular representations they were shown as young maidens. The point presented here is that as a woman may send a man into battle, she can also determine his survival.

In a similar fashion, a Norse woman could find magic in her spindle and distaff, and so not just a raven banner, but any woven and stitched cloth could in theory have magic woven into it, such as those shirts worn by our Norse heroes Ragnarr *loðbrók* and Örvar-Oddr. Ragnarr's magic shirt we have already discussed in the proper place. Oddr was presented with a magic shirt by an Irish princess named Ölvör. According to Ölvör, Oddr would never be cold at sea or on land while wearing the shirt, he would never become tired when swimming, never be harmed by fire and never be hungry, and swords would not wound him unless he ran away from battle. Oddr asked Ölvör about the circumstances of the shirt's tailoring, and she replied with the following verse:

> I have heard of a shirt of silk / made in six places: / one arm in Ireland, / the other in the north by Finnar, / Saxon girls began it, / and Hebrideans spun it, / Frankish brides wove it, / on the warp of Óþjóðan's mother.[45]

Oddr is now invincible until his life has run its course, as according to prophecy he cannot die until he returns to his birthplace, Berurjod, aged three hundred.[46] The involvement of Norse–Hebridean women in the spinning of Oddr's magic shirt probably derives from the depiction of them as sorceresses elsewhere in Old Norse literature. Not just a raven banner or a magic shirt, but any woven cloth could in theory have magic woven into it.

There is a strain in Old Norse mythology that holds that women have special powers, qualities of magic, and should be feared and mistrusted by men. The principal gods are all men. Furthermore, popular ideas of women contained a heavy element of suspicion. According to the *Hávamál*:

> A wench's words let no wise man trust, / nor trust the troth of a woman; / for on the whirling [potter's] wheel their hearts are shaped, and fickle and fitful their minds.[47]

In Norse society there was a division of power according to sex. Men ruled physical affairs; women, psychological matters.

Back to reality

To leave this section on Norse women on a more (and less misogynistic) note, though no Old Norse story or history depicts a woman as a warrior unless she has legendary or mythological characteristics, we do know of a Byzantine account, reporting on the Rus' defeat at Dorostolon (L *Durostorum*, today's Silistra) on the lower Danube in 971, which mentions the fact that the victors 'found women lying among the fallen, equipped like men; women who had fought against the Romans [viz. Byzantines] together with their men'.[48] This account, it should be noted, seems reliable and is completely independent of Norse texts. Conversely, Hjardar and Vike stress this Byzantine source does not prove the existence of actual female Rus' warriors, as the women described could just as well be females accompanying their warrior men in the Kievan forces, trying to defend themselves in the unavoidable situation of a battle.[49] They do not, however, dismiss the possibility that some females from the élite of Norse society, could actually have chosen to be warriors.[50]

In conclusion, women had a large opportunity to participate in warfare because military organization in our period of study was essentially domestic in character, or, to put it another way, the military, which we would consider the public sphere of life, coincided with the private sphere to an unusually large degree. The aforementioned figurine from Hårby may be a warrior woman of fact and not fantasy. What *is* clear is that the image of female fighters is not an invention of the mediaeval saga-writers and poets – it was definitely, unequivocally *there* in the Norse mind. Though it would be presumptuous of us to conclude that real Norse women were proverbial Amazon types, the possibility that a minority of them may have fought on the red field of battle is a serious one.

Endnotes

Introduction

1. Adam Bremensis, *Gesta Hammaburgensis ecclesiae pontificum* iii §16.
2. Turville-Petre 1968: 3–4.
3. Adam Bremensis, *Gesta Hammaburgensis ecclesiae pontificum* iii §16.

Chapter 1: War

1. The term 'Viking Age' as used by archaeologists means the period from about 780 to about 1100, during which raiding, trading and colonization from Scandinavia took place and during which there was a distinctive material culture – the same types of artefacts were used throughout the viking world. A word of warning, however. One should just keep in mind that though the so-called Viking Age comprises the final period of prehistory in Scandinavia, this definition in itself creates and enhances the differences between Scandinavia and contemporary early mediaeval Europe that actually did not exist. The absence of a written language and the fact that Scandinavia had yet to undergo Christianization constituted important and decisive differences indeed, but in many ways this region played an integral part in the broader cultural development of Europe and maintained an awareness of and contact with most parts of the then known world. Understandably, therefore, this classic term is the subject of much critique in viking studies today. Nonetheless, for sake of convenience I will use the term viking age (albeit in the lower case), as it is well-established in the terminology of Scandinavian historiography.
2. Adam Bremensis, *Gesta Hammaburgensis ecclesiae pontificum* iv §42.
3. *ASC*, s.a. 876.
4. *Brennu-Njáls saga*, 111.
5. *Hávamál*, st. 38.
6. *Brennu-Njáls saga*, 118.
7. Ibid. 19.
8. Ibid. 30.
9. *Egils saga Skallagrímssonar*, 46.
10. *Orkneyinga saga*, 105. For a good, lengthy saga account of summertime raiding, see *Vatnsdœla saga*, 7.
11. *Egils saga Skallagrímssonar*, 46.

12. *Brennu-Njáls saga*, 29.

13. See, for this, Crumlin-Pedersen 2002.

14. Jesch 2008: 197.

15. Lund 1985: 110–12. See also Lund 1997: 195–9.

16. DeVries 2003 [1999]: 204.

17. Biddle & Kjølbye-Biddle 1992: 42–8, 2001: 81–4.

18. Hansard, HL Deb, 6 July 2011, c. 303.

19. Bourke 2000: 92–3.

20. Du Picq 1946 [1903]: 137.

21. Bramley 1995: 149.

22. Ibid. 137, 139.

23. Hedeby 1 DR1, DR66, DR68, Sjörup DR279, cf. the later U391, Sö292, Vg112. For the texts of runic inscriptions mentioned in this book, see the Database of Runic Inscriptions http://www.nordiska.uu.se/forskn/samnord.htm.

24. *Annales Bertiniani* ('Annals of Saint Bertin'), s.a. 861.

25. Ibid. s.a. 861, 862. Eventually Weland's army 'separated into many fleets [*per plures classes se dividunt*]'.

26. *ASC*, s.a. 894.

27. *Heiðreks saga*, 1.

28. Burton 1884: xi–xii. Captain Sir Richard Francis Burton KCMG FRGS (1821–90) was possibly the most famous of all British explorers, having discovered the source of the Nile in 1856, and, two years later, with John Hanning Speke, becoming the first European to reach Lake Tanganyika. He was the first westerner to see the Ka'aba at Mecca, and to make the pilgrimage (in full disguise) from Mecca to Medina. He was also a treasure hunter, a captain in the East India Company, and a spy during the Crimean War. Between 1883 and 1886 he published his translations of the *Kama Sutra of Vatsyayana* (1883), the *Arabian Nights* (1885), and *The Perfumed Gardens of the Shaykh Nefzawi* (1886): he is said to have mastered thirty-five Oriental languages. Yet he could write, in middle age, 'The great solace of my life was the fencing room'. There survives a fine oil on canvas of Burton in full fencing rig, painted in 1883 by Albert Letchford during Burton's consular posting to Trieste (then part of Austria-Hungry). By then he was a fully qualified master, sufficiently pleased with his accomplishment to place *maître d' armes (breveté)* after his name on the title page of *The Book of the Sword*.

29. *Fóstbrœðra saga*, 3.

30. *Laxdæla saga*, 13.

31. Ibid. 30.

32. Ibn Rusta, *Kitab al-a'lak an-nafisa* 146.

33. The eddaic poems *Fáfnismál*, *Sigrdrífumál* and *Guðrúnarkviða*, as well as *Sigurðarkviða in skamma* narrate the different vicissitudes of Sigurðr's biography.

34. *Gísla saga Súrssonar*, 1, 11, 16, cf. 13.

35. *Heimskringla: Haralds saga hárfagra*, 40, cf. *Hákonar saga góða*, 28, 31.

36. *Ágrip af Nóregskonúngasögum*, §6.

37. This sword was given to Egill by his blood-brother and best friend, Arinbjörn Þórisson, who had received it from Egill's brother Þórólfr Skallagrímsson. Before him, Skalla-Grímr Kveldúlfsson, the brothers' father, had been given it by Þórólfr Kveldúlfsson, his brother and their uncle, who had received it from Grímr Hairy-cheeks, the son of Ketill *hœng* (Trout). Ketill was thus the original owner of *Dragvandil*, which he had used in duels because of its sharpness (*Egils saga Skallagrímssonar*, 61).

38. Ellis Davidson, writing nigh-on six decades ago, knew of approximately 200 sword names in Norse and European mediaeval literature (1962: 102).

39. *Hrólfs saga kraka*, 52.

40. *Laxdœla saga*, 57.

41. *Landnámabók*, S 174.

42. *Kormáks saga*, 9.

43. *Laxdœla saga*, 57.

44. Ibid. 58.

45. Ibid. 78.

46. *Sturlunga saga*, i. 261.

47. Ibid. i. 208.

48. Androshchuk 2014: 195–6.

49. *Laxdœla saga*, 77.

50. Ibid. 29.

51. *Heimskringla: Haralds saga hárfagra*, 40.

52. Petersen's twenty-six types and numerous sub-types have been reduced to just nine, viz. types I–IX. See, for this, Peirce & Oakeshott 2002: 3–5.

53. *Laxdœla saga*, 29.

54. Saxo Grammaticus, *Danorum Regum Heromque Historia* ii. 2.5–6.

55. *Egils saga Skallagrímssonar*, 64, cf. *Laxdœla saga*, 64, *Brennu-Njáls saga*, 17, 30, 45, 63, 72, 82, 129, 151.

56. *Beowulf*, ll. 2677–87 Heaney. The name *Nægling* derives from *nægl*, or nail, and may correspond to *Nagelring*, a sword from *Vilkina saga*, reputed to be the best sword in the world. It is possibly the sword of Hrethel, which Hygelac, lord of the Geats, gave to Beowulf (ll. 2190–4). Beowulf's first was the 'rare and ancient sword named *Hrunting*' (l. 1458 Heaney), which means 'Thrusting'.

57. Simpson 1967: 126.

58. Ibn Khurradadhbih, *Kitab al-masalik wa' l-mamalik* ('Book of Roads and Realms') 154.

59. Some of the *Ingelrii* blades bear the addition words ME FECIT, 'made me' and a few variations thereof (cf. list in Peirce & Oakeshott 2002: 8–9, who date the *Ingelrii* blades from 925). There are also the similar *Ulfberht*-inscriptions (ibid. 7–9, who date the *Ulfberht* blades from around 850).
60. Ibn Khurradadhbih, *Kitab al-masalik wa' l-mamalik* 154.
61. Franklin & Shepard 1996: 42.
62. E.g. *Heimskringla: Haralds saga hárfagra*, 43.
63. *Heimskringla: Hákonar saga Herðibreiðs*, 20, cf. *Heimskringla: Óláfs saga helga*, 228.
64. *Skjald* A I 468, B I 439. Preserved in its entirety (71 stanzas), this *drápa* is also called *Geisli*, 'Ray of Light'. *Drápa* is the technical term for the more formal type of skaldic praise-poem (usually to honour a mighty king) consisting of several stanzas and with a refrain or commonly more than one.
65. *Hávamál*, sts. 138–41.
66. *Laxdœla saga*, 55.
67. *Grettis saga Ásmundarsonar*, 19.
68. Gregory of Tours, writing on the murder of the Frankish king Sigibert I in 575, speaks of the two assassins using 'strong knives [*cultis validis*] with poisoned blades – of the sort commonly called scramasaxes [*scramasaxi*] – approached him on some pretext and stabbed him one on each side' (*Liber Historiae Francorum*, 4.51).
69. *Borgfirðinga sögur*, 243.
70. *Grettis saga Ásmundarsonar*, 89.
71. *Brennu-Njáls saga*, 63.
72. *Grettis saga Ásmundarsonar*, 18.
73. *Beowulf*, ll. 1545–6 Heaney.
74. Ibid. ll. 2703–4 Heaney, cf. l. 2904.
75. *Heimskringla: Haralds saga Sigurðarsonar*, 92.
76. Bayeux tapestry, scene 57, William of Malmesbury, *Gesta regum Anglorum* iii §§242–3, Henry of Huntington, *Historia Anglorum* bk. VI, s.a. 1066, cf. Guy d'Amiens, *Carmen de Hastingae Proelio* ll. 35–7, where Harold II of England is hacked to death by four nobles. For those of you interested in the possible controversy surrounding the death of Harold at Hastings, see Dennis 2009.
77. 1 Kings 22:34 NIV.
78. *Heimskringla: Óláfs saga Tryggvasonar*, 108.
79. *Skjald* A I 372, st. 14, cf. *Heimskringla: Haralds saga Sigurðarsonar*, 63.
80. *Brennu-Njáls saga*, 77, cf. 48.
81. See, for this, Roesdahl 1992: 131.
82. E.g. Bayeux tapestry, scenes 52–3, 56.
83. *Heimskringla: Óláfs saga Helga*, 207.
84. *Grettis saga Ásmundarsonar*, 40.
85. *Völuspá*, st. 50.

86. See, for this, http://www.hurstwic.org/history/articles/manufacturing/text/ viking_shields.htm.

87. *Y Gododdin*, B² st. 34 Koch. The tale is simple enough. *Y Gododdin* focuses upon the battle of *Catraeth*, which J.T. Koch (1997) proposes should be dated to about the year 570 rather than to the conventional date of around 600. King Mynyddog Mwynfawr of the Brythonic kingdom of Gododdin (the Votadini of the Romans) has raised a crack company of 300 Brythonic warriors, 'gold-torqued, noble youths'. After training, housing and feasting them for a year at his court in *Din Eidyn* (Castle Rock in Edinburgh), he unleashes them onto the Angles of Deira (roughly all of Yorkshire from the Vale of York to the coast) and Bernicia (Durham and Northumbria). The British take the Anglian settlement of *Catraeth* (probably the garrison town of Catterick in North Yorkshire), but are besieged by an Anglian host said to have numbered in the thousands (as this is heroic literature, we can assume this number is greatly exaggerated). The band of 300 Brythonic warriors ride out to their impending doom and their heroic deeds (including some incredible feats of weapon play) are recorded in *Y Gododdin*. After a fierce battle, only one of their number escapes with his life, the bard Aneirin. Although they went to their deaths, the Brythonic warriors butchered their enemies, and their ferocity and unrelenting savagery is celebrated by the bard. His comrades would 'sooner to a bloodbath than to a wedding feast', and their goal was to ensure that 'the clash of spears echoed in mothers' heads' as they 'paid for their mead' (or *talu medd* to give the Middle Welsh phrase, viz. mead was a stand-in for the hospitality, patronage and protection, which a warrior had received from his lord) with their lives. They were defeated, but their valiant attempt was regarded as being heroic, and not in vain. *Y Gododdin* survives in a late thirteenth-century manuscript known as *Llyfr Aneirin* ('The Book of Aneirin') in two quite separate hands, resulting in the so called 'A-text' of eighty-eight stanzas written in up-to-date Middle Welsh and the 'B-text' of forty-two stanzas which preserves a good deal of Old Welsh orthography. More recently scholars have established that the B-text actually seems to have been copied from two separate exemplars, the final nineteen stanzas being labelled B² by Koch in his fascinating, if controversial work. Most modern-day commentators ascribe the work to the poet Aneirin with the assumption that he composed a series of stanzas in a form of Old Welsh, commemorating his slain comrades in a collection of brief elegies (Wallace 2012: 9). We may see some shades of parallelism between *Y Gododdin* and Herodotos' account of the 300 Spartans who fought and fell at Thermopylae against a Persian host. While the Greek force included several thousand Greek hoplites in addition to the Spartans, Herodotos, who proudly says 'I have learned the names of all the three hundred' (*Historiae*, 7.224.1), concentrates heavily upon the actions and deeds of the modest force from Sparta.

88. *Grettis saga Ásmundarsonar*, 38, cf. 54, 57, 61.

89. *Fóstbrœðra saga*, 12.

90. *Heimskringla: Óláfs saga helga*, 205.

91. *Hávamál*, st. 156 Hollander.

92. Tacitus, *Germania* 3.1, cf. *Historiae*, 2.22, 4.18.3, 5.15, *Annales*, 1.65.1, 4.47.

93. Clausewitz, *On War*, bk. 1, chap. 3, p. 116 Howard & Paret.

94. *ASC*, mss. C & D, s.a. 1066, John of Worcester, *Chronicon ex chronicis*, s.a. 1066, Henry of Huntingdon, *Historia Anglorum* bk. VI, s.a. 1066. Note, John of Worcester's chronicle is sometimes ascribed to Florence of Worcester, a fellow monk at Worcester Priory.

95. *The Battle of Maldon*, ll. 19–21. The battle is recorded in three versions of the *Anglo-Saxon Chronicle* (mss. A, F & E, s.a. 991). Maldon also receives mention in *Vita Oswaldi* (839n, 843), a anonymous hagiographic text written within a decade of the battle, from which one learns that the vikings, so seriously mauled by their pyrrhic victory, 'they could barely manage to man their boats' for the voyage away from Maldon.

96. Kim Siddorn 2000: 38.

97. Marshall 2000 [1947]: 42

98. Ibid. 43.

99. Ibid. 42.

100. Sledge 1981: 315.

101. *Heimskringla: Óláfs saga helga*, 205.

102. Onasander *Stratêgikos*, 24.

103. War Office 1944: 57–8.

104. Ibid. 58.

105. C.S. Lewis, *The Allegory of Love: A Study in Medieval Tradition* (1936), p. 9.

106. *Hávamál*, st. 16 Hollander.

107. Sjörup DR 279.

108. *Hávamál*, st. 77 Larrington.

109. See, for this, Stewart Kinza 1991: 27–9, cf. King 2013: 35–8.

110. E.g. Spiller 1988.

111. *Sverris saga*, 47.

112. *Heiðarvíga saga*, 86.

113. Jesch 2008: 243–7, 2009: 71–8.

114. Cf. *The Battle of Maldon*, ll. 111–12.

115. Louis-Alexandre Berthier, general-in-chief of the Army of Reserve, to Napoléon Bonaparte, First Consul, Dijon, 5 *foréal* Year VIII (25 April 1800), quoted in Capt. G.J.M.R. de Cugnec, *La campagne de l'armée du reserve en 1800* (1900), vol. 1, chap. 5.

116. *Heimskringla: Óláfs saga helga*, 205.

117. Ibid. 216, 224.
118. *Heimskringla*: *Óláfs saga helga*, 49–50.
119. Ibid. 76.
120. *Heimskringla*: *Óláfs saga helga* 184, Theodoricus Monachus, *Historia de antiquitate regum Norwagiensium* 31.
121. Ibid. 209.
122. *Heimskringla*: *Magnúss saga ins Góða*, 7.
123. *ASC*, s.a. 1043.
124. Adam Bremensis, *Gesta Hammaburgensis ecclesiae pontificum* ii §59, John of Worcester, *Chronicon ex chronicis*, s.a. 1030.
125. *Morkinskinna* was most probably composed during the twelve-twenties. It is indubitably Icelandic, although it seems likely that the author or authors had some Norwegian court experience. It is a complex narrative, much concerned with personal relations between kings and subjects and with the ethics of kingship.
126. Thucydides 1.22.4.
127. *Heimskringla*: preface.
128. *Heimskringla*: *Óláfs saga helga*, 224.
129. Ibid. 235, repeating verbatim Adam Bremensis, *Gesta Hammaburgensis ecclesiae pontificum* ii §59.
130. Stiklestad co-ordinates 63° 47' 46" N 11° 33' 38" E / start of partial eclipse 12.59.14.9 / maximum eclipse 14.09.33.2 (obscuration 98.88%) / end of partial eclipse 15.16.31.4. See, for this, Eclipse Predictions by Fred Espenek (NASA GSFC).
131. Simpson 1964: 381
132. Theodoricus Monachus *Historia de antiquitate regum Norwagiensium* 20, *Heimskringla*: *Óláfs saga helga*, 235.
133. *Heimskringla*: *Óláfs saga helga*, 205–36.
134. Ibid. 238.
135. See, for this, Lindow 1976: 63–9.
136. *Gunnlaugs saga ormstungu*, 7.
137. *Skjald* B I 217–20, sts. 2:3–4, 14:1–2.
138. *Heimskringla*: *Óláfs saga helga*, 227, cf. 212, 226.
139. Per Sivle, *Tord Foleson* st. 6, ll. 1–2.
140. *Heimskringla*: *Óláfs saga helga*, 228.
141. *Heimskringla*: *Magnús saga góða*, 14.
142. *Orkneyinga saga*, 8.
143. *Heimskringla*: *Haralds saga Sigurðarsonar*, 52.
144. 2 Samuel 11:2–17.
145. *Heimskringla*: *Haralds saga Sigurðarsonar*, 1, *Morkinskinna*, 9 st. 45.
146. *Ágrip af Nóregskonúngasögum*, §32.

Chapter 2: Rus'

1. Leo Diakonos, *Historia* 9.11, cf. John Skylitzes, *Synopsis historiôn* 15.18 [309].
2. Madrid manuscript of John Skylitzes' *Synopsis historiôn*, Codex Matritensis Græcus, Vitr. 26-2, fol. 172v.-b.
3. *Primary Chronicle*, 6480 [972].
4. Kendrick 1930: 10.
5. In modern Slavonic *Povest' Vremennjkh Let* or 'The Tale of Bygone Years'. The work survives in two major versions, named from their earliest representative manuscript: the Laurentian after its fourteenth-century copyist Lawrence, and the fifteenth-century Hypatian, after the monastery where it was discovered. Compiled in Old East Slavonic, the original manuscript was once believed to have been composed by the monk Nestor of the Pechersk Lavra in Kiev soon after 1100 (whence its secondary name, *Nestor's Chronicle*). It is now more generally held that Nestor was either its first editor or just one of its compilers, internal evidence suggesting that the *Primary Chronicle*, instead of being a homogeneous work, is a compilation from several chronicle texts of greater and varying antiquity. It has been shown, for instance, that for the period up until the mid-tenth century the chronicle relies heavily on Byzantine texts, including biblical models, which are possibly overlaid with legendary accounts or traditions that survived from this period. A notable exception, however, are three treaties concluded between the Rus' and Constantinople during the course of the tenth century (911, 945, 971), that are considered to be authentic documents that were inserted into the text of the chronicle. As a final point, like the *Heimskringla* and the Old Norse sagas, the *Primary Chronicle* is written from a Christian perspective yet discusses the Russian people's pagan history. As such, it serves two primary purposes. One is to relate the history of Russia and the other is to relate the history of Russian Christianity. The figures who had converted to Christianity are discussed in greater detail than those who had not. Like many historical documents, the *Primary Chronicle* is the story of the leaders of Russia through time, and not the story of everyday folk.
6. *Primary Chronicle*, 6368–70 [860–2].
7. Liudprand served as an envoy of Otto I (duke of Saxony and king of Germany 936–73, Holy Roman Emperor 962–73) to Constantinople in 968, his second journey to the Byzantine capital. The first had been made in 949, when he served as an apprentice diplomat of Berengar II of Ivrea, king of Italy (r. 950–61), on a goodwill mission to the court of Constantinus VII Porphyrogenitus. The change of royal masters came about because in 951 Otto marched into Italy to assist Adelaide, the widowed queen of the Lombards, against Berengar, who had in truth usurped the throne. Defeating Berengar, Otto then married Adelaide and

took the Iron Crown of Lombardy (said to have been made from a nail of the True Cross) for himself in 952. Berengar thus became Otto's vassal, but later he resumed his aggression by invading the Papal States. Pope John XII (r. 955–63) appealed to Otto, who entered Rome in 962 and was crowned on 2 February 'emperor of the Romans', reviving the imperial title of the Carolingians and legitimizing the Saxon Ottonian claim to the Middle Kingdom. John quickly found Otto too powerful and, while the king was campaigning against Berengar, secretly negotiated with Berengar's son and co-ruler Adalbert (r. 950–63). Otto hastened back to Rome in 963, deposed John, and had Leo VIII elected in his stead. Otto sought to make Rome subordinate to the authority of the empire, and thus imposed the rule that no pope could be elected without the approval of the emperor. This proclamation opened the era of German domination of the papacy. Otto was also keen to control those lands in Italy which still owed allegiance to Constantinople, and so came into conflict with the hot-tempered Nikephoros II Phokas (r. 963–9); hence Liudprand's second journey to the capital with the objective to gain as a bride for Otto's son not just any Byzantine princess but, specifically, a Porphyrogenita, a girl born in the purple chamber of the Great Palace. However, Otto's campaign to gain control over southern Italy was unsuccessful, though a minor diplomatic coup was scored in 972 when the Byzantine emperor, John I Tzimiskès (r. 969–76), gave his niece princess Theophanu in marriage to Otto's son and successor, Otto II (r. 973–83). Considered by many scholars to be the founder of the Holy Roman Empire, Otto was an effective warrior king who restored kingship on the Carolingian model in the Middle Kingdom.

8. In Latin: *Rusios quos alio nos nomine Nordmannos appellamus*, Liudprand of Cremona, *Antapodosis* 1.11.
9. Ibid. 5.15.
10. See, for this, Hraundal 2013: 25–7.
11. Christiansen 2006 [2002]: 115.
12. For instance, Stender-Peterson (1953: 1–20), writing in the climate of the Cold War, went as far as to suggest that Soviet nationalism attempted to erase the Norse influences in place names and historical contact as an anti-Varangian theory became the popular historiographical method of accepted Soviet scholarship. Generally speaking, Soviet scholarship tended to significantly diminish or even eliminate the part played by non-Slavic peoples in the historical past of Russia. Sad to say, in addition to scholarly inertia, many Soviet scholars were coerced into writing a history that was looked upon favourably by the Stalinist state. One well-known example, which has been translated into English, is M.N. Tikhomirov's *Drevnerusskie goroda* ('The Towns of Ancient Rus"). Published in 1956, Tikhomirov was writing within an anti-Normannist framework, as well

as including an emphasis on a Rus' state separate from the rest of mediaeval Europe. Though Tikhomirov was not the only such Soviet scholar to write on this topic, he was emblematic of a viewpoint common in Soviet academia in the early years of the Cold War. He codified the idea that one could extend the modern east–west divide back into the mediaeval world. Sadly, the revolution that had seemed to promise such high hopes had developed under Stalin into a soulless, bloodsucking tyranny. Even today, almost three decades after the collapse of the USSR and the emergence of Russian investigators of the viking age from a stringent system of incarceration, anti-Normannist obsessions are still strong in nationalistic and Slavophil circles – with the occasional support from the political establishment – wherein Soviet style nationalists make strenuous efforts to rid of what they think as Russian history of Scandinavians and promote the belief that theirs was essentially a Slav country. For instance, Vladimir Putin, pursuant to the conflict and subsequent absorption of Crimea by Russia, stated that Kiev, which was the third largest Soviet city after Moscow and Leningrad, was 'the mother of Russian cities' (http://www.bbc.com/news/world-europe-26625476). Once again a historical shadow has descended upon Russia, and it is a process of selection, of preferring some pieces of the evidence to others, of discarding what does not easily fit. Nosov 1998 summarizes the trials and tribulations of Soviet archaeologists in this field.

13. *Annales Bertiniani*, s.a. 839.
14. Hedenstierna-Jonson 2006: 84.
15. See, for this, Blöndal/Benedikz 2007 [1978]: 33, fn. 1.
16. *Primary Chronicle*, preface 7.
17. Constantinus VII Porphyrogenitus, *De administrando imperio*, preface apud *CSHB* ix, 70–9.
18. Ibid. 60–1 apud *CSHB* ix, 70–9.
19. Ibn Rusta, *Kitab al-a'lak an-nafisa* 140, cf. the khagan Joseph, after noting that the Pečenegs live in the steppe, asserts that 'they all serve (me) and pay me tribute' ('The Reply of the Khazar Khagan Joseph', p. 102 apud P.K. Kokovtsov, *Evreisko-khazarskaia perepiska v X veke* (Leningrad, 1932), pp. 81–3 (the Short Redaction), pp. 98–102 (the Extended Redaction).
20. *Primary Chronicle*, 6480 [972].
21. Constantinus VII Porphyrogenitus, *De administrando imperio* I, 57–61, II, 38–52 apud *CSHB* ix, 70–9.
22. Pilgårds G280. See also, Pritsak 1981: 326.
23. *Guta saga*, 1.
24. Hallfrede G220.
25. The first rune stone is from Esta, Södermanland (Sö171), the second from Sjusta, Uppland (U687).

26. See, for this, Hedenstierna-Jonson 2009.
27. Constantinus VII Porphyrogenitus, *De administrando imperio* apud *CSHB* ix, 6.
28. See, for this, Mühle 1991.
29. See, for this, Nosov 1994: 190.
30. *Primary Chronicle*, 6465 [957].
31. Constantinus VII Porphyrogenitus, *De administrando imperio* I, 58 apud *CSHB* ix, 70–9.
32. Crumlin-Pedersen & Olsen 2002: 239.
33. Andersen & Andersen 1989, Andersen *et al.* 1997.
34. *Primary Chronicle*, 6388–90 [880–2], cf. preface 7.
35. SHM 29974:1, GM 3428, SHM 4171. For words of caution with regards to the realism of the ship motifs on the Gotlandic picture stones (as well as coins, graffiti and rune stones from the three Scandinavian countries), see Kastholm 2011.
36. *Heimskringla: Óláfs saga helga*, 181, *Magnús saga góða*, 1, *Haralds saga Sigurðarsonar*, 1, 71, 73, *Egils saga Skallagrímssonar*, 72.
37. For the much debated question of the dating of the Khazar conversion to Judaism, see Golden 2007: 151–7.
38. Al-Mas'udi, *Muruj al-dhahab wa ma'adin al-jawhr* ('The Meadows of Gold and Mines of Gems') §448.
39. Ibn Hawqal, *Kitab surat al-ard* ('Book of the Configuration of the Earth') 186.
40. Heb. II B6157.
41. See, for this, Golden 2007: 145–6.
42. 'The Reply of the Khazar Khagan Joseph', p. 102 apud P.K. Kokovtsov, *Evreisko-khazarskaia perepiska v X veke* (Leningrad, 1932), pp. 81–3 (the Short Redaction), pp. 98–102 (the Extended Redaction).
43. *Laxdæla saga*, 12.
44. Ibn Rusta, *Kitab al-a'lak an-nafisa* 142.
45. Al-Mas'udi, *Muruj al-dhahab wa ma'adin al-jawhr* §63.
46. Ibn Fadlan, *Risalah* §75. A *dirham* was an Arabic silver coin weighing usually about three grams (3.207 g) and produced in great numbers. They circulated in the Islamic caliphate and were exported as payment for goods in long-distance trade. Around half a million or so whole or fragmentary *dirhams* have been found across the vast trading networks of eastern and northern Europe. The name derived from the name of a Greek coin, the *didrachm* (two *drachmae*).
47. Mosfell Archaeological Project, inv. nos. 2007-21-142, -143, -144, -145.
48. In mainland Scandinavia 'eye beads' have been uncovered at Borg in northern Norway, Birka in Sweden, and Fyrkat in Jutland (Zori 2010: 471).
49. Leiruvogur was an ideal ship landing and winter beaching site. Leiruvogur's highly sheltered anchorage, deep inland at the eastern end of Faxaflói bay, offered

more protection for landed ships than other harbours in this part of Iceland. The natural barriers shielding the inner harbour at the seaward entrance and along the coast included breakwaters formed from a series of small islands and nesses. In the anchorage, ships could pass the winter safe from storms to await cargo and passengers, as was the custom for a spring or early summer departure. As *Flóamanna saga* suggests (cf. *Landnámabók* H/S 9, *Gunnlaugs saga ormstungu*, 10), it was a place to keep a ship anchored or beached for resale. It thus offered the chieftains at Mosfell considerable social and economic advantages.

50. Ibn Fadlan, *Risalah* §1 Montgomery. Arabic names work very much like Icelandic names: first the given name, then the father's name, then the grandfather's name, and after that any nickname – usually the place of birth or connected with.

51. Ibn Fadlan, *Risalah* §74 Montgomery.

52. Ibrahim ibn Ya'qub, apud Qazwini, *Athar al-bilad wa akhbar al-'ibad* ('Monuments of the Countries and Histories of their Inhabitants') 404.

53. Ibn Fadlan, *Risalah* §76 Montgomery.

54. Ibid. §2 Montgomery.

55. Op. cit., cf. §72 Montgomery.

56. Cf. ibid. §45 with fn. 40 Montgomery.

57. Jesch 1991: 123.

58. Ibn Rusta, *Kitab al-a'lak an-nafisa* 147.

59. E.g. Stenkyrka Lillbjärs III (G 268), Lärbro Tängelgárda I, Närr Stenkyrka Smiss I (GM 3428).

60. Ibn Rusta, *Kitab al-a'lak an-nafisa* 146.

61. Ibn Fadlan, *Risalah* ('Report') §74 Montgomery.

62. Ibn Rusta, *Kitab al-a'lak an-nafisa* 147, cf. Ibn Fadlan's obvious indignation (*Risalah* §76) about the Rus' of all ranks defecating (and copulating) in public.

63. Ibn Miskawayh, *Tajarib al-umam wa-'awaqib al-himam* ('Experience of the Nations, Consequences of Ambition') 62.

64. Ibid. 66.

65. Ibn al-Athir, *al-Kamil fi't-Ta'rikh* ('The Complete History') 8.412–15, 508, 9.43–4, 521, 10.65, 12.387.

66. See, for this, *Heimskringla: Ynglinga saga*, 9.

67. Hedenstierna-Jonson 2009: 168, cf. Hraundal 2013: 115–22, who promotes the hypothesis that the Rus' reported by the Muslim writers in the ninth and the tenth century, and are done so primarily as armed merchants in the region between the middle Volga, the Don and the Caspian Sea, had interacted with and were influenced especially by the Khazars and the Volga Bulghars, the two most prominent and powerful entities of this region in this period. Hraundal even suggests that the depiction of the Rus' in the Muslim written sources 'is significantly different from other early mediaeval written sources, even to the

extent that it is justified to speak of distinct eastern ("Volga-Caspian") and western (Kievan) groups of the Rus" (2013: 188–9).

68. Foote & Wilson 1970: 220.

69. Oikonomides 1997: 157–60.

70. Another tradition has Olga baptized in the church of Saint Elias in Kiev.

71. *Primary Chronicle*, 6415 [907].

72. Ibid. 6420 [912].

73. Ibid. 6453 [945].

74. According to the *Primary Chronicle* (6368–70 [860–2]) Askold (ON *Höskuldr*, cf. OEN *Haskuldr*) and Dir (ON *Dýri*) were two of Rurik's warlords (OCS *voyevodas*) in the eight-seventies. Oleg (ON *Helgi*), Rurik's son, is credited by the *Primary Chronicle* with unifying the territories of Novgorod and Kiev, consequently moving the capital of the Rus' from Novgorod to Kiev, having 'put Askold and Dir to death, and annexed Kiev to his sway, (6388–90 [880–2]). Significantly, here the *Primary Chronicle* describes Oleg (and Igor) pretending to be merchants travelling 'to the Greeks': this is the first mention of the Dnieper trade route 'road of the Varangians to the Greeks'. Kiev soon outshone Novgorod in importance: it became the capital of the Varangians and 'the mother of Russian towns' (in the eight-eighties); while the principality that took its name became the cradle of the first Russian state. Oleg's successor, Igor (ON *Ingar*), again according to the *Primary Chronicle*, is yet another son of Rurik. The very nature of all these members of the Rurikid dynasty is a matter of much controversy among historians, their lives (and deaths) being surrounded by the aura of legend. The semi-legendary Rurik (ON *Hrærekr*, cf. OEN *Rørik*), of course, is the famous first ruler of the Kievan Rus'. The last descendant of Rurik to rule was Fedor, the idiot son of Ivan the Terrible. He died in 1598, and his line was superseded by the Romanov dynasty.

75. *Primary Chronicle*, 6443–9 [935–41]. Liudprand of Cremona, whose account is based on the eyewitness report at of his stepfather, wrote that the Rus' fleet numbered only a thousand vessels, which does seem more credible. Liudprand's family involvement with Constantinople began with his stepfather, who had been given the post of ambassador from the court in Arles. His first task had been to deliver a pair of magnificent hounds to Romanos I Lekapenos (r. 919–44). It seems the gift was well received until the dogs turned around and nearly savaged the emperor.

76. John Skylitzes, *Synopsis historiôn* 10.31 [229], cf. Theophanes Continuatus 423–6.

77. A *chelandion* (from the Greek word κέλης, *kélês*, 'courser') was a bireme galley too, though the term *chelandion* is used interchangeably with *dromôn* (δρόμων, from the Greek word *drômein*, 'to run') in Byzantine primary sources, leading to much confusion as to the exact nature of the ship type and its differences

with the *dromôn* proper (this term appears already in Prokopios). This was a two-masted fully decked bireme with two banks of oars, one rowed from below the deck and one from above it. The vessel relied on oars for its tactical manoeuvring, while sails – two, sometimes three, lateen sails – were used for cruising when the wind direction was suitable. There were twenty-five oarsmen on each side of each deck, thus raising the total number of oarsmen to a hundred, all fully seated. The marines and the officers of the ship amounted to around fifty men, while the *ousia* (ουσία), the standard complement of a war galley (its crew excluding the marines and the officers) totalled 108 men (Constantinus VII Porphyrogenitus, *De ceremoniis aulae Byzantinae* apud *CSHB* i, 669–78). However, though the written sources do use the use the two terms indiscriminately, it is interesting to mention that Theophanes Continuatus, a ninth century chronicler, identifies the *chelandion* as horse transports. According to Pryor & Jeffreys (2006: 325–30) in the *chelandia* were indeed specialized horse transports, able to carry between twelve to twenty horses. By way of a comparison, a fourth century BC Athenian horse transport, rowed by sixty oarsmen, could carry thirty horses (*IG* 2² 1628.154–5, 161–2, 470, 475, 480, Thucydides 2.56.2, 6.43, cf. Aristophanes, *Knights* 595–610).

78. Liudprand of Cremona, *Antapodosis* 5.15: '*Denique miserator et misericors Dominus, qui se colentes, se adorantes, se deprecantes non solum protegere, sed et victoria voluit honorare, ventis tunc placidum reddidit mare; secus enim ob ignis emissionem Grecis esset incommodum*'.

79. *Primary Chronicle*, 6443–9 [935–41].

80. Leo Diakonos, *Historia* 9.2, cf. 6.10. 'Median fire', an alternative term for Greek fire, probably derived its epithet from the origins of naphtha, called 'Median oil' by Prokopios (*Wars*, 4.11.36).

81. Madrid manuscript of John Skylitzes' *Synopsis historiôn*, Codex Matritensis Græcus, Vitr. 26–2, fol. 130 v.

82. Ibn al-Athir, *al-Kamil fi 't-Ta'rikh* 9.521.

83. Michael Psellos, *Chronographia*, Constantinus IX 6.93.

84. Ibid. 6.94.

85. Ibid. 6.93.

86. Kekaumenos, *Stratêgikón* §22.

87. See, for this, Blöndal/Benedikz 2007 [1978]: 136–40.

88. *Heimskringla: Magnússona saga*, 13.

89. *Yngvars saga viðförla*, 6.

90. The latest Ingvarr-stone (U FV1992:157) was found in 1990 during road building at Arlanda airport (and now on display in the terminal there). No doubt further Ingvarr-stones will be discovered, and it is likely that some of those of whom it is only said that they 'died in the east' also perished with Ingvarr.

91. Note, however, the challenge to the Icelandic dating of Ingvarr's expedition based on the style of the monuments put up to commemorate the men who failed to return, which anchors it to the early ten-twenties. See, for this, Fuglesang 1986, 1993, 1998. Indeed, in the latter article, Fuglesang attempts an art-historical dating of the inscriptions and concludes they were carved 'around 1000–25', suggesting 'that the late Icelandic texts be disregarded' (1998: 206).

92. Gripsholm Sö179.

93. *Prose Edda: Skáldskaparmál*, 65.

94. E.g. Steninge U439, Ekilla U644, Varpsund U654, Råby U661, Svinnegarn U778, Alsta U837, Tierp U1143, Sö9, Sö107, Lundby Sö131, Tystberga Sö173, Sö335, Berga Vs19, Ög145, Sylten Ög155.

95. *Yngvars saga víðförla*, 5.

96. See, for this, Palsson & Edwards 1989, Jesch 2008: 104–6.

97. *Heimskringla: Haralds saga Sigurðarsonar*, 1, *Morkinskinna*, 9.

98. *Heimskringla: Haralds saga Sigurðarsonar*, 1, *Orkneyinga saga*, 7.

99. *Heimskringla: Haralds saga Sigurðarsonar*, 2.

100. *Orkneyinga saga*, 7.

101. *Heimskringla: Óláfs saga helga*, 72.

102. *Primary Chronicle*, 6523 [1015].

103. Ibid. 6532 [1024].

104. Op. cit.

105. Ibid. 6534 [1026].

106. *Heimskringla: Haralds saga Sigurðarsonar*, 2.

107. *Primary Chronicle*, 6539 [1031].

108. *Orkneyinga saga*, 7.

109. *Nóregs konunga tal*, 51.

110. *Eymundar þáttr Hringssonar*, 4. The *penningr*, penny, was the lowest unit of currency in Scandinavia up to the end of the thirteenth century.

111. *Orkneyinga saga*, 8.

Chapter 3: Varangians

1. Kitchen 1996: 7.

2. Quoted in Horn 2007/8: 35.

3. Horn 2007/8: 34.

4. Quoted in Horn 2007/8: 34.

5. *Væringjar* is cognate with Old English *wærgenga*, 'one who seeks protection, a stranger'. See, for this, Blöndal/Benedikz 2007 [1978]: 4–5. The Old English language originally came from the same roots as Old Norse, although these had already moved apart by the eighth century. The extent to which these two languages were mutually intelligible remains the subject of scholarly debate, but

it is likely that there was some shared understanding. See, for this, Townend 2002.

6. For a full discussion of the term *lið* and its compounds, see Jesch 2008: 187–94, 198–201.

7. E.g. al-Mas'udi, *Muruj al-dhahab wa ma'adin al-jawhr* §460.

8. Blöndal/Benedikz 2007 [1978]: 6.

9. Ibid. 28, 45.

10. Ibid. 128.

11. Ibid. 134–6.

12. See, for this, Treadgold 1992: 112, 1995: 79.

13. Shepard 2007: 377.

14. Constantinus VII Porphyrogenitus, *De ceremoniis aulae Byzantinae* apud *CSHB* ii, 579, 682. See, for this, Blöndal/Benedikz 2007 [1978]: 21, Shepard 2007: 377.

15. Constantinus VII Porphyrogenitus, *De ceremoniis aulae Byzantinae* apud *CSHB* i, 664.

16. Abu ar-Tayyib al-Mutanabbi, *Ode on the battle of al-Hadath*, l. 14.

17. *Hrafnkels saga freysgoða*, 9, cf. 3.

18. By comparison, Denmark has some two hundred viking-age rune stones, Norway has only about forty, and Iceland has as yet yielded no viking-age runic inscriptions. Elsewhere, from the Faeroes only a couple of rune stones are known, from Ireland there are only three or four, from England a handful, and likewise from Scotland. In contrast to this scarcity overseas is the remarkable case of the Isle of Man, which has nearly thirty rune stones.

19. Ed U112 A & B.

20. S. Sätra U101, U143, U147, U309, U310.

21. See, for this, Pritsak 1981: 393–4.

22. *Brennu-Njáls saga*, 81.

23. Blöndal/Benedikz 2007 [1978]: 45–6. Their argument rest on evidence in the anonymous late tenth-century Byzantine treatise *De re militari*.

24. Ibn al-Athir, *al-Kamil fi'l-ta'rikh* 9.43–4.

25. *Primary Chronicle*, 6494 [986].

26. Thietmar of Merseberg, *Chronicon Thietmari* 72.

27. Yahya ibn Sa'id apud Vasiliev-Kratchkowsky *Patrologia Orientalis*, t. xxiii, fasc. III, 423.

28. *Primary Chronicle*, 6494 [986].

29. 14 September 987, according to Yahya ibn Sa'id apud Vasiliev-Kratchkowsky *Patrologia Orientalis*, t. xxiii, fasc. III, 422. The number 6,000 is from the eleventh-century Armenian historian Stepanos Asoghik (*Universal History*, ii 164–5). However, Stepanos uses the same number on other occasions to denote a large army (e.g. ibid. 156).

30. Michael Psellos, *Chronographia*, Basil II 1.13.
31. 13 April 989, according to Yahya ibn Sa'id apud Vasiliev-Kratchkowsky *Patrologia Orientalis*, t. xxiii, fasc. III, 424.
32. Michael Psellos, *Chronographia*, Basil II 1.15–18.
33. John Skylitzes, *Synopsis historiôn* 15.7 [292–4].
34. Ibid. 16.8 [324].
35. Michael Psellos, *Chronographia*, Basil II 1.28.
36. Ibid. Basil II 1.14.
37. *Primary Chronicle* 6488, [980].
38. Anna Komnene, *Alexiad* 2.9.4, 2.12.4, 3.9.1, 4.6.2, 9.9.2, 12.6.3, Niketas Choniates, *O City of Byzantium* II, bk. 5, p. 98 [172] Magoulias, cf. Michael Psellos, *Chronographia*, Zoë & Theodora 6.3, Constantinus IX 6.87, Michael VI 7.22, Romanos IV 7.19.
39. In Latin: *securim Danicam in humero sinistro, hastile ferreum dextra manu gestantes*, William of Malmesbury, *Gesta regum Anglorum* ii §12, cf. John of Worcester, *Chronicon ex chronicis*, s.a. 1040.
40. Bayeux tapestry, scene 52. Plausibly commissioned by Odo bishop of Bayeux, Duke William's greedy and ambitious uterine half-brother and certainly present on the field, more than a quarter of the tapestry is devoted to the battle of Hastings. This most warlike cleric appears in scenes 43–4, 54. Alone among contemporary accounts the tapestry places Odo in the thick of the fighting, albeit wielding a mace not a lance or sword, a weapon favoured by martial bishops on the theory that it did not come under the canon law forbidding clerics 'to smite with the edge of the sword'. Odo would be arrested for treason in 1086. According to William de Poitiérs (*Gesta Guillelmi Ducis*, 125), for example, though the good bishop was present at Hastings, it was only for the purpose of aiding by prayer. As for the patronage of the tapestry, alternative explanations cannot be excluded. For the theory that Eustace II of Boulogne was a plausible candidate as the patron of the tapestry, see Bridgeford 2004: 304–9.
41. D'Amato 2005: 42, 2010: 36.
42. Bayeux tapestry, scenes 52–3, 56–8.
43. *Heimskringla: Magnúss saga ins Góða*, 28, cf. *Brennu-Njáls saga*, 120, 145, 146 where the axe belonging to Skarphéðinn Njálsson is called *Rimmugýgr*, Battle-hag.
44. Oakeshott. See also *Prose Edda: Skáldskaparmál*, 118 where Snorri Sturluson makes the the following observation: "People call axes by names of troll-wives, and refer to them in terms of blood or wounds, or forest or tree".
45. Guy d'Amiens, *Carmen de hastingae proelio* prologue, cf. *ASC*, ms. D, s.a. 1066, the misfortunes of the English were God's punishment of sin.
46. William de Poitiérs, *Gesta Guillelmi Ducis* 141.
47. Ibid. 129.

48. Bayeux tapestry, scene 53.
49. Wace, *Roman de Rou* l. 184. This Anglo-Norman chronicle covering the history of the dukes of Normandy in rhymed French verse was apparently commissioned by Henry II of England. A large part of the *Roman de Rou* is devoted to William of Normandy and the Norman Conquest.
50. Wace, *Roman de Rou* l. 185.
51. A sword, literally or figuratively, e.g. Eustathius of Thessaloniki, *Commentarii ad Homeri Iliadem Pertinentes* 6.166, Hesychius ῥομφαία, Souda Lexicon ῥομφαία, Plutarch, *Aemilius Paullus* 18. Again, in the New Testament, the word is used seven times, and in each instance it is translated as sword (Luke 2:35, Revelation 1:16, 2:12, 6:8, 19:15, 21).
52. Anna Komnene, *Alexiad* 14.3.8.
53. Michael Psellos, *Chronographia*, Michael VI 7.25.
54. See, for this, Dawson 1992, cf. D'Amato 2010: 37–8.
55. Michael Psellos, *Chronographia*, Michael VI 7.25.
56. Ibid. Michael VII 7.19.
57. Michael Attaleiates, *Historiae* 63.
58. Jordanes, *Getica* 30–2, 45, 123–5.
59. Prokopios, *Wars*, 4.5–6.
60. Niketas Choniates, *O City of Byzantium* VI, bk. 2, p. 298 [545] Magoulias.
61. Geoffroi de Villehardouin, *La conquête de Constantinople* pars. 171, 185.
62. Pseudo-Codinus, *De officiis* 209–10.
63. *ASC*, ms. D, s.a. 1052 [true date 1051].
64. The burghal network to defend Wessex had been established by Alfred (r. 871–99) in the eight-eighties after the damaging, free-ranging raids of the viking army known as the *mycel hæþen here* in the previous two decades. The *Burghal Hidage*, a remarkable ninth-century Anglo-Saxon document, lists thirty *burhs* established in Wessex as an integrated defensive system by Alfred before his death. These the king created by either fortifying or refurbishing old towns or building entirely new ones in strategic places. Rivers, of which there were many in Wessex, were a major strategic consideration. Alfred sited many of his *burhs* in locations where a small but armed and fortified unit could thwart riverine invasion. However, the full development of the burghal system, which also extended to Mercia and the Danelaw, and the development of these sites (e.g. pre-Roman Iron Age and Roman fortifications) into planned towns belong to the reigns of Alfred's successors, notably his son Edward the Elder (r. 899–924) and his grandson Æthelstan (r. 925–40).
65. *ASC*, mss. C & D, s.a. 1041.
66. ON *húskarl* (pl. *húskarlar*), 'house-man', as opposed to *húsbóndi*, 'master of the house', indicating that the housecarl shared his leader's roof, cf. OE/ON *þegn* (pl. *þegns*), 'one who serves', viz. the nobility.

67. Cf. *ASC*, ms. E, s.a. 1064 [true date 1065], mentioning *hiredmenn* both English and Danish, with *ASC*, ms. C, s.a. 1065, which describes these same men as housecarls.

68. *ASC*, ms. D, s.a. 1054, the housecarls of *eorl* Siward of Northumbria; *ASC*, ms. C, s.a. 1065, the housecarls of *eorl* Tostig Godwinson.

69. Orlest U335.

70. *Heimskringla: Haralds saga Sigurðarsonar*, 43.

71. *Heimskringla: Magnús saga góða*, 30.

72. *Flateyjarbók*, i. 203, 205, ii. 22.

73. Sveno, *Lex Castrensis* apud *Scriptores rerum Danicarum*, iii. 144.

74. *Anglo-Saxon Charter*, S 969.

75. *ASC*, ms. E, s.a. 1036 [true date 1035], mss. C & D, s.a. 1041, ms. C & D, s.a. 1054, ms. C, s.a. 1065.

76. Morillo 2008: 254.

77. Ibid. 251–2.

78. Ibid. 252–6.

79. John 10:11–13 NIV.

80. *Beowulf*, ll. 2490–6 Heaney.

81. Machiavelli, *Arte della guerra* bk. 1.

82. Machiavelli, *Il Principe* 12.

83. Op. cit.

84. *Magnússona saga*, 11.

85. Ibid. 12. See, for this, Jakobsson 2013.

86. *Magnússona saga*, 13.

87. Ibid. 1.

88. The son of the Norwegian nobleman Kolr Kalason and his Orcadian wife Gunnhildr Erlendsdóttir, Kali Kolsson had changed his name to Rögnvaldr because his mother said that Rögnvaldr Brúsason, he who had aided the young Haraldr Sigurðarson after Stiklarstaðir, was the most accomplished of all the jarls of Orkney, and believed the name would bring her son good fortune (*Orkneyinga saga*, 55).

89. *Orkneyinga saga*, 79.

90. *Skjald* A I 468, B I 439, st. 43.

91. *Heimskringla: Hákonar saga herðibreiðs*, 20. The historical Eindriði was probably a Norwegian nobleman related to Einarr *þambarskelfir* (Gut-shaker), the famed archer who fought by the side of the missionary king Óláfr Tryggvason at the battle of Svölðr (*Heimskringla: Oláfs saga Tryggvasonar*, 108). Eindriði probably transmitted his southern stories to the skald Einarr Skúlason in Björgvin (Bergen) around 1148 (Blöndal/Benedikz 2007 [1978]: 217). Einarr himself was a priest and prominent skald serving twelfth-century Norwegian monarchs. He

was descended from the family of the remarkable Icelandic poet and fearsome adventurer Egill Skallagrímsson. As we know, Egill was later made the hero/ antihero of a saga (by Snorri Sturluson himself, it seems), which includes verses (whether or not by Egill) that date to the tenth century.

92. The Old Norse word *máli*, or military service, may refer to any contract or agreement; the phrase *ganga á mála með* literally means 'takes service with'.

93. In Old Norse: *rjóðum gylðis góma*, *Orkneyinga saga*, 82.

94. Ibid. 83.

95. *Eiríks saga rauða*, 7.

96. Blöndal/Benedikz 2007 [1978]: 156–7.

97. Rögnvaldr (who was born in Norway, the home of skiing) the poet-*jarl* does not make any bones about his skills – he proudly claims: 'I'm a master of draughts, / And of nine kinds of sport. / I am adept at runes, / And in letters a scholar. / Glide I on ski; / Shoot and row well enough, / Play the harp and make verses, / Or toil in the smithy' (*Orkneyinga saga*, 58). Though he lived in the twelfth century, and his poem must date from this time, Rögnvaldr has retained the classic Nordic virtues. Thus, in his verse Haraldr III Sigurðarson *harðráði*, albeit more modestly, list eight skills: 'Eight arts I know; / To brew the drink of Ygg; / I'm fast and skilled to horse / Sometimes engage in swimming. / ....' Ygg is a name for Óðinn, so his drink is the mead of poetry (for how he acquired the mead of poetry – the draught that gave him the gift of tongues – from the giant maiden Gunnloþ, see *Prose Edda: Skáldskaparmál* 2, a tale that is also reflected in sts. 103–10 of *Hávamál*). Thus, Haraldr's verse boasts first his skill at versifying. Northmen were not ignorant roughnecks; they had their distinctive cultural activities, which an educated man was expected to take part in.

98. *Morkinskinna*, 42, cf. *Heimskringla: Haralds saga Sigurðarsonar*, 72.

99. Liudprand of Cremona, *Antapodosis* 1.12.42.

100. Högby Ög81, Harstad Ög94, Västerby Sö82, Västerby Sö85, Rycksta Sö163, Grinda Sö165, Nälberga Sö170, Ytterjärna Sö345, Sö FV1954:20, Sm 46, Vg 178, Hansta U73, Ed U104, Broby U136, Broby U140, Angarn U201, Skepptuna U358, Åshusby U431, Droppsta U446, Väster Ledinge U518, Ulanda Bridge U792, Uppsala U922, Ärentuna U1016, Lövsta U1087.

101. Rycksta Sö163, Grinda Sö165.

102. Ulanda Bridge U792.

103. Orderic Vitalis, *Historia ecclesiastica* iii §§160–1.

104. Kellett 1987: 206.

105. In Latin: *Angli vero, quos Waringos appellant*, Gaufredus Malaterra, *Historia Sicula* 3.27 apud Muratori, *Scriptores rerum Italicarum* v, 584.

106. Anna Komnene, *Alexiad* 4.6.2. Anna titles Nabites (or Nampites) ἄρχων τῆς Βαράγγοις. It has been postulated by Dawkins (1947: 44) that Nabites' name in

Old Norse was *nabitr* (corpse-biter, viz. hunting animal) and perhaps this was a nickname for someone whose real name was something like Úlfr.

107. In Latin: *caudatis bipennibus... nostris admodum importuni primo esse coeperunt*, Gaufredus Malaterra, *Historia Sicula* apud Muratori, *Scriptores rerum Italicarum* v, 584. As for the phrase *caudatis bipennibus*, this is perhaps better translated as 'double-tailed', the two 'tails' being the equal-armed sides of a single-edged axe (viz. Dane axe), as distinct from the asymmetrical bearded axe also in use at the time. The bearded axe was so named because the lower part of the head was flat instead of pointed. It should be noted that Malaterra's sources for his work, for he was not an eyewitness himself to the contemporary events he describes in his history, were primarily oral, gathered from people who had witnessed the events. He came to Sicily at the request of Roger de Hauteville, Great Count of Sicily (r. 1085–1101). See, for this, Shepard 1973: 74–5.

108. Anna Komnene, *Alexiad* 4.6.5. Anna puts into the mouth of Sichelgaita the Homeric line 'Halt! Be men!' (*Iliad* 5.529, 6.112 Lattimore, cf. *Odyssey* 6.199 Lattimore).

109. Anna Komnene, *Alexiad* 4.6.6. Ironically, the archangel Michael was a favoured saint among the Normans. In 1066, for instance, duke William's uterine half-brother, Robert of Mortain (d. 1090), had fought at Hastings '*habens in bello Sancti Michaelis vexillum*' (*Cartulary of Saint Michael's Mount*, vol. 5, p. 1), that is, while dutifully holding aloft a banner embroidered with an emblem of the saintly Michael.

110. *Heimskringla: Hákonar saga Herðibreiðs*, 21.
111. Ibid. 20.
112. *Skjald* A I 468, B I 439, st. 45.
113. John Kinnamos, *Deeds of John and Manuel Komnenos* apud *CSHB* i, 7–8.
114. *Skjald* A I 468, B I 439, st. 55.
115. Niketas Choniates, *O City of Byzantium* I, p. 10 [14–15] Magoulias.
116. *Skjald* A I 374, B I 344.
117. *Heimskringla: Hákonar saga Herðibreiðs*, 21.
118. Skjald B I 300–01, *Morkinskinna*, 65–6, *Heimskringla: Óláfs saga helga*, 245, cf. 230.
119. Kekaumenos, *Stratêgikón* §97.
120. Treadgold 1995: 115.
121. Bayeux tapestry, scenes 48–56.
122. E.g. *ASC*, s.a. 1016, where English horsemen pursue bands of Danes and slay them as they were overtaken.
123. *Battle of Maldon*, ll. 1–2.
124. E.g. Orderic Vitalis, *Historia ecclesiastica* vi §350.

125. John of Worcester, *Chronicon ex chronicis*, s.a. 1066, Orderic Vitalis, *Historia ecclesiastica* ii §196.

126. *ASC*, ms. E, s.a. 1066, John of Worcester, *Chronicon ex chronicis*, s.a. 1066.

127. Brown 1980, cf. Morillo 1997 [1994]: 27–8.

128. Orderic Vitalis, *Historia ecclesiastica* ii §§202–5. Born near Shrewsbury in 1075 to a Norman father and an English mother, Orderic's account of the history of the Norman conquest portrays a divided loyalty. Although he was sent to Normandy at the age of ten to become a monk, he always saw himself as an exile and he sympathized with the English suffering under the Norman yoke. However, he also justifies these events by arguing that England had fallen into a state of decay by the eleventh century that was rectified by the Normans. So, for example, in his monastic writings, he regards the Norman monasteries as the spiritual castles of the kingdom, manned by the true *militia Christi*. He wrote his history between 1115 and 1141.

129. Ciggaar 1974: 323.

130. Shepard 1973: 54, 55–7.

131. *Játvarðar konungs ins helga*, 10. The one other literary source that records this event, the thirteenth-century French *Chronicon Universale Anonymi Laudunensis*, calls the colony *Nova Anglia*, New England (Ciggaar 1974: 322–3, l. 74).

132. *Játvarðar konungs ins helga*, 10.

133. Ciggaar 1974: 321.

134. Shepard 1974: 20–2.

135. *Chronicon Monasterii de Abingdon*, 46.

136. John Kinnamos, *Deeds of John and Manuel Komnenos* 16, Niketas Choniates, *O City of Byzantium* III, p. 140 [248] Magoulias.

137. Robert de Clari, *La prise de Constantinople* par. 95, cf. 79. A vassal of Peter d'Amiens, Robert de Clari returned from Constantinople in 1205, and in 1216 wrote up, or dictated, his reminisces of the siege in Old French, rather than the Latin used by the clergy. His work, written from the perspective of an ordinary knight, is full of ideas and opinions as to how and why the Fourth Crusade took the turn it did and his frontline experiences at Constantinople.

138. George Pachymeres, *Historia*, ed. A. Failler (Paris, 1984), vol. 1, pp. 101, 485, 615.

139. Pseudo-Codinus, *De officiis* 209–10.

140. *Y Gododdin*, A st. 16, ll. 6–7 Clancy.

141. *Laxdæla saga*, 77. As well as his appearance in *Laxdæla saga*, Bolli has a separate *þáttr*, *Bollaþáttr*, devoted to him, which was later appended to the end of the saga in the early fourteenth century.

142. *Grágás*, St 361. Meaning 'grey goose', the origin of name is unknown; it first appears in an inventory taken in 1548 at the bishop's seat at Skálholt, but it may

be much older. Unlike other Scandinavian law, the *Grágás* was complied without concern for royal justice or prerogative.

143. *Reginsmál*, st. 25.

144. *Hávamál*, st. 61.

145. *Primary Chronicle*, 6415 [907].

146. When a reporter called them pearl-handled, Patton was quick to correct him about the grips on his revolver being of elephant ivory, not mother of pearl. He went on to make the statement that 'only a pimp in a Louisiana whore-house carries pearl-handled revolvers'. And for those of you interested in the history of Patton's two handguns, at first they were twin Colt Single Action Army .45 Model 1873 revolvers. After he gave one of that brace of six-guns to a Hollywood star he admired and appreciated having the courage to entertain his boys at the front, he backed up the remaining Peacemaker with a 3 1/2-inch barrelled Smith & Wesson Model 27 .357 Magnum.

147. *Heimskringla: Haralds saga Sigurðarsonar*, 91, cf. *Sneglu-Halla þáttr*, 4 where it is claimed *Emma* reached down to his shoes.

148. Find # 292 found in Ec VI 3 in the debris covering the pave street of the Great Palace. The excavations were carried out in 1935–8 under the direction of Professor J.H. Baxter of the University of Saint Andrews, Scotland.

149. See, for this, Dawson 1998: 43.

150. Basil II Psalter, Codex Marciana Græcus 17, fol. 3 r., now in the Biblioteca Nazionale Marciana in Venice.

151. Madrid manuscript of John Skylitzes' *Synopsis historiôn*, Codex Matritensis Græcus, Vitr. 26–2, fols. 11 v., 12 r.-v., 13 v., 16 r., 18 v., 22 v., 30 v., 31 r., 36 r., 54 v., 80 r. The *Synopsis historiôn* is a marvellous illuminated history covering the reigns of Michael I Rangabés to Michael VI Stratiotikos (viz. 811–1057), what is recognized as the second golden age of the Byzantine empire, an eventful era when the Byzantine military organization together with the art of war and diplomacy were at their highest. It was composed during the reign of Alexis I Komnenos (1081–1118), almost certainly towards the end of the eleventh century, by John Skylitzes, a Byzantine court official. Among the extant manuscripts of this work, the one held by the Biblioteca Nacional de España in Madrid must be mentioned. This copy, and the 574 warlike representations it contains, is currently dated to the late twelfth century. The codex (a book, as opposed to a scroll) was probably produced in Palermo, the capital of the Norman kingdom of Sicily, from a metropolitan original brought to Italy from Constantinople by the Greek Enrico Aristippo, as a gift from the Manuel I Komnenos (r. 1143–80) to William I of Sicily (r. 1154–66).

152. Hedenstierna-Jonson 2006: 55, 58. In the mass graves of Korsbetningen from the battle of Visby on the Baltic Sea island of Gotland, which took place on 27

July 1361 – Valdimarr IV Atterdag of Denmark having invaded the island – iron *lamellae* have been retrieved that are considered a fair parallel to those from the Garrison.

153. See, for this, Hedenstierna-Jonson 2006: 49–52.
154. Kitzler 1997.
155. *Grænlendinga þáttr*, 5.
156. *Brennu-Njáls saga*, 92.
157. Ibid. 157.
158. *Laxdæla saga*, 77. The Old Norse word *skarlet* is somewhat deceptive as the cloth could be red, but also dark brown, blue or grey. Nonetheless, coloured clothing was a sign of wealth.
159. *Flateyjarbók*, iii. 418, *Ljósvetninga saga*, 104, *Heimskringla: Haralds saga Sigurðarsonar*, 91.
160. Aristakes Lastivertsi, *Histories* 24.
161. George Kedrenos, *Compendium historiarum* ii, 643–4. John Skylitzes mentions the rumour that the blinding was done 'on Theodora's orders and against the emperor's wishes' (*Synopsis historiôn*, 21.5 [429]).
162. Anon., *Skylitzes Continuatus* 103, cf. John Skylitzes, *Synopsis historiôn* 22.12 [500].
163. Anon., *Skylitzes Continuatus* 105.
164. *Scripta minora*, 1.232–328.
165. For the author's own lengthy account of this important event, see Michael Psellos, *Chronographia*, Michael VI 7.20–32, cf. John Skylitzes, *Synopsis historiôn* 22.11 [496–7].
166. Doukas, *Historia Byzantina* 184–7 Bekker.
167. In Greek: Φράγγο, Μάραγγο [Βάραγγος], πίτζι, κακάραγγο, cited in Blöndal/Benedikz 2007 [1978]: 189. However, it should be noted that Blöndal himself believed Μάραγγο was not a corruption of Βάραγγος but was the same word as the modern Greek word for carpenter, μαραγγός, and thus the rhyme was no more than a scatological insult to some French carpenter.
168. George Pachymeres, *De Michaele et Andronico Paleologis* iv 529.
169. Ibid. v 12.
170. Setton 1975: 3.
171. Ramón Muntaner, *Crònica*, chap. 201. At the time the Catalan knight Ramón Muntaner (1265–1336) was one of the leading members of the Catalan Company, serving as its quartermaster. He is a delightful storyteller.
172. George Pachymeres, *De Michaele et Andronico Paleologis*, vi 24, vii 2, Ramón Muntaner, *Crònica*, chap. 215.
173. The contemporary Byzantine chronicler, Nikephoros Gregoras (*Historia byzantina* apud *PG*, cxlviii 414–15), records that more than 1,100 Ottoman Turks

were added to the Catalan Company before their invasion of Thessaly, central Greece.

174. Froissart 1978: 240 Penguin edition.

175. Quoted in Hale 1998: 128.

176. Franco Sacchetti, *Il libro delle Trecentonovelle* novella 178.

177. Anna Komnene, *Alexiad* 2.9.4.

178. Niketas Choniates, *O City of Byzantium* I, p. 6 [7] Magoulias.

179. John Kantakouzenos, *Opera* apud *CSHB* i, 200.

180. Anna Komnene, *Alexiad* 9.9.2.

181. *Veraldar saga*, ed. J. Benediktsson 1944: 65.

182. *Alfræði íslenzk*, ed. Kr. Kålund 1908, vol. I (*Hoc dicit Iohannes apostolus de Paradiso*), p. 10.

183. Robert de Clari, *La prise de Constantinople* par. 62.

184. Niketas Choniates, *O City of Byzantium* VIII, p. 314 [571] Magoulias.

185. Ibid. VIII, p. 314 [572] Magoulias.

186. Ibid. IX, p. 323 [587] Magoulias.

187. Odo de Deuil, *De profectione Ludovici VII in orientem* 57.

188. Niketas Choniates, *O City of Byzantium* IV, bk. 1, p. 167 [301–2] Magoulias.

189. Ibn Fadlan, *Risalah* §74 Montgomery.

190. Liudprand of Cremona, *Antapodosis* 5.6, cf. 1.11.

191. Michael Psellos, *Chronographia*, Michael IV 7.25.

192. *Heimskringla*: *Hákonar saga Herðibreiðs*, 21.

193. Ibn Fadlan, *Risalah* §80 Montgomery.

194. *Annales Bertiniani*, s.a. 865.

195. Michael Attaleiates, *Historiae* 294–6.

196. Liudprand of Cremona, *Relatio de legatione Constantinopolitana ad Nicephorum Phocam* 1 Henderson.

197. Blöndal/Benedikz 2007 [1978]: 115–16, 118–19.

198. Saxo Grammaticus, *Danorum Regum Heromque Historia* xii. 7 .7-9, cf. William of Malmesbury, *Gesta regum Anglorum* ii §486, where the author gives a similar story involving the Norwegian king Sigurðr I Magnússon *Jórsalafari*.

199. *ASC*, ms. C, s.a. 1012.

200. *Heimskringla: Haralds saga hárfagra*, 26.

201. For example, historical records document the existence of Hygelac, king of the Geats (and Beowulf's uncle in the story), who died in 521.

202. Halsall 2003: 34.

203. *Hávamál*, sts. 12, 14, 19.

204. *Ljósvetninga saga*, 8.

205. *Y Gododdin*, A st. 75, ll. 3–4 Jarman.

206. George Kedrenos, *Compendium historiarum* ii, 737–8.

207. John Skylitzes, *Synopsis historiôn* 19.4 [394].

208. Madrid manuscript of John Skylitzes' *Synopsis historiôn*, Codex Matritensis Græcus, Vitr. 26–2, fol. 208 v.-a.

209. Quoted in Richards 2002: 14 (with amendments).

210. *Heimskringla: Haralds saga Sigurðarsonar*, 99. Used in Iceland up to the thirteenth century, the Norse ell (*eln*) was the length from the elbow to the tip of the middle finger, which was thus equivalent to the ancient cubit. In modern terms, this equates to 18 inches (457 mm), which makes Haraldr seven-and-a-half feet (2.29 m) tall!

211. See, for this, Sanders 1999.

212. *Heimskringla: Haralds saga Sigurðarsonar*, 3.

213. *Morkinskinna*, 9.

214. Ibid. 10.

215. *Heimskringla: Haralds saga Sigurðarsonar*, 12, *Morkinskinna*, 13, *Nóregs konunga tal*, 51.

216. For Haraldr's Holy Land adventures, see Blöndal/Benedikz 2007 [1978]: 63–5.

217. *Heimskringla: Haralds saga Sigurðarsonar*, 5.

218. *Flateyjarbók*, iii. 290–304. Discovered in 1651, *Flateyjarbók* ('Book of the Flat Island') is an Icelandic manuscript compiled in the late fourteenth century by two priests. It is written on parchment, and additional pages were added to the manuscript in the sixteenth century. *Flateyjarbók* is in the Árni Magnússon Institute in Reykjavík (GKS 1005 fol.).

219. Kekaumenos, *Advice for the Emperor* §12.

220. *Nóregs konunga tal*, 51.

221. *Heimskringla: Haralds saga Sigurðarsonar*, 2, cf. *Skjald* A I 385, B I 355.

222. *Heimskringla: Haralds saga Sigurðarsonar*, 3, *Flateyjarbók*, iii. 291.

223. *Flateyjarbók*, iii. 296.

224. John Zonaras, *Epitome historiarum* iii, 589.

225. George Kedrenos, *Compendium historiarum* ii, 511–13.

226. *Skjald* A I 369, B I 339–40.

227. George Kedrenos, *Compendium historiarum* ii, 511–12.

228. John Zonaras, *Epitome historiarum* iii, 591.

229. It should be noted that Snorri Sturluson misplaces the date of Haraldr's journey to the Holy Land, that is, he places it *after* his return from the Sicilian campaign.

230. Amatus of Montecassino, *History of the Normans* 2.8, Gaufredus Malaterra, *Historia Sicula* apud Muratori, *Scriptores rerum Italicarum* i, 7.

231. The standard Byzantine foot was equivalent to 31.23 centimetres (cf. one Roman foot ≡ 29.60 cm). So by Psellos' reckoning, if taken at face value, Maniakes would have stood 3.12 metres in his stockinged feet!

232. Michael Psellos, *Chronographia*, Constantinus IX 6.77.

233. On Maniakes' humble origins, George Kedrenos, *Compendium historiarum* ii, 500.

234. On Stephanos' humble origins, Michael Psellos, *Chronographia*, Michael IV 4.26.

235. Michael Psellos, *Chronographia*, Michael IV 4.27.

236. *Skjald* A I 390, B I 329.

237. *Skjald* A I 390, B I 360.

238. *Skjald* A I 386, B I 355.

239. *Heimskringla: Haralds saga Sigurðarsonar*, 4.

240. George Kedrenos, *Compendium historiarum* ii, 522–3, John Skylitzes, *Synopsis historiôn* 19.20 [406].

241. *Skjald* A I 370, B I 340.

242. *Heimskringla: Haralds saga Sigurðarsonar*, 6–10.

243. According to the story, as told by Dudo de Saint-Quentin, Björn, flushed with his triumphs around the western Mediterranean, decided to attack Rome and become master of the world. His war band sighted a city, magnificent in its buildings and dazzling to their northern eyes. Under a shameless ruse Björn sent messengers into the city to say that he, in the last moments of life, desired baptism. The inhabitants allowed the entry of the Northmen into the city for this purpose. After his baptism, Björn 'died' and during the solemn obsequies the 'dead' Björn rose from his funeral bier and pierced the officiating bishop with his sword. Concealed weapons appeared and the war band lay waste the city. Only as they were leaving, we are told, did they discover that the city which they had seized by deceit was not Rome but the coastal town of Lúna, the ancient Roman town at the mouth of the Magra on the Gulf of Genoa, far in both distance and grandeur from Rome.

244. *Primary Chronicle*, 6454 [946]. An interesting, albeit bloody, tale, the Derevlians, a Slavonic people upon which Igor had imposed an exorbitant tribute, killed the greedy prince. The newly widowed Olga started her rule of Kiev by taking a fourfold revenge on the Derevlians: first, a Derevlian peace mission was buried alive; then a delegation of notables was locked in a bathhouse and burned alive; this was followed by another massacre, and lastly the main town of the Derevlians was burnt down. In due course she was canonized as the first Russian saint of the Orthodox Church.

245. Genghis Khan began the conquest of the kingdom of Xi Xia in 1209 and it was completed in 1227, within months of his death.

246. Fr. Giovanni de Plano Carpini, *Historia Mongalorum* cap. VI. Friar Carpini's report of his mission to the court of the *qaghan* in 1245–7 on behalf of the pope is a systematic survey of the Mongol's country, their dress, beliefs, customs, rise

to power, war gear and mode of fighting, together with a chapter proposing how they might be resisted.

247. *Skjald* A I 369, B I 339.
248. Jones 1984 [2001]: 407. See also *Króka-Refs saga*, 13 for another example of Haraldr's love of fire.
249. *Heimskringla: Haralds saga Sigurðarsonar*, 34, cf. *Morkinskinna*, 31, *Nóregs konunga tal*, 257–8.
250. *Heimskringla: Haralds saga Sigurðarsonar*, 34.
251. Crumlin-Pedersen 1997b: 94–5.
252. Michael Psellos, *Chronographia*, Michael IV 4.50.
253. *Heimskringla: Haralds saga Sigurðarsonar*, 13.
254. Michael Psellos, *Chronographia*, Michael V 5.15.
255. Michael Attaleiates, *Historiae* 11.5–10.
256. Michael Psellos, *Chronographia*, Michael V 5.21, cf. George Kedrenos, *Compendium historiarum* ii, 750.
257. Michael Psellos, *Chronographia*, Michael V 5.21.
258. Ibid. 5.26.
259. Michael Psellos, *Chronographia*, Theodora 5.46.
260. *Heimskringla: Haralds saga Sigurðarsonar*, 14, cf. *Sexstefja*, st. apud *Skjald* A I 370, B I 340. The kenning 'greedy-wolf-brood's-sater' is a warrior prince/king because his successful battles cheer the wolf with plenty of corpses to devour.
261. *Heimskringla: Haralds saga Sigurðarsonar*, 14, cf. *Skjald* A I 400, B I 368.
262. *Skjald* A I 391, B I 361.
263. *Heimskringla: Haralds saga Sigurðarsonar*, 2, cf. Kekaumenos, *Advice for the Emperor* §12.
264. *Sexstefja*, st. 7 apud *Skjald* A I 370, B I 340–1, cf. *Heimskringla: Haralds saga Sigurðarsonar*, 11.
265. William of Malmesbury, *Gesta regum Anglorum* iii §260.
266. *Heimskringla: Haralds saga Sigurðarsonar*, 16.
267. Constantinus VII Porphyrogenitus, *De ceremoniis aulae Byzantinae* apud *CSHB* i, 62/63. See, for this, Blöndal/Benedikz 2007 [1978]: 83–4, cf. 86.
268. Saxo Grammaticus, *Danorum Regum Heromque Historia* xi. 3.1.3.
269. Kekaumenos, *Advice for the Emperor* §12, cf. Saxo Grammaticus, *Danorum Regum Heromque Historia* xi. 3.17–11.
270. *Heimskringla: Haralds saga Sigurðarsonar*, 15.
271. See, for this, Erkal 2011: 198–200.
272. Niketas Choniates, *O City of Byzantium* VI, bk. 2, p. 297 [542] Magoulias.
273. Theophanes Confessor, Chronographia, *annus mundi* 6209 [717/18].
274. Leo Diakonos, *Historia* 5.2.
275. Niketas Choniates, *O City of Byzantium* II, bk. 7, p. 117 [205–06] Magoulias.

276. Frontinus, *Strategemata* 1.5.6, cf. John Zonaras (*Epitome historiarum* viii, 16) makes Hippo (probably Hippo(u) Acra, now Bizerta) rather than Syracuse the scene of this stratagem.
277. *Heimskringla: Haralds saga Sigurðarsonar*, 3.
278. Anna Komnene, *Alexiad*, 4.5.4, 6.2, 7.3.6 (with reference to the Northman Nabites).
279. Kekaumenos, *Advice for the Emperor* §12.
280. *Laxdæla saga*, 73.
281. *Sneglu-Halla þáttr*, 10, cf. 4 where Halli tells the king that porridge "When buttered, it's the best of food". This was not your porridge made with oatmeal, by the way, but that of barley meal.
282. Haraldr had previously married Elisaveta Yaroslavna of Kiev during the earliest weeks of the year 1043, and had by her two daughters, Maria (who was to die on the day – and, indeed, at the very hour – when her father had fallen in the fray) and Ingigerðr (later queen of Denmark and Sweden). Þóra Þórbergsdotter and Haraldr were married in the winter of 1047/8, and had at least two sons, Magnús (later Magnús II) and Óláfr (later Óláfr III). Some modern commentators (e.g. DeVries 2003 [1999]: 48–9, Marsden 2007: 171–2) have disputed this second marriage, since Haraldr in that case would be in a bigamous marriage, as he was still married to Elisaveta. Personally speaking, I believe this state of affairs would not have bothered Haraldr one whit. If this pagan kingly behaviour (more reminiscent of Vendel kingship rights than orthodox Christian behaviour) gave rise to criticism from the Church, we do not hear of it. Besides, by this 'bigamous marriage' Haraldr was surely hoping to secure a male successor. Þóra, of course, was the daughter of Þórberg Árnason, the youngest brother of the infamous Kálfr.
283. *Laxdæla saga*, 73.
284. *Eyrbyggja saga*, 65. Cf. Blöndal/Benedikz (2007 [1978]: 208), who argue that Bolli did not go abroad until 1032–3, and returned ten to fifteen years after that date.
285. *Morkinskinna*, 32.
286. *Laxdæla saga*, 73. However, according to *Laxdæla saga* (78) he returned home while his father-in-law was still alive (Snorri dies in 1031), but this leaves him very little time to win a place in the Varangian Guard, since he is said to have spent some time in Norway and Denmark before going on to Constantinople. Bolli must have spent a number of years in Byzantium, returning home a wealthy and sophisticated man.

Chapter 4: Northland

1. *Hávamál*, st. 58 Hollander.
2. Hassmyra Vs24.
3. See, for this, Appendix 3.

4. Adam Bremensis, *Gesta Hammaburgensis ecclesiae pontificum* iv §31.

5. In Scandinavia *fé* was used indifferently of a) cattle (in Iceland chiefly sheep), b) wealth and goods in general, c) money. Incidentally, the OE term *feoh*, fee, has precisely these three meanings.

6. This is probably the *lac concretum* of Tacitus (*Germania* 23).

7. *Landnámabók*, S 5.

8. Noonan 1987: 392.

9. Treadgold 1995: 43–4, 2005: 2–3.

10. *Heimskringla: Magnúss saga ins Góða*, 16.

11. See, for this, Bagge 2010: 165.

12. *Heimskringla: Haralds saga Sigurðarsonar*, 1.

13. Ibid. 3–4, 23.

14. *Rígsþula*, st. 34.

15. Smyth 1998: 27.

16. E.g. *Egils saga Skallagrímssonar*, 32, rune stones Simris DR334, Hablingbo Church G370, Bro U617, Härlingstrop Vg 61.

17. Etchingham 2014: 37, cf. Downham 2007: xv–xx.

18. For an in-depth discussions on the term viking and how it was used, see Jesch 2001: 44–68, Lind 2011.

19. *Landnámabók*, S 399. *Landnámabók*, 'Book of Settlements' derives from the noun *landnámsmenn* ('land-takers' or first settlers, a term that includes women). The original was written in the early twelfth century and is in part attributed to the Icelandic cleric and scholar Ari Þorgilsson (1068–1148), though the earliest version still extant is credited to Sturla Þórðarson 1214–84, the nephew of Snorri Sturluson, and thus known as *Sturlubók* (another major extant version is the later *Hauksbók*). Listing the events and characters of the original settlement of Iceland, it circles the coast in a clockwise direction, giving brief anecdotes of some 430 individual settlers (some 7 per cent coming from recognizably Celtic lands), among the 3,500 named people and their 1,500 farms. The book tells of how they moved from Norway, what they transported, why and how they established their boundaries and placated the land-spirits, what gods they worshipped, what laws they brought, and made, their feuds and killings, and who was descended from them. But this was no *Domesday Book*. It provides a perfect mirror of how the rulers of the island saw their past, and thus can be a snare for later historians if they do not step through the looking-glass. Nevertheless, it should not be forgotten that unlike other European peoples, who created for themselves timeless origins beginning with mythic descent from gods and semi-divine heroes, Icelanders knew their past, even the names of hundreds of the first settlers. In this unusual situation for Europe, they developed a historical, linear reckoning of the past that took into consideration a factual founding.

20. *Landnámabók*, 216.
21. *Hallfreðar saga*, 151–2.
22. *Landnámabók*, S 218.
23. *Örvar-Odds saga*, 17.
24. Ibid. 2.
25. Ibid. 31.
26. *Hávamál*, st. 81 Evans.
27. Louis' moniker *le Pieux*, the Pious, comes from self-description in official documents as *piisimus*, most pious, emphasizing the Christian nature of his empire.
28. The Monk of Saint-Gall, *De Carlo Magno* 2.19 [154]. Louis *le Pieux* also sponsored a mission to the Danes when in 823 he sped the papal legate, Ebo archbishop of Reims, in search of souls over the Eider. Ebo made a few converts, and it possible he was the catalyst for Haraldr Haraldsson (later known as *Klak*, the Harmful) and 400 of his followers being solemnly 'drenched in the wave of holy baptism' at Ingelheim in 826, thus becoming the first Danish convert-king (*Vita Hludovici*, s.a. 826, chap. 40, ll. 3–7). Haraldr, however, proved to be rather unpopular and was soon driven out of his kingdom.
29. *Eyrbyggja saga*, 54.
30. The *Æsir* were warlike gods of battle and conquest who lived in the beautiful realm of *Ásgard*. The *Vanir* gods existed long before the first *Æsir* gods appeared. They were beautiful beings of light and wisdom, brother and sister gods and goddesses who lived in their realm called *Vanaheim*, sending forth gentle sunshine and rain and fertility, but none the less powerful for all that. A war broke out between the *Æsir* and the *Vanir*, but neither side could win – or lose. Terms were discussed, and as a sign of good faith, the sides exchanged gods. Thus the *Vanir* god Freyr ('Lord') was sent to *Ásgard* as a peace token along with his twin sister Freyja ('Lady'), and his father, Njörðr. From thereon, the *Æsir* and the *Vanir* stood fast together against the common enemy, the Giants.
31. Adhémar, *Chronica* apud *PL*, cxli 37.
32. Kopytoff 1986: 66.
33. Widukind of Corvey, *Rerum Gestarum Saxonicarum* iii 65.
34. A number of Óðinn's many synchronic names are listed in *Grímnismál* (sts. 47–51, 55).
35. *Hávamál*, st. 138.
36. Ibid. st. 157
37. In Old Norse: *hanga Týr, hanga goð*, Prose Edda: *Gylfaginning*, 20.
38. *Gautreks saga*, 7.
39. Dumézil 1973: 121–2.
40. Ibid. 26.

41. Turville-Petre 1964: 35.
42. *Prose Edda: Gylfaginning*, 3.
43. Dumézil 1973: 28.
44. *Prose Edda: Gylfaginning*, 51–2.
45. Stenkyrka Lillbjärs III (G268) has a welcoming woman, Tjängvide I (G 110) has a woman and Óðinn and a domed hall, Ardre VIII (SHM 11118) has Óðinn and a hall.
46. See, for this, Wilson 1967.
47. 'Head-ransom' apud *Egils saga Skallagrímssonar*, 60.
48. Note other instances that more directly equate blood to drink, such as Þórðr Kolbeinsson's claim in one of his lays that 'The wolves enjoyed the grey beasts' ale' following a battle (*Eiríksdrápa*, 14).
49. Haraldr's sons are said to be twenty in *Heimskringla* (*Haralds saga Hárfagra*, 21, 33), but a few of the names, and many of the nicknames, differ. *Historia Norwegiæ* names sixteen of them, thirteen of which appear in *Ágrip af Nóregskonúngasögum* (2), which also names one not mentioned by Snorri Sturluson.
50. Theodoricus Monachus,*Historia de antiquitate regum Norwagiensiųm̃*, cf. *blekkir brœðra*, 'brother-killer', in Egill Skallagrímsson's *Lausavísur*, st. 22 apud *Egils saga Skallagrímssonar*, 57.
51. *Nóregs konunga tal*, 8.
52. *Historia Norwegiæ*, 105. It was the common Icelandic view, however, that Gunnhildr was the daughter of the more humble Qzurr *lafskegg/toti* (Dangling beard/Snout), but this may be due, at least in part, to Icelandic hostility toward her (e.g. *Heimskringla: Haralds saga Hárfagra*, 32, *Egils saga Skallagrímssonar*, 37, *Brennu-Njáls saga* 3).
53. *Heimskringla: Haralds saga hárfagra*, 43.
54. *Historia Norwegiæ*, 106, *Ágrip af Nóregskonúngasögum*, §7. It has been suggested that *Spán-* (from *Spáníalandi*, Old Norse for Spain) may be a corruption of *Stán-*.
55. *Nóregs konunga tal*, 8, *Heimskringla: Hákonar saga góða*, 4.
56. Theodoricus Monachus, *Historia de antiquitate regum Norwagiensium* 2.
57. *ASC*, mss. D & E, s.a. 954.
58. Roger of Wendover, *Flores historiarum* i §256, s.a. 950. However, the entry recording Eiríkr's death is wrongly dated 950.
59. Symeon of Durham, *Historia regum Anglorum et Dacorum*, *Opera*, ii, p. 382.
60. *Nóregs konunga tal*, 8.
61. Óðinn's relations to wolves should not be conceived as being exclusively hostile. *Prose Edda: Gylfaginning* (38) recounts that Óðinn has two wolves, Geri and Reki, who eat scraps from his table at Valhöll. They roam throughout the great hall, walking among the souls of the fallen. Warriors in battle, therefore, considered wolves to be signs of Óðinn's presence. A grey wolf on the battlefield was a positive

sign to warriors, for they believed it would guide their spirits to Valhöll if they died that day. In kennings, wolves are commonly referred to as corpse-eaters. These references make the image of wolves eating from the table of Óðinn reasonable, and would also explain why dogs, even wild ones, would be somewhat too tame for the rôle.

62. In Old Norse: *Konungar eru fimm – sagði Eiríkr – kenni ek þér nafn allra, ek em hinn sétti siálfr, Eiríksmál*, st. 9 Hollander.

63. E.g. Downham 2004: 63. Downham (ibid. 59–63, 2007: 115–20) believes Eiríkr of York was *not* Eiríkr Haraldsson *blóðøx*.

64. Thus Seeberg (1978–81), who also suggests that the topic of the 'five kings' ultimately derives from the Old Testament (*vide* Joshua 10:23–6).

65. *ASC*, ms. A, s.a. 937.

66. See, for this, Appendix 2.

67. *Annals of Ulster*, s.a. 870.

68. *ASC*, ms. D, s.a. 923 [true date 919].

69. *ASC*, ms. D, s.a. 925.

70. *Rex pius Æðelstan*, ll. 1, 3–6, cf. Psalm 58.

71. *Annals of Ulster*, s.a. 937.

72. *Annales Cambriae* (A), s.a. 937, *Chronicum Scotorum*, s.a. 937.

73. *ASC*, ms. D, s.a. 941.

74. *Egils saga Skallagrímssonar*, 52.

75. *Domesday* is the Middle English for Doomsday; the book was actually written in Mediaeval Latin and officially entitled *Liber de Wintonia* ('Book of Winchester'). A spectacular document, it was William's census of all peoples and goods in his newly conquered land.

76. Löfving 1991: 149.

77. *ASC*, ms. A, s.a. 991. The *Ánláf* mentioned in mss. C, D and E is probably Óláfr Tryggvason. However, his command of the invading Northmen passes unmentioned in Old Norse verse and saga. In an Ely church calendar the date of *ealdorman* Byrhtnoth's death appears as 10 August.

78. *ASC*, mss. C, D & E, s.a. 994.

79. In the anonymous *Ágrip af Nóregskonúngasögum*, written in the vernacular around 1190, it is said of Óláfr Tryggvason that 'he Christianized five countries: Norway, Iceland, Shetland, Orkney and the fifth, the Faeroes' (§19, cf. *Brennu-Njáls saga*, 100).

80. *Historia Norwegiæ*, 7, Theodoricus Monachus, *Historia de antiquitate regum Norwagiensium*, 14.

81. *Heimskringla: Óláfs saga Tryggvasonar*, 111, 112.

82. *Óláfs saga Tryggvasonar av Oddr Snorrason munk*, A 256, A 267–8.

83. *Heimskringla: Óláfs saga Tryggvasonar*, 112.

84. B 380, University Museum of Bergen, inv. BRM 000/34880.
85. Note, however, the monk Guillaume de Jumièges (*Gesta Normannorum ducum*, ed. E.M.C. van Houts [Oxford, 1995], vol. 2, pp. 26–8), which is accepted by Theodoricus Monachus (*Historia de antiquitate regum Norwagiensium*, 13) has Óláfr Haraldsson baptized in Rouen at the hands of archbishop Robert II *le Danois* (r. 989–1037) in 1013 (the ecclesiastical tradition), while Snorri Sturluson (*Heimskringla: Óláfs saga Tryggvasonar*, 44) has it performed twelve years earlier (viz. when Óláfr was just three years old) in Norway (the vernacular tradition).
86. E.g. *Heimskringla: Óláfs saga helga*, 13.
87. Ibid. 113.
88. Ibid. 121.
89. Ibid. 59.
90. Ibid. 226. However, a similar battle-cry is attributed to the twelfth-century Norwegian king Sverrir Sigurðarson (*Sverris saga*, 47).
91. Adam Bremensis, *Gesta Hammaburgensis ecclesiae pontificum* iv §32.
92. Skjald B I 300–01.
93. However, see Pentcheva 20014 [2006]: 79–80.
94. Geoffroi de Villehardouin, *La conquête de Constantinople* par. 228.
95. *Heimskringla: Hákonar saga Herðibreiðs*, 21.
96. *Heimskringla: Haralds saga Sigurðarsonar*, 17.
97. Ibid. 28, Theodoricus Monachus, *Historia de antiquitate regum Norwagiensium*, 27, *Ágrip af Nóregskonúngasögum*, §40.
98. Saxo Grammaticus, *Danorum Regum Heromque Historia* x. 22.3.2.
99. *Skjald* B I 339.
100. Cf. DeVries (2003 [1999]: 230, 236) who proposes that it was probably Tostig who was 'the prime instigator' of Haraldr's attempt to win England for himself, doing so by 'working on Haraldr Harðráði's pride'.
101. Theodoricus Monachus, *Historia de antiquitate regum Norwagiensium* 28. Theodoricus, who was writing in Latin, is probably a latinization of the Norse name Þórir.
102. *Beowulf*, ll. 5, 21–4 Heaney.
103. *Heimskringla: Haralds saga Gráfeldar*, 1.
104. *Heimskringla: Haralds saga Sigurðarsonar*, 19, *Morkinskinna*, 31.
105. *Heimskringla: Haralds saga Sigurðarsonar*, 61.
106. Ibid. 59.
107. Ibid. 60.
108. *Landnámabók*, H 268.
109. *Heimskringla: Óláfs saga Tryggvasonar*, 111.
110. *Heimskringla: Haralds saga Sigurðarsonar*, 63.
111. Op. cit.

112. Op. cit.
113. *ASC*, ms. E, s.a. 1069 & 1070.
114. Hansen 1914: 19.
115. *Heimskringla: Haralds saga Sigurðarsonar*, 64.
116. Ibid. 43.
117. Op. cit.
118. Ibid. 44.

Chapter 5: Conquest

1. Bede, *Historia Ecclesiastica* 4.16 (14).
2. *ASC*, s.a. 1002.
3. John Skylitzes, *Synopsis historiôn* 16.35 [349], cf. 38 [353].
4. See, for this, Rieck 2000: 60.
5. Prokopios, *Wars* 8.20.31.
6. *ASC*, mss. E & F, s.a. 793. Arguably the earliest account of a viking raid, when '*iii. scipu Norðmanna* [three ships of Northmen]' sailed into what is now Portland in Dorset, describes the death of a West Saxon royal official who treated the viking visitors as if they were traders and was killed for his trouble (ibid. MSS B, C, D and E, s.a. 787 [789], *Annals of Saint Neots*, s.a. 789). Indeed, the event may have begun as a trading expedition that turned violent, rather than being planned as a raid – there is no mention in our sources of plunder or uncontrolled violence. This unfortunate incident serves as a useful reminder that there is not always a clear-cut division between violent raiding and peaceful trading. Incidentally, an attack on Lindisfarne in 875 led to its abandonment, the monks undertaking an eight-year long peregrination from place to place in Northumbria with the precious relics of Saint Cuthbert, which terminated at Chester-le-Street, some eight kilometres north of Durham. There they remained for little over a century until moving to Durham in 995. It is at Durham that Cuthbert has rested ever since, Reformation notwithstanding.
7. Alcuin apud *EHD* 776.
8. *Annales Bertiniani*, s.a. 843.
9. Christiansen 2006 [2002]: 177–8.
10. Al-Ya'qubi, *Kitab al-buldan* ('Book of the Lands') 354.
11. In Old English: *mycel hæþen here*, *Anglo Saxon Chronicle*, s.a. 865.
12. *ASC*, ms. A, s.a. 896.
13. *Jomsvíkinga-saga*, 15, cf. 23. Vagn was obviously a precocious warrior, for the minimum age for signing up with the Jómsvíkings was eighteen (ibid. 12).
14. *Heimskringla: Óláfs saga Tryggvasonar*, 41. For a fuller version of the mass execution, see *Jomsvíkinga-saga*, 23. Note also *Jómsvíkingadrápa* by Bjarni Kolbeinsson, which honours the fallen Jómsvíkings at Hjörungavágr.

15. See, for this, Loe-Boyle-Webb-Score 2014, Chenery-Evans-Score-Boyle-Chenery 2014.

16. *ASC*, ms. C, s.a. 1011 & 1016.

17. Sellar & Yeatman 1999 [1930]: chap. 8.

18. *ASC*, mss. C & D, s.a. 1007.

19. *ASC*, ms. C, s.a. 1013.

20. Translated in *EHD* 416–18.

21. *ASC*, s.a. 1014.

22. *ASC*, ms. C, s.a. 1002.

23. Sawyer, no. 127, translated in *EHD*, no. 127.

24. *ASC*, ms. D, s.a. 1017.

25. *Heimskringla: Haralds saga hárfagra*, 24.

26. *ASC*, s.a. 1054.

27. *ASC*, ms. E, s.a. 1055.

28. *Heimskringla: Haralds saga Sigurðarsonar*, 91.

29. Ealdyð of Mercia should not be confused with the beautiful Eadgyð Swanneshals (Swan's neck), also known as 'the Fair', Harold's long-time mistress who bore him at least four sons and two daughters. Harold had one legitimate son, who was named after him, born to queen Ealdyð at Chester after his death at Hastings. Forced to flee Norman England in 1071, Harold Haroldson would be found fighting in 1098 off Anglesey alongside the Norwegian king, Magnús III Óláfsson *berfœttr*, against the Norman earls of Shrewsbury and Chester. Curiously enough, Magnús was the grandson of Harald *harðráði*.

30. *ASC*, ms. A, s.a. 1066.

31. Theodoricus Monachus, *Historia de antiquitate regum Norwagiensium* 22.

32. Shakespeare, *Macbeth* Act 1, scene 2, line 59.

33. *ASC*, mss. C, D, E & F, s.a. 1035.

34. John of Worcester, *Chronicon ex chronicis*, s.a. 1035.

35. Bayeux tapestry, scene 15. See, for this, Bridgeford 2004: 246–71.

36. McNulty 1980: 667–8, cf. Bridgeford 2004: 270–1.

37. *ASC*, ms. C, s.a. 1042.

38. *ASC*, s.a. 1014.

39. Óttarr svarti, *Knútrdrápa* apud *Knýtlinga saga*.

40. See, for this, Wallace 2012: 7.

41. *Heimskringla: Haralds saga Sigurðarsonar*, 80.

42. Bryggens Museum, inv. BRM 0/12274. Around 660 runic inscriptions, most of them cut into wooden sticks, have been found during archaeological excavations at Bryggen in Bergen. Many of them have served as letters or messages, and are genuine archival documents. Others are of a less formal nature, being just simple scribbles or idle doodles. See, for this, Spurkland 2005.

43. For example, the 'big ocean-going ship' of Þórólfr Kveldúlfsson 'was richly painted above the plumbline and fitted with a black-and-red stripped sail' (*Egils saga Skallagrímssonar*, 17). Ibn Idhari al-Marrakushi, in his history of the Maghreb and Iberia written in 1312, when describing the Norse arrival off the al-Andalus coast in the summer of 844, says: 'One might say they had, as it were, filled the ocean with dark red birds' (*Al-Bayan al-Mughrib*, AH 229 [30 September 843–17 September 844]), a rather poetic reference to the colour of the Norse sails.

44. Oxenstierna 1965: 264.

45. Crumlin-Pedersen 1997a: 191.

46. Lund 1996, 141.

47. Crumlin-Pedersen & Olsen 2002.

48. Cf. DeVries 2003 [1999]: 242, who estimates a fleet of 250 ships and an army of between 11,000 to 12,000 warriors. See also Campbell 1984.

49. *Heimskringla: Haralds saga Sigurðarsonar*, 80. Snorri Sturluson actually says 'nearly 200' ships, as do the anonymous authors of *Morkinskinna*, 49 and *Flateyjarbók*, iii. 118, but this number was probably based on the Old Norse numbering system (viz. the' long-hundred', *hundrað*), which means the total would actually be 240. The English and Anglo-Norman give higher numbers for Haraldr's fleet: 300 ships (*ASC*, mss. D & E, s.a. 1066, Henry of Huntingdon, *Historia Anglorum* bk. VI, s.a. 1066, William of Malmesbury, *Gesta regum Anglorum* i §§420–1); 470 ships (Geoffroi Gaimar, *L'estoire des Engleis* l. 5206); and 500 ships (John of Worcester, *Chronicon ex chronicis*, s.a. 1066, Symeon of Durham, *Historia regum Anglorum et Dacorum* ii §180). The lower number given by the Old Norse sagas is counted before Haraldr set sail from Norway, the higher number recorded by English and Anglo-Norman sources is from Haraldr's total after he had reached the coast of England and may reflect added vessels from Shetland and Orkney. Most modern commentators attach a number of 300 to the Norwegian fleet.

50. In Old English: *swa hy ær gesprecen hæfdon*, *ASC*, ms. C, s.a. 1066, cf. John of Worcester, *Chronicon ex chronicis*, s.a. 1066, who repeats this phrase, in Latin of course, verbatim, viz. '*ut prius condixerant*'. Mediaeval writers regarded the work of their predecessors or even contemporaries as common property. Thus, Anna Komnene, *Alexiad* 5.9, where she uses a passage taken directly from Michael Psellos, *Chronographia*, Romanos III 2–3.

51. *Heimskringla: Haralds saga Sigurðarsonar*, 83.

52. T.E. Lawrence, 2000 [1935]. *Seven Pillars of Wisdom*, p. 23 Penguin edition.

53. John of Worcester, *Chronicon ex chronicis*, s.a. 1066, Symeon of Durham, *Historia regum Anglorum et Dacorum*, ii §180.

54. York had been founded by Quintus Petilius Cerialis Caesius Rufus, then Roman governor of Britannia, in AD 71 as a legionary fortress for *legio* VIIII *Hispana*, his

old command. It was named *Eboracum* (probably 'the place of the yew trees' in the local Celtic tongue). This was turned into *Eoforwic* ('boar settlement') by the Anglo-Saxons, while the vikings changed the name to *Jórvík* ('horse town') when they captured it. In later Old Norse this became *Iork*, which was later adopted by the English as York.

55. So identified by the locally well-informed Symeon of Durham (d. *c.* 1130) as 'on the northern shore of the river Ouse at Fulford near York' (*Historia regum Anglorum et Dacorum*, ii §180), the only source to do so. All other written sources mention only the distance from York, and as these do not differ with Symeon's position, it is commonly believed that Gate Fulford is where the battle was fought.
56. *Heimskringla: Haralds saga Sigurðarsonar*, 85.
57. Jones 1987: 106.
58. DeVries 2003 [1999]: 256.
59. *Heimskringla: Haralds saga Sigurðarsonar*, 84.
60. John of Worcester, *Chronicon ex chronicis*, s.a. 1066.
61. Op. cit.
62. *Heimskringla: Haralds saga Sigurðarsonar*, 85. Snorri uses here a regular topos when major man-slayings occur. One example must serve for many. The description of the aftermath of the victory of Ecgfrith (r. 670–85), ruler of the Anglian kingdom of Bernicia, over Drust, king of the Verturian Picts: 'He slew an enormous number of people, filling two rivers with the corpses of the slain, so that – marvellous to relate – the slayers, passing over the rivers dry-foot, pursued and slew a crowd of fugitives' (Stephan, *Vita Sancti Wilfrithi* §19).
63. *ASC*, ms. C, s.a. 1066.
64. The date is recorded in *ASC*, ms. C, s.a. 1066.
65. Napoléon, *Corespondance*, vol. XVIIII, no. 14707, p. 218.
66. Victor Hugo, *Les misérables*, trans. Charles E. Wilbour (1992), p. 271.
67. *Heimskringla: Haralds saga Sigurðarsonar*, 87.
68. In Old Norse: *catir mioc*, *Morkinskinna*, 50.
69. *ASC*, ms. C, s.a. 1066.
70. Hildr is a valkyrie; the whole kenning for 'proud woman'. Hildr is the personification of strife, and this is why her name is popular in kennings where poets tell of battles and conflicts, such as *él Hildar*, 'Hildr's storm' (battle), *hyrr Hildar*, 'Hildr's flame' (sword), or *hjól Hildar*, 'Hildr's wheel' (shield).
71. *Heimskringla: Haralds saga Sigurðarsonar*, 91. See, for this, Turville-Petre 1968: 19.
72. Crammed with entries describing battles fought, kings, earls and warriors slain, town besieged, and whole regions plundered and burned, the *Anglo-Saxon Chronicle* is the most important and trustworthy narrative source, or more properly group of narrative sources, for the history of what should be called

Anglo–Scandinavian England between the years 1042 to 1066. For this period it survives in four principal manuscripts: A, C, D, and E. None of these manuscripts can be considered as an original text for they are all copies of texts that are now lost, and they were written in different religious houses. Manuscript A contains only brief, isolated entries and for 'contemporary' evidence for Stamford Bridge we are dependent upon manuscripts C, D, and E. Manuscript C was probably compiled at Abingdon in the middle of the eleventh century, manuscript D possibly at York, Worcester, or Evesham during the twelve century, and manuscript E although transcribed at Peterborough Abbey during the twelve century is largely based for the period up to 1121 on a version compiled at Saint Augustine's Abbey, Canterbury. Although manuscripts D and E are northern compositions, it is manuscript C that best reports the events of Haraldr's invasion of England.

73. William of Malmesbury, *Gesta regum Anglorum* ii §228.
74. Henry of Huntington, *Historia Anglorum* bk. VI, s.a. 1066.
75. *Ágrip af Nóregskonúngasögum*, §42, Theodoricus Monachus, *Historia de antiquitate regum Norwagiensium* 30.
76. *Heimskringla: Haralds saga Sigurðarsonar*, 90, *Morkinskinna*, 50, *Nóregs konunga tal*, 44.
77. *ASC*, ms. D, s.a. 1066.
78. *Heimskringla: Ynglinga saga*, 6.
79. See, for this, Simek 1995: 47.
80. *Grettis saga Ásmundarsonar*, 2, cf. 40, *Nóregs konunga tal*, 8, *Egils saga Skallagrímssonar*, 9.
81. *Vatnsdæla saga*, 9.
82. *Skjald* A I 68–71, B I 60–2, st. 6.
83. See, for this, Ellis Davidson 1986: 149.
84. Saxo Grammaticus, *Danorum Regum Heromque Historia* vii. 2.7.4.
85. *Grágás*, K 7.
86. London, British Museum, Iv. Cat. 123–5, Edinburgh, National Museums of Scotland, NS 29. Found on the Isle of Lewis, Outer Hebrides, these twelfth-century, high quality chess pieces are thought to be of Norse manufacture, probably the product of a single workshop in Nidaros, Norway. Every piece is different. They are among the most iconic images of both the Isle of Lewis itself and the Norse heritage of the whole of the British Isles. The Scandinavians who settled and ruled the Hebrides until they were ceded to the Scottish crown in 1266, called the islands *Suðreyjar*, Southern Islands, which nicely reflects their position in the Norse-settled islands relative to Orkney and Shetland.
87. *Egils saga Skallagrímssonar*, 64. See also *Vatnsdæla saga*, 46 for two berserks who "howled like dogs and gnawed the ends of their shields".
88. See, for this, Price 2002: 368.

89. *Egils saga Skallagrímssonar*, 1.

90. Ibid. 27.

91. In ON *hamhleypa*,or 'skin-leaper', viz. one who leaps from his/her own human skin into that of e.g., a wolf.

92. *Landnámabók*, H 223.

93. *Heimskringla: Ynglinga saga*, 7. The belief is of course found in every age and land. In India the shape shifter becomes a tiger; in Japan a fox; in Africa a hyaena, less commonly a lion. The Greek word is *lykánthôpos*. A rather skeptical Herodotos was told "that once a year every Neurian [northern neighbours of the Scythians] turns into a wolf for a few day, and then turns back into a man again" (4.105). In Europe the shape is generally of wolf or bear.

94. See, for this, Breen 1997, 1999, Price 2002: 78–84, 366–74.

95. Fabing 1956: 232–7.

96. In French: *comme bonnes à penser*, Lévi-Strauss 1962: 89.

97. *Heimskringla: Haralds saga Hárfagra*, 18.

98. *Egils saga Skallagrímssonar*, 9.

99. *Heimskringla: Haralds saga Hárfagra*, 9.

100. *Heimskringla: Haralds saga Sigurðarsonar*, 88.

101. Ibid. 92.

102. Op. cit.

103. For an in-depth literary critique of Haraldr's death, see Salvucci 2005: 53–85.

104. *Egils saga Skallagrímssonar*, 88, *Víga-Glúms saga*, 28.

105. Henry Purcell, *King Arthur, or the British Worthy* Act 1, scene 2 (chorus).

106. *Morkinskinna*, 50.

107. *Heimskringla: Haralds saga Sigurðarsonar*, 92.

108. *ASC* ms. D, s.a. 1066.

109. Baxter 2009: 118.

Epilogue

1. Adam Bremensis, *Gesta Hammaburgensis ecclesiae pontificum* iii §16.

2. *Morkinskinna*, 40.

3. The dwarfs made the mead of poetry from the blood of Kvasir, a god formed from the mixture of the spittle of the *Æsir* and *Vanir*, and a giant held them to ransom for it. Óðinn, after a night of love making, was allowed a sip of the mead by the giant's daughter who guarded it. However, he drank the lot and then flew back, in the guise of an eagle, to the gods and spat it out for them into three huge wooden vats.

4. Turville-Petre 1968: 5. See also *Sneglu-Halla þáttr*, 1 where Haraldr is said to have taken "great pleasure in poetry and always had people about him who knew how to compose poetry".

5. *Heimskringla: Haralds saga Sigurðarsonar*, 36.
6. R.L. Stevenson (1896), 'Faith, Half-Faith, and no Faith at all', *Fables* XVII, 59–60.
7. *Morkinskinna*, 28.
8. *Heimskringla: Haralds saga Sigurðarsonar*, 90.
9. *Chronicle of Man*, s.a. 1066.
10. Ibid. s.a. 1098, cf. Orderic Vitalis, *Historia ecclesiastica* v §225.
11. Marsden 2007: 231–3.
12. *Ágrip af Nóregskonúngasögum*, §51.
13. *Heimskringla: Magnúss saga berfœttr*, 16.
14. Saxo Grammaticus, *Danorum Regum Heromque Historia* xiii. 1.1.3–2.1, cf. *Heimskringla: Magnúss saga berfœttr*, 14, *Nóregs konunga tal*, 310–11.
15. *Heimskringla: Magnúss saga berfœttr*, 16.
16. Ibid. 7.
17. According to the *Chronicle of Man* (s.a. 1102) Magnús sent his shoes to Muirchertach for him to wear on his shoulders in his hall on Christmas Day as a token of submission, and the high king replied that he would not only wear them but eat them if it prevented the Norwegian king from despoiling a single province of Ireland. It has been suggested that this anecdote may contain a vague reference to Magnús' curious cognomen, *berfoettr*. See, for this, Power 2005: 15 n. 12.
18. Ibid. 24.

Appendix A: Skald, saga, serpent slayer, son of Óðinn

1. *Heimskringla*: *Óláfs saga Helga*, 234.
2. *Heimskringla:* preface.
3. At the Althingi in 1262, and then during the next two years at local assemblies held throughout the country, the Icelanders agreed to become subjects of the Norwegian crown. Each *þingfararkaupsbóndi* (literary, 'Thing-tax-paying-farmer') was to pay to the Norwegian king a nominal tribute (in perpetuity) in return for the king's respect for Iceland's laws and a promise to maintain peace.
4. *Brennu-Njáls saga*, 129.
5. Ibid. 128.
6. *Sögubrot*, 10. The term *álfar* needs explanation. The word *álfr* is akin to our 'elf' but it has quite different connotations, lacking the 'elfin' quality of English. Indeed, in Old Norse literature the *álfar* are closely linked to the great gods, the *Æsir* (sg. *Áss*), and the two nouns form an alliterating pair that is common in verse texts. However, the *álfar* were subsidiary deities whose cult seems to have been a group rather than an individual one. They were connected to specific localities, and had some similarity to the *landvœttir*, land spirits, recorded in other written sources. The help of these local semi-deities was welcomed to bring success to a family.

7. *Ragnars saga loðbrókar*, 3, cf. *Þáttr af Ragnars sonum*, 1, Saxo Grammaticus, *Danorum Regum Heromque Historia* ix. 4.6-8. In the Russian folktale of Nikita the Tanner, the hero takes thirty hundredweight of flax, smears it with pitch, and wraps himself up in it. Thus protected, he fights and defeats a dragon. See, for this, McTurk 2015 [1991]: 13.

8. Saxo Grammaticus, *Danorum Regum Heromque Historia* ix. 4.8.1–4.

9. *Krákumál*, st. 1.

10. *Ragnars saga loðbrókar*, 4, cf. Saxo Grammaticus, *Danorum Regum Heromque Historia* ix. 4.12–13, 17.

11. *Ragnars saga loðbrókar*, 15, 16, cf. *Þáttr af Ragnars sonum*, 3, 'silken shirt'.

12. *ASC*, s.a. 871, 874–6, 878.

13. *Annals of Ulster*, s.a. 877.

14. *Annales Fuldenses*, s.a. 873.

15. For Ragnarr and his family, see Smyth 1977: 17–35, McTurk 2015 [1991]: 39–50.

16. *Chronicon Fontanellense*, s.a. 845.

17. Though it has often been claimed (e.g. Graham-Campbell 2001: 119, Ferguson 2010: 96), this was not the first recorded payment of official tribute to Northmen. Thus, *Annales Bertiniani*, s.a. 841: 'Danish pirates devastated and plundered along the banks of the Seine, or else took large payments and left them thoroughly terrified'. Again, *Annales Bertiniani*, s.a. 842: 'a fleet of Northmen made a surprise attack at dawn … [t]hey left nothing in it except for those buildings which they were paid to spare'. See, for this, Turner 2014: 18–19.

18. *Annales Bertiniani*, s.a. 845.

19. In Latin: *diffusa… sunt omnia vicera ejus in terram*, Heiric d'Auxerre, *Miracula sancti Germani*, cf. *Annales Xantenses*, s.a. 845, *Annales Bertiniani*, s.a. 845, Saxo Grammaticus, *Danorum Regum Heromque Historia* ix. 4.22.1–8.

20. The prose sagas do not mention Ragnarr raiding in this region, but Saxo Grammaticus mentions several episodes of raiding here – and even goes so far as to have him dying in snake-free Ireland (*Danorum Regum Heromque Historia*, ix. 4.38.1) – as does *Krákumál* (st. 21).

21. See, for this, McTurk 1976: 94–5, 121–3, 2015 [1991]: 1–6.

22. Abbo Cernuus, *Bella parisiacæ urbis* apud *PL*, cxxxii.

23. The Icelandic priest Ari Þórgilsson (1068–1148), known as 'the Learned', appears to be the first to provide the earliest known instance of the use of the names *Ragnarr* and *loðbrók* in combination in his *Íslendingabók*, written between 1120 and 1133. His great-grandmother was Guðrún Ósvífursdóttir, the heroine of *Laxdæla saga*. See, for this, McTurk 1976: 95.

24. McTurk 2015 [1991]: 1–50.

25. Saxo Grammaticus, *Danorum Regum Heromque Historia* ix. 4.15.4.

26. Ibid. ix 4.38, cf. Adam Bremensis, *Gesta Hammaburgensis ecclesiae pontificum* i §37, where the authors says: 'Inguar, *filius Lodparchi*, who everywhere tortured Christians to death'.

27. *Ragnars saga loðbrókar*, 15 Waggoner, cf. *Krákumál*, st. 27, Saxo Grammaticus, *Danorum Regum Heromque Historia* ix. 4.38–9. *Ragnars saga loðbrókar* is now regarded as one of the sagas about olden times, a legendary saga or *fornaldarsaga* (pl. *fornaldarsögur*), based as much on folktale and legend as on dimly remembered historical fact. Typically, the hero undertakes a series of exciting but improbable adventures, which involve raiding, killing and conquering. The supernatural plays an important part in *fornaldarsögur*, with the pagan Norse gods occasionally putting in an appearance, as do giants, trolls and other monsters, and, of course, dwarves, wizards and dragons. It also allows Sigurðr *Fáfnisbana*, the most famous of all Germanic heroes who would have lived in the fifth century (insofar as he can be dated at all), to father a daughter who would marry Ragnarr in the ninth century.

28. Saxo Grammaticus, *Danorum Regum Heromque Historia* ix. 5.5.2.

29. Frank 1984: 336–40, cf. Smyth 1977: chaps. 14 & 16. Note also in Old Norse poetry the eagle can be known as a 'corpse-scorer' (e.g. *Gunnlaugs saga ormstungu* 13).

30. *Annals of Ulster*, s.a. 841.

31. *Eyrbyggja saga*, 1.

32. *ASC*, s.a. 865.

33. *Annals of Saint Neots*, s.a. 878, cf. Asser, *Vita Alfredi Regis* 54B.

34. *ASC*, mss. B, C, D & E, s.a. 878.

35. *Encomium Emmæ Reginæ*, 2.9.

36. *Brennu-Njáls saga*, 157.

37. *Flateyjarbók*, ii. 186.

38. *Brennu-Njáls saga*, 157.

39. Op. cit.

40. Sigurðr's father was Hlöðver, who married Eðna Kjarvallsdóttir, the daughter of Kjarvall, the king of the Ívar. Eðna, as she is named in the *Brennu-Njáls saga*, is probably the Irish name Eithne. Kjarvall is the Cerball mac Dúnlainge of the Irish annals, who was, as the king of Dublin (r. 872–88), a major player in viking affairs in the latter years of the ninth century. He is mentioned in the opening chapter of the Icelandic *Landnámabók* as ruler of Dublin when Haraldr *hárfagri* ruled in Norway, though it should be noted that no Irish source claims him as such. The two branches of the ruling clan of Ívarr (*Uí Ímair*, children of Ívar, as the Irish called them), kings of Dublin and Limerick, were the descendants of the Dane Ívarr *inn beinlausi*, one of the sons of Ragnarr *loðbrók*. Alternatively, if we confine ourselves to Irish annalistic sources, Cerball is the king of Osraige, a native kingdom in the southeast of Ireland, and in one is described as 'a man who was worthy to possess all of Ireland because of the excellence of his form and his

countenance and his prowess' (*Fragmentary annals of Ireland*, §260). The facts, if that is what they are, can be made to fit either hypothesis, but go more generally with the second. So much for his ancestry and authority.

41. *Flateyjarbók*, ii. 186.
42. In Old Norse: *hrafna seðja, hrafna gleðja*, e.g. *Nornagests þáttr*, 6. The French structural anthropologist Claude Lévi-Strauss (1958: 224–5) proposed a theory that suggests the raven obtained mythic status because it was a mediator animal between life and death.
43. *Orkneyinga saga*, 22.
44. *Heimskringla: Haralds saga Sigurðarsonara*, 9.
45. Ibid. 22.
46. *Prose Edda: Gylfaginning*, 38.
47. *Grímnismál*, st. 20.
48. Heyerdahl & Lillieström 2001.
49. Ovid, *Metamorphoses* 2.536–65, 596–611.
50. *Iliad* 11.518, cf. 2.731, 4.194, 219.
51. Pindar, *Pythian Ode* 3.55–8.
52. Hyginus, *Poetic Astronomy* 2.14.

Appendix B: Mosfell Archaeological Project

1. Byock & Zori 2013: 126.
2. Ari Þorgilsson's *Íslendingabók* records that at the time of settlement, forests covered Iceland from the sea to the mountains. Pollen research has confirmed that about 25 per cent of Iceland would have been covered by relatively small birch (*Betel*) woods. As evident by the pollen record, Iceland was quickly deforested primarily to create pastureland for the settlers' cattle and sheep. But the Icelandic soils, geologically young and low in nutrients, were different from the Norwegian soils and erosion quickly set in with devastating effects. See, for this, Byock 2001: 56–9.
3. Hrísbrú means causeway or bridge (*bur*) made of branches of bushes (*his*) placed over swampy ground. The farm sits on a series of small knolls on the south slope of Mosfell mountain.
4. The longhouse was built before 940 and abandoned sometime in the eleventh century. The church was built in the late tenth or early eleventh century with a concentration of burials in the eleventh century. The Hulduhóll cremation took place in the late tenth or early eleventh century (Zori 2010: 311–15).
5. Byock & Zori 2013: 129.
6. Zori 2010: 431–40.
7. Adam Bremensis, *Gesta Hammaburgensis ecclesiae pontificum* iv §36.
8. Byock 2001: 67–8.

9. The Althingi (ON *Alþingi*, literary 'meeting of all') was Iceland's semi-democratic, quasi-parliamentary annual gathering of regional leaders and their retinues where laws were debated and revised, business deals arranged, conflicts mediated and grievances settled, often celebrated as the world's first democratic parliament (Byock 2001: 170–4). It met for two weeks around the summer solstice at Þingvellir, 'Thing-plains', a watered plain some fifty kilometres northeast of Reykjavík (British place names such as Dingwall in Cornwall, Thingwall in Cheshire, Tingwall in the Shetlands, and Tynwald in the Isle of Man have the same meaning, and are lexical borrowings from Old Norse). An elected official, the Lawspeaker mediated the yearly Althingi, recited one-third of the laws every year, but had no executive power. Outside of the Althingi the Lawspeaker held no power to make decisions or exercise authority and therefore possessed no power on the local level. Lawspeakers came from the most prominent and highly cultured families in Iceland. They served for a number of years. It should be noted that in Iceland there were three types of annual assemblies, including two regional assemblies held in the spring and the autumn, and the island-wide assembly, the *Alþingi*. Of course it is not easy in this first half of the twenty-first century to recapture the spirit of the early mediaeval period, yet so far as institutions are concerned we are its heirs. For all their glamour and glory the Athenian Assembly and the Roman Senate are mere names today, and the governments of Britain and France have their roots, not in the systems that flourished on the Acropolis or by the Tiber, but in those that were slowly and painfully evolved by Saxons, Franks and Northmen, in a stage of civilization which to the cultured Athenian or Roman would have appeared little, if at all, removed from barbarism.

10. *Egils saga Skallagrímssonar*, 79.

11. Ibid. 77, 79.

12. The Mosfell chieftains controlled the area known as Nesin (the Nesses), the headlands or promontories of the southern coastal region that stretched out from the valley's mouth past modern Reykjavík and farther west. The people of the Nesses are referred to in the sagas as the *Nesjamenn* ('the Men of the Nesses').

13. *Egils saga Skallagrímssonar*, 81.

14. Tjaldanes, the site of the mound, lies in the wide valley below Hrísbrú at a distance of about 900 metres. For the archaeological investigation of a mound associated with Egill Skallagrímsson, see Zori 2010: 502–4.

15. See, for this, Byock 1995. The site of the turf church at Hrísbrú is today called Kirkjuhóll, 'church knoll'. Around 130 or so years later, a new, timber/stave church was built about 500 metres to the east from the old one. In accordance with the saga information that bones were moved to the new churchyard, the archaeologists found several emptied graves in the old Hrísbrú graveyard. The emptied graves are witnessed by shafts containing small pieces of isolated human bone, apparently missed when the remains were removed from the grave. Such a

transfer of bones is consistent with accounts of exhumations found in the sagas and in *Grágás*, the oldest collection of Icelandic law (first complied in 1117/18 from oral laws). As noted, *Egils saga Skallagrímssonar* mentions the reburial of pagan ancestors at the Mosfell/Hrísbrú site.

16. According to the *Landnámabók*, Skapti's parentage is traced directly through six generations to Egill: Skapti – Æsa – Helga Þórsteinsdóttir – Geirlaug – Skúli – Þorsteinn – Egill. Skapti was a man involved in feuds, and in *Þorgils saga ok Hafliða*, he is credited with the famous statement: 'Costly would be all of Hafliði, if this should be the price of each limb' (*Þórgils saga ok Hafliða*, 31). The statement refers to the large sum demanded by Hafliði for the loss of a finger. This episode took place in 1121. The same Skapti is named by Ari Þórgilsson in *prestatál*, a list of important Icelandic priests in 1143.

17. *Egils saga Skallagrímssonar*, 86. For a full analysis of this particular account from *Egils saga Skallagrímssonar*, see Zori 2010: 514-19.

18. The earliest mention of Skapti at Mosfell is in *Þórgils Saga ok Hafliða*, where he appears at the end of the saga in 1121. The aforementioned register of priests also lists Skapti as one of the forty noteworthy and highborn priests in the year 1143. The historical authority of this document is substantial since scholars attribute it to the respected historian Ari Þórgilsson, who also wrote *Íslendingabók* between 1120 and 1133. Based on this basic chronology Icelandic scholars have suggested that the church at Hrísbrú was moved to Mosfell at some point between 1130 and 1160. See, for this, Zori 2010: 247–8.

19. *Eiríks saga rauða*, 8.

20. Byock 1993, 1995 (Paget's disease), Weinstein 2005 (skeletal fluorosis).

21. *Egils saga Skallagrímssonar*, 50.

22. Byock 1993: 30. The Icelandic term for *prima signatio* was *prímsigning*.

23. *Egils saga Skallagrímssonar*, 50.

24. Zori & Byock 2014: 45.

25. Ibid. 50.

26. Ibid. 78, cf. *Jomsvíkinga-saga*, 15 for Vagn Ákason, who had killed three men "by the time he was nine years old".

27. Thus, Turville-Petre calls Egill 'greatest of all the scalds' (1953: 40).

28. *Egils saga Skallagrímssonar*, 31.

29. Ibid. 40.

30. Kirkjuhóll cemetery, Burial 2.

31. *Beowulf*, ll. 1384–5 Heaney.

32. Önundr was related to the Norwegian king and future royal saint, Óláfr II Haraldsson: 'Önundr was the brother of Guðbjörg, who was the mother of Guðbrandr *kula* (Ball), who was the father of Ásta, the mother of king Óláfr the Saint' (*Grettis saga Ásmundarsonar*, 1). Before he had moved to Mosfell, Önundr

and his father Eilífr had been drawn into a famous feud recounted in *Brennu-Njáls saga* (75, 77) that results in the slaying of Njáll's good friend, Gunnarr Hámundarson of Hliðarendi in 992, a warrior without equal who disliked killing.

33. *Gunnlaugs saga ormstungu*, 13.
34. For nationalism and its effect on saga interpretation, see Byock 2001: 151-6.
35. Byock 2001: 43–62, Zori *et al.* 2013.

Appendix C: He, her, hero, heroine

1. *Brennu-Njáls saga*, 116. This phrase also appears in *Gísla saga Súrssonar* (19) and *Laxdæla saga* (65). Its use by Chaucer's Nun's Priest – Wommennes conseils been ful ofte colde / Women's counsels are very often fatal (l. 3256) – indicates that it may have been a common proverb.
2. *Laxdæla saga*, 48.
3. See, for this, Byock 2001: 196–203.
4. *Laxdæla saga*, 78.
5. *Heimskringla*: *Óláfs saga helga*, 123. Disguised as a vagrant, Ásbjörn Sigurðarson had decapitated, before Óláfr II Haraldsson, the royal steward Þórir *selr* (the Seal); the king was splattered with the steward's blood. This honour killing had not only earned him the king's utmost displeasure, but also the moniker *selsbani*, Slayer of Seal (ibid. 118, 120).
6. *Gísla saga Súrssonar*, 32.
7. Ibid. 37.
8. Christine de Pizan, *Le Livre de la cité des dames*, I.1.2.
9. Christine de Pizan, *Le trésor de la cité des dames*, chap. viii.
10. Christine de Pizan, *Ditié de Jehanne d'Arc*, st. 33, ll. 4–8 Kennedy.
11. Saxo Grammaticus, *Danorum Regum Heromque Historia* vii. 6.8.2.
12. Jesch 1991: 176–7.
13. Saxo Grammaticus, *Danorum Regum Heromque Historia* vii. 4.7.1–3.
14. In Latin: *virilem in virgine animum gerens*, ibid. ix. 4.2.1.
15. Ibid. ix. 4.2.1–11.4
16. Ibid. ix. 4.9.2.
17. *Sögubrot*, 6, 10.
18. Saxo Grammaticus, *Danorum Regum Heromque Historia* viii. 3.
19. *Cogadh Gáedhel re Gaillaibh*, 36.
20. *Laxdæla saga*, 35. See also Jesch 1991: 193–4, 199.
21. *Grænlendinga saga*, 7.
22. *Eiríks saga rauða*, 11.
23. *Grágás*, K 254.
24. Holmqvist-Larsen 1983: 24–8.
25. *Guta lag*, 21.12–23 Peel.

26. Ibid. 23.20–30 Peel.
27. Ibid. 1.3–9 Peel.
28. *Heimskringla*: *Óláfs saga helga*, 7, cf. *Guta saga*, 2.
29. *Heimskringla*: *Óláfs saga helga*, 192, cf. *Nóregs konunga tal*, 198–9.
30. For the possible visit of Óláfr Haraldsson to Gotland, see Peel 2010 [1999]: xxxvi–xl.
31. Denmark: grave BB from Bogøvej in Langeland, as well as the Gerdrup grave and grave A505 from Trekroner-Grydehøj, both in Sjælland (Gardeła 2013: 277–84); Norway: a grave from Løve, near Larvik in Vestfold, and grave 2 from the cemetery at Mårem, Telemark (ibid. 286–8). At the cemeteries in Kaupang, Vestfold, are at least thirteen out of a total of forty-one datable female graves that contained weapons, nine of which contained axe heads and brooches – one burial in particular (grave IXb) contained a Petersen type K axe head, which is categorized as a weapon not a tool (Furan 2009: 43–5). There are several examples from southern Sweden of female burials containing arrowheads (Gardeła 2013: 296).
32. Oseberg tapestry fragments nos. 1, 2 & 16. See, for this, Ingstad 1992: 176–85.
33. See, for this, Price 2008.
34. See, for this, Henriksen & Petersen 2013.
35. *Hákonarmál*, st. 11.
36. See, for this, Price 2002: 331–46.
37. *Darraðarljóð*, sts. 1–3 apud *Brennu-Njáls saga*, 157, cf. *Skjald* A I 419–21. The same concept is found in *Beowulf*, l. 697 Heaney, 'war-loom' (OE *wig-speða gewiofu*).
38. *Darraðarljóð*, st. 8, ll. 1–2, apud *Brennu-Njáls saga*, 157.
39. For an in-depth discussion on the *Darraðarljóð*, see Poole 1991: 116–56.
40. *Táin Bó Cúailnge*, 4.
41. *Heimskringla: Ynglinga saga*, 7.
42. See, for this, Clunies Ross 1994: 206–11, Jochens 1996: 73–4.
43. *Lokasenna*, st. 24.
44. *Völuspá*, sts. 19–20.
45. *Örvar-Odds saga*, 12. See also *Vatnsdæla saga*, 19 for the magic cloak of Hróðleifr woven by his sorceress mother "and which iron could not pierce", and *Brennu-Njáls saga*, 155 for Bróðir, who was "skilled in sorcery" and wore "armour which no iron could bite".
46. *Örvar-Odds saga*, 2.
47. *Hávamál*, st. 84 Hollander.
48. John Skylitzes, *Synopsis historiôn* 15.14 [305]). On Rus' warrior women, see Price 2002: 332.
49. Hjardar & Vike 2014: 104–5.
50. Ibid. 107–8.

Abbreviations

Ar.	Arabic
ASC	D. Whitelock, *Anglo-Saxon Chronicle* (London, 1961)
bk.	book
BMGS	*Byzantine and Modern Greek Studies* (Birmingham, 1975—)
BZ	*Byzantinische Zeitschrift* (Leipzig & Munich, 1892—)
c.	circa
cf.	compare
chap(s).	chapter(s)
CIL	T. Mommsen *et al.*, *Corpus Inscriptionum Latinarum* (Berlin, 1862—)
cod.	codex
CSHB	B.G. Niebuhr, *Corpus scriptorum historiae byzantinae* (Bonn, 1828–97)
d.	died
DOP	*Dumbarton Oaks Papers* (Washington DC, 1958—)
ed(s).	editor(s), edited (by)
EHD	D. Whitelock, *English Historical Documents*, vol. 1, c. 500–1042 (London, 1979)
fl.	floruit
fol(s).	folio(s)
Fr.	Frankish
Gr.	Greek
IG	*Inscriptiones Græcae* (Berlin, 1923–)
JRS	*Journal of Roman Studies*
L	Latin
l(l).	line(s)

MW	Middle Welsh
ms(s).	manuscript(s)
OE	Old English
OEN	Old East Norse
OES	Old East Slavonic
OI	Old Irish
ON	Old Norse
p.	page
PG	J-P. Migne, *Patrologiae cursus completus: Series græca*, 161 vols. (Paris, 1857–66)
PL	J-P. Migne, *Patrologiae cursus completus: Series latina*, 221 vols. (Paris, 1844–63)
pl.	plural
r.	recto
REB	*Revue des études byzantines* (Bucharest & Paris, 1944—)
rev.	revised (by)
rev. edn.	revised edition
s.a.	*sub anno* ('under the year' – for annals or chronicle references)
sg.	singular
Skjald	F. Jónsson, *Den norsk-islandske skjaldedigtning*, A I–II, B I–II (Köbenhavn, 1967–73 [1912–15])
st(s).	stanza(s)
trans(s).	translator(s)
v.	verso
vol.	volume
VV	*Varangian Voice*

Bibliography

Abels, R.P., 2008. 'Household men, mercenaries and vikings in Anglo-Saxon England', in J. France (ed.), *Mercenaries and Paid Men: The Mercenary Identity in the Middle Ages*. Leiden: E.J. Brill, 143–65.

Ahola, J. (PhD thesis), 2014. *Outlawry in the Icelandic Family Sagas*. Helsinki: University of Helsinki.

Alcock, L., 2003. *Kings and Warriors, Craftsmen and Priest*. Edinburgh: University of Edinburgh Press.

Andersen, B. and Andersen, E., 1989. *Råsejlet – Dragens Vinge*. Roskilde: Vikingeskibsmuseet.

Andersen, E., Crumlin-Pedersen, O., Vadstrup, S. and Vinner, M., 1997. Roar Ege. *Skuldelev 3 skibet som arkaologisk eksperiment*. Roskilde: Vikingeskibsmuseet.

Anderson, S.M. and Swenson, K. (eds.), 2002. *Cold Counsel. Women in Old Norse Literature and Mythology. A Collection of Essays*. London: Routledge.

Androshchuk, F., 2013. *Vikings in the East: Essays on Contacts along the Road to Byzantium (800–1100)*. Uppsala: Uppsala University Library (Studia Byzantina Upsaliensia).

Androshchuk, F., 2014. *Viking Swords: Swords and Social Aspects of Weaponry in Viking Age Societies*. Stockholm: Statens Historiska Museum.

Ardent du Picq, C., 1903 (trans. Col. J. Greely and Maj. R. Cotton 1920, repr. 1946). *Battle Studies: Ancient and Modern*. Harrisburg, PA: U.S. Army War College.

Auden, G.A., 1927. 'The strategy of Harold Hardrada in the invasion of 1066'. *Journal of the Society for Army Historical Research* 6: 214–21.

Bagge, S., 2005. 'Christianisation and state formation in early medieval Norway'. *Scandinavian Journal of History* 30: 107–34.

Bagge, S., 2006. 'The making of a missionary king: The medieval accounts of Olaf Tryggvason and the conversion of Norway'. *The Journal of English and Germanic Philology* 105/4: 473–513.

Bagge, S., 2010. *From Viking Stronghold to Christian Kingdom: State Formation in Norway, c. 900–1350*. Copenhagen: Museum Tusculanums Forlag.

Bagge, S., 2014. *Cross and Sceptre*. Princeton, NJ: Princeton University Press.

Bardill, J., 1999. 'The Great Palace of the Byzantine emperors and the Walker Trust Excavations'. *Journal of Roman Archaeology* 12: 216–30.

Baxter, S.D., 2007. *The Earls of Mercia: Lordship and Power in Late Anglo-Saxon England*. Oxford: Oxford University Press.

Baxter, S.D., 2009. 'Edward the Confessor and succession question', in R. Mortimer (ed.), *Edward the Confessor: The Man and the Legend*. Woodbridge: Boydell Press.

Beatson, P., 1998. 'Byzantine lamellar armour: conjectural reconstruction of a find from the Great Palace in Istanbul based on early mediaeval parallels'. *VV* 49: 3–8.

Beatson, P., 1999. 'A warrior with a "Danish axe" in a Byzantine ivory panel'. *VV* 52: 14–17.

Beatson, P., 2000a. 'Relics of the Varangians – Part 1'. *VV* 55: 14–16.

Beatson, P., 2000b. 'Relics of the Varangians – Part 2'. *VV* 56: 20–1.

Beatson, P., 2001a. 'Relics of the Varangians – Part 3'. *VV* 57: 16–20.

Beatson, P., 2001b. 'Relics of the Varangians – Part 4'. *VV* 59: 20–3.

Beeler, J., 1971. *Warfare in Feudal Europe 730–1200*. Ithaca, NY: Cornell University Press.

Benedikz, B.S., 1969. 'The evolution of the Varangian regiment in the Byzantine army'. *Byzantinische Zeitschrift* 62: 20–4.

Biddle, M. and Kjølbye-Biddle, B., 1992. 'Repton and the vikings'. *Antiquity* 66: 36–51.

Biddle, M. and Kjølbye-Biddle, B., 2001. 'Repton and the "great heathen army", 873–4', in J. Graham-Campbell, R. Hall, J. Jesch and D.N. Parsons (eds.), *Vikings and the Danelaw: Select Papers from the Proceedings of the Thirteenth Viking Congress*. Oxford: Oxbow, 45–96.

Birkenmeier, J.W., 2002. *The Development of the Komnenian Army*. Leiden: E.J. Brill.

Blaum, P.A., 1994. *The Days of the Warlords: A History of the Byzantine Empire, AD 969–991*. Lanham, MA: University Press of America.

Blöndal, S., 1939a. 'The last exploits of Harald Sigurdsson in Greek service: a chapter of the history of the Varangians'. *Classica et Mediaevalia* 2: 1–26.

Blöndal, S., 1939b. 'Nabites the Varangian'. *Classica et Mediaevalia* 2: 145–67.

Blöndal, S., 1954. *Væringjasaga*. Reykjavík: Ísafoldarprentsmiðja.

Blöndal, S., (trans., rev. and ed. B.S. Benedikz, 2007 [1978]). *The Varangians of Byzantium*. Cambridge: Cambridge University Press.

Bourke, J., 2000. *An Intimate History of Killing*. London: Granta.

Bozhkov, A., 1972. *The Miniatures of the Madrid Manuscript of Johannes Scylitzes*. Sofia: Bulgarian Academy of Sciences.

Bramley, V., 1995. *Two Sides of Hell*. London: Bloomsbury.

Breen, G., 1997. 'Personal names and the recreation of *berserkir* and *úlfhéðnar*'. *Studia Anthroponomica Scandinavica* 15.

Breen, G., 1999. 'The wolf is at the door'. *Arkiv for nordisk filologi* 114: 31–43.

Bridgeford, A., 2004. *1066: The Hidden History of the Bayeux Tapestry*. London: Fourth Estate.

Brøgger, A.W. and Shetelig, H., 1951. *Viking Ships, their Ancestry and Evolution*. Ósló: Dreyer.

Brown, R.A., 1980. 'The battle of Hastings'. *Proceedings of the Battle Conference on Anglo-Norman Studies* 3: 1–12.

Buckler, G., 1968. *Anna Comnena, a Study*. Oxford: Clarendon Press.

Bugarsky, I., 2005. 'A contribution to the study of lamellar armours'. *Starinar* 55: 161–79.

Burton, R.F., 1884. *The Book of the Sword: Being a History of the Sword and its Use in all Countries, from the Earliest Times*. London: Chatto & Windus.

Burton, R.F., 1911. *The Sentiment of the Sword*. London: Horace Cox.

Byock, J.L., 1982. *Feud in the Icelandic Saga*. Berkeley/Los Angeles, CA: University of California Press.

Byock, J.L., 1993. 'The skull and bones in *Egil's Saga*: a viking, a grave, and Paget's Disease'. *Viator: A Journal of Medieval and Renaissance Studies* 24: 23–50.

Byock, J.L., 1995. 'Egil's bones'. *Scientific American* 272: 82–7.

Byock, J.L., 2001. *Viking Age Iceland*. London: Penguin.

Byock, J.L., 2003. 'Feuding in Viking-Age Iceland's Great Village', in W.C. Brown and P. Górecki (eds.), *Conflict in Medieval Europe: Changing Perspectives on Society and Culture*. Farnham: Ashgate Publishing, 229–41.

Byock, J.L., 2004. 'Social memories and the sagas: the case of *Egils saga*'. *Scandinavian Studies* 76/3: 299–316.

Byock, J.L., Walker, P., Erlandson, J., Holck, P., Zori, D.M., Guðmundsson, M. and Tveskov, M., 2005. 'A Viking-age valley in Iceland: the Mosfell Archaeological Project'. *Medieval Archaeology* 49: 195–218.

Byock, J.L. and Zori, D.M., 2013. 'Viking archaeology, sagas, and interdisciplinary research in Iceland's Mosfell Valley'. *Backdirt – Annual Review of the Costen Institute of Archaeology at UCLA* 124–41.

Campbell, M.W., 1984. 'An inquiry into the troop strength of King Harald Hardrada's invasion fleet of 1066'. *American Neptune* 44: 96–102.

Cavill, P., 2015. 'The battle of *Brunanburh* in 937: Battlefield despatches', in S.E. Harding, D. Griffiths and E. Royles (eds.), *In Search of the Vikings: Interdisciplinary Approaches to the Scandinavian Heritage of North-West England*. Boca Raton, FL: CRC Press.

El Cheikh, N.M., 2004. *Byzantium Viewed by the Arabs*. Cambridge, MA: Harvard University Press.

Chenery, C.A., Evans, J.A., Score, D., Boyle, A. and Chenery, S.R., 2014. 'A boatload of Vikings?' *Journal of the North Atlantic* Special Volume 7: 43–53.

Christensen, E., 2006 [2002]. *The Norsemen in the Viking Age*. Oxford: Blackwell Publishing.

Ciggaar, K.N., 1974. 'L'émigration anglaise a Byzance apres 1066'. *REB* 32: 301–42.

Ciggaar, K.N., 1981. 'England and Byzantium on the eve of the Norman Conquest'. *Anglo-Norman Studies* 5: 78–96.

Ciggaar, K.N., 1996. *Western Travellers to Constantinople: The West & Byzantium, 976–1204*. Leiden: E.J. Brill.

Clunies Ross, M. 1994. *Prolonged Echoes: Old Norse Myths in Medieval Northern Society, Volume I: The Myths*. Odense: Odense University Press.

Clunies Ross, M., 2005. *A History of Old Norse Poetry and Poetics*. Cambridge: D.S. Brewer.

Clunies Ross, M., 2010. *The Cambridge Introduction to the Old Norse–Icelandic Saga*. Cambridge: Cambridge University Press.

Cooper, D., Guðmundsson, R. and Muir, T., 2005. *Destination Viking SAGALANDS: The Icelandic Sagas and Oral Tradition in the Nordic World*. Reykjavík: The Institute of Regional Development in Iceland.

Cooper, J. (ed.), 1993. *The Battle of Maldon: Fiction and Fact*. London: Hambledon Continuum.

Coupland, S., 1998. *From Poachers to Gamekeepers: Scandinavian Warlords and Carolingian Kings, Early Medieval Europe*. Oxford: Oxford University Press.

Crumlin-Pedersen, O., 1997a. 'Large and small warships of the North', in A. Nørgård Jørgensen and B.L. Clausen (eds.), *Military Aspects of Scandinavian Society in a European Perspective, AD 1–1300*. Copenhagen: National Museum, 184–94 (Studies in Archaeology and History 2).

Crumlin-Pedersen, O., 1997b. *Viking-Age Ships and Shipbuilding in Hedeby/ Haithabu and Schleswig*. Schleswig/Roskilde: Wikingermuseum Haithabu/ Vikingeskibsmuseet Roskilde.

Crumlin-Pedersen, O., 2002. 'Splendour versus duty – 11th century warships in the light of history and archaeology', in A. Nørgård Jørgensen, J. Lind, L. Jørgensen and B.L. Clausen (eds.), *Maritime Warfare in Northern Europe. Technology, Organisation, Logistics and Administration 500 BC – 1500 AD*. Copenhagen: National Museum, 257–70.

Crumlin-Pedersen, O. and Olsen, O. (eds.), 2002. *The Skuldelev Ships I. Topography, Archaeology, History, Conservation and Display*. Roskilde: Vikingeskibsmuseet (Ships and Boats of the North 4:1)

D'Amato, R., 2005. 'A *prôtospatharios*, *magistros*, and *stratêgos autokratôr* of 11th century'. *Porphyra* supplemento 4: 1–75.

D'Amato, R., 2010. *The Varangian Guard 988–1453*. Oxford: Osprey (Men-at-Arms 459).

D'Amato, R., 2012. *Byzantine Imperial Guardsmen 925–1025: The* Tághmata *and Imperial Guard*. Oxford: Osprey (Elite 187).

D'Amato, R., 2013 'The betrayal: military iconography and archaeology in the Byzantine paintings of the 11th – 15th c. AD representing the arrest of our Lord'. *Wratislavia Antiqua* 18: 69–96.

Daly, K.N., 2010 (3rd ed.). *Norse Mythology, A to Z*. New York: Chelsea House.

Danylenko, A., 2004. 'The name "Rus' ": In search of a new dimension'. *Jahrbücher für Geschichte Osteuropas* 52: 1–32.

Dawkins, R.M., 1947. 'The later history of the Varangian Guard: some notes'. *JRS* 37: 39–46.

Dawson, T., 1992. 'The "Varangian Rhomphaia": a cautionary tale'. *VV* 22: 28–31.

Dawson, T., 1995. 'The myth of purple pants'. *VV* 37: 24–6.

Dawson, T., 1998. '*Kremasmata, Kabadion, Klibanion*: some aspects of middle Byzantine military equipment reconsidered'. *BMGS* 22: 38–50.

Dawson, T., 2007. '"Fit for the task": equipment sizes and the transmission of military lore, sixth to tenth centuries'. *BMGS* 31: 1–12.

Dawson, T., 2009. 'The *Walpurgis Fechtbuch*: an inheritance of Constantinople?'. *Arms & Armour* 6: 79–92.

Dawson, T., 2013. *Armour Never Wearies: Scale and Lamellar Armour in the West, From the Bronze Age to the 19th Century*. Stroud: Spellmount.

DeVries, K., 2003 [1999]. *The Norwegian Invasion of England in 1066*. Woodbridge: Boydell Press.

Decker, M.J., 2013. *The Byzantine Art of War*. Yardley, PA: Westholme.

Dennis, C., 2009. 'The strange death of King Harold II: propaganda and the problem of legitimacy in the aftermath of the battle of Hastings'. *The Historian* Spring 2009: 14–18.

Dennis, G.T., 1997. 'The Byzantines in battle', in K. Tsiknakes (ed.), *Το εμπόλεμο Βυζάντιο, 9 – 12 αι*. Athens: Εθνικό Ιδρυμα Ερευνών, 165–78.

Dijkstra, J. (MA thesis), 2013. *Rulers of Jorvik: A Critical Examination of the Contemporary, Anglo-Norman, and Scandinavian Sources Pertaining to the Rulers of Anglo-Scandinavian York*. Utrecht: University of Utrecht.

Dinter, E., 1985. *Hero or Coward: Pressures Facing the Soldier in Battle*. London: Frank Cass.

Divjak, A., 2014. 'Constantinople – a proto-tourist destination in medieval Icelandic tradition?' *Quaestus* 5: 48–65.

Dobat, A.S., 2015. 'Viking stranger-kings: the foreign as a source of power in Viking Age Scandinavia, or, why there was a peacock in the Gokstad ship burial?' *Early Medieval Europe* 23/2: 161–201.

Docherty, F., 2013. *The Fighting Seax: The History and Combat Methods of the Fighting Seax*. London: Seax Publishers.

Downham, C., 2004. 'Eric Bloodaxe – axed? The mystery of the last Scandinavian king of York'. *Mediaeval Scandinavia* 14: 51–77.

Downham, C., 2007. *Viking Kings of Britain and Ireland: The Dynasty of Ívarr to AD 1014*. Edinburgh: Dunedin Academic Press.

DuBois, T.A., 1999. *Nordic Religions in the Viking Age*. Philadelphia, PA: University of Pennsylvania Press.

Duczko, W., 2004. *Viking Rus': Studies on the Presence of Scandinavians in Eastern Europe*. Leiden: E.J. Brill.

Duczko, W., 2014. 'Viking-age Wolin (Wollin) in the Norse context of the southern coast of the Baltic Sea'. *Scripta Islandica* 65: 143–51.

Dumézil, G., 1973 (trans. and ed. E. Haugen). *Gods of the Ancient Northmen*. Berkeley/Los Angeles, CA: University of California Press

Durham, K., 2002. *Viking Longship*. Oxford: Osprey (New Vanguard 47).

Earle, T., 1997. *How Chiefs Came to Power: The Political Economy in Prehistory*. Stanford, CA: Stanford University Press.

Ellis Davidson, H.R., 1962. *Swords in Anglo-Saxon England*. Oxford: Oxford University Press.

Ellis Davidson, H.R., 1976. *The Viking Road to Byzantium*. London: Allen & Unwin.

Ellis Davidson, H.R., 1986. 'Shape-changing in the Old Norse sagas', in C. Otten (ed.), *A Lycanthropy Reader*. Syracuse, NY: Jefferson.

Erkal, N., 2011. 'The corner of the Horn: an architectural review of the leaded magazine in İstanbul'. *METU JFA* 28/1: 197–227.

Etchingham, C., 2014. 'Names for the Vikings in Irish annals', in J. V. Sigurðsson and T. Bolton, (eds.), *Celtic-Norse Relationships in the Irish Sea in the Middle Ages 800–1200*. Leiden: E.J. Brill, 23–38.

Edberg, R., 2009. 'Experimental "viking voyages" on eastern European rivers 1983–2006'. *Situne Dei* 35–46.

Fabing, H.D., 1956. 'On going berserk: a neurochemical inquiry'. *Scientific Monthly* 83: 232–7.

Faundez Rojas, G.A. (MA thesis), 2012. *'The English Exodus to Ionia': The Identity of the Anglo-Saxon Varangians in the Service of Alexios Comnenos I (1081–1118)*. Arlington, VA: Marymount University.

Featherstone, M., 2006. 'The Great Palace as reflected in the *De ceremoniis*'. *Byzas* 5: 47–6.

Fell, C., 1974. 'The Icelandic saga of Edward the Confessor: its version of the Anglo-Saxon emigration to Byzantium'. *Anglo-Saxon England* 3: 179–96.

Fields, N., 2017. *God's City: Byzantine Constantinople*. Barnsley: Pen & Sword.

Flori, J., 2007. *Bohémond d'Antioche, chevalier d'aventure*. Paris: Éditions Payot-Rivages.

Foot, S., 2011. *Æthelstan: The First King of England*. New Haven, NJ: Yale University Press.

Foote, P.G. and Wilson, D.M., 1970. *The Viking Achievement: The Society and Culture of Early Medieval Scandinavia*. London: Sidgwick & Jackson.

Frank, R., 1984. 'Viking atrocity and skaldic verse: the rite of the bloodeagle'. *English Historical Review* 99: 332–43.

Franklin, S. and Shepard, J., 1996. *The Emergence of Rus', 750–1200*. London: Longman (Longman History of Russia, vol. 1).

Frye, R.N. and Blake, R.P., 1949. 'Some notes on the *Risala* of Ibn-Fadlan'. *Byzantina Metabyzantina* 2: 7–37.

Fuglesang, S.H., 1986. 'Ikonographie der Skandinavischen runensteine', in H. Roth (ed.), *Zum Problem der Deutung frühmittelalterlicher Bildinhalt*. Sigmaringen, 183–210.

Fuglesang, S.H., 1993. 'Viking art', in P. Pulsiano (ed.), *Medieval Scandinavia. An Encyclopaedia*. New York/London, 694–700.

Fuglesang, S.H., 1998. 'Swedish runestones of the eleventh century: ornament and dating', in K. Düwel (ed.), *Runeninschriften als Quellen interdisziplinärer Forschung*. Berlin: De Gruyter, 197–218 (Ergänzungsbände zum Reallexikon der Germanischen Altertumskunde, 15).

Furan, N.P.F. (MA thesis), 2009. *Våpnenes biografier – en fruktbar tilnærmning til våpengraver i vikingetid?* Ósló: University of Ósló.

Ferguson, F., 2010. *The Vikings: A History*. London: Penguin.

Gaiman, N., 2017. *Norse Mythology*. London: Bloomsbury.

Gardeła, L., 2013. '"Warrior-women" in Viking age Scandinavia? A preliminary archaeological study'. *Analecta Archaeologica Ressoviensia* 8: 273–314.

Garipzanov, I. and Tolochko, O. (eds.), 2011. *Early Christianity on the Way from the Varangians to the Greeks*. Kiev: Institute of Ukrainian History (Ruthenica Supplementum 4).

Gelsinger, B., 1988. 'The battle of Stamford Bridge and the battle of Jaffa'. *Scandinavian Studies* 60: 13–23.

Genç, U., 2010. *The Golden Horn Chain*. Istanbul: Askeri Müze ve Kültür Sitesi Komutanlığı.

Godfrey, J., 1977. 'The defeated Anglo-Saxons take service with the eastern emperor'. *Proceedings of the Battle Conference on Anglo-Norman Studies* 1: 63–74.

Golden, P.B., 2007. 'The conversion of the Khazars to Judaism', in P.B. Golden, H. Ben-Shammai and A. Róna-Tas (eds.), *The World of the Khazars: New Perspectives*. Leiden: E.J. Brill, 123–62.

Grabbar, A. and Manoussacas, M. (eds.), 1979. *L'llustration du Manuscript de Skylitzes de la Bibliothèque Nationale de Madrid*. Venise: Institut Hellénique d' Études Byzantines et Post-byzantines de Venise.

Graham-Campbell, J., 2001 (3rd edn.). *The Viking World*. London: Frances Lincoln.

Griffith, P., 1998 [1995]. *The Viking Art of War*. London: Greenhill Books.

Guilland, R., 1959. 'La chaine de la Corne d'Or'. *Etudes Byzantines* 263–97.

Haldon, J.F., 1999. *Warfare, State and Society in the Byzantine World, 565–1204*. London: University College London Press.

Haldon, J.F., 2000. *The Byzantine Wars: Battle and Campaigns of the Byzantine Era*. Stroud: Tempus Publishing.

Haldon, J.F., 2003. *Byzantium at War, 600–1453*. London: Routledge.

Bibliography   341

Haldon, J.F. (ed.), 2007. *Byzantine Warfare*. Burlington, VT: Ashgate Publishing.

Hale, J.R., 1998. 'The viking longship'. *Scientific American* 278: 56–63.

Hall, R., 2007. *Exploring the World of the Vikings*. London: Thames & Hudson.

Halsall, G., 1992. 'Playing by whose rules? A further look at Viking atrocity in the ninth century'. *Medieval History* 2/2: 3–12.

Halsall, G., 2003. *Warfare and Society in the Barbarian West, 450–900*. London: Routledge.

Harris, J., 2001. 'Looking back on 1204: Nicetas Choniates in Nicaea'. *Mésogeios* 12: 117–24.

Harrison, M., 1999 [1993]. *The Viking Hersir, 793–1066 AD*. Oxford: Osprey (Warrior 3).

Hazzard Cross, S. 1929. 'Yaroslav the Wise in Norse tradition'. *Speculum* 4/2: 177–97.

Head, C., 1977. 'Alexios Comnenos and the English'. *Byzantion* 47: 186–98.

Heath, I., 1994 [1979]. *Byzantine Armies, 886–1118*. Oxford: Osprey (Men-at-Arms 89).

Hedenstierna-Jonson, C. (PhD thesis), 2006. *The Birka Warrior: The Material Culture of a Martial Society*. Stockholm: Stockholm University.

Hedenstierna-Jonson, C., 2009. 'Rus', Varangians and Birka warriors', in L. Holmqvist Olausson and M. Olausson (eds.), *The Martial Society: Aspects of Warriors, Fortifications and Social Change in Scandinavia*. Stockholm: Stockholm University Press, 159–78.

Helms, M.W., 1993. *Craft and the Kingly Ideal. Art, Trade, and Power*. Austin, TX: University of Texas Press.

Henriksen, M.B. and Petersen, P.V., 2013. 'Valkyriefund'. *SKALK* 2: 3–10.

Heyerdahl, T. and Lillieström, P., 2001. *Jakten på Odin – På sporet av vå fortid*. Óslò: Stemersens forlag.

Hjardar, K. and Vike, V., 2014. *Vikinger i krig*. Århus: Turbine Forlaget.

Hill, J., 1993. 'Pilgrimage and prestige in the Icelandic sagas'. *The Saga-Book of the Viking Society* 23: 433–53.

Holck, P, 2006. 'The Oseberg ship burial, Norway: new thoughts on the skeletons from the grave mound'. *European Journal of Archaeology* 9/2–3: 185–210.

Hoffmeyer, A.B., 1966. 'Military equipment in the Byzantine manuscript of Skylitzes in Biblioteca Nacional in Madrid'. *Gladius* 5: 7–160.

Hollister, C. Warren, 1998 [1962]. *Anglo-Saxon Military Institutions: On the Eve of the Norman Conquest*. Oxford: Sandpiper Books.

Holmes, C., 2005. *Basil II and the Governance of Empire (976–1025)*. Cambridge: Cambridge University Press.

Holmqvist-Larsen, N.H., 1983. *Møer, skjoldmøer og krigere*. Copenhagen: Museum Tusculanums Forlag.

Hooper, N., 1985. 'The housecarls in England in the eleventh century'. *Anglo-Norman Studies* 7: 161–76.

Horn, B., 2007/8. '"Love 'em or hate 'em": learning to live with elites'. *Canadian Military Journal* 8/4: 32–43.

Hraundal, T.J. (PhD thesis), 2013. *The Rus' in Arabic sources: Cultural Contacts and Identity*. Bergen: University of Bergen.

Hudson, B.T., 2005. *Viking Pirates and Christian Princes: Dynasty, Religion, and Empire in the North Atlantic*. Oxford: Oxford University Press.

Ingstad, A.S., 1992. 'Hva har tekstilene vært brukt til?', in A.E. Christensen (ed.), *Osebergdronningens Grav*. Ósló: Chr. Schiebsteds Forlag, 176–257.

Jacoby, D., 2014. *Travellers, Merchants and Settlers in the Eastern Mediterranean, 11th – 14th Centuries*. Farnham: Ashgate Publishing (Variorum Collection Studies series: CS1045).

Jakobsson, Á., 2013. 'Image is everything: The *Morkinskinna* account of king Sigurðr of Norway's journey to the Holy Land'. *Parergon* 30/1: 121–40.

Jakobsson, S., 2008. 'The schism that never was: Old Norse views on Byzantium and Russia'. *Byzantino-Slavica* 66: 173–88.

Jansson, S.B.F., 1962 (trans. P.G. Foote). *The Runes of Sweden*. London: Phoenix.

Jansson, S.B.F., 1987 (trans. P.G. Foote). *Runes in Sweden*. Stockholm: Gidlunds.

Jesch, J., 1991. *Women in the Viking Age*. Woodbridge: Boydell Press.

Jesch, J., 2002. 'Eagles, ravens and wolves: beasts of battle, symbols of victory and death', in J. Jesch (ed.), *The Scandinavians from the Vendel Period to the Tenth Century: An Ethnographic Perspective*. San Marino.

Jesch, J., 2008 (rev. edn.). *Ships and Men in the Late Viking Age: The Vocabulary of Runic Inscriptions and Skaldic Verse*. Woodbridge: Boydell Press.

Jesch, J., 2009. 'The warrior ideal in the late Viking age', in L. Holmquist Olausson and M. Olausson (eds.), *The Martial Society: Aspects on Warriors, Fortifications and Social Change in Scandinavia*. Stockholm: Stockholm University Press, 71–8.

Jesch, J., 2013. 'Earl Rögnvaldr of Orkney, a poet of the Viking Diaspora'. *Journal of the North Atlantic* Special Volume 4: 154–60.

Jochens, J., 1996. *Old Norse Images of Women*. Philadelphia, PA: University of Pennsylvania Press.

Jochens, J., 1998. *Women in Old Norse Society*. Ithaca, NY: Cornell University Press.

Jones, G., 2001 [1984] (2nd edn.). *A History of the Vikings*. Oxford: Oxford University Press.

Kastholm, O.T., 2007. 'Viking age iconography and the square sail'. *Maritime Archaeology Newsletter from Denmark* 22: 8–12.

Kastholm, O.T., 2011. 'The rigging of the Viking Age warship: the Skuldelev find and the ship motifs', in L. Boye (ed.), *The Iron Age on Zealand: Status and Perspectives*. Copenhagen: The Royal Society of Northern Antiquities, 175–83 (Nordiske Fortidsminder, ser. C, vol. 8).

Kellett, A., 1982. *Combat Motivation: The Behavior of Soldiers in Battle*. London: Kluwer-Nijhoff.

Kellett, A., 1987. 'Combat motivation', in G. Belenky (ed.), *Contemporary Studies in Combat Psychiatry*. London: Greenwood.

Kendrick, T.D., 1930. *A History of the Vikings*. London: Methuen & Co.

Kim Siddorn, J., 2000. *Viking Weapons & Warfare*. Stroud: Tempus Publishing.

King, A., 2013. *Combat Soldier: Infantry Tactics and Cohesion in the Twentieth and Twenty-First Centuries*. Oxford: Oxford University Press.

Kitchen, M., 1996. 'Elites in military history', in A. Hamish Ion, K. Neilson and R. Legault (eds.), *Elite Military Formations in War and Peace*. Westport, CT: Praeger, 7–30.

Kitzler, L., 1997. *Rapport från utgrävningen av Garnisonenpå Björkö*. Stockholm: Stockholms universitet.

Koch, J.T., 1997. *The Gododdin of Aneirin: Text and Context from Dark Age North Britain*. Cardiff: University of Wales Press.

Koestler, A., 1976. *The Thirteenth Tribe: The Khazar Empire and its heritage*. London: Hutchinson

Kopytoff, I., 1986. 'The cultural biography of things: commoditization as process', in A. Appadurai (ed.), *The Social Life of Things. Commodities in Cultural Perspective*. Cambridge: Cambridge University Press, 64–91.

Lévi-Strauss, C., 1958. *Anthropologie structurale*. Paris: Éditions Plon.

Lévi-Strauss, C., 1962. *Le Totémisme aujourd'hui*. Paris: PUF.

Liberman, A., 2005. 'Berserks in history and legend'. *Russian History* 32: 401–12.

Liebeschuetz, J.H.W.G., 2003. *The Decline and fall of the Roman City*. Oxford: Oxford University Press.

Lind, J.H., 2011. ' "Vikings" and the Viking Age', in N. Yu. Gvozdetskaja *et al.* (eds.), *Stanzas of Friendship: Studies in Honour of Tatjana N. Jackson*. Moscow: Dmitriy Pozharskiy University, 201–22.

Lindow, J., 1976. *Comitatus, Individual and Honor: Studies in North Germanic Institutional Vocabulary*. Berkeley, CA: University of California Publications in Linguistics.

Livingston, M. (ed.), 2011. *The Battle of Brunanburh: A Casebook*. Exeter: University of Exeter Press.

Loe, L., Boyle, A., Webb, H. and Score, D., 2014. *'Given to the Ground': A Viking Age Mass Grave on Ridgeway Hill, Weymouth*. Oxford: Oxford Archaeology and Dorset Natural History and Archaeological Society (DNHAS Monograph 22).

Löfving, C., 1991. 'Who ruled the region east of the Skagerrak in the eleventh century?', in R. Samson (ed.), *Social Approaches to Viking Studies*. Glasgow: Cruithne Press, 147–56.

Logan, F.D., 1991 (2nd edn.). *The Vikings in History*. London: Routledge.

Loud, G.A., 2000. I*he Age of Robert of Guiscard: Southern Italy and the Norman Conquest*. London: Longman.

Lund, A.B. (MA thesis), 2016. *Women and Weapons in the Viking Age*. Aarhus: Aarhus University (http://www.academia.edu/28281242/).

Lund, J., 2008. 'Banks, borders and bodies of water in a Viking Age mentality'. *Journal of Wetland Archaeology* 8: 53–72.

Lund, N., 1985. 'The armies of Swein Forkbeard and Cnut: *leding* or *lið*?' *Anglo-Saxon England* 15: 105–18.

Lund, N., 1996. *Lið, leding og landeværn*. Roskilde: Vikingeskibshallen.

Lund, N., 1997. 'Is *leidang* a Nordic or European phenomenon?', in A. Nørgård Jørgensen and B.L. Clausen (eds.), *Military Aspects of Scandinavian Society in a European Perspective, AD 1–1300*. Copenhagen: National Museum, 195–9 (Studies in Archaeology and History 2).

Lunde, P. and Stone, C., 2012. *Ibn Fadlan and the Land of Darkness: Arab Travellers in the Far North*. London: Penguin.

McLaughlin, M., 1990. 'The woman warrior: gender, warfare and society in medieval Europe'. *Women's Studies* 17: 193–209.

McLynn, F., 1999 (2nd ed.). *1066: The Year of the Three Battles*. London: Pimlico.

McNulty, J.B., 1980. 'The Lady Ælfgyva in the Bayeux Tapestry'. *Speculum* 55: 659–68.

McTurk, R.W., 1976. 'Ragnarr *loðbrók* in the Irish annals?', in B. Almqvist and D. Greene (eds.), *Proceeding of the Seventh Viking Congress, Dublin 1973*. Dublin, 83–123.

McTurk, R.W. (ed.), 2007 [2005]. *A Companion to Old Norse–Icelandic Literature and Culture*. Oxford: Blackwell Publishing.

McTurk, R.W., 2015 [1991]. *Studies in "Ragnars Saga Loðbrókar" and its Major Scandinavian Analogues*. Oxford: Society for the Study of Mediæval Languages and Literatures (Medium Ævum Monographs XV).

Marren, P., 2006. *Battles of the Dark Ages: British Battlefields AD 410 to 1065*. Barnsley: Pen & Sword.

Marsden, J., 2007. *Harald Hardrada: The Warrior's Way*. Stroud: Sutton Publishing.

Marshall, S.L.A., 2000 [1947]. *Men against Fire: The Problem of Battle Command*. Norman, OK: University of Oklahoma Press.

Martin, J., 1986. *Treasure of the Land of Darkness: The Fur Trade and its Significance for Medieval Russia*. Cambridge: Cambridge University Press.

Mason, E., 2003. *The House of Godwin: The History of a Dynasty*. London: Hambledon Continuum.

Miller, W., 1908. *The Latins in the Levant: A History of Frankish Greece 1204–1566*. London: John Murray.

Molke, E., 1985 (trans. P.G. Foote). *Runes and their Origin, Denmark and Elsewhere*. Copenhagen.

Montgomery, J.E., 2000. 'Ibn Fadlan and the Rusiyyah'. *Journal of Arabic & Islamic Studies* 3: 1–25.

Morillo, S., 1997 [1994]. *Warfare under the Anglo-Norman Kings, 1066–1135* Woodbridge: Boydell Press.

Morillo, S., 2008. 'Mercenaries, Mamluks and militia: Towards a cross-cultural typology of military service', in J. France (ed.), *Mercenaries and Paid Men: The Mercenary Identity in the Middle Ages*. Leiden: E.J. Brill, 243–59.

Mühle, E., 1991. *Die Städtischen Handelszentren der nordwestlichen Rus'*. Stuttgart.

Myklebus, M., 1997. *Óláf: Viking and Saint*. Ósló: Norwegian Council for Cultural Affairs.

Nicol, D.M., 1974. 'Byzantium and England'. *Balkan Studies* 15: 179–203.

Noonan, T.S., 1986. 'Why the Vikings first came to Russia'. *Jahrbücher für Geschichte Osteuropas* 34: 321–48.

Noonan, T.S., 1987. 'The monetary history of Kiev in the pre-Mongol period'. *Harvard Ukrainian Studies* vol. XI, no. 3/4: 384–443.

Noonan, T.S., 1991. 'The Vikings and Russia: some new directions and approaches to an old problem', in R. Samson (ed.), *Social Approaches to Viking Studies*. Glasgow: Cruithne Press, 201–6.

Noonan, T.S., 1997. 'Scandinavians in European Russia', in P.H. Sawyer (ed.), *The Oxford Illustrated History of the Vikings*. Oxford: Oxford University Press, 134–55.

Noonan, T.S., 1998. *The Islamic World, Russia and the Vikings, 750–900: The Numismatic Evidence*. Burlington, VT: Ashgate Publishing.

Nordeide, S.W., 2006. 'Thor's hammer in Norway. A symbol of reaction against the Christian cross?, in A. Andrén (ed.), *Old Norse Religion in Long-term Perspectives*. Lund: Nordic Academic Press, 218–23.

Nosov, E.N., 1994. 'The emergence and development of Russian towns: some outline ideas'. *Archæologia Polona* 32: 185–96.

Nosov, E.N., 1998. 'The Varangian problem', in A. Wesse (ed.), *Studien zur Archäologie des Ostseeraumes*. Neumünster, 61–5.

Novello, G., 2007. 'Giorgio Maniace'. *Porphyra* 9: 83–99.

Nurmann, B., Schulze, C. and Verhülsdonk, T., 1999 [1997]. *The Vikings: Recreated in Colour Photographs*. Marlborough: Crowood Press (Europa Militaria Special 6).

O'Connell, R.L., 1989. *Of Arms and Men: A History of War, Weapons, and Aggression*. Oxford: Oxford University Press.

O'Donoghue, H., 2004. *Old Norse–Icelandic Literature: A Short Introduction*. Oxford: Blackwell Publishing.

Oakeshott, R.E., 1991. *Records of the Medieval Sword*. Woodbridge: Boydell Press.

Oakeshott, R.E., 1994 [1960]. *The Archaeology of Weapons*. Woodbridge: Boydell Press.

Obolensky, D., 1994. *Byzantium and the Slavs*. Yonkers, NY: Saint Vlademir's Seminary Press.

Ostrowski, D., 1999. 'Who are the Rus' and why did they emerge?' *Palaeoslavic* 7: 307–12.

Oxenstierna, E., 1965 (trans. and ed. C. Hutter). *The Norsemen*. Greenwich, CT: New York Graphic Society.

Page, R.I., 2014 [1995]. *Chronicles of the Vikings: Records, Memorials and Myths*. London: British Museum.

Palsson, H. and Edwards, P., 1989. *Vikings in Russia: Yngvar's Saga and Eymund's Saga*. Edinburgh: University of Edinburgh Press.

Pearce, M., 2013. 'The spirit of the sword and spear'. *Cambridge Archaeological Journal* 23/1: 55–67.

Peel, C. (trans. and ed.), 2009. *Guta Lag: The Laws of the Gotlanders*. London: University College London Press (Viking Society for Northern Research Text Series XIX).

Peel, C. (ed.), 2010 [1999]. *Guta Saga: The History of the Gotlanders*. London: University College London Press (Viking Society for Northern Research Text Series XII).

Peel, C., 2015. *Guta Lag and Guta Saga: The Laws and History of the Gotlanders*. London: Routledge.

Peirce, I.G., 1987. 'Arms, armour and warfare in the eleventh century'. *Anglo-Norman Studies* 10: 237–57.

Peirce, I.G. and Oakeshott, R.E., 2002. *Swords of the Viking Age*. Woodbridge: Boydell Press.

Pentcheva, B.V., 2014 [2006]. *Icons and Power: The Mother of God in Byzantium*. University Park, PA: Pennsylvania State University Press.

Petersen, J., 1919. *De Norske Vikingesverd: En typologisk-kronologisk studie over vikingetidens vaaben.* Kristiana/Ósló: Jacob Dybwad.

Petrukhin, V., 2007. 'Khazaria and the Rus': an examination of their historical relations', in P.B. Golden, H. Ben-Shammai and A. Róna-Tas (eds.), *The World of the Khazars: New Perspectives*. Leiden: E.J. Brill, 245–68.

Phillips, J., 2005 [2004]. *The Fourth Crusade and the Sack of Constantinople*. London: Pimlico.

Piltz, E., 1998. 'Varangian companies for long distance trade. Aspects of interchange between Scandinavia, Rus' and Byzantium in the 11th and 12th centuries', in E. Piltz (ed.), *Byzantium and Islam in Scandinavia: Acts of a Symposium at Uppsala University June 15–16 1996*. Uppsala: Uppsala University, 85–106.

Poole, R.G., 1991. *Viking Poems on War and Peace: A Study in Skaldic Narrative*. Toronto: University of Toronto Press.

Poss, J.M. (MA thesis), 2010. *Behind the Shield-wall: The Experience of Combat in Late Anglo-Saxon England*. Clemson, SC: Clemson University.

Power, R., 2005. 'Meeting in Norway: Norse-Gaelic relations in the Kingdom of Man and the Isles, 1090–1270'. *The Saga-Book of the Viking Society* 29: 5–66.

Price, N.S., 2002. *The Viking Way: Religion and War in Late Iron Age Scandinavia.* Uppsala: Uppsala University.

Price, N.S., 2008. 'Dying and the dead: Viking Age mortuary behaviour', in S. Brink and N.S. Price (eds.), *The Viking World.* London: Routledge, 257–73.

Pritsak, O., 1981. *The Origin of the Rus'.* Cambridge, MA: Harvard University Press (Harvard Ukrainian Research Institute).

Pryor, J.H. and Jeffreys, E.M., 2006. *The Age of the Δρόμων: The Byzantine Navy ca. 500–1204.* Leiden: E.J. Brill.

Raffensperger, C., 2014. 'The place of Rus' in medieval Europe'. *History Compass* 12/11: 853–65.

Richards, J., 2002. *Landsknecht Soldier, 1486–1560.* Oxford: Osprey (Warrior 49).

Richards, J.D., 2003. 'Pagans and Christians at the frontier: Viking burial in the Danelaw', in M.O.H. Carver (ed.), *The Cross Goes North: Processes of Conversion in Northern Europe, AD 300–1300.* York/Woodbridge: York Medieval Press/Boydell Press, 383–95.

Richardson, F.M., 1978. *Fighting Spirit.* London: Leo Cooper.

Rieck, F., 2000. 'Seafaring in the North Sea region, AD 250–850', in P. Pentz, *et al.* (eds.), *Kings of the North Sea, AD 250–850 AD.* Newcastle: Tyne & Wear Museums, 55–66.

Riley-Smith, J.S.C. (ed.), 1991 [1990]. *The Atlas of the Crusades .* London: Guild Publishing.

Roesdahl, E., 1992. 'Princely burial in Scandinavia at the time of conversion', in C. B. Kendall and P. S. Wells (eds.), *Voyage to the Other World: The Legacy of Sutton Hoo.* Minneapolis, MI: University of Minnesota Press, 155–70.

Runciman, S., 1962. 'The schism between the Eastern and Western churches'. *Anglican Theological Review* 44: 337–50.

Salvucci, G. (PhD thesis), 2005. *'The King is Dead' The Thanatology of Kings in the Old Norse Synoptic Histories of Norway, 1035–1161.* Durham: Durham University (Durham E-Theses, http://etheses.dur.ac.uk/2204/).

Sanders, A., 1999. 'Anthropology of warriors', in *Encyclopaedia of Violence, Peace and Conflict,* vol. 3. London, 773–84.

Sävborg, D. and Bek-Pedersen, K. (eds.), 2014. *Folklore in Old Norse – Old Norse in Folklore.* Tartu: University of Tartu Press (Nordistica Tartuensia 20).

Sawyer, B., 2000. *The Viking-Age Rune-Stones: Custom and Commemoration in Early Medieval Scandinavia.* Oxford: Oxford University Press.

Sawyer, P.H., 1971 (2nd edn.). *The Age of the Vikings.* London: Arnold.

Sawyer, P.H., 1989 [1982]. *Kings and Vikings: Scandinavia and Europe AD 700–1100.* London: Routledge.

Self, K.M., 2014. 'The valkyrie's gender: Old Norse shield-maidens and valkyries as a Third Gender. *Feminist Formations* 26/1: 143–7.

Setton, K.M., 1975 (rev. edn.). *Catalan Domination of Athens, 1311–1388*. London: Variorum.

Ševčenko, I., 1965. 'Sviatoslav in Byzantine and Slavic miniatures'. *Slavonic Review* 24: 709–13.

Ševčenko, I., 1984. 'The Madrid manuscript of the Chronicle of Skylitzes in the light of its new dating', in I. Hutter (ed.), *Byzanz und der Westen, Studien zur Kunst der europäischen Mittelalters*. Wien: Österreichischen Akademie der Wissenchaften, 117–30.

Shafer, J.D. (PhD thesis), 2010. *Saga-accounts of Norse Far-travellers*. Durham: Durham University (Durham E-Theses, http://etheses.dur.ac.uk/286/).

Shaw, B.D., 2001. 'War and violence', in G. W. Bowersock, P. Brown and O. Grabar (eds.), *Interpreting Late Antiquity: Essays on the Postclassical World*. Cambridge, MA: Harvard University Press.

Shepard, J., 1973. 'The English and Byzantium: a study of their role in the Byzantine army in the later eleventh century'. *Traditio* 29: 53–92.

Shepard, J., 1974. 'Another New England?' *Byzantine Studies/Études Byzantines* 1: 18–39.

Shepard, J., 1993. 'The uses of the Franks in eleventh-century Byzantium'. *Anglo-Norman Studies* 15: 275–305.

Shepard, J., 1995. 'The Rhôs guests of Louis the Pious: whence and wherefore?' *Early Medieval Europe* 4: 41–60.

Shepard, J., 2007. 'Rus´', in N. Berend (ed.), *Christianization and the Rise of Christian Monarchy: Scandinavia, Central Europe and Rus´ c. 900–1200*. Cambridge: Cambridge University Press.

Shepherd, D.J., 1999. 'The elusive warrior maiden tradition: Bearing weapons in Anglo-Saxon society', in J. Carmen and A; Harding (eds.), *Ancient Warfare: Archaeological Perspectives*. Stroud: Sutton Publishing, 219–43.

Short, W.R., 2010. *Icelanders in the Viking Age: The People of the Sagas*. Jefferson, NC: McFarland & Co.

Simek, R., 1995. *Lexicon der germanischen Mythologie*. Stuttgart: Alfred Kröner.

Simpson, J., 1967. *Everyday Life in the Viking World*. London: B.T. Batsford.

Sledge, E.B., 1981. *With the Old Breed: At Peleliu and Okinawa*. New York: Ballantine.

Smyth, A.P., 1977. *Scandinavian Kings in the British Isles, 830–850*. Oxford: Oxford University Press.

Smyth, A.P., 1998. 'The emergence of English identity, 700–1000', in A.P. Smyth (ed.), *Medieval Europeans: Studies in Ethnic Identity and National Perspectives in Medieval Europe*. New York: St Martin's Press, 24–52.

Speidel, M.P., 2004. *Ancient Germanic Warriors: Warrior Styles from Trajan's Column to Icelandic Sagas*. London: Routledge.

Spiller, R., 1988. 'SLA Marshall and the Ratio of Fire'. *Royal United Services Institute Journal* 133: 63–71.

Spurkland, T., 2005 (trans. B. van der Hoek). *Norwegian Runes and Runic Inscriptions*. Woodbridge: Boydell Press.

Steinsland, G., Sigurðsson, J.V., Rekdal, J.E. and Beuermann, I. (eds.), 2011. *Ideology and Power in the Viking and Middle Ages: Scandinavia, Iceland, Ireland, Orkney and the Faeroes*. Leiden: E.J. Brill.

Stender-Petersen, A., 1953. *Varangica*. Århus.

Stephenson, P., 2003. *The Legend of Basil the Bulgar-Slayer*. Cambridge: Cambridge University Press.

Stewart Kinza, N., 2002 [1991]. *Mates & Muchachos. Unit Cohesion in the Falklands/ Malvinas War*. Washington, DC: Brassey's Inc.

Straubhaar, S.B., 1998. *The Varangian Guard in the Nordic Imaginary*. Tempe, AR: Society for the Advancement of Scandinavian Studies.

Theotokis, G. (PhD thesis), 2010. *The Campaigns of the Norman Dukes of Southern Italy Against Byzantium, in the Years between 1071 and 1085 AD*. Glasgow: University of Glasgow (Glasgow Theses Service, http://theses.gla.ac.uk/1884/).

Theotokis, G., 2012. 'Rus', Varangian and Frankish mercenaries in the service of the Byzantine emperors (9th–11th C.): numbers, organisation and battle tactics in the operational theatres of Asia Minor and the Balkans'. *Βυζαντινά Σύμμεικτα* 22: 125–56.

Thompson, L., 1999. *Daggers and Bayonets: A History*. Staplehurst: Spellmount.

Thompson, L., 2004. *Ancient Weapons in Britain*. Barnsley: Pen & Sword.

Toynbee, A.J., 1973. *Constantine Porphyrogenitus and his World*. Oxford: Oxford University Press.

Townend, M., 2002. *Language and History in Viking Age England*. Turnhout: Brepols Publishers.

Treadgold, W.T., 1995. *Byzantium and its Army, 284–1081*. Stanford, CA: Stanford University Press.

Treadgold, W.T., 1997. *A History of the Byzantine State and Society*. Stanford, CA: Stanford University Press.

Treadgold, W.T., 2001. *A Concise History of Byzantium*. New York: Palgrave.

Treadgold, W.T., 2005. 'Standardized numbers in the Byzantine army'. *War in History* 12/1: 1–14.

Tsamakda, V., 2002. *The Illustrated Chronicle of Ioannes Skylitzes in Madrid*. Leiden: Alexandros Press.

Turner, D., 2014. 'A change in northern winds: a modern review of the viking siege of Paris in 845'. *Noter* 203: 16–22.

Turney-High, H.H., 1991 [1949]. *Primitive Warfare: Its Practice and Concepts*. Columbia, SC: University of South Carolina Press.

Turville-Petre, E.O.G., 1953. *Origins of Icelandic Literature*. Oxford: Oxford University Press.

Turville-Petre, E.O.G., 1968. *Haraldr the Hard-Ruler and his Poets*. London: H.K. Lewis & Co.

Turville-Petre, E.O.G., 1975 [1964]. *Myth and Religion of the North: The Religion of Ancient Scandinavia*. Westport, CT: Greenwood Publishing.

Turville-Petre, E.O.G., 1976. *Skaldic Poetry*. Oxford: Oxford University Press.

Underwood, R., 1999. *Anglo-Saxon Weapons and Warfare*. Stroud: Tempus Publishing.

Vasiliev, A.A., 1937. 'The opening stages of the Anglo Saxon immigration to Byzantium in the eleventh century'. *Annales de l'institute Kondakov* 9: 39–70.

Vasiliev, A.A., 1946. *The Russian Attack on Constantinople in 860*. Cambridge, MA: Mediaeval Academy of America.

Vasiliev, A.A., 1948. 'The monument of Porphyrius in the Hippodrome at Constantinople'. *DOP* 4: 27–49.

Vasiliev, A.A., 1951. 'The second Russian attack on Constantinople'. *DOP* 6: 163–225.

Vasiliev, A.A., 1964 (2nd edn.). *History of the Byzantine Empire*, 2 vols. Madison, WI: University of Wisconsin Press.

Verbruggen, J.F., 1954. *De krijgkunst in west-europa in de middeleeuwen (IXᵉ tot XIVᵉ eeuw)* . Brussels.

Vernadsky, G., 1953. 'The Byzantine–Russian War of 1043'. *Sudost-Forschungen* 12: 47–67.

Volkoff, V., 1984. *Vladimir the Russian Viking*. Woodstock, NY: Overlook Press.

Walker, G., 1994. ' "The Varangians of Byzantium": problems with the Blöndal/ Benedikz book'. *VV* 33: 34–7

Walker, G., 1995. 'Kiev and the supplies of Norse mercenaries to Constantinople, 838–1043 AD'. *VV* 37: 3–5

Walker, G., 1999. 'Genesis of the emperor's Varangians: a new theory'. *VV* 50: 6–13

Walker, G., 2001. 'Everyday life with the emperor's Varangians'. *VV* 58: 6–16

Walker, I.W., 1997. Harold: The Last Anglo-Saxon King. Stroud: Sutton Publishing

Wallace, B. (PhD thesis), 2012. *Warriors and Warfare: Ideal and Reality in Early Insular texts*. Edinburgh: University of Edinburgh

War Office, 1944. *Infantry Training. Part VIII: Fieldcraft, Battle Drill, Section and Platoon Tactics*. London: War Office Publications

Weinstein, P., 2005. 'Palaeopathology by proxy: the case of Egil's bones'. *Journal of Archaeological Science* 32: 1077–82

Whaley, D.E., 1998. *The Poetry of Arnórr jarlaskáld. An Edition and Study*. Turnhout: Brepols Publishers.

Whaley, D.E., 2003. 'Arnórr, earl's propagandist? On the techniques and social functions of skaldic eulogy', in D.J. Waugh (ed.), *The Faces of Orkney. Stones, Skalds and Saints*. Edinburgh: Scottish Society for Northern Studies, 18–32.

Williams, G., Pentz, P. and Wemhoff, M. (eds.), 2014. *Vikings: Life and Legend*. London: British Museum.

Wilson, D.M., 1967. 'The Vikings' relationship with Christianity in northern England'. *British Archaeological Association* 30: 37–46.

Wilson, D.M., 1989 [1970]. *The Vikings and their Origins*. London: Thames & Hudson.

Wilson, N.G., 1978. 'The Madrid Skylitzes'. *Scrittura e civiltà* 2: 209–19.

Winroth, A., 2014. *The Age of the Vikings*. Princeton, NJ: Princeton University Press.

Wood, M., 1980. 'Brunanburh revisited'. *Saga-Book of the Viking Society* 20: 200–17.

Wood, M., 1986. *Domesday: A Search for the Roots of England*. London: BBC Publications.

Wood, M., 1987 [1981]. *In Search of the Dark Ages*. Oxford: Facts on File Publications.

Woolf, A., 1998. 'Erik Bloodaxe re-visited'. *Northern History* 34/1: 189–93.

Wyley, S., 1995. 'The Gjermundbu mail shirt'. *VV* 37: 27.

Yewdale, R.B., 2010 [1924]. *Bohemond I, Prince of Antioch: A Norman Soldier-of-Fortune and Crusader 1050–1111*. Milton Keynes: Leonaur.

Zori, D.M. (PhD thesis), 2010. *From Viking Chiefdoms to Medieval State in Iceland: The Evolution of Social Power Structures in the Mosfell Valley*. Berkeley/Los Angeles, CA: University of California.

Zori, D.M., Byock, J.L., Erlendsson, E., Martin, S., Wake, T. and Edwards, K.J., 2013. 'Feasting in Viking Age Iceland: sustaining a chiefly political economy in a marginal environment'. *Antiquity* 87: 150–65.

Zori, D.M. and Byock, J.L. (eds.), 2014. *Viking Archaeology in Iceland: Mosfell Archaeological Project*. Turnhout: Brepols Publishers (Cursor Mundi 20).

Index

'Abbasid caliphate, 18, 53, 56, 66–8, 76, 86, 91
Abbo Cernuus of Saint-Germain-des-Prés, Neustrian Benedictine monk, 251
Abd ar-Rahman III, 'Umayyad caliph of Qurtubah (912–61), 65
Abu ar-Tayyib al-Mutanabbi (d. 965), Muslim poet, 87
Abydos, battle of (13 April 989), 90
Adam of Bremen, 11th-century Saxon cleric and chronicler, xvii, 1, 45, 161–2, 191–2, 197, 237
Descriptio insularum aquilonis, 161–2
Adelaide of Italy (Saint), Holy Roman Empress (962–99), 291–2 n.7
Advice for the Emperor, 46, 143, 156–8
Aegean Sea, 144, 153–4, 161
Ælfgar, *eorl* of Mercia, 216
Ælfgifu of Northampton, mistress to Knútr I Sveinsson and mother of Sveinn Knútsson, 44, 51–2, 216–17
sexual scandal, 217
Ælfheah, archbishop of Canterbury (1006–12), 135
Ælla (d. 867), king of Northumbria, 249, 251–2
see also blood-eagle
Æsir, Norse gods of battle and conquest, 172, 175, 281, 314 n.30, 323 n.3, 324 n.6
Æthelred, king of the Northumbrians, 204
Æthelred II *unræd*, king of England (978–1016), xiv, 14, 100, 201, 209–13, 218
Saint Brice's Day massacre (13 November 1002), 201, 211
Æthelstan *æðeling*, son of Æthelred II *unræd*, 14
Æthelstan, king of Wessex (925–39), 13, 181–2, 210, 265, 301 n.64
conquerors Northumbria, 183
foster father to Hákon Haraldsson *góði*, 13, 15, 179
rex totius britanniae, 183–4
see also Brunanburh, battle of (937)
Ágrip af Nóregskonúngasögum ('Epitome of the Sagas of the Norwegian Kings'), 51, 227, 286, 290, 315 n.49, 316 n.79
Ahmad ibn Abi al-Ya'qub (d. 897/8), Muslim geographer, 206
Ahmad ibn Fadlan, 10th-century Baghdadi envoy and traveller, 65, 67, 70, 134
Ahmad ibn Rusta, 10th-century Persian traveller and geographer, 12, 57, 65, 69

Aifur (1992), Swedish replica viking-age ship, 62–3
Alcuin of York (d. 804), Northumbrian monk and scholar, 204–205
Alexios I Komnenos, emperor (1081–1118), 74–5, 104, 107, 108, 114, 115–16, 131, 135, 165
Alexios III Angelos, Byzantine emperor (1195–1204), 132
Alexios IV Angelos, Byzantine emperor (1203–4), 132
Alexios V Doukas (Mourtzouphlos), Byzantine emperor (1204), 132
álfr / álfar, 'elf(ves)', 248, 324 n.6
Alfred, king of Wessex (871–99), 207, 209, 301 n.64
Anastasius II, Byzantine emperor (713–15), 156
Anatolia, 90, 128, 137, 141, 144–5, 154
al-Andalus, 67, 206, 320 n.43
Andronikos II Palaiologos, Byzantine emperor (1282–1328, d. 1332), 127–8
Andronikos III Palaiologos, Byzantine emperor (1328–41), 131
Anglesey, Isle of, 251, 319 n.29
Anglo-Saxon Chronicle, 3, 100–101, 181, 184, 207, 210–11, 214, 216–17, 226–7, 233–4, 250, 254, 289, 321–2 n.72
Anna Komnene (1083–1153), Byzantine princess and chronicler, 97, 107–108, 130–1, 158, 300–301, 303 n.106, 304 n.108, 308, 312, 320 n.50, 336
Anna Porphyrogenita (963–1011), sister of Basil II, xii, 89–90
Annales Bertiniani ('Annals of Saint Bertin'), 10, 56, 325 n.17
Annals of Ulster, 183, 254
Apollo, Greek god of prophecy, 258–9
Aquae Seravenae, battle of (24 March 979), 91
Aristakes Lastivertsi (d. 1080), Armenian chronicler, 124–5
Armour, body, 10, 21–2, 24, 31, 61, 71, 119, 141
aventail(s), x–xi, 26, 28
byrnie(s), 26–9, 32, 122
iron / ring mail, xi, 21, 24, 26, 28–9, 64, 95, 121–2
construction, 27–8
Gjermundbu mail shirt, 27–8
lamellar, 95, 119–22
'plate', 122

Arnórr Þórðarson *jarlaskáld*, skald, 196, 256
  Þorfinnsdrápa, 256
Artemis, Greek goddess of boundaries, 259
Arthur, king, 249
Ásbjörn Sigurðarson *selsbani* (Slayer of Seal), 49,
  271, 330 n.5
Ásgard, abode of the *Æsir*, 314 n.30
Asklepios, Greek god of healing, 259
Áslaug, daughter of Sigurðr *Fáfnisbana* and third
  wife to Ragnarr *loðbrók*, 250
Assandun, battle of (18 October 1016), 212
Ásta Guðbrandsdóttir, mother of Óláfr II
  Haraldsson and Haraldr II Sigurðarson, 42
Athenagoras I, patriarch of Constantinople
  (1948–72), 126
Axe(s), 2, 7, 21, 23, 30, 32–4, 70, 103, 110, 123,
  136, 195, 208, 239–40, 256, 264–5, 267–8, 276,
  278, 280, 331 n.31
  bearded, 304 n.107
  breiðox, 'broad axe', 92
  Dane axe, 28–9, 92–100, 108, 110, 116–17, 119,
    122, 125, 131, 141, 218, 226–7, 304 n.107
  named, 95, 300 n.44
    Hel, 95
    Rimmugýgr, 300 n.43
  short or wood-axe, 3, 11, 136, 160
Azov, Sea of, 80–1

Baghdad, 18, 53, 64–8, 76, 91, 164
  see also 'Abbasid caliphate
Baldwin I (of Boulogne), count of Edessa
  (1097–1100), king of Jerusalem (1100–18), 104
Baldwin IV Fairbeard, count of Flanders
  (987–1035), 222
Baldwin V, count of Flanders (1035–67), 222
Bardha'a (Barda, Azerbaijan), 70
Bardas Phokas (d. 968), father of Nikephoros II
  Phokas, 87
Bardas Phokas (d. 989), nephew of Nikephoros II
  Phokas and Byzantine usurper, 90–1
Bardas Skleros (d. 989), brother-in-law of John I
  Tzimiskès and Byzantine usurper, 90–1
Basil II, Byzantine emperor (976–1025), vi, 89–91,
  113, 124–5, 136, 144, 152, 201
  Psalter of, xi–xii, 120, 306 n.150
Basil Pedidiates, Byzantine admiral, 148
Basilica di San Marco, Venice, 120, 190
Basilika Therma, battle of (978), 91
Bayeux tapestry, vii, xiii, 26, 28, 93, 96, 112–13,
  214, 217, 287, 300 n.40, 301, 304, 319, 335, 344
Bayonet(s), 8–10
Beads, glass, 66, 294 n.48
Bear(s), 71, 227–8, 230–1, 274, 323 n.93
  see also berserkir, 'berserkers'
Beer, 134, 162, 171, 261
Beowulf, 16–17, 23, 102, 193, 268, 286 n.56, 287,
  308 n.201
  Beowulf, 3, 23, 136, 193, 218–19, 302, 317, 329,
    331 n.37

Benfleet (*Beamfleote*), 11
Berengar II, king of Italy (950–61), 291–2 n.7
Bergljot Hákonsdóttir, wife to Einarr *þambarskelfir*
  (Gut–shaker) of Lade (*Hlaðir*), 198
Beroë (Stara Zagora, Bulgaria), battle of (1122),
  19, 109–10, 190
  Panagía Varangiotissa, 190
Berserkir, 'berserkers', 34, 227–31, 267, 322 n.87,
  335
  berserksgangr, 228–30
  magic mushroom, 230
  see also wolf(ves)
Berthier, Louis-Alexandre (1753–1815), French
  marshal, 40, 289
Biddle, Martin and Kjølbye-Biddle, Birthe,
  archaeologists and academics, 7, 285, 335
Birka, Swedish trading town, 56, 58, 71, 120–1,
  253, 294 n.48
Bjarkamál, pagan poem, 47
Björgvin (Bergen), 104, 187, 302–303 n.91
  Bergen rune stick, 220–1, 319 n.42
Black Sea, 18, 53, 57, 62–4, 68, 71–4, 80, 98, 116,
  141, 156–7
Blöndal (Sigfús, 1874–1950) and Benedikz
  (Benedikt Sigurðr) Icelandic scholars and
  librarians, 86, 89, 106, 299, 307, 312 n.284
'blood-eagle', 252
Bolesław I Chrobry (the Brave), duke of Poland
  (992–1025), first king of Poland (1025), 80, 81
Bolli Bollason, Icelandic Varangian, 14, 89, 158–9,
  271, 305 n.141, 312 n.284, n.286
  attire of, 117–18, 122, 124
  death of, 158–9
Bolli Þorleiksson, father of Bolli Bollason, 20,
  159, 271
Bölverkr Arnórsson, Icelandic skald, 143, 147
bóndi/bœndr, 'free farmer(s)', 4, 19, 39, 41–2,
  44–5, 76, 161, 166, 178–9, 198, 221, 261
  see also farms, farming
The Book of the Fruits, Byzantine satire, 135
Bosporus, 132, 143, 156–7
Bourke, Joanna, historian and academic, 9
Bow(s), 6, 11, 23–5, 31–2, 278
Brádvellir, battle of (*c.* 750), 274–5
Brân the Blessed, Welsh hero, 258
Brennu-Njáls saga, 3, 5, 22–3, 147, 270, 280,
  326–7, 329–30 n.32, 331 n.45
  Bergþóra, wife to Njáll Þorgeirsson, 247
  Bróðir, 331 n.45
  Flosi Þórðarson, 247, 270–1
  Gunnarr Hámundarson, 3, 5, 22, 25, 247,
    329–30 n.32
  Hallgerðr, wife to Gunnarr Hámundarson, 25
  Hallvarðr the White, 5
  Hildigunnr, niece of Flosi Þórðarsson, 270
  Höskuldr Þrainsson, 3, 270–1
  Kolr Egilsson, 22–3
  Kolskeggr Hámundarson, Icelandic Varangian,
    22–3, 88, 106

Mörðr Valgarðsson, 147, 247
Njáll Þorgeirsson, 3, 247, 271, 329–30 n.32
Skarphéðinn Njálsson, 300 n.43
Þorsteinn Siðu-Hallson, 123–4, 225
Brian Bórumha mac Cennétig, king of Munster (978–1014), high king of Ireland (1002–14), 242–3, 280
Brown, Reginald Allen, mediaevalist and academic, 112
Brunanburh, battle of (937), xiii–xiv, 181–2, 184
location of, 184
Byock, Jesse, archaeologist and academic, 260, 266, 269, 327–30, 336, 351
Byrhtnoth (d. 991), *ealdorman* of Essex, 35, 112, 209, 316 n.77
see also Maldon, battle of (11 August 991)
Byzantium, *see* Constantinople
Bulgaria, xi, 68, 109, 141, 149–52, 154, 157, 201
Bulghar(s), 60, 64–6, 68, 89, 149, 151, 295–6
Danube, 60, 149, 151
Volga, 64–6, 68, 89, 295–6 n.67
Burke, Edmund (1729–97), Irish politician and philosopher, 194
Burton, Richard Francis (1821–90), English explorer, soldier and scholar, 12, 285 n.28, 336

Cædwalla, king of Wessex (685–8, d. 689), 201
Caspian Sea, 18, 57, 64, 66, 68, 70, 75, 141, 295–6 n.67
Catalan Company (*la Companya catalana*), 127–8, 307 n.171, 307–308 n.173
Cattle, 6, 12, 38, 43, 65, 162, 313 n.5, 327 n.2
dairy products, 162
hide, 29–30, 120
rustling, 200, 246
Causantín mac Áeda (Constantine II), king of the Scots (900–43), 181–2
Cereals, 65, 162
barley, 41, 134, 162, 312 n.281
oats, 162
rye, 162
Charente, river, 206
Charlemagne, King of the Franks (771–814), Holy Roman Emperor (800–14), 52, 171, 200–201, 204
Charles *le chauve*, king of the West Franks (843–77), king of Italy (875–7), 206, 250
Charles III *le simple*, king of the West Franks (898–923, d. 929), 213
Charles VII *le Bien-Servi*, king of France (1422–61), 273
Chaucer, Geoffrey (1340–1400), English poet and writer, 246, 330 n.1
chelandion, horse transport, 296–7 n.77
Chrétien de Troyes, 12th-century French romance writer, 246, 266

Christianity, 45, 50, 60, 64, 89–90, 127, 167, 169–72, 176–7, 185–9, 201, 237, 247, 261–5, 277–8, 291, 340, 351
baptism, 60, 89, 169–76, 182, 185, 187–8, 201, 278, 310 n.243, 314 n.28
conversion to, 89–90, 169, 172–3, 176, 185–7, 247, 262, 265, 277–8
Jesus Christ, 50, 126, 174–5, 187
Christ (*Kristr*)/White Christ (*Hvitakristr*), 172, 190
prímsigning, 'prime signed', 265
Christiansen, Eric (1937–2016), English polymath and academic, 55, 206, 292, 318
Christine de Pizan (b. 1364), writer, 272
Le Livre de la cité des dames (1404), 272–3
Le trésor de la cité des dames (1405), 272–3
Chronicon Monasterii de Abingdon, 116, 305
Chronicon Universale Anonymi Laudunensis, 114–15, 305 n.131
Chrysopolis, battle of (14 September 987), 90
Chudes, 79, 81
Clausewitz, Carl von (1780–1831), Prussian general and military theorist, 33–4, 38, 150, 289
Clontarf, battle of (23 April 1014), 78, 123, 243, 255–7, 280
Cogadh Gáedhel re Gaillaibh, 275, 330
Constantinople, *passim*
Blachernai, palace of, 98, 130
Golden Horn, 98, 156–7
chain, 156–7, 340
Great Palace, x, 87, 106, 120, 130, 135, 153, 291–2, 306 n.148
Chalke gates, 130
purple chamber, 291–2 n.7
Hagia Irene, 190
Hagia Sophia, 79, 125–6, 131
graffiti, x, 131–2
Hippodrome, x, 130, 152
Latin sieges (1203, 1204), 98, 116–17, 133
Rus' sieges (860, 907, 941, 978, 1043), 72–4, 79, 91
chapel of Saint Óláfr, 19, 190
'Umayyad siege (717), 157
walls of, 98
Constantinus I, Byzantine emperor (306–37), 143
Constantinus VII Porphyrogenitus, Byzantine emperor (913–59), 57–61, 87, 152, 291–2 n.7
De ceremoniis aulae Byzantinae 86–7, 155, 297, 299, 311
Constantinus VIII, Byzantine emperor (1025–8), 152
Constantinus IX Monomachos, Byzantine emperor (1042–56), xi, 152, 156, 162
Constantinus Laskaris, 132–3
Constantinus, Byzantine *nobilissimus*, 127, 153
Crichton, Michael (1942–2008), American author and screenwriter, 68–9

Eaters of the Dead (1976), 68

Crumlin-Pedersen, Ole (1935–2011), Danish
naval architect and nautical archaeologist, 221,
285, 294, 311, 320, 334, 337

Cuthbert (d. 687, Saint), 167, 204, 318 n.6

D'Amato, Raffaele, author and academic, 93,
300–301, 337

Dag Hringsson, 41

Danegeld, 209–10, 212

Dante Alighieri (1265–1321), Florentine
politician, poet and writer, 246

Danube, river, 53, 60–1, 98, 282

Denelagu, Danelaw, 182, 207, 301 n.64

DeVries, Kelly, mediaevalist and academic, 6, 285,
312 n.282, 317 n.100, 320 n.48, 321, 338

Derwent, river, xiii–iv, 226

Dirham(s), 65–6, 164, 294 n.46
coin hoards, 164

Divorce, 271–2, 275

Dnieper, river, 18, 53, 56–60, 62–4, 72, 79, 81,
141, 189, 296
cataracts of, x, 53, 58–9,
portage along, 56–9, 296 n.74

Dorostolon (Silistra), 53, 282
battle of (971), 282

Drœngr, 'like men', 76

Dryden, John (1631–1700), English poet,
playwright and literary critic, 232

Dublin (*Dubh-linn*), 1, 123, 169, 182–4, 189, 242,
251, 253–5, 280, 326–7 n.40, 344
foundation of, 253
Norse-Hibernian kings of, 169, 182, 184, 253–4

Dvina, river, 58–9, 62

Dyrrhachium (Durazzo, Dürreš), 87, 107–108
Italo-Norman siege of (1081), 107–109

Eadgyð Swanneshals (Swan's neck), mistress to
Harold II Godwinson, 319 n.29

Eadmund, king of Wessex (939–46), 181, 209

Eadmund II Ironside, king of England (1016),
211–12

Eadred, king of Wessex and Mercia (946–55),
179–80, 184, 209

Ealdred Ealdulfing, lord of Bamburgh (913–33), 183

Ealdyð of Mercia, wife to Harold II Godwinson,
216, 319 n.29

East Anglia, kingdom of, 42, 207, 209, 253

Edgar *œdeling*, son of Edward the Exile, 197, 214

Edward the Elder, king of Wessex (899–924), 11,
209, 211, 301 n.64

Edward Æthelredsson 'the Confessor' (Saint),
king of England (1042–66), 100, 115, 214–16,
218–20, 234–5

Edward the Exile (1016–57), son of Eadmund II
Ironside, 215

Edwin, *eorl* of Mercia (1062–6), 216, 223–4

Egils saga Skallagrímssonar, 4, 181–2, 184, 231,
262–3, 265, 267, 284, 286, 294, 313, 315–316,
320, 322–3, 328, 329 n.17
Arinbjörn Þórisson, 267, 286 n.37
Egill Skallagrímsson, 4–5, 13, 16, 178, 181,
228–9, 232, 239, 262–7, 271, 286, 303, 315,
328, 329 n.16
abnormal bones of, 264–5, 266
as a berserker, 229, 266
as a poet, 178, 239, 267, 302–3 n.91, 329
n.27
as a warrior, 16, 181, 263
burials of, 263–6, 328 n.14
character of, 262, 266–7
Arinbjarnarkviða, 267
his swords, 13, 286 n.37
Grímr Svertingsson, Mosfell chieftain and
Lawspeaker (1002–04), 262–4, 266, 268
Kveld-Úlfr, 229
Ljot the Berserker, 16, 228
Skalla-Grímr Kveldúlfsson, father of Egill
Skallagrímsson, 262, 286 n.37
Skapti *prestr* (the Priest) Þórarinsson, 264–5,
329 n.18
Þórdís, niece and stepdaughter of Egill
Skallagrímsson, 262–4
Þorgerðr Egilsdóttir, 271
Þórólfr Kveldúlfsson, brother of Skalla-Grímr
Kveldúlfsson, 286, 320 n.43
Þórólfr Skallagrímsson, elder brother of Egill
Skallagrímsson, 5, 13, 181, 262, 265, 286
n.37
Þorsteinn Egilsson, 262–3, 329 n.16
see also Brunanburh, battle of (937)

Einarr Skúlason, 12th-century Norwegian skald
and priest, 19, 105, 109, 302–303 n.91
Óláfrsdrápa, 19, 105

Einarr *þambarskelfir* (Gut-shaker) of Lade
(*Hlaðir*), Norwegian *jarl*, 24, 100, 197–8,
302–303 n.91

Eindriði Einarrson (1003–50), son of Einarr
þambarskelfir (Gut-shaker) of Lade (*Hlaðir*),
198

Eindriði *ungi* (the Young), Norwegian Varangian,
19, 104–106, 109–10, 302–303 n.91

Eiríkr I *ejegoð*, king of Denmark (1095–1103), 135

Eiríkr Hákonarson of Lade (*Hlaðir*), Norwegian
jarl and regent for Sveinn I Haraldsson
tjúguskegg, 24, 48, 186, 195, 198

Eiríkr Haraldsson *blóðøx* (Eric Bloodaxe), king of
Norway (930–4), king of York (947–8, 952–4),
166–7, 178–81, 184, 209, 224, 254, 315, 316
n.63
death of, 180, 315 n.58
Eiríksmál, 180–1, 316 n.62

Eiríkr *rauða* (the Red), 167, 275–6

Elisaveta Yaroslavna of Kiev, first wife to Haraldr II Sigurðarson, xii–xiii, 79, 147, 191, 312 n.282

Emma of Normandy (d. 1052), queen consort of England, Denmark and Norway, 196, 216–18
Encomium Emmæ Reginæ, 217, 254, 326
her marriages, 218

Estrið Svendsdóttir of Denmark, mother of Sveinn II Estriðsson, 196, 218

Eustace II, count of Boulogne (1049–87), 300 n.40

Eymundar þáttr Hringssonar, 80, 298
Eymundr Hringsson, Norwegian mercenary, 80–2

Eysteinn Orri (d. 1066), betrothed to Maria Haraldsdóttir, 233

Eysteinn Meyla (d. 1177), Norwegian pretender, 45

Eyvindr Finnsson *skáldaspillir* (the Plagiarist), 10th-century Norwegian skald, 193, 228, 279
Hákonarmál, 279

Exemption Charters, 114

Fagrskinna, 'Beautiful Vellum', 45, 165

Falklands/Malvinas War (2 April – 14 June 1982), 8–10, 38, 38
3rd Battalion the Parachute Regiment, 8–10
Mount Longdon, battle of (11–12 June), 8–10

Farm(s), farming, vii–viii, 2–6, 11, 19, 26, 32, 41–2, 44, 46, 50, 66, 76, 78, 143, 161–3, 165, 169–70, 178–9, 187–8, 194, 199, 218, 246–7, 260–1, 263–6, 277, 313 n.19, 327
see also bóndi, bændr

Feast(s), feasting, 12, 38, 46, 125–6, 135–6, 172, 178, 238, 261–2, 267, 269, 288
Christmas/Yuletide, 125, 238, 324 n.17
Easter, 125

félagi, 'fellows/comrades', 10

Fenrir, killer of Óðinn, 180

Flateyjarbók ('Book of the Flat Island'), Icelandic manuscript, 100, 302, 307, 309 n.218, 320, 326–7

Florence of Worcester (d. 1118), English monk and chronicler, 289 n.94

Foote, Paul, archaeologist, 71, 296, 339, 342, 344

Fóstbræðra saga, 12, 32

Frank, Roberta, philologist and academic, 252, 326

Frankia, Carolingian kingdom of, 10, 56, 177, 200, 205, 207, 251

Frederick II (or III), king of Sicily (1296–1337), 127

Freydí Eiríksdóttir, 275–6

Freyja, Norse goddess of sex, 281, 314 n.30

Freyr, Norse god of fertility, ix, 45, 170, 314 n.30

Friesland, 181, 205, 267

Frigg, Norse goddess and wife to Óðinn, 177

Funen (Fyn), Danish island, 49–50, 279

Fur(s), 27, 56, 65, 71, 270
as trade, x, 18, 58–9, 64–6

Gabriel, archangel, xi

Gambeson, 29

Garðaríki/Garðar, 'the kingdom of fortified towns', 77–8, 83
see also Kiev

Gate Fulford, battle of (20 September 1066), 34, 223–4, 321 n.55

Gaufredus Malaterra, 11th-century Italo-Norman chronicler, 107, 303 n.105, 304 n.107, 309

Genghis Khan (1155–1227), 149, 248, 310 n.245

Geoffroi de Villehardouin, 12th/13th-century French crusader and chronicler, 98, 190, 317

George Kedrenos, 11th-century Byzantine historian, 137, 144–5, 307–309, 310 n.233, 311

George Pachymeres (b. 1242), Byzantine cleric and historian, 117, 127, 305, 307

Georgios Maniakes (d. 1043), Byzantine *stratêgós*, xii, 111, 145, 151, 310 n.233
campaign in Sicily, 145, 147–8
campaign in southern Italy, 148–9
physical appearance, 145–6, 309 n.231
rebellion of, 152

Giant(s) and giantess(es), 39, 170–1, 175, 177, 248, 251, 314 n.30, 323 n.3, 326 n.27
Gunnloþ, 303 n.97, 323 n.3
Mímir, 175
Surtr, 177

Gibbon, Edward (1737–94), English politician and historian, 125

Gisèle (*fl.* 911), Frankish princess and wife to Rollo of Normandy, 213

Gísla saga Súrssonar, 13, 272, 286, 330 n.1
Auðr, wife to Gísli Súrsson, 272
Eyjólfr the Grey, 272
Gísli Súrsson, outlaw, 272
Þórdís, sister of Gísli Súrsson, 272

Gnézdovo, 59, 71

góði/góðar, 'chieftain(s)', 48, 262, 265
goðorð, 'chieftaincy', 262

Y Gododdin, Welsh heroic poem, 31, 117, 136, 288 n.87

Godred Haraldsson *crovan* (d. 1095), Norse-Gael king of Man and the Hebrides, 240–1

Godwin Wulfnoðsson, *eorl* of Wessex (1020–53), 196, 219–20, 233

Gormr *gamli* (the Old), king of Denmark (936–58), 179

Gotland, Baltic island, x, 27, 30, 44, 54, 58–9, 62–3, 69, 164, 174, 177, 249, 276–8, 294, 306–307, 331 n.30, 346
merchants, x, 58–9, 164
picture stones, 27, 30, 62–3, 69, 174, 177–8, 294 n.35
Alskog Tjängvilde I (SHM 29974:1), 62
Ardre VIII (SHM 11118), 315 n.45
Lärbro Stora Hammars I (SHM 4171), 62
Närr Stenkyrka Smiss I (GM 3428), 62
Stenkyrka Lillbjärs III (G 268), 315 n.45

Tjängvide I (G 110), 315 n.45
  see also Guta lag, Gotlander law code
Grágás, Icelandic law code, 118, 276, 305–306,
  322, 328–9 n.15
  on cross-dressing, 276
Greek fire, 73–5, 297 n.80
Greenland, 167, 220, 276
Gregory of Tours (d. 594), Gallo-Roman
  historian, 21, 287 n.68
Grettis saga Ásmundarsonar, 22–3, 29, 287, 289,
  322, 329
  Grettir Ásmundarson, 20, 22–3, 29, 32
a Grikklandi, 'in Greece'/grikkfari, 'the Greece-
  farer', 87–8, 107
  see also rune stones
Gruffydd ap Llywelyn, king of Gwynedd and
  Powys (1039–55), king of Wales (1055–63), 216
Guillaume de Jumièges, 11th-century Anglo-
  Norman cleric and chronicler, 214, 317
Gunnhildr konungamóðir (Mother of Kings), wife
  to Eiríkr Haraldsson blóðøx, 179–80, 315 n.52
Gunnhildr, niece of Knútr I Sveinsson, 44
Gunnlaugr ormstungu (Worm's Tongue), Icelandic
  skald, 48, 268
Gunnlaugs saga ormstungu, 268, 290, 294–5, 326,
  329 n.29
  Illugi svarti (the Black), Borgarfjörður chieftain
    and father of Gunnlaugr ormstungu, 268
  Önundr Eilífsson, Mosfell chieftain, 268,
    329–30 n.32
Guðrum, Danish warlord and king of East Anglia
  (879–90), 149
Guta lag, Gotlander law code, 276–7, 330
  on molestation, 277
Guy d'Amiens, bishop of Amiens (1058–75), 96,
  287 n.76, 300
Gyða Þorkelsdóttir (1001–69), wife to Godwin
  Wulfnoðsson of Wessex, 196
Gyrth Godwinson, 220

al-Hadath (Adata, Turkey), battle of (954), 87,
  299
Hákon Eiríksson, Norwegian jarl and regent of
  Norway (1028–30), 44, 188–9, 277
Hákon Haraldsson góði (the Good), king of
  Norway (934–61), 12, 13, 15, 179, 187, 279
Hákon Hræreksson (fl. 844), Swedish king, 56
Hákon Ivársson of Lade (Hlaðir), 198
Hákon Sigurðarson of Lade (Hlaðir), Norwegian
  jarl and regent (975–95), 92, 186, 197–8, 208
Hálfdan svarti (the Black), king of Ringerike and
  father of Haraldr I hárfagri (Fine-hair), 165
Halldór Snorrason, Icelandic Varangian, 256–7
Hallr of Síða, 123, 255
Haraldr grænski (d. 995), father of Óláfr II
  Haraldsson, 42
Haraldr hilditönn (War-ooth), legendary Danish
  king, 274–5

Haraldr I hárfagri (Fine-hair), king of Norway
  (870–933), ix, 15, 45, 135, 165–7, 179, 228,
  326–7 n.40
  'hárfagri–dynasty', 165–6
Haraldr II gráfeldar (Greycloak) Gunnhildarson,
  king of Norway (961–70), 166, 193
Haraldr III Sigurðarson harðráði, king of Norway
  (1046–66), passim
  'burner of Bulghars', 149–50
  death at Stamford Bridge, 231–3
  Emma, xiv, 119, 124, 306 n.147
  his character, 192–3, 238
  in the Holy Land, 142–3, 309 n.216, n.229
  Landøyðan, 'Land-waster', 223, 231, 233,
    240–1, 256–7
  physical appearance, 215, 309 n.210
  poetry of, xii–xiii, 198, 225–6, 237–9, 323 n.4
  promotions in Byzantine service, 149, 157–8
  use of stratagems, 149, 156–7
  war with Denmark, 193–7
Hárekr of Þjóttu, 46
Harold I Harefoot, king of England (1035–40),
  216–18
Harold II Godwinson, king of England (1066),
  99–100, 196–7, 220, 223–5, 319 n.29
  at Hastings, xiii, 113, 218, 287 n.76
  at Stamford Bridge, xiv, 215, 225–6, 233–4
  kills (?) his brother Tostig, 96
  his claim to the English throne, 214–16
Harold Haroldson, son of Harold II Godwinson,
  319 n.29
Hasdai ibn Shaprût, foreign minister serving Abd
  ar-Rahman III, 65
Hastings, battle of (14 October 1066), xiii, 96,
  112–13, 218, 234–5, 287 n.76, 300 n.40, 304
  n.109, 319 n.29, 336, 338
Hauteville, de (family)
  Bohémond, prince of Antioch (1098–1101,
    1103–04, d. 1111), 108, 339, 351
  Drogo, second count of Apulia and Calabria
    (1046–51), 111, 145
  Robert Guiscard, duke of Apulia and Calabria
    (1059–85), xii, 107–108, 114, 149
  Roger I, Great Count of Sicily (1085–1101),
    xii, 304 n.107
  Tancred, father of William, Drogo and Robert, 145
  William bras-de-fer, first count of Apulia
    (1042–6), 111, 145
Hávamál ('The Sayings of Hárr'), 3, 33, 37–8,
  118, 136, 160, 171, 174, 175, 244, 282, 303 n.97
Hawkwood, John (d. 1394), English condottiere
  and commander of the White Company, 129
Hebrides, the, 5, 180, 207, 241, 253, 322 n.86
  Isle of Lewis, 168, 228, 322 n.86
Hedeby, Danish market town, 10, 23, 24, 67–8,
  124, 150, 253
  burning of (1051), 150
  Hedeby 1 wreck (c. 985), 150, 205, 208

Heiðarvíga saga, 22, 39, 289
  Gestr Þórhallason, 22
  Þorsteinn Víga-Styrsson, Icelandic Varangian, 22
Hel, Norse goddess of the shameful dead, 95
Helgeä river, battle of (1026), 42–3, 196
Hellespont, 90
Helmet(s), vii–xi, 7, 24–7, 28, 31, 32, 34, 64, 95, 96, 113, 119, 225, 228–9, 242, 257, 263
  Byzantine, x–xi,
  conical, vii, viii, 26, 119
  Gjermundbu, 'spectacle' helmet, viii–ix, 26
  spangenhelm, 26
  Vendel period, 228
Henry I, king of England (1100–35), 116
Henry II, king of England (1154–89), 301 n.49
Henry of Huntingdon (d. 1157), Anglo-Norman chronicler, 184, 226–7, 289, 320
Herodotos, 5th-century BC Greek historian, 97–8, 288 n.87, 323 n.93
Heyerdahl, Thor (1914–2002), Norwegian adventurer and ethnographer, 258, 327, 341
Hiberno-Norse, 65, 169, 182–4, 209, 254, 280
  see also Dublin (*Dubh–linn*)
hirð, 'king's retinue', vii, 48–9, 100
  hirðmenn, 158, 302 n.67
hirðmaðr, 'personal retainers', 41, 48, 189
Hjörungavágr, battle of (986), 208, 318 n.14
Homer, Greek bard, 40, 97, 238, 259, 272, 304 n.108
Hörða-Knútr, king of Denmark (1035–42), king of England (1040–2), 52, 100, 124, 196, 216–18
Hörik I Godofredsson, king of Denmark (827–54), 200
Horses, 6, 25, 54, 57, 62–3, 96, 111–13, 118, 146, 188, 205–206, 226–7, 297 n.77, 303 n.97, 304 n.122
  as food, 6, 54
Housecarl(s), 43, 93, 96, 99–101, 113, 218, 301–302, 314
  Anglo-Scandinavian (*huscarl/huscarlas*), 93, 96–7, 99–101, 113, 218, 302 n.67–8
  Scandinavian (*húskarl/húskarlar*), 43, 100, 218, 301 n.66
Hrafn-Flóki Vilgerðarson, 163
Hrafn *rauða* (the Red), 255
Hrólfr *kraki*, king of Denmark, 13, 47
Humbert de Mourmoutiers, cardinal of Silva Candida (1051–61) and papal legate, 125

Ibn Khurradadhbih, Baghdadi courtier and chronicler, 18, 67, 286–7
Ibrahim ibn Ya'qub, Andalusian merchant and chronicler, 67
Iceland, 12–14, 66, 77, 117, 124, 132, 158–9, 162–3, 166–7, 170, 207, 228–30, 238, 245–7, 249, 256, 260–1, 263, 265, 267–9, 271, 276, 295,

299 n.18, 309 n.210, 313 n.5, n.19, 316 n.79, 327–8, 336–7, 349, 351
Althingi, 260, 262, 324 n.3, 328 n.9
  Grímr Svertingsson, Lawspeaker (1002–04), 262–4, 266, 268
  Borgarfjörður, 262–4, 268
  Leiruvogur, 66, 294–5 n.49
  Mosfell valley (Mosfellsdalur), 66, 260–9, 294–5 n.49, 327, 328 n.12, 329–30 n.32, 336, 351
    Mosfell Archaeological Project, 260–9, 294, 327
    Hulduhóll, 261, 327 n.4
    Hrísbrú (Old Mosfell), 66, 261–4, 267–8, 327 n.3, 328–9 n.15, n.19
    Kirkjuhóll, 266, 328–9
Saga(s), *passim*
  Íslendingabók ('Book of Icelanders'), 262, 325 n.23, 327 n.2, 329 n.18
  Íslendingasögur ('Sagas of the Icelanders'), 75, 132, 246, 266–7, 269
  Íslenski skólinn, 'Icelandic School, 269
  Settlement of, 13, 169–70, 246–7, 262, 313, 327 n.7
    Landnámabók ('Book of Settlements'), 161, 169, 195, 313 n.19, 326–7 n.40, 329 n.16
    Glúmr, 169
    Helgi Eyvindarson *inn magri* (the Skinny), 169–70
    Oddr Arngeirson, shape shifter, 229–30
  see also Egils saga Skallagrímssonar
Igor I, ruler of Kievan Russia (912–45), 53, 55, 72–4, 149, 296 n.74, 310 n.244
Ilevollene, battle of (27 May 1180), 39
Ilmen, Lake, 57, 63
Infantry Training (1944), British Army pamphlet, 37, 350
Ingigerðr, daughter of Haraldr II Sigurðarson, xii, 312 n.282
Ingigerðr Óláfsdóttir (d. 1050, Saint Anna of Novgorod), wife to Yaroslav of Kiev, 79
Iron smelting/smithing, 16–18, 20, 32, 41
Isaakos I Komnenos, Byzantine emperor (1057–9), 97, 125–6
Isaakos II Angelos, Byzantine emperor (1185–95, 1203–04), 14, 98
Ishbiliyya (Seville), 206
Italo-Norman(s)/Norman(s), xi–xiii, 96, 107–108, 111–16, 124, 134, 145, 148–9, 151–2, 169, 213–14, 304 n.109, 305 n.128, 319 n.29
  in Constantinople, 134
  in Italy and Sicily, 107, 111, 145, 148–9, 151–2, 306 n.151
Iustinianus I, Byzantine emperor (527–65), x, 131, 143
Izz ad-Din ibn al-Athir (1160–1233), court chronicler of the Zengid dynasty, 70, 89

Yggdrasil, great cosmic ash tree, 19, 177, 249, 281
Ynglinga saga, 174, *295*, 322–3, 331
Yngvars saga víðfǫrla, 75, 77, 248, 297–8
    Ingvarr the Far-Traveller, 75–6, 88, 221, 297
        n.90, 298 n.91
    see also rune stones

Jansson, Sven Birger Fredrik (1906–87), Swedish
    scholar and runologist, x, 132, 342
Játvarðar konungs hins helga, 115–16, 305
Jeanne d'Arc (d. 1431, Saint), 273, 275
Jerusalem, 104–106, 143, 186
    shrines of the Holy Sepulchre, 142
    True Cross, 142, 292
Jesch, Judith, historian and academic, 5, 39, 69,
    285, 289, 295, 298, 299 n.6, 313 n.18, 330, 335,
    342
John the Baptist (Saint), 186
John I Tzimiskès, Byzantine emperor (969–76),
    53–4, 61, 90–1, 292 n.7
John II Komnenos, Byzantine emperor (1118–43),
    19, 109
John VI Kantakouzenos, Byzantine emperor
    (1347–54, d. 1383), monk and historian, 131,
    308
John the Orphanotrophos, 125, 146
John XII, pope (955–63), 291–2 n.7
John Kinnamos, 12th-century Byzantine courtier
    and historian, 109, 116, 304–305
John Raphael (or Rafayl), catepan of Italy (1046),
    114
John Skylitzes, 11th-century Byzantine court
    official, x, xii, 54, 73–4, 120, 137, 291, 296–7,
    300, 306 n.151, 307 n.161, 309–310, 318, 331
John of Wallingford (d. 1258), English
    Benedictine monk and chronicler, 118
John of Worcester (d. 1140), English monk and
    chronicler, 45, 217, 223, 289–90 n.94, 300, 305,
    319, 320 n.50, 321
John Zonaras, 12th-century Byzantine theologian
    and chronicler, 144, 309, 312 n.276
Jómsvíkings, 208, 318 n.13
    Vagn Ákason, 208, 318 n.13, 329 n.26
Jones, Gwyn (1907–99), Welsh scholar and
    academic, 150, 223, 311, 321
Jones, James (1921–77), American combat veteran
    and author, 85
    From Here to Eternity (1951), 85
    The Thin Red Line (1962), 85
Joseph ben Aaron, 10th-century khagan of the
    Khazars, 65, 293 n.19, 294
Judith de Flandre (d. 1095), wife to Tostig
    Godwinson, 222

Kálfr Árnason, 46, 48–50, 312 n.282
Kálfr Arnfinsson, 49
Kasplya, river, 62–3

Kendrick, Thomas Downing (1895–1979), English
    archaeologist and art historian, 54, 291, 343
Khazar(s), 18, 57, 64–5, 68, 80–1, 294, 295–6 n.67
    conversion to Judaism, 64, 294 n.37
Kherson, 18, 62
Kiev (*Kœnugarðr*), xi–xii, 43–4, 50–3, 57–60,
    72–3, 78–81, 143, 147, 157, 188, 291, 293 n.12,
    296 n.74, 310, 345, 350
    church of Saint Elias, 296 n.70
    church of Saint Sophia, 79
    see also Rus'
Kjarvall, Hiberno-Norse king of Dublin (872–88),
    326–7 n.40
Knútr I Sveinsson, king of England (1014,
    1016–35), king of Denmark (1014–35), king
    of Norway (1028–35), 5–6, 42–4, 47, 51, 78,
    99–101, 113, 124, 188–9, 195–7, 209–12,
    216–19, 222, 254
    his character, 218–19
    conquers England, 5, 113, 209–12, 218
    North Sea empire, 44, 209, 211, 222, 240

Ladoga, Lake, 56–7, 63
Lagertha, shield maiden and first wife to Ragnarr
    loðbrók, 250, 273–5
landvættir, 'land spirits', 195, 324 n.6
Laxdœla saga, 20, 65, 158, 161, 271, 275, 285–7,
    294, 305, 307, 312, 325 n.23, 330 n.1
    Breeches-Auðr, 275
    Geirmundr *gnýr* (Thunderer), 12, 14–15
    Guðrún Ósvífursdóttir, mother of Bolli
        Bollason, 159, 271, 325 n.23
    Helgi Harðbeinsson, 20
    Kjartan Óláfsson, 271
    Þuríðr Óláfsdóttir, wife to Geirmundr *gnýr*, 12
leiðangr, 'levy of ships for war', 5–6
Leo V the Armenian, Byzantine emperor
    (813–20), x
Leo VIII, anti-pope (963–4), pope (964–5), 292
    n.7
Leo Diakonos, 10th-century Byzantine historian,
    53, 74, 157, 291, 297, 311
Leo Phokas, father of Bardas Phokas, 90
Leo Phokas (the younger), brother of Bardas
    Phokas, 90
Leofric, *eorl* of Mercia, 219
Leofwine Godwinson (d. 1066), younger brother
    of Harold II Godwinson, 220
Lewis, Clive Staples, British writer and lay
    theologian, 37, 289
Lévi-Strauss, Claude (1908–2009), French
    structural anthropologist, 230, 323, 327 n.42,
    343
Liber Vitae, 219
Liffey, river, 123, 253, 255
    see also Dublin (*Dubh-linn*)
Lindisfarne, island of, viii, 21, 167, 204, 318 n.6

lið, 'host', 85, 147, 299 n.6
Liudprand of Cremona (d. 972), envoy of Otto I
    and historian, 54–5, 73–4, 106, 134–5, 291–2
    n.7, 296–7 n.75, 303, 308
Loire, river/valley, 205–206, 273
    Noirmoutier, island of, 205–206
Loki, Norse god of chaos, 95, 177, 180, 249, 281
London, viii, 11, 42, 100, 113, 135, 187, 206, 212,
    224, 322
    London Bridge, vii, 42, 187
    Tower of London, vii, 113–14
Longship(s), vii, ix, xvii, 5, 202, 205–206, 220,
    221–2,
    Gokstad ship (895/900), ix, 30, 202–203,
        221–2, 338
    Crane, 195
    Long Serpent, 186, 195
    Short Serpent, 195
    Nydam Mose boat (310/320), 201–202
    see also Hedeby 1, Skuldelev 1, Skuldelev 5,
        Roskilde 6
Louis *le Pieux*, King of Aquitaine (781–814), Holy
    Roman Emperor (813–40), King of the Franks
    (814–40), 56, 67, 171, 205, 314 n.27, n.28
Louis VII *le Jeune*, King of the Franks (1137–80),
    133
Lovat, river, 57, 62–3
Lund, Niels, historian and academic, 5–6, 221,
    285, 320, 344

McTurk, Rory, translator and academic, 251, 325,
    344
Machiavelli, Niccolò (1469–1527), Florentine
    politician and polymath, 38, 102–103, 137, 302
Madonna *Nicopea*, 9th/10th-century Byzantine
    icon, 190
Máel Sechnaill mac Domnaill, king of Mide
    (976–1022), high king of Ireland (980–1002,
    1014–22), 243
Magnús I Óláfsson *góði* (the Good), king of
    Norway (1035–47), king of Denmark (1042–7),
    52, 59, 79, 100, 166, 189, 191, 198, 216, 218–19,
    240, 257
    death of, 191–2
Magnús II Haraldsson, king of Norway (1066–9),
    312 n.282
Magnús III Óláfsson *berfœttr* (Barefoot), king of
    Norway (1093–1103), 104, 241–2, 319 n.29,
    324 n.17
    death of, 104, 242
Magnússon, Eiríkr (1833–1913), Icelandic scholar
    and academic, 244
Magyar(s), 64, 80
Mälar, Lake, 62, 75–6, 121
Maldon, battle of (11 August 991), 35, 112, 185,
    209, 289 n.95
Man, Isle of, 180, 240–2, 299 n.18, 328 n.9
    Chronicle of Man, 241, 324 n.17

Manuel I Komnenos, Byzantine emperor (1143–80),
    105, 109, 120, 157, 306 n.151
Maria Haraldsdóttir (d. 1066), daughter of
    Haraldr II Sigurðarson, xii–xiii, 312 n.282
Mária, sister of Michael IV and wife to Stephanos
    the Paphlagonian, 151, 155
Marsden, John, author, 241, 312 n.282, 324, 344
    Fairy Flag, 241
Marshall, Samuel Lyman Atwood (1900–77), US
    Army combat historian, 35–6, 38
    Men against Fire (1947), 35, 344
Marx, Karl (1818–83), 242, 247
al-Mas'udi (d. 957), Baghdadi chronicler, 64, 294,
    299
Mathilde de Flandre (d. 1083), queen consort of
    William I of England, 222
Mead, 34, 135, 177, 193, 288–9 n.87
    mead of poetry, 238, 249, 303 n.97, 323 n.3
Mercenary(ies), x–xi, xviii, 42, 47, 50, 53, 71,
    73, 80–2, 84–92, 99–107, 111, 115–16, 121–2,
    127–30, 132–4, 136–7, 140–3, 154, 163–4, 181,
    191–2, 208, 210, 212, 222, 237, 265, 334, 345,
    349–50
    definition of, 99–103, 104–107
    Landsknecht, 137–9
    Papal Guard, 163
    Swedish/Rus', xi–xii, 71, 73, 80, 86–7, 88–9,
        90, 91–2
    Swiss *reisläufer*, 103, 128–9, 137
    wages of, 81–2, 92, 164
Mercia, Anglo-Saxon kingdom, 179, 182, 207,
    216, 219–20, 223, 253, 301 n.64, 319, 335
Michael, archangel, xi–xii, 72, 107–108, 120, 304
    n.109
Michael I Keroularios, patriarch of
    Constantinople (1043–59), 125–7
Michael I Rangabés, Byzantine emperor (811–13),
    306 n.151
Michael IV the Paphlagonian, Byzantine emperor
    (1034–41), xii, 46, 143, 144–6, 151, 154–5, 157,
    165, 308, 310–11
Michael V Kalaphates, Byzantine emperor
    (1041–2), 127, 129, 137, 151–3, 155–6
Michael VI Stratiotikos, Byzantine emperor
    (1056–7), 306 n.151
Michael VII Doukas, Byzantine emperor (1071–8),
    114
Michael VIII Palaiologos, Byzantine emperor
    (1259–82), 99
Michael Attaleiates (d. 1080), Byzantine courtier
    and historian, 135
Michael Psellos (d. 1078), Byzantine courtier and
    chronicler, vi, 74, 90–1, 97–8, 126, 134, 145–6,
    151, 153, 320 n.50
Mikligarðr, see Constantinople
Ibn Miskawayh (932–1030), Baghdadi civil
    servant, philosopher and historian, 70, 295

Morkere, *eorl* of Northumbria (1065–6), 216, 223–4

Morkinskinna ('Rotten Vellum'), 45, 142, 165, 196, 225, 233, 238, 290 n.125, 298, 303–304, 309, 311–12, 317, 320 n.49

Morillo, Stephen, mediaevalist and academic, 101–102, 302, 305, 345

Mórrígan, Irish goddess of war and fate, 258–9

Morris, William (1834–96), English textile designer, poet, translator and activist, 244

Mstislav, prince of Chernigov (1024–36), 80–1

Muhammad ibn Hawqal (d. 986), Muslim traveller and geographer, 64

Muirchertach Úa Briain, king of Munster (1086–1119), high king of Ireland (1101–19), 242–3, 324 n.17

al-Mu'tamid, 'Abbasid caliph (870–92), 18

al-Muqtadir, 'Abbasid caliph (908–32), 68

mycel hæpen here, 'great heathen army', 7, 10, 207, 253, 301 n.64
    capture York (1 November 866), 253

Nabites/Nampites, Varangian commander, 107–108, 303–304 n.106, 312 n.278, 335

Napoléon Bonaparte (1769–1821), 9, 40, 43, 140, 224–5, 289, 321

Nemesis, Greek goddess of justice/retribution, 234

Nicolle, David, mediaevalist and academic, 93

Nidaros (*Niðaróss*, today's Trondheim), vii, 36, 39, 41, 46, 48, 140, 176, 185, 189, 197–8, 240, 322 n.86
    church of Saint Clement, 189
    church of Saint Mary, 240

Nikephoros II Phokas, Byzantine emperor (963–9), 87, 90, 157, 165, 292

Nikephoros III Botaneiates, Byzantine emperor (1078–81), 135

Nikephoros Diogenes, son of Romanos IV, 131

Nikephoros Gregoras (d. 1360), Byzantine historian and theologian, 307–308 n.173

Niketas Choniates (d. 1217), Byzantine courtier and historian, 98, 110, 116, 132–3, 300–301, 304–305, 308, 311

Níza (Niså, Sweden), battle of (9 August 1062), 25, 194, 196, 198

Noonan, Thomas Schaub (1938–2001), American historian, Slavicist and anthropologist, 164, 313, 345

Normans *see* Italo-Normans/Normans

Norns, Norse goddesses of fate, 259, 281

Norse language, xv, 167, 213
    kenning(s), 38, 226, 228, 249, 280, 311, 316 n.61, 321 n.70

Norse numbering system, 46, 144, 320 n.49

Novgorod (*Hólmgarðr*), 53–4, 56, 58–9, 62, 73, 79–80, 189, 278, 296 n.74
    church of Saint Óláfr, 19, 45, 59, 278
    church of Saint Sophia, 79

Nóregs tal konungr, 'List of Norwegian kings', 45, 81, 143, 154, 179, 298, 309, 311, 315, 322, 324, 331

Fagrskinna, 'Beautiful Vellum', 45, 165

Northmen *see* viking(s)

Northumbria, Anglo-Saxon kingdom, xiv, 3, 179, 180, 182, 184, 204–205, 207, 209, 215–16, 251–3, 288, 302, 318 n.6

Oakeshott, Ronald Ewart (1916–2002), English collector and historian, 95, 286–7 n.59, 300, 345–6

Oddr Arngeirson, Icelandic shape shifter, 229–30

Oddr Snorrason, 12th-century Icelandic Benedictine monk and chronicler, 77, 186, 316

Óðinn, supreme Norse god, xiv, 19, 33, 39, 71, 170, 174–5, 177–80, 187, 201, 288, 230, 232, 238–40, 244–5, 247–50, 256–8, 265, 267, 275, 279–81, 303, 315 n.45, 316–17 n.61, 323
    and *seiðr*, 281
    as god of poetry, xiv, 249, 266–7, 303 n.97, 323 n.3
        named: *Heriafòðr*, 'Father of war bands', *Alðafòðr*, 'All-father', *Yggr*, 'Terrible', *Grímnir*, 'Hooded One', *Harbarðr*, 'Grey Beard', etc., 174, 303 n.97, 314 n.34
    as a shape shifter, 230, 249, 258, 265, 323 n.3
    proto-Christ, 174–5

Odo (d. 1097), bishop of Bayeux, 300 n.40

Odo, count of Paris (882–8), king of the West Franks (888–98), 251

Odo de Deuil (1110–62), chaplain to Louis VII of France, 133

óðöl, 'family land', 42, 165–6

Offa, king of Mercia (757–96), 14

Óláfr II Haraldsson *inn digri* (the Stout), king of Norway (1015–1030), *passim*
    canonisation of, 189–90
    death at Stiklastaðir (1030), 45, 48, 50, 78
    miracles of, 48, 50, 110, 189, 190
    vitae of, 190

Óláfr III Haraldsson, 242, 312 n.282

Óláfr Guðrøðsson, Hiberno-Norse king of Dublin (934–41), king of York (939–41), 182–4, 254

Óláfr *Cuarán* (the Red) Sigtryggsson, Hiberno-Norse king of York (941–4), king of Dublin (945–7), 182, 184

Óláfr *sköttkonungr* (d. 1022), Swedish king, 79, 186, 188, 191, 196

Óláfr Tryggvason, king of Norway (995–1000), 24, 166, 185–7, 189, 195, 197–8, 209, 265, 302–303 n.91, 316
    at Maldon (991), 185, 209, 316 n.77
    Christianity of, 187, 265, 316 n.79
    death at Svölðr (1000), 186

Oleg the Prophet, prince of Kiev (882–912) and founder of Kievan Russia, 72, 171, 296 n.74

Olga (Saint), princess of Kiev and widow of Igor I, 60, 72, 89, 149, 296, 310 n.244
conversion to Christianity, 60, 72, 296 n.70
Onasander, 1st-century Greek military writer, 37, 289
Onund Jakob, Swedish king (1022–50) and brother-in-law of Óláfr II Haraldsson, 41–2, 44,
Orkneyinga saga, 5, 49, 81, 104–105, 284, 290, 298, 302–303, 327
Eðna Kjarvallsdóttir, mother of Sigurðr Hlöðvirsson *inn digri* of Orkney, 256, 326–7 n.40
Gunnhildr Erlendsdóttir, 302
Rögnvaldr (Kali) Kolsson (d. 1158), *jarl* of Orkney, 104–105, 302 n.88
Sveinn Ásleifarson, 5
Orderic Vitalis (b. 1075), English monk and chronicler, 114, 303–305 n.125, 324
Orkney, 185, 207, 222, 234, 280, 316 n.79, 320 n.49, 322 n.86, 349–50
Örvar-Odds saga, 171, 314, 331
Ölvör, Irish princess and sorceress, 281–2
Örvar-Oddr (Arrow-Odd), 12, 170–1, 281–2
Ósló, viii, xiv, 27, 198
Ostrabos (Ostrovo, Bulgaria), battle of (1043), 152
Otto I, duke of Saxony and king of Germany (936–73), Holy Roman Emperor (962–73), 291–2 n.7
Otto II, Holy Roman Emperor (973–83), 291–2 n.7
Otumba, battle of (7 July 1520), 110
Ouse, river, 222–4, 226, 321 n.55
Outlawry, outlaw(s), xvii–xviii, 22, 228, 246, 267, 272, 334
Owen (Owain ap Dyfnwal), 10th-century king of Strathclyde, 182

Pagan(s)/paganism, 1–2, 47, 50, 67–8, 72, 89, 149, 167–70, 172–80, 187–8, 193, 200, 204, 219, 230, 232–3, 261, 263, 265, 277, 291 n.5, 312 n.282, 326 n.27, 329 n.15
Pankaleia, battle of (978), 91
Paphos, 86
Paris, xiv, 134, 250–1
see also Ragnarr *loðbrók* (Hairy-Breeks)
Patton Jr, George Smith (1885–1945), US Army general, 119, 306 n.146
Paul VI (Saint), pope (1963–78), 126
Pečeneg(s), 53, 57–8, 61, 64, 79–81, 92, 109–10, 152, 293 n.19
Petersen, Jan (1887–1967), Norwegian archaeologist, viii, 15, 93, 286 n.52, 331 n.31, 346
du Picq, Ardent (1821–70), French army officer and military theorist, 9, 285, 334
Plato, 4th-century BC Greek philosopher, 127, 238

Poetic Edda, 244, 258
Codex Regius, Icelandic manuscript, 244
Grímnismál, 19, 244, 314 n.34, 327
Vafþrúðnismál, 244
Völuspá ('The Prophecy of the Seeress'), 30, 177, 244, 251, 287, 331
see also Snorri Sturluson
pólútasvarf, 155
Polyphemus, HMS (1881), 157
Porridge, buttered, 158–9, 312 n.281
Primary Chronicle, 54, 57, 60, 62, 72–4, 80–1, 89, 91, 98, 291 n.5, 293–4, 296 n.74, 297–300, 306, 310
Prudentius, bishop of Troyes (843–61), 10
Putin, Vladimir Vladimirovich, President of Russia (2000–08, 2012–), 293

Qur'an, 68–9, 164
Qurtubah (Córdoba), 65, 67, 206

Ragnarök, 177, 180, 249
Ragnarr *loðbrók* (Hairy-Breeks), 149, 167, 206, 248–54, 274–5, 281, 325 n.23, 326 n.27, 326–7 n.40, 344
death of, 249, 250–1, 252
Krákumál ('Words of the Raven'), 249, 325 n.20
Ragnars saga loðbrókar, 248, 326 n.27
his siege of Paris (845), 250–1
sons of, 325 n.15
Agnar, 250
Björn *járnsíða* (Ironside), 149, 206–207, 250, 310 n.243
Eiríkr, 250
Hálfdan Ragnarsson/Hvítserkr (White Shirt), 207, 250
Ívarr *inn beinlausi* (the Boneless), 7, 182, 207, 250, 252–4, 326–7 n.40, 338
his nickname, 252
Rögnvaldr, 250
Sigurðr *ormr í auga* (Snake–in–the–Eye), 167, 250
Ragnvaldr Ingvarsson, Swedish Varangian, 88
Rán, Norse goddess of the sea, 172
Raven(s), 110, 175, 178–9, 181, 188, 249, 254–9, 279, 327 n.42
Huginn and Muninn, 257–8
Repton burials, 7
Grave 511, 7–8
rhomphaia, myth of, 97–8
Riccall, 222–4, 226
Richard fitz Gilbert de Clare (Strongbow), first lord of Clare (1066–90), 169
Ridgeway Hill mass grave, 207–208, 343
Robert II *le Danois*, archbishop of Rouen (989–1037), 317 n.85
Robert de Clari, French crusader and chronicler, 116–17, 132, 305 n.137, 308
Rodrigo Díaz de Vivar (*El Cid*), xvii

Rögnvaldr Brúsason, *jarl* of Orkney, 49, 78, 81, 83, 302 n.88

Rollo (*Göngu*-Hrólfr), count of Normandy (911–27), 172, 213
    Treaty of Saint-Clair-sur-Epte (911), 213

Romanos I Lekapenos, Byzantine emperor (919–44), 296 n.75

Romanos II, Byzantine emperor (959–63), 57, 90, 152

Romanos III Argyros, Byzantine emperor (1028–34), 89

Romanos IV Diogenes, Byzantine emperor (1068–71), 131

Romanos Skleros, 152

Roskilde Fjord, ix, 61
    church of Saint Lucius, 196
    Roskilde 6 (*c.* 1025), 195, 205
    see also Skuldelev wrecks

Rutger von Blum (1267–1305), *condottiere* and commander of the Catalan Company, 127–8

Rune stones, ix–x, 10, 39–40, 75, 77, 87–8, 100, 203, 294 n.35, 299 n.18, 347
    Gotland
        Hallfrede (G220), 59
        Pilgårds (G280), x, 58, 293
    Östergötland,
        Ledberg (Ög 181), vii
    Södermanland
        Esta (Sö171), 293 n.25
    Uppland
        Ed (U112 A & B), 88, 299
        Sjusta (U687), 293 n.25
    Västmanland
        Hassmyra (Vs24), 161, 312
    Västergötland
        Smula (Vg 184), ix–x
        Sparlösa (Vg 119), 177–8
    í/með Grikk(j)um 'among the Greeks'/*til Grikk(j)a* 'to the Greeks', 106–107
    með Ingvari on Ingvarr-stones, 75–7, 88, 297 n.90

Rurik, first prince of Novgorod (862–79), 54, 56, 296 n.74

Rus', 12, 18, 53–7, 59–61, 63–75, 81, 85–92, 119, 123, 134, 157–8, 206, 282, 291–3, 295–6 n.74, n.75, 331 n.48, 338–9, 341–2, 345–9
    appearance, 66–71, 79, 123, 134, 295 n.62
    Byzantine treaties with (861, 907, 911, 945, 957, 971), 72–3, 86–7, 118–19, 291 n.5
    name and origin, 54–5, 79, 85, 292–3 n.12
    Rhôs, 54–6, 87, 98
    trade and commerce, 18, 57, 61, 65, 295–6 n.67

sækonungr, 'sea-king', 179, 220, 250

Særkland, 75–6, 145

Saxo Grammaticus, 12th/13th-century Danish theologian and historian, 16, 101, 155, 192, 228, 242, 248, 252, 273–6, 286, 308, 311, 317, 322, 325 n.20

Schism, Great (1054), 125

scramasax(es)/seax(es), viii, 16, 21–3, 287 n.68, 338
    Kársnautr (Kárr's gift), 22–3

Sheep, 6, 102, 162, 313, 327 n.2

seiðr, 'magical practice', 278, 281
    and homosexuality, 281
    magic arrows, 171
    magic raven banner(s), 254–6, 281
    magic cloak, 331 n.45
    magic shirt(s), 12, 170–1, 250, 252, 281–2, 325 n.11
    sorceress(es)/witch(es), 230, 256, 270, 331 n.45
        Norse-Hebridean women, 282
    warlock(s)/wizard(s), 230, 326, 331 n.45

Seine, river, 111, 213, 250, 325 n.17

Serpent(s), 133, 190, 230, 249–51
    Jormungundr, 249
    Níðhöggr, 249

Shetland Isles, vi–vii, ix, 167, 207, 222, 280, 316 n.79, 320 n.49, 322 n.86, 328 n.9
    Lerwick, vi, 167

Shield(s), viii, x–xi, 15–16, 20–1, 24–5, 29–35, 40, 64, 70, 87, 92–3, 96–7, 110, 113, 117, 119, 160, 181, 225, 263, 280, 321 n.70
    biting of, 227–8, 322 n.87
    boss, 30–1
    Gokstad, 31, 203

Shield maiden(s), 250, 270, 274, 278, 347
    Hervör, 275
    Rusila, 273, 275
    see also Lagertha

Shield wall, 23, 33–5, 37–8, 40, 45, 95, 112, 189, 223, 233, 270

Sichelgaita, wife to Robert Guiscard, 108, 304 n.108

Sigtryggr (d. 927), Hiberno-Norse king of York, 182

Sigurd (*fl.* 1075), *eorl* of Gloucester, 115–16

Sigurðr I Magnússon *Jórsalafari* (Jerusalem-farer), king of Norway (1103–30), 74–5, 104, 242, 308 n.198

Sigurðr *Fáfnisbana* (a.k.a. Siegfried), 13, 250, 285 n.33, 326 n.27

Sigurðr Hlöðvirsson *inn digri* (the Stout), *jarl* of Orkney (991–1014), 78, 123, 255–7, 280, 326–7 n.40

Sigurðr *hringr* (Ring), father (?) of Ragnarr *loðbrók*, 274–5

Sigurðr Oddsson *grikkr* (the Greek), 12th-century Icelandic Varangian, 14

Sigurðr *sýr* (Sow) Hálfdanarson, father of Haraldr II Sigurðarson, 42–3

Sigvatr Þórðarson, Icelandic skald, 45, 48, 51, 166, 188, 252
    Bersöglisvísur ('Out-spoken Verses'), 166

Sivle, Per (1857–1904), Norwegian poet and novelist, 49, 290
Siward, Danish warlord and *eorl* of Northumbria (1041–55), 215, 219, 302 n.68
skáld, skald, poet, 244–5
Skis/skiing, 63, 303
Skuldelev wrecks, 61, 211
  Skuldelev 1 (*c.* 1030), 204, 211
  Skuldelev 2 (*c.* 1042), 204–205, 208, 211
  Skuldelev 3 (*c.* 1040), 61, 211
    Roar Ege (1984), 61–2, 334
    Sif Ege (1990), 62
  Skuldelev 5 (*c.* 1040), ix, 5, 211, 221
    Helge Ask (1991), 221
    Sebbe Als (1969), ix
  Skuldelev 6 (*c.* 1030), 211
Skuthai, 'Scythians', 109, 152
Slav(s), 53, 55, 61, 68, 72, 81, 149, 162, 292–3, 310 n.244
Smolensk *see* Gnëzdovo
Sneglu-Halla þáttr, 158–9, 306, 312, 323
  Sarcastic Halli, 11th-century Icelandic skald, 158–9, 312 n.281
Snorri Sturluson (1179–1241), Icelandic saga writer, *passim*
  Heimskringla, 19, 45–6, 49, 112, 155, 165, 189–90, 208, 224, 244, 286–7, 289–91 n.5, 294–5, 297–8, 300, 302–304, 306–313, 315–24, 327, 330–1
    Haralds saga Sigurðarsonar, 166, 197, 287, 290, 294, 298, 302–303, 306–307, 309–313, 317–24, 327
    Magnússona saga, 104, 297, 302
    Óláfs saga helga, 46, 49, 189–90, 277
  Prose Edda, 76, 244, 258, 298, 300, 303, 314–15, 327
    Gylfaginning, 314–15 n.61, 327
    Skáldskaparmál, 76, 298, 300 n.44, 303 n.97
Soviet nationalism, 292–3 n.12
Normannist dispute, 55–6, 292–3
Spear(s), vii–viii, x–xi, xiv, 6, 11, 18–22, 25–6, 31–5, 37, 70, 93, 95–7, 100, 103, 108, 112, 122, 131, 137, 160, 195, 218, 226, 242, 255, 263, 274, 278–9
  Gungnir (Swaying One), 19
  Selshemnaren (Seal's Avenger), 11, 49, 272
Stamford Bridge, battle of (25 September 1066), vii, xii–xiv, 34, 50, 96, 112–13, 140, 167, 192, 214 223–34, 239–41, 322 n.72, 340
Staraja Ladoga (*Aldeigjuborg*), 54, 56, 59
Starship Troopers (1997), film, 34
Steinn Herdísarson, skald, 196
Stephanos the Paphlagonian, Byzantine admiral, 146, 148, 151, 155, 310 n.234
Stevenson, Robert Louis (1850–94), Scottish novelist and travel writer, 239–40, 324
Stiklarstaðir, battle of (31 August 1030), vii, 19, 29–30, 33, 36, 41–2, 45–52, 78, 154, 188–9, 222, 272, 302 n.88

Sturlunga saga, 18, 286
Sveinn I Haraldsson *tjúguskegg* (Forkbeard), king of Denmark (986–1014), king of Norway (986–95, 1000–14), king of England (1013–14), 5–6, 100–101, 113, 185–6, 195–6
  invades England, 210–11
Sveinn II Estriðsson, king of Denmark (1047–76), 61, 115, 150, 197–8, 218, 237, 257
  war with Haraldr II Sigurðarson, 191, 192–6
Sveinn Hákonarson, Norwegian jarl, 186
Sveinn Hákonsson, Norwegian *jarl*, 42
Sveinn Knútsson, regent of Norway (1030–35), 44, 51–2, 217–18
Sven Aggesen (*fl.* 1150), Danish historian, 101
Sverrir Sigurðarson, pretender–king of Norway (1184–1202), 39, 317
Sviatopolk I, prince of Kiev (1015–19), 80
Sviatoslav I, ruler of Kievan Russia (945–72), 53–4, 58, 60–1, 74, 80, 89, 92, 348
  death of, 57–8, 92
  rejects Christianity, 60, 89
Svölðr, battle of (1000), 24, 186, 195, 198, 302–303 n.91
Sword(s), vii, xvii, 3, 7, 11–24, 28, 31–3, 58, 69–70, 74, 87, 93–6, 100, 103, 106, 113, 119, 124, 131, 136, 171, 173, 195, 201, 256, 268, 278–9
  Frankish, vii–viii, 16, 18, 70
    Ingelrii blades, 18, 287 n.87
    Ulfberht blades, 287 n.59
  as heirlooms, 12–13
    Brynjubítr (Byrnie-biter), 14, 18
    Dragvandil (Slicer), 13, 286 n.37
    Fjörsváfnir (Life-taker), 13
    Fótbítr (Foot- or Leg-biter), 12, 14
    Grásiða (Grey-sides), 13
    Gunnlogi (Battle-flame), 13
    Hneitir (Cutter?), 19, 105
    Hrunting (Thrusting), 286 n.56
    Hvítingr (White One), 13
    Jarlsnautr, (Gift of the earl), 13
    Kvenbítr (Quern-biter), 13
    Langr (Long), 13
    Naðr (Viper), 13
    Nægling (Nailer?), 16–17, 286 n.56
    Sköfnungr (Shinbone?), 13–14
    Skrýmr (Boaster), 13
    Týrfingr (Týrfing), 11–12
  Persian, 137
  xiphos, 97, 301 n.51
Symeon of Durham, 11th/12th-century English monk chronicler, 180, 184, 315, 320–1 n.55

Tacitus, 1st/2nd-century Roman historian, 33, 251, 289, 313 n.6
The Thirteenth Warrior (1999), film, 68–9
  see also Crichton, Michael
Theodora Porphyrogenita (d. 1056), sister of Zoë Porphyrogenita and empress, 156, 307 n.161

Theodoricus Monachus, 12th-century Norwegian Benedictine monk and historian, 46, 179, 193, 227, 290, 315–16, 317 n.85, n.101, 319, 322
Theophano Porphyrogenita, empress and mother of Basil II, 90
Theophanu Skleraina (d. 991), Byzantine princess and wife to Otto II, 292
Theophilos, Byzantine emperor (829–42), 56, 67
Thietmar of Merseberg (975–1018), Ottonian cleric and chronicler, 89, 299
Thucydides, 5th-century BC Greek soldier and historian, 46, 97, 290, 297
Tiberius II Constantinus, Byzantine emperor (578–82), 156
Tiberius III Apsimar, Byzantine emperor (698–705), 156
Tostig Godwinson, *eorl* of Northumbria (1055–65, d. 1066), 96, 196, 215, 220, 222–4, 233, 302 n.68, 317 n.100
  at Gate Fulford, 223–4
  at Stamford Bridge, 233
Trading ship(s), 61, 203–204
  see also Skuldelev 1, Skuldelev 3
Treadgold, Warren, Byzantist and academic, 111, 299, 304, 313, 349
Trøndelag, district of Norway, 44, 185, 197–8
Turville-Petre, Gabriel (1908–78), English scholar and academic, xvii, 238, 284, 321, 323, 329 n.27, 350
þegn(s), 'thegn(s)', 112, 214, 301 n.66
Þjóðólfr, 9th/10th-century Norwegian skald, 135
Þjóðólfr Arnórsson, 11th-century Icelandic skald, 25, 78, 100, 143, 148–9, 153–4, 192, 194, 196
  Sexstefja, 153, 192
Þóra Þórbergsdotter, second 'wife' to Haraldr II Sigurðarson, 159, 197, 312 n.282
Þóra, first wife to Ragnarr *loðbrók*, 249
Þórarinn *loftunga*, 11th-century Icelandic skald, 190
Þórarinn Skeggjarson, 11th-century Icelandic skald, 154
Þórberg Árnason, brother of Kálfr Árnason and father of Þóra Þórbergsdotter, 312 n.282
Þorfinnr Sigurðarson *inn ríki*, *jarl* of Orkney, 256
Þorkell Eyjólfsson, 13–14
Þorkell *inn hávi* (the Tall), Danish warlord, 210
Þorkell Leira, 10th-century Vík chieftain, 208
Þorkell Þjójstarsson, 10th-century Scandinavian mercenary, 87
Þórir *hundr* (the Hound), 46, 49, 271–2
Þórir *selr* (the Seal), 330 n.5
Þormóðr Eindriðason, Icelandic Varangian, 106
Þormóðr *kolbrúnarskáld* (Coal-brow's-skald), 11th-century Icelandic skald, 45, 47, 244
Þórólfr smjör (Butter), 163
Þórr (Thor), Norse god, 8, 39, 170, 187–8, 201
  Mjöllnir, 8, 170
Þorsteinn *knarrarsmiðr* (Shipbuilder), 49

Úlfr Óspaksson, marshal of Haraldr III Sigurðarson, 159, 256
Úlfr Þorgilsson, Danish *jarl* and father of Sveinn II Estriðsson, 42, 196
Ulfric, English Varangian, 116
Uppland, district of Norway, 25, 41–2, 198–9
Uppland, region of Sweden, 75, 77, 87–8
Uriah the Hittite, 50

Valgarðr á Vellir, Icelandic skald, 147, 154, 194
Valhöll, home of Óðinn, 2, 19, 175, 177, 180, 226, 315–16 n.61
  einherjar, 'those who fight alone', 177
valkyrja/valkyrjur, 'valkyrie(s)', xiv, 19, 178, 259, 270, 279–80, 321, 347
  in *Brennu-Njáls saga*, 280
    Brynhildr (a.k.a. Brünnhilde), 'Bright Battle', 250
    Hildr, 'Battle', 226, 280, 321 n.70
    Hjörþrimul, 'Sword Warrioress', 280
    Sanngriðr, 'Very Violent', 280
    Svipul, 'Changeable', 280
Vanaheim, abode of the *Vanir*, 314 n.30
Vanir, Norse gods of light and wisdom, 172, 281, 314 n.30, 323 n.3
Varangian Guard/Varangians, *passim*
  arms and armour, 92–5, 119–24
  in battle, 95–7, 107–11
  drinking habits, 134–6
  'Inglínoi, 'English', 114, 116
  Tauroskuthai, 'Scyths from the Taurus', 98, 153
  væringjar, 'varangian', 85, 154, 298–9 n.5
Vendel period, 17, 26, 177, 312 n.282
Vietnam War (1 November 1955 – 30 April 1975), 8–9, 38
Viking(s), *passim*
  hygiene, 68, 118
  name, meaning of, 167–8
  wintersetl, 'winter bases', 7, 205–206
Vinland, 276
Visby, Gotland, 59, 306–307 n.152
Vita Oswaldi, 289 n.95
Vladimir (Saint), ruler of Kievan Russia (980–1015), xi, 79–80, 88–92, 113, 350
Vladimir Monomakh, prince of Novgorod (1036–52), 79, 88
Volga, river, 18, 56–7, 64–8, 70, 75, 121, 134, 295
  portage along, 64–6
Völsunga saga, 174, 244

Wace, Anglo–Norman poet, 96, 301 n.49
Wagner, Richard, 13, 177, 250, 279
War band(s), 2, 10, 134, 144, 174, 177, 201, 205, 275, 310 n.243
Weaving, 124, 280–1
Weland, viking warlord, 10, 206, 285 n.25
wergild, 'man-price', 268
Wessex, Anglo-Saxon kingdom, 182, 209, 212, 219, 253, 301 n.64

William I, king of Sicily (1154–66), 306 n.151
William I the Conqueror, duke of Normandy
     (1035–87), king of England (1066–87), 96,
     112–15, 197, 213–14, 222, 234–5, 300 n.40, 301
     n.49, 304 n.109, 316 n.75
  his claim to the English throne, 96, 214, 234–5
William de Poitiérs (d. 1090), chaplain to William
     I the Conqueror, 96, 214, 300 n.40
William of Malmesbury, 12th-century Anglo-
     Norman monk and chronicler, 93, 155, 226–7,
     235, 287, 300, 308 n.198, 311, 320, 322
Wilson, David Mackenzie, archaeologist and
     academic, 71, 296, 315, 339, 315
Wolf(ves), vii, 102, 154, 177–81, 228–9, 279, 311
     n.260, 315 n.48, 315–16 n.61, 323 n.91, n.93
  werewolf, 229, 267, 299
  úlfhéðinn/ úlfhéðnar, 'wolf-skin(s)', 228–9, 231
  see also *berserkir*, 'berserkers'
Women, 4, 7–8, 10–11, 24, 66–7, 85, 118, 127,
     161–2, 170, 173, 194, 201
  armed, 137, 270, 273–5, 278–9, 282–3
  Hårby figurine, 279
  Oseberg burial, 278
  on picture stones, 315 n.45
  as rulers, 51
  on rune stones, 76, 161
  in sagas, 161, 245–6, 270–2, 275
  see also shield-maiden(s)
Wood, xi, 11, 15, 19, 21–4, 29–31, 61, 94, 123,
     201–203, 211–12, 220–2, 230, 327
  ash, xi, 19, 21, 23, 94, 212, 221
  birch, 24, 230, 327 n.2

Cornelian cherry, 21
elm, 23–4
fir, 29
juniper, 220–1
linden, 29–30
oak, xi, 61, 201–203, 221–2
pine, xi, 29, 31, 221, 230
spruce, 29
yew, 23, 25, 320–1 n.54
Wystan (Saint), Mercian *æðeling*, 7

Xenophon, Greek mercenary and historian, 92

Yahya ibn Sa'id of Antioch (d. 1066), Egyptian
     Melkite Christian chronicler, 89, 299 n.29, 300
     n.31
Yaropolk, ruler of Kievan Russia (972–80), 92
Yaroslav I (the Wise), ruler of Kievan Russia
     (1019–54), xii, 43, 50–2, 59, 78–83, 88, 143,
     155, 157, 188, 341
York (*Jórvík*), xiii, 1, 167, 179–80, 182–4, 197,
     209, 223–5, 234, 253–4, 320–1 n.55
  foundation of, 320–1 n.54
York, Vale of, 288 n.87

Zoë Porphyrogenita (d. 1050), niece of Basil II and
     Byzantine empress, 142, 143, 151, 155–6
  exiled, 152–3
  recovers the throne, 153
Zori, Davide, archaeologist and academic, 260–1,
     266, 269, 294, 327–9, 230, 336, 351